Charkin Blog

The Archive

Richard Charkin

Charkin Blog

The Archive

Macmillan

First published 2008 by Macmillan
an imprint of Pan Macmillan Ltd
Pan Macmillan, 20 New Wharf Road, London N1 9RR
Basingstoke and Oxford
Associated companies throughout the world
www.panmacmillan.com

ISBN 978-0-230-74202-4

Visit **www.panmacmillan.com** to read more about all our books
and to buy them. You will also find features, author interviews and
news of any author events, and you can sign up for e-newsletters
so that you're always first to hear about our new releases.

Preface

It was towards the end of 2005 that the IT department of Macmillan in London complained about the rapidly diminishing free space available on its servers. Apparently I was one of the worst offenders and my greatest offence was sending all employees a fairly regular email newsletter about the business. A colleague proposed a solution. If I wrote the newsletter not as an email but as a blog then those who were interested could simply log on to the site thus eliminating all the emails sitting on the system. The next question was whether to make the blog public or private. Obviously it would have been better as an intra-company and confidential service. However, the IT system was such that it would have been very difficult to include overseas employees (and Macmillan is predominantly made up of businesses outside the UK). Secondly, I was pretty sure that if I ever wrote anything interesting, damaging or controversial (and what's the point of a blog if it isn't one of these?) someone would copy and paste the offending item and send it to the book-trade press.

We launched the blog publicly on 12 December 2005 with absolutely no hoohah. It began more as a personal diary than a commentary but then the competitive spirit stepped in. I discovered a statistics package which allowed me to track the quantity and source of visitors to the site. I was hooked and determined to learn how to improve traffic. I moved gradually from posting on a pretty regular basis to never missing a day. The diary became less personal and more general. I discovered various themes which generated comments and/or traffic and I found myself revisiting these frequently.

I left Macmillan at the end of September 2007 and the blog ceased. I had no idea that somehow or other I'd filled hundreds of pages, nor that so many people would write to say thanks or good riddance and even less that anyone would think it would be worth producing as a book. But here it is, warts and all.

I've tried very hard not to abuse anyone's copyright without permission. If I have done so, please let the publishers know and, through the wonder of on-demand technology, the mistake will be corrected.

Finally, a big thank you to the team at Macmillan who supported this endeavour, to the guest bloggers who allowed me a day off from time to time, to the hotel receptions around the world who lent me access to their Internet connections in the early hours of the morning, and to the commenters who made the blog a two-way experience for me.

Richard Charkin
Soho Square, 20 August 2008

P.S. Because it's impossible to render hyperlinks in a printed book and because it is impractical to include the comments I think it's important to use this book in conjunction with www.charkinblog.macmillan.com for maximum enjoyment. It's like watching cricket on TV with the sound off while listening to the radio commentary.

Charchive

≤ **December 2005** ≥

Mon	Tue	Wed	Thu	Fri	Sat	Sun
28	29	30	1	2	3	4
5	6	7	8	9	10	11
12	13	14	15	16	17	18
19	20	21	22	23	24	25
26	27	28	29	30	31	1
2	3	4	5	6	7	8

🌙 12 December 2005

Monday – MDL, Wottakars, the Archers

Morning – MDL (Macmillan Distribution) Executive meeting – detailed discussions on new investments, new client publishers, better use of technology, slow-paying retailers, how to improve accuracy, how to stay ahead of the competition. Publishing services is an increasingly important part of our strategic direction. It's not easy, because competition is lifting people's expectations and demands. But we are beautifully positioned to respond to the changes because we understand the publishing process, and we ourselves expect the very best from our service departments.

Afternoon – teleconference about Wottakars, the proposed takeover of the UK bookshop chain, Ottakars, by HMV, which the Publishers Association – of which I am President – is opposing on grounds of retail dominance leading to reduction of consumer choice. The deal has now been referred to the UK Competition authority which will grind on for months before making a decision.

I have been quoted in some newspapers as saying the most important thing now is for the book trade to get 'get off its arse and sell books in the run-up to Christmas'. I think I've been misquoted – but applaud the sentiment anyway.

Evening – annual Christmas party chez Lord and Lady Archer where we drink Krug, scoff that British delicacy, shepherds pie, and run into a mixture of Tory politicians who tend to be rather overweight, and sports people, who tend not to be.

🌙 13 December 2005

Tuesday: Cricinfo/Friday Project

Morning – Finance Committee (don't ask). Then Wisden/Cricinfo Board meeting where the euphoria of beating Australia in the Summer has been replaced by the reality of being thrashed in Pakistan . The most memorable factoid about our cricket website is that on the last day of the last India/Pakistan series, Cricinfo came within a whisker of having more downloads than Google. Who would have thought that cricket would be the most popular sport on the Internet bar one?

Afternoon – celebrate with the Friday Project (see blogroll) who helped with the development of this blog, and whose first list is in the shops now, sold in by our own Pan sales force and distributed by MDL.

🌙 14 December 2005

Wednesday: Stuttgart

Morning – off to my second favourite city, Stuttgart, where the Holtzbrinck executive team is discussing the threats and opportunities of the Internet world – newspapers, reference works, children's books, textbooks etc. I have my opinions but I won't repeat them all here. Instead you can read the piece I wrote on this subject for Palgrave Macmillan's excellent author magazine.

Evening – dinner with Holtzbrinck colleagues to discuss how best to grow our business in Russia. This has always been a difficult market for all the reasons you can imagine, but we have been making good progress the last few years and want to build further.

☀ 15 December 2005

Thursday: . . . Kings Cross

Being filmed for a promotional video for the property development going up next to our main King's Cross building. It looks like the area which was once as famous for its prostitutes and drug dealers as for its station is changing fast. The new development will include a concert hall, a sculpture gallery, two flash restaurants and any number of trendy businesses, including the Guardian newspaper.
http://www.kingsx.co.uk/kx7.htm

Friday: Gill & Macmillan/Publishers Association

The annual London Board meeting with our good Irish friends at Gill & Macmillan. They are having a spectacular year, which should make the meeting go with a swing. And then off to the Publishers Association to see how we can fund next year's budget. Any ideas?

☀ 19 December 2005

Children's Books lead the way

I'm pleased to see Macmillan leading the field again, with Macmillan Children's Books launching the first webcast in Children's Publishing to communicate with its partners. I-NEWS is going to run from January 2006, delivering news about the children's market, children's media and Macmillan Children's Books to UK and international retailers, UK librarians, co-edition customers and agents. Making full use of webcasting possibilities, I-NEWS will be a mix of videos, animated slides and downloads.

The first webcast is going to include video clips of Julia Eccleshare, Guardian Children's Books Editor, Emma Hopkin, MD of Macmillan Children's Books and children from Upminster Junior School. There will also be several animated title specific presentations which will give information about the books and the publishing strategy behind them. Using data from Childwise, it will also give an overview of how the children's market in general is evolving.

As well as giving information about Macmillan Children's Books and news about the children's market, I-NEWS will give the opportunity to download reading guides and activity sheets and will also invite its audience to communicate directly with Macmillan Children's Books via several email links.

4

Recommended read / recommended listen

I've just left the BBC, where I was the studio guest for a phone-in on You and Yours on Radio 4 about the current and future shape of the book industry. We heard from independent booksellers who spoke feelingly about working hard to maintain their position on the high street, from book buyers who want to continue to be offered choice as well as volume of titles, from authors dismayed at the impact high discounting is having on their income levels and from publishers working to develop new business models for the upcoming digital generation. You can listen in at http://www.bbc.co.uk/radio4/youandyours

I note my former colleague Michael Gill is continuing the active life even in retirement. He's written an article in the Irish Times looking back over 'A life in Books'. Worth a read. http://www.ireland.com/newspaper/weekend/2005/

On another note, if you thought our stand at the Frankfurt Book Fair was big, take a look at Macmillan's presence at the Guadalajara Book Fair recently. Here are some pix.

Castillo team on the Macmillan stand

Palgrave Macmillan's Jim Papworth talks the talk

A view of the stand

Run-up to Christmas

Huge party in posh London stately home to say au revoir to David Young, Managing director of Time Warner Books UK who has been promoted to run TW Books worldwide out of New York. Apparently (although I am sure my American colleagues would disagree) publishing in the USA is a doddle compared with the UK. The authors are constantly charming and not in the least demanding, agents are more interested in long-term career development for their clients than in large advances and booksellers are only concerned with ensuring the long-term viability of their publisher suppliers. Sounds good to me. Left early to prepare for next round of discussions with UK authors, agents and retailers.

🕊 24 December 2005

Still running

I just wrote a piece about today and managed to lose it. It might reappear so I won't try to recreate it in full. Who said blogging was easy! Grrr.

Long and short of it was – slow trading in shops in London, thank God no transport strike a la New York, Macmillan company results look OK, first two in are records (Ireland and New Zealand), Jeffrey Archer's new novel selling like mad in Australia (out elsewhere early in 2006),lots of coverage of digital versus 'real' books with most of the arguments being luddite, pseudovisionary, subjective and ill-informed – the normal high standards of the British media.

more later . . .

🕊 25 December 2005

Puerto de Palos

Happy Christmas everyone.

Macmillan never sleeps. Late last night (Christmas Eve, which is the big day in Latin America) we signed an agreement to acquire Puerto de Palos, one of Argentina's leading Spanish language textbook publishers. I recommend you switch on the sound on your computer and go to www.puertodepalos.com.ar. It's not traditional Christmas music but none the worse for that.

Puerto de Palos was founded in 1996 and has grown rapidly to a position of leadership in Spanish language curriculum publishing. The company is particularly strong in Spanish language publishing and also owns the successful Cántaro imprint, which publishes readers and supplementary materials for schools.

Macmillan already has a significant presence in Argentina through Macmillan Publishers S.A., a company founded in 1998 which is the clear market leader in materials for teaching the English language. Macmillan's acquisition of the assets of Ediciones Castillo, Mexico's second largest school textbook publisher, in 2003, marked the group's first entry into Spanish language curriculum publishing, and this is now complemented and strengthened by the acquisition of Puerto de Palos.

The Puerto de Palos educational publishing activities will be run separately from those of Macmillan Publishers in Argentina and Raúl González, the company's founder, will continue to be Chairman and Managing Director.

Through this acquisition we expect to consolidate Macmillan's position in the Argentine educational market, sharing resources to improve the quality of our publishing and marketing, while respecting the different cultures prevailing in Macmillan's two investments in Argentina.

This investment reaffirms the strong commitment of Macmillan to Argentina and to international educational publishing in Spanish.

The scope of Puerto de Palos' and Cántaro's publishing can be explored by visiting www.puertodepalos.com.ar and the award-winning www.cantaro.com.ar

And now to cook my goose.

🕊 26 December 2005

Boxing Day

Boxing Day is a matter of tidying up, watching the cricket in Melbourne (well done South Africa), avoiding soccer fans arriving for the Chelsea-Fulham derby near my house, catching up with other family members etc. The papers are full of economic predictions for 2006 and justifications for the wrong predictions of 2005. What amazes me is the certainty of the judgements made. I am becoming less and less certain of anything except the innate unpredictability of everything. Pip pip.

🕊 29 December 2005

Alumni

This is not just the peak time for greetings cards, it is also when alumni magazines arrive. I've received three so far.

Hearts and Wings come from my secondary school – www.haileybury.com. When I was at school it was single sex, pretty well monocultural and the word 'alumni' hadn't crossed anyone's mind, let alone a magazine. The main link was the annual cricket match between old boys and the school first eleven (who invariably won easily). I was pleased to see that the cover picture was of two boys playing rugby (a touch of tradition) but the rest was entirely changed from my days – and all for the better.

Then the Green College (Oxford) Record (www.green.ox.ac.uk). I was a Supernumerary Fellow there for a few years when I worked in Oxford. Green is only 25 years old but has already built a very high reputation particularly in medicine and life sciences. The magazine rightly uses much space to cover the death of Sir Richard Doll, the founding Warden of the college. He was a wonderful guy but he'll be remembered for devising the epidemiological experiment which proved conclusively the link between lung cancer and smoking. It was an elegant experiment from a scientific point of view. It was also probably the most important public health discovery of the twentieth century and his insistence on the use of randomised controlled clinical trials has led to many other important linkages between health and environmental factors. A rather popular recent discovery was that alcohol in moderation is good for you.

Finally the very austere Trinity College (Cambridge) Annual Record (www.trin.cam.ac.uk) mainly still black and white with a one-colour cover. The ghoulish interest here is to check out how many of one's undergraduate colleagues have died in the previous year. This pastime is one of the few which improves with age. The best thing about this magazine (apart from the excellence of its contributions) is that there are no begging-letter inserts. Trinity is in an almost unique position among educational establishments in having more money than it can spend on itself although I am sure the University of Cambridge would like to get its hands on some of it. In any event, not only do they not ask alumni for money but they go out of their way to advise us of free dinners to be had. That's what I call a great establishment.

30 December 2005

Cool or what?

I am told reliably that in the text messaging community the word 'cool' is often shown as 'book' (the 'b' and 'c' are on the same key as are the 'k' and 'l'). Hence it has become perfectly acceptable, indeed desirable, to use the word 'book' when referring to 'cool'. This would seem to be a good omen for our industry although it could lead to some serious confusion if this letter replacement became widespread.

≤ January 2006 ≥

Mon	Tue	Wed	Thu	Fri	Sat	Sun
26	27	28	29	30	31	1
2	3	4	5	6	7	8
9	10	11	12	13	14	15
16	17	18	19	20	21	22
23	24	25	26	27	28	29
30	31	1	2	3	4	5

Scotland the Brave

Macmillan is a Scottish company historically. Two crofters from the tiny Isle of Arran – http://www.undiscoveredscotland.co.uk/areaarra/ – set it up in 1843 – http://www.macmillan.com/history1.asp – and it has expanded ever since.

But it is not just historically Scottish. Much of its ethos is Scottish – commitment to education and the highest educational standards, being careful with money, being pragmatic, being analytical are all typically Scottish characteristics.

I was therefore interested when I saw a Times newspaper article by one of Britain's leading literary agents and an old friend and sparring partner, Michael Sissons, on Scottish devolution – http://www.timesonline.co.uk/article/0,,1072-1964167,00.html.

He argues that Britain is no longer a viable or meaningful concept and that England and Scotland should be allowed to govern themselves as independent sovereign states. I'm not sure whether this means that Macmillan's HQ will have to relocate back to Scotland but worse things happen at sea. I am looking forward to the debate on all this and wish Michael well in his campaign.

🦢 04 January 2006

Balderdash and Piffle

Pleased to see that the good old Beeb has launched a programme investigating the fascinating stories behind commonly-used words and phrases in our own English language. I wonder whether the idea for this programme was in any way influenced by the huge and unexpected success of Lynne Truss's book, 'Eats, Shoots and Leaves,' but in any case all this popular interest in language and words can't be bad for publishers.

This week's programme saw guest presenter Ian Hislop trying to come to grips with one of modern life's worst maladies and one of my own bug-bears: 'management-speak'. Equally intriguingly, Victoria Coren travelled the country on the trail of the mysterious origins of the 'full Monty', investigating whether it first referred to male nudity, an impossibly substantial breakfast, the strategic genius of Field Marshal Montgomery or to the full three piece suit from Montague Burton's . . .

I will also be interested in the results of this programme's 'Wordhunters' appeal. Viewers are being invited to find an earlier appearance of a word than is currently quoted in the OED. You can log in to http://www.bbc.co.uk/balderdash to track the progress of words such as 'bog-standard' (earliest verified usage currently 1983), 'bonk' (1975), 'cyberspace' (1982) and 'phwoar' (1980). You may even be able to help the OED discover the origins of words such as 'jaffa', a cricketing term, that to this date remain a mystery.

Another programme aired by the BBC over Christmas took a rather different but equally loving look at words – focusing as it did on the wit and verbal dexterity of the now departed Ian Dury. You can listen in at http://www.bbc.co.uk/radio4/factual/pip/jm01b/?focuswin

🦋 05 January 2006

Guilt and indulgence

There is much concern around the world about the potential demise of small independent bookstores.The best thing to do is to buy books from them. Sometimes that is not possible and you may be wracked with guilt. Lorem Ipsum might offer you the reprieve you need. Purchase one of their 'Indulgences' at http://www.loremlabs.com/projects/indulgences/

🦋 06 January 2006

The Pan Bookshop

This blog isn't here for advertising or plugs but I may not be able to hold myself back. After yesterday's piece about the demise of independent bookstores and all the stuff in the UK about the chains selling the same books and restricting choice I did some research in this Macmillan-owned small retail bookshop in London's Chelsea district – http://www.allinlondon.co.uk/directory/1278/3012.php. It's a beautiful and idiosyncratic shop which is custom-made for the sort of people who live and shop in Chelsea.

The question I asked the staff was to establish the top ten most in demand Christmas titles for them and for fun the four titles whose Christmas sales had disappointed them the most. The list is entirely different from all other bestseller lists and suggests that diversity does indeed exist albeit in a rather rare and well-heeled environment. Here we go:

The winners

1. Untold Stories by Alan Bennett

2. Now we are Sixty (and a bit) by Christopher Matthew

3. Journeys of a Sufi Musician by Kudsi Erguner

4. Wall and Piece by Banksy

5. City of Falling Angels by John Berendt

6. Kitchen Diaries by Nigel Slater

7. Silver Spoon

8. Lunar Park by Brett Easton Ellis

9. A Little History of the World by E. H.Gombrich

10. Kings Road by Max Decharne

Only one Macmillan title and no mention of Jamie Oliver or Sharon Osbourne!

And the most disappointing

1. Talk to the Hand by Lynne Truss

2. Grumpy Old Men

3. Two Lives by Vikram seth

4. A Long way Down by Nick Hornby.

I recommend you visit the shop but alternatively you can order these or any other books by emailing them at <u>panbookshop@btclick.com</u>. They also produce an excellent newsletter which you can order from the email address. Enjoy.

07 January 2006

A message from Susan Hill: Small bookshops

This message is from the author and publisher, Susan Hill. You can find more about her and her works at <u>www.susan-hill.com</u> and <u>www.thewomaninblack.com</u>.

What is all this about small independent bookshops being everything wonderful ? Some may be. But on a recent small independent survey I found nothing to cheer me, much that was either depressing, infuriating or both. Whenever I hear people shouting 'Save the village store' I wonder if they have been in one lately and the same goes for the bookshops. There are honourable exceptions . . . the nearest one to me is The Bookshop, Chipping Norton, as good as you can get. Otherwise, come with me on a miserable tour.

Shop one used to be superb. It is tiny and ten years ago it was my favourite place in the world, crammed with new books from floor to ceiling, and wall to wall. The ingenuity with which the proprietors used to fill every nook and cranny with such an astonishing variety of titles made you start and stretch your eyes and I never came out of it empty handed. Yes, there were the Big New Bestsellers, prominently displayed in the window or on a table, but it was the rest of the stock that delighted and surprised, books you did not dream of, wonderful, unusual books, about Spanish Art or Heraldry, Medieval Music or 18th century poetry, military books, quirky little titles on wild flowers or celtic prayer, books of wood engravings from tiny publishers, Everyman classics, rows of unusual paperback novels by little-known authors, biographies, memoirs, history, and travel, children's books you never saw anywhere else, as well as diaries, calendars, maps, guide books and that volume privately published by the local poet which the owners were trying their best with. Oh, if that little shop were the same today. But a new broom has swept clean and decided to de-stock. The window is still OK, but inside I doubt if there are a quarter the books there were and you can't really browse because they are almost all turned face forwards. A quick glance round and you've seen the lot. According to the proprietiors, 'People don't buy books that are shelved spine-out, only if they can see the covers, face-on.' Not any book buying people I know.

Shop two, twenty miles away in another market town, looks more promising. The place is crammed with books, shelved spine-facing as well as covers-up on tables and well displayed two or three deep in the window and an excellent assortment too. Most enticing. The stock is certainly not the problem here. But do you remember when you were a child and librarians and ladies who kept bookshops were witches ? Well Ding dong, the witches are not all dead.

I went into Shop Two and started to browse while an elderly gentleman handed over a copy of Lynne Truss's book about manners. 'I'm buying this for my grand sons. They have no manners.'

The witch – sorry, lady behind the counter said sharply, 'Well it isn't a children's book you know. And anyway it isn't doing nearly so well as her first one, about punctuation. They're just trying to cash in.'

Do you know, he actually bought that book, in spite of her best efforts to dissuade him ? Then it was my turn. The shop had a second, inner room, even more crammed with interesting books, a browser's paradise but I didn't get to enjoy its fruits for more than a nano second because she came in to watch me like a hawk while pretending to dust. I tried to browse on but my heart wasn't in it once she had told me they did not usually allow people with shopping bags through here. You may not be wholly surprised to learn that I left without making a purchase.

The third shop, in a town I had never visited before, was run by not a witch but a sad looking man who said that until recenntly the shop had sold shoes. 'But it had to close.' You could see why. Location, location, location. It's a wonder I found the bookshop at all, in its dismal side street which was also a rat run for lorries. The whole place was run-down and peeling, its inhabitants looking too care-worn and harassed to spend time or money on new books. Had our new bookseller done any market research ? He told me he had always wanted to own a bookshop but it seemed clear that having acquired the over-large premises he had no money left over for stock. Too few books were randomly spread out like too few sandwiches on a big buffet table. They were mainly the latest bestsellers in expensive hardback. But there is a large W.H.Smith five miles away where Jamie's Oliver's Italy and friends can be bought half price. A few children's picture books were fanned out loosely on a table. The man said sadly, 'I'm afraid I don't know anything about them but I thought I ought to have a few.'

I left before I burst into tears.

Yet I daresay each of those bookshop owners joins the loud chorus blaming Waterstones, Amazon and the supermarkets for snatching their customers and has never looked to themselves for either the reason or the remedy.

There is room for small independent bookshops. There is room for the tiny room bursting at the seams with stock, where you can browse happily for hours in a treasure-trove of the books you do not find in the supermarket and in which no one suspects you of being a potential shoplifter and asks children if they have washed their hands. But there is only room for them if they do not try and beat the big chain bookstores and the internet sellers at their own game. They can't. They can probably knock a pound off the recommended retail price of a new hardback but that is no good when Waterstones is doing three for two and Amazon is selling at 45% off and post free. But only a small percentage of the books out there attract big publicity and big discounts. There are thousands of books which could be stocked by small independents to their advantage, books from the back list, unusual books, books from the many, many small publishers, books which are at the back of the catalogues from the big publishers, who stick the bestsellers at the front. Books you will not know about until you browse and discover, books which tempt you, quirky books, novels you had forgotten, biographies of un-obvious people, the book-road less travelled. If I owned a small bookshop I would not even bother to stock the top ten, the latest blockbusters, the new Harry Potter and Dan Brown, though any of them could be obtained the next day to special order. The book wholesalers give a superb service to independent shops.

Unless they take a long hard look at themselves, none of the small shops I visited can survive the next two or three years. And when I hear authors telling the public not to buy their books at half price from Amazon or in Waterstones I am appalled. If I have twenty pounds, I can go to a small independent bookshop and buy one copy of Alan

Bennett's latest at full price. Or I can go to a chain bookstore or online, get it for half price and have a tenner left over with which to buy at least one other book. How can that be bad ?

There has never been such a boom in book buying and reading. Look at the eReading Group phenomenon. Look at the surge in popularity of children's books, thanks almost entirely to J.K. Rowling. Books have never been cheaper, there has never been such a wonderful variety of new titles from smaller publishers, unusual books, books that the chain stores do not give much shelf space to but which the small independents can focus on, stocking just one of hundreds of different titles rather than hundreds of just a few.

I wish I had the chance to stock a small independent bookshop in a market town somewhere. There would be neither a Da Vinci Code nor a witch in sight.

09 January 2006

Nature in the Asia Pacific region

Scientific research in Japan, Korea and China is having a growing international impact. Nature Japan K.K. was established in 1987 with three staff built around an editorial news bureau for *Nature* set up in 1984. It has since grown to 30 staff focused primarily on marketing and sales operations and contributes a significant portion of the Nature Publishing Group's global turnover. In addition to covering news for *Nature*, the company now produces Japanese pages for the Japan edition of *Nature*, a Japanese monthly supplement for *Nature*, *Nature Digest*, Chinese pages for the China edition of *Nature* and Japanese pages for several *Nature* research journals as well websites in Japanese, Chinese and Korean.

In response to these seismic shifts, NPG has today announced plans to transform its representative company in Japan into the hub of a scientific, technical and medical publishing powerhouse in the Asia-Pacific region, with several major new initiatives already in development.

Following a strategic review of its activities in the region, Nature Japan K.K. along with NPG offices in Hong Kong and Melbourne, Australia, have now merged to become NPG Nature Asia-Pacific, handling editorial, marketing, sales, print and web production for the Group in the region. This new organization will develop the *Nature* brand in the Asia-Pacific, as well as developing society-owned publications and creating a new custom publishing service.

2006 marks the first placement of *Nature* journal editors in the Asia-Pacific region, in response to the growing output of high quality research. Editors of two new *Nature*-branded primary research journals, *Nature Nanotechnology* and *Nature Photonics*, will be located in Tokyo to help the region's researchers in these disciplines publish their best research. For *Nature Photonics*, this will extend to the Editor-in-Chief and the core editorial staff. It is anticipated that more editors will follow in Japan and in China.

In a major new initiative, NPG Nature Asia-Pacific will partner with scientific societies in producing high-quality journals. From January 2006, NPG will partner with the Shanghai Institutes for Biosciences (SIBS) to publish their premier journal *Cell Research*, which has the highest impact factor of all life science and medical journals in China. Also in 2006, NPG Nature Asia-Pacific will produce a quarterly Japanese translation of *Kidney International*. This move coincides with NPG taking over publication of *Kidney International,* on behalf of the International Society of Nephrology. Further top journals from the region will join the program shortly.

NPG Nature Asia-Pacific will also be launching a new custom publishing service to help institutions in the Asia-Pacific region raise their profile and awareness of their best research. The first contract will be signed shortly.

With science in the region moving ahead so quickly, we have to move forward as well. David Swinbanks, NPG Publishing Director, has recently returned to Tokyo to implement the new strategy after a four-year stay in London.

www.natureasia.com

www.nature.com

10 January 2006

The Shipping News

Continuing yesterday's Asia theme, our man in Hong Kong, Colin Bond, just sent me some pretty gob-smacking statistics which provide a real measure of our business growth in the region. In 2005, Macmillan Production (Asia) Ltd (MPAL) shipped 1034 containers of books in comparison to 459 containers in 2000. This is almost 20 containers a week. We produced approximately 5,500 titles for publishing clients all over the world, equating to approximately 47 million books. All these books required 24,000 pallets – which would, if laid end to end, easily span the English Channel between Dover and Cape Gris-Nez. Go check out http://www.macmillan.com.hk/ for more on our Asian developments.

11 January 2006

Railway stations

When I joined Macmillan my office was based just by Victoria Station in Central London. I had mixed memories of that particular station as it was the departure point for my prep school in Kent. The terror and abject misery of saying goodbye to my parents on the platform at Victoria at the age of nine remains with me. But that was not the reason we moved our main London location to next door to Kings Cross station in North London. The real reason was, as usual in publishing, cost. Some publishers have very grand buildings. We reckon our authors and our customers would rather we had efficient and economic work environments and spent the money on better and better value books and journals.

In any event we moved amid much concern from staff that the Kings Cross area is more famous for its prostitutes and drug pushers than publishing. And since the move things have changed radically. The main terminal for trains to and from Europe is being built and the whole area is being redeveloped in the biggest reconstruction project in Western Europe.

Right next door to us a new building complex is emerging from the clay as I write and following this link – http://www.kingsplace.co.uk/ – will give you some idea of the new Kings Cross environment with a concert hall, sculpture gallery, posh restaurants and the Guardian newspaper (http://www.guardian.co.uk/) as founding tenants.

Of course, all this activity means that our properties in the area are increasing in value – but I don't think we can face another move to an alternative London railway station just yet.

And now to Africa

Macmillan is a truly global company, and its staff in every corner of that globe constantly amaze me with their determination and ballsiness – not only in their working lives. I have just discovered that a group of colleagues from Macmillan Education in Oxford recently trekked to the summit of Mount Kilimanjaro. Publishing Manager Dorothy Robertson, Sales Director Steve Tweed, Publisher Tom Hardy, Commissioning Editor Jon Beck, Web Manager Tim Oliver, Mr. Khalaf Rashid, MD of Macmillan Aidan in Tanzania and Iain Baxendine, Group Project Accountant, as well as some of their partners, all braved the effects of the extreme altitude and proved their strength as a team in aid of charity projects that will really benefit the region: an agricultural project in Malawi; an education project for teenage girls in Zambia; a village project in Mozambique and a scheme to rebuild a school in Swaziland.

13 January 2006

Walking back to happiness

It's Friday and thoughts turn to weekend activities. In a few Sundays' time some of you might like to consider the 'Flirt Walk,' organized this year by the British Heart Foundation in conjunction with my King's Cross co-inhabitants, PARSHIP. Whether you are a fearless flirt or a hopeless romantic, the Flirt Walk offers an opportunity to 'find the mate of your dreams' whilst taking part in the 'biggest outdoor matchmaking event in the UK!' The Flirt Walk takes place on Sunday 12th February 2006 in London's Hyde Park. Register now at www.bhf.org.uk/events. For more information about Parship see www.parship.co.uk or read about it in The Times at http://women.timesonline.co.uk .

15 January 2006

Independent bookselling

Susan Hill's piece on this blog (also in the Guardian newspaper http://books.guardian.co.uk/comment/story/0,,1685920,00.html) has certainly stirred up the British book-loving and book-selling population. Last Friday the British Publishers Association were invited by the Competition Commission committee investigating the proposed takeover of the Ottakars bookshop chain by HMV who also own the Waterstones chain. The committee was extraordinarily well-informed and perceptive in their questioning but I had the impression that they found the whole book business overcomplicated and slightly apart from normal economic principles. What was not in doubt was the importance of books to the cultural and educational environment and that diversity of choice in the type of book and the type of retailer is vital. Somehow we have to ensure that diversity through sustainable unsubsidised economic models. Susan's argument is about how to improve the independent sector through better bookselling. My argument would be how do we make the independent sector more economically viable without publishers sacrificing their and their authors' viability.

PS This blog has now had its 5000th visitor in less than a month. No big deal compared with my favourite site (www.cricinfo.com) but I am pleased. I've been hurt by one remark that I write and look like Michael Winner (http://www.waitrose.com/food_drink/wfi/foodpeople) but by and large people have been remarkably kind. Thanks.

16 January 2006

E-Read all about it

I have been quoted in an Observer article by Robert McCrum all about the future of the book, digitisation and all that – see http://books.guardian.co.uk/ebooks

The article describes the book trade in Britain as vigorous and supports this with statistics. The article quotes 161,000 titles being published in the UK in 2005 a near tripling since 1990. I am sure the bare facts are correct but they are not a reflection of the truth. The unit of measurement is the ISBN – the international standard book number. Every book has one. And so does every audiobook. And every variation of that audiobook – tape, CD, tape and book. And every variation of the book – hardback, airport paperback, posh format paperback, mass-market paperback, compact hardback etc. And so does every academic monograph with a print run of 200. And every rejacketed film tie-in and re-issue. As publishers search for every nook and cranny to promote and repromote their authors' titles so there has been hyperinflation of the ISBN. Someone somewhere will know what the actual increase of title output is (and I am sure there has been an increase). I wish there was an accurate measure if only to show the world that the publishing industry actually knows what its business is.

17 January 2006

Reasons to be Cheerful Part 2

Quite apart from being pleasantly surprised by my blog statistics, the real reason to be cheerful is that Souvenir Press (which does not have a website but whose titles are listed at http://isbndb.com/d/publisher/souvenir_press.html) is 55 years old this year. It is an entirely idiosyncratic general publisher and wonderful because of that. But the real reason for being cheerful is that Ernest Hecht, its founder and Arsenal supporter has clearly discovered the secret of eternal youth. This is him aged three:

. . . and as photographed recently:

🗓 18 January 2006

Bits and bytes and things that go bump in the night

I attended a very constructive meeting yesterday with the Society of Authors (http://www.societyofauthors.net/). the Association of Authors' Agents (http://www.agentsassoc.co.uk/) and the Publishers association (http://www.publishers.org.uk/).

The agenda was digital rights and how authors and publishers can work together to ensure that creativity is both rewarded and protected while still allowing us to take advantage of the enormous opportunities offered by the Internet and other digital distribution channels. This is easier said than done. The issues are complex and far-reaching and all constituents have a slightly different perspective. Fortunately our industry is populated with intelligent and patient people. My worry is that we are too patient. The successful inhabitants of the Internet deal in nanoseconds. Book publishing deals in Spring and Autumn (Fall) lists. We're going to have to change our perceptions of time and timeliness if we are to succeed in helping our authors reach out to readers electronically as well as in print – and the authors will need to work with us to achieve this.

PS During the meeting which was held in the boardroom of a major publisher I noticed (surprisingly for the first time) that boardroom is an anagram of Broadmoor, the British establishment for the imprisonment of mentally ill criminals. I wonder whether this explains some of the decisions made in the higher levels of most companies.

🗓 19 January 2006

Tim Waterstone

There has been a huge amount of newsprint (and blog space) in the UK dedicated to the proposed takeover of Ottakars chain of bookshops by the Waterstone's chain, owned by HMV (http://www.hmvgroup.com/).

The Waterstone's chain was founded in 1983 by Tim Waterstone. He also founded the toyshop chain, Daisy and Tom (http://www.daisyandtom.com/) which is now part of Early Learning Center (http://www.elc.co.uk/).

The thing about Tim's career is that at almost every point he followed his instincts rather than the herd. For instance,when he opened the first Waterstone's store books clearly had little growth potential – the market then proceeded to grow by 5% per annum.

He is publishing a book about how to create your own business and and make your life. It's called Swimming against the Stream. Waterstone's stores are stocking it of course but you can also get it from Amazon or from the Pan Bookshop by emailing panbookshop@btclick.com.

🐦 20 January 2006

Write for Africa

Various themes seem to be emerging on this blog. One of them is a taste for all things African, which I guess is only natural with Macmillan's commitment to the region. First time writers from Ghana and Nigeria and a midwife from Uganda have triumphed as winners of the third Macmillan Writer's Prize for Africa, the only prize to promote the best in unpublished African fiction for children and young people. This year some 600 entries were submitted by writers from 19 different countries across the continent and from African writers living overseas. You can read more about the prize and the winners at www.write4africa.com but as a taster, here are a couple of the award-winning illustrations by Enoch Yaw Mensah, who won the Macmillan Children's Illustrator Award this year.

🐦 21 January 2006

Rapture

Poetry is a very small part of contemporary publishing in money terms but generates debate, controversy and emotion. Remember when Oxford University Press cancelled its poetry list? It is also regarded as an essential part of being a literary publisher and Picador has therefore been investing heavily in building a very special poetry list and in working with the very best poets around. The announcement therefore last week that Carol Ann Duffy had won the highly prestigious T.S.Eliot poetry prize cheered everyone at Picador as well as Carol Ann's growing following.

The judges said, 'This year's TS Eliot prize highlights a (some would say) rare moment of agreement between the critics and the booksellers as to what constitutes great poetry'. The judges' chairman, David Constantine, called Rapture 'a coherent and passionate collection'.

Who killed the Whale?

Something happened in London this weekend which brought out everything which is silly and somehow loveable about the British. A 19 foot female northern bottle-nosed whale strayed into the River Thames . . . and instantly caused a silly-season style media frenzy at the same time as bringing a state of anarchy to the capital.

Joining the crowds who rushed to the river banks, willing the now dubbed 'Thames Whale' to live with an ardency that only a nation of animal lovers could summon, I was amazed to note the complete disregard for the rules and behaviours that govern our usually polite society. The scenes would have been rich pickings for anthropologists such as Kate Fox, whose brilliant book, 'Watching the English' makes such acute observations on the qualities of being English. Apparently a slew of parking tickets were issued as whale-crazed citizens stranded their cars willy-nilly to get a sighting of the whale. But perhaps only in Britain could the resulting outrage lead to those parking tickets being overturned . . .

This morning I read that 'Thames Whale is to stay in London'. The mammal's remains are to be given to the Natural History Museum after a post-mortem examination has been carried out by the Zoological Society of London. Newspaper articles with headlines such as 'Who killed the whale' fuelled speculation that sonar from Royal Navy vessels made the whale disorientated and led to it straying into the Thames. The British media's requirement to find a scapegoat is clearly as strong as ever.

Perhaps the funniest story of all, though, is that the red watering can used to douse Thames Whale during the 36 hour rescue attempt is being sold on eBay in order to raise money for further rescues of stranded marine life. As of this morning there have been 101 bids, with the latest bid putting it at £6,450. The auction page features the headline, 'Own a symbol of hope and a piece of history.' So, as sales of watering cans rocket nationwide, I wonder, will sales of Moby Dick increase exponentially as well? Maybe, but what I really hope is that every parent will now realize the importance of purchasing a copy of The Snail and the Whale by Julia Donaldson and Axel Scheffler (wrong kind of whale I know, but still . . .). It's published by Macmillan Children's Books of course and available from your local bookstore or from Amazon.

🐦 24 January 2006

Of whales and amazon

My last posting has upset a reader, excellent commentator and quality bookseller because I recommended buying a book from 'your local bookstore or from Amazon'. The sin I committed was to link the book title to Amazon. Okay, I am guilty as hell. Can I plead mitigation? I was editing the piece on a Blackberry. I wanted to link to the Pan Macmillan website but it was being upgraded so the link didn't work. I then thought of the Pan Bookshop but I had done that before and I didn't want to appear one-sided. And then I thought of independent bookstores, but which one? And then I thought 'your local bookstore'. And then I thought but I'd better make it easy for bloggers to link to a website and so I added Amazon – but the link doesn't go direct to the book because that was too hard to do on a Blackberry. So mea culpa but it wasn't exactly thoughtless . . .

🐦 25 January 2006

Even more on whales and things

Latest bulletin. The watering can used to keep the Thames whale comfortable when beached is being auctioned on eBay for charity. Latest bid is £112,600. I don't know the meaning of all this but the watering can seems to have joined the whale in the pantheon of iconic marketing images. Some enterprising souls have also put Thames

Whale magnets, commemorative T-shirts and even a cross-stitch kit up for sale on eBay. There must be a lesson here on how to seize the opportunity – suggestions welcome. Unfortunately it seems that the bidding for the watering can contains some phoneys – that's life – see The Inquirer

Electronic publishing is the focus of attention in the world of publishing right now. I was, therefore, pleased to notice that Macmillan's worldwide sales of slates, abacuses and chalk exceeded $5m last year. Perhaps the abacus is the new marketing icon?

28 January 2006

Record downloads and a sponsorship deal for Nature podcast

I don't want this blog to become a repository for Macmillan press releases – apparently that would make this a 'plog', half way between a 'blog' and a 'plug' – but this one from Nature Publishing Group somehow appealed to me . . .

The Nature podcast from Nature Publishing Group (NPG) has successfully completed its pilot phase with a record number of downloads and a sponsorship agreement with Bio-Rad Laboratories. This signals its graduation from an innovative experiment to a fully-fledged service for the scientific community.

The Nature Podcast was launched in October 2005, making it one of the first scientific podcasts to be released by a journal. It quickly climbed into the iTunes Top 50 in the US, the UK and other countries, and since then has continued to enjoy rapid week-on-week increases in popularity. The number of weekly downloads is now well over 30,000 and continues to grow.

This marks the end of the pilot phase for the Nature Podcast, which NPG now intends to provide as a regular service, while continuing to evolve the content and format in response to audience feedback. (A listener survey is currently underway.)

This week's show also marks the beginning of sponsorship by Bio-Rad Laboratories. Timo Hannay, NPG's Director of Web Publishing, said: 'We are delighted that Bio-Rad shares our vision for this exciting new medium. We have already received a hugely positive response from listeners. Bio-Rad's support will allow us to continue making the show even better.'

31 January 2006

Delhi Book Fair

Just back from a two-day trip to Delhi for board meetings of Macmillan India, MPS Technologies and Charon Tec (http://www.macmillanindia.com/) – and a quick visit to the Delhi Book Fair. I have a prejudice against book fairs. They seem to cost a lot and achieve a little. Publishers meeting publishers. Publishers lying to publishers. Booksellers complaining about publishers. Literary agents hyping books. Much gossip little action. But Delhi was different. Its primary purpose is to stimulate interest in books among children and to sell books to the general public. Hurray. A simple concept but it seems to work. Eighteen halls were packed and the book trade was outnumbered by real people for a change. Pictures will appear on this blog in due course.

The rest of the trip was all about our business and how we can grow it even faster. We have more employees in India (2500) than any other country and the number is increasing rapidly. Education is seen as the highest priority and every state government is committed to improving literacy at the primary level, general skills at the secondary level and the highest standards of research and scholarship within universities. We are investing in new courses for schools at all levels and in many languages, in textbooks for universities, in the creation of Nature Publishing Group India, in developing electronic infrastructures for publishers within MPS Technologies and bulding a significant operation in book and journal text processing in Bangalore, Chennai, Delhi and elsewhere.

The scale of India is frightening. The opportunities are immense – which reminds me . . .

At a recent meeting in Basingstoke a colleague remarked that a particular initiative by a competitor was 'awesome'. Another colleague responded by saying that we don't want to be awesome, we want to be professional. Macmillan studiously avoids having a mission statement (thank God) but if we were to I would favour: Macmillan – awesome ain't us.

≤ **February 2006** ≥

Mon	Tue	Wed	Thu	Fri	Sat	Sun
30	31	1	2	3	4	5
6	7	8	9	10	11	12
13	14	15	16	17	18	19
20	21	22	23	24	25	26
27	28	1	2	3	4	5
6	7	8	9	10	11	12

Charchive

Spectator goes digital

Some very old friends of mine have started Exact Editions http://www.exacteditions.com – a new system for digital magazines. Their service has been in beta-test for a couple of months and today the shop opened with one title – The Spectator. Plenty more to come apparently.

The current issue of the magazine is in the shop as a free sample so follow the link to see how the service works

http://www.exacteditions.com

A subscription to the online Spectator costs £57.50 and for the price you get a steadily growing archive – right now 30 back issues are in the collection. The searching is fast and effective. A quick test drive confirms my suspicion that the Conservative party is on a new wave . The Spectator has 7 mentions of 'Dave Cameron' but 'David Cameron' features 118 times. I suspect the 'Dave' will wither on the vine as he seeks weighty status. There are 53 sightings of 'Margaret Thatcher' but only 14 for 'Harold Macmillan'. It is clear that the editors are not giving enough attention to Supermac . . . . . .

The principals of Exact Editions previously founded xrefer http://www.xrefer.com the leading reference book aggregator. I think they may have found another new business using the web to find new readers and new income streams for publishers. I don't suppose may non-British readers have ever seen the 'Speccy' – so enjoy!

🐦 04 February 2006

Mission Statements

I was at a conference on search technology in Munich last week and my thoughts turned to the mission statements of the big webonaut companies.

Google's mission is to organize the world's information and make it universally accessible and useful.

AOL's Mission is to build a global medium as central to people's lives as the telephone or television . . . and even more valuable.

Yahoo's mission is to be the most essential global Internet service for consumers and businesses.

To enable people and businesses throughout the world to realize their full potential.

The word which comes to mind is 'immodest'. Do the people who work in these companies actually think their mission is achievable? Do they want to achieve it? Does anyone else want them to achieve it? Perhaps we would be less suspicious of these organisations' motives if they toned down (or, perish the thought, abandoned) these absurd and ultimately meaningless strings of words.

And then I thought I'd better check out some publishers:

'Reed Elsevier's Science & Medical mission is to be an integral partner with the scientific, technical and medical communities, delivering superior information products and services that foster communication, build insights, and enable individual and collective advancement in scientific research and health care.' This seemed OK until I dug a bit more and found 'To fuel a continuous cycle of exploration and discovery and inspire meaningful action' on a later page.

'Pearson help people of all ages to get the most out of their lives.' More modest than Google but I'm not sure that books and newspapers come first on most people's life wishlist.

Hachette's is much more down-to-earth, albeit somewhat strange grammatically – 'Its mission as a publisher of quality works for all audiences is concentrated on the general literature, textbook and illustrated book market segments.'

I'm afraid that Macmillan doesn't have a mission statement at all. Perhaps we should – and all suggestions welcome. Meanwhile my favourite (after last weeks 'Awesome we ain't') is 'We're doing our best'. Seems a pretty reasonable mission.

06 February 2006

Nature's Mission

Maxine Clarke has reminded me through her comment on Saturday's blog that at least one part of Macmillan (Nature, the world's top science journal) has a mission statement. The current one is practical and fine but I prefer the original one from 11 November 1869 which can be found at
http://www.nature.com/nature/about/mission.pdf

It clearly says what the journal aims to achieve and how it will achieve these objectives. Hooray.

I also like the line-cut illustration and the quote from Wordsworth.

09 February 2006

Copyright, competition and collegiality

It's been an interesting couple of days. A conference on the future of copyright including an address by the James Purnell who isMinister for the Creative Industries inthe Department of Culture, Media and Sport of the British Government. The conference was organised by a think tank- the IPPR.

There is little doubt that the digital revolution is making some aspects of copyright legislation look clunky. There is also little doubt that there is pressure from some quarters for information to be universally available and free of charge. My own view is that copyright has been an amazingly effective tool for encouraging and rewarding creativity and for ensuring mass distribution of information largely unfettered (at least in most Western countries) by political or sectarian interference. We should do everything possible to ensure that copyright legislation is held where it isand strengthened in places. Any weakening of copyright would severely damage culture, education, commerce and freedom of speech.

And then the Publishers Association second hearing with the Competition Commisssion on the question of the HMV Group's proposed takeover of its rival bookshop chain, Ottakar's.

Our argument is that the merger would reduce competition in the quality or specialist bookselling arena. The trouble with that is in defining specialist bookselling. We all know how a 'real' bookshop differs from a retail outlet which happens to sell a few books but economists need definitions not descriptions. Our second argument is that the merger would reduce consumer choice – the number of titles readily available to be purchased would diminish. And our third argument was that it would be much harder for new talent to emerge. We are all sending in slews of information to help the Commission come to its conclusion.

Yesterday afternoon and evening saw an excellent and productive meeting between publishers and literary agents where we discussed openly the challenges facing our industry and how we can work more closely together to ensure authors can reach the widest audience and be rewardedappropriately notwithstanding the quantity and severity of the challenges.

But what struck me most about the meeting – and indeed the other meetings was how lucky we are in the book industry to have so many articulate, intelligent, open, committed and personable colleagues. I was dreading being President of the Publishers Association and I will, frankly, be relieved when I hand over to my successor in the Spring but the job has been made hugely enjoyable by the interactions with my fellow publishers, booksellers, authors and agents – I never thought I'd say that!

11 February 2006

Octopus Stew

I liked what my friend Adam Hodgkin of Exact Editions had to say about copyrights and the web so much that I asked him whether I could use it as a guest entry on my blog. Here's what he said:

Interesting to have the link to the IPPR think tank on your blog. Apparently, 40 years ago a Harvard Law Professor anticipated something like the web and postulated that copyright would need to 'bend' as copying became easier and computer networks became more powerful. He wrote a book, 'An Unhurried View of Copyright', published by Columbia UP and now republished by Matthew Bender.

Isn't this a rather brilliant visionary quote?

'You must imagine, at the eventual heart of things to come, linked or integrated systems or networks of computers capable of storing faithful simulacra of the entire treasure of the accumulated knowledge and artistic production of past ages, and of taking into the store new intelligence of all sorts as produced. . . . Lasers (and) satellites (among others) will operate as ganglions to extend the reach of the systems to the ultimate users . . . .'

But it is interesting to note that Professor Kaplan's thoughts still merit a reprint and the book carries a $95 price, even though the powerful system he prophesies has come to pass.

It's a wonderful passage, but I am glad that Tim Berners Lee thought of the metaphor of the 'world wide web'. Somehow I don't think the invention would have taken off if he had called it the 'global ganglion gallimaufrey'. Sounds more like octopus stew . . . .

Tradition

You may notice that this appears to be from tomorrow but that's because I'm in Sydney where, as everyone knows, you get up before the rest of the world (apart from New Zealand of course) goes to bed. Anyway, I'll keep this short because it isn't easy writing a blog on makeshift hardware in a hotel room.

A tradition is about to be broken at Wisden (www.wisden.com or www.cricinfo.com) of which I am proud to be a director. For the first time in history, an edition of the revered work is going to be published in a more traditional book format and with type which its average purchaser can actually read. There is an article about it in yesterday's London Times – http://www.timesonline.co.uk/article/0,,22669-2038005,00.html

There are bound to be complainants but I have seen specimen pages and I think the simple idea of increasing the size will be a huge success and that much of the excellent non-statistical articles will be read by a significant audience for the first time. Of course the original small format yellow editions will still be published but I hope this larger version will become an alternative and friendly non-traditional competitor.

Incidentally, I had a small bet on England to win the Ashes last Summer. Any advice on whether I should double or quits? This will all be incomprehensible to most American readers of this blog for which my apologies.

14 February 2006

Valentine's Day

I know it was Valentine's Day yesterday because nearly every restaurant in Melbourne was booked out. Love was in the air clearly which reminded me of a very strange book we are publishing this April, proofs of which I read on the plane coming here.

The book is called Lonesome George: The life and loves of a conservation icon by Henry Nicholls. It is the fascinating and gripping story of George, the last of a particular species of giant tortoises who lives on one of the Galapagos islands. Efforts to find him a mate in order to perpetuate his genes (not the exact same species but similar) have failed. He may be gay. He may just not know how to do it although he has been shown many times – live tortoise sex shows feature. That is the light-hearted side. The real story of extinction, environmental damage, evolution is completely absorbing and worrying.

But apart from the content there is a publishing story. This is part of a series called Macmillan Science which publishes popular science. The trouble with popular science is that it is hard to get literary people excited about it and to achieve economic sales levels. This problem has been compounded by one or two authors selling very well and a few publishers then offering absurdly high advances because science might be trendy for a nanosecond.

Macmillan Science does not offer advances but it does pay very competitive royalties. It does not attempt to fill bookshops with more copies than they can possible sell. It only acquires world rights and thus can publish in English simulatneously in the main markets of the USA and UK. We believe that promoting the books through our own publications – Nature and Scientific American – is the way to stimulate word of mouth which in turn is by far the best marketing tool available. This all, I hope, sounds obvious. But persuading the various bits of the book trade that not buying books through auctions, that not dividing up territorial rights, by dealing with the authors direct rather than through literary agents makes sense has been tough. The other thing we do, of course, is to have a brilliant and knowledgeable editor committed to her authors and committed to ensuring that the books get maximum exposure in spite of the lack of traditional hype.

We haven't made a profit yet (but not a loss either) but I am hoping that Lonesome George will become the new Longitude. It deserves to. Read more about him at http://www.macmillanscience.com/1403945764.htm

15 February 2006

An offer from Susan Hill

Susan Hill of Long Barn Books asked me to post the following – and I thought I'd oblige, because I like her style:

Word seems to be out that I hate small independent bookshops. Rubbish. People who actually read what I said know I hate BAD small indies. Good ones are terrific. And to prove it, I am making them an offer they ought to look at twice. Last year, Long Barn Books started looking for a first novel to publish in 2006. There were 3,741 entries, out of which the head and shoulders winner was THE EXTRA LARGE MEDIUM by HELEN SLAVIN. It will be published on May 9th and has a fantastic quote from Beryl Bainbridge on the cover because BB loved the book and thinks highly of Helen's writing. There will be loads of media coverage . . . . can a good small independent afford to be without this novel ?

Not when the discount is 50% they can't.

The offer is for 3 or more copies ordered at one time and it is for all the GOOD SMALL INDEPENDENT BOOKSHOPS out there.

If you think you qualify, e-mail me editorial@longbarnbooks.com to pre order.

16 February 2006

Aussie News

I thought you'd like to be kept abreast of the most important news stories from down under.

Front page business story – Ansell has paid $24.7m for a 75% stake in condom distributor Jissbon (Wuhan) sanitary Products. Jissbon is a Chinese translation of James Bond, reported CEO James Tough.

Pamela Anderson has written to Prime Minister John Howard asking him to tackle the practices of live export and mulesing, in which skin is cut from a sheep's rump to prevent maggot infestation.

The upright Australian Government is a little embarrassed by its monopolistic Wheat Board's paying of bribes to Sadaam and his cronies. Nobody seems very surprised. The PM expects the people of Iraq to sympathise with the agonies that Australia's little farmers will suffer if sales fall. If the people of Iraq do indeed feel the need to bail out Mr Howard there might be a surprise.

Apparently James Packer thinks his dad is enjoying an afterlife in spite of Kerry's earlier assertion that he'd been to the other side and there's nothing there. More surprising is that James thinks his dad is in heaven rather than anywhere else.

17 February 2006

The point of no return

Arrived in Auckland this morning. New Zealand is famous for many things – kiwis, Lord of the Rings, sailing, rugby, kauri trees, Edmund Hillary, Rachel Hunter, Russell Crowe (although many New Zealanders would rather he became Australian officially) and of course Kiri Te Kanawa.

In order to overcome the 'tyranny of distance' and to compete in global markets New Zealanders have had to become street wise. Imagine a book retail market where supplies are eight weeks away by ship, where competing editions arrive unannouced, where the total market is one sixtieth of the USA and one fifth of Australia, where consumer expectations of currency and choice are as high as anywhere in the world.

How have publishers managed to serve bookshops and readers without going bust? Well, one explanation is that New Zealand is essentially a firm sale market. When a bookshop orders a book the responsibility for selling it is theirs. If it does not sell, the cost of the mistake belongs to the bookseller not to the author.

Are there millions of unsold books washing around New Zealand bookshops? No. Booksellers have had to develop a sense of their market and they have – New Zealand booksellers are the best in the world and they sell the most books per head in the English-speaking world.

If only . . . .

20 February 2006

Don't Cry for Me

Continuing my down-under trip I've arrived in Argentina to review our two businesses. I'd heard the route from Auckland to Buenos Aires via Santiago would take me over (under?) the South Pole – it's all a rumour, there was nothing but sea, not even an iceberg. I'm delighted to see that I seem to have returned to the same date as most of the world but it hasn't done great things for my jetlag. So I'll keep it short.

If you want to visit one of the most beautiful countries in the world at a ludicrously favourable exchange rate, Argentina is the place. And if you want to experience creative publishing in a difficult environment go visit:

http://www.cantaro.com.ar/

http://www.macmillan.com.ar/

http://www.puertodepalos.com.ar/

Incidentally. Puerto de Palos is the port in Spain from where Christopher Columbus set off to discover the Americas. The company's logo represents the ship in which he sailed and is in my view and in the words of Goldilocks 'just right'. And don't forget to switch up the volume when you open the last link.

With Chris West, Regional Director Latin America (centre) and Raul Gonzalez, Chief Executive of Puerto de Palos, at Estancia Villa Maria, Buenos Aires.

With the Puerto de Palos and Mexico teams, Buenos Aires

26 February 2006

Size isn't everything

I thought the physical effects of travelling around the world in just over a week were pretty shattering . . . but not as shattering as the shock of Scotland beating England at rugby yesterday. I was watching it in a bar in Kilkenny in Ireland. It was made worse by my losing €10 betting on England to win by 15 points. And the agony of seeing Willie Anderson of John Smith's bookshop chain picking up €55 betting on Scotland. The populations of Scotland, Ireland and New Zealand (where I was the previous weekend) together total less than a fifth of the England and yet it looks like they are all going to beat us (Ireland play us on March 18 but I fear the worst).

Kilkenny (http://www.kilkennytourism.ie/) is famous for its castle. Wolfe Tone and an insightful limerick:

There once were two cats of Kilkenny,
Each thought there was one cat too many,
So they fought and they fit,
And they scratched and they bit,
Till, excepting their nails
And the tips of their tails,
Instead of two cats, there weren't any.

I was there for the annual conference of Irish Branch of the Booksellers Association – an event well-known throughout the book trade for its serious discussion, valuable insights, and most importantly its late-night parties. The optimism of most of the Irish trade is in contrast to the UK and it really lifts the spirits. The gala dinner was memorable for three events:

1. The award of an iPod to Michael Gill for services to the Irish book trade and for being a great guy. Michael has just retired as Managing Director of Gill and Macmillan (http://www.gillmacmillan.ie/) but remains Chairman while Dermot O'Dwyer replaces him.

2. An after-dinner speech by John McGahern (http://www.laoisedcentre.ie/LENGLISH/engrwww/mcgah.html) which was wonderfully witty, poetic . . . and short. If only every speech combined those qualities.

3. Having hot gravy poured down the back of my suit (serves me right for bowing to dress orthodoxy and wearing suit and tie).

28 February 2006

False Impression

On most matters most people are indifferent – at least in Britain, which is what makes this country such a great place. There is , however, one author on whom nearly everyone has a view – he is a best seller, he is a star raiser of funds for charity, he is an advocate of radical prison reform, he is hugely successful businessman, and at one time a political heavyweight. He is, of course, Jeffrey Archer, Baron Archer of Weston-super-Mare and we publish his latest novel in Britain this week. You can find information on False Impression at http://www.false-impression.co.uk/.

The book has already appeared in the Southern Hemisphere and has broken all his previous records. We were very nearly able to announce that England had won a second Ashes series when he came close to toppling Steve Waugh's autobiography from the number one slot in Australia. (For non-cricket-understanding citizens of the world, Steve Waugh was captain of the finest Australian cricket team ever and, amazingly, a good guy too). For more information go to:

http://content-uk.cricinfo.com/ci/content/player/8192.html

In any event, Jeffrey is one of the most professional authors and promoters around and we are proud to be his publisher worldwide. False Impression is the best novel he's ever written and we are looking forward to amazing sales.

I can also add that he is a pleasure to work with and a good friend. I also predict that my writing this might generate an interesting dialogue with those who only want to look back rather than forward and who like to think the worst of people.

≤ **March 2006** ≥

Mon	Tue	Wed	Thu	Fri	Sat	Sun
27	28	1	2	3	4	5
6	7	8	9	10	11	12
13	14	15	16	17	18	19
20	21	22	23	24	25	26
27	28	29	30	31	1	2
3	4	5	6	7	8	9

01 March 2006

The right to publish

I am involved in this conference:

http://www.publishinginnovation.com/

It is an eclectic mix of themes from national security to diversity. It sounds a bit politically correct for my taste but these are clearly issues of interest to the students at the London College of Comunications. The College is a fantastic place and in addition to the highest standards of teaching I can recommend the sausage sandwiches in their canteen.

Incidentally, for those of you interested in electronic publishing here's a link to a revived electronic journal with a very interesting article on Google and Trust.

http://www.hti.umich.edu/j/jep/

02 March 2006

World Book Day

I'm just back from a Tony Blair attending event to launch World Book Day (http://www.worldbookday.com/). It was packed and a tribute to all the people – authors, publishers, trade associations, librarians, booksellers, Arts Council, UNESCO, Book Tokens, sponsors etc – who put in so much time, effort and in many cases money. WBD is a really great institution which encourages reading at all ages and at all levels. I am sure it helps improve literacy in the UK.

What I'm not quite sure about is why it's called World Book Day. There is hardly a mention of it anywhere in the world except the UK. Now I know we think that Britain is the centre of the universe but . . .

The other mystery is how so many publishers (including me) found time to be there. What is it about the presence of a senior politician that attracts even the most cynical anarchists to rub shoulders with the mighty. Actually, you don't even get to rub shoulders. You get to see the great man on a video screen because the main room is overflowing with the real VIPs. Ah well, it's all in a good cause although I sometimes wonder whether it would be better not to have a launch and spend the money on more events in schools and libraries or even more books for libraries . . . .

03 March 2006

Good news week

Congratulations to John Banville on winning the first Irish Book Award for Irish Novel of the Year for The Sea:

http://www.rte.ie/arts/2006/0302/irishbookawards.html

This follows, of course, his triumph in the Man Booker. I have always loved John's books ever since The Book of Evidence but my favourite has to be The Untouchable for the entirely egocentric reason that one of the characters is called Charkin – the only Charkin in literature I am certain.

There are two words I occasionally use on this blog which seem to generate the most correspondence, verging on hate mail – Amazon and Archer. Well, the two came together this week when Jeffrey's False Impression went straight to number one on Amazon. It is now number two behind a Lennart Nilsson picture book and ahead of the new Stephen King. And in spite of one or two literary zealots the reviews are excellent.

Yesterday I had my most fun day of the year, interviewing the latest crop of would-be Macmillan graduate recruits. What happens is that the several hundred applications are weeded by two very expert colleagues, then a longlist of interviews and then I get to see the last few. They were (and usually are) all terrific and we shall be offering them all a place in the scheme. Goodness knows what it is about publishing which tickles their fancy or what we do to deserve such great entrants when they could earn twice as much in banking or law. I am simply grateful that publishing can still attract the very best people.

Finally, this week's good news must include the launch of University College London's Centre for Publishing – http://www.publishing.ucl.ac.uk/. As our industry moves from paper-based to digital, from content to context, from national to global, from instinctive to analytical there is a growing need for proper research and understanding. The academic team being assembled is excellent and the facilities and support of the university are strong. We are very lucky to have this resource to add to the several other educational and research establishments in the UK.

05 March 2006

London Book Fair

Today sees the opening of the London Book Fair (http://www.lbf-virtual.com/) if London Transport allows visitors to reach the exhibition hall in less than two hours.

Book Fairs tend to coincide with journalists scraping barrels for something bookish to write about. At a time when the industry is undergoing fundamental change, threats and opportunities the distinguished literary editor of the discriminating and excellent Observer newspaper has decided that the key issue is a list of the fifty most powerful people in British publishing – http://books.guardian.co.uk/comment/story/0,,1723699,00.html.

It is an entertaining list and shows some insight and will no doubt generate debate – but it also underscores the narrow vision of most publishing commentators. With due respect to Amanda Ross (Richard and Judy TV show), Caroline Ridding (buyer at the Tesco supermarket chain) and Diana Guy (Chair of the Competition Commission investigating the takeover of one bookshop chain by another) who are the top three in Robert's list this is simply nonsense. Each of them has a significant role in the book trade (mainly time limited) but it is patently absurd (inverted snobbery at play?) and plain silly to pretend they are the most powerful people in a trade which encompasses scholarship, education, literacy, technology and creativity.

Robert describes me (over-promoted at number 23) as provocative. I suspect he is trying to gain a similar reputation. He cannot possibly believe his list has any meaning at all. I don't even suppose it will sell many newspapers.

Yours ever

Pooter

07 March 2006

Letter from Germany

This comes from snowy Stuttgart where my blog seems to have transmogrified itself into German – ain't technology wonderful?

The main conversations here all relate to the chances of the German football team in the upcoming World Cup. People are pretty pessimistic but we English know better. Apart from a glitch (or should it be glitsch) in 1966 Germany always wins – at least against England, and everyone knows that that is the only match which really counts.

And while on global domination it seems that my friends at Google have been doing some excellent public relations at the London Book Fair. I introduced several Google managers to the joys of the Chelsea Arts Club on Sunday evening and am hoping that the experience will have shocked them into understanding publishers' concerns, changing their policy with regard to the digitisation of in copyright books and maybe even changing their overblown mission statement!

I've been asked to plug my friend Susan Hill's new website, so here goes: http://www.longbarnbooks.com/.

I've also been sent instructions on how to hyperlink which I'll do as soon as I learn the ropes.

And yesterday was the highest visitor numbers for this blog. Hooray for Robert McCrum.

The joy of walking

You may see that I have added a link to London Cross. This is strange but appealing idea for a 'book' describing absolutely everything you see if you walk across London in a straight line from two staring starting points. I walk a huge amount in London and so naturally empathise with the idea.

I have yet to find a better way to get round London or most other cities. It takes very little longer than a taxi or a bus. It makes you (slightly) fitter. It allows you to make phone calls and send emails without being arrested (although there is admittedly a risk of being run over). It increases the chances of unexpectedly meeting old friends. It forces you to minimise the amount of paper transported. It allows you to listen to great music or Test Match Special without feeling guilty.It is very cheap.

When I have a spare weekend I'm going to attempt Paul K Lyons's routes in London Cross.

On a completely separate note, there was much wringing of hands when we announced a new fiction imprint, Macmillan New Writing. Dedicated solely to publishing authors' first novels submitted to Macmillan in the UK – usually direct rather than through an agent – the initiative was attacked by some sections of the press as a commercial gimmick and was called 'the Ryanair of publishing' by The Guardian.

However, it has since attracted widespread support from authors, the book trade and the publishing business press, and I'm pleased to see that as we near the launch of the first six novels, my fellow blogger the Grumpy Old Bookman has offered his <u>sanguine opinion.</u>

09 March 2006

Indian Ink

One of the most dynamic areas of business right now is India, where Macmillan India is already a leading provider of typesetting, copyediting, project management, digitisation, graphics, software and technology services to major publishers in UK, Europe and the US. The company is already a global leader in services to scientific journal publishers. With its recent acquisition of <u>Interactive Composition Corp (ICC)</u> – and before that <u>Charon Tec</u> in Chennai – it is now also a major supplier of full services to book publishers.

ICC is based in Portland, Oregon with a wholly owned subsidiary in Delhi. It employs 300 people and provides typesetting and other services to major book publishers in the US. This is a strategic acquisition . It enables us to achieve two major objectives of having a significant presence in the US to maintain close and efficient service levels for our customers, and enhancing our Indian management and workforce.

<u>Macmillan India</u> now employs more than 3000 people in Bangalore, Chennai, Delhi, Kolkata, Mumbai and many other cities. Unlike many publishers following the herd into India, Macmillan has been there since 1893, fifty years after the original foundation of the firm, and it is a real part of the social, educational and informational infrastructure of the country.

11 March 2006

Powerplay

Predictably, the Observer's silly list of powerful people in the UK book trade has generated a fair degree of comment, debate and enhanced the traffic to this blog. I have been sent two alternative lists (top ten only, most people don't have the leisure time to dream up fifty). I wonder how many people can without reference name the jobs of each of the people in this first list but I reckon it is a lot closer to the truth than the Observer one.

1. Sir Crispin Davis

2. Dame Marjorie Scardino

3. Richard Harrington

4. Professor Sir Ron Cooke

5. Kate Swann

6. Arnaud Nourry

7. Peter Olson

8. Peter Rigby

9. James Purnell

10. Kit van Tulleken

And the second is more literary but again more realistic than the Observer:

1. Scott Pack

2. Amanda Ross

3. Nigel Newton

4. Victoria Barnsley

5. Gail Rebuck

6. Richard Charkin

7. The bookbuyer at WHS whoever that is

8. Jamie Byng

9. Caroline Gascoigne

10. Martin Goff – still!

Remembrance of things past

Marcel Proust's multi-volume work was once described in a book club catalogue as the Great French work of comic genius. And I remember OUP once published Humour in the Works of Proust but that's not the point of this blog.

My past was brought back to me by a flurry of articles and books about a close friend of my young adulthood, Nick Drake. Over the years his music has grown in popularity and he now appears to be up there with the other 60s and 70s dead pop icons.Do try out his music if you haven't yet. It has stood the test of time.

And just recently I tripped over a website dedicated to another dead friend from that era, Julian Allen. We travelled together across the USA in an open-top Ford Mustang and thought we were really cool. Julian was really cool and his art only tells half the story. He was a professional illustrator working to deadlines and for money but I think he's captured the spirit of the times better than anyone.

 13 March 2006

Tapping the wisdom of crowds

The Nature Publishing Group recognizes that in today's digital environment it must constantly strive to provide more than well-filtered information; it must also provide valuable digital services for scientists and clinicians that help them to communicate with one another more effectively. I asked Timo Hannay, NPG's Director of Web Publishing, to guest on the blog as he can describe the group's latest web initiative much better than I can:

'One of the most important roles of a publisher is to help readers to find writers with something interesting and relevant to say. The arrival of the web means that we are no longer limited to doing this by the traditional means of filtering and editing content by hand (though that will remain an essential part of the process for a long time to come). Increasingly we can also help readers to help themseleves — and each other — when in search of information or entertainment.

One important experiment we've been conducting in this area is <u>Connotea</u>, Nature's free social bookmarking service for scientists and clinicians. For the last year-and-a-half or so, it has allowed users to post web links of interest and to 'tag' them with one or more keywords in order to make them easy to retrieve later. (For example, you might choose to save a bookmark to this blog entry under the tags 'social bookmarking', 'Connotea' and 'Macmillan'). Also, by storing everyone's links on a central server, it can generate recommendations based on people's overlapping interests, which is where the 'social' part of 'social boomarking' comes in.

With usage growing daily, it's clear that a lot of people already find Connotea a valuable service. But we've only scratched the surface of its potential. In particular, we're keen to make the underlying data useful to other sites. That's why, with generous funding from the UK Joint Information Systems Committee (<u>JISC</u>), we have just <u>released</u> software that adds Connotea functionality to <u>EPrints</u>, an institutional repository platform developed at the <u>University of Southampton</u>. By installing this software on their own repositories, administrators can allow their users to bookmark and tag content in Connotea, and to browse Connotea's recommendations, all without leaving the repository website. This adds useful new functionality to the repository, makes the content held there easier to discover, and makes Connotea more useful to everyone by adding more information to its data pool. For further details see <u>this blog post</u> by Ben Lund, who runs Connotea.

Where will all this lead? Frankly, we're not sure. But the use of communal data such as shared bookmarks and tags (and the collective taxonomies, or 'folksonomies', that arise from them) is already attracting a lot of interest among clever researchers who are developing ways to manage information in this era of over-abundance. We at Nature think that collaborative services like Connotea will become an important part of the answer, and when that happens we want to have a role to play. That's how publishers can stay relevant even as the world around us passes through its most disruptive period since our industry came into being.

14 March 2006

Access Africa and the Publishers Association

Some of you may know that I am President of the <u>UK Publishers' Association</u>. Fortunately this post only lasts for a year and I hand over to my successor, Stephen Page who is head of one of the world's great literary publishing houses <u>Faber and Faber</u>.

The trouble with Trade Associations is that by their nature they spend a lot of time stopping things – stopping piracy, stopping governments meddling, stopping censorship, stopping restrictive practices. Stopping these things is vital to a healthy industry but it all gets a bit negative.

But from time to time the PA can try to do something positive and the Council of the PA is wholeheartedly backing an innovative attempt to kick start college textbook publishing in Africa with the help of the British Government. The attached article (AccessBooks.pdf (75.92 KB)) which appeared in The Bookseller by Sonny Leong, Managing Director of the innovative legal publishers, Cavendish, says it better than I ever could.

All support for this from all quarters would be much appreciated. There is an opportunity to help improve vocational and university education in Africa on a sustainable basis. This will be the basis of improved economies and health in the impoverished countries of sub-Saharan Africa.

15 March 2006

Of SBNs and Germinating Sprouts

Our print sourcing operation in Hong Kong (Macmillan Production Asia Ltd) received an order this morning for 2000 deckchairs. As everything we do requires a standard book number in order to satisfy our computer requirements, these will probably be the first literary deckchairs in history.

Which reminds me of an early lesson in interpreting publishers' stock systems. During my first week at the Octopus Publishing Group I was checking the list of overstocks (all publishers have them) and came across 10,000 unsold copies of 'Chinese Food the Wok Way' (or similar) which had been written down to zero value. 'Crazy!' I screamed. 'It must be possible to remainder them and get some price however small'. 'No!' the distribution director screamed back: 'the beansprouts have germinated'. It was a food pack for Marks and Spencer masquerading as a book and brought a new meaning to old stock.

And I should mention to readers that MPA can and will source almost anything from China for you – from cherry blossom to shampoo bottles – as long as the quantities and your credit rating are good.

17 March 2006

Salon du Livre

It is of course trite to say the French are different. If there is another way of doing things they'll discover it and probably make it work. it wasn't until I started typing this that I realized that a French keyboard layout is almost entirely different to an Anglo-Saxon one and entirely non-intuitive to an Anglo-Saxon person (qwerty becomes azerty, full stop is on shift and the rest of the punctuation marks are scattered randomly). One more blow for globalization and American hegemony. Ah well, please forgive the typos.

I am here in Paris on behalf of British publishers to defend our authors' copyrights from the threat of digital kleptomania (Quelles modalités d'accès aux textes numériques sous droits?). Digital technologies offer the greatest opportunities for centuries for publishers but only if we can ensure our authors a proper income from the distribution of their works and develop business models which genuinely work for the reader and user of information.

Scientific and legal publishers have invested heavily in digital infrastructure which has enabled them to offer their authors faster and more enhanced publication; their readers lower cost, better designed and more universal access; and their owners enough cash to continue to invest. These publishers work closely with the new digital giants (Microsoft, Yahoo, Google, Amazon etc) and their aims seem to be aligned.

On the contrary typical book publishers have yet to create the necessary platforms and the new 'players' see that as an opportunity to move into the book business and a moral justification for turning a blind eye to the niceties of copyright.

Book publishers need to fight vigorously to maintain strong copyright protection for their authors. Copyright not only rewards authors for their creativity and labour, it also is a protector of freedom of speech.

But book publishers must do more than simply fight on principle and by turning to lawyers. They must show that they are willing to invest money as well. They must build digital warehouses which can protect the copyrights. They must build digital delivery systems which can work with search engines to present and sell their authors' work to new markets in new forms. They must be willing to take investment risk. They must work with authors and distributors to help build new and better business models.

All this and continue to sell books too. Bonne journée.

John Watson

On Sunday I attended the memorial service for a long-time Macmillan (and various other publishing company) employee, John Watson. Ian Taylor's obituary in the Guardian says it all. Apart from the budget-saving orders he managed to extract I'll always remember him as being the gentlest off-spin bowler I have ever faced – and he still got me out. In work too the combination of his huge size and his rather Nigerian pace of life still resulted in enough energy to succeed thus proving that E really does equal mc squared.

The turn-out at the service in Oxford and the warmth of the addresses were indicators of his friends' and colleagues' respect and affection for him. It also reminded me how lucky we are to be in an industry which cherishes people like John who break most of the corporate rules. Thank God.

21 March 2006

Transparent imprint and Lady Chatterley

Mike Barnard, publisher of Macmillan's almost equally derided and applauded 'first novels' imprint, Macmillan New Writing has written and published a book about the genesis of the imprint. 'Transparent Imprint' tells the story of 'how a publisher's decision to tell the truth to authors stirred up a storm'. The choice of cover quote given by Jonny Geller of literary agent Curtis Brown says it all: 'I don't think there's a hope in hell of this succeeding.' When the imprint was launched there were stories that authors would have to pay for their own editing, the books would only be printed on demand, and bookshops would not touch them. A year on, bookshops are taking stock, libraries are buying them and the initiative is gathering momentum and press coverage. The book's publication coincides with the launch of MNW's first titles. You can purchase a copy for £10 direct from the MNW website or, if you work at Macmillan, you can download a PDF version from the company intranet .

And perhaps some of MNW's detractors would like to follow this piece by Michael Fuchs to read what one of the authors thinks of us.

And talking of innovative new imprints, BBC4's drama 'The Chatterley Affair' broadcast on Monday evening was an interesting interpretation of the 1960 obscenity trial over the publication of Lady Chatterley's Lover and a great reminder of the origins of the Penguin imprint. It used a fictional love affair between two jurors on the trial to illuminate the subtle moral arguments and the social impact of this great English novel. The two jurors in question, a beautiful upper class young woman and a working class clerk, play out the book as they embark on their own love affair, which, crudely interpreted, could just prove the prosecution's case . . . but a colourful array of witnesses for the defence including bishops, professors and new graduates, argue the case for the novel's literary merits and ethical standpoint. Particularly enjoyable was the moment when Penguin's founder stands up in the witness box to state that he is willing to go to prison if the book is banned, as he 'believes it was right to publish this book,' proving that publishers have always been a contrary and ideological bunch.. And the subtle layers of hypocrisy are played out beautifully as two conservative male jurors deride the book as 'dirty' whilst simultaneously leering jealously over the affair of the two young lovers.

🌠 22 March 2006

'Love Libraries'

Here's a guest blog from Ronnie Williams, Chief Executive of the Publishers' Association. It's about the new 'Love Libraries' campaign being launched by the government, and I believe it needs no further introduction . . . .

I went to the launch of the 'Love Libraries' campaign by David Lammy, Minister of Culture on 22 March. It is a first initiative by The Future Libraries Partnership in which nine major UK publishers are involved, together with the government department (DCMS), the Society of Chief Librarians, the Museums Libraries and Archives Council, and the Reading Agency. There is also support from authors.

The atmosphere was very positive and reflected clearly how strongly people feel about the future of libraries and the clear priority that books are the very core of the library service. Although Lammy stuck to his constitutional position that the actual management of libraries, and specifically the balance of book stocks and new acquisitions, depends on decisions at the local level, there was a very strong message from the floor that these issues are central to the public's perception and therefore use of the library service.

The initiative is rather modest insofar as it focuses on the 'transformation' of three libraries only, but the stated intention is that these should provide a replicable template for libraries all over the country. Representatives of these 'showcase' libraries emphasised that in addition to refurbishment, they would review book stocks and acquisitions to ensure a good range of new best-selling titles as well as an extensive backlist. They would be looking to publishing 'marketing mentors' to advise them on this balance. The publishers are also closely engaged with the Reading Agency in developing 'live events' and authors' tours to liven up the library experience and involve consumers in book related activities.

It remains to be seen whether this small beginning can be developed into a more ambitious programme and whether these related initiatives can be harnessed into a practical and forward looking plan. While librarians were admitting to an image problem, a lot of practical marketing expertise is going to be needed. The three 'showcases' are promoted as a start, but if the decline which many people perceive is to be reversed, then reforms must reach a very much wider library constituency and a more ambitious programme will need to follow. The words at the launch offered comfort, but it is what is actually done across the larger scale which will determine whether this is the first real step on what may be a long journey !

RW

Trade Associations

Yesterday saw me chairing my last Publishers Association Council meeting. The next one will be chaired by my successor, Stephen Page. Phew!!!

The thing about trade associations is that they were established as a means of protecting businesses. Frequently their aim was to ensure 'fair' ie 'high' prices. They were effectively legal cartels rather like OPEC. But times have changed. And the PA has changed with the times.

The key role of our trade association today is to help our members navigate through the complexities of the new digital world. This means revisiting business models, relationships with authors and distributors, established technologies and ways of working.

The strength of British publishing is in its diversity – large, small, general, specialist, domestic, global. The PA can help all its members to find their position in the digital world and ensure that authors are both protected and rewarded. I'll continue to do my best to help but am relieved I can now concentrate even more on steering Macmillan. At some moments in the last year it has been running automagically. Now we are back on full manual steering.

24 March 2006

Storm in a teacup

If you follow this link you will be able to read an exchange of broadsides between Encyclopaedia Britannica (EB)and our very own Nature. Nature published some material suggesting that in some areas of science Wikipedia entries can compete with those in the magisterial Encyclopaedia. I trust the guys in Nature totally and I am sure their assessment was both objective and correct but even if they were being unfair the last thing I'd do at EB would be to publicise the affair. This can only damage EB's reputation and that would be really unjust. Nowt so queer as folks.

As Timo says in his blog, judge for yourselves.

26 March 2006

Elephants never forget

Dinner last night with the managing directors of our businesses in Greece, Brazil and Argentina.

What do the businesses have in common apart from all being run by exceptionally talented women? There is a deep desire to learn English. In spite of Chirac's histrionics last week when he walked out of a EU Council meeting because a fellow Frenchman addressed him in English, most people recognise that English is the language of business and essential in the modern world. The books used in schools differ significantly because of local curricula and culture but they are all demanding higher and higher standards of pedagogical and production quality and better value for money. They are all challenged by local piracy and illegal photocopying. The businesses are all growing their market share by working closely with teachers to make better teaching materials.

I was going to follow this with a description of the differences – the apostilas in Brazil, the Israeli competitors in Greece, Britsh English in Argentina – but realised that knowing the differences is what sets Macmillan apart from its competitors and I want us to remain apart.

So I'll end with a publishing quandary. We all know that elephants never forget. We also know that if publishers remembered all the times a book failed to live up to expectations nobody would ever publish anything new again. Additionally, we often try to remember a slight or a piece of betrayal. Perhaps Arthur Balfour got it right: 'I never forgive. I always forget.'

And from the source of quotations a truth from Auberon Waugh: ' Generally speaking, the best people nowadays go into journalism, the second best into business, the rubbish goes into politics and the shits into law.' I suppose publishing lies somewhere between journalism and business. I hope so.

Transparency Again

Some things serve to cheer me up. A few blogs ago I wrote that Mike Barnard had written a book, Transparent Imprint, about the fun and games he had setting up Macmillan New Writing to the derision of many in the literary world. Well, the first review has come out on the Grumpy Old Bookman blog and its a humdinger. So congratulations Mike and two fingers to the detractors. And to see the novels themselves go to the MNW website.

28 March 2006

Blogs, coffee and literary prizes

'Blogs are the new phone in modern society', according to online coffee retailer Boca Java. In a report issued by the company it states that there are now around 50 million blogs on the Web – with the blogging community expanding by around 65,000 a day. So significant a group is this new breed that the company has decided to target bloggers as a consumer market with a new line of coffee called Blogger's Blends. They're holding a contest where bloggers get to design and name a new blend of coffee. The climax of the contest is a prize – a free year of coffee. Certainly some form of energy-giving drug is required to keep up a blog, but my efforts pale into insignificance when compared to those of the anonymous Iraqi woman whose blog, Baghdad Burning, has been nominated for a literary prize. The blog, started in 2003, recounts how the Iraq war has affected the daily lives of ordinary citizens and has been nominated for the most valuable award for non-fiction – the Samuel Johnson Prize. Baghdad Burning is being published by the independent publishers Marion

Boyars and is among 19 candidates for the award. Other contenders include Untold Stories by Alan Bennett, After The Victorians by A. N. Wilson, and a biography of Mrs Beeton by Kathryn Hughes.

31 March 2006

New writing

As March comes to an end we've seen the Nibbies, an annual publishing event of acquired taste and little import (although I'm told it is at the heart of our industry which worries me rather), come and go; India squeeze a one-day victory over England at cricket, and the UK Competition Commission give provisional clearance for the takeover of the Ottakar's bookshop chain by HMV.

April kicks off with a literary question. Are there more people who want to write a book than who want to read one? There is a a three-hour debate at the London College of Communications which looks like it will be quite lively. If you have a moment I'd recommend you look in. You can find more details here.

PS Back to the Nibbies, it is clearly excellent getting TV coverage for books and authors and this must sell books. My back of an envelope calculation suggests the industry has to sell an additional two million books to cover the costs of the televised dinner. Hmmmm?

≤ April 2006 ≥

Mon	Tue	Wed	Thu	Fri	Sat	Sun
27	28	29	30	31	1	2
3	4	5	6	7	8	9
10	11	12	13	14	15	16
17	18	19	20	21	22	23
24	25	26	27	28	29	30
1	2	3	4	5	6	7

A word from Tim Coates

Libraries are part of global culture, as British as fish and chips, as American as apple pie and as Jewish as chopped liver. I've known Tim Coates from the time he was Managing Director of the then up-market, fiercely independent and anarchic up-and-coming Waterstone's bookshop chain. He is currently involved in a highly personal campaign to encourage the British Government and local authorities to spend library budgets on books – a simple, obvious but difficult objective. Not everyone agrees with Tim's in-your-face approach to campaigning but at the very least he has made the topic unignorable. I asked him to write a guest blog for me and here it is:

'Half the management in this country is public sector. The rules are different: income does not depend on judgment, efficiency or performance; cash is available; there is no such thing as bankruptcy and nor are there the disciplines, anxieties, skills and systems which are used to avoid it. Employment is secure and very well paid. Projects thrive on persuasive plans but rarely on actual outcomes. To a private sector manager, the regime is unfamiliar.

We have become used to the idea that only a small portion of charitable donations reach their intended recipients; we should get used to the idea that the great part of the money we thought was for public service will never reach any public beneficiary. We live in an economy which is the travelling equivalent of a crowded roundabout. Huge amounts of public funds travel on a journey which goes nowhere in an unpleasant and wasteful manner.

For seven years I have studied the public library service in both central and local government where most of the operation is managed. This is a £1.2bn pa operation which has no accounts, no boards of directors, no planning or budgeting, no measurement of performance and no management of the kind a garage mechanic would recognise. It is a disaster from the tip of its branches to the lengths of it ancient roots. Use of the service has fallen to half its rather successful level of twenty years ago and no one can even agree whether that is a good thing or a bad one. No junior manager learns the basic skills of 'yes' or 'no' from his senior – because he, or she, never learned those skills either. The operation is a national disgrace and nobody even knows.

We have an extremely and potentially devastating problem of the economy in this country and it is the management of public sector activities. We worry about political incompetence, global warming and the management of our soccer team. We should be sensible and start worrying about the management of public services. That really is frightening.'

Scientific and medical publishing

A very good friend of mine in the publishing business has always described himself as a science publisher rather than a publisher. This means he won't be harassed by dinner party acquaintances into reading their new novel or discussing the latest novel from a Guatemalan genius. The idea of discussing science publishing nearly always moves the conversation on to soccer or supermodels immediately.

However, science publishing is probably the most vibrant part of the modern world of information dissemination and is a hugely successful British industry. At Macmillan we are blessed by being the publisher of a wide range of scientific journals with Nature at its head. By investing in quality and in technology we have been able to grow this business in partnership with learned societies, scientists, advertisers and subscribers. The business is global of course but there is a local dimension too and we are announcing today the formation of new operations in India, Latin America and Spain.

This is yet another investment in what we do best and we have hired the best people to help us do it.

🥏 04 April 2006

When gamers and ELT publishers collide

Fiona Mackenzie of Macmillan English Campus has been filling me in about the new MEC language CD-ROM which is published tomorrow:

'We wanted 'real' games created by real gamers not 'educational' games – we wanted people to play the games because they were fun and to use their English because they needed it in order to win. We didn't know what we were getting into. Games developers brainstorm ideas then they make the games up as they go along. We ELT editors and authors brainstorm then plan and organize – word sets, sentence structures, suitable language for different language levels. The gamers were helpful. If our words were too long, they changed them for shorter ones. If a sentence didn't fit, it was cut to fit. If there wasn't enough text they added more words . . . any words. The alpha versions of the games were exciting. We never quite knew what text was going to emerge, explode, ooze or bounce on to the screen. We explained it wasn't quite that simple. They did listen. There was a game with past tenses of verbs: 'dry', 'cry' and 'try' have three red stars in the Macmillan English Dictionary – they are high frequency words for language learners. Imagine the pride of the ex-teacher mingled with the despair of the ELT editor as the joyfully apt and wondrously inappropriate 'beatify' slid into view.

We cracked it though – when a developer suddenly said, 'I know – we need to treat the English like we do the text for a website in French. We don't touch a thing.'

And when an ELT editor understands that the 'stickiness' of a game depends on the sensuous satisfaction of drawing an 'elastic band' round words as opposed to the tedium of clicking on dozens of individual letters and a gamer halts a discussion with the words, 'Pedagogically, this isn't right for our learners . . . ', you're know you're on to something special.

Language Games CDROM is published by Macmillan English Campus on April 7th. It features over 150 English language games – about 54 hours of game-play for the average language learner. Combining real language practice with a sophisticated level of gaming challenge, it is great value at only £19.95 for the single user. For schools and institutions, a network edition is also available for 1-25 users.

To buy Language Games please visit the Macmillan English Campus website.

Funny old world part 93

We had a great party here in <u>Kings Cross</u> yesterday evening to celebrate the publication of the first six titles in the <u>Macmillan New Writing</u> fiction imprint. As followers of this blog or readers of the Guardian, Observer etc newspapers will know, our announcement of this initiative last year caused something of a stir amongst what the British call 'the chattering classes'. Thomas Hardy was going to turn in his grave because Macmillan was proposing not to rewrite an author's work if it wasn't up to scratch. Macmillan was sinking into becoming a 'vanity press' (in spite of the fact that we have rejected well over 99% of all submissions and absolutely do not accept money from authors wishing to be published). Macmillan's standards of editing would fall because the person running the scheme was a 'marketing guy' (actually that is one job Mike Barnard has never done and he is a damned sight more literate than many of the editors I see hanging around in the Groucho Club). And so on.

As a matter of courtesy we invited every journalist, literary agent and commentator who had written on the subject and expressed concern to a debate on new writing at the London College of Communications and to the party. Not one showed up in spite of both events being hugely successful with authors, publishers, printers and booksellers mixing and discussing new ways to stimulate creative writing. I suppose the commentators were too busy protecting their reputations and trying to spike other initiatives which might threaten their comfortable and elitist status quo.

Most of our industry is decent and professional but clearly not as unified and unbitchy as for instance <u>beekeepers</u> – a thousand great places to bee on the web!

It's (nearly) Summertime

Here in Britain there is little sense of global warming as Spring (let alone Summer) seems reluctant to arrive. However, next Tuesday evening will definitely presage a new season. It is the traditional dinner to celebrate the publication of the latest edition of Wisden Cricketers' Almanack and the start of another cricket season.

Cricket in England had been on a downward (some would say nihilistic) trend for a couple of decades and then last Summer a miracle . . . England won back <u>The Ashes</u> from a normally triumphant Australia. And suddenly, as the Almanack says, cricket became the new football with sell-out crowds, newly converted fans, and national excitement. Such an upsurge in interest initiated some changes in the venerable reference book. Perhaps the most obvious is that, alongside the traditional pocket-sized edition, there will appear a <u>large-format edition</u>. For the first time in my memory the articles have become easily readable and their content more accessible.

Another tradition is the naming of five players of the year and one 'Leading cricketer in the world' as written up in <u>the Times</u>. You'll have to wait a couple of days for the choice to be public.

Finally, on the subject of Wisden (for the time being at least and I should declare an interest as I am a director of <u>the Wisden Group</u> which owns <u>cricinfo</u>) I'd like to mention Matthew Engel, its editor. He has done a fantastic job as usual – a mixture of hard work, humour, scholarship, cunning – but he also suffered a personal tragedy which is best described by <u>him</u>. There is now a website dedicated to a fund set up in Laurie Engel's memory. Do go look at <u>it</u>.

Buildings

A <u>huge hole in the ground</u> has appeared next to our King's Cross building. This is one of the first parts of Western Europe's largest building development. The hole will house an underground car park, a concert hall, a sculpture gallery, the Guardian newspaper, several restaurants and I don't know what else.

Most importantly it will ensure that Macmillan will be no more than two and a half hours from the centres of Paris and Brussels door to door by train. It won't necessarily make me any more sympathetic to Eurocracy and a 'federal' Europe but it should certainly be good for business and communications.

And <u>this</u> is what the hole will look like when completed in 2008 – the sooner the better.

🐦 11 April 2006

Italian Cream Buns

This morning's leader in the Times described the Italian election as an <u>Italian fudge</u>. I think cream buns might be the more appropriate confectionery as the contenders sling insults at each other like clowns at the circus. Clearly this non-result is bad for Italy and the Italian economy.Equally clearly the German result last year did nothing for European economic liberalisation. And Chriac's pathetic climb-down yesterday was equally unhelpful.

These were the down-sides of some political stalemates. But the joy of all these results is that they confirm the intrinsic differences between the nation states of Europe and make federalisation even more obviously absurd. Gloria Italia.

On a more bookish theme I was amazed to discover that <u>Oxfam</u> in the UK sells £60m (roughly a third of Ottakar's total book sales) of used books a year through 750 outlets of which 112 are book and music specialists. It's great that so much money is raised to help alleviate famine and disease in the developing world but if I were a second-hand bookseller I'd be pretty worried.

And here is a <u>link</u> to an article by commentator Clive Keble.

🐦 13 April 2006

More cricket, sorry

The weather shows no signs of improving in Britain in spite of the beginning of the cricket season.

As I mentioned here earlier in the week, the latest edition of Wisden is published this week, and is the 143rd consecutive annual since the first one in 1864. This is a remarkable achievement, especially when you consider that it came out in every year of both world wars, despite there being virtually no cricket played anywhere between 1915 and 1918, and wartime paper shortages as well.

However, this year there is a significant online development to go with the new edition: the Cricinfo website has launched the Wisden archive online. It is free, but subject to a simple registration process. So for the first time it is now possible to find online a large selection of Wisden's articles, including the annual Editor's Notes, the Cricketer of the Year essays and obituaries, or track down Wisden's contemporary reports of virtually every Test or one-day international match. And it is searchable, allowing you to select a particular year, or perform a text search across the entire archive.

As a taster, you can look at the 1916 obituary of WG Grace or the 1965 obituary of Peter, the Lord's Cat. Alternatively the 1982 Almanack will bring you the report of Botham's Ashes, and you can click on the 2006 edition to read about this year's Five Cricketers of the Year.

And Wisden was number one in Amazon this week and number two (briefly) for the large format edition. Two reasons to be cheerful – the third would have been had minnow Bangladesh beaten Australia but fairy tales don't happen every day.

And for non cricket lovers a publishing mention of significance – Simon Master most recently of Random House has retired. There was a huge reception in London on Tuesday – the great and the good, the less great and the less good, the famous and the unsung heroes of the book trade were all there. It was a generous tribute to a generous man. I'm sure we haven't seen the last of Simon though.

15 April 2006

Easter links

This comes to you from a rainy and grey South-West France. I've been checking out some links which I'd like to share.

First an interview with Stephen Page, Chief Executive of Faber and my successor as President of the Publishers Association – and the best thing to happen to independent publishing in years.

And then feast on an interview with Tom Turvey who is in charge of Google's Booksearch program. Tom is the acceptable face of Google and has had to put up with all sorts of publisher attacks beginning at the 2005 PA AGM debate and continuously since then. He's still smiling which says a lot for his character and commitment.

And whilst on character and commitment I forgot to mention that the mother of Laurie Engel,then known as Hilary Davies, for Macmillan for ten years until 1991 as editorial director of Sidgwick & Jackson and then Pan.

And finally, if you want to set yourself a difficult task which will bring cheer try to track down a Costa Rican group called el Cafe Chorale and in particular the track Ojala que llueva cafe. I'm listening to it right now and the skies have already brightened.

Still Spitting at Sixty

About a million years ago when I was an undergraduate I was introduced to a bearded giant called <u>Roger Law</u>. He was married to my then girlfriend's sister and was working as an illustrator-cum-troublemaker on the unbelievably trendy Sunday Times Colour Magazine. He is now sixty and still an illustrator-cum-troublemaker and his <u>sort of autobiography</u> is about to come out in paperback from HarperCollins (who says I only plug Macmillan books?). It is absolutely brilliant and is not only addressed to friends and enemies (including media moguls, smoking nuns, Mrs Thatcher, all South Africans and the Queen, God bless you and happy eightieth birthday, Ma'am) but also to all those interested in the sex life of the platypus. Go get it (and I won't dare give you a link to Amazon in case I get pilloried again by independent booksellers).

And the latest health scare is that blogging is definitely a communicable disease. My friend, Susan Hill, has clearly caught the disease and is <u>blogging away</u> merrily – do check her out. Apart from anything else, she can write English.

🐦 20 April 2006

Libraries

A little while ago Tim Coates wrote a guest blog here on waste in Government-funded activities. It hit quite a few nerves and the response has been interesting. Tim has meanwhile contracted blogitis and it's worth checking out his <u>good library blog</u>.

Also, a little while ago I mentioned a book we were about to publish about Lonesome George the last of a species of giant tortoise who lives a long but celibate and lonely life on an island in the Galapagos. Hardly likely to be a bestseller you might think but here is the list of publicity to date which augurs rather well. Do read Henry Nicholls's book. It really is a marvellous story blending science, good writing and a gripping story.

quote from lovely review in this week's *NewScientist*

'Read this fascinating book — it skillfully blends historical derring-do with cutting-edge conservation biology.' *NewScientist*

John Vidal, *Guardian* Environment editor promises us that his pages in Wednesday 19th's Society section should contain a full page interview by Nicholls of the new head of research on the Galapagos.

the *Guardian* have an interview with Nicholls in the can which they plan to use in their hugely successful podcast any day soon. I'll let you know when that airs.

MacSci's new editorial assistant Lisa Hayden has managed to get Nicholls onto BBC Radio 4's premier science show *Material World* on 27th April 16:30-17:00 [http://www.bbc.co.uk/radio4/science/thematerialworld.shtml]

He's appeared twice on *'The Naked Scientists'* radio show, syndicated across BBC Essex, Cambridgeshire, Northampton, Norfolk, Suffolk, and BBC Three Counties Radio, and in the itunes top 100 podcasts: http://www.thenakedscientists.com/HTML/shows/2006.03.19.htm

The book is the subject of a 2 page feature in the major German newspaper the Sueddeutsche Zeitung:

http://sz-magazin.sueddeutsche.de/front_single/front_content.php?idside=1662&idcat=90&sid=60c956f5b6206be8ff473f0636c618a7

Meanwhile, Henry is doing lots of gigs in London, Cambridge, Oxford, Hay and beyond. For details see:
http://www.macmillanscience.com/archive.asp?view=archive&year=2006

🦢 23 April 2006

Entente cordiale

I spent Friday as a guest of La bibliothèque nationale de France. Every day one learns something and today I have learned how to type an e with a grave accent.

The bibliothèque is an extraordinary series of interlinked buildings housing not just books but a wholly Gallic philosophy of culture. Whilst it clearly shares many aims, objectives and practices with the British Library there is equally clearly a peculiarly French tinge to everything – and thank goodness for that. During the course of the visit I was able to see the manuscript of Samuel Beckett's En attendant Godot. For some reason the French guide didn't seem very interested in the fact that Beckett is the only Nobel prize winner ever to have appeared in Wisden – strange these French. Well worth following the Wisden link for details of the great man's prowess with bat and ball.

One strange thing is that researchers have to pay to use the bibliothèque. It seems perfectly sensible to me but I am certain that, if adopted in Britain, there would be an outcry about abandonment of cultural values, open access etc. The French who are as committed (some would say much more so) to the preservation of culture, language, scholarship, freedom of information have absolutely no problem with the idea of paying for a cultural service – and nor should we in Britain.

And finally on French matters, if you can get to Paris this Spring do try to visit Les lumières exhibition. Apart from fascinating Voltaire and Rousseau materials there is a wonderful collection of Hogarth cartoons – well worth it.

🦢 24 April 2006

Waterstone's

Tim Waterstone, the founder of the eponymous British bookshop chain, has today made a £280m offer to buy it back from its prsent owners, HMV. Who knows what the outcome of this will be although it certainly adds another chapter to the roller coaster of British bookselling over the last year. Anyone wishing to predict or to bet money on the outcome would be well advised to check out Tim's book Swimming against the stream for clues. One thing is clear – Tim is not a quitter.

🔖 25 April 2006

Neuer Eintrag

The blog has come up in German this morning as I'm in Stuttgart – hence the title.

But back to Britain and the significant coverage for Tim Waterstone's attempt to buy back the bookshop chain he founded. I mentioned it briefly yesterday and it resulted in a debate between two highly articulate correspondents. The debate brings out the arguments for both 'sides'. I just wish that the bookselling corporate deals could be over and we can all get back to focussing on selling more good books and investing in authors and marketing rather than lawyers and merchant banks.

On a more prosaic level I have also been wondering why the majority of bestseller lists exclude manuals, reference books etc. Aren't bestseller lists there to indicate which books sell best notwithstanding their subject matter? This musing was stimulated by the absence from bestseller lists of one of the bestselling titles of last week – my favourite Wisden Cricketers' Almanack which (in spite of Clive Keble's tirade against Amazon for selling it at a heavy discount) is selling better than ever through independent and chain booksellers alike.

🔖 26 April 2006

Everyman's Rules for Scientific Living

I'm delighted that Carrie Tiffany's first novel has been shortlisted for the Orange prize. She is competing with some well established authors such as Sara Waters and Hilary Mantel but it's marvellous that a debutante author can make it on to the list. Carrie's own story is worth reading as is this interview.

Here is a quote from a review in the Times Literary Supplement:

'Carrie Tiffany's first novel . . . is about love. Beautifully written in a naive register, it is kindly, sometimes hilarious and ultimately very sad. The setting is 1930s rural Australia, a country where the typical economic model of expanding population prompting agricultural revolution, has been reversed. It is a sensual novel, both in what it tells us about the couplings and appetites of animals and humans; and in the way the book has been produced with the corn-coloured, wheaty smelling paper; photographs of plump animals; and tactial stitchwork on the dust jacket.'

For more information go here.

🔖 29 April 2006

On change and creativity

I spent the last couple of days in Mumbai at board meetings of our various Indian businesses. We now have more than 3000 people in Macmillan India spread over I don't know how many offices and operations (well over fifty anyway). Our first quarter closed with sales 30% ahead of the previous year and there is plenty more growth to come – from local publishing, from imports of books from all round the world which feed the intellectual curiosity of a rapidly growing educated middle class, from services developed to help other publishers benefit from the high-quality labour force available, and from innovation. Such a welcome change from the problems facing the UK book trade as it grapples with a mature market, increasing regulation, resistance to change in some quarters and overcomplexity.

While on the subject of innovation we were all very pleased to read this about Nature. Just in case you can't be bothered to follow the link, this is the last paragraph of the article:

'In a market where a few large companies control access to much of the critical information, Nature is a shining star for their flexibility, their willingness to test new technologies and their efforts to keep the 'community' in scientific community. Nature and NPG are clearly one of the 50 Content Companies that Matter.'

You can imagine what we thought of this accolade, but enough of that self-congratulation, back to work and a further plug for Susan Hill's blog. The thing about her blog is that it's written by a real writer – and the difference, to my embarrassment, shows.

30 April 2006

Marcus Aurelius

I have been described as many things in my career. I either agree, disagree or don't care. Only occasionally, as today, have I had to resort to reference works to check out what the description means.

Robert McCrum's regular feature on the world of books in the Observer newspaper adds colour to Sunday mornings. Today he is reviewing the development of a new publishing company, the Friday Project, which Macmillan helps to sell and distribute and which I personally have tried to support. Its aim is to turn concepts and brands on the Internet into world-class books. Anyway they've just hired an excellent new director, Scott Pack. According to Robert McCrum, this guy makes me look like Marcus Aurelius. Should I be flattered or offended?

I've checked out Wikipedia and the Columbia Encyclopedia gave me:

'Devoted to his duty and humanitarian in his conception of it, Marcus Aurelius was concerned with improving living conditions for the poor, particularly minors. He was always lenient with political criminals and tried to decrease the brutality at gladiatorial shows. He did, however, persecute the Christians, whom he regarded as natural enemies of the empire.'

And Chambers Biographical Dictionary:

'He was retrospectively idealized as the model of the perfect emperor, whose reign and style of rule contrasted with the disastrous period that began with the accession of his son Commodus, the disturbed age of the Severan emperors, and the imperial anarchy that followed in the 3rd century.'

I'm still not sure but one thing is for certain. I couldn't have done this research as quickly and effectively without great reference works brought together through the Internet by xrefer – the very opposite of the Friday Project concept, but none the worse for that.

May 2006

≤   ≥

Mon	Tue	Wed	Thu	Fri	Sat	Sun
24	25	26	27	28	29	30
1	2	3	4	5	6	7
8	9	10	11	12	13	14
15	16	17	18	19	20	21
22	23	24	25	26	27	28
29	30	31	1	2	3	4

May Day musings

This blog has been running for four months (plus a bit of experimenting in December). We set it up with three objectives:

To communicate to Macmillan staff worldwide without clogging up our servers;

To generate debate about specific publishing issues as our trade grapples with what can only be described as the digital revolution (forgive the cliché);

To help me understand the power (or otherwise) of blogging and learn a few technotips on the way.

Objective one seems to be working OK although there are still places where the blog's existence is unknown. Time will sort this.

Number two is a disappointment. The principal debate has been around discounts that UK publishers grant to supermarkets, chains, Amazon etc. I can understand why small independent booksellers feel that their businesses are threatened when they see massive discounts being granted by supermarkets on, for instance, Harry Potter but that is out of the hands of publishers. The discounts we publishers grant are as low as feasible in a highly competitive market. But the real disappointment is that this argument is as old as the hills and incapable of resolution or new thinking. Surely the opportunities and challenges of the Internet are more relevant.

Number three is more positive. I've learned how to hypertext, how to spell words with accents and how to check out the blog statistics.

Visitors in January were 9036, in February 8492, in March 18724, and in April a record 19257. The highest day was 900 visitors. I'm working on crossing the 1000 barrier. The audience is genuinely global. The biggest uptick on a single day was when we ran a story about the whale being stranded in the Thames. This is a fairly typical page of the searchers people undertook to reach this blog:

parship reviews (www.google.com)	4
charkin blog (www.google.co.uk)	2
Charkin blog (www.google.co.uk)	2
charkin (www.google.co.uk)	2
'cell research' npg bought (www.google.com)	2
charkin blog (www.google.co.uk)	2
earth chark (www.google.com.tr)	2
MacMillans Publishers Kings Cross London UK (www.google.co.uk)	2
charkin Blog (www.google.com.hk)	2
independent bookshops, central london (www.google.co.uk)	2

charkin blog (www.google.co.uk)	2
elc daisy & tom new board (www.google.co.uk)	2
richard charkin blog (www.google.co.uk)	2
Ernest Hecht Editor (www.google.co.in)	2
richard charkin (www.google.com)	2
book fair +auckland (www.google.co.nz)	2
richard charkin blog (www.google.co.uk)	2
list best mission statements of all time (www.google.ca)	2
charkin (www.google.co.uk)	2
'crispin davis' and speech (www.google.com)	1
false impression (www.google.com)	1
tim waterstone (search.bbc.co.uk)	1
toby charkin (www.google.co.uk)	1
'the friday project' (www.google.co.uk)	1
jeffrey archer + false impression + blog (www.google.com)	1
whale that got killed in london (www.google.com)	1
'wicked witch of publishing' (www.google.com)	1

If you celebrate May Day in your country, have a good one. If not, still have a good one.

02 May 2006

May Day musings part 2

My musings yesterday seemed to have stirred up a lot of comment and it's worth reading the contributions if you're interested in the problems and opportunities affecting the British book trade.

What I find interesting in all this (and from private emails I receive not for publication) is how publishers are blamed by absolutely everyone. Independent booksellers complain because we give too much discount to everyone. Supermarkets complain because we don't give enough to their intermediaries who regularly go bust as a result. Chain booksellers complain because we don't give enough to support their marketing efforts. Authors and agents complain that discounts are too high and this affects their royalty earnings. Illustrators, translators, indexers, copy-editors complain that they aren't paid enough and don't get enough recognition. Printers complain that publishers don't pay them enough. Readers think books are too expensive and blame publishers. Libraries think they should receive bigger discounts. Google thinks information (if supplied by them) should be free. Everyone thinks books should be produced to higher standards. Everyone wants better levels of service.

Meanwhile we have price deflation, higher author costs, higher energy costs, higher technology and innovation costs, shorter print runs, more competitive media for spend and leisure time.

Something has to give.

But in spite of everything the business continues and let's celebrate Macmillan having two of the five shortlisted titles for the James Tait Black Memorial prize for biography:

Max Egremont's Siegfried Sassoon and Nigel Farndale's Haw-Haw, The Tragedy of William and Margaret Joyce.

📝 03 May 2006

Book 2.0

Putting the final touches to a talk I am giving tomorrow for the STM organisation. It occurred to me that the list of speakers at this conference might give a flavour of how book publishing is changing in the 21st century. Many of the companies did not exist a decade ago and yet I suspect that the debates at this meeting may prove more relevant to our future than the retail 'controversies' we are suffering in the UK right now. I have also pasted in the aims of the conference which set out very clearly some of the challenges facing book publishers today.

- Keynote Speaker: Richard Charkin, Chief Executive of Macmillan and President of the Publishers Association 'The Internet Changes Everything – Not!'

- Chris Armstrong, Managing Director, Information Automation, Ltd

- Louise Breinholt, Marketing & Communications Manager, Wiley Interscience

- Paul Carr, Editor-in-Chief of The Friday Project and Editor of 'The Friday Thing' and 'London by London'

- Warren Cowan, CEO, Greenlight

- Adrian Driscoll, Publishing Consultant, Caxtonia

- Richard Fisher, Executive Director, Humanities and Social Sciences, Cambridge University Press

- Suzanne S. Kemperman, Director, Publishing, NetLibrary (a division of OCLC)

- Sara Lloyd, Business Development Director for BookStore, MPS Technologies

- Ray Lonsdale, Reader in Information Studies, Department of Information Studies, University of Wales, Aberystwyth

- Jayne Marks, CEO, Global Operations, MPS Technologies

- Dan Penny, Account Manager, Electronic Publishing Services, Ltd

- Marika Stauch, Marketing Manager, Mathematics & Computer Science, Springer

- Wim van der Stelt, Vice President Global Marketing, Springer

While STM journal publishers have been driven to 'go digital' by market need, the market and business models for digital book content delivery have been far from clear.

It has been difficult to assess if and when students, graduate students, academics, and the general reader, will begin demanding digital delivery of the content they want. Publishers have questioned which formats and business models will dominate, and, crucially, how we can unlock the revenue potential of digital delivery.

During the past year book publishers have recognized the need to resolve the answers to some of these questions. This has been driven partly by non-traditional, Internet-based competitors such as Google and Amazon stealing the march on publishers, launching their own initiatives enabling readers to get to the content they need. Also new 'non-publisher publishers', such as Wikipedia, are introducing innovative content development and delivery mechanisms playing to markets where 'good enough' content is increasingly acceptable.

There is also a sense that, particularly in academic and professional markets, at least a proportion of readers are actively beginning to seek digital engagement over print content, delivered in the simplest, fastest and most cost-efficient way. The key question for publishers is: how to remain at the heart of the relationship between author and reader in this new digital environment? In other words, how do we continue to add value for authors and readers in the digital delivery chain?

04 May 2006

The Whitechapel Project

I'm going to take a risk today and celebrate the closure of a public library.

For a period in the 1990s I was Chairman of the Whitechapel Art Gallery. It was established in 1901 to bring great art to the people of the East End of London. At the time (and it is still true today) Whitechapel was home to recent immigrants. In 1901 the imigrants were largely Jewish. Today they are largely Asian. The impact of these immigrant comunities has been enormous and beneficial and the area continues to thrive as a creative catalyst for London, Britain and the world.

The gallery has premiered international artists such as Pablo Picasso, Jackson Pollock and Lucien Freud. It is financed by public bodies, private individuals and companies, and through the hard work and entrepreneurism of its staff.

Next door to the gallery is a public library with a rich history, particularly from the 'Jewish' times but in recent years it had become run down through lack of investment and changing social needs. The library is being moved to a new site close and merged with another library. I really believe that one first-class library is better than two second-class ones in this case.

And the gallery acquired the freehold in the library and last night celebrated the launch of the Whitechapel Project which will turn this beautiful and historic building into a beautiful space for creative artists, students, art lovers and coffee lovers to use and enjoy. Losing the Whitechapel Library is sad but extending the Gallery is a cause for celebration and support.

The Director of the gallery is Iwona Blazwick. She used to work at the famous art publisher Phaidon and she brings to the leadership of this project everything that is best about publishing – optimism, shrewdness and charm. This project deserves to succeed.

05 May 2006

Children's Books

The great thing about children's publishing is that everything about is worthwhile. The authors and illustrators, not to mention the editors, designers andf salespeople, are all committed to an important set of objectives – making great books to help literacy, stimulate creativity, enhance enjoyment and to educate. Even when individual titles fail commercially at least they had a good reason to exist which cannot be said of all types of books.

It is therefore with enormous pride and pleasure that I heard today of Macmillan's success on the prize front today.

Frank Cottrell Boyce's second novel **Framed** has been shortlisted for the Carnegie Medal. Published by Macmillan Children's Books, Frank won the Carnegie Medal last year with his debut novel **Millions**. Described as original, charming and funny, Framed has achieved great acclaim and was also shortlisted for the Whitbread Medal.

Emily Gravett's **Wolves** has been shortlisted for the Kate Greenaway Medal. This is Emily's debut picture book, which was also awarded a bronze medal in the Nestle Children's Prize. It was published to great acclaim last year.

Emma Hopkin, MD of Macmillan Children's Books says: 'We are delighted to have a book on each shortlist – something that we have not achieved for years. Both Emily and Frank are masters of their craft and both thoroughly deserve to be on the shortlists. Both the Carnegie and Kate Greenaway awards are very important to us as publishers, because the books featured on them are chosen by librarians for outstanding work.'

Full shortlists are available at www.carnegiegreenaway.org.uk

06 May 2006

Literary Euphemisms

My favourite columnist of the moment is Ben Macintyre in the Times (of London). Today's Last Word piece is a fine example. For those who can't be bothered to click, here is his glossary of literary euphemisms. I think we should add to this list so that in time OUP will be able to publish a truly scholarly, magisterial, authoritative and comprehensive Dictionary of Literary Euphemisms which might just fill the much-needed gap in the market.

Mesmerising This word is traditionally deployed by the non-specialist reviewer to describe a specialist book, for example: 'Hawking's *A Brief History of Time* is quite mesmerising.' It translates as: 'I didn't understand a word, but I'm not going to admit it because I need the money, and I've already sold the book.'

Edgy Any author under the age of 30, being reviewed by someone over 30, is likely to be described as edgy. The edginess factor will increase in proportion to whether the author is non-white, female and attractive, and the reviewer is white, male, and fat. Drugs, sex and racial conflict are also contributory factors. Edgy is also a synonym for glue-sniffing, necrophilia, lap-dancing and Michel Houellebecq.

Exquisite sensibility Gay.

Veiled sensibility Closet gay.

Shot through with mordant wit This phrase tends to be used by reviewers to describe books written by other reviewers. It means: 'Extremely nasty, but I don't want this bastard to work me over next.'

These are minor quibbles (mere cavils) This is a favourite of the weedier academic reviewers. It usually crops up towards the end of the review, when the reviewer has suddenly realised that he may have put the boot in too hard at the start, and feels guilty.

Writing reminiscent of Probably plagiarised.

It is a truth universally acknowledged . . . that any review touching, however tangentially, on the life, times, writing or recipes of Jane Austen must begin with this knackered introduction.

X meets Y This is the single greatest contribution of publishers' marketing departments to modern literature. It shackles together two more famous authors or books in the hope of making a hybrid, and can lead to some unlikely couplings: 'Henry James meets Hunter S. Thompson' or 'Virginia Woolf meets Naomi Wolf meets *Steppenwolf* meets Peter and the Wolf'. The offspring of such unions are almost always stillborn. (qv *The next Dan Brown / Brick Lane / Shakespeare* etc.)

Exhaustive Exhausting.

Wears its scholarship lightly Author is not a real scholar. But I am.

Triumphant return to form I was expecting this to be as abysmal as the last one, but it was only mildly disappointing.

Gnomic Baffling.

Imaginative Fiction reviewers use this to describe a book that they wish they had written; nonfiction reviewers use it to describe a book they do not believe.

Compelling I managed to finish it.

Painfully funny / sad / poignant / long Demonstrates the deep sensitivity of the reviewer. A health warning also attaches to any book described as *achingly, eye-wateringly* or *heart-stoppingly* anything.

Arch I'm not sure if this is funny *Detailed* Has footnotes.

Richly detailed Has lots of footnotes.

Densely detailed Has footnotes, endnotes, acknowledgements, epigrams, foreword, preface, bibliography, appendices, indices, and marginalia. Translation: unreadable. qv *panoramic, workmanlike, painstaking, extensively researched.*

Quaint Eccentric.

Eccentric Author should be sectioned immediately.

Vertiginous So clever and showy that it made me feel a bit sick.

Vibrant Usually used to describe a young author that the reviewer met when drunk at the Martin Amis launch and thinks he might have fancied. (See also *accomplished debut.*) *Important* Worthy.

Crucial Worthier.

Seminal Worthiest.

A colourful cast of characters The author is trying to be P. G. Wodehouse

This curate's egg of a book . . . The telltale mark of the indecisive reviewer

Whips along, zips along, rattling yarn, high-octane, page-turner I usually review books about classical music, but the literary editor has given me this ghastly potboiler and I am putting a brave face on it

Smorgasbord, potpourri, salmagundi, etc are typical literary show-off terms intended to demonstrate the international learning of the reviewer. Translation: mixture.

Schadenfreude 'The book of mine enemy hath been remaindered, and I am glad' (Clive James).

Tightly plotted Has a beginning and a middle, and you find out whodunnit at the end.

 07 May 2006

Tetsworth and Bournemouth

I have just been sent this link to a review by <u>Grumpy Old Bookman</u> and couldn't resist posting it.

Subject to weather, today will see the first game of the 2006 season for <u>Baldons Cricket Club</u>. We play <u>Tetsworth</u> in the second round of the Cricketer <u>Village Cup</u> – our opponents in the first round were clearly intimidated by our reputation and waved us through without playing. I've spent the morning rummaging for my whites, box, strapping etc. In the olden days I was always keen to win. Now survival seems a worthwhile objective. The competition ends up with a final at Lords on 3rd September. Betting on cricket is very popular. Don't bet on Baldons CC to reach the final.

Which leads clearly to today's Sunday Telegraph. The headline is a joyous example of misleading in order to increase sales:

Out of the shadows: It's a church wedding at last for Kate and William.

William is Prince William and Kate is his girlfriend. You might think they'd announced their wedding plans but no, merely that they are going together to someone else's wedding. Priceless.

In the same issue there is an article about seismic changes in publishing. More inaccurate stuff about the industry and digitisation and self-publishing blah blah.

After the cricket I'm heading off to the gorgeous seaside town of Bournemouth for the Booksellers Association annual meeting where I suspect the industry will be spending a few days discussing digitisation, self-publishing blah blah and . . . . trading terms. Plus ça change.

09 May 2006

We're all searching for something

Keeping a blog is bringing out all my trainspotter tendencies. For instance, I spend a probably unhealthy amount of my time looking at my web statistics to see how many hits the blog has had, and so on. The bit that really fascinates me though is the referring searches that bring web surfers to the blog. A cursory look today shows the usual Google searches for 'Charkin' and even for 'Charkin blog', which just goes to prove that new-fangled ideas like 'viral marketing' really do work. But it also reveals the interests so common to us all right now – for example the number of searches on 'e-books' or 'digital publishing'. Perhaps more interestingly it conclusively proves that cricket is the new football with searches for 'Wisden' rating highly. One lone search saddened me to my boots, though – the one looking for 'Elsevier mission statement.' But I guess the most disappointed searchers will have been all those looking for 'condom.'

10 May 2006

Bestsellers?

The latest bestseller list seems unintentionally ironic. Here are the top five non-fiction bestsellers in the UK this week.

1 Jade My Autobiography

2 Jordan A Whole New World

3 Ugly – Constance Briscoe

4 The Other Side of Nowhere – Danniella Westbrook

5 Is It Just Me Or Is Everything Shit?

No further comment required.

Digitalia and Bookselling

I attended the annual Booksellers Association conference earlier this week. There were a number of highlights including Richard Dawkins' attack on religion in his new book The God Delusion based on the TV series <u>The Root of all Evil?</u> Go buy the book when it comes out in the Autumn.

There were discussions on whether or not to print prices on books, whether or not the London Book Fair should be in Earl's Court or Docklands, whether all publishers should be buried alive for their iniquitous discount policies or just some of them, and so on.

The most important thing from my point of view related to the future of independent (and not so independent) bookselling in a digital environment.

Nobody doubts that the book has a future and that booksellers will continue to find a decent market for fiction and popular non-fiction. However, some areas of publishing have already moved to a completely new distribution mechanism which eliminates the role of the traditional bookseller. The first movers were scientific and legal publishers, rapidly followed by business information providers. Schools business could be hugely affected by the BBC's plans for a digital curriculum. Right now reference books and travel guides are moving rapidly to a web-only model. Other areas of non-fiction, particularly high-level academic works, will follow.

One can certainly paint a picture of doom for the small book retailer. But I came away from the conference convinced otherwise. Provided publishers digitise their material and make it available to all at a price. Provided booksellers are willing to take risks and learn new skills. Provided that authors allow fast and effective re-use of their copyright works. I believe the small bookseller can build a profitable and growing business selling traditional books on the web and still serving their local community; building deeper communities of interest among readers; building digital delivery websites for text and audio books. The more book retailers enter this business the more we and our customers will all be protected from the dangers of monopolistic or oligopolistic distribution channels.

In Britain and Ireland we are hugely fortunate in having an organisation which can facilitate this future and who have proved its worth time and time again. Now the <u>BA</u> needs to encourage all its members to seek advice in order to harness the potential of these powerful new digitalia (as a colleague calls it).

Bureaubscurity

This quote from my French bank statement may make sense to someone with better French than me – but I've been completely baffled this morning.

Si votre compte courant à été ouvert avant le 28/01/2003, sans établissement d'une convention de compte, vous pouvez obtenir un project de convention et proceder à sa signature en vous adressant à votre agence habituelle.

In the world of British books last week's London Book Fair event overshadowed much else. The outcome – the existing good managers of the London Book Fair announced that next year the Fair will move back to a more central location – is excellent for most exhibitors. Unfortunately the catalysts for this change of mind, the team from the Frankfurt Book Fair, were thus excluded. It was a complicated series of events with a number of parties and I'm sure many people will feel let down, misled and double-crossed.

The coverage in the Independent newspaper – **The World Cup has not even started yet but already it's England 1, Germany 0** – was typically chauvinistic and anti-German. It's strange how the most liberal British commentators become quietly xenophobic where Germany is involved.

14 May 2006

Asia

I feel as if there's been simply too much on this blog about the UK. For Macmillan the UK represents about 15% of our people and about the same proportion of our sales. Of course it's important and the issues affecting the UK quite often have global implications but my mind turned elsewhere – to Asia where we have seen and are continuing to enjoy exceptional growth across a range of activities and territories.

Earlier this year we launched a web landing page for these operations which you can find here. I'll mention just four of the many new initiatives.

Just over a year ago Pan Macmillan Asia opened its doors as a sales and distribution agency for all Macmillan and Holtzbrinck USA and for a number of highly successful third-party publishers such as Rodale and Granta. The next step is rapidly to build our service for Australian publishers who rightly see Asia as a natural export market for them.

A little earlier we established a mainland Chinese publishing operation with the top Chinese publisher FLTRP. Our joint textbook programme, New Standard English, already has sales of more than 50 million copies a year and is growing alongside a raft of other initiatives.

Macmillan Production Asia has sourced print for Macmillan companies in Asia for decades but only recently have we offered this service to non-Macmillan companies. The year has begun with excellent new business in Germany, Greece, Mexico, and Australia. And it's not just books – MPA can supply globes, diaries, MP3 Players and deckchairs.

And finally Nature Asia Pacific which is launching new journal services in Chinese, Korean and Japanese; working with scientific and academic societies; building websites for better dissemination of both Western and Asian research and helping industrial companies comunicatte with their markets.

There is a great calypso, London is the place for me, but Asia is where it's happening.

16 May 2006

On outselling Dan Brown

Further to my Asia posting on Sunday, it was serendipitous that The Times ran an article yesterday, 'How to eat peas and then outsell Dan Brown' featuring Macmillan Education and FLTRP's New Standard English (NSE) series of text books for primary school children that has sold 105 million copies in China. NSE has set a new standard for English teaching text books in the region due to a radical new approach using cartoons, songs, funny stories and games which are engaging a new generation of school children in China.

17 May 2006

Publishing without frontiers

Our international sales teams acknowledge no frontiers: Charles Jenkins, International Sales Manager at <u>Palgrave Macmillan</u> has just sent me these dispatches after his recent trip to the Kurdistan region in Northern Iraq..

'After overcoming considerable logistical and security challenges, the first International Book Fair to take place in Iraq for nearly 30 years went ahead last week in Erbil, the administrative capital of the Iraq Kurdistan region which is located in the North of Iraq, not far from Mosul. Held in a specially constructed exhibition hall in a beautifully landscaped park, amid tight security, it was formally opened by the newly-appointed Minister of Higher Education from the Kurdish Regional Government(KRG).

It had been hoped the President of Iraq, Jalal Talabany, the first non-Arab President of an Arab country would attend, but his visit was called off at the last minute for security reasons. Many officials from various Iraqi and KRG Ministries were in attendance along with representatives from every University and library in the country, starved for so long of good quality English and local language books and materials for the educational sector.

The Book Fair provided an excellent opportunity for foreign and Arabic academic publishers and suppliers to display and sell their latest textbooks, library books and materials. The Iraqi government had budgeted about £700,000 for the purchase of books relating to Higher Education in the English Language; cash sales were brisk, and in the purchasing frenzy one could witness the unusual sight of boxes of books being hauled away in supermarket trolleys by librarians, academics, students and private individuals, under the watchful eye of the ubiquitous, gun-toting Peshmerga soldiers . . . theft was not a problem at this Fair! Most popular subject areas included medicine, engineering, sciences(particularly geology), English language/linguistics/literature and business.

Kurdish National flags fluttered proudly at the entrance to the Fair, something which would not have been possible before Saddam's overthrow. The event was widely heralded as a great success and one that is hoped will become established as an important annual event in the educational and cultural development of the country in the future.

No other foreign publisher's representatives attended. Many were not permitted by their companies to visit or, if they were, were unwilling to do so because of the perceived security risks, despite Erbil being much safer in reality than most of the rest of the country provided sensible precautions are taken. The US monitor all commercial and military flights in and out of Iraqi airspace and two American F16 Jets were in close radio contact with my plane from Amman 'guiding' us in to Erbil airport. It's still very much uncharted territory from a business travel perspective and it was in fact the first time these particular Royal Jordanian pilots had ever flown into Erbil!

Erbil, believed by many to be the oldest continuously-inhabited city in the world is definitely 'back on the map' and eager to reintegrate itself into the international business community.'

🕊 18 May 2006

Letter from America

Just back from two days on the East Coast of the USA. First stop Boston for meetings at Bedford St Martins where we discussed the rapidly changing US college textbook market. As in most markets, students are demanding more and more and are willing (or able) to pay less and less. However, what is clear is that how we deliver information for students is becoming almost as important as what we deliver – and that the winners will be those who innovate, learn and change fast.

One lesson I learned and I am happy to share with you – don't go to Anthony's Pier 4 restaurant. Apparently it was good 25 years ago – but they don't seem to have adapted.

Second stop New York and meetings with our cousinly trade publishing houses. I do love America. When you get a bestseller you REALLY get a bestseller. I'm not at liberty to disclose how many copies Farrar, Straus and Giroux have sold of The World is Flat and in any event I've already forgotten but it sure makes a difference.

But for me the most personal sales figure is that yesterday this blog exceeded 1000 (1152 to be precise) visitors for the first time. I feel just like an author when a bookshop places a re-order.

And whilst in self-congratulatory mood, some months ago I rabbitted on about Lonesome George, a bizarre but IMHO brilliant book about a celibate giant tortoise called George. Well, I'm not alone. The Guardian reviewer loved it too and the headline, The Fire in Lonesome George's Loins, says it all.

🕊 20 May 2006

Wormsley

Yesterday I was able to visit one of the most beautiful places in England in the Spring. Being England, it rained on and off. I have also been experimenting with loading picture files and so I hope this works. It didn't work for this printed version and so I've edited out further references to the pictures!

Paul Getty, an American but an anglophile, fell in love with cricket and decided to create a cricket ground exactly as it should be in the grounds of his estate in the Chiltern Hills. The Wisden Group has been allowed to host an annual tournament there and I was lucky enough to be invited.

Cricket may not be the most universally comprehensible sport but at least it is played in beautiful surroundings.

More on Google

I was going to do a piece on Google today following an article entitled Scan This Book by Kevin Kelly in last Sunday's (May 14) New York Times Magazine which was an apologia for Google and its plans to digitise all the world's knowledge (without asking permission from copyright holders). The problem is that the article (of May 14) is now more than seven days old and the NYT charges for access to its archive. I couldn't be bothered to go to the hassle of paying – hence no in-depth review (which is probably a relief to you all). I was slightly pissed off at being asked to pay.

Nevertheless thank goodness the NYT company IS charging. The Times is trying to build an economically sustainable model to help pay for its present and future investments in web technology and editoprial standards and they are protecting copyright by establishing that content has a value.

It is strange that the NYT has adopted a strictly commercial and proper arrangement when it comes to protecting its own copyright – and yet it sees no inconsistency in supporting 'cool' Google which appear to be bent on undermining the very sort of commercial arrangements being developed by book publishers.

It is really a very strange world where those who are arrogant or mad enough to think they can build a 'perfect search engine (which) would be like the mind of God' (Google co-founder, Sergey Brin) are treated as cool and honourable and publishers such as Random House, Bloomsbury, Reed Elsevier, Blackwell, Macmillan etc are regarded as dinosaurs when they spend money and creativity developing new ways to support their authors and excite their readers. Go figure.

PS I've now found a link to the KK article. Enjoy but treat with care – it's full of assertions about Google's 'do no evil' sentiment. Never forget that Google is a huge ($90 billion revenue) public company whose job is to maximise returns to its shareholders.

📝 23 May 2006

The world of Macmillan

Yesterday saw our twice a year board meeting. We reviewed last year's results, first quarter 2006 performance and our projections for the rest of the year. Or that's what we pretended to do. Actually it was an opportunity to collect our thoughts and focus on what really matters – where do we want to take the business, where are the opportunities for growth, where are the pratfalls, where the genuine strategic threats, are we investing enough in people, publishing, are we taking enough risks? It reminded me of the enormous breadth of the world of Macmillan – children's publishing, learned journals, software development, science, Picador, Papua New Guinea, Sao Paulo, Greece, On-line learning, site licences for academic content, books on memory sticks, online communities, mass-market paperbacks, growth in Russia, support for African education, sourcing slates from China, new authors versus existing blockbusters, building blogs for authors, developing sales analysis tools, serving US college publishers with text processing, selling New Zealand-developed literacy schemes to the USA and so on. All this is what makes publishing so exciting, interesting and fulfilling.

And meanwhile the Google debate continues and we have a new concept, the literati/technorati divide which you can read about at http://www.washingtonpost.com/wp-dyn/content/article/2006/05/21/AR2006052101349_pf.html.

Incidentally a googly (from which the great organisation may have derived its name – OED please check) is a delivery by a right arm spin bowler which to a right hand batsman appears as if it will spin from leg to off, however, spins in the opposite direction. This may well be the problem with Google too.

🗓 24 May 2006

BookStore goes international

I can't help admire the Boersenverein des Deutschen Buchhandels , Germany's association for the book trade, which yesterday launched its 'full-text search online' project. This collaborative initiative to develop a digital content storage and delivery platform, in which all German booksellers and publishers will be invited to participate, is a forward-thinking approach for sure. Germany certainly looks like it's wisely gearing up for an increasingly digital future.

Of course I am particularly pleased that MPS Technologies and Hamburg-based sister company HGV, both Holtzbrinck companies, have been chosen as development partners for the project. MPS Technologies and HGV launched their 'digital warehouse' concept, BookStore, at the Frankfurt Book Fair last year. Since then a prototype has been developed and demonstrated to many publishers in the UK, Germany and the USA. A beta site will be available in late June. A bespoke version of the BookStore platform will be developed for the Börsenverein which will be offered to publishers across Germany and launched at the Frankfurt Book Fair 2006.

Yet one more step in publishers and booksellers opening their eyes to the imperative of adapting to a digital future.

🗓 25 May 2006

Best film quote

I've been waiting for an opportunity to use my favourite film quote of all time. There were one or two moments in my sojourn at the Publishers Association and quite a few at Macmillan but they're not bloggable. So I'm going to give it to you anyway. I suspect it only works in English, so apologies to non-native speakers. It comes from one of the great non-arthouse films, Carry on Cleo (original idea by William Shakespeare), and was spoken by the brilliant and camp Kenneth Williams playing Julius Caesar as the plotters encircle. The line was lifted from an earlier series, Take it from here, by Frank Muir and Denis Norden.

And the quote?

Infamy, infamy, they've all got it in for me.

As a commentator points out, it gives 'Et tu, Brute' decent competition.

Hearts and minds

Three years ago Nature Publishing Group decided to invest heavily in clinical medical publishing. We were well-established in science, particularly biology, and thus our medical focus was on the scientific rather than clinical end of health care. Of course clinical medicine is a very heavily published area and there are many very old and well-established competitors. (I was the editor of Oxford Medical Publications back in 1975 – and a great job it was.) If we were to succeed in this field we'd have to do things a bit differently and better. Peter Ashman who has driven the project from its inception tells us a bit about it:

'About two and a half years ago, Nature Publishing Group made our first foray into Nature-branded medical publishing with the launch of the first four Nature Clinical Practice (NCP) journals. Since then we've launched a further four with more in the pipeline.

Quite apart from the achievement of launching eight journals in 12 months – an incredible feat in itself – one of the great successes of the Nature Clinical Practice series has been our ability to attract some of the world's leading medical specialists and opinion leaders as Editors-in-Chief and on to Advisory Board members. Doctors such as Vincent T DeVita (NCP Oncology) and Valentin Fuster (NCP Cardiovascular Medicine) are frequently approached by publishers asking them to endorse or to lend their weight to some medical publishing project or other. For NPG, we have been delighted by the willingness of so many key global figures to embrace the NCP concept and to give so freely of their time and knowledge.

One of our Advisory Board members is the pioneering heart surgeon Professor Sir Magdi Yacoub who, despite 'retiring' in 2001 is still a major influencer in the world of heart transplantation. An example of his continuing influence is the recent case of 12 year old Hannah Clarke who suffered from cardiomyopathy (a condition in which the heart can inflame to double its size before, frequently, giving up) on whom Professor Yacoub performed a heart transplant in 1995. During the operation Yacoub took the unplanned decision that, rather than remove the girl's heart, he would leave it in situ and place the donor heart on top – a 'piggy-back' procedure.

This turned out to be a visionary decision as, ten years on, doctors discovered that Hannah's body was rejecting the donor heart and it needed to be removed. Doctors called on Professor Yacoub to come out of retirement and advise on what to do. The decision was taken that Hannah's own heart, having had a 10-year rest, could now be re-started – the operation was undertaken and has proved to be a resounding success with Hannah now being able to stop taking her anti-rejection drugs. Had Professor Yacoub removed Hannah's heart in 1995 as was the norm for this type of condition ten years ago – Hannah would probably be dead by now. You can read more on this heart-warming story on the BBC site and here at CORDIS.

It's an honour for us at Nature to be working with people who make such a difference to our lives.'

Book and media statistics

The Publishers Association has just published its <u>Statistics Yearbook for 2005</u>. It's well worth getting a copy if only to marvel at the divergence between popular perception and reality.

Next week Macmillan is welcoming a group of top German booksellers to London to learn what's going on in the UK and perhaps to avoid some of the British mistakes. And I'm hoping we can learn something from them. As part of the preparation we have been digging in to swathes of statistics on consumer behaviour in relation to reading etc. I thought I'd share some of the nuggets.

In Germany Internet users have increased from 7% of the population in 1997 to 58% now. The over 60 year olds have increased from 0 in 1997 to 18% now.

In UK Internet advertising now represents 7% of total media spend up 73% on the previous year.

In USA 27% of online users buy or sell in online auction sites.

On average across the world people spend 6.5 hours a week reading. The most of amount time spent reading is in India (10.7 hours), the least Korea (3.1 hours). UK is very near the bottom at 5.3 hours, Germany and USA a little higher at 5.7 hours.

The Chinese listen to radio less than any other nation (2.1 hours a week), Argentina the most (20.8 hours).

On average people now spend more time on the Internet for leisure (not work) than reading – 8.9 vs 6.5 hours. Mexico uses the Intenet for leisure least (6.3 hours) and Taiwan the most (12.6 hours).

Internet use reduces the time people have for reading by around 20%.

40% of Europeans do not read books.

More people use the Internet for leisure than read books in the developed world.

And people wonder why publishers are spending so much time and effort on digital developments . . .

28 May 2006

Exact Editions

The joy of electronic publishing is that new ideas can sometimes be turned into real businesses without huge capital investments. Take for instance <u>Exact Editions</u>. I quote from their description of themselves:

Exact Editions was founded in the summer of 2005 by Tim Bruce, Adam Hodgkin and Daryl Rayner. The founders have backgrounds in software, publishing and marketing and they are all veterans of the first wave of web publishing. Their aim with Exact Editions is to build a web service which works for publishers and readers to make magazines as useful, simple and pleasurable as any other web service. The starting point is that a magazine on the web can be exactly as it is on the page. The web page should look like the magazine and it should be there when you search for it.

No downloads, no flash, no 're-purposing', no messing around. Just straightforward click and search, point and browse.

The founders are all friends of mine and so I should declare an interest but it seems to me that they are doing everything absolutely right. A straightforward business model, a clean website, effective software functionality, a genuine market – and low overheads to run the business. Do try out some of the specimen issues and see what you think.

If they succeed (which I think they will) they will have done the magazine industry a huge favour in expanding their readership internationally as well as to their core domestic market. I'm not sure what Americans will make of the Spectator.

29 May 2006

Kathrin's first blog

As I mentioned a couple of blogs ago we are welcoming colleagues and friends from the book trade in Germany this week. Kathrin Berger from Stuttgart is the key organiser. Because things have gone so smoothly she has found the time to guest blog for me. Over to you, Kathrin.

We arrived yesterday and so far my spirit has lifted – London is always lively and overwhelming. There is no other city in Europe where you meet so many different cultures. We went for a walk in the city and for we Germans it was great because all the shops were open on a Sunday!

We're staying at a pretty hotel with flowers everywhere in the room – that's what we call typical English. Today it is a holiday in the UK but nevertheless we will start our conference. I am really curious what we will learn about the UK book market and the current trends there.

Tonight we will meet some authors at the Chelsea Arts Club – Clare Francis, Peter James, and Wilbur Smith and then tomorrow real work trying to get to grips with the absurdities and charms of English-language bookselling.

30 May 2006

All Blacks and Kiwis

I've been blessed by good bosses throughout my career – honestly! One of the very best was Dan Davin who was responsible for hiring me to Oxford University Press in 1975. Apart from teaching me most of what I know about scholarly publishing he also introduced me to the expatriate New Zealand community in Oxford and London. To this day I marvel at the creative, literary and sporting output of that tiny country. Not only that but in the Macmillan world New Zealand is always at or near the top of our league of best performing businesses. How come? Because we have the very best people. I asked our NZ Managing Director, David Joel, to tell us what's happening over there.

Dispatches from New Zealand

With the advent of the blog we seem to have mixed the boundaries of the formal business and the personal. At work the perfunctory 'Good Morning' may be enough without giving away all the personal issues or delight in our lives –the blog and perhaps the internet seem to have changed that. If I mentioned in a blog I was really disappointed in the Super 14 final (a Rugby Union competition between Australia, South Africa and New Zealand) was held in such foggy conditions in Christchurch last Saturday it was as hopeless as the 'mist' spectacle. you may not be surprised. If I mentioned this in a business report I might be considered loopy. Of course the final was between two New Zealand teams. I can tell you the failure of the Rugby spectacle was more than made up for on Sunday afternoon at a Beethoven concert conducted by my brother's son which was spectacular. The soloist for the Violin Concerto was nothing but brilliant. I have about 8 CDs of the Beethoven Violin Concerto by different violinists (I can't seem to get the Campoli one though) and I have to believe this young man was nothing but the best. Or is it that a live performance cannot be beaten by a CD? In any case Eugene Lee is a violinist to look out for. Beethoven's 5th was excellent too.

On a more mundane note the recent NZ budget here was criticized because it did not offer personal income tax cuts. It was named the Bondi budget because the place to obtain a tax cut is in Australia (Oz is a three hour flight away and is not joined to Auckland by the Sydney Harbour Bridge as some who live in the Northern Hemisphere believe) where they recently announced tax cuts in their budget. The prime NZ budget announcement was preempted from the budget night because a government courier had leaked the proposed budget announcement of the deregulation of Telecom two weeks early to Telecom themselves. Because it is the most significant NZ listed company Telecom felt they had to let the government know they had this information. So much for NZ Government security! To think we might obtain better ADSL prices and speed by deregulation? Why am I so cynical about central government's ability to deliver?

In the book publishing industry the big news is that Penguin are moving their distribution to Australia in a few months along with Hachette Livre. The plane might take three hours but airfreight seems to take a week and a ship a month. At Macmillan NZ we should be smiling as we are in the process of installing a mezzanine in our warehouse which will give us 50% more floor space. We will be the only publisher/distributor in NZ which stocks tertiary titles.

Richard Charkin astutely pointed out before we put in the mezzanine we should just reduce the stock by half – we could reduce it totally if we distributed from Australia. Only time will tell which publishers are making the right move. In the meantime we are going to play on the concept our books are sent from NZ and not packed by people in Australia (You'll note the rivalry between the countries does not stop on the Rugby field).

The other issue in New Zealand is the price of petrol (we are part of the global community after all) The price has risen 70% this year and we now pay about $1.80 per litre.(60p) This might not be so bad compared with the UK but it is a real shock to us all here.

We are blaming this for our difficulty meeting expected sales as we can't seem to find another reason. It would be stretching credibility to believe that the demise of our 5c piece (sixpence in the old currency) was the reason. Surely everyone realizes $29.95 is about twenty dollars whereas $30.00 is thirty dollars without dispute?

It has been said those of us who live in Auckland know the price of everything but the value of nothing. Well I paid the price for the new Blackberry model 8700 in the belief the irritating button on the side would be remedied (and it has) but they didn't tell me the screen backlight would go off after not more than 2 minutes and I could see nothing unless I pressed a button – so much for my nonchalance in meetings now. New models are supposed to be an advancement in critical areas but the new Blackberry demonstrates this is not always the case. I'm still not disposing of the old model yet. I thought I might put it on Trademe (NZ's eBay). I could give you a blog on the story of TradeMe and NZ's Gullivers Travels – in fact I have just thought of about 100 things I could blog on about but who would be interested?

Greetings to all from New Zealand.

31 May 2006

HMV (Waterstone's) buys Ottakar's

It seems that the deal is done although has the fat lady sung? Check out BBC news.

I calculate that HMV has paid £35m less than they originally offered. This reduction was caused by a deterioration in Ottakar's trading between the original offer and now. The delay was caused by the referral of the deal to the Competition Commission. I suspect that the whole affair has cost HMV (and everyone else) a huge amount of money in legal and economist fees (not to mention management time) but at least HMV shareholders have a better deal than they might have done.

Let's now hope that the book trade can get back to selling more books more economically and that the lessons of this sorry affair are well and truly learnt.

≤ June 2006 ≥

Mon	Tue	Wed	Thu	Fri	Sat	Sun
29	30	31	1	2	3	4
5	6	7	8	9	10	11
12	13	14	15	16	17	18
19	20	21	22	23	24	25
26	27	28	29	30	1	2
3	4	5	6	7	8	9

Stats and things

A new month means I can't resist checking out the number of visitors to this blog. Here we go:

January 9036

February 8492

March 18724

April 19257

May 22868

I suspect numbers will fall during the (Northern Hemisphere) Summer months as people rush off to their Tuscan villas . . . but you never know. The public is unpredictable.

The visit by our German bookseller and publisher colleagues finished yesterday. I'm not quite sure what they made of the British book trade scene as they were treated to excellent but not altogether consistent discussions with leaders of bookshop chains, Internet gurus and retail market experts. I think the overwhelming theme is one of confusion and complexity. Finding a way through will require good will as well as foresight – and with profit margins for most participants in the general book supply chain very low good will tends to take second place to achieving budget.

02 June 2006

More digitalia

This week has been ever more focussed on matters digital. Bookseller concerns, librarian concerns, authorial concerns, publisher concerns.

Macmillan New Writing in India

When we launched Macmillan New Writing a couple of months ago one of the authors, Suroopa Mukherjee, came to London with her husband for the launch. You can see and listen to her talking about her book here.

The book (along with the others in the series) is selling well on the back of excellent reviews and by present-day standards reasonable stock in bookshops.

The series was greeted with varying degrees of enthusiasm in the British media but I think this article in India's leading newspaper Daily News and Analysis is the best balanced.

Incidentally, if you go to the MNW website you'll see that a number of the titles are showing as out of stock. We have had to reprint just about every one – but new stock will be available soon and there are copies in bookshops – both independents and chains.

🦋 04 June 2006

Gordon Brown

For those who don't know (or don't care) Gordon Brown is the Chancellor of the Exchequer in the UK (Finance Minister in most other countries). He is trying to become Prime Minister and as a consequence spends a deal of time sucking up to foreign heads of state and cuddles a lot of African babies in order to show what a great guy he is. He also wishes to maintain a reputation as a 'prudent' chancellor and a scourge of tax dodgers.

His main attack on 'tax dodgers' has been to steal billions of pounds from pension funds thus discouraging prudent saving and personal responsibility.

His latest attack is described in the Sunday Times today. Essentially he seems to have decided that authors' agents are not a tax-deductible business expense. Now I am one of the first people to decry the role of the literary agent in contemporary publishing but to pretend they are not a legitimate business expense is absurd. I'm sure this tax-raising nonsense will fail but it is symptomatic of current British politicians to think they might get away with it. As they say in the Drones Club, harrumph.

🦋 05 June 2006

Are Books Dead?

RajAT commented on an earlier posting here (27 May) that:

'The most connected country in the world that is Korea is spending least time reading books. Now there lies the juice. Does this mean that internet is going to kill the books as we know. Has it become an outmoded means of communicating information.'

He goes on to quote from Jeff Jarvis of the Buzz Machine about some of the problems with books:

- They are frozen in time without the means of being updated and corrected.

- They have no link to related knowledge, debates, and sources.

- They create, at best, a one-way relationship with a reader.

- They try to teach readers but don't teach authors.

- They tend to be too damned long because they have to be long enough to be books.

- They are expensive to produce.

- They depend on scarce shelf space.

- They depend on blockbuster economics.

- They can't afford to serve the real mass of niches.

- They are subject to gatekeepers' whims.

- They aren't searchable.

- They aren't linkable.

- They have no metadata.

- They carry no conversation.

- They are thrown out when there's no space for them anymore.

Of course there are plenty of positives about books. We'd better make sure our marketplace understands – or we'd better address some of the book's shortcomings using technology.

🕐 06 June 2006

Change change change

It was not so long ago that Google was revered as a whiter than white crusader against evil, an upholder of right against might, of menschlichkeit against corporatism. That image has changed. Has it changed permanently?

They have managed to alienate nearly all of the publishing industry. A colleague has now alerted me to Bob Cringely writing on the PBS website. It appears that now they have pissed off their advertising clients. 'Click fraud' is an obvious and very dangerous development. Google seems ill-equipped or unwilling to deal with it. The very basis of their prosperity and credibility is being challenged.

They are also bloody awful at communication. Weren't they meant to be helping the world not creating a job's-worth humourless soviet e-bureaucracy?

And on the subject of change, one of the key planks of scholarly research is peer review. The advent of the Internet is potentially opening up possibilities for wider, deeper, more open review. Nature is undertaking trials and running a debate. Even if you are not a scientist I do recommend you check this out. It is a sign of more change but a change which is being thoroughly road-tested. Google, please note.

Tonight I am attending the awards ceremony for the Orange Prize for the woman who, in the opinion of the judges, has written the best, eligible full-length novel in English. Our shortlisted author is Carrie Tiffany. Fingers crossed for her this evening.

And back to Nature. The editor, the esteemed Dr Phil Campbell, has just received a bottle of white wine in the post. At the risk of breaking a confidence or breaching copyright I am pasting in his email on the subject:

I have on my desk a bottle of white wine – unopened, so far. It is called 'Nature!' The typography is almost identical to our logo, though the first letter is upper case.

The full label reads:

Nature!

According to Gabriel Escande

It's different. Under the capsule, no bubbles, no foam. No cheating, just fruit.

Savour it, devour it, drink it. Fruity, cool, smooth, lively, easy and simply good. No fuss.

A taste from the aromatic Mediterranean 'garrigue'. This is because it's made in the vineyards, not in factories. By men, not by machines. Because it does you good.

Because our body is thirsty but our spirit is hungry. Because nature's like that . . . .

Recommendation: we have two options:

1. Sue them to hell and back.

2. Hire their copywriters and set up an exchange subscription.

My recommendation is that we drink it at the next board meeting and then decide.

🦎 07 June 2006

Orange

Literary prizes always generate a pile of back-biting among the gliterati of the book world. Whilst biting and scratching backs we often forget to say thank you. So here it is – THANK YOU ORANGE FOR SUPPORTING WOMEN'S FICTION.

We at Macmillan were disappointed that Carrie Tiffany did not win. This disappointment was soon moderated by the pleasure of Zadie Smith deservedly winning with On Beauty. But general book publishing is strange and complicated. The German edition of On Beauty will be published in August by one of our sister companies in Germany – Kiepenheuer & Witsch. White Teeth and the Autograph Man were also published in German by a sister company, Droemer Knaur. So hooray for Zadie.

People say that publishers must be optimists. Searching for good news like this is a symptom of that optimism.

I talk a lot about innovation in publishing. It's very hard to define but you know it when you see it. Take a look at the Think Publishing website and see if you agree.

And finally another piece of innovation, Nature Network Boston, an example of how scientific publishing is moving away from a content-supply business towards becoming a facilitator of communications for scientists.

🦎 08 June 2006

Reaching the parts other publishers . . .

Our print sourcing office in Hong Kong, MPAL, is challenged by its publisher customers every day. The latest is a request to quote for the delivery of textbooks to Sulaymaniyah. It is just possible that not everyone knows where Sulaymaniyah is – it's more or less due East of Kirkuk. You will notice the preponderance of neighbouring towns with (destroyed) beneath their name. As I say, we face challenges every day.

A colleague has just reminded me of the apposite motto of the New York postal service:

'Neither snow nor rain nor heat nor gloom of night stays these couriers from the swift completion of their appointed rounds.'

BookStoreMore

Before getting into the main part of today's blog I thought you might enjoy this link to the distinguished medical journal <u>Annals of Internal Medicine</u>. The guy on the left has clearly fallen asleep while reading the journal resting on his chest. You may notice that the journal's title has been grayed out. The journal in question is our very own <u>Nature Clinical Practice Endocrinology</u> and one wonders why someone bothered to gray out its title. Because they don't want to publicise another publisher's journal? Can you imagine the hordes of people who might cancel their subscription to Annals in order to subscribe to Endocrinology because of the picture? Or because they think we might sue them for implying that our journal has sedative side-effects? Who knows? The email telling me about this was simply headed 'weird' and indeed it is.

From time to time (perhaps too often for the more light-hearted) I have mentioned our new investment in <u>BookStore</u>. It is progressing well with really encouraging discussions with publishers, retailers, wholesalers, and printers in a number of countries. When we decided to set it up we wondered whether it would be better to wait until the whole book trade had agreed on standards for the delivery of digital information. It would really make sense for there to be a standard but speed is also important and we all know how long it takes any industry to agree on anything. However, a reader of this blog wrote to me about all this and as he was an author at our sister company <u>St. Martin's Press</u> and as he seems to make sense here's what he has to say:

Could the BookStore digital warehouse actually end up more standards-compliant than Amazon or Google – and thus gain the moral high ground? OpenReader, a new consumer-level e-book format that's a turbocharged version of the existing OEBPS production standard, is worth a close look. dotReader, the first implementation of OpenReader, will even allow blogs and forums to show up in specified locations in e-books. It will also permit interbook deep linking.

As an author, I look forward to interactivity for appropriate books. For example, the Complete Laptop Computer Guide (St. Martin's Press, 1990) could have appeared with forums to let my readers update the guide with their insights. Likewise, medical, legal and scientific books could be kept timely, and classes could jointly mark up textbooks. The notes would be accessible even off line.

dotReader will also offer optional DRM and even let interested publishers insert advertising, one way to drive down textbook costs and protect margins. Moreover, translation houses such as Rosetta Solutions like the philosophy of the accompanying OpenReader format.

For more information – and I hope that BookStore and publishers follow up – people can reach me at 703-370-6540 or davidrothman@openreader.org. I can arrange for guided virtual demonstrations of the new technology, regardless of your time zone.

Helpful URLs: OpenReader Consortium (openreader.org), dotReader (dotReader.com), a mock-up of dotReader (http://www.dotreader.com/site/?q=node/45), why dotReader stands out (http://www.dotreader.com/site/?q=node/18), dotReader's Dorothy Thompson connection (http://www.dotreader.com/site/?q=node/17), and OSoft (osoft.com).

Thanks,

David Rothman, co-founder of OpenReader.

🦅 10 June 2006

Ravi Dayal

I've been lucky enough in my career to have worked for and with amazing people. It's impossible for me to create league tables as they do at the Nibbies but the former Managing Director of Oxford University Press in India, Ravi Dayal was definitely premiership. He was the real editor, the real publisher, the real thing – and a gent to boot. I have just heard about his death and wanted to write about him but Amitav Ghosh says it so much better.

🦅 11 June 2006

Publishers becoming writers

Before today's piece I need to add a link about Ravi Dayal.

I was reminded of a long tradition this morning when reading an excellent review of Simon Winder's The man who saved Britain. The book is all about James Bond and his impact on British and global culture. By all accounts the writing and insights are brilliant.

Simon Winder is the editorial director of Penguin Press, the up-market non-fiction part of Penguin – and he does a great job as you can see from, for instance the history section of the Penguin website (I couldn't find a link to Penguin Press itself except on the US website and I don't think Simon is responsible for that imprint – ain't publishing strange?).

It got me thinking about publishers who became authors or really were primarily authors. We publish a few. Robin Robertson is a superb picker of contemporary fiction for Jonathan Cape but he manages to put aside his business head from time to time and produce some of the finest poetry of our time. Tim Binding worked successfully for Simon and Schuster before deciding to go into full-time writing. I'm sure there are plenty of others.

It sometimes goes the other way too. Stephen King has been known to become a publisher of his own novels on the web. And Susan Hill launched Long Barn Books some years ago and is still going strong.

My instincts are that writers should stick to writing and publishers to publishing but as usual the evidence suggests otherwise. Perhaps someone can find something to support my contention.

Book scanning and best seller lists

A wonderful article in Slate about how journalists have fun telling the truth about book sales through Book Scan as opposed to the hype is worth reading if only for the last pastiche Bob Dylan line. The article explains why writers pick on enemies not friends when revealing abysmally poor sales figures because 'the scanner now will later be scanned'.

This article also coincides with Joel Rickett explaining in the Guardian about the new independent booksellers' bestseller chart. The point is that sales of mass-market books through supermarkets in the first couple of weeks after publication are a function of where the supermarket chooses to display rather than whether the book has really caught the imagination of the reading public. This can sound like an elitist argument but it is a genuine concern. The new chart reflects what is selling in 'real' bookshops and is almost certainly a better indication. All strength to the new chart and I hope it is taken up by national newspapers.

12 June 2006

It had to happen

I was waiting for it – and it has happened. Nature has a special section on the science of football. Enjoy!

13 June 2006

Spin

A strange thing happened yesterday. I attended a meeting along with several other publishing colleagues with a major Internet company. We were discussing a number of issues. In particular how publishers need to protect their authors' intellectual property rights while making the most of the opportunities of the web etc.

The strange thing was that there were two highly articulate and clever senior representatives of the company but accompanied by two 'communications consultants' who no doubt were intelligent and knowledgeable (not to mention well paid) but who said little apart from commenting on the time schedule.

Presumably somebody felt that we were more likely to agree if the message we received was suitably communicated. It is possible, however, that the knowledge that we were being 'spun' might make us just a tad more resistant to the arguments. It confirms my view that big corporations rarely show any degree of common sense or human understanding.

Fortunately, and in spite of the lack of expensive advisers on our side, the Publishers Association held firmly to the position that copyright law is not to be amended and distorted simply to suit the aspirations of a very big Internet company which claims to do no evil.

14 June 2006

Colm Toibin – a deserved winner

Picador Publisher Andrew Kidd gave me his take on last night's IMPAC win for Colm Toibin:

Yesterday Picador's Colm Toibin won the IMPAC Dublin Literary Award for his splendid novel THE MASTER. The prize is the richest in the world, and Colm received a cheque for 100,000 Euros. But what was most notable about last night's black tie ceremony, held in Dublin's beautifully restored City Hall, was not the pomp of the occasion but rather the extraordinary warmth that filled that high-ceilinged room. The excitement that an Irish writer was winning this prize for the first time and the deep admiration for THE MASTER were two reasons for it. But most of all the genuine love for Colm himself was the cause. Unlike some prize ceremonies, where the glamorous frocks, the (minor) celebrities and the overwrought canapes obscure the real reason for being there, last night was all about a wonderful writer (and a great champion of other writers) getting the recognition he deserved. The Irish have always taken their artists more seriously than we do in the UK, and treated them with greater respect, and it was both humbling and inspiring to witness.

15 June 2006

Censorship and Humpty Dumpty

Some censorship is evil. Some is downright silly. Here's a piece of wonderful silliness courtesy of the BBC. I guess Alice in Wonderland will also have to be banned in case anyone notices the similarities between it and the actions of some politicians.

This afternoon England play Trinidad and Tobago in the World Cup Football tournament. The major trade union in the publishing world (and in many other worlds), Amicus, has got into trouble for allegedly giving out information on how to 'throw a sickie'. This would allow employees to watch the match while still being paid. A major supermarket chain, Asda, has apparently offered staff two weeks unpaid leave on the grounds that they won't be working anyway. I'm in two minds on all this. On the one hand winning would cheer the country up. But early elimination might well be good for the economy. Losing to T&T would be a national humiliation but the British do have a reputation for enjoying a touch of masochism.

Whatever else the Cup seems to have killed off High Street book sales except that there are three soccer books in the top five non-fiction bestseller list – Gazza, Pele and our very own Match World Cup book.

16 June 2006

Hawk-Eye

My friends at Wisden have forged a brilliant partnership with which you can read about here. They have acquired Hawk-Eye which is the computer simulation that tennis and cricket followers have been enjoying for several years and which is now extending to other sports.

I never dreamt when I first joined the Board of Wisden some ten years ago that we would be measuring our market in the hundreds of millions worldwide and would have extended to other sports and other media. Even had I foreseen that I would then not have believed that the original Wisden Cricketers Almanack would not only be thriving (2006 has been a record sales year) but that its editorial standards have never been higher.

It can be done. Merging innovation, technology, good business practice, vision, strategy with traditional literary, scholarly and editorial values. Hooray.

🗐 17 June 2006

Madrid

Dateline 17 June . . . staying at the formidable <u>Westin Palace Hotel</u> for the annual Georg von Holtzbrinck management meeting. Last year was in <u>Trier</u> where we were treated to EU propaganda from a European commissioner for information and culture. What I remember best was that the reason given for France and Netherlands voting against the proposed European Constitution was the ignorance of the electorate. And that the EU was intending to remedy this by setting up marketing offices throughout the Community. What an excellent way of spending citizens' taxes.

Restaurant tip – go try <u>Botin de Madrid</u> if you're into black pudding, pigs' trotters, baby lamb and peppers. Fantastic.

As we're in Madrid we've taken the opportunity of showcasing our <u>Spanish</u> and <u>Latin-American</u> operations which have been growing at a startling rate.

Off to work now . . .

🗐 18 June 2006

More Madrid

For an amazing collection of various schools and types of art do go to <u>Thyssen Bornemisza Museum</u>. We went there for a reception and dinner last night and shivered over tapas outside – I thought Madrid was meant to be hot hot hot.

As I write Brazil have just scored against Australia. Up to that point Australia looked the equal of the might Brazilians and my prediction of an unlikely Australia England world cup football final a little more likely – but now?

I seem to have upset my good friend Anne from the Federation of European Publishers with yesterday's remarks about EU commissioners. Sorry, Anne, I can't help disliking centralism of any sort.

🗐 19 June 2006

Why blog?

This blog started as an in-house newsletter on email. The IT department complained that it was causing too many people to hold large amounts of data in their in-boxes thus slowing down the system. Then someone suggested I do it as a blog. Then the question as to whether it should be internal to Macmillan or open to the world. We decided to go public on the grounds that if I wrote anything of interest someone would forward it to the trade press anyway!

Having decided to go this route I then tried to justify it post hoc as a means of learning about modern communication. So what have I learned?

How to type letters with accents. Café olé.

How to <u>hyperlink</u>.

How a <u>social network</u> operates.

How to respond to a comment.

How to upset people.

And a few other things I dare not mention.

Today is business plan day for Latin America – so head down to scrutinise the numbers.

20 June 2006

Mexican democracy

Yesterday's blog generated a few comments about the purpose of blogging itself. Do give them a look.

This morning's work has been focussed on planning with our Mexican colleagues. The trouble is nobody knows the result of the July presidential election – or at least I hope nobody knows the result in advance of the poll.

Mexico seems to be following the rest of the democratic world in having a neck and neck contest – think Germany, USA, Italy. The two candidates are politically miles apart but are equally likely to win according to the pollsters. The result affects many things in Mexico not least the direction of publishing. The uncertainty is compounded by the likelihood of the third candidate's votes being split equally between the front runners.

If you're interested in this election do check out this article and in particular note the health warnings.

Disfruten!

21 June 2006

What makes an old blogger tick?

'Anon' commented on this blog yesterday that the first law of blogging is that 'all blogs before too long stop addressing the issues for which the blog was established and start talking about the act of blogging.' Apparently this makes me a 'true blogger', a label which I happily accept. And I suppose that like any 'type', we bloggers do like to discuss and debate the very activity to which we are so committed. But I hope it doesn't indicate that this blog has become a navel-gazing exercise in any way. The thing that continues to motivate me to blog is the chance to talk about the issues and challenges of publishing today and to engage with others who are excited and challenged by the same things.

Speaking of which, one of the things challenging most publishers right now is how we continue to provide services and products that ensure we are relevant and useful to the communities we serve. One such initiative is Macmillan Medical Communications (MMC), which launches this month. A strategic medical communications agency, MMC is set up to provide customized products and services for partners in the pharmaceutical, healthcare, and biotechnology industries. It uses the full range of communication and publishing strategies to develop high impact campaigns and services including novel internet-based approaches.

MMC will specialize in the creation and localization of content for target audiences throughout the world, including some of the fastest growing pharmaceutical markets such as Far East Asia, India and Latin America. MMC will offer a broad range of services including local language reprints of Nature Publishing Group (NPG) articles, website development, targeted supplements, seminars, and strategic consultancy on publication and information dissemination strategies.

As the division of the Macmillan Group servicing the pharmaceutical and healthcare industries, MMC has exclusive access to some of the world's leading journal content, including journals from our own Nature Publishing Group <http://www.nature.com/> (NPG), publishers of Nature <http://www.nature.com/nature/> the international journal of science, Nature Medicine <http://www.nature.com/nm/> , the Nature Clinical Practice <http://www.nature.com/clinicalpractice/index.html> series of journals, and a large number of major medical society titles.

MMC's first live service is an experimental collaborative medical news site called Dissect Medicine (www.dissectmedicine.com), developed as a joint initiative with Nature Clinical Practice. MMC's activities will also include identifying local language sponsorship opportunities for Nature Clinical Practice titles, organizing seminars and conferences in regions where MMC teams are active. MMC will also work with some of NPG's society journals to help develop special projects outside the regular publication of their journals. These may include training and advocacy related projects. MMC will also run the production of local language editions of existing titles such as Kidney International, which is currently published in Japanese, Spanish and Portuguese.

 22 June 2006

Yes, but is it good for the Jews

Jonny Geller is a well-known literary agent working at (or is it 'with'?) Curtis Brown. He is well known for being 'cool' and 'sharp' and getting good deals for his clients. What isn't so well known is that he trained as a rabbi and is publishing his own book later this year. I was very keen for Macmillan to publish it but Jonny, being used to getting the top deal for his clients, managed to get great contracts from Bloomsbury in the USA and Penguin in the UK. I still reckon he should have come to us for the best if not the top deal. Nevertheless the book should be read and enjoyed as widely as possible and here is a link to a blog Jonny has created as a taster for the book.

Of course Jonny's advance didn't compare to Alan Greenspan's $8.5m from Penguin but as he says: This much money for a Jewish banker? Can this be good for the Jews? I'm worried..

Enjoy.

 23 June 2006

Chennai

This comes to you from Chennai (formerly known as Madras) which is the headquarters of our Indian operations. It was the Annual General Meeting this afternoon after a series of executive and Board meetings this morning. We now employ more than 3000 people in India and it is our fastest growing market. The shareholder issues today included complaints about the colour of the paper in our annual report, the lack of takeaway presents for attendants and the lack of a bonus shares or a share split. On the other hand there was enthusiasm for our strategy and our brilliant and diligent Indian team.

During the course of the day I came across some wonderful words and phrases. I particularly like:

Blamestorming – a meeting to decide who to blame for bad performance.

PDCA – plan, do, check, act – the antithesis of most publishing procedures.

Strategy without action is daydreaming; action without strategy is a nightmare.

And as I left the meeting an ex-employee grabbed me and said that the difference between Indian and American (or British) business is that the Indians don't 'go with a smile'. My experience says the opposite.

Back to the plane – incidentally free advice, avoid Delta Airlines.

 24 June 2006

Grumpy old air traveller

There are different opinions about President Charles de Gaulle of France. But there can be little argument that right now the airport named after him has turned itself into a premiership class rotten airport. The present design involves huge distances for travellers, impenetrable signage, unhelpful staff, lousy acoustics. Chennai was a place of peaceful efficiency in comparison. Is there or should there be a good airports guide so that people can plan their trips around avoiding particular black spots such as LAX, Lagos, and now league leader Paris. Incidentally, the PC in the lounge has only some of the keyboard working and no way of linking to another site – so please forgive lack of hypers and any spelling mistakes.

26 June 2006

Parallel universes

I seem to have bored one of our regular visitors by moaning about the airport in Paris. He has a fair point. Whingeing travellers are a pretty boring lot. In mitigation I had spent 10 hours in the air flying to Chennai, a day's solid work and then ten hours back.

But where I disagree with the correspondent is that international travel has nothing to do with understanding book buyers. My critic runs an antiquarian bookshop in middle class England and I have no doubt he understands his clientele. My job is to manage an international publishing house and our most important clients are school teachers and scientists in emerging markets such as India, Latin America and sub-Saharan Africa. The universe in which I travel is very different from Clive Keble's but I'd contend that kids in India represent the real world just as much as traditional book lovers in England – and maybe just maybe it's more important to work on developing these markets than on specialist antiquarian bookselling in Middle England.

Incidentally, who said anything about first class? A rule in Macmillan is that we seek the lowest cost travel wherever feasible.

And finally . . . . Macmillan's imprint for first novels, Macmillan New Writing, has attracted a great deal of attention, some positive, some negative, but most of it serving only to promote it further with authors and booksellers, all of which is very helpful. But one somewhat amusing trend is now emerging – a stream of submissions from, how shall I put it, 'incarcerated' individuals, hoping that somehow their artistic endeavours might serve as a 'get out of jail free' card . . . .

I'm posting here a letter recently received at the MNW offices:

'I am an artist and I've recently written two (2) books. One of the books is completed the other is still in the works. The completed one is Hot! (Not to toot my own horn) . . . .

The problem is this- I am incarcerated (since 2004) in a California state prison, on some bogus conviction. Due to the fact that I wasn't financially able to afford a 'real' attorney I was given a court appointed 'dump truck' thus the results being a 16 year conviction.

What I offer is this – I will give you the completed book, original manuscript, copy rights, and all the profits from the book sales.

What I want is this – I want a lawyer that can get me out of this position I am in. If he / she can't get me 'out', at least get me a sentence reduction (although I know nothing in guaranteed through the courts) I want to be recognized as the author and a flat 10.000 (ten thousand dollars).

So basically there is no loss for your company. To make it even better, I will give you the book in hand, manuscript, copyrights, and al the profits as well as the 'author' title for a flat 20.000 (twenty thousand dollars).
That's without the lawyer.

As you can see my main focus is getting out of prison and/or getting a real lawyer. If that means I have to give up 'all' my rights to the book just to get enough money for a lawyer then that's what I'm willing to do.'

Now that's what I call a tempting offer . . .

27 June 2006

Danger in Kings Cross

There are many things that can blow a publishing programme off course – late delivery of manuscripts, legal challenges, rows with retailers, stock deliveries going astray etc. Yesterday we suffered a new one.

Apparently part of the Kings Cross development programme suffered a fire. On the site there are fuel containers which might explode potentially sending toppling cranes onto one or both of our buildings. Pretty Hollywood. In any event the outcome is that we had to evacuate the buildings yesterday and probably today as well. That means we'll have lost some 1000 person days at a crucial time of the year. Fortunately many people are working from home or from our other UK sites – Oxford, Basingstoke, Swansea – but even so . . . The other plus is that our disaster recovery plans moved smoothly into action and all business-vital activities performed perfectly. What might have been seen as a bureaucratic exercise has proved its worth – not for the first time.

And Nigel Beale wrote a comment yesterday. It appears that the software on my comments won't allow hyperlinking and so please check out www.nigelbeale.com where you can find some really interesting interviews with authors, publishers and other literary figures alongside interesting blog critiques and debates.

And I want to show off a bit more about Macmillan Science. This is an experiment to see if we can take a particularly difficult part of general book publishing (popular science is in some senses a contradiction in terms) and create a different business model and still publish well. The model is that we only publish books where the author grants us world rights (no territorial restrictions, no arguments about who owns the Turkish book club rights etc), there is no advance but a high gross income related royalty, low expectations of bookshop support and hence lowish discounts, simultaneous global English-language publication, promotion to the scientific community through Nature and Scientific American, and most important of all an editor who understands popular science, scientific journalism and how to help authors promote their own work.

You only have to click on any of the covers on the website to get a feel for the quality of what we're publishing and we're doing it without all the hype of 'traditional' general book publishing. It's a simple formula. Spend money only where it's necessary. Keep editorial headcount to a minimum but make sure the editor is the very best. Reward authors who sell and don't reward (via unearned advances) those who do not. And don't forget that the world of books is global and that they do speak English in a little place called America.

28 June 2006

APT

Yesterday's blog (the bit about Macmillan Science) elicited a comment from Peter Collingridge who runs a design consultancy for publishing clients called APT. It's well worth reading as a constructive critique of the way Macmillan and others are approaching web marketing and the use of the Internet.

I have discovered one way of increasing traffic to this blog is to write the words 'Jeffrey Archer'. However, on this occasion I am not interested in increasing the number of visitors here but to encourage you to look at Jeffrey's blog which is part of his official website.

And while on the use of the Internet as a marketing vehicle, President Chirac has inaugurated a French version of Google Earth (although they deny that this is what it is). It launched last week and the interest has been so great that the following page comes up

http://www.geoportail.fr/excuses.htm.

I've left the url as it stands because there's something about the word 'excuses' which is perfectly fine in French but in English says it all. And some governments still think they can do a better job of web publishing than private enterprise . . . .

And finally an excellent article in Nature which analyses the financial standing of the most important open access organisation The Public Library of Science. What the article shows is that the 'author pays' model for scientific publishing is likely to be unsustainable without charitable support. I don't think that scientific publishing should be a charitable enterprise. Its innovation and growth has been driven by commercial market pressures to improve which have always been the best guarantee of high-quality service. The alternatives nearly always end in bureaucracy and protection of the status quo.

🦜 29 June 2006

Oxford university presses

I was in Oxford yesterday at the Macmillan Education offices in the former car-building (and now new Mini building) area of Cowley. Driving back I thought I might indulge in one of my favourite pastimes – listening to international cricket on the radio (Test Match Special). Unfortunately the English team were so dreadful and unprofessional in being beaten for the fourth time in a row by Sri Lanka I couldn't bear to listen.

Instead I tried to calculate the size of the publishing industry in Oxfordshire (Oxford and its surrounding area). It is a really impressive bunch of companies. Big daddy in terms of employees, sales and profits is probably Oxford University Press itself. Reed Elsevier has two major units – Elsevier Science in Kidlington (which incorporates the famous and brilliant Pergamon Press of Robert Maxwell fame) and Harcourt Education in Jordanhill (incorporating Heinemann Education, Ginn, Rigby etc). Blackwell Publishing is up the road from our offices and, not to be confused with its retailing cousins, is a hugely successful and profitable academic and scientific publisher. A little further South near Abingdon are the main offices of the academic divisions of Informa (Taylor & Francis, Routledge etc). Also in Abingdon we can find Hodder's distribution centre Bookpoint. And there are scores of smaller but no less significant specialist and general publishing firms scattered around the area.

I estimate total sales of publications emanating from these companies at well over €3 billion and profits close on €500m. I reckon this is more than the total profit emanating from London and maybe even New York. Explanations please.

≤ July 2006 ≥

Mon	Tue	Wed	Thu	Fri	Sat	Sun
26	27	28	29	30	1	2
3	4	5	6	7	8	9
10	11	12	13	14	15	16
17	18	19	20	21	22	23
24	25	26	27	28	29	30
31	1	2	3	4	5	6

🗓 01 July 2006

Ann Cleeves and The Author

I have been quite rightly chided for failing to celebrate Thursday's triumph at the Crime Writers' Association awards. Ann Cleeves the Duncan Lawrie Dagger award for her book Raven Black. This is the biggest crime writing prize in the world, completely deserved and wonderful for one of Macmillan's (and Pan's) favourite authors.

Another Macmillan author, Malcolm Mann, has written twelve English language teaching texts for us and there are more in the pipeline. He has just launched a new website called Manifesto UK which is an experiment in online democracy. Do try it out.

The number of visitors to this blog in June was 27169, 19% ahead of May. I'm sure the world cup, soaring European and North American temperatures and the holiday season will slow the growth over the next few months. Nonetheless in the interests of finding out more about the web by doing rather than theorising I've been trying to register with Google Adwords in order to generate revenues to pay for my overheads. So far the process has defeated us but we're trying – so expect to see some ads at some point.

This morning I've been reading my favourite magazine – the Summer issue of The Author published by The Society of Authors. It is, in my opinion, by far the most important reading material for publishers. Of course I don't agree with everything in it but if we don't understand authors' concerns we'll never get anywhere. It also has the merit of being written mainly by professional authors and so the literary quality is superior to other such association publications. It's not obvious hoow to subscribe but perhaps an email to theauthor@societyofauthors.org might do the trick. A flavour of the contents of this issue – Publishers internet strategies, A positive view of the Wottakars bid, The long-anticipated development of e-paper, Authors as limited companies etc.

🗓 02 July 2006

LibraryThing

Those of you who, like me, are concerned about the activities of some organisations challenging authors' rights might like to see an organisation which is wholly positive for authors and the book industry. LibraryThing was invented and built by Tim Spalding and you can read some notes from him and others on his blog. There is also an article in the Wall Street Journal which is open access for thirty days – so read it fast.

Everything about this project makes sense. I do sometimes worry that publishers' legitimate requirement to protect copyright can be interpreted as luddism. It is not but we can do ourselves and our authors a service by wholeheartedly supporting technology where it really does support comunication and sharing of ideas.

Incidentally, Tim Spalding is also the publisher of Isidore of Seville which I'm incapable of describing but which again seems to offer simplicity, service and information. Three cheers.

Shame about England's inability to score penalties in soccer but at least we can stop worrying now and take down the flags of St George which were a little too nationalistic for my liking. This prediction from one of yesterday's papers was foresightful:

Should the quarter-final go to penalties, Hargreaves believes England will reverse a trend that has seen them go out of four major tournaments on shoot-outs.

Hargreaves, who scored one of England's penalties when they lost against Portugal in Euro 2004, said: 'I fancy our chances on penalties. For example, I don't think a German could take a better penalty than an Englishman. We've got dead ball specialists such as David Beckham, Frank Lampard and Steven Gerrard and they are some of the best in the world.'

England lost shoot-outs against Portugal (Euro 2004), Argentina (World Cup 1998), Germany (Euro 96) and West Germany (World Cup 1990). Their only victory on penalties came against Spain at Euro 96.

Hargreaves, Beckham, Gerrard, Lampard, Ashley Cole, Wayne Rooney and John Terry are known to be keen to take a penalty but Eriksson will not nominate in advance.

03 July 2006

Macmillan English Campus and technofrustration

I spent the morning trying to issue the following internal announcement about an important promotion:

Dear all,

I am delighted to announce that as from 1 September Emma Shercliff will become Managing Director of Macmillan English Campus (MEC). Peter Mothersole, who has managed MEC since Ian Johnstone left, will continue to work with the Division during the present intensive development phase, which will show a considerable expansion of the activities of both the MEC and onestopenglish.

Emma joined Macmillan as a graduate recruit in 1997 and worked in Southern Europe, Latin America, and Australia as well as in the UK. She temporarily abandoned us for a stretch of unpaid leave in Teheran where she helped us with Palgrave Macmillan sales and at one point joined Hodder but saw the light and returned to become Sales and Marketing Director of MEC (and onestopenglish) a year ago and is currently advertising for her successor in that post.

Please join me in wishing Emma all the very best in her new position and wishing the whole MEC team a bright future.

Richard Charkin

The technofrustration derived from the first line 'Dear All'. Who is all? Where does all live? Is anyone in all who should not be in all? How does one construct the list? How does one keep it up to date (my inbox was flooded with bouncebacks – return to sender, address unknown, no such number, no such home – for full lyrics click here). The no doubt ineffective solution involved four people, several coffees, a map of the world, a speaker phone and several hot towels.

But it was all worth it to celebrate the growing success of the Macmillan English Campus under Peter Mothersole's brilliant leadership and his ability to nurture top managerial talent. Peter held many senior jobs at <u>Oxford University Press</u> all of which he managed successfully and he left them last year. OUP's loss is Macmillan's gain.

🥀 04 July 2006

The power of the database

Publishers, booksellers, academics and librarians have always known the power inherent in a really useful database. Now England's footballers have learned the hard way that they really ought to do their homework using a powerful database of collated knowledge. Yesterday's <u>Guardian</u> explained how Germany's goalie applied database technology to winning a quarter final football match (and probably all the way to the final). If only . . .

And for those of you who are interested in boosting traffic and commerce on your blogs or websites I recommend you try a spot of <u>Feng Shui 2.0</u>. Never forget that:

Earth is the layout, fire is the colour, air is the HTML, space is name of the site, and water is the font and graphics.

🥀 05 July 2006

Grand designs

Emma Giacon of Pan attended a meeting today about further developments at King's Cross. Here's her report:

'Peter Millican from the <u>King's Place development</u> and Richard Thompson from architects <u>Dixon Jones</u> popped in at lunchtime to give us all a bit more info on what's going on in the building site next door. After last week's events, first on most people's minds was 'Can we expect to be evacuating our offices again any time soon?' The answer, happily, was no, with Peter apologising profusely for the inconvenience. Apparently it was a very small fire, and didn't slow down the building work too much . . . lucky them!

Development on the site is coming on apace, and we were told that the building will begin to take shape properly around Christmas. By all accounts it will be an impressive space: two concert halls (the larger of which will seat 425 people), sculptures (that will be visible from York Way as well as throughout the building), and a floor devoted to visual arts (that will house a permanent collection of portraits) will all be open to the public. A colonnade along the York Way side of the development will provide some glamour to a currently unappealing road, while an internal street will lead visitors from York Way right through the building to the canal. I should mention that this will be a very 'green' building, producing only half the CO_2 per square metre that most offices produce.

The York Way side of the building will also benefit from a glass façade – which as well as looking very striking – will also provide a noise barrier for the building within. Dixon Jones (who have worked on notable projects including The Royal Opera House, National Gallery and National Portrait Gallery) have also included a rotunda building that will sit on the corner of the canal basin. The ground floor of the rotunda will house a huge brasserie restaurant with inside and outside dining, and there will also be a private events section canalside.

We will certainly be gaining illustrious neighbours renting the offices on site. As well as 1500 staff from The Guardian, the Sinfonietta Orchestra and The Orchestra of the Age of Enlightenment will be in residence, and New Music groups such as NMC, SPNM and BMIC will likely be based there. We also hear that Central St Martin's Art College is moving to Kings Cross, so our bright new authors from Pan will be joined by bright young artists – very appropriate!

The thing to remember about all this is that as well as this particular development, the area in general will be completely overhauled by Argent (beginning late 2007 when the Channel Tunnel link is completed). It really feels as though we are witnessing of something very exciting and refreshing, of which all locals, residents and business, will be able to take advantage.'

06 July 2006

A long walk for a good cause

It was an evening for nostalgia last night as a team from Macmillan Distribution (MDL), ably supported by their colleagues at Palgrave Macmillan, paraded around the streets of London, masquerading as Bobby Moore and the boys from the 1966 world cup winning team. (*MDL: A Winning Team.*) David Smith, MD of MDL, took the part of the referee in leading his team round the course and even took the opportunity to send off one of the 'Wayne Rooneys', from the HarperCollins team. For the evening I became an honorary member of MDL and adopted the persona of Geoff Hurst (he was the guy who scored the winning goal against Germany in 1966), joining the boys and girls in red. We certainly made plenty of noise with our football rattles and *World Cup Willie* blaring out of the loud speakers.

And the reason for all this was a charity walk on behalf of BTBS known as Walkies. BTBS is the book trade's own welfare charity and Walkies is their yearly sponsored walk around checkpoints that include the likes of the Publishers' Association, Foyles bookshop and Bloomsbury. MDL were not the only ones to send up a team and a variety of costumes and themes were on display. In the end the prize for best team went to Vista who were dressed up in medical outfits with 'Vista Cures' on the back. The Macmillan team were very proud to come an honourable second although I have had to point out that being a good loser sucks.

The Guardian has an in-depth article about Google and publishers. There's not much new in the piece although it's well written and informative. What I found most interesting is that it is clearly the result of a public relations exercise by Google to influence public opinion in their favour. I can quite understand this but I do wish that such a great organisation would spend less money on spinning their story and concentrate on finding solutions to their impasse with copyright owners. And incidentally, one might think that Google is the only search engine in the world. Thank goodness it is not (monopolies are rarely beneficial) and perhaps newspaper journalists should talk to some of the other organisations in the business. They seem to be able to cope with copyright.

🖋 08 July 2006

A lucky break

Driving on the A20 just South of Limoges in the middle of France I spotted an enormous BMW motorbike with a gendarme with sunglasses aboard waving me down. Off to an 'air' along with several other foreign cars accompanied by similar policemen.

You were exceeding the 130 km per hour speed limit.

But it's not raining. It's 110 when it rains but 130 in the dry.

Not on this stretch.

How would I know that?

Use your eyes.

What now?

You have two choices. Pay a fine right now (no credit cards allowed) or I confiscate your driving licence, you stay the night here until someone rescues you, you go to court and then we fine you. It is your choice.

How much? €90. Okay. Here's two €50 notes.

I don't have any change.

Okay, don't worry. Keep the €10.

I am not an Italian policeman, I am French.

Sorry. How about borrowing the €10 and betting it on France to beat Italy on Sunday. If France wins (which please God they do) we could split the winnings. If not, tant pis.

He didn't go along with this suggestion, borrowed €10 from a mate to give me and let me go. I was so relieved. I suspect that if I were Italian I'd have had a lot tougher session.

Bon weekend tout le monde et allez France.

🖋 09 July 2006

Non-fiction

At a recent meeting of British general book publishers there was a general moan about the state of the non-fiction market. Quality history, biography, politics, economics hardbacks sell between 2000 and 20,000 copies in hardback. UK sales of totally brilliant books such as Tom Friedman's The World is Flat are a tiny fraction of US even allowing for population differences. It appears that Americans are more prepared to purchase and read challenging books than the British.

At the more popular end of the market there are some huge sellers – Sharon Osborne, Katy Price etc – but there are large numbers of failures too. And these failures are usually very expensive. Every second-rate Big Brother famous-for-five minutes celebrity is demanding (and frequently getting) ludicrous advances from publishers desperate to find something to sell through supermarkets to the mass market.

And so neither the up-market nor the mass market is performing. Add to this the demise of backlist sales, the pitifully small paperback sales and the legitimate demands of authors for a fair reward for their work. Furthermore in order to achieve this unsatisfactory state of affairs publishers are spending big marketing budgets and granting special discounts to retailers thus undermining their low profitability further.

In the words of the great Russian sage when asked how to solve the problems of their great Tsarist empire: I have the solution. Something must be done about it.

🥄 10 July 2006

More on non-fiction

Please have a look at yesterday's entry on the difficulties of publishing non-fiction. Probably because it was a Sunday and people have some spare time or because there are some soccer-and-tennis phobes wanting to escape TV we had a great postbag.

In short, the solution from the comments is to publish fewer better titles, reduce prices, give better discounts to independent retailers and worse ones to supermarkets, chains and Amazon, not accept returns, not pay advances, spend money on editorial and design overheads but overall reduce publishing costs.

All good stuff. I remember a management accountant at OUP wondering aloud why on earth we didn't stick to publishing best selling expensive titles with low unit costs. He was, of course, right.

I believe Macmillan Science is a legitimate attempt to find a new model which can benefit all 'stakeholders' but en passant our average UK subscription (the support given by booksellers in terms of advance orders ensuring visibility in store) is around 200 copies across 4000 accounts. And these are returnable!

Ah well, soccer must be tough too – Ronaldo sneaks on his team-mate, Zidane nuts someone in the chest, the Argentinean team assaults the Germans after the final whistle, the apparently corrupt Italians win, and Germany doesn't make the final to the disappointment of the advertising community. Now we can concentrate on Pakistan beating England at cricket.

And while on cricket this is by Mike Hopkin a reporter for News at Nature. We feel the match should have been reported on cricinfo and I am still hopeful. Meanwhile charkinblog will have to do:

Cricketing glory for NPG

Arguably one of the few things more complicated than calculating journal impact factors is cricket, so it made sense for *Nature* to challenge its perennial citation competitors *Science* to a match.

Science were hoping to avenge their crushing defeat of three years ago, whereas for *Nature*, a British institution playing that most venerable of English sports, defeat against an American journal (albeit its British staff) was unthinkable.

The select band travelled to Cambridge to be greeted by a tropical downpour and the very real possibility of spending the whole afternoon in the clubhouse. But as the rain relented we realized the battle for scientific and sporting supremacy was on.

With *Nature* first to bat and clouds still looming, a strong start was vitally important. Thankfully the intensity of the first two overs was unmatched by anything that followed, with *Nature*'s openers Adam Rutherford and captain Andy Douglas smacking *Science*'s surprisingly pacy attack to all quarters of the field.

With the scoreboard ticking along nicely and plenty of wickets in hand, *Nature* finished with a score of 152 for 9. Good, but would it be enough to defend against a *Science* batting line-up with obvious hunger in their eyes (and not just for the sandwiches)?

Science, needing to score at more than 6 runs per over to win, were on the back foot as soon as they came up against *Nature*'s devastatingly fast opening attack pairing of Neil Smith and Rob Dicks. Smith combined with Mike Hopkin to produce arguably the scalping of the day, dismissing former *Nature* staffer Pete Wrobel with a fizzingly fast delivery and slip catch hailed by spectators as 'just like proper cricket, like you get on TV'.

Any hope the home side had of matching *Nature*'s total evaporated when man of the match Chris 'the Wizard' Townson then produced a simply unplayable spell of bowling, finding pace and bounce on a rapidly drying pitch to claim two victims at a cost of just one run (for those more familiar with baseball, almost the equivalent of pitching a no-hitter).

In the end it was a comfortable victory for *Nature* by some 70 runs, *Science* finishing all out for 82. Honourable mentions go to Rutherford for his top score of 40, Douglas for inspiring captaincy, Richard Charkin for unrelenting commitment (including a full-length dive to avoid a run-out), and Peter Collins for overcoming an almost total lack of prior cricketing ability to inflict damage with both ball and bat. Great work also from Gerard Preston, Arran Frood, Quinton Creighton and Robin Brown in ensuring victory.

11 July 2006

Cory Ondrejka

One of the advantages of having a world-beating science journal in the Macmillan stable is that one can invite extraordinarily interesting people to come and talk to our staff. We've had a series of fascinating presentations by scientists, politicians, authors. Today sees a talk by Cory Ondrejka who is CTO of Linden Lab, the developers of Second Life. The concept is both fascinating and scary. An article is this week's Observer newspaper describes things better than I could but I do recommend you take a look at Second Life if only out of fear for the future of cyberhumanity.

 12 July 2006

Children's publishing

In contrast to the problems associated with adult non-fiction publishing, children's books are flourishing. At Macmillan we are still celebrating with Emily Gravett her winning the Kate Greenaway medal for Wolves.

This was closely followed by this press release suggesting that even more good things are on the way. It's really great working with the professional authors, illustrators, designers and editors who seem to proliferate in children's publishing and the results speak for themselves.

A new transatlantic partnership

Macmillan Children's Books UK teams up with US publisher Jean Feiwel in her new role at Holtzbrinck Children's

Macmillan Children's Books UK will be teaming up with Jean Feiwel, recently appointed Senior Vice President and Publisher of children's books at

Holtzbrinck USA, to acquire jointly and to co-publish select titles. In particular, books acquired by Macmillan Children's Books will play a role in Feiwel's new imprint, Feiwel & Friends; and Feiwel's projects are already starting to cross the Atlantic to MCB.

Macmillan Children's Books' big Spring 2007 title THE BLACK BOOK OF SECRETS by F. E. Higgins will be on the Feiwel & Friends Fall 2007 launch list, and Kate Saunders' THE LITTLE SECRET will be published in Spring 2008. From Feiwel's list Macmillan Children's Books will be publishing a new series by bestselling Australian author Andy Griffiths, as well as Lily Archer's debut novel THE POISON APPLES.

Sarah Davies, Publishing Director of Macmillan Children's Books, said: 'It's great to have the opportunity to forge stronger links with our Holtzbrinck sister companies and – when the occasion's right for us both – to have the potential to acquire rights together. The arrangement is entirely flexible, but there are times when standing together will make us even stronger. Jean Feiwel is a dynamic publisher with a stellar track record and it's very exciting to work with her.'

Jean Feiwel said: 'My mandate coming to Holtzbrinck has been to make the whole even stronger than the sum of our parts. I believe it is in the best interests of our authors, our books, our company to work together in a way that allows us to accomplish a global reach, using the best ideas and talents from both countries. Sarah and I immediately connected on commercially like-minded projects. I am very excited to be working with her and the entire MCB team.'

Macmillan Children's Books, a division of Pan Macmillan UK and part of the Holtzbrinck group, is a leading children's publisher in Britain. It publishes fiction and non-fiction, picture books and novelty books, and the leading preschool imprint, Campbell Books. It has had both commercial and critical acclaim with authors such as Meg Cabot, Georgia Byng, Frank Cottrell-Boyce, Eva Ibbotson, and with Julia Donaldson and Axel Scheffler's GRUFFALO titles and new picturebook star Emily Gravett.

Jean Feiwel joined Holtzbrinck USA in February 2006 to start a broadly defined children's effort and to guide strategy within the group. As well as creating new imprints she will also be publishing into paperback and other formats the backlists of fellow Holtzbrinck companies Farrar Straus & Giroux, Henry Holt and Roaring Brook Press. Prior to this she spent more than 20 years at Scholastic where she invented the children's series market with THE BABYSITTERS CLUB, GOOSEBUMPS and DEAR AMERICA, and designed the editorial strategy for all Scholastic's successful imprints.

For further information contact:

Emma Hopkin, Managing Director, Macmillan Children's Books: 0207 014 6071

Sarah Davies, Publishing Director, Macmillan Children's Books: 0207 014 6109

13 July 2006

More on Second Life

Further to the short mention I gave to Second Life (SL) the other day, Sara Lloyd, Pan's new Head of Digital Publishing, felt inspired to email me this guest entry on her impressions of the SL revolution . . . .

'Second Life is (IMHO) one of the most fascinating, inspiring – and somewhat terrifying – social, cultural and technological phenomenons of Web 2.0. If people ask me where it's at right now, this is one of the first examples I give.

Second Life is a virtual world. Membership is free. 'Subscription models suck', as Cory Ondrejka, head of Linden Labs, creators of SL, commented when he visited us the other day. Instead, the payment model is based on buying 'property' or 'land' in the world, on which you can build . . . whatever you like. It is explicitly NOT a game. Second Life has 350,000+ users, a number that is rising at about 15% per month. Of these users, about two thirds are actually 'building stuff' on a regular basis. i.e. the proportion of active – or engaged – users to users who just pass through, is *very* high. Only about 0.1% of Wikipedia users actually write stuff. And it's a lot more complicated to build something in SL than it is to post a Wikipedia entry. SL users are seriously committed. And some of them are making a pretty serious living entirely through this virtual world. (See article from Business Week.) SL has its own currency, Linden dollars, which are exchangeable in the real world for real currency. Hundreds of thousands of 'real life' dollars of business are conducted through SL every week. Perhaps more interestingly, the profile of users is not as geeky as you would think: the user base is around 50/50 male to female in terms of hours of use; the average age is 33; older users and women tend to continue to use Second Life – perhaps because they are able to get more out of it; the majority of users do not apparently consider themselves to be 'game players.'

SL is inspiring because its creators, like so many other successful Web 2.0 businesses, developed a space where people could do interesting stuff, provided the tools for them to do it, then just waited to see what cool things happened and responded to developments. It is also a little frightening because of this. No one, including its creators, really knows what the full potential (or even full repercussions) of SL might be. But hey, it sounds like a great place to conduct some edgy experiments for individuals or businesses with the creativity and willingness to invest (time and money) in it.

For publishers, some of the thought-provoking things that are already happening on SL are: virtual book signings (authors like Cory Doctorow have done this in SL); the development of virtual libraries; the use of virtual communities to test real life business concepts or products before 'real life' launch; the presence of publishing companies such as John Battelle's Federated Media Publishing – which has set up an office in the virtual world; the fact that the BBC have broadcast SL versions of their shows; the idea that students can now do a university course entirely virtually through one of the sixteen or so US universities running virtual classes . . . . I could go on. Check it out for yourself.

A few blog entries ago I posted a comment in response to some pertinent remarks that Peter Collingridge made about what dinosaurs publishers can be when it comes to web site development: 'Some very basic things need to be addressed in order to move general publishing businesses from Web 1.0 companies to Web 2.0 companies and beyond. First of all, we need to educate our own staff to be more 'e'-savvy, effect cultural and process change internally and change our thinking about some of the qualities we look for when hiring new staff; then we need to get the basic 'building blocks' right – develop a digital platform for delivery of our e-content, work out how to budget and resource for new 'strategic' web developments which do not deliver traditional cash flows, develop leaner, swifter decision-making processes . . . and that's all before we do anything creative or 'blue sky' with our content or services', and I wondered aloud, 'How on earth do we move away from some of the bricks and mortar, historically-inherited constraints that prevent us moving fast enough for the pace required in this new digital age?' SL is one of those web developments that make these concerns sound like massive understatements. Whilst we are still at the stage of wondering whether we should hire some more web developers maybe we should really be wondering how many 'avatar reps' we need on SL . . . '

N.B. For more info, Timo Hannay, NPG's Web Publishing Director, has also blogged his notes of Cory Ondrejka's talk on Monday here.

14 July 2006

Crime and Indexation

About a month ago a burglar broke into the Pan Bookshop, lifted (rather little) cash from the till and then proceeded to urinate and defecate over the stock. This is apparently common behaviour among burglars in the UK (and perhaps elsewhere too). Fortunately the stupid and unpleasant criminal cut himself on some broken glass and the police were able to track him down. He has pleaded guilty which saves us the trouble of having to go to court. But the affair leaves a nasty taste in the mouth.

On a brighter note Hazel Bell has won the Wheatley Award for the index in W. B. Yeats's Mythologies. In these days of Yahoo, Google and other automatic indexing machines it's great that the Society of Indexers still exists to promote professional indexing by intelligent human beings. The quality of an index is rarely appreciated by the general reader but it can frequently turn an informative book into a real information resource. Let's hear it for the unsung heroes of the book world.

🐦 16 July 2006

Nothing new under the sun

Forgive me, I have just written today's blog only to have it disappear into cyberspace. I'm working on a very slow line on an unfamiliar laptop and can't make hyperlinks work – and maybe I'll fail again. So fingers crossed as I try to remember my grumpy old man piece.

When I started in the UK publishing industry in 1971 (I think it was then but it was such a long time ago . . .) all books were published on Thursdays. When I asked why the answer was clear – in order to optimise the chances of a publication day review in the Times Literary Supplement – http://tls.timesonline.co.uk/.

Like many things in our industry this practice fell into disuse and books were published on any day of the week – normally to suit an author's publicity schedule or to suit a particular retailer – or most likely just when the book arrived at and was despatched from the publisher's warehouse.

In parallel the tracking of sales through retailers improved immeasurably as did the importance of best seller lists. Publishers would try to get the best position for their authors' books by publishing on the day which gave the best chance of a high entry – obviously. However that was not necessarily the best or most efficient day for retailers as a whole. A committee of leading booksellers and publishers was established to address this issue. After many hours of discussion (sometimes heated) over a period of many months the committee agreed and signed up to Mondays for all books to be published. Within a week the agreement was broken by publishers wishing to steal a march on their competitors.

How to deal with this problematic development? Reconvene the committee. The solution? All books to be published on Thursdays. I think it was the British Prime Minister, Harold Wilson, who resigned because he couldn't bear the same old problems coming around time and time again.

But some things are new. This article from last week's Nature – http://www.nature.com/news/2006/060710/full/060710-8.html – about a quadriplegic man controlling some important actions through thought seems to come from science fiction but is real, truly amazing and really important.

🐦 17 July 2006

champion du monde de cracher de bigorneau

The heat gets to everyone I suppose.

Story of the day in the paper I bought this morning, La depeche du midi (http://www.ladepeche.com/contenu/cache/depeche_id1.asp) is about Alain Jourdren who has won his fifth world championship. There have been ten tournaments in all, so he really has towered over the sport. This year there were 178 contestants from all round the world. The Germans had by far the most gender-equal participants and indeed Narion Zahn from Germany won the women's event with a length of 5.61 metres. In the 12-16-year-old junior championship the winner was Alain's son, Thierry, with 9.58 and was indeed Alain's strongest overall challenger. However, Alain triumphed with 10.41 metres which he modestly ascribes to 'une capacite respiratoire hors de commune . . . '

The sport is, of course, winkle spitting. This year Roscoff next year the world. Watch out soccer lovers.

And in the real world we at Macmillan were delighted to welcome back Graham Swift (http://www.contemporarywriters.com/authors/?p=auth93) with his new novel Tomorrow. Writers of his calibre are rare indeed and the team at Picador are justifiably thrilled that he has entrusted them with furthering his literary career.

19 July 2006

Beating back blockbuster culture: the Long Tail

Chris Anderson's new book The Long Tail has been eagerly anticipated. Why? He blogged it first, of course. Partly due to the blogosphere effect and partly because it explains a concept that holds an innate attraction for many of us, it has been greeted with enormous enthusiasm and has been fallen upon as a kind of gospel for our age by content creators in many media. The Long Tail suggests that in this culture of the blockbuster in which we seemingly live, the wonder of the Internet is that it enables – no, encourages, even – the niche interest to flourish as well as the mass market. So, online retailers can afford to 'stock' thousands of titles and are therefore able to benefit from the 'long tail' of small scale sales; niche interest groups can indulge their interests, networking with the comparatively few others that share their passion. Natasha Walter has explained it all much more cogently here at Guardian Unlimited and Chris Anderson himself discusses his book on the Guardian's Newsdesk podcast.

20 July 2006

Blogging is good for books

Have you noticed a rise in great blogs about books? My attention has recently been drawn to bookbar.com and to Danuta Kean's web site and associated blog both of which are well worth taking a look at. There was a thoughtful guide to the UK's book bloggers in The Bookseller last week, too.

I also just wanted to highlight The Guardian's recent coverage of German bestseller Measuring the World, which has been a runaway sensation selling 600,000 copies in hardback since last September and is published by one of the Holtzbrinck Group companies, Rowohlt. Not only has it delighted readers but it has also been universally praised by Germany's 'famously grudging critics' . . . . Its author – 31-year-old Daniel Kehlmann – has been hailed as 'a literary wunderkind'.

22 July 2006

ISBN 13

Before the world as we know it publishers invented systems for numbering their titles for reasons of identification and book-keeping. I don't have access to the exact historical records but my understanding is that a bunch of British publishers got together and invented the 9-digit standard book number (SBN). One of the major publishers (Macmillan as it happens) stood out against it (doubtless on the grounds that they considered their internal system the best and that they wanted to be different). Everyone came into line when the powerful retailer, W H Smith, refused to stock any book without an SBN – game, set and match to the SBN.

Shortly afterwards the rest of the world joined in and the ISBN (with a language digit introduced) became ten digits and became ubiquitous. Surprisingly, book publishing had become a leader in identifier technology which set it up well for the computer age.

More recently retailers have been demanding a 13-digit ISBN so that many other products can have a similar identification structure – magazines, DVDs etc. It makes sense and the industry has been working away to implement ISBN-13 on January 1 2007.

This blog and many of its commentators have dealt with the inadequacies of book publishers – not enough risk-taking, too little investment, picking the wrong books, luddism, declining standards, ignoring the small retailer, copyright problems, etc, etc.

ISBN-13 may not get the juices running like literary argumentation but it is a brilliant example of publishers working together on a hugely difficult project (it affects every system in a publishing company – billing, royalties, production, editorial, sales, finance and more). It has taken large amounts of cash, millions of technical person-hours, imagination and insight.

If all goes well, what will it achieve? A total non-event. Next year books will be ordered and sold as normal. And it will be because publishers' IT departments have worked hard and well. The people involved don't get headlines in the trade press and definitely they don't have awards ceremonies. Nobody writes about them when they change jobs and they don't flounce. Thank God for them all.

23 July 2006

Are books too expensive?

A few days ago one of the commentators on this blog exonerated copyright thieves on the grounds that publishing companies are greedy money-making organisations who don't deserve protection. This may be the case in rare instances but by and large general publishing is a low-margin business particularly when compared with other high-risk investments such as oil exploration, aviation manufacture, films – or even low-risk ventures such as investment banking, legal services, accountancy etc.

One reason for the low margins might be pricing. I think that current prices are unbelievably low by almost any criterion – yet people still think they're expensive.

A full-price quality paperback is £7.99 in the UK. A cinema ticket in London is the same price unless you go to a posh place where it'll be more. The average price of a main course at a moderate gastropub is £12. A not very distinguished bottle of wine is £8.99.

And the £7.99 paperback is the result of months or years of authorial creativity, 500 pages of sophisticated printing and binding, a complex distribution and marketing network – and something to keep, re-read, lend, refer to, argue about, enjoy.

And this fantastic value is not just confined to works of fiction. When I was a medical editor at OUP one of our best sellers was Sir Zachary Cope's Early Diagnosis of the Acute Abdomen. It was then in its 13th edition having originally been published during World War I. The original price was one guinea – at the time around $4. Back in 1980 we were selling most of the copies in the USA (apparently British textbooks were lousy at therapy but okay at diagnosis, particularly that requiring clinical discernment rather than technological excellence) and the price was $4.95. Applying inflation the price should have been $100.

So what is it that makes people

a) think books are overpriced

b) think publishers make too much money?

Answers on a blogcard, please.

24 July 2006

Winkle spitting 2 and Media Mogul

A few days ago I ran a story about the world winkle-spitting championship and the winner, Alain Jourden. Here he is shortly after his moment of glory.

On a more serious note the St James Partnership is an investment banking consultancy specialising in the media sector. They produce a regular newsletter on media deals. The newsletter always comes with an interesting introduction by its editor, Niko Jaakkola. With his permission I attach his latest thoughts which need no further gloss from me.

Dear Reader,

Last time I mused over 'decisions, decisions for the media mogul of tomorrow' – presupposing there would be some!

A favourite game of the media world 20 years ago was to guess which six, of the then twenty, big groups would emerge globally on top; again, presupposing there would be groups, competing together, essentially doing the same thing.

The twin functions of historic publishing have been editing content, and distributing it. With the inexorable rise of online distribution, the latter function is becoming redundant. More interestingly, Google is a working example of how the former function, too, may eventually become automated. An editing machine of power unimaginable less than 10 years ago, it is starting to cause serious worry in the minds of not only academic publishers, but traditional book publishers as well. What will the landscape look like after ten more years of developing clever algorithms, driven by serious financial incentives?

The work of The St James Partnership team has been to talk to media owners, large and small, and we sense everyday the joy that owning media brings. But, 20 years into the future, will we still see the media mogul of old? Or will it just be Google and their ilk – not to forget the good old state-funded Aunty! – with all of us posting our tuppence worth up on to the net, just as I am doing now!

Best wishes,

Niko Jaakkola

25 July 2006

Are books too expensive 2?

This question I posed a couple of days ago which was described by one of our most polite commentators as stupid has generated quite an amount of correspondence.

One argument is that price should be linked to value. Am I getting enough out of the hours spent reading the book. That would suggest that short books should (all other things being equal be more expensive than long ones. There are of course those who think that fat books are good value and there are many retailers who encourage 'bulking out' of novels.

Another argument is that people think books are too expensive because British publishers are money-grabbing idiots who love dishing out huge discounts to some retailers who then discount. I don't understand the argument because the issue I was trying to address is universal, not just British and not related to pricing in supermarkets versus independent stores. And discounts granted to retailers (incidentally) is only one factor in the business relationship between publisher and retailer. Other factors such as the cost of servicing, freight, speed and ease of payment, returns rates, author support also weigh heavily in publishers' commercial thinking.

One commentator thought I was out of touch suggesting £7.99 was a typical price for paperbacks. He cited some Penguin classics at higher price. I could quote back many many classics at £1 – give us a break!

Then there is the argument about whether prices should be printed on covers. And I don't want to get involved in that debate but it does seem a rather trivial matter for our industry compared with the threats of competing media, changing social behaviour and challenges to copyright.

And finally a question about the pricing of textbooks where the US market has seen significant price inflation which is then exported. It's hard to argue against the idea that students find paying $100 for a book difficult. The problem has arisen, in my view, because college textbooks have become over-engineered (rather like American cars of the 1950s and 1960s). Too much colour, too much ancillary material, too long, too slow to market. Perhaps the answer is a return to shorter less flashy textbooks geared to specific courses and being revised annually.

But to finish on a positive note <u>Book Marketing's</u> latest update reports research that shows that for adults in the UK reading is an important activity for 79% and more popular than sex (69%), watching TV (67%), gardening (49%) and computer games (15%). Or the interviewees could have been lying.

And while browsing this excellent document I couldn't help noticing another statistic which confirms the views of most of my female and many of my male colleagues. On average men manage to take out 41.5 hours a week from their busy schedules to enjoy themselves whereas women only manage 23 hours. No comment needed.

I have just spent £8 on two replacement heads for my electric toothbrush. How does that compare to a 400-page book?

📑 26 July 2006

On blogs and the future

For those of you who can read French and for those of you who can make intelligent guesses <u>here</u> and <u>here</u> are interesting links on blogger statistics sent in by a regular reader.

I suppose a few years ago the very concept of blogging would have been considered futuristic. One of Macmillan's authors, Ray Hammond, produces a monthly futurology <u>newsletter</u> which is well worth studying. Ray must be wrong quite a lot of the time but I bet he's right too – as usual picking the winner is the tough thing.

I don't get too carried away by technopredictions but I do reckon that some people in the book trade could do with a little bit more open-mindedness when it comes to thinking about the future of their own businesses – judging by some of the comments received on this blog over the last few days.

📑 27 July 2006

Nature Statistics

I've just come out of an excellent <u>Nature</u> meeting. Of course most of the documents we were addressing are company confidential and I cannot share them. It is, however, no secret that the Nature Publishing Group has successfully moved from being a magazine publisher with one flagship journal to being a scientific information and communication organisation whose lifeblood is on the internet. Two million registered users, ten million visits per month, 35 million page views per month and about 50% of its sales entirely electronic – not to mention 95% of manuscripts received electronically and 100% refereed, edited and designed electronically.

But the factoid I thought you'd appreciate, which I'm allowed to share and which, I think, says a huge amount about the concerns of the contemporary world is the list of top terms sought by users on the site.

Stem cell – 2997

HIV – 1877

Global warming – 1460

Cancer – 893

I should add that the Independent newspaper has just given a great plug for Nature's weekly podcast which competes with Madonna for top billing in the podcast ratings.

🐦 28 July 2006

Amazon woes and Hamlyn Foundation

I have been reading about Amazon's latest problems with Wall Street in Publishers Weekly. Most of us would be more than content with sales growth of 16% but it is amazing how an organisation the size and quality of Amazon can show operating income of just 2.5% (and I bet that's before all sorts of dadeda – as in EBITDA – and one-offs). On the other hand, for Wall Street to savage a company for investing in its future does seem a bit harsh. Perhaps Amazon should pay a bit more attention to the bottom line by focussing less on the price 'flywheel' and more on range and service – at least when it comes to books.

But while reading this article my eye skipped to an ad for big bad book blog which is an excellent, informative and entertaining site put together by the Greenleaf Book Group who look to be a really sensible publishing company except for one thing. Why pay for an ad on PW Online when they could have had this plug for free?

Someone who never failed to understand the bottom line was my old boss, Paul Hamlyn. I was delighted to see that his Foundation is still going strong and dishing out money intelligently and generously – typical of the man whom I and many others miss enormously.

🐦 29 July 2006

Manga manga manga and Glyndebourne

Pan Macmillan have just announced a Manga distribution contract with the Japanese publisher leading the Manga revolution, Tokyopop. The market for Manga is doubling every year and Pan are aiming to gain the largest market share.

A rather different experience when I attended a wonderful production of Die Fledermaus at the equally wonderful opera house at Glyndebourne last night. The only problem is the time it takes to get there from London. The show also starts quite early to allow a very long interval for picnics in the beautiful gardens.

This entails leaving London shortly after lunch. There is a story of the late great Australian media tycoon Kerry Packer. He was doing a deal in London involving a bunch of bankers and lawyers. At 2.30 several of them upped and left, explaining they had to get to Glyndebourne. He is said to have remarked (language softened) that 'this is typical of the bloody Poms. They charge an arm and a leg for doing f all and then b . . . . r off to the races at the drop of a hat.'

🦉 30 July 2006

Good Library Blog

Last year an old friend of mine, Tim Coates, launched a campaign to save British public libraries from politically-correct destruction. He was able to produce evidence showing that library expenditure on books was being devastated by explicit or implicit government policy in favour of 'outreach centres' etc. His campaign has not made him popular with government or parts of the library establishment. As part of his campaign he set up a Good Library Blog which I linked to. This blog has now been hijacked by some variety of loonies. Tim is putting it straight and will announce when things are back to normal. But it is really sad that something so self-evidently worthwhile should be attacked for no reason.

🦉 31 July 2006

Charles de Gaulle 2

Last time I was stuck in this godforsaken place and blogged it I was chastised as a a first-class travelling plutocratic publisher of no worth. So I'd better not moan about delays, lousy service, lousy signage, grumpy staff and attitudes more reminiscent of 1960s Britain than I care to remember. So let's celebrate Tim Coates's recovery of his own blog Good Library Blog – see Blogroll – which he's managed to hijack back from the dastardly hijackers – and has celebrated the doubling of book purchases by libraries in Ulster. The scandal of diminishing book budgets in libraries (as opposed to the burgeoning of 'other outreach activities') would never have been noticed without Tim's crusade. and it matters – see the comments on my previous blog. Aux barricades mes amis pour les bibliotheques – and please will someone privatise Air France properly as soon as possible.

Charchive

≤   **August 2006**   ≥

Mon	Tue	Wed	Thu	Fri	Sat	Sun
31	1	2	3	4	5	6
7	8	9	10	11	12	13
14	15	16	17	18	19	20
21	22	23	24	25	26	27
28	29	30	31	1	2	3
4	5	6	7	8	9	10

Brands and branding and July blogstats

In July this blog had 31151 visitors, 15% up on June which was 19% ahead of May. Still going in the right direction but Summer lassitude must surely slow the growth soon.

We work closely with the world's leading branding organisation, Interbrand. They did an excellent job helping us with the launch of Palgrave Macmillan as a an established imprint with a new name. We also publish with them across a range of titles. I therefore take a particular interest in their annual report on global brands which has had quite a bit of press attention of late.

For those of you who can't be bothered to click to the report and scroll down here are the top ten global brands:

Coca-Cola

Microsoft

IBM

GE

Intel

Nokia

Toyota

Disney

McDonald's

Mercedes

Only one 'media' company, Disney. Google appears at 24, Sony at 26, Apple at 39. Amazon is 65. The first professional publisher is Reuters at 78. There is not a single consumer publisher in the top 100. No Penguin, no Random House, no Hachette, no HarperCollins – definitely no Macmillan. And yet I cannot remember an annual report of a publishing company which did not shout about the strength of its brand and the protection this gives a publisher from the challenges of a changing technological world.

And an old chestnut from British politics but I like it. Someone once asked a colleague why everyone took an instant dislike to Peter Mandelson (now the EU Trade Commissioner, whatever that is) and the answer was 'Because it saves time.'

🐦 02 August 2006

Prizes and charges

This caught my eye this morning in the Book2Book newsletter:

The Crime Writers' Association has announced that it is to start charging publishers for any of their books that are shortlisted for its annual Dagger Awards.

The charges for each shortlisted title will be £500 per title for the Duncan Lawrie Dagger, £200 for the Duncan Lawrie International Dagger and Ian Fleming Steel Dagger, and £100 for the New Blood and Non Fiction Daggers. As previously, there is no entry fee for books submitted for the Dagger Awards.

CWA Chair Robert Richardson said: 'This is not a money-making move, but a way to reduce the considerable financial costs we face in organising and promoting the Dagger Awards. We are not a wealthy organisation and it is an increasing burden on our limited finances. Authors and publishers benefit from being shortlisted – and especially winning – while there is no gain to the CWA. The income these charges generate will not cover the full costs of the operation, but will leave us with a balance that we can afford. This is solely a CWA committee decision.'

Higher profile prizes such as the Booker and Orange prizes charge as much as £2000 per shortlisted title.

Macmillan has always been a strong supporter of the CWA and we were, of course, delighted at Ann Cleeves's success this year. However I found my eyebrows raising at the idea of being charged to be shortlisted. And then a bit higher when I was informed that the Booker and Orange prizes also charge. I quite understand the desire to defray the costs of organising the prize and the winners certainly benefit from the exposure but I have one question. If an author or publisher refuses to pay when shortlisted what then happens? To exclude a book for reasons other than literary surely devalues any literary prize? Or am I just being naive?

03 August 2006

Google Adsense

You may notice down the right-hand side of this blog some ads. One of the purposes of this blog was for me to learn how things work. It's taken about a month to set up the deal with Google. when we first did it our server crashed just as Google went in to check our validity. And then it just seemed to take forever for them to re-check. However, all is now well although I'm hoping the ads might become a little more interesting. I'll keep you in touch with how the income stream develops. I'm not anticipating this to be Macmillan's profit salvation but it should be interesting.

Incidentally, I notice that one of the ads which appears from time to time is for Macmillan – but I do not intend to pay myself if anyone links – and I don't remember authorising Google to sell any ads for us. A mystery. Can anyone illuminate me?

04 August 2006

Literary agencies

I was talking to an author this morning who changed his literary agent. The one he dumped was, apparently, very good at extracting large advances from publishers but he didn't show enough care in commenting on the author's work as he completed it.

This reminded of a long-held ambition of mine to start a new-look literary agency. The concept is twofold.

First, every author is different and is looking for different things from an agent. Some want love. Some want money. Some want accounting help, some don't. Some want an auctioneer, others simply want someone to negotiate fair terms with an existing publisher.

The second part of the concept is not to charge a percentage commission (on all sales until 70 years after the author's death in the UK) but to charge a fee in the same way that other professional advisers charge (lawyers, accountants etc).

Whenever I've discussed this idea with an agent it has been dismissed on the grounds that all authors want everything all the time and that I'd never be able to charge enough to cover my expenses without the cross-subsidy from easy money rolling in from the 'backlist' authors. They are probably right but I've had fun drawing up a draft a la carte menu for authors signing up with the imaginary new firm.

Opening file (cover charge) £100 (compulsory)

Reading manuscript and giving opinion £100 per hour

Reading manuscript and giving brutally frank opinion £500 per hour (but normally this only takes 15 minutes)

Phoning author to reassure £200 per hour subject to a minimum annual payment of £2000

Submitting an unknown author to appropriate publishers £500

Submitting a well-known author to publishers and conducting an auction £5000

Submitting a well-known author to her existing publisher £500

Drawing up contract and negotiating small print with publisher £200 per page of contract

Checking royalty statements and arguing with publisher £100 per hour

Complaining about sales and promotion on behalf of the author £100 per hour

Avoiding repayment of advance when author fails to deliver £500 per hour

Tendering legal advice £500 per hour plus direct outgoings and the cost of indemnity insurance

Transferring files to new agency £5000.

Please feel free to amend or add to these. I was also thinking of creating a menu touristique which gave a basic all-round (but not very good) service for £200 per annum.

I've had a lot of flak about running the Google ads. The next step in my learning is working out how to cancel it. I'll keep you informed.

05 August 2006

On commentators

I think I mentioned that my admission that we were taking Google ads on this blog generated flak from commentators. All well and good. That's why there is a comments section – and I've never felt the need to monitor or referee it.

However, I suspect that most of the comments are overlooked. So here are a few recent ones. And I'd love to have more.

Some of the comments are rather pompous. For instance my jokey piece yesterday on a new form of literary agency elicited:

I can't quite decide if this post displays a complete contempt for agents, a complete contempt for publishers, a complete contempt for authors, or a complete contempt for all three. Quite funny though.

For goodness sake! On the other hand this next commentator clearly understands more about marketing than the average publisher:

Is it any wonder that us 'ordinary readers' have become increasingly cynical about the whole kitten caboodle and now blog amongst ourselves about great reads and pass the word around? Most of us are ignoring the review pages, the 3 for 2's and increasingly the prizelists.Plenty of us have been quietly exchanging great reads through international online reading groups for years and there's a potential audience that no one seems to have taken any notice of, do publishers even know they exist? Have you typed 'reading group' into Yahoo groups lately?
Word of a good read spreads around these like a bush fire and likewise we telegraph the turkeys well in advance!

The Book Bloggers Book Prize when it comes to fruition will have a far bigger audience than many people realise and I don't think it will cost a penny to be shortlisted. The awards dinner won't wreck your cholesterol because it will be virtual, no new outfits to be bought, but just wait; the book that wins will truly deserve to be read.

And here are some wise words about brands in publishing and their importance or non-importance:

Very few consumers walk into a bookshop or browse Amazon and select a book on the strength of the publisher's brand. Penguin used to have that influence, but I would doubt that many book buyers would know if they have bought a Virgin book (Losing my Virginity excepted) even though Virgin has such strong brand recognition. Product reliability and quality is a major factor in the success of many of the companies in this list and this drives consumer loyalty. With a product as varied and variable as a publisher's booklist it is difficult to meet consumer expectation on each and every title (based on the last one read), making loyalty to one publisher brand extremely unlikely.

Please keep the comments coming. I really appreciate them.

The open access debate

I know that many of the readers of this blog are more interested in literary publishing than scientific research. However, the debate about how best to use the Internet to disseminate information about the latest scientific and medical findings is, I believe, relevant to all types of publishing in one way or another.

There are a number of criss-crossing arguments. In essence, the open-access advocates believe that the fruits of research should be made available through the Internet free of charge to every citizen. This is particularly true where the research has been funded by taxpayers (the bulk of research is funded this way). The business model proposed is that the author (or more likely funding agency) would pay the publisher a fee to cover the costs of publication and access would then be 'open'.

The counterargument is that an 'author-pays' model increases the likelihood of less vigorous refereeing; less investment by publishers in improving the processes of editing, storing and distributing; the proposed business model is intrinsically more administratively burdensome than the present one (collecting fees from tens or hundreds of thousands of authors is harder than collecting subscriptions from a thousand university libraries); and is commercially unsustainable.

In any event, a number of open-access publishers have been established and are carving a niche for themselves. In some cases they are achieving very respectable 'impact factors' (a measure of quality). Nature recently published an article (which I linked too in an earlier posting) suggesting that a well-known open-access pioneer, Public Library of Science, is a bit wobbly financially. This caused a fair amount of comment and has generated some really interesting views and discussion on Nature News Blog. I really think the debate is important and has implications for copyright, for freedom of information and for future publishing investment strategies. Do read it. It is one of the strengths of the web and publishing that dangerous and difficult arguments can be freely expressed and everyone can participate.

If this is all too serious for you perhaps you'd enjoy my entry for the worst song lyrics of the month.

07 August 2006

E-books the options

A second posting in a day but I'm afraid it's a business one. The Publishers Association has just released an excellent primer on e-books which I wanted to let you know about – details at the PA website. At £100 for 70-odd pages for non-members (half that for PA members) it appears rather expensive but, as someone pointed out in a previous discussion about book prices, it's the quality not the quantity that matters.

08 August 2006

Plagiarism, imitation and flattery

Every now and again the book industry is convulsed by a bout of plagiarism. Someone is suspected of lifting material from another author, there is a court case, someone wins, someone loses and the loser not only loses the case but is typically subjected to abuse from the literary police force. This is not much different from athletes being caught taking performance-enhancing drugs. It used to be otherwise.

I was listening to a Prom (an annual series of concerts broadcast by the BBC) last night and heard for the first time Michael Haydn's Requiem pro defuncto Archiepiscopo Sigismundo which was first performed in 1771 when Mozart was fifteen years old. The introducer of the prom mentioned the friendship between Michael Haydn and Mozart in spite of the near twenty year age difference. He also mentioned the similarities between the Haydn Requiem and the later Mozart Requiem. There are references in various sources to the fact that the Haydn work 'greatly influenced' Mozart. I wonder what is the difference between being greatly influenced and pinching.

Go listen. If this were raised in a contemporary court I reckon Mozart would be branded a top-class plagiarist and would have to hand over his gold medal and a chunk of his reputation to Michael Haydn.

And for today's light relief go to Scott Pack's blog. He was the chief buyer at Waterstone's book chain for a period and he tells the inside story of his departure. He is now working for the innovative Friday Project who might well become the exemplar of a modern book publishing company.

09 August 2006

There was a ghastly groundhog day moment when I was listening to the news yesterday about a team from the Arab League flying to New York to persuade the UN to amend the peace plans for Lebanon. At the end of the bulletin the programme presenter whispered (on air) to his colleague 'I think that was *yesterday's* news bulletin'. And so it was. But I hadn't noticed (and nor presumably had the BBC technicians). A sad commentary on the Middle East situation.

A happier day for England cricket where a brilliant test match ended in an England victory. The really good news was that the two heroes of the final day were Mudhsuden Singh Panesar (Monty) and Sajid Iqbal Mahmood (Saj) whose names tell a story. British Asians are becoming mainstream sports stars which will further enhance respect for the first and second-generation immigrants who have done so much for Britain.

A publishing statistic – worldwide sales of textbooks increased 8% year on year according to a recent study from EPS. This is not so surprising. Although mature markets such as the UK have constrained spending on school materials many developing countries have recognised the importance of education as a necessary forerunner of economic and social development (thank God) and have increased budgets for textbooks.

The more telling statistic is that online educational sales increased 18%. In parallel I saw that in Australia teachers are being encouraged to retire earlier in order to bring forward a new cohort of younger teachers more sympathetic to electronic learning systems. In the USA every college course is supplemented with or indeed driven by electronic materials for learning, testing and administration.

The electronic revolution in educational publishing has been slower to arrive than in, say, scientific or legal publishing but it's coming and it's coming fast.

10 August 2006

Creative Economy

August in the UK (and I imagine elsewhere) is known as the silly season. So many people are away on holiday. Parliament closes down. Schools are shut. So little happens that newspapers constantly have to concoct absurd stories to fill their pages (even more than usual). Practical jokes are played too.

I received an email yesterday from someone in the British Government asking me to review the draft reports from the CEP working party groups. CEP is the Creative

Economy Programme and it is a government-sponsored (ie tax-payer funded) project to 'make the most out of the great creative talents thriving all round the country, and is the first step in the Government's goal of making the UK the world's creative hub.' Truly a worthy objective and in line with many of the Government's policies. The question is how they intend to go about achieving this objective.

On the assumption that not too many of you will want to plough through these documents I thought you might like a flavour taken from the executive summary of the infrastructure working group.

This document provides an overview of the key themes and recommendations from the Creative Economy Programme Infrastructure Working Group. It introduces a set of essential and actionable ways forward to maximise the UK's cultural and creative infrastructure offer as a key driver for creative competitiveness and growth. These ways forward are encapsulated in the concept of the Creative Grid. The Creative Grid represents a new way to connect our creative asset base, broker and coordinate new relationships and partnerships, and provide vital market-driven intelligence, in order to give the UK a competitive edge as the knowledge broker of the global creative economy.

The Creative Grid and its component parts provide the strategic framework for each of the other Creative Economy Programme Working Groups, connecting their targeted policy recommendations through the following three main themes:

Global Competitiveness: Our creative critical mass and knowledge advantage is based around the connectivity of concentrations of infrastructure and activity seen most prominently in our Core Cities, London and the South East. A key challenge is to focus these assets outwards – towards global markets and partners – to ensure the UK is recognised as a global creative leader.

Convergence: It is in the connectivity of these concentrations of infrastructure and activity that ideas are shared, that technology meets content, that culture meets commerce. A key challenge is to build effective links between different parts of the creative value chain and across traditional sectoral, institutional and locational boundaries.

Stimulation: Progressive creative senses of place are formed, and creative people are stimulated, by connectivity of concentrations of infrastructure and activity. A key challenge is to position cultural and creative infrastructure at the heart of place and community, which will allow our cities to flourish as creative hubs that work together and with London and the South East for increased UK creative competitiveness.

Well, that clarifies things. I imagine this will set our authors well on the way to lead the world in creativity. Or, given the silly season, is this a practical joke? I was also glad to find out that book publishing is a product business as opposed to a process business (eg architecture) or media (eg newspapers). Hmm.

11 August 2006

Foo Camp

My colleague Timo Hannay looks after Nature's blue-sky developments in technology and most of the blue skies are turning out be real.

He also contributes to the Nascent blog and yesterday he was hoping to get on a plane to San Francisco for a science Foo Camp. Foo is an abbreviation of Friends of

O'Reilly. Tim O'Reilly founded O'Reilly Media, a hugely successful technology publisher. Tim is viewed as one of the most far-sighted publishers in the world and has forged close relations with the movers and shakers of the Web 2.0 generation. His Foo camps have become legendary events for open discussions among top practitioners in any number of fields. Nature is proud to have been working with O'Reilly and Google to organise a Science Foo Camp today and tomorrow at the famous Googleplex. There are 200 of the world's top scientists and knowledge engineers discussing the future. Goodness knows what will be the outcome but for sure it will be interesting and for sure Timo will write it up for us.

On a more parochial but interesting historical note, Matthias Mueller, a student in publishing studies at City University in London is writing a dissertation on the Net Book Agreement (whatever that is). He's asked me to encourage interested people to fill in his questionnaire which can be found on his blog.

🐦 12 August 2006

Garbology

After last week's utterances from the British government about building creative hubs blah blah I was pleased to see that the Macmillan English Dictionary's Word of the Week was garbology. I was hoping that this was the new science of studying verbal garbage as practised by civil servants, management consultants and politicians throughout the world. Unfortunately it is the much more prosaic but possibly more interesting 'study of a person or group of people by examining what they throw away'.

Anyway, this led me to look more closely at how our English Language Teaching websites and electronic resources have been developing. Given the importance of English in the world. Given the importance of language to international understanding. Given the importance of education to economic prosperity I am delighted that Macmillan is leading the industry. You just have to check out a few sites to see what I mean.

One Stop English

Macmillan English

Dictionary Magazine

Macmillan English Campus

Macmillan English for India

We've had quite a bit of interesting correspondence on the need for scientists to communicate better. I think it applies to everyone and particularly in the UK where reticence and inability to speak other people's languages are considered virtues. Maybe this will change with better education.

🐦 13 August 2006

Moaning about publishers – and others

There's a guy called Gerard Jones who sends emails around the publishing industry about his website. I think he's probably a talented writer. I think he's also extremely assiduous judging by the amount of time and effort he has dedicated to creating a huge database of people in the publishing and related industries. Here's an example of his email style:

EWA, Fifth Edition, September 2006

The Fifth Edition of 'EVERYONE WHO'S ANYONE IN ADULT TRADE PUBLISHING, NEWSPAPERS, MAGAZINES, BROADCASTING AND TINSELTOWN, TOO: A Writer's Guide to The All-Pervasive Nazi Propaganda Network' is finally finished. Phew.

EWA (everyonewhosanyone.com) is a free, searchable, 1.2 GB online e-mail and web address directory of around fifteen thousand (15,000) of the most influential ignoramuses in the media, entertainment and academic industries whose perverse job it is to keep themselves and others brainwashed beyond belief. Here's the page you're listed on: http://everyonewhosanyone.com/eduk.html

During the four years EWA has been online I found a good agent, sold one of my books (*Ginny Good*), got it published the way I wanted it published and made it into a fifteen-hour, multimedia audio book all on my own. *The Audio Book of Ginny Good* is easily and by far the single greatest literary achievement of the 21st Century. Listen to it and see. It's free. Like me.

http://everyonewhosanyone.com/ggsyn.html

Or not. Stay safe in your creepy cave with money-grubbing Nazi thought thugs keeping you from reading, writing, seeing, hearing or saying anything worth reading, writing, seeing, hearing or saying. Land of the free, home of the brave, yes . . . as long as you don't do anything brave or free. Ignorance is bliss, but calling slavery 'freedom' is absurd. There's plenty of other worthwhile stuff on the rest of the site, as well. Click some links. Let 'em take you where they take you. Or not.

Finally, if you don't want me to send you any more e-mails, let me know and I will gladly put a little mark (666) by your name to remind me not to send you any more e-mails. Thanks. G.

Gerard Jones
http://everyonewhosanyone.com/audio/GGch00introm.mp3

Why does he do it? Making enemies can't be the best way to help his efforts to be published. He can't make money from it (or can he?). Perhaps it's a way of creating a community of like-minded people. He seems to think there is a conspiracy among publishers to avoid new talent, to promote rubbish and in general to do a very bad job. All this might be true but I'd like to reassure Gerard and anyone else who thinks similarly that there is no conspiracy – it is merely incompetence. Perhaps the publishing industry should adopt a mission statement – WE'RE DOING OUR BEST.

Having posted this I went to get my weekly fix of book browsing – in an independent bookshop – all right, not that independent, the Pan Bookshop. I picked up a copy of Bad Faith by Carmen Callil. It is history of the guy in the Vichy Government responsible for 'controlling the Jewish population' in Southern France. I haven't read it yet but it is clearly a work of scholarship about a fascinating period of French history. It must have taken the author years of research, tears and trouble to produce this 600-page treatise. It is beautifully designed and produced by the team at Jonathan Cape, part of Random House UK, part of Random House Worldwide, part of Bertelsmann Media Worldwide. The book's audience is clearly not mass market and yet, in spite of the consolidation, gloabalisation and commercialisation of the industry it has seen the light of day and found a market (I bought a copy and so, according to the bookshop manager, have another forty people, helped by a signing session).

Alongside this book were hundreds (possibly thousands) of similarly excellent titles – a great range, beautifully produced, idiosyncratic but tailored to the local market – at great prices. Bad Faith was £20 in hardback which elsewhere in the Fulham Road in London buys a bunch of asparagus, 100g of Brie and two glasses of wine. The point of this is to suggest that maybe (just maybe) the industry is doing a great job and is getting better by becoming more professional and more market-aware. If so, then perhaps a little credit should go to the dedicatee of Bad Faith – 'To PBH' – Paul Hamlyn who, extraordinarily does not have a Wikipedia entry and so you'll have to make do with a link to one of his legacies – another reason to be cheerful.

14 August 2006

Moaning about publishers 2

I wrote about Gerard Jones and his directory of trade publishers. This has generated a few comments which say what a good thing he is – and I am sure he is – but I asked a question: Why does he bother? He hasn't responded in the comments section but he has emailed me this reply and in the interests of freedom of speech and assuming he has no objection here it is:

'Richard Charkin has a blog, upon which he had this to say about one of my innocent little e-mails and this to say about me:

I don't think anyone hates Gerard and certainly no-one that I know of minds his publishing names etc. Actually nobody gives a damn about him. The question is why does he bother?!

Why he bothers is that books have become 'product,' merely another means to make nothing but money . . . not art, not truth, not beauty, nothing worth anything but money. Books themselves don't matter a whit, how much money they generate is all. With the right packaging, enough endorsements, a fair amount of expensive hype and a modicum of proof-reading, any piece of unreadable drivel can make some short-term money. That's the publishing industry's stock in trade. It's the same as the salami industry. There are truly great salamis out there that nobody's ever going to get to eat 'cause you don't see 'em advertised on the telly. The Audio Book of Ginny Good is a greater literary experience than everything Macmillan has published in the last twenty years combined but nobody's ever gonna listen to it 'cause nobody can make any money off it. It's free. That's anathema. G.'

Well, I think Gerard is wrong. The publishing industry is full of people who care about books. He wants to believe the opposite simply because his proposals haven't been accepted as widely as he'd have liked. There are always two explanations of failure. One is that you need to try harder or get better. The other is that the world is conspiring against you. The latter is better for the ego. The former is probably the more likely.

Man Booker long list 2006

I was at a celebration yesterday afternoon to welcome <u>Graham Swift</u> back to <u>Picador</u>. His last book was published by Penguin. He told a nice story of how he was in a very swanky Madrid hotel recently. Apparently this was the hotel where bullfighting stars stayed when preparing for an event. So perhaps unsurprising but uncomfortable to share the lift with two fully-uniformed <u>picadors</u>. As he pointed out, this is still more likely than sharing a lift with two penguins.

There was a certain tension in the air because we (and Graham's agent) were awaiting the announcement of the <u>Man Booker prize long list</u>. We were delighted that books by two authors published by Picador, <u>Claire Messud</u> and <u>Edward St Aubyn</u> were selected. The trouble with the longlist is that it must really hurt not to be on it if you think you have a chance but that being on it is still a huge distance from winning the prize itself. Fingers crossed that these two make it to the next round to be announced on 14 September and then they can both suffer the agony of awaiting the final announcement on 10 October. Authors published by Picador have won the prize the last two years (<u>Alan Hollinghurst</u> and <u>John Banville</u>). I'm not sure any publisher has ever achieved a <u>hat-trick</u> but records are there to be set.

🦅 16 August 2006

Cairo

Arrived in <u>Egypt</u> for the first time at 1.00am this morning after coping with Heathrow security etc etc. First impressions:

They drive on the right in spite of still using pounds as their currency;

They identify the quality of fruit by naming the best quality after film stars and worst quality after George Bush;

They claim that more <u>Mercedes</u> are sold in Egypt than in Germany;

On arrival at the airport we were whisked into a luxury lounge, had our passports and luggage tickets taken away and suddenly everything (customs, passport control, luggage carousel) was fixed – nowhere else in the world that I've experienced . . .

We're here because the Egyptian Government has decided to encourage competition among publishers to produce the best quality textbooks for schools and colleges. <u>Macmillan</u> has worked in Egypt for more than thirty years and intends to be part of the massive opportunities of a country with 15 million schoolchildren, 4 million university students and a commitment to education as a driver of economic and social progress. There are many many problems but as usual we follow our new mission statement – We're doing our best.

🦅 17 August 2006

Potpourri

Just back in London from the Cairo day trip (where I failed even to glimpse the pyramids) and a few miscellaneous items.

1. Someone will be able to make a lot of money by working out how to have Egyptian hotels, restaurants and cafes serve decent espresso. I'm told that it's something to do with the water but really . . .

2. An Egyptian author asked how best to get her book sold in the UK given that wholesalers and retailers weren't in the least bit interested in Egyptian Homes and so it is only available through the online bookseller which I'm not allowed to mention. Do have a look at the website – it's very special.

3. And from Egypt back to an excellent interview about our burgeoning medical publishing arm, Nature Clinical Practice.

4. Tracy Hofman has written an interesting piece (apart from the fact that she describes me as silver-haired – accurate but do I need to be reminded?) on blogging. She can't see why I bother to do this blog and sometimes I wonder too. However, the original reason which still stands is that our IT department were getting fed up with my internal email newsletter clogging up the Macmillan servers. The blog solved that issue at least. And if you want to know more about corporate blogging I see that Piatkus publishers are offering a free download chapter from Debbie Weil's new book The corporate Blogging Book (it presumably does what it says on the tin).

5 and finally,phew. I can't resist pasting in the attached press release from Wisden which suggests that A&C Black have done a great sales job, MDL an excellent distribution effort, Matthew Engel a brilliant editorial tour de force and the England team – thank you for the Ashes and the extra sales.

This year's edition of *Wisden Cricketer's Almanack* has seen record sales, and the standard hardback version is to be reprinted for the first time since 1982. The Almanack, which has been published every year since 1864, is an annual bestseller and is described as 'the most famous sports book in the world'.

Wisden 2006 records the 2005 Ashes, which it describes as the greatest-ever Test series. The Ashes factor has clearly boosted sales, just as it did 24 years ago when *Wisden 1982* featured the series known as 'Botham's Ashes'. Since then *Wisden* has revamped its format to include more top-class writing, pictures and the quirky facts cricket followers love. Gavyn Davies, in *The Guardian*, called *Wisden 2006* 'the best edition ever', while in *The Spectator*, Frank Keating described it as 'the most compelling must-have for many years'.

This year, for the first time, *Wisden* published a large-format edition as an alternative to the standard hardback and soft-cover versions. Combined sales of all three has reached 50,000, nearly 20% up on recent years and far ahead of recorded sales for previous editions.

Christopher Lane, *Wisden*'s managing director, commented 'One of the articles in this year's *Wisden* asks whether the Ashes boom is real. Sales of *Wisden* suggest that it certainly is. Our challenge now is to convert those new readers into *Wisden* collectors. And to achieve that we are striving to make next year's edition even better.'

October sees the publication of the *Wisden Anthology 1978–2006*, covering the best of the Almanack from the past three decades. This is a long-awaited sequel to the highly successful *Wisden* anthologies published in four volumes in the early 1980s.

For further information please contact Christopher Lane on 01420 83415 or e-mail: chris.lane@wisdengroup.com

Barry Turner

There are two Barry Turners in Wikipedia. The first one is a Canadian politician in favour of freedom for ducks and the vital conservation of wetlands in North America. The second is a friend of mine, a former Macmillan employee and a prolific author and editor.

He is the editor of the invaluable and enormous Statesman's Yearbook which improves with every annual edition and this year comes with a free single-user online licence.

He is also celebrating the twentieth birthday of another of his brainchildren The Writer's Handbook which has become the leading resource for professional and would-be professional writers. He has written a piece in the London Times on the difficulties and issues around new writers getting published. Judging by the amount of correspondence I get on this whenever it's mentioned I thought I'd encourage readers to visit the associated debate which is getting a fair response.

I reckon that saving the Canadian wetlands is really important for the world but I reckon that Barry does his bit too.

And a propos ducks I came across a wonderful quote from Colin Haycraft, ex owner of the idiosyncratic publishing house Duckworth, cited (his name wrongly spelt) in the Bookseller magazine by Anthony Cheetham: 'A publisher who writes books is about as much use as a pregnant midwife.' In researching him I also came across his wonderful: 'A publisher is a specialized form of bank or building society, catering for customers who cannot cope with life and are therefore forced to write about it.' Have a good weekend.

Brian Martin

The last few days have seen a renewed flurry about the impossibility of new writers getting published and/or the inequity of the process of selection and/or the inanity of publishers in general and big publishers in particular. I am pasting in a piece by Brian Martin which appeared in this weekend's Financial Times.

Better late than never

By Brian Martin

Published: August 19 2006 03:00 | Last updated: August 19 2006 03:00

There are writers whose work is not published until late in their lives. Fanny Trollope published Domestic Manners of the Americans, her first of more than 40 books, at the age of 52. That was from financial necessity. Her husband had died and she had a family to support. Perhaps her son Anthony gained his discipline of writing, in his case novels, from her. He wrote his first book, The Macdermots of Ballycloran, aged 32, while working for the Post Office.

Earlier this year my first novel, North, was published. There is nothing particularly remarkable about this except that I am 68. Admittedly I had written a couple of academic books, but fiction was new to me. Now I have joined a coterie of novelists who started late: Mary Wesley, who first saw her fiction in print at 70; Charles Chadwick, whose book It's All Right Now appeared when he was 72 – it took him three decades to write; and Marina Lewycka, whose prize-winning novel A Short History of Tractors in Ukrainian was published when she was 58.

My career has been spent teaching. I taught English at the same school in Oxford for 40 years and could have continued for another two, but release was too tempting. (Only one of my predecessors, a Victorian named Brownrigg, exceeded my tenure at the 500-year-old school.) At the same time, over a period of 14 years, I taught English literature at the university. But by 2001 I was free and spent a year contemplating and considering what I should do next.

As it happened Mary Wesley proved an inspiration. I remembered that she had once said: 'I have no patience with people who grow old at 60 just because they are entitled to a bus pass. Sixty should be the time to start something new, not put your feet up.' For more than 30 years I had been reviewing fiction, first for the New Statesman, then for The Times, Spectator and FT. It occurred to me that I should try my hand at a novel. So, intellectually refreshed by a year of freedom, I turned my attention to writing fiction. Here, Graham Greene was my mentor. I wrote every morning until lunchtime, and only if the mood took me would I return to the typescript. Otherwise, like Dr Johnson (but only in this respect), I was available for tea or coffee. After about 10 months, North was born.

It is certainly not easy to find a publisher in your late sixties. I spent a couple of years approaching agents, finding people who liked what I had written but who doubted its marketing potential. Then I found an innovative fiction-publishing scheme, Macmillan New Writing, which took to North without hesitation, and a deal was struck.

At the same time as trying to find a publisher, I continued to write. At the present time, I have three more novels completed. The publisher David Fickling said to me with characteristic enthusiasm, 'Test yourself. If you want to go on writing most of the time, if it's a habit, almost an obsession, then you are a writer in the proper sense.'

I reckon I pass the test.

I wrote North because I am interested in the ways people think and behave towards one another. It is a psychological novel, a drama of suspense. Three of the main characters are young. Others are older, professionals, more sceptical and circumspect. All are caught up in the turmoil of emotion and events. The novelists whom I have admired are Greene, Henry James, Joseph Conrad and Iris Murdoch. There is no telling what their influence has been, but the agent Giles Gordon, to whom I showed the North manuscript just before his death, said it reminded him, 'at different times of C.P. Snow and Iris Murdoch'. I make no such claims, but pay tribute to their craft and power.

Readers should take heart. Even in your sixties, it is not too late to start a new career. A few weeks ago Joanna Trollope, a mature novelist, and Charlotte Mendelson, a young, distinguished newcomer to the art, discussed on the Today programme the contention that novelists should not start writing till they are at least 35 because they lack experience and authority. Naturally, I inclined to Trollope's point of view.

Some journalists have accused Macmillan New Writing of cheapening the publishing process for novels, likening it to Ryanair inasmuch as there are standardised conditions and no advances. The novels it publishes stand or fall on their own merits. When it came to the stage of editing the final page proofs, my editor was on sabbatical in Languedoc. I was flown down to Carcassonne to pass the pages. As my publisher put it, 'North goes south on Ryanair.'

On libraries

I am attending the September annual conference of National Acquisitions Group, which, to quote:

' . . . exists to create and encourage dialogue and improvements for all involved in the acquisition process. Members include organisations in publishing, bookselling and library systems supply as well as librarians in academic, public, national, special and government institutions.'

In preparation I'm keeping my ears open for library relevant material. I'll be making a presentation on the key issues affecting publishers today and how these may impact on both the public and academic library sector. So please send me anything you think is relevant.

Working with libraries seems to me an essential part of a publisher's support for authors and for dissemination of information as freely as possible. In the midst of the tectonic shake-up of our industry it is vital that the library and librarians remain at the heart of what we do.

Amazing cricket events

It's not often even in England that cricket makes the front pages. The reason is best summed up in the Guardian or cricinfo report on the test match between Pakistan and England which was meant to finish today but finished yesterday when Pakistan were deemed to have forfeited the game.

For the many people who are uninterested in cricket or don't understand it the essence is that an Australian (and thus apparently neutral) umpire penalised Pakistan for cheating by tampering with the ball illegally. Pakistan were definitely ahead in the match and more likely to win. The Pakistan team then staged a protest by refusing to play and the umpires then declared England the winners. After negotiation the Pakistan team then agreed to play but the umpires 'spat the dummy' and refused to have their prior decision overturned and would not restart the game.

All very silly. But there were (and are) two really unpleasant undertones or suspicions.

The first, I hope, is highly unlikely. Before the cheating penalty England were huge outsiders to win the match with the bookmakers (and a lot of money is gambled on cricket worldwide). Immediately afterwards the odds shortened dramatically. Anyone who bet on England to win on Sunday morning stood to make a large amount of money – which always raises eyebrows in sport.

The second relates to bias. Asian cricket teams have been known to suspect that the umpire in question, Darrell Hair, did them no favours. This particular penalty has never been applied before in international cricket. And so on. The bit that really worries me is that this has happened at a time of acute tension between the West and the Islamic world. Cricket is only a sport but in Pakistan and India it is an obsession. To accuse their players of cheating is a grave insult.

God knows where this will all lead but I think that even non-cricket lovers whould follow the story.

PS An excellent piece on the affair by Andrew Miller.

22 August 2006

Creative commons

The Friday Project, which I have mentioned before, is experimenting, yet again, with a new business model. I asked Clare Christian of the FP to tell us about it:

Some of you will have already heard of a Creative Commons licence as many websites and blogs are published under this agreement. There are a number of licences that can be complex in places but essentially a CC licence means that the content provided under that licence can be downloaded for personal and other non-commercial use while the copyright holder remains the author.

Although many publishers will throw up their collective hands in horror at the thought of giving away content (see the ongoing Google debate) is it really such a bad idea?

At The Friday Project, we don't think so. On Monday we released the creative commons edition of Blood, Sweat and Tea, a book based on the blog of Tom Reynolds a London EMT who has been writing about his life and work for the last three years. The publication of the online version coincides with the print edition and we believe that by offering the book in this way we will widen its audience and so increase the potential market for purchases of the print version.

Tim O'Reilly once said 'Obscurity is a far greater threat to authors and creative artists than piracy' and I agree. Certainly, as far as this book is concerned, obscurity is not a problem. Already the launch of the CC version is generating comment across the web, including the highly influential Boing Boing and the Telegraph blog which states 'it's encouraging to see a publisher taking such an innovative approach. It's the ones who experiment that will survive the online world, not the ones who stick rigidly to the traditional business models'.

Of course, time will tell if we are right or wrong, but what do you think?

The creative commons edition of Blood, Sweat and Tea can be found here). Download it, enjoy it – and buy the book too.

23 August 2006

More creative commons

Yesterday's guest posting on Creative Commons by Clare Christian has generated some interesting comments. Are the risks of undermining traditional copyright protection greater than the benefits? Is traditional copyright unsustainable in this new environment? By NOT embracing the new environment are we in danger of creating a copyright-hostile environment? By embracing the new environment are we simply encouraging copyright piracy? By allowing free access are we undermining the value of intellectual property or are we increasing its reach and hence its importance? These are, I believe, some of the important issues for writers, publishers and retailers today (not whether in the UK we print prices on covers or use stickers!).

I thought you might also be interested in yesterday's improbable letter received by one of the editors at Nature:

You better watch it trying to tell the world that humans evolved from chimps. We didn't – and I will pray for you and ask God to open your eyes to see the ridiculousness of your articles. The Apostle Paul wrote about people like you in the Book of Romans, explaining that due to your rebellion and the refusal to accept God, He has taken away any capacity that you may have had to see Him. Paul explains it as, brilliant men who cannot see the wonders of creation in front of them become morons. Evolution is being ditched, it cannot be proven, and is a perverse religion. You will never find an answer other than God.

Thanks for your time.

Ah well, at least it ended politely.

🦎 24 August 2006

Crockatt & Powell

On the way home earlier this week I popped in to see the bookshop co-owned by one of our regular commentators, Adam Powell. The shop is absolutely great – just what an independent bookshop should be. Good but not flash design. Interesting stock range. Intelligent and engaging staff. The problem is that Adam's customers want the best quality, the best range, the best service and the lowest prices – a difficult business proposition. From a publisher's point of view and with the best (honest) will in the world it is hard to fulfil all the needs of such a bookshop when their purchases are inevitably so much lower than those of the big chains and supermarkets. Who knows what the solution is but committed booksellers like Adam are absolutely part of it.

But he's not always right. In his latest comment he says that record companies and publishers are reacting to rather than engaging with technological change. I guess that might be true in some instances but I don't believe it's true in general. British publishers in particular are at the forefront of embracing, using and experimenting with new models. The most difficult area in which to move quickly is where there are the most constituents with a voice. That is probably literary publishing where everyone has a vested interest, an opinion, and a right to veto – authors, agents, retailers, reviewers etc. We do need to open this up to change but, believe me, it's hard!

🦎 25 August 2006

Spelling and all that

I know that this blog sometimes has spelling mistakes – mea culpa. I do try to eliminate them but I type badly and fast and make mistakes. Does it matter? Yes, it upsets me. We are a publishing company and should know how to spell and we should care about getting things right all the time. More importantly (and even more importantly in a computer age where successful searching by and large depends on accurate spelling) bad spelling causes problems.

For instance roughly half of Macmillan's internal reports used to spell Ottakers (sic). Which meant that to find out the total Ottakars sales you had to search on both spellings. It's also a bit insulting billing a customer twice because we can't decide how to spell him/her. Of course this is now a lot easier, although is it Waterstones or Waterstone's?

However, that is nothing compared to the horror I found on the main Macmillan website this morning (which I hope will be corrected by the time you read this):

Picador celebrates the inclusion of two of it's authors on the Man Booker Prize for Fiction 2006 Longlist

It was like a knife to my heart. Can everyone in Macmillan please learn the difference between it's and its – please. And if the rest of the world would follow suit I'd be a happier guy. Or is this yet another sign of fast-approaching grumpy old bookman-itis? Aaaargh.

26 August 2006

Teaching English

My grumpy old man blog of yesterday touched a few nerves. After the enormous success of Eats, shoots & leaves I shouldn't be surprised that the subject of spelling and use of English is a popular issue. I suppose the problem starts in schools. And if it's difficult to teach British kids how much harder is it to teach English to non-native speakers.

About five years ago Macmillan Education launched onestopenglish to offer teaching resources, tips and support to teachers of English throughout the world. It has been a huge success with 350,000 registered users who come back time and again. The material is free and usage has not been restricted at all.

Fine and dandy and very web 2.0 but we needed to develop the site further, to pay top-class professional writers, teachers and developers and to create a web 3.0 level of service. This requires an income stream but we could not risk losing our loyal users. We therefore developed a subscription site, the Staff Room where we have responded to user feedback gathered via questionnaires, workshops and focus groups by generating new 'missing' material, enhanced search, comprehensive support materials and much else.

Teachers of English are not wealthy and we have therefore kept the subscription price to the lowest possible level – £2 per month – and onestopenglish users have already begun to convert in good numbers (we launched last Thursday). Do have a look at onestopenglish and if you are a teacher of English do take out a subscription to the Staff Room – it's worth a go.

Logos

If you google (note lower case initial, the sign of brand domination) 'Logos' you find a number of logo companies, a journal of modern society and culture, a foundation dedicated to music in Flanders, a magazine about research at Argonne National Laboratory, a journal of Catholic thought and culture and so on, page after page of things called Logos. At last I found the Logos I was hunting.

Logos is the premier journal of the world publishing and book community. Unlike other trade journals, *Logos* is international in scope and focuses primarily on the deeper issues and challenges facing publishing and the book world. Appearing quarterly since 1990, *Logos* has featured hundreds of essays by many of the leading figures in publishing and the library community.

If Publishing News is the Daily Mirror of the publishing industry, The Bookseller is the Daily Mail, Publishers Weekly is the International Herald Tribune then Logos is the Economist.

Logos doesn't have a website. It is run as an independent charitable foundation which has an email for service and ordering – logos-Marlow@dial.pipex.com. I rung up its editor, Gordon Graham, for permission to use a review he wrote and published about Mike Barnard's Transparent Imprint. Gordon was a very successful publisher as MD of McGraw-Hill in the UK and then CEO of Butterworths and President of the Publishers Association. He is a brilliant speaker and I remember some of his bons mots such as: 'The secret of success in a corporate environment is always to let your owners have better returns than they expected but less than you could afford'; and in defence of charging for scientific information 'Wherever information is free there will be no freedom of information'.

In any event, the only problem with Logos is that its circulation is small (please do subscribe) and therefore not many people will see this review. I apologise in advance because printing it might be seen as immodest and self-serving (which it is) but I think Mike's book is excellent and I want to tell the world – or at least the readers of this blog.

LOGOS

The Journal of the World Book Community

BOOK REVIEWS

TRANSPARENT IMPRINT: How a Publisher's Decision to Tell the Truth to Authors Stirred Up a Storm

Michael Barnard

Macmillan, 2006 208 pp

ISBN 1-400-9242-4

£10

If you work in a large publishing corporation, how do you win sanction to start a new publishing programme which has no promise of profit? The answer is by conviction, persuasive power, tremendous energy and faith. Michael Barnard has all of these qualities. His energy even enabled him to write this book about the new publishing programme just before it was launched.

The new programme was built on that notorious graveyard of literary aspiration – unsolicited first novels. So many of these are received by trade publishers that they have no time to acknowledge, let alone read, them. In fact, the Macmillan website until 2005 warned, 'We do not accept unsolicited manuscripts.' However, one day Mike Barnard – a career executive whose responsibilities embrace production, distribution and information technology – wondered aloud at a meeting whether 'a streamline system' could he devised to handle unsolicited manuscripts, not only to encourage and do justice to authors, but in the hope of achieving an occasional bestseller which might pay for the programme.

From this casual remark was born Macmillan New Writing, with the blessing of CEO Richard Charkin. At the beginning Barnard thought that his problems would be to harness the powerful resources of the many departments inside Macmillan who would tend to regard the new programme as an orphan without a future. What he did not expect was to be scorned by forces outside of the company. Viewed inside the company as working on a shoestring budget, his 'streamlining' was called, particularly by literary agents, publishing on the cheap and exploitation of authors.

The books certainly don't look cheap – each printed in hardcover and full colour, with individually designed jackets, reasonable quality of paper, head and tail hands, ribbon markers and modest retail prices (£12.99). What is missing is invisible to the outside observer or reader – no author advances, minimal print runs, standardised contracts, standard designs. Those with long memories may well feel that Barnard has resurrected fiction publishing as it used to be.

Of course, the first problem for Barnard and his team was somehow to arrange that all of the manuscripts would be read. This labour was dispersed among a team of freelance readers, and eased by requiring that all manuscripts be submitted as electronic files. Another rule was that there would be no dialogue with authors except those whose manuscripts were accepted.

The scheme was immediately popular with authors, including the 99 per cent who were rejected, because they knew they were in with a chance. And they would rather accept the formulaic terms – same royalty for everybody (20 per cent of net receipts), no rewriting, take-it-or-leave-it contract, no cash advances – than have no chance at all of being published.

Barnard was content with the usual fate of those with bright ideas: 'You thought of it. Now do it. But don't spend any money.' What he did not reckon with was the enormous public criticism that the announcement of the programme would attract. But he was clever enough to see this as welcome publicity. The first report, appearing in *The Guardian*, quoted views that 'the scheme is a scam', is 'atrocious and wrong', and that Macmillan was guilty of requiring authors to bear their own editing costs.

A vigorous public debate ensued in both the trade and national press. The major assault in the latter came from Robert McCrum, literary editor of the *Observer*, who told his readers that the launch of Macmillan New Writing meant that the 'days of taste and literary discrimination at Macmillan are over.' Barnard's written reply to McCrum's article, calling it 'a bizarre outburst', was not published.

Nicholas Clee in *The New Statesman* wondered whether Macmillan was 'exploiting authors' desperation'. Under the heading 'Publishing on the budget plan', *The Washington Post* announced that Macmillan New Writing was 'the talk of Britain's book world'.

Meanwhile, Barnard's team had read three thousand manuscripts and decided to publish just six. The programme would continue at the rate of one publication a month.

The second half of *Transparent Imprint* deals with the nuts and bolts of bringing together all of the elements in the publishing process through what Barnard calls 'horizontal management'. His book thus has elements of a publishing primer, written in a lively, conversational way which makes the reader feel it was written as it happened – as it was. Through the whole of the adventure Barnard somehow continued his regular executive responsibilities, including trips to Asia, where the books are typeset, printed and bound.

Macmillan New Writing kindly sent LOGOS copies of their first six books along with Barnard's *Transparent Imprint*. We don't review fiction. I don't even read it. My wife does. But I do study publishing. To me, the most encouraging feature about this book is one that Barnard does not mention, but which is implicit on every page: individual enterprise can indeed flourish in the corporate environment. It just needs the right individual to take the initiative – and the right boss to lend support.

Gordon Graham

28 August 2006

Another reason to be cheerful

There are many upsides to being in the publishing industry. You work with (mainly) intelligent people; your objectives are (mainly) laudable; your products are (mainly) at worst harmless and at best inspirational; your lifestyle is (mainly) free of physical danger; and you may, if you're lucky and/or reasonably able, earn a living wage.

The downsides are that most people you meet have an opinion about publishing and publishers. I wouldn't say we get a completely bum rap (I suspect arms dealers, drug runners, secret policemen, dictators do worse) but I (and I hope it's not just me) get a fair amount of flak essentially pointing out the general inanity or foolishness of the industry.

From booksellers – why don't you give more discount to me? Why don't you give less to others? Why aren't books more expensive? Why don't you make books cheaper?

From authors – why don't you pay me more? Why don't your editors love me more? Why do your editors interfere so much? Why do you give booksellers such big discounts? Why isn't my book in Waterstones in Dulwich?

From would-be authors – why won't you publish my book? Why did you publish that other guy's book? Why has nobody spotted my brilliance? Why is there a conspiracy against me?

From agents – why don't you print my client's books on better paper? Why aren't they designed better? I want to know in advance before you sell Serbian rights. Why do you insist on exclusive European rights when you know the Americans want to sell into Europe? I don't like the jacket.

From friends – have you thought of publishing other books like Harry Potter? I don't think this book is good as her last one. Why don't you advertise more? Publishers must make lots and lots of money because I spend lots on books – and they're very expensive. Why did you publish that heap of rubbish?

But on Friday a miracle happened. I was having my annual medical check-up and was wired up for the treadmill heart test. I rather enjoy it because it's an opportunity push yourself to the limit knowing that there's a consultant cardiologist by your side. If you're going to have a coronary there's no better place or time.

While I'm hammering away on the treadmill the doctor asks me what I do. Publishing. What sort? All sorts including scientific and medical. What sort of medical? Nature Clinical Practice. 'Aha', he said, 'you must work for Macmillan. The medical profession was concerned when you launched that series. The worry was that you were simply using the Nature brand to con us into buying a bunch of new journals. We were wrong. I subscribe to Cardiovascular Medicine and it's absolutely terrific. The articles are excellent, the editor is the best possible person in the world, production is excellent, pricing is fair. I'm also a contributor and the in-house team have been complete professionals in every way.'

You could have knocked me down with a feather or a myocardial infarction.

29 August 2006

Japan

The thought of Japan makes me nostalgic. I used to visit once or twice a year when I worked at Oxford University Press. We had two companies there, TOPELL which sold English Language Teaching books and TOPMAST which sold the rest (you can puzzle out the acronyms for yourself). I was a director of TOPMAST. The nostalgia comes not just from fond memories of a wonderful country but from a time when publishers could make money from a rich and vibrant economy. Our standard discount to retailers was 25% (30% for very large orders). There were no returns whatsoever. Orders were substantial, placed in good time and the quantities ordered were meant to keep the book available for several years (rather than several hours as in much of the UK today). Accounts were paid absolutely on time. Business courtesy was everything. The ethics of business remain the same. It says a lot about a culture when the two owners of a major book importer committed suicide recently because they could not meet their financial obligations. However, the market is not what it was. A combination of demographics, economic slow-down and regional shifts have all served to push Japan down the league of publishing hotspots.

But books still appear and one of our directors, Richard Nathan, has just published a new edition of his Frequently Asked Questions about Corporate Japan and I attach his notes about it:

The new revised edition was published on the 28th of August by Kondansha (http://www.kodansha-intl.com) eight years after the first edition, which sold more than 17,000 copies after six re-printings. The first edition also came out in audio format and believe it or not was licensed to Microsoft for use in research they were conducting on translation software. Apparently, according to the Microsoft boffins, the Japanese-English bilingual structured format was ideal for computers to try to mimic. I doubt the research came to much and I haven't noticed any improvement in translation software or seen a Microsoft branded product like the Babel Fish in the Hitchhiker's Guide to the Galaxy, but you never know it might just be round the corner!

Many of the original questions in the book came from the mouths of visiting Macmillan executives to Japan when I was based in Tokyo. Such as 'Why do Japanese businessmen exchange business cards so often?'; 'How are annual pay rises negotiated in Japan?' and 'Is sexual harassment a problem at Japanese companies?' Not sure why they asked the last question, but we did have some pretty faces in the office.

It is quite amazing how much Japan has changed over the last 8 years. For example, the finance and banking industry has been completed restructured. In the early 1990s there were 23 major banks including retail banks, long-term credit banks, and trust banks in Japan, but this number has now fallen to 8, and three groups now dominate the market. The largest bank Mitsubishi UFJ Financial Group (http://www.mufg.jp/english) which has the rather odd slogan 'Quality For You' is now the world's largest bank and manages a staggering 40 million accounts. It doesn't compare well to US and European banks in terms of profits. Nevertheless, it is still amazing how much has changed since the last edition of the book.

One thing that hasn't changed is that Maruzen (http://www.maruzen.co.jp/home-eng) is still the oldest surviving company listed on the stock exchange in Japan, despite all the changes and disruption to traditional publishing activities in Japan following the collapse of the economic bubble and the entry of Amazon and others into the Japanese market. Maruzen was founded in 1869, the same year that Macmillan published the first edition of Nature (www.nature.com), and today Maruzen sells print and online editions of Nature to universities and libraries across Japan. In its early years Maruzen imported and sold Burberry rain coats and the Encyclopaedia Britannica.

The book (ISBN 4-7700-4035-0) is available from Amazon Japan at: www.amazon.co.jp/gp/product/4770040350/sr=1-2/qid=1156779250/ref=sr_1_2/250-0114605-6236240?ie=UTF8&s=books and probably at all good bookstores in Japan including Maruzen.

🐦 30 August 2006

Paris Hilton meets Jeffrey Archer

I came across this headline on the blog of a celebrated British journalist Bryan Appleyard. He has written about Jeffrey Archer in the past and still writes about him a lot nowadays never favourably. But what interested me about the headline was the complete lack of connection between the two people mentioned. The only explanation I have is that Bryan Appleyard knows a thing or two about marketing as well as about journalism and that he reckons that those two names juxtaposed will bring more traffic to his site.

This site averages 1500 visitors a day at the moment. Let's see if my pinching Mr Appleyard's idea can improve this number. A simplistic form of Google manipulation but most marketing ideas are pretty simplistic! I'll let you know the results of this scientific experiment although I am aware that Bryan Appleyard has written extensively about the threats to society of science itself.

Of course the problem is that if the results prove positive just about every book blurb will contain the words Paris, Hilton, Jeffrey and Archer, such is the me-too-ism of publishers' copywriters.

I've just received this extract from a marketing flyer about the forthcoming Frankfurt Book Fair: Record number of 7,223 exhibitors from 101 countries took part in the Frankfurt Book Fair 2005. 284,838 visitors came to the Fair from 121 countries, 6.3 % more than in 2004. About 30 per cent of visitors were from abroad. With these credential the fair needs to no introduction. This fair is the most important platform for the books and publishing industry to feel the pulse the market and open itself to the new opportunities.

What this says is that approximately 100,000 visitors came from overseas. I estimate that the average cost per person of attending the fair from overseas (airfares, hotels, food and drink, transport, cost of stand, opportunity cost etc) is of the order of $5,000. That means a total of $500 million. If the average margin from selling books is, say, 10% it would be necessary to sell an additional $5 billion just to pay for attending the fair. Hmm.

31 August 2006

Another googly

When some executives of Google came to the Publishers Association to discuss their plans for digitising in copyright material they brought with them two 'communications consultants' better known in English as spin doctors. I wondered why. I now know.

I do not know the business editor of the Times, James Harding. I assume he's an intelligent and diligent journalist who does his best to report and comment accurately. What then explains this article? How does an announcement that Google is digitising some classic and out of copyright books make the main leader in the business section of a great newspaper? The business impact is close to zilch. The books mentioned have already been digitised many times over and so it's really not news. Google have already press released any number of times about their various library scanning projects. And purple prose such as this:

Google may have just done for book-reading what e-mail has done for letter-writing. Yesterday the internet search engine started making classic, out-of-copyright books available to download and print free. The service makes available to everyone the dusty pages of old tomes that once were reserved only for those with privileged access to the likes of the Bodleian library in Oxford and Harvard University in Cambridge, Massachusetts. Google likes to boast that its mission is to organise the world's information, but it is doing something better than that: it is is democratising it.

But the bit that's really got my dander up is where he (or a spin doctor?) says: 'Inevitably, the Google service has been greeted by the book industry with the kind of welcome normally reserved for a can of kerosene and a box of matches.' This is garbage. The industry has no quarrel at all with Google over the digitisation and searchability of out of copyright works. We quarrel with them over the use of the copyright material produced by authors whose copyright we are obliged to protect. They wish to usurp that copyright without prior permission. That is our argument and it is straightforward to understand. Presumably the 'communication consultants' failed to make that clear to James Harding and he didn't think it worth finding out why publishers have reacted the way they have. The positive publicity – e.g. the headline of the article, 'Google does book-reading a huge favour' – will certainly have justified the spin doctors' doubtless exorbitant fees but, frankly, it makes me feel a bit queasy and I wonder what else I should recognise as complete rubbish in the Times.

Coincidentally in the same issue of the paper there are big articles on page 2 of Times 2 on Paris Hilton and Jeffrey Archer. After yesterday's blog should I begin to suspect a conspiracy? I also wondered yesterday whether juxtaposing the names would increase traffic? The answer is no. We had 1628 visitors yesterday against an August average of just over 1500 a day. In scientific research, negative results can be just as valuable as positive ones, albeit slightly less fulfilling.

≤ September 2006 ≥

Mon	Tue	Wed	Thu	Fri	Sat	Sun
28	29	30	31	1	2	3
4	5	6	7	8	9	10
11	12	13	14	15	16	17
18	19	20	21	22	23	24
25	26	27	28	29	30	1
2	3	4	5	6	7	8

✒ 01 September 2006

Silence is golden

Yesterday's entry about Google digitising out of copyright works has generated quite a few supportive emails in my in-box. Today in The Times Ben Macintyre has written a great piece in support of copyright, the need to protect authors' rights and the continued requirement for would-be users of intellectual property to seek permission to offer digital versions rather than Google's posited offer to take down material if the rights holder complains. Ben describes what I think more eloquently than I ever could:

'For centuries, artists have fought to protect their work from being copied and disseminated without payment: in 1623 the composer Salomone Rossi wrote a setting of the Psalms that included a curse on anyone who copied the contents. These days authors can rely on more than a curse.

The tutting librarian should be replaced by another authority figure policing the stacks: the copyright lawyer, ensuring that every new addition to the online collection comes with the express permission of the writer, and a royalty.

Silence is golden in a library; but the law of copyright is beyond price.'

As this is the first of September I have been totting up the numbers of visitors in August. I was expecting a fairly quiet month given the holiday season etc. We had 42944 visits, up 38% on July. Here's a graph attempting to show progress through the year:

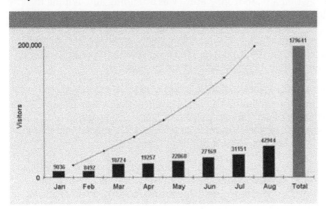

✒ 02 September 2006

Waterstone's and BCA

I've just taken a look at Waterstone's new website. It's a cause for celebration. One of my concerns for the industry is that the excellence of Amazon and its clear customer benefits might result in their becoming wholly dominant. Waterstone's have shown that it's quite possible to build an attractive, clean, professional alternative on-line bookstore. And it doesn't stop with Waterstone's. Many book retailers – independent, chain, specialist, clubs – are experimenting with on-line selling and many more will do so. Some will try to compete on price (which is probably a forlorn exercise) but most will use the web to reinforce their existing skills of selection, service, local knowledge and building customer loyalty. The more routes to market the better.

One route to market which has disappointed in recent years but which we're told is turning a corner now is Book Club Associates in the UK. I think everyone in publishing wants to give them the benefit of the doubt. We all hope that they will return to the glory days when they helped build new authors such as the early titles from Wilbur Smith; where they underwrote many great non-fiction series such as Antonia Fraser's Kings and Queens of England; where they helped reintroduce classic books, such as the Oxford History of England, to a new audience. So good luck to them but I was rather concerned by a recent quote from their Chief Executive (perhaps misquoted) in Publishing News. Are Bernard Cornwell and the Sharpe series really an example of a new author and new fiction?

'Particular successes have been facsimile editions of Enid Blyton and Agatha Christie, and collections of Danielle Steel and James Patterson. 'We're continually testing new authors – Bernard Cornwell's *Sharpe* series for example – and I think there are real opportunities for us with combined author collections under subject groupings such as crime and thriller, science fiction, true life adventure . . . We're only limited by our imaginations.'

03 September 2006

Scifoo camp and Beijing

I blogged a little while ago that a team from Nature was attending and helping to organise a foo camp along with O'Reilly and Google. In spite of transatlantic flight problems and delays it happened. Timo Hannay, our director responsible for this project (and many others of course) has his own blog, Nascent, where he reported on the meeting and has promised further updates. This is one of many examples of the 'good' Google can do. If only they'd lay off their attack on copyright.

The 2006 Beijing Book Fair has just closed. I wasn't able to attend – a strategy conference in Europe – but Macmillan had a good presence. It was, apparently, bigger and better than ever. The most feted foreign publisher was Jane Friedman of HarperCollins. I don't suppose this has anything to do with HC's refusal to publish Chris Patten's East and West but I imagine it did little harm.

We launched Picador Asia, our new company for publishing the very best of Chinese writing in English (and other languages) for the rest of the world. Meanwhile our existing publishing such as New Standard English continue to grow at rates and in volumes which dwarf almost all other activities. However prices are very low and it will be some time before our sales in China exceed the UK.

04 September 2006

Start-up #1

In a day full of meetings and similar distractions I asked Clare Christian of The Friday Project if she could offer a few words covering the challenges of setting up a small independent publishing company. Her comments follow.

Well, Richard offered me three paragraphs to cover the various challenges-i-mean-opportunities presented in setting up a new company, which is clearly not quite enough. Instead I thought I would offer a few of the stages that we went through prior to becoming TFP proper and hopefully Richard will allow me the space later to elaborate.

1. **Plan**. In March 2005 I went to Anthony Cheetham with a forward list. Yes, just a forward list. Most people in publishing know that Anthony is an experienced publishing entrepreneur, but to look at a list and see an entire business is a skill that Anthony has for which I am extremely grateful.

2. **Money**. A great idea is not enough. You apparently need to put your money where your mouth is so I remortgaged my house. No, no, please don't worry about Jake, 5 and Edie 3 – the cardboard box is fine.

3. **People**. All of a sudden there is an office and some contracts with authors and you're in business. The office is good as it means there is an option beyond the cardboard box but we do have to pay for it and all of a sudden we have people in it. They are 'staff'. Another terrifying concept, for me at least.

I'm not oversimplifying. A plan, money and people is really all that you need to start a publishing company, or any company, and this is where I found myself a few months ago.

At this stage though, I found myself with some great books (in theory at least) but no sales and distribution channel. I looked at a few distribution options but they were expensive and not very satisfactory. We went to Macmillan and were lucky enough to be accepted onto their third-party sales and distribution system, but what would we have done otherwise? What should we have done? What would *you* do? As a bookshop, does it matter? As a Publisher, does it? As a consumer I guess it makes no difference? Is there an alternative?

I've failed to squeeze even a fraction of the issues I face as a new publisher into this post so I started with this initial one. I'm genuinely interested in your thoughts on the distribution issue. There are a million and one other things we face every day as a new start-up. I might cover them at www.thefridayproject.co.uk/vox but perhaps Richard might allow me to mention them here too. Who knows?

05 September 2006

Of this and that

Some interesting statistics from Oxford University Press about the reaction to their open access experiment for publication in the journals they publish. In essence they offer authors whose research has been accepted for publication the option of paying £1500 (or £800 if their institution already subscribes to the online version of the journal in question) to have their paper made available absolutely free to anyone in the world. Open access is being encouraged by a number of research-funding organisations and this 'mixed-economy' response is clever. OUP benefit from being seen to be scholar-friendly, they earn money from the author fees, they encourage institutional subscriptions and they still retain the vast bulk of their subscription income. They are also seen to be transparent in publishing the results of the experiment widely. However, none of this answers the fundamental question of why paying for publication is likely to result in better scientific literature than the existing subscriber sytem. Time will tell and it's great to see practical experimentation rather than hypothetical debate.

From some interesting experimental findings to a report documenting the 'bleeding obvious'. Google have discovered that 16% of visitors to the Google BookSearch web page then move on to a bookshop site (Amazon, WHS etc). Well, shiver my timbers. Who would have thought that some of the people who visited a book page on Google might have wanted to see more about the book and perhaps even buy it? Much more interesting is why on earth the remaining 84% did not visit an online bookshop.

At a dinner last night I was asked what the successful British TV show, Richard and Judy, could do to encourage even more new writing and enjoyment of literature. Their book club has been enormously successful in every way and it was really hard to see how they could do better what they already do. But there is one thing. They could invite their millions of viewers to visit their local public library and demand that the library stocks more books, particularly those by new authors. Libraries seem to have been hijacked by some politicians as out-reach centres or IT retraining camps. Libraries are there for readers and for books. Richard and Judy could be a huge force for good if they marshalled their troops accordingly. They could start by asking how much the library service has spent on management consultants, PwC, compared with their book purchasing budget over the last few years. Libraries are very definitely open access (see above) but there's no point having open access if the choice of books is limited and inappropriate.

06 September 2006

On political incorrectness but Pan trumps Penguin

Here are some excerpts from a review of Hugh Paxton's novel Homunculus in the The Star newspaper in Johannesburg (I cannot find the link to the review itself):

Apologies for starting with the back end of this novel, but Hugh Paxton's afterword bears quoting. 'I'm proud to say' writes this splendidly immodest British journalist, "that Homunculus is probably the most bizarre work of fiction ever to emerge from the African continent (African presidents' memoirs and autobiographies excepted).' Bizarre it certainly is. Also horribly political incorrect and remorselessly downbeat on our current continent.

In Paxton's defence, let me say at once that he's cynical not only about Afro-lunacy, but also about everyone who sticks their nose into our affairs, do-gooders not excepted. These include foreign mercenaries (South Africans especially); foreign intelligence agencies, foreign correspondents (such as Paxton himself); UN aid agencies and 'peacekeeping' forces; and the Japanese doomsday cult Aum Shinrikyo (remember Tokyo subway sarin gas attack?). Even those with frankly commercial – okay, homicidal as well – involvement are not spared Paxton's satire . . .

. . . I well recall the impact Tom Sharpe made on the literary scene in 1971 with his first novel, *Riotous Assembly*, set in the 'Piemburg' of those days. Where Kommandant van Heerden of the SAP longed for the heart of an English gentleman. Published at the height of apartheid, its fierce mockery exposed the idiocy at the heart of the system.

If only *Homunculus* could do the same for West Africa . . .

. . . Quite simply, *Homunculus* is outstanding, the best piece of new fiction I've seen for a long time. However, although Paxton threatens a 'Homunculus II. More of the same', I Hope this doesn't happen. The pace of this one is too frenetic to bear repetition. Let's hope for something totally different, for a novelist of such skill can surely tackle another genre with equivalent success.

We at Macmillan are proud to be the publishers of what I hope will turn out to be the most politically incorrect book of the year.

At the launch last night for Dick Francis's latest I ran into John Makinson, the head of Penguin. He told me that there was an article in yesterday's London Evening Standard about a Penguin launch party where there were none of the author's books for sale – yet another example of Penguin's poor distribution record etc etc. The truth was, of course, more complex. Penguin had arranged for an independent bookseller to run the book stand. The bookseller had confused the dates and hadn't turned up. John Makinson arranged for a car to go to the bookshop, pick up the books and the bookseller, return same to the party and rescue the situation. There was a slight frisson when he told me that the independent bookshop in question was . . . er the Pan Bookshop, owned by Macmillan. Sorry John and sorry excellent Pan Bookshop team for exposing what must have been an extremely rare error to public scrutiny. I just couldn't resist.

On a more serious note this link about the problems faced by a Lebanese book warehouse may put some of our concerns into perspective.

🦝 07 September 2006

Science again

If I write an entry about new writing (average readership of a first-time novelist maybe 500 people if they're lucky) or UK bookselling (average value of an account to an independent bookseller for Macmillan Distribution thus including publishers such as Bloomsbury, Walker Books, Guinness etc but excluding sales through wholesalers, less than £2000 per annum) we get a full postbag of comments and private emails to me. Whenever I write about science (average readership of a highly complex paper in Nature 15,000, total registered users 2 million) there is a resounding silence. The two cultures still operate. Why is it that book publishing only rarely closes the gap?

In any event I promised you more about our Science Foo Camp and here is the link. For those who can't be bothered to go there here is one para that sums it up:

Science Foo was the best conference I can remember in my life, and I've been to a lot of them . . . Thinking about what made this Foo different from all other conferences, I realized that people brought their whole selves to this conference, their hopes, foibles, humor, outrageousness, brilliance, good intent, and little to no ego in the 'look at me' sense. It was fantastic.

🦝 08 September 2006

Indecent proposal

Before anything else I thought I'd share with you an old piece of news which I'd hate to think you might have missed.

Greetings from sunny Stuttgart. Last night I had dinner with colleagues from the finance and M&A departments of Holtzbrinck. The 'controller' for Macmillan was there and here are his memories:

'Having had dinner in a typically Swabian Weinstube in down-town Stuttgart we were just about to leave. At that moment a very attractive, open-minded lady came to our table just having been eavesdropping our conversation. She introduced herself and conceded that she was listening to our talks for quite a while. She told us that she was looking for a British man to take her to the UK – and she made very clear that she knows what she wants: A British man, middle-aged, grey-haired, living in London and by the way, he should be wealthy. She seemed to be quite desperate. Last year she got to know a British man looking like Hugh Grant, living near Basingstoke. She found her presumed love for life via the online partner agency <u>Parship</u> – what are the odds? But in the end (after 4 weeks) it didn't work out.

Richard, the landlord of Parship UK, couldn't really bring himself to take her with him to London and to offer her a job (maybe as his new assistant?) and of course free living. So he made a deal with her: He promised her to get a three months' free access to Parship to find the right British man.

Will see what happens . . . for further report.'

🐦 09 September 2006

Two cultures more

My <u>post</u> about the disparity in interest between science and publishing generated some interesting comments. However, I know that most readers don't go back to previous postings and read the comments. So I am going to paste in one from Timo Hannay which says what I think but much more coherently:

(Disclosure: I wrote the blog post that Richard links to above and co-organised Science Foo Camp. I'm also a Nature Publishing Group, and hence Macmillan, employee.)

I take Richard to be asking not 'Why don't scientists show an interest in my blog?', but rather 'Why don't (book) publishers take an interest in science?'. Susan's comment implies that only scientists are interested in science, which is probably true but no less tragic for that.

I couldn't blame anyone for being indifferent to publishing any more than I could blame them for a lack of interest in steelmaking – it's just an industry after all. But anyone with half a brain and an ounce of curiosity, whether a publisher or something else, ought to have an interest in science (as well as literature, music, philosophy, technology and history).

Whatever your area of expertise, if you don't understand Darwin then you don't understand fully what it means to be human. If you don't appreciate Einstein then you don't appreciate the wonder of the universe we inhabit. And if you haven't read up on Godel's Theorem (arguably the most profound discovery a human mind has ever made) then you have a gap in your experiences the size of a Beethoven or a Shakespeare. If I – a humble neurophysiologist – can subscribe to the Literary Review and read the works of Joyce then any publisher can occasionally digest the contents of Nature (or, if you must, some other scientific publication).

Funnily enough, the single greatest personal discovery that I made at SciFoo was just how much the invited writers – in particular, a small posse of eminent science fiction authors – added to the debates. Perhaps their eloquence and originality shouldn't have surprised me (though it did). But most of all I was taken aback by the depths of their insights. I'm no particular fan of sci-fi, but I am now a fan of those authors. They showed, among other things, that it's possible to hold a fascination for both reason and its artful expression; that a true love of knowledge doesn't stop at arbitrary borders; and perhaps that ignoring the very idea of 'two cultures' makes for a more complete and interesting human being.

PS Two very nice comments from the women in the Weinstube mentioned in yesterday's Stuttgart blog.

10 September 2006

Being British

I hate nationalism, jingoism, chauvinism, patriotism and all the isms which have led to human misery. As a result I find it hard to get excited by being a citizen of the country of my birth. However, there are certain things which make me (in spite of myself) proud to be British. Yesterday evening the BBC broadcast The Last Night of the Proms, the final concert in the 2006 season. Of course there are similar concerts elsewhere and I suspect the standards are as high or higher. Of course some of the flag-waving and cheering is silly. But there is something about the BBC's continuing commitment to supporting music and musical appreciation that is neither self-righteous nor patronising. It is simply the right thing to do and they do it brilliantly.

Incidentally the guy who runs the Proms is Nick Kenyon. I first met him around 1980 when I was responsible for Oxford Journals. One of the key journals was Early Music. It was edited by its founder, a brilliant musicologist from New Zealand called John Thomson. He edited the journal brilliantly but it constantly lost money and there were innumerable glitches and feuds. He had a staff of ten including picture researchers, in-house copy editors etc – all for a quarterly journal. My job was to try to turn round the finances of the journal which inevitably involved cutting staff. Every suggestion I made was met by the assertion that all cost savings would result in the collapse of editorial standards. After any number of rows and heart-searching John eventually decided to leave and by the best luck in the world we were able to hire Nick Kenyon to replace him. He cut the staff from ten to two, regularised the publication schedule, maintained editorial standards and turned the journal from a cash leaker into a cash generator within two years. The journal is still the best in its field and I bet it still makes money. You don't have to lose money to have the highest editorial standards – it just takes a good editorial manager.

My two book recommendations of the moment are both transatlantic, both by women and both titles incorporate an apostrophe. Go check out Elisabeth Hyde's The Abortionist's Daughter and Claire Messud's The Emperor's Children.

I am in the middle of preparing for a speech I am giving this week to a big conference of librarians. If you want to have input into what I'm going to say let me know fast.

11 September 2006

Another sad end-of-Summer moment. The last cricket match of the season at Marsh Baldon in beautiful Oxfordshire. It has not been a vintage season – played 9, won 4, lost 4, drawn 1. Honours go to Paul Denning (438 runs from 7 innings including a 173 not out and an average of 87.6); James Cookson (69 overs, 13 wickets average 15.46); Geoff Penington (our youngest player who took 7 wickets at 6.43); and our oldest newcomer Tim Coates (5 wickets from 11 overs at 9.4). And the greatest honour and thanks to the team's only full professor and almost full-time organiser <u>Robert Denning</u>. We won this last game resoundingly – always important to end on a high.

A busy week ahead. A speech at <u>National Acquisitions Group Annual Conference</u> in Reading; participating in a panel on the development of the Asian market at the grandly titled <u>Global Information Industry Summit</u> in Amsterdam; a meeting of the <u>British Library Strategy Advisory Committee</u>; and of course the usual round of Macmillan businesses including the launch of the 20th edition of Barry Turner's <u>Writer's Handbook</u>.

12 September 2006

Joachim Fest

I had dinner last night with the editor-in-chief of <u>Tagesspiegel</u>, Berlin's leading newspaper. On searching for the link I came across this <u>article</u>. I met <u>Joachim Fest</u> when he came to London to promote his book about the last days of the Third Reich <u>Inside Hitler's Bunker</u>. He was a brilliant man, a brilliant historian and a brilliant writer. Amazingly, his entry in Wikipedia has already been updated.

At the dinner we were discussing the <u>Natascha Kampusch</u> TV interview and the widely held belief that no person could have been so composed after such an ordeal and that therefore this was not her but an actress. I suppose this falls into the conspiracy theory genre which includes the (non)moon landing, Elvis Presley is dead, Lady Diana was murdered but who knows . . .

Later today we have the first international sales conference of <u>Macmillan Medical Communications</u>, our newest publishing venture. Our first wave of launches are in Latin America, India, Japan, Spain, Turkey and Asia-Pacific. Our aim is to become the number one in this field within five years and the number one for quality from day one. I'll keep you up to date with our progress.

13 September 2006

Reading University

The things I do to keep this blog fresh! My PC at home didn't work this morning and so I drove to <u>Reading University</u> early and persuaded the helpful IT team to let me have use of one of their computers. Thanks Reading.

Last minute jitters before my speech as usual. Do you have to be controversial to be interesting? How many toes will I step on? Someone described my speech <u>here</u> would be like Joshua addressing the walls of Jericho. My biblical knowledge is too scant for me to understand fully what he meant but it sounds bad for me. More later if a) I survive and b) I can find a free computer terminal at Heathrow.

Incidentally here are the words of the British politician responsible for libraries, David Lammy. The bit I really like is his attack on self-appointed, unelected, unrepresentative groups. In other words he's sick of people who disagree with his vision. Aren't we all?

Books V Computers

Which brings me to another issue that is regularly kicked around in library circles. What are libraries for?

The Concise Oxford Dictionary describes a library as a 'collection of books for use by the public . . . . . . .or a similar collection of films, records, computer routines {sic}, etc'.

That's a dry definition of course. What I really think libraries are about are people; both as individuals and as members of communities. And libraries are there to serve a multiplicity of people's needs.

So I get heartily tired of self-appointed, un-elected, un-representative groups who dogmatically say that libraries are for this and not for that.

I love reading. Coming from a household where you could count the number of books on the fingers of two hands, I celebrate libraries' central mission of the promotion of the enjoyment of reading. Bookstart – great! Summer Reading Challenge – fantastic! Adult reading groups in public libraries – absolutely wonderful!

But libraries are not just about books. They never have been. And the digital resources at our disposal today have broadened immeasurably the kind of public services that they can provide.

Again, let's look at this in a 'House' context. The last time you wanted to check a reference in Hansard, did you wade through a 6 inch pile of paper copies? What you probably did is to search on a database capable of bringing up a series of matches in seconds. I repeat, why should the public want anything less efficient for their information needs.

Post script – I survived.

14 September 2006

Amsterdam

A hundred delegates from the information industries have gathered here to network and listen to pearls of wisdom from the likes of Helen Alexander. I'm on a panel discussing opportunities in Asia which I suspect may descend (or elevate) to disagreements about the real (as opposed to the perceived) potential of China.

Very different from yesterday's UK library discussions which Susan Hill has commented on already. The argument is all about libraries but the underlying concern is about local government and freedom of expression.

Karen Christensen was passing and I persuaded her to write a few words: Richard said last night that the zeitgeist is anti-authoritarian, which means that these debates – whether about what libraries are for, or whether China is threat or opportunity – are just what people crave. I hope so, because I think only good can come of these hot discussions!

Statistic of the day – there are more Internet users in China than in the USA. In other words more than 200 million people.

And back in Britain the bookmaker William Hill has announced the odds for the forthcoming Man Booker prize. I remember Paul Hamlyn telling me that he moved a title from 20/1 to 4/1 by betting a mere £50. By coincidence the title went on to win which was typical of Paul's good fortune or canniness. In what is probably an appalling breach of blogiquette I have highlighted the two Picador titles in order to encourage you to bet on them, read them, and tell all your friends about them.

5/1 Sarah Waters – 'The Nightwatch',

5/1 David Mitchell – 'Black Swan Green',

6/1 Peter Carey – 'A Love Story',

8/1 Andrew O'Hagan – 'Be Near Me',

10/1 Barry Unsworth – 'The Ruby In Her Navel',

10/1 Howard Jacobson – 'Kalooki Nights',

12/1 Clare Messud – 'The Emperor's Children',

12/1 Hisham Matar – 'In The Country Of Men',

12/1 Kiran Desai – 'The InheritanceOf Loss',

14/1 Edward St Aubyn – 'Mother's Milk,

14/1 Kate Grenville – 'The Secret River',

16/1 Naeem Murr – 'The Perfect Man',

16/1 Jon McGregor – 'So Many Ways To Begin',

16/1 Mary Lawson – 'The Other Side Of The Bridge',

16/1 M J Hyland – 'Carry Me Down',

20/1 Bar the rest

15 September 2006

Pan nostalgia

Anyone who is in the least bit interested in the history of publishing will enjoy Tim Kitchen's brilliant First 25 years of Pan Books website. In particular, the covers are sensational. Here is one. The site has scores – all evocative.

Yesterday I encouraged you to bet on our two Man Booker longlist titles. The shortlist is now out and we are very sorry (and fed up) that Claire Messud has not made the cut. However, delighted that Mother's Milk by Edward St Aubyn is still in the running and his odds are shortening.

At the Global Information Summit yesterday in Amsterdam there was much talk of the competition between India and China for leadership in the 21st century. My trivial observation was that India's population will inevitably exceed China's because of its obsession with cricket where the highest score always wins. China's only hope is to take up cricket with immediate effect (and with great benefits to the Wisden Group).

And meanwhile Macmillan India has completely upgraded its very impressive website. We now employ twice as many people in India as in the UK or the USA.

🦅 16 September 2006

Many unhappy returns

I've always marvelled that anyone not brought up speaking English can make any sense of it. For instance, the noun 'return' has 19 separate meanings in the OED (the verb has a further 21) and many of these are further subdivided by nuance. One meaning is 'Pecuniary value resulting to one from the exercise of some trade or occupation' – in other words 'return' equals 'profit'. In the book trade 'return' has nothing to do with profit, it is all to do with loss. The distinguished writer and part-time publisher Susan Hill has agreed to guest a piece for this blog on that old adage 'Gone today here tomorrow' which plagues the book trade.

RETURNS

Probably I should be a better environmentalist. I recycle the bottles and don't drive many miles a year. I use no air miles as I have no passport. We grow some fruit and vegetables. Otherwise, I tend to switch off when the talk contains too many words like environment, ecology, global and warming.

There is one thing which has been exercising me on several fronts lately – RETURNS, as in books and Sale or Return but the front which struck me especially today can be summed up by the word WASTE. Waste of fuel, waste of paper, waste of road miles, waste of resources, waste of time, waste of energy.

In no other retail business are there Returns except for 'returns of damaged goods.' But in the book trade, everyone buys books on S or R. As a publisher, I preach to authors every time I take them on, that a sale is not a sale INTO a bookshop, it is only a sale when it goes OUT of the bookshop in the hands of a customer. No one listens.

So let me tell you what has happened this week in this topsy-turvy, Alice-in-Wonderland world of publishing.

Earlier this year my company Long Barn Books, published a book. 2,000 copies were printed. The books came to me on a lorry on pallets. Waterstones did a scale-out from Head Office of some 1,400 copies. So parcels of books were packed into cartons and sealed with brown tape and labeled and send off to 160 odd stores around the country by courier. More van journeys.

The system of invoicing is quaint and involves a great waste of paper. I am obliged to put an invoice into each carton, and to send a copy of that invoice, a paper copy, to the Finance Department. They eventually pay me – though they do this via BACS, which at least saves some paper.

The books stay in the Waterstones stores for some 3 months. I then get a request to authorize Returns. I agree. This involves the sending of a single e-mail to which I reply. More efficiency.

During the 'Returns Window' cartons start to arrive back to me, on courier vans, with unsold copies of the book. The cartons contain requests for Credit. I have to pass these pieces of paper on to the Accounts Department. But a considerable number of the books are returned carelessly packed so that they come back to me bumped, cover-damaged or, worst of all, with 3 FOR 2 WATERSTONES stickers plastered over them. I refuse to give credit for these, which involves a bit of a battle and more paperwork.

I sent out some 1,400 copies and some 600 have come back. This is what I mean when I tell the author that they are not SOLD they have only been on offer.

This is waste enough. BUT there is worse. Out of approximately 40 branches which have returned books some fifteen have RE-ORDERED THE SAME TITLE, sometimes on the same day that the RETURNS were dispatched to me. They have Returned FIVE and re-ordered FOUR. So four books are sent back on their way via yet another van, travelling more miles, to the same shop. I have to process the paperwork for the returns and then raise new- paper – invoices for the new orders.

I was told there was no alternative though everyone realizes it is a nonsense, and a WASTE.

On environmental grounds alone, this is madness. Multiply those books to-ing and fro-ing by however many separate titles from however many publishers there are in the UK, at least twice a year – around the end of January (post-Christmas de-stocking) and around now (pre-Christmas de-stocking) and you see the waste involved.

I think the government should step in the outlaw this nonsensical and wasteful practice on environmental grounds alone.

And I never ever thought I would hear myself say anything like that.

🗑 17 September 2006

Used books

I quote from <u>VSS Communications Industry Forecast</u> just released.

Total spending on new, used and online books will increase 2.7 percent in 2006 to $21.88 billion. The rise of used books is expected to alter the spending pattern on consumer books in the years to come. Spending on used books is projected to grow at a 25.0 percent compound annual rate over the next five years, reaching $2.25 billion in 2010. Record-setting demand for Harry Potter and the Half-Blood Prince, plus strong spending on titles related to the movie The Chronicles of Narnia, helped to boost total consumer spending on new books by 3.6 percent in 2005 to $20.48 billion. The used book market, limited primarily to small retail outlets, libraries and the neighborhood tag sales in the past, has become a more important factor in the consumer book market due to the Internet, jumping 25.0 percent in 2005 to $736.0 million. Used book spending pushed total spending on consumer books to $21.31

billion, a 4.4 percent increase over the 2004 level. The Consumer Book publishing industry is forecast to have total spending in 2010 of $24.9 billion.

What this suggests is that spending on new books might actually decrease in real terms in the next five years with customers turning more and more to the second-hand market. This trend is already apparent in the college textbook market in the USA and is accelerating in Europe and elsewhere. Yet another challenge to how we do business in this changing world. What do you think?

On a more positive note my friends at the Pan Bookshop have launched their own blog. All power to them.

18 September 2006

Independent Bookselling Chapter 94

I know that many British independent booksellers feel that bigger publishers are ignoring them in the fight for shelf space in supermarkets and chain bookstores. There has been much debate in the comments part of this blog over the last few months and Macmillan has taken its share of criticism. I was pleased therefore to discover that we sponsored a Small Business Forum dinner in Bristol last week. Organised by The Booksellers Association, the SBFis a forum for independent booksellers to debate the issues affecting their businesses as well as sharing ideas to help then thrive. The evening event was attended by eighty independents together with Alison Penton Harper, Beth Webb, Kate Long and Clive James who made an extremely funny after-dinner speech. This is exactly the sort of event which supports independent bookselling and which helps authors and publishers understand the issues of bookselling today.

This week is full of budgeting for next year. It sometimes feels that we might as well simply slaughter a goat and hope for the best! Any other suggestions?

19 September 2006

Big Mac

This is being composed on the early flight to Stuttgart where I have a board meeting later today. I try not to make this blog too Macmillan-centric but for every rule there must be exceptions and this is one.

For those who don't already know we have two new main board directors, Julian Drinkall and Steven Inchcoombe. I won't bore you with reporting lines, structures and responsibilities. That'll come through the normal channels. What they will have to do is fill the enormous gap which will be left by the upcoming retirements of two of the most important people in the history of Macmillan, Geoff Todd and Mike Barnard. These are not household names in the British book trade like Gail or Gillon or Vicky or Caradoc (why are industry celebs by and large known by one name, like Pele or Fangio?) They have, however, contributed as much or more by being at the forefront of introducing modern management to the running of the business – in forecasting, in logistics, in production, in IT. Thank goodness they have also taught us the wisdom of planning ahead and we've allowed a sensible handover period to ensure continuity and the maintenance of Macmillan's culture.

On the publishing side of Macmillan there has never been greater activity. Just a few examples.

We're working literally 24/7 in London and Gurgaon putting the finishing touches to the prototype BookStore which we're launching at Frankfurt. This is an electronic storage and selling vehicle to help publishers and booksellers take advantage of digital information delivery without the risk of losing control of authors' copyright material.

Results are coming in from Spain where it seems we've had our most successful school season ever.

In Mexico our children's books have won more selections for the government school library project and this in spite of the appalling political nonsense going on there – road blocks, demos etc.

We've even managed to publish successfully in Zimbabwe!

At Palgrave Macmillan frantic activity working on two huge projects – the new complete edition of Shakespeare's works with the Royal Shakespeare Company and the new edition of the multi-volume and world-renowned Palgrave Dictionary of Economics.

In Oxford editors and designers are ploughing through the creation of some 500 new titles this year for markets as disparate as Nigeria, Egypt, Russia, and China.

We're working like mad turning our audio business based on CDs into a download business. We've built a podcasting studio in our London office.

At Pan Macmillan, our Picador imprint has a contender on the Booker Prize shortlist for the third year running (the remarkable Mother's Milk by Edward St Aubyn). This is a tremendous feat, especially considering that we have won the prize for the past two years. Fingers crossed for a hat trick.

At Nature it seems there's a new initiative every week.

Note to Macmillan people – if you'd like your achievements or initiatives listed send it in as a comment to this blog. Also, corrections welcome.

Note to non-Macmillan people – apologies if this is boring or show-offy but I am really proud of Macmillan and every now and again I want to tell people. Normal service will be resumed.

20 September 2006

Google ads and dreaming spires

Transparency is all. I told you that I'd be monitoring the income from the Google ads which appear (fairly unintrusively) on the right of this blog. It's proved harder than I thought to get the information, to do with tax declarations etc, but I can now reveal our total earnings to date – $22. This is not actually paid over until the account reaches $100 so celebrations are for the time being rather muted. I know some of you think we should drop the ads but I do think it's worth claiming the first $100 at least.

I'm off to Oxford today to visit our principal educational publishing operation. The offices are in the former home of the Potato Marketing Board and when we took over the lease the signage reflected the organisational structure – crisps, chips, new potatoes etc. I suppose our structure (Europe, Middle East, Africa and Caribbean, Latin America) is just as baffling to an outsider. The building is also famous for starring in Bill Bryson's Notes from a Small Country where he describes it as one of worst architectural warts in Britain. I think we've improved it a little but the best bit was and is the (albeit distant) view of the dreaming spires. And if we use binoculars we can just about see (from a superior position) the offices of our fiercest competitor, Oxford University Press.

🐦 21 September 2006

Made in China

In the late 1970s or maybe early eighties there was an article in Publishers Weekly about a new company called Dictronics which had acquired the rights to produce floppy-disk versions of a number of their reference books in the USA. I was head of reference at Oxford University Press at the time, called them, blagged a return ticket to New York and visited them to see if we could join whatever electronic party was about to happen. We did a deal with a substantial advance to OUP($600k if my memory serves me right) and Dictronics began work. Their editorial director ('the guy who can spell and things like that') was a young guy from Chicago, Andy Rosenheim, who then emigrated to England to work on the stuff and stayed here. He got a full-time job at OUP and then at various London trade houses including four years at Penguin, wrote a few top-notch novels, got married, had children,became a great friend and now has taken over as editor of my favourite magazine, The Author, which does not have a website but is run by The Society of Authors. This is a long preamble to justify my reprinting a piece which will appear there by Simon Greenall, one of the Macmillan team of authors. And please take out a subscription to the Author to help fund the new editor's desire to make the magazine even greater.

It's about 8.30am, and I leave for the office, about fifteen minutes' walk away. I go past the uniformed security guards and into the large open plan office where I greet my friends. Someone brings me a coffee and the latest gossip, then I sit down, sometimes with one editor, sometimes with another, and we start work checking proofs. I could be with any ELT publisher in the UK . . . but this is the Foreign Language Teaching and Research Press (FLTRP) in Beijing, and it's the start of a very typical day.

About seven years ago, Christopher Paterson and Yiu Hei Kan of Macmillan Education began to explore a possible partnership with FLTRP, one of the largest educational publishers in China. China was soon to be admitted to the World Trade Organisation and would sign the International Copyright Agreement. These events coincided with an important curriculum reform in primary and secondary education.

The first fruits of this partnership were a textbook series for primary schools. The Chinese Ministry of Education curriculum reform now requires English to be taught from the age of eight. No one in China had produced books for this age group before, and while Macmillan has published primary school books elsewhere in the world, no one was certain if this experience was relevant for China. A team of UK-based writers, with Printha Ellis as Chief Editor, worked with an editorial team in FLTRP to publish a series of textbooks. Sadly, Printha died before she could see the extraordinary success of *New Standard English for Primary schools*, which soon became the best seller in China.

In December 2000 I went to Beijing to discuss plans for the continuation of the *New Standard English* series in junior middle and senior high schools. I sat through my first nerve-wracking meeting, one of three people from Macmillan facing twenty Chinese editors, publishers and professors. It was the start of many meetings.

Since then, we've spent much time discussing the kind of English that China would need for the 21st century. We've researched the traditions of teaching and publishing in China, and we've explored how Macmillan's international expertise can be used in the Chinese context. The Chinese Ministry of Education imposes many requirements on the grammar, vocabulary, pronunciation and the social and cultural content. Our final course design has had to work within these constraints, as well as to have a story line, and to be interesting and motivating for the schoolchildren. Above all, we've had to submit the seventeen main coursebooks to the Ministry of Education for approval. About forty books, including teachers' books and supplementary material, have had to be ready for the start of the school year.

There have been up to fifteen authors and editors in the Macmillan team, and about twenty editors and professors in Beijing. As co-editor in chief, my role in Beijing is to help interpret feedback from both the market and the FLTRP team, and to develop the course design. Back in the UK, I then brief the Macmillan team, monitor the writing progress and help edit or rewrite, if necessary.

It's not always easy. One problem has been the Ministry wordlist, a list of about 3500 words which are considered to be the most frequently used and which need to be taught. While it is relatively easy to think of unconnected sentences to illustrate the meanings of these words, we need to ensure they are presented in a more extended context, within the general topic of the lesson, and in a way which practises different language skills. At times it has meant trying to write an exciting dialogue for teenagers which includes such disparate words as *Ottawa, dumpling, goldfish* and *shabby.*

The Beijing team has to ensure the dialogues and passages that we write are appropriate for schoolchildren. Only positive moral values and role models can be portrayed, respect for parents and older people is maintained at all costs, and negative feelings about, for example, upcoming exams is unacceptable. More specifically, there are certain words which, if we include them in a reading passage, will be questioned. These include not only the most obvious ones, such as *human rights, Taiwan,* or *God,* but also names, places and events. Apparently innocent (to a westerner) words, such as *change, exile, boss,* need to be treated with care, and even the word *communism* would trigger attention to the context in which it's used.

One particular difficulty in our working relationship has been our different understanding of the concept of time. There is a theory that all societies gradually move from a concept of *appropriate* time (I'm hungry, so I'll have lunch) to one of *clock* time (It's 1pm so I'll have lunch). This is usually related to some transition in their economic, trading or business life. Cultures which are at different stages in this transition may experience conflict between the two contrasting views of the same concept. Perhaps this explains why, for our project, schedules were often unrealistic, quality was initially compromised, and there has been a lot of urgent rewriting. Although the UK and the Beijing teams share the consequences of any setbacks, and give each other endless support, we have never entirely overcome this cultural difference.

But on the whole, the experience has been overwhelmingly positive. On the personal side, I've seen regions of China I would never have visited otherwise. Part of my work involves visiting provinces which have adopted our books. My visits usually include a presentation, a question-and-answer session, the inevitable fifteen course banquet with the provincial ministry officials, and some of the most welcoming hospitality you could imagine. These trips have taken me all over the country, from Ningxia, a Muslim, semi-autonomous province in the desert in the north, via Guilin, with its rocks rising vertically from the river in scenes photographed for travel books everywhere, to the tropical island of Hainan, with its water buffalos and rice fields.

A substantial part of the marketing budget is assigned to teacher training. FLTRP, for example, holds seminars all over the country, and runs training courses at its purpose-built conference centre just outside Beijing. The facilities here include a 1500-seater auditorium, two or three smaller lecture halls, break-out rooms, a hotel and other accommodation for all the delegates or trainees. There's also an entertainment complex with a bowling alley, karaoke room, gym and a 25-metre swimming pool fed by the hot springs which were discovered while the centre was being built. It's extravagant and visible proof of FLTRP's commitment to developing best practices in education.

Above all, the relationship between FLTRP and Macmillan seems to be a model of intercultural co-operation, with both teams learning from and supporting each other. And together, we've been fortunate. The New Standard English course is now one of the best selling courses in China, and sells tens of millions of copies every year. However, the price of each textbook is low, sometimes 40 pence for a book for which the UK list price might be £9 or £10. Recently, in order to make the main course textbooks for Primary and Junior Middle Schools even cheaper, the government has decided to allow publishers to print and distribute their competitors' books under licence within their own provinces. The licence is subject to a bidding process: the lower the bid, the cheaper the title, and so a more attractive proposition to the provincial ministry. It's like OUP being obliged to sell a licence to CUP to print and distribute OUP books in Cambridgeshire, for a low royalty. Fortunately, the licence bidding process should increase overall sales and its net effect on revenue should be neutral. But it's a decision which shows some of the unpredictability of doing business in China.

Over five years of almost monthly visits by me, our mutual trust and affection has grown. FLTRP is a first-rate publisher and a model employer, and has welcomed me as one of the family. Among my friends and colleagues, we recognise, enjoy and even celebrate the cultural differences between us. I've had the privilege of an insight on life in China which is denied to most visitors from the West. But above all, I've learnt that I should not always view a different culture or society through my own Western eyes.

It's now six pm, and the last evening of my stay. Someone has booked one of the many rooms in Partyworld, where we have something to eat, and then sing karaoke for three hours or more. Any song by the Beatles or from the Sound of Music are favourites. It's surprising how much fun we can have with our own poor singing and without any alcohol to give us courage. When I say goodbye, I already begin to miss my friends, although it won't be more than a few weeks before I come to Beijing again. We sit together, we work together and at the end of the day, we play together. We will remain friends for life.

Simon Greenall is an ELT writer, and a committee member of the Educational Writers Group. He lives in Oxford . . . and in Beijing.

And while on the subject of China please follow this link and click on Picador Asia Brochure to see the amazing progress that new imprint has made in a very short period of time.

Libya

We have decided to make this editorial linked to this news story in Nature open to everybody to read. I quote from the opening paragraphs of the editorial.

Imagine that five American nurses and a British doctor have been detained and tortured in a Libyan prison since 1999, and that a Libyan prosecutor called at the end of August for their execution by firing squad on trumped-up charges of deliberately contaminating more than 400 children with HIV in 1998. Meanwhile, the international community and its leaders sit by, spectators of a farce of a trial, leaving a handful of dedicated volunteer humanitarian lawyers and scientists to try to secure their release.

Implausible? That scenario, with the medics enduring prison conditions reminiscent of the film *Midnight Express*, is currently playing out in a Tripoli court, except that the nationalities of the medics are different. The nurses are from Bulgaria and the doctor is Palestinian.

This is something worth making a noise about in my opinion. Stories generated by the editorial are being collected on Connotea by Declan Butler.

This week also saw a sad event for Macmillan, the retirement of Alastair Gordon after a 21 year distinguished career in publishing sales. I asked Charles Jenkins and Jim Papworth to pen a few words about him:

Alastair studied PPE at Oxford and after short stints in the wine trade and as a stockbroker, entered the publishing industry with Pergamon Press being interviewed by Robert Maxwell (as was I, RC).He subsequently joined Macmillan Publishers in 1985.

For the last decade he has been International Sales Director at Palgrave Macmillan. Alastair built up enormous reserves of respect and genuine affection amongst colleagues and the international publishing and bookselling communities around the world. Modest and unassuming by nature, his achievements have been considerable, overseeing significant sales growth in our international markets for academic, reference and professional books, especially in Europe, Middle East, South Africa, Asia, Australia and Latin America, and encouraging and guiding literally hundreds of staff under his wise and humane leadership. His presentations at sales conferences were legendary for their panache!

On his last day he sold a 30 volume set of Collected Writings of John Maynard Keynes to a customer in Chile. Truly characteristic.

More on public libraries

After I made a speech to the National Acquisitions Group recently which I described here, The Bookseller magazine invited me to write a piece. For those of you who cannot be bothered to access the link or want to see the unedited version here it is:

A few months ago I was asked if I would be willing to address the National Acquisitions Group (NAG) of leading librarians at their annual conference. Although I knew little about the politics and economics of the library world the partnership between librarians and publishers is important and I agreed. They didn't (quite reasonably) tell me at the time that I was second choice to the government minister responsible for libraries, David Lammy. Coincidentally and at about the same time Ronnie Williams (Chief Executive of the PA) and I (wearing my PA President hat) had a meeting with Lammy and his civil servants. Thus began my introduction to the world of British public libraries.

Here are some of the things I learned while doing my research.

The Minister for Libraries has no power to administer libraries. This is handled entirely by local authorities.

Expenditure on books has fallen from **14.4% to 8.5%** of the budget over the last decade.

The book collection has been **reduced in the same time by 20m** books.

100 libraries have been threatened with closure in this year alone.

1000 library buildings in England **are no longer fit for use**, 30% of the total.

The acronymic quango which tries to oversee library policy, MLA, has spent £4m with various consultants since they were formed. In particular these include in the past 2 years £0.5m with accountancy firms PwC and PKF who have come up with a plan which at best will produce savings of just 1% of the budget.

Libraries are chronically short of books and (surprise surprise) libraries with poor book stockholding fail to attract users.

The government and the MLA whilst mouthing support for books seem bent on turning libraries into community centres, outreach posts, and IT training camps.

The total UK public library book acquisition annual budget is **£90m**, the cost of 'selectors' is **£45m**, the total cost of acquisition processes is **£200m**, the total annual revenue and capital cost of the library service is £1.3bn. During the last decade overhead costs have risen by 5% per annum, book purchasing has fallen at the same rate.

The solution is not simple but here are a few suggestions:

1. Re-establish that the prime objective of libraries is to lend books and that book stocks need to be increased and improved significantly by an initial doubling of the budget.

2. With the support of our excellent wholesale distributors work with libraries to ensure that the money is efficiently spent thus eliminating multiple classification systems in local authorities and ensuring rapid dissemination of new books through the system.

3. Use the publishing industry's media contacts and authors to generate a wave of support for libraries and front-line librarians.

4. Back an initiative from Tim Coates (former Managing Director of Waterstone's and the leading nearly lone voice in the wilderness) to work with three or four local authorities to act as exemplars for the rest of the library network – with or without the support of the MLA or any other quango. He needs the help of the industry. His email address is timcoatesbooks@yahoo.com and his blog is www.goodlibraryguide.com/blog.

Of course publishers and authors arguing for higher expenditure on books will be seen as special pleaders but sometimes change benefits everyone and the changes required will benefit readers as well as authors, particularly non-blockbuster authors. I suspect that my support for books in libraries will get me into serious trouble with the Minister for Libraries because, to quote him: 'So I get heartily sick and tired of self-appointed, unelected, unrepresentative groups who dogmatically say that libraries are for this and not for that.'

I also get heartily sick of certain things. My list includes bureaucratic waste, missed opportunities to improve education in deprived areas, vandalizing through inaction a great national treasure and civil servants and government officers whose jobs and final salary pension scheme are to be protected ahead of the needs of the public at large.

In short, public libraries are in crisis. They are there for making books available to all. **The book purchase budget should be doubled and the costs of that recovered through administrative savings not by more strategy consultations.** The government and all those connected with it should cease pretending things are fine and justifying past decisions and take action now.

24 September 2006

Copyright news from Brussels and Washington

Readers may have ascertained that I'm not a great lover of bureaucracies, least of all the rapidly-developing eurocracy. However, some good things do come out of Brussels and this week's good (and bad) news comes from the Director of the excellent Federation of European Publishers, Anne Bergman-Tahon. The Belgian courts have found against Google and its traffic diversion activities.

French speaking and German speaking (Belgium has a 60,000 German-speaking community) newspaper publishers represented by Copiepresse, an association who looks after their interest in the field of reproduction (especially for reprography), had decided to take action in order to stop Google copying and reproducing their content on its cache sites. They claimed that doing so, the 'do no evil' company was infringing their copyright and causing them to lose control of their websites and their content.

A Belgian court ruled on 5 September against Google in a case associated with Google News. The ruling cited both copyright and the EU database directive in ordering Google to remove articles from its service. Whilst Google News links to an article on the newspaper publishers' servers, once the publishers removed the article it still remained accessible on Google News via the link to the Google cache. The appearance of automatically generated headlines on Google news means that users may avoid or by-pass the newspaper sites, resulting in a reduction of traffic and therefore loss of advertising revenue to the publishers and their authors and journalists. Also, Google News circumvents other protections for the publisher such as copyright notices and terms of use.

Google was told to remove stories from certain publications on its Belgian news website or face a daily fine of €1m.

At first Google decided not to obey the Court ruling arguing they never received the citation to Court.

Friday 22 September, a Brussels civil Court has again ruled in favour of the newspapers and confirmed that Google must publish the Court ruling on its website which they refused to do considering it 'completely disproportionate'. Finally, Saturday morning the judgement was published on www.google.be. It should remain there till Wednesday.

In retaliation (frequently referred to as throwing toys out of the pram – RC), Google has stopped referencing the newspapers and they no longer appear on either www.google.be or www.googlenews.be. The websites of Le Soir, La Libre Belgique ou La Derniere Heure no longer appear as main references and if you type Le Soir on google.be, you can access jobs or houses pages but not the front page.

Perhaps the new motto for Google should be: 'Do not get in our way'.

On a brighter note good news on copyright from the United States. This is a joint press release from the Association of American Publishers and Cornell University:

Jointly Written Guidelines Affirm That Copyright Law Applies to Electronic Course Content

New York, NY, September 19, 2006: As part of ongoing discussions over the manner in which Cornell University provides copyrighted course content to students in digital formats, the Association of American Publishers (AAP) and Cornell recently announced a new set of copyright guidelines to govern the use of electronic course materials on the library's electronic course reserves system, on faculty and departmental web pages, and through the various 'course management' websites used at Cornell. The guidelines affirm that the use of such content is governed by the same legal principles that apply to printed materials.

The guidelines, which were jointly drafted by Cornell and AAP, make it clear that faculty must obtain permission to distribute such works to the same extent as permission is required with respect to reproductions and distributions of publishers' copyrighted works in hard-copy formats.

'Cornell and AAP concur that instructional use of content requiring the copyright owner's permission when used in a printed coursepack likewise requires permission when used in an electronic format,' said John Siliciano, Vice Provost of Cornell.

'The Publishers and the authors they represent are gratified that Cornell has responded positively to their concerns and has taken a leadership role on this issue in the academic community,' said Pat Schroeder, former Congresswoman and head of the AAP. 'With more and more content now available in digital form, it is important to clarify the copyright responsibilities that accompany use of that content – and to be sure that colleges and universities are enforcing the rules they adopt.'

Mrs. Schroeder continued, 'AAP hopes that Cornell's actions will set an example for other colleges and universities and provide them an opportunity to review their own practices and institute similar guidelines.'

Discussions are ongoing between AAP and Cornell concerning additional approaches that may be appropriate to encourage compliance with copyright law so that instructors' postings of electronic course content conform with legal requirements.

If only Google . . .

🗓 25 September 2006

Johannesburg

Arrived first thing this morning for strategy and board meetings of Macmillan Southern Africa. Issues include:

Only 45% of the Mozambique population is literate.

South Africa itself can only boast a reading age of a 9-year old or better for 85% of its people.

Life expectancy ranges from 31 in Swaziland to 47 in South Africa.

There are only 30 university campuses for a population larger than Germany's and not one appears on the top 200 list of universities.

Apparently computers in schools remain in the classroom for no longer than one term before reappearing on market stands etc.

Two retail book chains control 70% of the consumer market (CNA and Exclusive Books).

I could go on about the difficulties and challenges of the region but of course these things don't take account of the gees (or siel) of the people. You'll need to brush up your Afrikaans to check these out.

Now the good things:

151,000 copies of the Macmillan English Dictionary sold last year and which is also available free of charge on the Department of Education website.

More than 1 million books sold in Mozambique.

Wilbur Smith's Triumph of the Sun sold more copies in South Africa than any of his previous titles (and that's saying something). Incidentally he was in Swaziland recently researching the reed dance which will feature in his new book, The Quest.

I could go on but have to return to the boardroom to work out how we can fulfil our mission – To offer learner and teacher support for all in Southern Africa.

🗓 26 September 2006

Dutch rugby

Still in Johannesburg where Spring is bursting out and sports fans are bemoaning South Africa's bottom place in the Tri-Nations Tournament in spite of being the only team to beat the New Zealand All Blacks. Whenever I am here and talking rugby I ponder one of the mysteries of the world. Why isn't Holland a major rugby-playing country? With respect to the Dutch Rugby Union Association Holland makes almost no impact. And yet . . . sponsorship would be huge (internationals are played in Dublin, Edinburgh, Cardiff, London, Paris and Rome – why not Amsterdam?); the fans would love another opportunity for rugby chauvinism; the Dutch team could be filled with Afrikaners and nobody would be any the wiser from a language or a physique point of view – and if by a miracle Holland were to win the Northern Hemisphere tournament then I'm certain that Germany would have to join in, thus adding a further 100 million to the rugby-watching world.

We're still working through the plans for our Southern African businesses for the next few years. The most surprising thing to me has been the realization that broadband technology has so far had so little penetration and the debate about this is <u>hot</u>. When it does happen, as it surely will, there will be an explosion of digital creativity, learning and publishing adventure. It will happen fast and <u>Macmillan in Southern Africa</u> will be the leader in the new world as it has always been in the traditional worlds of publishing and education.

Flying back to London on <u>Virgin</u> this evening all being well.

 27 September 2006

Stand and deliver

Back in the London office and spent a happy hour deleting the 311 emails which had accumulated in the two days I was away from my laptop. It's a good feeling when the still-to-be-answered emails fit onto a single screen.

Prior to the <u>Frankfurt Book Fair</u> everyone in London, New York, Oxford, Melbourne, Delhi, Bangalore,Mexico, Tokyo and Basingstoke is putting finishing touches to sales material, appointment and schedules and travel plans. One of our most important presentations is <u>BookStore</u> and the prototype I've seen looks great. Fingers crossed for a successful fair in every way – more next week from the floor.

Today's potpourri:

Adam Ant's <u>Stand and Deliver</u> has instigated a wedding. A fan went down on one knee in front of where Adam was signing at Borders in Glasgow yesterday and proposed! I don't suppose you can see the happy event on this <u>link</u> but it gives an idea of his popularity.

Another author, Lisa Scottoline, invented a new publicity wheeze. She has been in London promoting her new hardback <u>Dirty Blonde</u>. While here she managed to fit in some detective work in the best style of one of the characters from her novels. Finding out from the in-house hairdresser at the Ritz that Bill Clinton was staying there, she charmed his bodyguards into getting a copy of her book to him. Two days later she was summoned to his room, and they sat chatting while he was packing his socks!

Last week saw the pub quiz launch of the latest edition of Barry Turner's <u>Statesman's Yearbook</u>. I thought some of you might like to test yourselves with some of the questions. Incidentally, the team from the BBC won. Here you go:

1. How many people are there aged 100 or over in the world
a) 29,000 b) 290,000 b) 2.9 million?

2. What is particularly notable for Brits about Liechtenstein's national anthem?

3. In 1999 how did a recently suspended Air Botswana pilot die?
Did he
a) Jump out of the air traffic control tower into the path of an incoming plane
b) Crash an empty passenger plane into the airline's two serviceable aircraft at the main airport or
c) Die in a shoot-out with the airline's chief executive

4. What does 'Venezuela' mean?

5. In 2001 did King Mswati I of Swaziland order all virgins in the country a) to abstain from sex for five years
b) to have five children each to help boost the population or
c) to come to the royal palace a week later for a panel of experts to find him a suitable bride?

6. On which island in the Atlantic Ocean is McDonalds banned?

7. In which country were the handful of traffic lights removed a few years back because they were considered to be eyesores?

8. For how many years did the longest-serving editor of the Statesman's Yearbook edit the book?

28 September 2006

Spitting Image

Dinner last night with a very old (old in years we've known each other, not in any other sense) friend, Roger Law, who co-founded (with Peter Fluck) Spitting Image, a satirical TV series featuring puppets made by the team. The final series was aired over ten years ago but it still remains in people's consciousness – evidenced not least by the length and depth of the Wikipedia entry I linked to above and which is constantly updated and amended. If you have the capacity to view video links I do recommend that you follow the links to the songs. Some of them are offensive (I don't think my South African colleagues will thank me for reminding them of the Apartheid-era South Africa song), all of them are politically incorrect and all brilliantly performed.

Later today I'm seeing another old (this time even younger) friend, Charlotte Mendelson, to discuss her new book due out on 4 May next year, 'When we were bad'. She works for a competitor publisher (boo) as an editor at Headline Review but she still finds time to write the most brilliant fiction. Her first two novels are already in Picador in paperback and there was some debate about whether she was too young to write such important books. Bah phooey I say and if you go this link and scroll down you can hear her (and Joanna Trollope) being interviewed on that subject.

29 September 2006

Friday plugs

Simon Greenall's piece about publishing in China (which I blogged here) prompted Macmillan's archivist, Alysoun Sanders, to dig into our records. This is what she found.

'Unlike the relationship with India, the history of Macmillan in China has not been documented at all, but I found evidence that the first rep and school traveller for Macmillan & Co Ltd in China, Fred G Whittick was appointed on 1 July 1907 – almost a century ago – and according to the agreement with him sales to China in the previous year, 1 July 1906 to 30 June 1907, were approximately £2,700. Enough to justify employing a traveller, I suppose.'

£2700 in 1906 when inflated in line with the retail price index equates to £193,396.72. I wonder how many general publishers have that much invoiced business in China today?

And now for the plugs. From Pan Macmillan – Picador to be precise. Cormac McCarthy's new book, the post-apocalyptic The Road, has received a rave review from the New York Times. Too long to include in its entirety, but this will give you an idea of the reception that we're expecting for this astonishing novel.

'In The Road a boy and his father lurch across the cold, wretched, wet, corpse-strewn, ashen landscape of a post-apocalyptic world. The imagery is brutal even by Cormac McCarthy's high standards for despair. This parable is also trenchant and terrifying, written with stripped-down urgency and fueled by the force of a universal nightmare. The Road would be pure misery if not for its stunning, savage beauty.

This is an exquisitely bleak incantation — pure poetic brimstone. Mr. McCarthy has summoned his fiercest visions to invoke the devastation. He gives voice to the unspeakable in a terse cautionary tale that is too potent to be numbing, despite the stupefying ravages it describes. Mr. McCarthy brings an almost biblical fury as he bears witness to sights man was never meant to see.'

This, from a bookseller review on Waterstone's Online, says it all: 'Both terrifying and beautiful, it is about us all, about the best and worst of humankind, and it would be impossible to recommend it too highly.'

And some more from Pan Mac, courtesy of Camilla Elworthy. In a brilliant address to the assembled ladies at the Windsor Festival on Wednesday, Major General Barney White-Spunner, talking about his forthcoming history of the Household Cavalry, Horse Guards, shared the following information from the book: In Windsor in the 1850s 'nine soldiers would sleep, eat, wash and store their equipment in a room measuring 28 by 16 feet. They were allowed one roller towel per week between them and their bedding – straw stuffed into palliases – was only changed every two months. Washing facilities included a wooden tub, which stood in the middle of the room and also passed as a urinal at night. There was no running water and no washrooms and even as late as the 1860s the regiment opposed the introduction of water closets as they became blocked with the bundles of hay issued instead of lavatory paper. This last commodity was eventually issued on the basis of one sheet per soldier every four days.'

No wonder we were so often victorious in battle – the enemy probably ran away from the stench.

30 September 2006

The Dubliners

Yesterday I was in Ireland for a board meeting of Gill and Macmillan. This involves getting up at 5am, suffering the indignities of Terminal 3 at Heathrow and the airline BMI (whose motto is 'The UK's most punctual airline' – it was punctual and that is really important but everything else was . . .), hanging about at Dublin airport for the traffic to lighten (I do think Dublin has the worst traffic jams in all of Europe – up there with Bangalore on a bad day), and then an hour to the office.

But it's all worthwhile to spend time with a highly professional, highly creative, and totally engaging team determined to do the best possible job in what is intrinsically a small market.

To fully understand modern Dublin you need, in my opinion, just two guides. First you should grab a copy of David McWilliams brilliant book on modern Ireland The

Pope's Children, so called because nine months to the day after the Pope's 29th September 1979 speech to the Irish people in Dublin's Phoenix Park there was the largest ever number of births – a tribute either to Pope John Paul's virility or the aphrodisiac effect of religion. This signalled the beginning of the Celtic revival. And second, to understand the true vibrancy of modern Dublin simply click on this video about Dublin coastal development.

Earlier in the week I wrote about the potential for Dutch rugby. Amazingly I now discover that the brightest young hope in English rugby is Dutchman Tim Visser. Watch this space.

I also received this from an occasional commentator on this blog. I wonder when it will dawn on Gerard that it may not be a media conspiracy which is blocking his success but that readers aren't that interested in buying his book.

Just got my 'royalty' statement from the publisher. GINNY GOOD sold 24 copies worldwide in the last six months and I bought at least four of the copies, myself . . . so that's what? Less than one copy a week? Yes! I get a dollar for every copy sold, though, so in six months I made enough to pay for almost two of the four of my own books I bought. Yippee! Oh, but wait, I didn't actually *get* the twenty-four bucks 'cause I still owe $1,800 on the $2,000 'advance.' Rats. At that rate I won't have the advance paid off until I'm a hundred and eighteen years old. Oh, well. Here's the latest 'review' of *The Audio Book of Ginny Good*: http://thommalyn.blogspot.com/2006/09/audio-book-of-ginny-good.html Here are four more . . . and a bunch of other reviews of the real book: http://everyonewhosanyone.com/ggrev.html

When you write a great book, whether it makes money or not is superfluous. The morons who run the media and entertainment industries will understand that one of these days. Or not. G.

Gerard Jones
http://everyonewhosanyone.com/audio/GGch0ointrom.mp3

And finally a link to a brilliantly funny website promoting a book published by a brilliant (albeit competing) London publisher Piatkus Books. Have a good Saturday.

≤ **October 2006** ≥

Mon	Tue	Wed	Thu	Fri	Sat	Sun
25	26	27	28	29	30	1
2	3	4	5	6	7	8
9	10	11	12	13	14	15
16	17	18	19	20	21	22
23	24	25	26	27	28	29
30	31	1	2	3	4	5

🦆 01 October 2006

Product placement in publishing

To start a new month I propose a new monthly award to be judged and given by one of the great organs of the trade press – Publishers Weekly, The Bookseller, Publishing News – for the best piece of product placement. I'd like to submit the picture below as an example of how the marketing team at Henry Holt really used their imagination in the promotion of Noam Chomsky's Hegemony or Survival and generated a significant sales uplift. We had the Oprah Effect and now the Chavez Efecto.

I've just calculated the visitor numbers to this blog for September – 41738, slightly down on August which was a very strong month, and bringing the total visitors for the year to 221379. Comments have been quiet except on matters concerning the UK book trade and discounts and things. It's quite surprising and worrying (to me at least, but I'm sure wiser people will tell me that I am misguided) that nobody seemed interested in the entry about copyright news from Brussels and Washington – both really important for the future stability of literature, research, education, publishing and retailing but perhaps too theoretical for most people.

🦆 02 October 2006

La Petite Anglaise

This is one of the most engaging and popular blogs which generates literally thousands of comments a month and I imagine hundreds of thousands of visitors. It is funny and insightful and the author is clearly a talented writer with a good future. She has just signed various deals for a book she will publish in 2008 and here's a precis of the business so far from Media Bistro.

So much for the 'blogger book deal' bandwagon being over

PETITE ANGLAISE will be published in the UK in the spring of 2008, and will also be published by **Spiegel & Grau** in the US and with **Doubleday** in Canada, through **Zoe Pagnamenta** at PFD New York. **RCS/Sonzogno** has also bought rights through **Nicki Kennedy** at ILA.

Because the latest to step right up to the deal plate is **Catherine Sanderson**, whose blog **Le Petite Anglaise** caused a furore this past summer when her employers, the accountancy firm **Dixon Wilson**, decided to fire her for what she said on the blog – even though she never named them directly. And so, the Bookseller reports, **Katy Follain** at **Michael Joseph/Penguin** signed Sanderson up in a two-book deal, paying a sum approaching the mid six figures. The deal was done after a heated auction conducted by **Simon Trewin** and **Sarah Ballard** at PFD.

Follain describes Sanderson as 'a very talented writer, one that we are very keen to build so that she becomes a household name with Petite Anglaise and future books.'

I'm not quite sure what a mid six figure sum is but let's imagine £500k and let's assume that non-UK rights are about the same. This means a total advance of at least £1m which represents a brilliant deal by the literary agent. It also means that the book will have to sell around a million copies to earn back the advance. I wonder whether Simon Trewin and Sarah Ballard might like to try raising a similar advance for a book loosely based around my experiences as recorded on this blog.

I was reminded that things weren't like this in the old days by the death of the wonderful Alan Maclean whose obituary appeared in today's Guardian.

🦋 03 October 2006

British Library

Flew to Frankfurt last night. Prior to the opening of the Book Fair on Wednesday there are a number of meetings, conferences, arrangements to be fixed. I'll report later in the week.

Meanwhile on the plane I spent time reading the British Library's IP Manifesto. Here is a summary of the main recommendations:

* Existing limitations and exceptions to copyright law should be extended to encompass unambiguously the digital environment

* Licenses providing access to digital material should not undermine longstanding limitations and exceptions such as fair dealing

* The right to copy material for preservation purposes, a core duty of all national libraries, should be extended to all copyrightable works

* The copyright term for sound recordings should not be extended without empirical evidence of the benefits and due consideration of the needs of society as a whole

* The US model for dealing with 'orphan works' should be considered for the UK

* The length of copyright term for unpublished works should be brought into line with other terms (ie: life plus 70 years).

Lynne Brindley, Chief Executive, went on to say:

'The World Intellectual Property Organisation, the body that frames intellectual property law internationally, is clear that limitations and exceptions such as fair dealing and library privilege are as relevant tothe digital environment as they are to the its analogue equivalent. However, out of thirty licensing agreements recently offered to the Library for use of digital material, twenty-eight were found to be more restrictive than the rights existing under current copyright law . . . Our concern is that, if unchecked, this trend will drastically reduce public access, thus significantly undermining the strength and vitality of our creative and educational sectors – with predictable consequences for UK plc.'

I am a member of the Strategy Advisory group of the British Library and so I guess a bit conflicted but my suspicion is that the outcome of this debate will have significant repercussions for the publishing community as well as for libraries. The heart of the matter is the tension between the rights of the content user as a member of society versus the rights of the content creator. Difficult stuff but vital to get it right.

🦋 04 October 2006

Frankfurt day one

For those who have had the honour of never attending the Frankfurt Book Fair it's hard to describe the enormity of the experience. Probably the most worrying statistic is that there are more than 10,000 journalists reporting on the fair – and there really is very little news to report so far. I guess they'll just have to make something up as usual.

There is surprisingly little technology in the main hall and I have had to beg the use of a terminal to write this from the wonderful Thomson team. On the other hand the amount of hot air is at normal levels.

The Macmillan team is assembling. One delay so far where a guinea fowl ran into the engine of a jet leaving Zimbabwe thus delaying our key director's arrival. One other logistical nightmare unfolding is our need to supply large quantities of books for Kurdistani primary schools. Our plans were initially wrecked by the Israeli invasion of Lebanon, made worse by the row between the Turks and the Kurds and finally delayed by the start of Ramadan.

One issue which doesn't seem to be going away is the price differential between US and UK editions of college textbooks. Because of the very high used-book market in the USA publishers need to build in to the price the decline in sales over the life of an edition. The used-book issue in the UK is less severe (although growing at a frightening rate helped on by traders on ebay) and thus prices have been kept down. This disparity will have to close if we are not to see significant international arbitrage and the resulting diminution of authors' royalties. Yet another challenge for our industry to resolve.

05 October 2006

Google ads

A few months we had a debate here as to whether I should allow Google ads to appear. Those who disapproved told me so. Those who couldn't care less didn't. I decided to let the ads run a bit just to see what happened. I can now report that we've earned a princely $30 from people clicking through – but Google keep the money until we pass $100. They have however forwarded us 40 pence just to check that the system works and I am very proud of this first fruit of a new income stream for Macmillan. The ads rotate but yesterday one in particular caught my eye:

'Buy Macmillan Publishing, Full Range available now online: fast, reliable, secure.'

As a colleague remarked, The only thing that matters in publicity is that they spell your name right (which remarkably they have) but are we really fast, reliable and secure?

http://www.auravita.com/ is where to go if you're really interested. These guys could put the investment banks out of business if they succeed in selling us!

06 October 2006

Question: What links Jeremy Clarkson, Rupert Murdoch and avian flu?

Answer: Nature. Why, you ask? At the UK Association of Online Publishers awards last night, Nature's Avian flu Google Earth mashup won in its category, Best Use of New Digital Platform.

Other winners on the night were mostly from seriously large scale operations, such as the BBC's Top Gear (Jeremy Clarkson) and The Sun's bingo site (Rupert Murdoch).

For those of you wondering what on Google Earth a mashup is, it involves one set of data being put into a format that wasn't designed for it. So, in this case, Nature enables you to obtain information about avian flu by scrolling the various locations of the outbreaks on Google Earth.

The judges singled it out as 'perfectly demonstrating the intersection of content and technology' – which is no more than its due. It really is a remarkable resource, and has been noted as such by researchers in the field.

Congratulations to the team involved: Oliver Morton, Angela Bird, Arran Flood and Alex Thurrell, and particularly to Declan Butler, who conceived and produced the mashup.

Further congratulations are in order for Robin Robertson, one of Picador's list of award winning poets (and an ex-colleague of mine from Secker in the olden days of Michelin House), whose collection Swithering won the Forward Prize for poetry on Wednesday night.

07 October 2006

Much preening in the Messe

I leave my 33rd Frankfurt today. As usual, the logistics were impeccable. It's quite amazing how little goes wrong given the complexity, size and innate likelihood of Murphy's Law taking effect.

Business seemed pretty well in line with expectations. There were the usual number of non-events, non books of the fair, missed appointments, preening opportunities, job interviews, deals concluded or initiated, authors wandering about looking dazed and wondering why they were there, consultants, ex industry superstars prowling the aisles in search of just one more challenge. And then there are the parties and dinners and late night drinks in smokey (yes, people still smoke in Frankfurt) and crowded bars. The slightly (or hugely) jaded people at breakfast the following morning. The perpetual discussions about stand design and cost. But every year we come back for more. We are a strange industry.

If you're feeling up to it and want a framework in which to think about the changes in publishing today check out this article on Thomas Kuhn. The word 'paradigm' has been debased by over- and inaccurate use but I believe we are seeing the 'normal' way of publishing being challenged from many directions and we are finding it hard to address the issues with our current structures and understandings. We are undergoing a paradigm shift which is what makes our industry so interesting right now. I'm not sure how far we are in developing a new 'theory' to replace the old but I supect we need to find it fast or suffer some harsh consequences.

Have a good weekend.

Postscript on Frankfurt 2006. Not mentioned in any of the statistics issued about the fair (numbers of visitors, deal done, awards granted, parties enjoyed etc) was one significant fact. There is only one postbox in the whole enormous complex. Ten years ago there would have been at least twenty.

The Book People

I'm going to take a chance and risk offending all sorts of book retailers by writing about the prize-winning booksellers, The Book People. The company was founded by Ted Smart and Seni Glaister in 1988. I remember the first time I met them when I was at Reed International Books and we had to decide whether to offer them credit terms. We did and I fixed a lunch for Ted and Paul Hamlyn. They got on like a house on fire. At that time a number of major publishers resisted supplying the Book People – concerns about credit-worthiness, impact on book club and trade sales etc. Ted and Seni proved their detractors wrong by consistently generating more sales into channels which had been underdeveloped. Their importance to the book trade (and to many readers who have been introduced to books buying habit) is illustrated by the dinners they host on every evening at Weideman's restaurant during the Frankfurt Book Fair. The guests are everyone with whom they deal on a day-to-day basis (specials sales managers etc) and the high and mighty of the industry who pay homage to Ted and Seni. I can't help thinking back to traditional publishers' attitudes to them in 1988 and I'm sure Ted and Seni do too.

I've managed to upset a very senior civil servant, John Dolan who works at the Museums, Libraries and Archives Council by criticising how the UK public library system is run. In a letter to the Bookseller he accuses me of distorting statistics. I'm not going to reply but this link has generated a lot of interesting debate. It seems to me that the underlying problem of library funding is that we're arguing about statistics and paying consultants to support a point of view rather than getting down to work to sort out what is rapidly becoming a national disgrace.

New Kid on the Block

More than thirty years ago Macmillan instituted a scheme to attract the very best people from universities to the publishing industry. Today former graduate recruits hold some of the most senior positions in the company and dozens are working their way up. Some leave immediately when they decide publishing is not for them. Others use the scheme as a way of launching a career – e.g. Nigel Newton and Tim Hely Hutchinson – and going on to great things in the industry.

Kristin Annexstad joined us three weeks ago as one of the first of the 2006 intake. Here are her thoughts:

'After being frightened during my undergraduate days with bedtime stories of psychometric testing, in-tray exercises, and absurd scenarios during interviews, and even sitting through interviews designed to make me cry at some of the big boys in the city, the Macmillan applications process was unnervingly easy. During my Christmas holidays I decided that, despite my lack of an English literature background, I would investigate jobs in publishing, something I had considered for some time. I wasn't sure whether my social science background would be appropriate but decided my love of books must count for something. Trawling the internet I discovered Macmillan ran a graduate scheme. Could it be? Was there really an obvious entry into the industry? With five days to go before the deadline I gave it my best but wasn't wildly optimistic, although it was the most sunny and sincere cover letter I had ever written. About a month later I got a phone call asking me to come in for an interview. Fully expecting a battery of proofreading and intense grilling, I instead had a pleasant chat about publishing and books, and the obligatory 'give us an example of a time when you . . . ' I left feeling confident – too confident? Had I been too relaxed? Biting my nails, I convinced myself I had seemed arrogant and informal. I didn't hear from them for ages and assumed I was out, but about a month later I was asked to come and see the CEO. Preparing myself for a brutal interrogation I was kept standing in Richard Charkin's office for about ten minutes while he conducted an urgent phone call about a recent golf championship. Finally allowed to sit I was asked why in God's name I wanted to go into publishing, whether I had ever been to the Vietnamese restaurant in my neighbourhood, and abruptly was told I had the job. I wasn't really sure what had just happened but I was pleased. Of course I accepted the job, and turned up in September fresh-faced and bright-eyed, knowing only that I would be working with the Strategy Director, whatever that was. Apparently I was a Research Associate, which sounds very grand, but occasionally means someone who uses Google a lot and counts the number of books in a catalogue. It also means someone who writes reports which get sent to the CEO, which was not a little exciting. Unlike many of my classmates who started graduate schemes in the City I was given real tasks to begin with, and not busywork, which had been my fear. I wasn't quite wined and dined but lunch dates were set up for me with my predecessors and I am promised meetings with division bigwigs to help me figure out my next step, which is apparently decided not just by the powers that be but also based on my own interests and talents. I have even been promised a tour of the warehouse in Basingstoke, which has me feeling very much like Charlie before his trip to the Chocolate Factory. So what do I do all day, my friends ask. I can't talk about it, I say, after having had the fear of God put into me about confidentiality. I try to assure them that I have no delusions of grandeur but that since I work on The Top Floor it's all very hush-hush, don't you know. Finally I look around suspiciously, before tapping my nose and lowering my voice conspiratorially: 'I write competitor reports and research the market. Sometimes I count books.' But I am very smug that I have been given my own responsibilities, and despite this have never stayed much later than required. Perhaps I should be? I did stay later than the boss once evening last week, which had me feeling very superior. I made sure to email him what I had been working on so that he would know I had been there at 19:30. Unfortunately, in my excitement, I sent the wrong attachment. He was very nice about it though, so no tears shed by me yet. That may, of course, change, should I incur the wrath of RC, who occasionally comes out of his office wtih the sole purpose, seemingly, of intimidating me, or stumping me with obscure facts about the industry. But I am watching and learning, and planning my takeover bid.'

🐧 10 October 2006

Booker day

Going to Basingstoke for a series of forecasting and budget meetings, and catch-ups with a number of my colleagues. I remember once a dinner in Gaborone where the Botswanan politician next to me asked what I thought of his city. I said that it was hard to comment as I had just arrived having driven from Johannesburg. But what did you think of the architecture and in particular the ring road? Well, I said, I have to say that it reminds me of a town in England called Basingstoke. Yes, he said, precisely. We decided that Basingstoke was so excellent that we've tried to copy its layout and in particular its roundabouts. I was stunned.

If I get back in time from Basingstoke I'll have to don the penguin and trip off to the Guildhall for the annual Booker prize dinner ordeal. Fingers crossed for Edward St

Aubyn. If every reader of this blog could wish him to win . . . . Essay on book prize dinners tomorrow, tenor dependent on result.

🕮 11 October 2006

The inheritance of loss and the emergence of profit

Huge congratulations to Kiran Desai for her book winning the Booker Prize. We were, of course, sad for Teddy St Aubyn but the judges had a really tough job and I'm sure, judging by her speech, that Ms Desai is a great person as well as a great writer. I'm off to India this morning and I have no doubt the country will be celebrating yet another national hero.

I should have known that this particular title would win when, earlier in the evening, I was asked whether Macmillan was committed to publishing literary books. I asked what is meant by a literary book. Apparently it is a work of fiction which loses money. It seemed rather an odd definition and I tried to argue that publishing companies tend to do a better job when they are solvent. In addition I'm not quite sure why literary publishing should deserve more support than, say, educational publishing in Zimbabwe. That said, of course we are committed to literary publishing and to the continued growth of Picador in all its markets – UK, USA, Australia, South Africa, India and most recently Asia. But I should not want to leave future publishers at Macmillan with an inheritance of loss whatever the definition of literature.

During the 1990s the foundations were laid for the terrific success of the Nature Publishing Group. The strategy was to launch the highest-quality 'sister' journals in subjects close to Nature's core expertise and audience. This resulted in many top life science journals being launched – Genetics, Medicine, Cell Biology etc. The group was begining to be seen purely as a life science publisher. This is changing and the recent launch of Nature Nanotechnology prompted me to ask Jason Wilde, its publisher, to describe what is happening in the Nature world of physical sciences.

What a difference a year makes

Over the past year Nature Publishing Group (NPG) has quadrupled its portfolio of physicals science journals by launching three new titles: Nature Chemical Biology, Nature Physics and Nature Nanotechnology. These launches came on the back of Nature Materials (our first physical science research journal) which was launched in 2002 and has become the number 1 research journal in the physical sciences.

The reason for these launches is simple; it is to ensure NPG is at the forefront of serving all of science including the physical science community. Ten years ago NPG expanded its program from just Nature to include 7 primary research journals in the biomedical and life sciences. These became essential titles for each of their fields and ensured that NPG was seen as a leading publisher in the life sciences.

Many people have forgotten that Nature is as strong in the physical sciences as it is in the life sciences publishing a number of firsts including: The discovery of X-Rays (1896); the development of the particle accelerator (1932) and the production of the first LASER (1960). More recently Nature has led the way publishing research on: the formation of C60 (1985); the first paper on electronic ink (1998) and only last year new research from INTEL on LASERs made from silicon.

The launch of Nature Materials, Nature Chemical Biology, Nature Physics, and Nature Nanotechnology ensures we continue this tradition and that NPG provides the physical science community with the same high quality journals that the life sciences have enjoyed for the past decade.

Not only have we launched new titles but we have also expanded our editorial operations to include Asia. The decision to have one of the editors for Nature Nanotechnology in Tokyo reflects the strengths of the Asia-Pacific region. Japan is second only to the US in terms of investment in nanotechnology research, and South Korea is ranked fifth in the world. China is also emerging as a force in nanotechnology and scientific research.

12 October 2006

Mumbai

Arrived late last night. Traveller's tip – go Jet Airways who remind me of the early days of Virgin Atlantic – better, cheaper and trying harder. Given the ever-growing importance of the Indian market the other airlines had better wake up.

The last few months have seen a stream of British and American publishers turning up in India to announce grand plans for the development of publishing in India. The latest pronouncements have emerged from HarperCollins during a presidential visit by Jane Friedman and Victoria Barnsley. I'm sure that they will find interesting opportunities here and will rapidly understand the Indian market and character. We've been here for over a century and every day brings fresh surprises.

Macmillan India was founded in 1892 and has grown every year since. It now employs more than 3000 people all over the country and is publicly traded on the Mumbai and National Stock Exchanges. On the publishing front we focus on education at all levels and serious non-fiction. We have recently set up Picador India which is carving a niche in high-quality Indian literature as part of the overall efforts of Pan Macmillan. Palgrave Macmillan has its own office to promote academic works and college textbooks and Nature Publishing Group has embarked on a programme of publishing and marketing in India with the aim of finding the very best Indian scientific work needing to reach an international audience.

The other area of growth comes from our publishing services activities in Information Processing, MPS Technologies and Software Development Services. At Macmillan we have a tradition of working for other publishers as well as for ourselves in order to spread the costs of staying at the cutting edge of new developments. The alternative strategy as followed by several of our competitors is to retain these activities to themselves in order to maintain competitive edge. Both strategies are legitimate but we prefer the more social version.

The papers here today are full of Kiran Desai's triumph at the Booker but the headlines are really about the row between the BCCI and the ICC – acronyms only of interest to followers of cricket – which is really a post-imperial flare-up of the very best nostalgic kind – much hot air but no bloodshed.

13 October 2006

Cat o' nine tales

I mainly resist using this blog to promote individual titles or authors. That's not what blogs are for IMHO but a comment here a couple of days ago has tempted me to write about <u>Cat o' nine tales</u> by <u>Jeffrey Archer</u>. The comment from an excellent independent bookseller said how pleased he is NOT to be selling books by Archer. I've never worked in a bookshop but I reckon I'd be pleased to be selling books by anyone.

Of course there are many people who have decided that Jeffrey Archer's prison sentence (one of the longest ever handed down for perjury) was not enough of a punishment for his crime (no violence involved, no theft, no damage to an individual apart from himself). This is probably because people simply don't like success combined with a lack of shyness but that's not justification for unrelenting vilification and censorship.

Outside Britain people see Jeffrey simply as a writer and his popularity is growing with every book he publishes. His latest book of short stories augmented by the world's greatest illustrator <u>Ronald Searle</u> is a case in point. I notice on Jeffrey's <u>blog</u> someone asking when he could buy a copy here in Mumbai. Here in India they care not a jot for British Archer-baiting. They just want good books from a brilliant story-teller. Try it out for yourself before sounding off, my bookseller friends.

By permission of Pan Macmillan, London.

14 October 2006

Back from Mumbai this morning to enjoy ploughing through a full email inbox. Here's an edited piece from the <u>Times Higher Educational Supplement</u> where an author praises us for not overselling his books into book stores – makes a change:

Publish and be damned wasteful
THES
Dave Reay
Published: 13 October 2006

'Dave Reay is pleased to see his book on climate change in the shops but chastened by the harm publishing causes the environment.

The university bookshop is crammed full. Every corner not occupied by stacked boxes of new books is filled with reading list-toting students frowning at price tags on required texts. It's Christmas come early for the textbook publishers. But it's also something of a minor tragedy for the planet . . .

For, like Christmas, this first-term feeding frenzy at the bookshop will be short-lived. Soon the returns will begin flowing back to the publishers, vanload after vanload of unwanted stock hauled off to become a vast reservoir of fodder for the pulping machines.

For authors of books about the environment, such as myself, this is not a little embarrassing. Publishers are unsurprisingly cagey about providing figures on how many books are sent back to them. But one of the largest publishers in the UK has admitted that the return rate for some of its titles topped 50 per cent. That's an awful lot of pulp . . .

What with production and transport, the average paperback has eaten its way through 4.5kWh of energy by the time it gets to a reader. In terms of climate impact, this is equivalent to about 3kg of carbon dioxide emissions for every glossy new textbook. So, for a print run of 10,000, there is a cost of 30 tonnes of carbon dioxide not mentioned on the dust jackets. But this is a best-case scenario. The sale-or-return system virtually guarantees that the damage is much more severe. If half the books delivered to bookshops then have to be trucked back to the publisher and pulped, there's yet another great belch of greenhouse gases to ultimately heat up the cheeks of both publisher and author . . .

Assume that the average print run for those 200,000 titles is just 1,000 copies. That's 200 million books coming off the presses in a year – 600,000 tonnes of carbon dioxide emissions and, even if we assume very low return rates, enough pulped book to fill the dining hall at Hogwart's several times over.

In terms of its contribution to global warming, UK publishing in effect puts an extra 100,000 cars on our roads. Our esteemed seats of learning are a sizeable cog in this engine: the average undergraduate buys at least three volumes per course, while most academic offices are crammed from floor to ceiling with dusty tomes . . .

The sale-or-return system is outdated and thoroughly wasteful. It is not uncommon for bookshops to return copies of a title to a publisher on the same day that they reorder more copies of the same book.

At least the number of returns for my book has been tiny. Palgrave Macmillan is trying to do something to cut waste by distributing small numbers and then responding to demand. Of course, e-books might end waste, but I would miss the smell and texture of printed books. It's the vats of pulp and the global warming I could do without.

As long as waste is cheap and the environmental impact of a book fails to be reflected in its cover price, the pulping machines will continue to work overtime. It stinks. Someone should write a book about it. Or then again, maybe not.

Dave Reay is a research fellow in the School of Geosciences at Edinburgh University and author of Climate Change Begins at Home published by Macmillan, £8.99.'

On another subject altogether Erica Wagner in today's Times, Do writers belong to one country – or to the world?, where she aske whether it matters where literary archives and manuscripts reside. This was prompted by the forthcoming British-Library hosted conference Manuscripts Matter where I am chairing a discussion on Collecting Electronica. Given the concerns of librarians, scholars, authors and publishers I sense an 'interesting' debate.

The 'interesting' Google debate continues with Google seeming to make some friendlier gestures towards copyright. I quote;

'Notwithstanding its contention that Google News and Google Books do not infringe copyright, Google promised yesterday that it would work with a new global coalition of newspaper groups and European publishers, which is planning to develop technology that will make it possible to automatically license content to search engine sites and news aggregators.'

It reminds me of the great Billy Bunter when found guzzling a stolen toffee in class: 'There wasn't a packet of toffee on the table. If there was, I never saw it. Besides, I never touched it. I left it there just as it was.'

🌂 15 October 2006

On libraries, technology and politics

I'm not sure why but yesterday was this blog's best day ever as measured by unique visitors – 2570. I'm equally unsure (and slightly worried) as to why http://www.used-aircraftsales.com/ should be the top referrer.

More movement on the issues around the dissemination of scientific research using the web and its impact on researchers, funding bodies, libraries and publishers. The Research Information Network in the UK has published a very full report on the operations and costs of scholarly publishing. The idea was to take some of the heat out of the open-access debate and replace it with some light and informed debate. I've been invited to chair a workshop on November 14 in London and everyone is welcome. There are many sides to this discussion but at least this report has been prepared properly, thoughtfully and impartially. Not least because the Chair of the overseeing panel is an old acquaintance from the days when I was a medical commissioning editor and signed him up to co-author the Oxford Textbook of Clinical Pharmacology.

And more on public libraries. The Libraries Minister, David Lammy, has dismissed those trying to focus libraries on books (as opposed to community centres or worse) as:

Those that want to turn the clock back to some highly-selective and rose-tinted vision of libraries from their own childhoods are out of luck. I'm with them as far as putting the written word at the heart of the library service. And I'm with them on the campaign to keep the book stock fresh and relevant. But there's more to this than nostalgia.

His solution is to commission a White Paper on Communities, presumably supported by many very wise (and expensive) consultants. Fortunately the importance of libraries and books has been recognised by politicians outside the junta and pressure is building for the implementation of genuine management improvements, genuine investment and genuine recognition of the centrality of the printed word in a modern society. More on this at the excellent Good Library blog.

Incidentally, I must confess that I was rather worried when I spotted Mr Lammy at the Man Booker Prize dinner last week. It might have confirmed his prejudice that the book trade was populated by white, penguin-suited, public-school-educated middle-class (or worse) men entirely cut off from the real multicultural Britain. Thank goodness then that the prize was won by an American-domiciled Indian woman.

Books and accounts

Back in the office today I was greeted by a pile of management accounts for our various companies. I get approximately fifty separate sets of accounts a month and nearly all of them have different formats. The formats are in line with the needs of the company but serve to make my life doubly hard – are these dollars or yen, is that last year or this year, is that profit or contribution, is that cash or sales? C'est la vie. However, I managed to postpone the accounting ordeal by scanning the pile of new books which arrived. This was much more fun and probably more enlightening too. I've deliberately selected books which most readers are unlikely to come across in the normal course of events.

From Ireland comes the number one hardback bestseller This is Charlie Bird, having ousted U2 from the perch. We have sold 20,000 copies so far which would be pretty good for a UK hardback non-fiction title let alone in a country with a population of only four million. Charlie Bird has been the face of RTE news for the last 25 years and clearly has a dedicated fan base.

And from Australia an outstanding scholarly book The Great War by Les Carlyon. The joy of this book is that it is written by a 'writer' not by a 'scholar' although the scholarship shines through. It makes a change to read about a familiar story from an alternative perspective. World War I was Australia's (as well as Europe's) greatest tragedy and they suffered 179,000 dead or wounded and they still remember. The book is not published in Australia until 1 November and it's not listed on the Bantam website (who published his previous book) or on Amazon UK. The desire to sub-divide territorial rights on this sort of book seems to me an absurdity of value to no-one least of all to potential readers.

Also in my in-tray was Picador Asia's first book February Flowers by Fan Wu. I have yet to read the novel but it is getting rave reviews across Asia but I can say that the paperback edition I have been sent is one of the most beautiful productions I've seen in years which is why I've linked to the Asian edition. I think British publishers and printers are going to have to up their game in production standards as well as everything else if we wish to compete and attract more book buyers. I've asked Fan Wu's literary agent to contribute to this blog to describe the whole process of being published out of Asia rather than the traditional Western route.

Finally a doorstep of a book from Rodale whom we represent in many territories. It is The Encyclopedia of New Medicine from the Duke Center for Integrative Medicine in the USA. I am deeply sceptical about all forms of 'alternative' health regimes but for once there is a book which objectively tries to offer solutions from all sources and tries to deal with the person as an integrated system. It deals with 200 conditions and all the ones I checked out have been totally sensible and helpful.

Enough books – back to the accounts.

National Blog Day

Today in the UK is National Blog Day when people are invited to record their day for posterity – and the duller the better. Here's mine which I'll post at the British Library later today (just in case something unpredicted happens).

Got up 5.30, lamented the passing of the BBC Radio 4 British folksong theme which used to open the day and lift the spirits, did 300 kcals on the exercise bike, shower(s), breakfast, bus to Tottenham Court Road, walk to King's Cross, email while I walk and listen to Janacek's Lachian Dances. Write blog.

Meetings this morning with various Macmillan directors and a brilliant editor who has decided to move back into selling rights for another company. I think it's called an exit interview. Lunch in Islington with an old friend, Bob Gavron, who is or has been involved in all aspects of the book trade – printing (St Ives), publishing (Carcanet), retailing (Folio Society) and much else.

This afternoon a catch-up session with our personnel director and then a discussion with new joiners. I try to get to meet all new joiners in the UK to share with them some of our aims as an organisation. One of the main (and beneficial) changes of the last thirty years in publishing is that people have become more specialised and professional. The downside is that it's very hard for anyone to understand the full scope of the company which employs them. I'll try to redress the balance.

Finally a dinner with the past and current managing directors of the Macmillan English Campus to say thanks for what's been achieved so far and good luck for what will be achieved.

And so, in the words of A. A. Milne, to bed. I went to check that it was A. A. Milne and you may be interested to know that a Google search on that phrase throws up Hot hotels to take your lover.

🗓 18 October 2006

Macmillan New Writing Chapter 2

It's been a while since I've written about our experimental model for discovering new fiction talent. Here's an update prepared with the help of the MNW team. Several things didn't go as planned. I wanted uniform jackets but was over-ruled. We didn't succeed in persuading Ryanair to lend us a plane in which to hold the launch party. None of the authors has won the Man Booker Prize or hit number one in the best-seller lists (yet) but neither has Jonny Geller's prediction – 'I don't think there's a hope in hell of this succeeding' – come about.

This month sees the launch of the twelfth debut novel to be published under the New Writing imprint, Macmillan's streamlined publishing scheme for first-time novelists. The imprint's launch in April induced some unusually shrill denunciations from the broadsheet press – apparently, Macmillan was not only abdicating cultural responsibility but taking advantage of 'vulnerable young authors' – but six months down the line, MNW has become established as part of Pan Macmillan's mainstream publishing operation, submissions continue to pour in from around the world (well over 5000 complete novels in the past year), and the list itself is going from strength to strength, with some excellent review coverage.

Some MNW titles have reprinted several times and have sold thousands in the UK market. A US distribution deal is to follow next year. Roger Morris (author of *Taking Comfort*) has – wisely or unwisely – published the contents of his first royalty statement on his blog. Audio, large print and translation rights have been sold in several titles; one is about to be optioned for film rights; and the German rights to a forthcoming title have just been sold for an advance which would have many established authors breaking out the champagne.

Highlights for 2007 include a crime debut by young Northern Ireland author Brian McGilloway. Borderlands (April) is set on and around the Irish border, and is the first in a projected series, 'The Inspector Devlin Mysteries'. August 07 will see the publication of a novel which is already causing a buzz at Macmillan: *The Great North Road*, by former professional vocalist Annabel Doré, is a beautifully written literary saga set in post-war northern England.

Follow-up novels from authors who made their debuts with MNW will also be published by the imprint in 07. Michael Stephen Fuchs's philosophical techno-thriller *Pandora's Sisters* will be published in July, alongside a Pan mass-market paperback of his debut *The Manuscript*, while Edward Charles's historical epic, *In the Shadow of Lady Jane*, will be followed in May 2007 by a Pan paperback, and the sequel, *Daughters of the Doge*, set amongst the world of artists and courtesans in a vividly imagined Renaissance Venice.

The truth is that agents serve a very valuable function in the publishing world, but they do not have an exclusive on good new books. It is commercially and culturally unwise to ignore the potential of unrepresented writers. For an entertaining account of how the imprint can look at over 5000 unsolicited manuscripts a year, read MNW founder Mike Barnard's book Transparent Imprint.

Pan Macmillan Deputy Publisher Maria Rejt has recently taken the helm in preparation for Mike's impending retirement, working with Commissioning Editor Will Atkins. As the editor behind *Richard & Judy*'s 'How to Get Published' scheme, run in conjunction with Macmillan, Rejt has an unparalleled reputation as a publishing innovator and champion of new writing, and so the success story promises to continue.

What the press *also* said . . .

'For lonely authors, the level playing-field now feels like a choppy shark pool. In such a climate, Macmillan's much-abused plan to publish first-time novelists in its 'New Writing' series seems almost like a model of fair dealing . . . . These are decent novels: low-key, quietly engrossing, and more worthwhile than some of the meretricious drivel that famous houses now select.' Boyd Tonkin, 'A Week in Books' 7 April, *The Independent*

'North is one of six first novels to be published by Macmillan's New Writing, a project that has had many brickbats showered upon it, the *Guardian* calling it 'Ryan Air publishing' . . . if the other five are as entertainingly written as Martin's the *Guardian* will have to eat its words.' – Digby Durrant, on Brian Martin's *North, The Spectator*, 1 April 2006

'Macmillan has launched its books and they are being bought by libraries, stocked by book shops and read with enjoyment.' – Charles Howard, 'Macmillan Unveils First of its New Writers', *Writers Forum*, May 2006

'I have been spending some time with my royalty statement and a calculator, and I have worked out that royalties from sales of my book are lower than they would have been under the terms of the Macmillan New Writing list. Given that MNW has been described as 'the Ryanair of publishing', and that my contract benefited from the expert negotiations of my agent and conformed roughly to industry standards, this is a surprising discovery.' – Nicholas Clee, 'Dividing the spoils', *The Bookseller*, 14 July 2006

'This 'streamlined model' – standard format, minimal editing, no advances – was dismissed by some as sharp practice, but it is hard to see what is wrong in giving aspiring authors a helping hand that might otherwise be denied them.' – Barry Turner, 'Another Turn of the Screw', *The Times*, 17 August 2006

'If you have a ms in your bottom drawer, you really ought to take a long hard look at the Macmillan offer, and at the Guardian article. But my personal view is that the Macmillan deal sounds like a bloody good offer, and it is the most attractive piece of new thinking that I've come across in a long time.' – Michael Allen, 'New Thinking by Publisher – World Grinds to a Halt'. Grumpy Old Bookman has several entries on the experiment.

19 October 2006

Children, politics and electronica

I spent some happy hours yesterday with our children's books teams from Spain, Mexico, UK and US. It reminded me of the importance and vitality of that part of the publishing spectrum. Take a look at the Priddy Books website or Julia Donaldson's or Macmillan Children's Books. The interface between traditional educational publishing and children's books is blurring and we are publishing books to entertain children and help educate them too. This requires great authors and great publishing teams and across our group we are lucky enough to have both.

Another thing we've been developing is News at Nature which helps explain the latest research and scientific developments to a wider audience than pure scientists. In particular we now have a tradition of in-depth analyses of upcoming elections and the impact of various outcomes on science policy and hence our lives. For the next week or so we are making available a special on the US mid-term elections. Well worth a click.

This afternoon, as I mentioned a couple of days ago I'm chairing a conference session on collecting electronica. Here's the press release for the conference which is also being covered by BBC Radio 4 this morning.

Save our written heritage:

Making UK writers' archives available to future generations

The Right Honourable Lord Chris Smith of Finsbury and Poet Laureate Andrew Motion are addressing an international conference at the British Library, *Manuscripts Matter* on 19 -20 October 2006 to discuss the importance of UK institutions acquiring the archives of living writers.

Increasingly, manuscripts of modern and contemporary UK authors are being sold abroad, despite the best endeavours of UK public institutions and funding bodies. Public institutions find themselves unable to compete with organisations abroad, primarily in the United States, in terms of readily available and accessible funds. The Working Group aims to ensure that authors know that UK funds may be made available if enough time is given and that they should approach UK libraries and archives to discuss the sale of their works.

The cultural benefits of retaining the archives of pre-eminent UK authors within the UK for research, educational and creative use are significant and wide-reaching. As well as national collections, regional and university libraries collect papers with local connections and international reputations. The acquisition of significant modern literary papers enhances the reputation of collecting institutions throughout the UK, raises their profile worldwide, and in turn encourages new writing as the nation is seen to value its writers.

Primary sources are increasingly valued to inspire young writers; there is no substitute for being able to consult manuscripts first-hand to gain an insight into the processes that created the most important modern works of literature.

This conference is an opportunity for authors, publishers, dealers, funders, academics and collecting institutions, and other experts to discuss a range of issues:

☐ the perception and reality of UK markets,

☐ the national funding position and tax incentives

☐ the value of manuscripts as a research resource

☐ developing a national and international policy for collection, preservation and access to archives both nationally and internationally

Rt Hon Lord Smith of Finsbury said 'Despite wishes of authors that their manuscripts are available to UK institutions, the financial allure of selling abroad is often too great as they depend on this income to continue writing. Living authors are not eligible for current tax incentives. Funders such as the HLF make a significant and valuable contribution, but the process can be lengthy in the face of international competition. '

For further information or images from the collection, contact Catriona Finlayson at the British Library Press Office: 020 7412 7115 or Catriona.finlayson@bl.uk or Eileen Kinghan:

NOTES FOR EDITORS

The UK Literary Heritage Working Group was established in March 2005 to develop and implement a national strategy to benefit the UK cultural and intellectual environment by ensuring that archives of pre-eminent modern and contemporary authors are retained and made accessible to UK audiences. Led by Rt Hon Lord Smith of Finsbury, its members drawn from across the sector, including authors, publishers, dealers, funders, academics and collecting institutions, and other experts join as guests. It works with the Group for Literary Manuscripts and Archives (http://archives.li.man.ac.uk/glam/index.html), who are carrying out a survey into collection development policies throughout Britain and Ireland, are encouraging collaboration and making these policies more widely known. The activities of the Working Group focus on three main areas of concern

- ¨ Funding available nationally, and the funding processes

- ¨ Tax incentives to benefit living writers who sell papers to public institutions

- ¨ Provision of guidelines for authors selling papers, on financial incentives currently available, and on appropriate collecting institutions.

In November 2005, the Working Group formally submitted two proposals to HM Treasury which, it believes, will encourage pre-eminent UK authors who are considering selling their literary archives to choose to approach UK institutions:

- ¨ **To extend the douceur arrangement** with regard to inheritance and capital gains tax to income tax for living authors selling their papers to a designated UK public institution by private treaty

- ˜ **To extend the Acceptance in Lieu of tax** scheme to living writers

These proposals, although of minimal cost to Treasury, would benefit intellectual and cultural life beyond literary heritage, as they would apply equally to the archives of contemporary historians, scientists, economists and political scientists. Support for the measures has also been found among these communities. No formal response has been received from HM Treasury. The working group continues to pursue the proposals.

The issues were raised during debates in the House of Lords on 13 December 2005 and on 24 July 2006 (http://www.publications.parliament.uk/pa/ld199900/ldhansrd/pdvn/lds05/text/51 213-01.htm#51213-01_star0 and http://www.publications.parliament.uk/pa/ld199900/ldhansrd/pdvn/lds06/text/60 724-1052.htm#06072410000015).

20 October 2006

A formal release of the recently published Palgrave Macmillan book Foreign Capital Inflows to China, India and the Caribbean, took place last week in New Delhi in the presence of the Indian Minister of Defence(and former Finance Minister), Mr. Pranab Mukherjee, in his private parliamentary offices. Kalpana Shukla, General Manager of Palgrave Macmillan in India was in attendance along with co-authors, Dr. Arindam Banik and Dr. Pradip Baumik. We're hoping that the Minister will write a book for us now. Given India's fantastic growth and success the rest of the world has much to learn from his experiences.

My friend, Nick Clee was editor of the The Bookseller magazine for several years, after Louis Baum (who got very irked at me once when we added an 'e' to Louis on the cover of his book), and before the incumbent Neill Denny. Nick has become a cookery author with Don't sweat the aubergine published by the small but growing and excellent Short Books. Nick has recently launched The sceptical cook blog. The recipes sound delicious and the advice soundly based on practical experience of an ordinary person. It also makes a change from book trade gossip.

The conference at the British Library yesterday seemed to go very well. The session I chaired was all about the archiving of electronica. If my email filing system is typical, a better descriptor would be chaotica a word already bagged by an electronic rock group. In any event I was reassured that every word uttered and every powerpoint shown yesterday will certainly be archived to the highest standards and I believe the BL is even archiving this blog for the delectation of future generations. Good luck to them.

21 October 2006

A memorable birthday party

Just back from Munich which is one of my favourite cities. It also has one of the most beautiful (and efficient) airports.

Amongst other things I was invited to a party at the <u>Haus der Kunst</u> to celebrate the 150th anniversary of the great publishing house of <u>Langenscheidt</u>. It's hard to describe exactly what it is that makes this sort of event in Germany so special – probably the fact that everything is done so well, the serious bits, the fun bits, the setting, the hosts and the guests. It was a great party.

If you read German (which I don't) you'll find <u>this website</u> invaluable. It started life in 1966 and is still going strong run by <u>Christian von Zittwitz</u> whom I met for the first time.

And today there will be great parties all over India to celebrate <u>Diwali</u>. I imagine the celebrations will be very different from the Bavarian ones of yesterday but no less enjoyable.

Next week I'm hoping to put together some words about Alan Maclean who worked for Pan and Macmillan for many years and died recently. For now I thought you might like to see a handsome picture of him.

 22 October 2006

Mushrooms and Roses

Roger Phillips is one of Pan Macmillan's most successful authors/photographers with a number of <u>books</u> on gardening and plants. His latest book on <u>mushrooms</u> arrived on my desk a couple of weeks ago just in time for the height of the mushrooming season. It is beautiful as well as scientifically accurate and will sell very well indeed, I think. However, it caused me to check what progress Roger had made in converting his expertise to the Internet. We have had on-and-off discussions about what to do over the years. Here's the <u>link</u> to the mushroom site and to the <u>Roses</u> one. I'm meeting Roger soon to discuss web trends and how to 'monetise' (I hate that word) his million visitors a year. I thought readers of this blog might like to see how traditional books and photos can be transformed into wonderful websites with a bit of imagination and web intelligence. Also I'd appreciate any thoughts for improvements which I can pass on to Roger. For those who can't be bothered to click through here are some mushrooms to whet the appetite (but I bet some of these are not to be eaten).

Oxford publishing investment committee

At some point in the 1970s there was a Christmas party where the hosts served mulled wine in their flat in Woodstock near Blenheim Palace. Unfortunately the wine was left to mull for so long that the desired level of intoxication for a successful Christmas party was not achieved. There was a drift to a local pub where several of the partygoers discovered that they shared a common passion for poker. Thus began the first of the publishing investment committee meetings. They still happen.

The cast of characters has changed over the years and I won't list them in full for fear of legal action but perhaps the first names and descriptor may help identification for those versed in the history of British publishing:

Alan (lexicographer), Simon (academic marketing), Jon (international sales), Iradj (academic publisher), Ivon (managing director), Marshall (educational software), David (legal sales), Stephen (ELT sales), Tim He (author), Adam (philosophy editor), Robert (history editor), Tim H (medical publisher), Tony J (accountant), Anton (actor), David C (academic publisher), Bob C (science publisher), Mike (science and legal publisher), Denis (IT inventor), Andrew S (textbook editor), John D (editor) and many others. A clue – there are three current members of the Publishers Association Council in this list.

Having set the scene I can now share with you the confidential minutes of one of the early meetings as supplied by the Secretary to the Investment Committee:

An Episode of Asquith

Polstead Road, Oxford, Friday, 3 November 1978, 11 pm. Fog.

A light is dimly visible from the basement window of a large house. The house is otherwise dark. You make your way through the rhododendrons and crouch to look in. To the left you see a heavy Victorian press, its top crowded with bottles. Beside it seven men are gathered round an oval mahogany table that fills most of the room. Each appears to be taking turns at throwing notes into a large pile of money in the centre of the table. There is a pause followed by loud groans. Long arms reach out to gather in the money. They belong to a lanky young man sitting opposite the window. He has a pipe dangling from one corner of his mouth and his features are half-hidden by a black hat tilted jauntily over his forehead.

Time to go in.

'Ah, there you are. Nice to see you. Glass of wine? Red OK? Squeeze in here between Washbag and Sharkfin. Need some change? Twenty OK? You know these reprobates? Richard, Simon, Jon, Bob, Alan, Adam. Right, it's my choice of game I think. A round of Asquith?'

'Oh not bloody Asquith, Ivon. Sue's going to kill me as it is.'

'It's your choice next Richard. Does everyone know the rules? You don't? Well, it's basically two down three up pass the card eights wild high low two changes the first free the second the last bet for an up card and twice for a down. You'll soon get the hang of it. It's your deal. Don't forget the ante. Just a fiver at this stage. Oops, no, deal one card at a time. Sorry, yes I'm afraid it's double for a misdeal. Try again. Well done. Try to keep your voices down Simon and Bob. The landlady's asleep on the next floor.'

By the last round of the hand everyone has dropped out except Ivon and Adam. Ivon is now showing a five, a two, and a wild eight. Adam shows a six and an ace, and also has an eight. They appear to be going low. It is Ivon's bet.

'I think I'll pass.'

Adam opens his wallet and takes out two ten pound notes.

'Twenty.'

There is a long pause while Ivon scrutinizes his cards.

'I'm not sure I believe you. You've got a dirty hole. Your twenty and raise you thirty.'

'O.K. Asquith, just this once I'll be kind. Your thirty and see you.'

'Damn. All right then. Under the table.'

Both take two coins and put their hands under the table. A few minutes pass. 'Get on with it you two can't you?'

Eventually each extends one clenched fist across the table and at the same moment they open their hands with a flourish. There is a single coin on both outstretched palms.

'Good grief. Going high. Hard luck Ivon. Nice try.'

Adam flips over his two down cards to show an ace and a six.

'Full house. Aces on sixes.'

'Oh well done Adam. What a fantastic concealed high.' Ivon turns over his cards. He has an eight and a five. 'But I seem to have four fives. What jolly hard luck.'

Later . . .

'You've all got to go? So soon? It's only 3.30. OK who wants notes for coins? Noone has any coins? Yes, I do seem to have rather a lot. I'll keep them as change for the next meeting, and what about the next? 24th? and what about a pre-Christmas game on 22nd December? Thanks Bob, I did do reasonably well this evening. Luck of the cards.' He takes out a slim black book. 'I'll just note down the total. Oh Jon, I've got an IOU here for £30.'

'I haven't got £30, Ivon. How's your hifi?'

'I haven't got a hifi.'

'Have mine.'

'Does it work?'

'Yes.'

'OK.'

'I'll bring it to the next meeting. I don't know why I bother. You'll just fleece me again.'

'Nonsense. You won last time. OK chaps see you soon. Could you see yourselves orff quietly please? The landlady sleeps.'

More on Libya and a few bestsellers

A little while back I highlighted a piece in Nature about the plight of the Bulgarian nurses and the Palestinian doctor under threat of death in Tripoli. The story has moved on and there is an excellent piece in yesterday's Times about the efforts of scientists to show that the defendants are clearly innocent. Gaddafi is using the defendants as hostages to obtain $6billion and the release of one of the Lockerbie bombers. The article concludes:

'What matters, of course, is the science; Libya will not allow it into the courtroom. Without it, a murderous miscarriage of justice remains a dreadful possibility.'

On a happier note, Julia Donaldson, the author of my favourite book of the decade The Gruffalo is touring Southern Britain. If you have kids (or if you don't) do try to see her at one of her events. And if you haven't yet met the beast get a copy of the original for yourself and enjoy.

If you're in London you might also like to pop in to Chris Beetles Gallery where he is showing a marvellous exhibition of the works of Ronald Searle, famous for St. Trinian's School illustrations. as I mentioned before, he has also illustrated a special gift edition of Jeffrey Archer's Cat O'Nine Tails.

And Macmillan is celebrating a number one bestseller in hardback fiction with James Herbert's latest, The Secret of Crickley Hall. Worldwide the Pan Macmillan teams are gearing up for plenty more number ones in the run-up to Christmas.

© John Davey.

Evidence-based publishing

One of the key tenets of modern medicine is to develop treatments based on collected evidence rather than intuition. While the very best physicians do have a streak of intuition this is based on experience and data (sometimes accumulated subconsciously). Publishing can be a pretty intuitive business. What market research would have identified Eat, Shoots and Leaves? However, there is always a place for reviewing the outcomes of publishing initiatives.

A couple of years ago we announced the formation of Macmillan Science, an experiment in non-fiction publishing. The idea was to publish popular science books globally and simultaneously in the key English-language markets. Authors would receive no advance but royalties would be based on publisher's receipts rather than retail price (as retail price is completely variable) at a higher than normal rate. We would not anticipate high subscriptions for the books because this might lead to high returns from booksellers. Our print runs were intended to be conservative with reprints the norm rather than the exception. We used our academic rather than our trade sales forces in general. The books would be supported by promotions in our various science-related journals and websites including Nature and Scientific American. And perhaps most importantly the person publishing the books is a specialist in scientific journalism and comunication rather than an all-rounder general editor.

So here's the evidence so far from the publisher, Sara Abdulla:

'Of the 13 hardbacks and 3 paperbacks we've published to date, one is currently longlisted for the Guardian First Book Award (_Lonesome George_) and one is currently shortlisted for the Times Higher Academic Author of the Year Award (_Climate Change Begins At Home_). One of the launch titles was longlisted for the 2005 Royal Society Aventis Prize (_Venomous Earth_) and another was shortlisted for the 2005 Medical Journalists Association Open Book Award (_Whole Story_). I was shortlisted for the 2005 Booktrust Kim Scott Walwyn Women In Publishing Award at the end of the first full year of publishing. One of these days, fingers crossed, the list will actually win something!

Our tenacious global Palgrave Macmillan sales and marketing force has sold 60,000 hardbacks to date and 6000 paperbacks (these are only just coming through now). The bestseller (_The Science Of the Hitchhiker's Guide to the Galaxy_) moved 12,426 hardbacks. Average hardback sales are now 4,443 per title. Thanks to our amazing rights folks, we have 11 translation deals, two extract deals, 7 bookclub deals, two film options, two TV adaptations and a museum exploitation rights arrangement.

Macmillan Science books have received more than 140 great reviews to date, appearing regularly in _Guardian, THES, BBC Radio 4, NewScientist, Discover, Focus, Seed Magazine, Booklist_ and innumerable specialist journals. MacmillanScience authors have done at least 125 events at venues including Hay Festival, Edinburgh Literary Festival, Chichester Science Festival, British Library and the Royal Institution. There have been at least 170 print, online and email adverts for the titles in _Scientific American_ and in _Nature_ journals. A couple of authors are now writing for Macmillan Children's and several are preparing their second books for Macmillan Science. I haven't signed up any existing popsci stars, I admit, but I think I've found a couple!

The main strategic focus now is to offer the books in flexible digital formats via BookStore. Obviously, we also need to keep signing up kickass authors, especially in the US — sales there really pick up when we give them some home-grown talent. UK sales are modest, given the strength and breadth of the books' critical reception, but they are creeping up now that the list is more of a known quantity to the force, Amazon and the high street. Hardback EU/ROW sales are sluggish too, but giving these territories more paperbacks helps.

So all in all, I'd say our high royalty/no advance/all rights experiment is working — at least for popular science. And plenty more great books to come.'

🗐 26 October 2006

Schapelle Corby

This book story broke yesterday in Australia and Tom Gilliatt of Pan Macmillan Australia shared this internal note with me.

Sitting in her cell in Kerobokan Jail in Bali (shared with a minimum of five other prisoners, and sometimes as many as fifteen), Schapelle Corby has been writing her story. In appallingly primitive conditions, and despite the crushing weight of a 20 year sentence, Schapelle has written something quite extraordinary. It's harrowing, it's deeply moving, it's utterly compelling and it presents an almost unarguable case for her innocence. For once the publisher's blurb on the cover is not hyperbole: it's simply the most unforgettable book you'll ever read.

The book is now at the printers, with a first print run of 120,000 copies, and I suspect we'll be returning to the press a few more times before the year is out. The book is still officially a secret until Wednesday 25th October, when it will feature on the cover of The Women's Weekly, and there's a complete embargo on any material from the book till the weekend of 11/12 November.

This is going to be a bestseller in Australia and elsewhere – more on the book here.

And some internal (and frightening) statistics from our IT department in the UK – in short 94% of emails sent to us were invalid for one reason or another.

In the past month:

- 78% of email received (nearly 6.5 million emails) were rejected by our mail systems as the servers attempting to send the emails had poor reputations, meaning they have been classified as highly likely to be sending spam.

- 12% of email received (just under 1 million) had invalid recipients.

- 4% of email (about 300,000) was classified as being spam emails

- 6% of email (about ½ million) were clean emails and were delivered.

27 October 2006

Down-under pole dancing

I seem to be in Australian mode right now. We're publishing Richard Flanagan's new book in Picador Australia next Tuesday. Paul Kenny, who is possibly Australia's greatest book marketeer has had to pay out of his marketing budget for a pole dancer in a Hobart night club. He claims this is the first time but I'm not absolutely sure.

However, what he has created for the book is one of the most innovative online campaigns for a literary work that I've ever seen. The book is The Unknown Terrorist and don't forget to turn off your mute button.

And while innovation occurs in the real world of publishing there is tremendous activity in the slightly unreal world of mergers and acquisitions, IPOs, private equity, leveraged buy-outs, Uncle Tom Cobleigh and all. Springer is trying to buy Informa; Riverdeep and Houghton Mifflin are 'merging'; Wolters Kluwer has hired Lehman to sell its Education Division; and now Thomson is threatening to sell its Learning Division. I'm certain that all these assets will fetch very high prices but can't help feeling that the real winners will be, as always, the bankers and the lawyers. I wonder whether authors,students, academics and educational organisations will benefit as much.

28 October 2006

Sumertime, Wintertime, Europe and India

Clocks go back (or is it forward?) in the UK tonight (or tomorrow morning). I think what it means is that I'll wake up even earlier than ususal and fall asleep even earlier (hardly possible). There is some discussion about whether we should move to European time. Apparently this would save lives (not quite sure why) and would make communication within the EU easier. I'm not sure about the latter. Lisbon and Dublin are on the same time as London. Would they change too? And it would be odd to change your watch when driving from Belfast to Dublin. Still, the forces of European homogenisation are strong.

Whilst I disagree with the need for uniformity of time across countries I do think India could do us and itself a great favour if it would abandon Indian Standard Time. Given the huge latitudinal spread I can understand the need for compromise over which time zone to adopt but to compromise with a 30-minute shiift seems unnecessary,unhelpful and perverse. But not as odd as Kathmandu which has a 45-minute difference.

My entry about the amount of email spam we are intercepting generated a comment from the head of Macmillan IT with these statistics:

January 2002, 400,000 emails received
January 2003, 960,000 emails received
January 2004, 1.6 million emails received
January 2005, 2.2 million emails received
January 2006, 6.5 million emails received

If only our sales had increased in proportion.

One of my favourite writers is John Banville. He has written any number of high-quality 'literary' novels, the last of which, The Sea, won the Man Booker prize. My recommendation is The Untouchable for the entirely inappropriate reason that one of the characters is called Charkin and I suspect that is the only literary character in world literature with that name. But I digress. John has decided to pursue a writing career in parallel to his literary novels with the launch of Christine Falls by 'Benjamin Black'. I think this review from Guardian says it all.

29 October 2006

The elephant and the rat and Pergamon Press

On Tuesday I am giving a talk at Oxford Brookes University in their International Centre for Publishing Studies. The subject is Innovation in Publishing and the title is an allusion to the R and K strategies for the survival of species.

The typical R isn't as cuddly but might very well be more successful in the long run. For more on reproductive strategies try this site.

Apart from being happy to discuss innovation with some of the brightest publishing students the other reason for going is nostalgia. This grand building is now part of Oxford Brookes University but it was where I worked in 1974.

It was the home of Robert Maxwell and the headquarters of Pergamon Press.

I was called senior publishing executive, life sciences and my job was to commission and publish about 200 books a year, look after 100 journals and launch as many new journals as possible. Maxwell's (correct) theory was that the fastest areas of research paper growth would be in the biological (rather than physical) sciences because each experiment was cheaper to fund and therefore there would be more literature per funding dollar.

They were exciting times. Every morning we editors and marketing people were summonsed to open the post under Maxwell's tutelage. 'Every piece of paper is a publishing opportunity.' 'Every letter contains a lesson.' 'Don't assume anything except that you will die.' Every morning new edicts would be issued. 'No green covers'. 'Henceforward all textbooks will be designated paperback even if they are hardback.''No more billing in pounds. Tell Blackwell's they have to pay in dollars.' 'All books are journals. Reduce the discounts from 30% to 10%.' 'You're sacked.'

The amazing thing is that Maxwell transformed the company from a rather staid and sleepy business (he'd been away fromt the company for a few years) into an innovative and successful scientific information provider. It was only his disastrous forays into newspaper publishing and his absurd war with Rupert Murdoch which forced him to sell what was the real jewel in his corporate crown. His demise was Reed Elsevier's gain. And somehow his death was inevitable.

Of course Bob Maxwell was a terrible guy in many ways but he did build a great publishing company and working in Headington was a great (albeit not always fun) experience.

30 October 2006

Climate change

This morning's headlines in the UK are all about the publication of a Treasury-commissioned report on the economic aspects of climate change. It's pretty hairy stuff and particularly so as it comes from Nick Stern who has held a number of very influential posts including Chief Economist at The World Bank. The conclusions are stark and require politicians to sacrifice votes in some instances – an almost impossible act for most of them.

I fear we'll have to wait a long time (perhaps too long) for governments to get their acts together. Meanwhile, we can do things as individuals. Get your hands on a copy of Climate change begins at home by Dave Reay. This quote from Popular Science says it all:

'This is one of the most easily readable popular science books I've seen in several years, it's practical rather than ridiculous, it puts the case without being preachy – it really is a wonderfully effective description of the realities of climate change, how it will affect us and our families, and what we as individuals can do about it. So go out and buy one. In fact, buy two and send one to the world leader or large company CEO of your choice.'

While on matters environmental, you might care to look at Landmine Action campaign to prohibit the manufacture, sale and use of cluster munitions whose effects impact decades after a war has been resolved. The main sufferers are children. I delivered a signed petition by hand yesterday to the House of Commons – it was very difficult as they don't have a letterbox.

🐦 31 October 2006

News and spin, spin and news

A short quiz. The Bookseller headline announces 'Outstanding Penguin pushes Pearson to record'. Sales at Penguin are up 2%, 10% or 20%? The answer can be found here.

There is so much corporate activity going on right now that I thought the best thing I could do for those interested would be to reprint here the latest issue of EPS Headlines from Electronic Publishing Services which is my weekly Bible. Like the law-abiding citizen I try to be I called them for permission to reproduce. They graciously granted it on the grounds, I suppose, that they may pick up some new subscribers from this promotion. They deserve to. It is the best news service around. I strongly recommend you go the final item if nowhere else.

EPS HEADLINES DIGEST :: 30/10/2006

_ _ _ _ _ _ _ _ _ _ _ _ _ _ _ _ _ _ _-

** Pearson on course to produce record full-year profits **

** Riverdeep plans to buy Houghton Mifflin **

** Microsoft reported better than expected Q3 results **

** Google launches customisable search engine service **

** Scirus partners with CrossRef **

_ _ _ _ _ _ _ _ _ _ _ _ _ _ _ _ _ _-

Company News

_ _ _ _ _ _ _ _ _ _ _ _ _ _ _ _ _ _-

23/10/2006

Non-profit copyright licensing solution provider Copyright Clearance Center (CCC) has announced that medical publisher BMJ Publishing Group, Ltd has selected Rightslink as its automated, online permissions licensing solution. BMJ Publishing is the fifth STM publisher to have implemented Rightslink for online permissions or reprint ordering.

KnowledgeSpeak ::

http://www.knowledgespeak.com/newsArchieveviewdtl.asp?pickUpID=2967&pickUpBatch=490#2967

24/10/2006

The entire editorial board of the Elsevier journal Topology resigned in August in protest at Elsevier's refusal to lower the journal's subscription price. The editors' letter to Elsevier talks of their concerns with the price of Topology since Elsevier gained control of the journal in 1994, and their belief that the price has had a significant and damaging effect on Topology's reputation in the mathematical research community, which they say is likely to become increasingly serious in the future.

SPARC e-News :: http://www.arl.org/sparc/pubs/enews/aug06.html#partner

24/10/2006

Wolters Kluwer is planning to move many of its pre-press and data conversion jobs from the US to India. The move is projected to make the Indian subsidiary play a key role in the company's global operations. The company will also start selling tax, accounting and law books in India early in 2007.

Knowledgespeak ::

http://www.knowledgespeak.com/newsArchieveviewdtl.asp?pickUpID=2975&pickUpBatch=491#2975

25/10/2006

Pearson is planning to combine the Financial Times Group's newspaper and magazines businesses, in an attempt to both sharpen the FT's focus on niche audiences and to expand the magazines' international and online presence. The proposal will involve no redundancies but will see FT Business titles such as The Banker and Investors Chronicle move into the same offices as the FT newspaper and FT.com. The combined businesses are expected to look for shared opportunities in the events market.

FT.com (subscription required) ::

http://www.ft.com/cms/s/149f02ac-63c6-11db-bc82-0000779e2340.html

27/10/2006

Factiva has announced that it has enhanced its Taxonomy Warehouse, a community directory and information source for taxonomies, thesauri, and classification schemes. The service provides enterprises and academic and government organizations with information to categorize internal and external data collections, listing more than 650 taxonomies arranged in 73 subject domains.

E-Content Mag ::

http://www.econtentmag.com/Articles/ArticleReader.aspx?ArticleID=18511

_ _ _ _ _ _ _ _ _ _ _ _ _ _ _ _ _ _ --

Financials

_ _ _ _ _ _ _ _ _ _ _ _ _ _ _ _ _ _ --

26/10/2006

The publisher of Yellow Pages directories, R.H. Donnelley, has reported a third-quarter loss, compared with profits in 2005, even as revenue more than doubled. The company posted a loss of USD35.4 million, or 51 cents a share, compared with year-earlier net income of USD27.1 million, or 62 cents a share. The company reported revenue of USD524 million, up from USD255 million a year earlier.

Reuters ::

http://today.reuters.com/news/articleinvesting.aspx?view=CN&storyID=2006-10-26T121847Z_01_WEN8096_RTRIDST_0_MEDIA-RHDONNELLEY-EARNS-URGENT.XML&rpc=66&type=qcna

27/10/2006

Microsoft reported Q3 results that were better than expected, with overall revenues climbing 11 per cent to USD10.8bn. Net income also rose 11 per cent to USD3.5bn. The strong results were boosted by solid sales in two of its newer businesses, servers and video games. The company reported that USD136 million losses in Q3 within its online-services group were due to its investment in a product aimed at competing with Google.

SearchEngineWatch :: http://blog.searchenginewatch.com/blog/061027-085703

30/10/2006

Pearson is on course to produce record full-year profits, and has announced a 15 per cent rise in underlying operating profits for the first nine months of the year. The company is entering its busiest selling period 'confident' of increasing margins and growing faster than its markets. Headline sales growth was 11 per cent across the group in the first nine months, and reported operating profits rose 26 per cent.

FT.com (subscription required) ::

http://www.ft.com/cms/s/d5390b04-67f2-11db-90ac-
0000779e2340,_i_rssPage=cbad994c-3017-11da-ba9f-00000e2511c8.html

_ -

M&A

_ -

23/10/2006

ProQuest, the publisher of information and education solutions, reported that it has signed an agreement to sell its ProQuest Business Solutions segment to Snap-on Incorporated for approximately USD500 million. ProQuest Company will use most of the proceeds from the sale to pay down outstanding debt. Snap-on Incorporated is a manufacturer and marketer of tools, diagnostics and equipment solutions for professional users in industry, government, agriculture and construction.

Press Release (Proquest) ::

http://phx.corporate-ir.net/phoenix.zhtml?c=93447&p=irol-
newsArticle&ID=919430&highlight

24/10/2006

Dublin-based education and consumer software company Riverdeep is planning to buy Houghton Mifflin, the US-based educational publisher. Houghton Mifflin is currently owned by Thomas H. Lee Partners, Bain Capital and Blackstone. Its Promissor division was sold to Pearson PLC for USD42 million in January 2006.

BostonHerald.com ::

http://business.bostonherald.com/businessNews/view.bg?articleid=163852

24/10/2006

Digg, the user-submitted and reviewed news site, is reported to have been in acquisition discussions with a number of companies, including News Corp. It is suggested that the company is looking for at least USD150 million, and that that price has resulted in no formal written offers for Digg. One point of controversy is around

Digg's claim of 20 million unique monthly visitors.

TechCrunch ::

http://www.techcrunch.com/2006/10/24/digg-does-the-acquisition-dance-with-news-corp/

24/10/2006

Apax Partners and Veronis Suhler Stevenson are reported to be considering bids for VNU's European business magazines division. A deadline of the end of October has been set for first-round bids, which are expected to be in the region of UKP335 million. Apax is backing a UKP199 million management buyout of Incisive, the publisher of Legal Week and Investment Week.

The Times Online ::

http://business.timesonline.co.uk/article/0,,13130-2418228,00.html

_ _ _ _ _ _ _ _ _ _ _ _ _ _ _ _ _ _ _-

New Products & Services

_ _ _ _ _ _ _ _ _ _ _ _ _ _ _ _ _ _ _-

23/10/2006

Yell.com and Thomasglobal.com have formed a partnership to offer global industrial search results. Yell.com will now be able to offer business-to-business search results from outside the UK for the first time, while New York-based Thomasglobal.com will now be able to offer its business-to-business search and industrial classifications to Yell.com's customers.

European Association of Directory and Database Publishers ::

http://www.eadp.org/index.php?q=node/14984

23/10/2006

Google has launched a customisable search engine service for users to integrate with their own blogs and web sites. Users of Google Custom Search Engine will be able to select the web sites they want to be included in their searches, and add to this list in future by 'tagging' web sites they visit. Any searches will then return results just from that slice of the Google search index, which will carry context-relevant advertising from Google's AdSense network.

FT.com (subscription required) ::

http://www.ft.com/cms/s/a53ea278-62e9-11db-8faa-0000779e2340.html

24/10/2006

Elsevier's science-specific search engine, Scirus, has signed an agreement with publisher linking services provider CrossRef which allows Scirus to collect metadata from hundreds of participating publishers via CrossRef's new Web Services protocol. The partnership is expected to improve how researchers, academics, students and librarians search authoritative, scientific published content.

Press Release (Elsevier) ::

24/10/2006

Adobe has released a beta edition of Adobe Digital Editions, an application for digital publishing and reading. The product enables users to acquire, read, and manage content such as eBooks and other digital publications. The final version of the new software will be out early in 2007 and will run on Windows, Mac and Linux machines, as well as various mobile devices.

Adobe :: http://labs.adobe.com/technologies/digitaleditions/

– – – – – – – – – – – – – – – – – – –-

Legal

– – – – – – – – – – – – – – – – – – –-

23/10/2006

IBM has filed two infringement lawsuits for five patent violations against Amazon, which relate to Amazon's online product recommendation systems and other features Amazon uses at the foundation of its business. IBM says it developed similar systems as early as the 1980s, and has been speaking with Amazon since 2002 on reconciling the alleged infringement through licensing.

Wall Street Journal Online ::

http://online.wsj.com/google_login.html?url=http%3A%2F%2Fonline.wsj.com%2Farticle%2FSB116161475467500836.html%3Fmod%3Dgooglenews_wsj

– – – – – – – – – – – – – – – – – – –-

Wireless and Telecoms

– – – – – – – – – – – – – – – – – – –-

26/10/2006

Spending on mobile marketing is expected to reach USD2.90 billion by 2011 according to a report released this week by JupiterResearch. The report also said that by the end of 2006, 22% of online advertisers and 29% of online agencies will be using mobile marketing campaigns. Mobile phone penetration in the U.S. was found to have reached 76%, with 11% of mobile phones having video capabilities.

BtoB online ::

http://www.btobonline.com/toc.cms?productId=6&issueDate=2006-10-26

– – – – – – – – – – – – – – – – – – –-

China STM

– – – – – – – – – – – – – – – – – – –-

24/10/2006

China's minister of Science and Technology, Xu Guanhua, has announced a data-sharing plan which will cover the entire country. He said that over 80 per cent of data relating to China's research into pure science will be freely available on the Internet, via 40 openly accessible scientific data centres that will be established by 2010.

SciDev.net ::

http://www.scidev.net/content/news/eng/china-unveils-plans-to-boost-scientific-data-sharing.cfm

_ _ _ _ _ _ _ _ _ _ _ _ _ _ _ _ _ _ -

And Finally..

_ _ _ _ _ _ _ _ _ _ _ _ _ _ _ _ _ _ -

27/10/2006

The record-holder for fast thumb text messaging has lost his first ever head-to-head contest, against a new piece of voice-recognition software. Ben Cook took on a program from Nuance Communications, and his first message – 'I'm on my way. I'll be there in 30 minutes' – took him 16 seconds to send by text. However, the voice recognition software finished it in under 8 seconds. The final round in the competition was the phrase on which Cook had previously won his title: 'The razor toothed piranhas of the genera Serrasalmus and Pygo centrus are the most ferocious freshwater fish in the world. In reality they seldom attack a human.' The Nuance program finished 32 seconds ahead of its human rival – but then, it had already been programmed to recognise the Latin.

Physorg.com :: http://www.physorg.com/news80933892.html

< **November 2006** >

Mon	Tue	Wed	Thu	Fri	Sat	Sun
30	31	1	2	3	4	5
6	7	8	9	10	11	12
13	14	15	16	17	18	19
20	21	22	23	24	25	26
27	28	29	30	1	2	3
4	5	6	7	8	9	10

Innovation and size

My talk to the MA students of <u>Oxford Brookes</u> which I mentioned <u>recently</u> passed without anyone throwing bad eggs or rotten tomatoes at me – which is always a relief. Apart from the students there was a generous sprinkling of old friends which is reassuring in one sense but worrying in another – their memories of my anecdotes from the olden days might differ from mine. Various journalists from the trade press asked me to send them my notes of the talk or to write it up. The combination of a very full schedule and natural indolence meant that my notes were very sketchy but they were the only facts in the talk! Here they are. The numbers relate to headcount. The companies are all mainly English language except one.

Albatros 4; Profile 16; Faber 82; Bloomsbury 271; Informa 7000; McGraw-Hill 18,000; News Corporation 30,000; Pearson 32,000; Reed Elsevier 37,000; Thomson 40,000, Bertelsmann 93,000.

The conclusion was that size is not in itself an inhibitor nor a catalyst for innovation in publishing although the larger (and more publicly owned) the company the harder it is (obviously) to remain nimble and innovative. At Macmillan we try to encourage innovation by devolving responsibility to small creative units. For instance <u>Palgrave Macmillan</u> has set up a three-person team to help us identify new opportunities in academic and textbook publishing and then take them to market. Here is their latest success described by Alison Jones.

The Study Stick leads, the rest follow

Nice to see publishing leading the music industry for a change. The recent 'ground-breaking' <u>announcement</u> that Keane are to release a limited run of 1,500 USB memory sticks pre-loaded with their latest single has generated lots of chat in the blogosphere, sadly none of it commenting on the fact that Keane were simply following the trail blazed by Palgrave Macmillan last month.

<u>The Study Stick</u> is a 512MB memory stick preloaded with an ebook of the best-selling The Study Skills Handbook, with a link to a protected online site with more resources, community areas, competitions and special offers. We spent a lot of time gently introducing dazed booksellers to the idea and meeting their concerns – for example by supplying dummy packs for display, and by reclassifying part of the stock to make it amenable to Amazon's overloaded systems. The site currently has over 50 registered users and the number is growing quickly – the challenge now is to capitalize on this innovative move by creating a community in which the students benefit from our authors' expertise and we learn more about our market and the possibilities for reaching it.

Finally, an update on this blog's visitor statistics. After no growth in September we had 54793 visitors in October, a 31% increase. Total visitors since January are now 276172.

🗓 02 November 2006

John Wisden and Co Ltd

The last time I wrote about the Wisden Group there were lots of negative comments from independent booksellers about the fact that Amazon was promoting and selling the Almanack at a huge discount thus making it impossible for them to compete. Of course, in the UK every retailer is able to decide what level to price at and what customer benefits it wishes to offer. The job of the publisher is to maximise sales and this year has been an absolutely outstanding year for Wisden through Amazon and through just about every retail outlet and chain we supply. Obviously winning The Ashes in 2005 helped but so did the launch of the large format edition and the brilliance of the editorial content. All parts of the book trade benefited if they wished to participate.

The company was founded by John Wisden in 1864 and I'm certain he wouldn't recognise it today. Apart from the Almanack there is a magazine (in fact several in different countries including South Africa), the most popular sports website in the world, the leading sports technology organisation, Hawk-eye, and any number of books.

Three recent books have caught my eye for different reasons. The first is the Wisden Dictionary of Cricket by Michael Rundell who is also (thank goodness) the brains and lexicographic brawn behind the best-selling Macmillan English Dictionary range.

And then a grave turner for the blessed JW, The Cricinfo Guide to International Cricket 2007 which is the only book to contain biographies and statistics about every international cricketer likely to be playing in the forthcoming World Cup in the West Indies – book your flights and hotels now and coloured pyjamas too, just in case . . .

Finally, the blockbuster – not in unit sales but in size, price, scholarship and insight – Wisden Anthology 1978-2006, a truly boring title but with a glimpse of what's within in the sub-title, Cricket's Age of Revolution. It is 1300 plus pages of meticulously edited nostalgia, fascination, social history and global economics. I think it's underpriced at £40 let alone whatever some booksellers choose to discount it to. Here's the press release for anyone interested:

'The last three decades of cricket have produced more tumult and controversy, heroism and villainy, thrills and scandal than anything seen since shepherd boys on the downs first turned their crooks into cricket bats.

First the game's genteel world was convulsed by the intervention of the Australian tycoon Kerry Packer, who bought up nearly all the top players. Suddenly, cricket was played at night in pyjamas, with searingly fast bowlers aiming at the heads of helmeted batsmen.

From that, a new world emerged – one that produced England's amazing Ashes triumphs of 1981 and 2005 (and much misery in between), the heyday of Caribbean pace, the rise of Indian influence, the match-fixing scandals . . . and extraordinary players such as Ian Botham, Viv Richards, Imran Khan, Brian Lara, Shane Warne, Steve Waugh, Sachin Tendulkar and Andrew Flintoff.

Through it all, Wisden Cricketers' Almanack has been there. Just as it has since 1864, this unique sporting institution has tried each year to make sense of a fast-changing global sport.

Now this anthology does the same, but for an entire generation of change.

Nearly a quarter of a century ago Wisden published four popular anthologies that celebrated the best of Wisden stretching back to its first edition. They were edited by the late Benny Green, who saw the almanack partly as 'a social history of England'.

Now the Wisden Anthology 1978-2006 brings the story up to date, painting a coherent, compelling picture of cricket's evolution – and revolution. A story that was charted in more than 40,000 Wisden pages is distilled into this 1,328-page anthology. It is a portrait of the age – and of the great players and contests that ushered the game into a brave new century, and beyond. It offers a chance to replay the greatest moments of the era, from Headingley 1981 to The Oval 2005 – and assess what they all add up to.

But Wisden is not just days like that. The book tells the stories of Merv the mongrel and Hansie the rabbit, of Bill Wyman's one-handed catch, of the sale of No.10 Dulka Road, and of the marijuana-laced cup cakes.

The obituary section includes not just Don Bradman, Herbert Sutcliffe and Jim Laker -but also 'The Master', Anthony Ainley, 'who despised cheeses of all kinds', the fantasist Donald Weekes, and the cricket-mad fireman, Jeff Wornham, who died trying to save a woman in a burning tower block. Wisden itself has changed in that time. In 1981 John Woodcock became editor. He ensured the book became far more than a conscientious record of facts, and made it a volume of unprecedented literary quality and cricketing authority.

Now, under Matthew Engel, it has evolved into an almanack for the internet age, with a sense of fun and a hint of subversion – without losing its reputation for accuracy, robust comment and flinty integrity.

Stephen Moss, who loves and understands both the game and the book, has synthesised the best of 29 Wisdens into one outstanding volume.

The editor

Stephen Moss has been in love with cricket for 40 years, ever since a chance sighting of a game in Barry, South Wales, cured a sun-induced headache as a child. It has been balm for the soul ever since. He has played for many teams, always ineptly, and still turns out for an Observer newspaper XI. He has scored three fifties in a 30-year career, and has occasionally propelled the perfect leg-break. When he is not sneaking off to The Oval, watching his beloved (though ever-challenging) Glamorgan or poring over battered copies of Wisden, he is a feature writer for The Guardian.'

Stephen Moss is available for media interviews by contacting Christopher Lane on 01420 83415 or email chris.lane@wisdengroup.com

03 November 2006

Macmillan hires new marketing director

Many years ago (July 1987 to be precise) Heinemann were all set to publish another ho-hum spy memoir by a not-very-famous spy, Peter Wright. The history of what

215

happened next is best described in The Spycatcher Trial by the distinguished Australian lawyer (and now politician) Malcolm Turnbull. At some point (and I'm really not sure when or why) the British Prime Minister of the time, Margaret Thatcher, decided she'd like a bit of publishing limelight and appointed herself marketing director for Heinemann by trying to have the book banned.

She was a spectacular success and within weeks Spycatcher was an international bestseller. Overall I think about 4 million copies were sold. I imagine the initial estimate was for 5000 copies. It showed the power of prime ministers in marketing roles.

I was therefore particularly pleased to see that Tony Blair has decided to follow Thatcher's lead not just in economic and social policies but in supporting the book trade. He has been appointed marketing director for our latest title from Boxtree and here is a link to his first effort in the new role – about 12 minutes into the speech.

Today is the publication day of Giant Leaps, a collaboration between The Sun newspaper (this morning's typically glorious headline – 'PC gone mad – racist jelly baby farce – £1/4m black sweets trial'), the Science Museum and Boxtree. The idea is to attract more people to understand science through the use of catchy headlines supported by impeccable educational and scientific text. The book is being backed by the great and the good of science (see below) and politics as part of Britain's desire (and need?) to become the global hub for research and development and the prior requirement for a scientifically literate population.

Go for it, Tony.

What the
experts say

BARONESS GREENFIELD

HEAD of the Royal Institution of top scientists says: 'It teaches people about science without being pious. It is highly readable – and highly look-at-able.'

SIR DAVID ATTENBOROUGH

THE broadcaster, author and naturalist says: 'I read Giant Leaps from cover to cover. I found it a very innovative and exciting book.'

SIR PATRICK MOORE

THE astronomer says: 'I enjoyed it immensely. It is beautifully put together and imparts a lot of knowledge in an attractive way. Above all, it is FUN.'

JON SNOW

THE newscaster says: 'If only I'd had a book like this – compelling. It's a genuine come-on to kids to log-in to science. Well done The Sun. Go to the top of the class!'

ROBERT WINSTON

THE science presenter says: 'An inventive, appealing, really riveting way to depict science and technology. It will excite young people . . . and oldies like myself.'

PROF COLIN BLAKEMORE

THE Chief Exec of the Medical Research Council says: 'It captures the magic of science. I hope it also captures the imagination of young people.'

Quotes, Misquotes and Sex

I owe Philip Jones at The Bookseller Online an apology. In my blog of 31 October I joked about his piece describing Penguin's sales increase of 2% as 'outstanding'. He quite rightly corrects me:

Richard, you neglected to put quotation marks around the word 'outstanding' in the headline you reference from The Bookseller. It was Pearson's interpretation of Penguin's 2% growth, not The Bookseller's.

Still, I expect I've misquoted you in the past.

Philip

You could say he was being oversensitive but I know how he feels. I recently wrote the following light-hearted piece about a conversation at the Booker Prize dinner referring to Kiran Desai's Inheritance of Loss:

'I should have known that this particular title would win when, earlier in the evening, I was asked whether Macmillan was committed to publishing literary books. I asked what is meant by a literary book. Apparently it is a work of fiction which loses money. It seemed rather an odd definition and I tried to argue that publishing companies tend to do a better job when they are solvent. In addition I'm not quite sure why literary publishing should deserve more support than, say, educational publishing in Zimbabwe. That said, of course we are committed to literary publishing and to the continued growth of Picador in all its markets – UK, USA, Australia, South Africa, India and most recently Asia. But I should not want to leave future publishers at Macmillan with an inheritance of loss whatever the definition of literature.'

This was reprinted in the excellent US newsletter Publishers Lunch. Unfortunately this is what they reprinted – spot the difference:

'I should have known that this particular title would win when, earlier in the evening, I was asked whether Macmillan was committed to publishing literary books. I asked what is meant by a literary book. Apparently it is a work of fiction which loses money. It seemed rather an odd definition and I tried to argue that publishing companies tend to do a better job when they are solvent. In addition I'm not quite sure why literary publishing should deserve more support than, say, educational publishing in Zimbabwe . . . But I should not want to leave future publishers at Macmillan with an inheritance of loss whatever the definition of literature.'

I was alerted to this 'minor' piece of editing by complaints from US friends and colleagues that the piece showed my disdain for literary publishing and that this could damage our reputation with literary authors and agents. This was quite a blow given our huge commitment to publishing the best in literature and my best efforts to support these activities in deed and in word. Michael Cader, the editor of Publishers Lunch was unrepentant. I can understand his position on his freedom to edit and he pointed out that the dots showing that something had been edited out might not have shown up properly. I felt misrepresented and I still do. Boohoo. I'll get over it but hence my genuine apology to Philip.

On a more cheerful note I was reminded by this morning's Book section of The Times that this day in 1992 saw the publication of one of my better commercial decisions, Madonna's Sex. We paid an advance of $750k for UK and Commonwealth (Warner published in USA) for this book and another untitled (and still unpublished). It was essentially in print for only two days – publication day and the day we released the only reprint. The combined sales of the two printings were 360,000 at £25 and we were really tight with discounts. We launched at Books Etc in Charing Cross Road. I was scared out of my mind at the shenanigans at the New York launch where the scenes from the book were (practically) re-enacted. MPs tried to have it banned. The printer in the USA nearly lost a contract to print Bibles. My mum thought I'd have to go to jail. Paul Hamlyn thought it was all okay except the picture with the dog. What interests me is whether the second book will ever come and whether (as I jokingly predicted at the time) it will be about Madonna discovering God . . .

05 November 2006

Bears and things

While looking for a photo on the web I tried to remember the Edward Lear limerick about Kamchatka – and as is the way took a detour into Edward Lear sites and found this marvellously comprehensive one. It's corny I know but ain't the web wonderful for rediscovering forgotten treasues? Here's the limerick in question.

There was an Old Man of Kamschatka,
Who possessed a remarkable fat cur;
His gait and his waddle
Were held as a model
To all the fat dogs in Kamschatka.

Just in case I might be considered too frivolous for a Sunday here are some sobering statistics about public libraries in England between 1995/6 and 2004/5 (the latest audited year). Total gross expenditure on libraries rose from £603 million to £1021 million. The proportion spent on books fell from a miserable 11.56% to a disastrous and reprehensible 7.37%. You can find more, much more, on this issue at the Good Library Blog.

While this blog has been in existence one of the most opinionated commenters has been an independent (in business and in spirit) retailer, Clive Keeble. Essentially he gruntles on about Amazon, supermarkets, publishers' terms, unfairness, stupidity of publishers, despicability of corporates etc. It is with immense pleasure therefore that he made the following positive comment about one of our books a couple of days ago. This means more to me than any review in the Times Literary Supplement in spite of the predictable sting in the tail.

'The book is very well designed and hopefully will succeed in helping to make science an appealing subject to the younger generation : hopefully – speaking as an indie shopkeeper – the corporates will resist the temptation to heavily discount the title.'

Corpspeak

Luke Johnson is Chairman of Britain's most innovative TV station, Channel 4. He has also been involved in the restaurant trade (Belgo, Pizza Express etc) and a number of other businesses. But I know him only though his weekly 'Maverick' column in The Sunday Telegraph. He has written on publishing in the past (and with some insights) but yesterday he wrote a rough guide to corporate language. One of the commenters to this blog pointed me to a videocast of Dick Harrington of Thomson explaining why they have decided to sell Thomson Learning. It contains quite a lot of corporate language but not as insightful as this selection from Luke Johnson's corporo-lexicographic database. I do hope that you might like to add your own gems.

Safety droids – tedious Health and Safety managers who go around highlighting the tiniest risks.

Melpew – the language of the fast-food industry – a contraction of the phrase – Can I help you?

Elephant Man strategy – a scheme simply too scary to back even if it sounds incredibly exciting. The Channel Tunnel is an example.

Moonshine shop – the research and development department.

Bobbleheading – mass nodding by staff in a meeting at a remark by the boss that no-one understands.

Greenwash – a company that touts its environmental credentials to deflect attention from other, less attractive aspects of its operations.

I must go. I have a blamestorming meeting to attend.

Back from the meeting where I was reminded that our very own new word dictionary for the 21st century, From al desko to zorbing is out any day now – al desko means eating lunch in the office and zorbing is a thrills and spills extreme sport which I'd rather never experience.

Wind of change

A fortnight ago an important publisher, Charles Clark, died. He worked at Sweet and Maxwell (now part of Thomson Legal and Regulatory), at Penguin (where he was among other things MD of Penguin Education, now part of Pearson Education), at Hutchinson (which has no website presence but nestles within Random House UK) and for the Publishers Association where he was legal consultant. He was the keeper of the flame of copyright and was 'theological' in its defence. He was also very generous and a mover and shaker in all matters of general book trade importance. He was part of a fast disappearing generation of all-round publishers which has been replaced by specialists focussing on one field of publishing – education or science or literary fiction or children's books. I suspect the new structures are more efficient and more profitable but they do leave a gap for cross-trade issues – and copyright is the foremost one.

So change is all around us and three events this week and one historical one illustrate it.

This evening at the Royal Society is the Autumn Reception of the Academic and Professional Division of the PA (whose website is going to undergo a serious overhaul in the New Year). The guest of honour is the British politician, writer and editor Boris Johnson and there will be representatives from government, higher education, academia, research funding bodies, research councils and the library world. The conversation will be all about digital delivery – not whether or why or how but what are the next steps? Change is accepted and welcomed albeit with some trepidation and some very real concerns.

Tomorrow sees the retirement dinner for the CEO of HMV, the Reading FC supporter and former MD of Waterstones (and several other jobs in book retailing), Alan Giles. I can't say I've always agreed with Alan, not least over the takeover of Ottakars by HMV but he's always been a supporter of bookshops and of book sales in the UK and always straight. Yet another change for the 'traditional' book trade.

On Thursday there is the launch of the Booksellers Association Digitisation of Content report. I guess it will address the role of the traditional bookseller in a digital world, how they can participate, what are the threats and what are the opportunities. Unlike the PA meeting there is still a sense of resistance to change and deep fear for the future. However, the BA and some enlightened retailers are investing in understanding more and finding new business models and ways to continue to serve their customers.

All this change reminds me of Macmillan's heritage and in particular Harold Macmillan's famous speech to MPs in the Houses of Parliament in South Africa. If you do nothing else today spend five minutes listening to what he had to say – it's brilliant, compassionate and still relevant.

08 November 2006

Alan Maclean

I promised a fuller tribute to the great publisher and person, Alan Maclean. Our archivist, Alysoun Sanders, has written this piece with links to some of the obituaries.

Alan Maclean, who died last month, aged 81, is well remembered by colleagues and others in the publishing world for his kindness, his wit, his charm and courtesy as well as for his positive influence on the success of Macmillan during the 30 years he worked for the company.

Alan started at Macmillan in 1954, when Dan Macmillan ('Mr Dan') was Chairman of the company and the Macmillan building in St Martin's St was, as he described it, a 'rabbit warren of offices, some with clerks crouched on high stools at tall ledger desks'. During Alan's distinguished career at Macmillan he was a Director of both Macmillan & Pan Books. In 1965 he married Robin Empson, who had been his secretary. When he retired in 1984 he was credited with having a great influence on the building up of the firm.

Some of his accounts of this time, which were renowned for making old hands weak with laughter, are recorded in his book of reminiscences published in 1997: No, I tell a lie, it was the Tuesday – a title devised during an editorial meeting in the 1970s as a suitable title for an outstandingly boring autobiography. His is anything but. Instead it brings life to this period of the company's history, much of which was under the leadership of Harold Macmillan.

Colleagues have spoken of his capacity for building devoted and lasting friendships. His authors, who included many great writers of the twentieth century, became great friends and the friendship never wavered whatever their latest offering. C P Snow, Frank Tuohy, Muriel Spark, Jane Duncan, John Wain, Barbara Pym, Lilian Hellman and many others, valued him for his wisdom, humour and integrity. His opinion on editorial & publishing matters was often sought, even after he retired, by Margaret Laurence and others and he became literary executor to Rebecca West.

Fuller tributes can be found in the obituaries in The Times, The Telegraph, The Guardian and The Independent whose archive is unavailable to non-payers but who published an excellent piece by my former boss and mentor, Robin Denniston and by Robin Baird Smith, and from which I've extracted some quotes:

Robin first met him after he had been 'shooed out of the Foreign Office' . . . and rescued by Billy Collins and went to work in the Glasgow factory as assistant to the deputy Chairman. Robin was a trainee there. The 'two poor Englanders' were thrown together and used to eat heavy and boozy high teas with each other at his landlady's residence.

'Muriel Spark called him 'the best-liked editor in London"

'He became famous as an excellent editor – not only of Muriel Spark, but of Lillian Hellman, Rebecca West, CP Snow, Pamela Hansford Johnson and Joyce Grenfell. He was the heart and soul of Macmillan London, a much older and more prestigious firm than Collins, and became the favourite of 'Mr Dan', the elder brother of 'Mr Harold'. ..

'He was a truly friendly, delightful and deeply good man'

Robin Baird Smith says that it was thanks to him that he became a publisher.

'He was the last of a breed of publisher, now extinct, best described as the equivalent of the actor manager: At the heart of his personality and energy was a passionate editor of the old school. He acted on instinct and hunch, excelled at spotting new talent and kept accountants at bay. Unusually for the manager of a large publishing house, he made the people who worked for him happy. And this was his avowed intention.'

'Maclean knew talent when he saw it and backed it with relentless energy'

'His authors loved him dearly and he shared their lives'

But it is amongst his colleagues that he will be remembered as a splendid person to work with, and as a shoulder to lean on, for his ability to smile at life with a wry but affectionate air as well as his patience, and his self-deprecatory humour. He was a charming man who will go down in Macmillan folklore.

🗓 09 November 2006

More change

I was meant to be in Bangalore this week for a board meeting of the Wisden Group but had to be in autumnal London instead. The reason for the Bangalore meeting was that Wisden has moved its Cricinfo headquarters and its group CEO, Tom Gleeson, there. EFY Times, The Hindu and various other newspapers covered the event. There are few things more English than Wisden and yet the move is completely logical. Market size, enthusiasm for the game, availability of high-quality, committed and techno-savvy people make the move exciting and inevitable. Fortunately the Almanack itself will continue to be edited by the English Matthew Engel, published by the English John Wisden & Co, printed in England by the English Richard Clay and sold to the UK book trade by the very English A&C Black sales team. Plus c'est la meme chose, plus ca change.

Last night I attended a wonderful farewell dinner for Alan Giles who is retiring from being CEO of the HMV Group which owns Waterstone's bookshop chain.

The great and the good (and some of the not so good) were all there to wish Alan well. In spite of various fracas over central buying, demands for ever greater discounts from booksellers, the takeover of Ottakar's Alan was always forthright, professional and a pleasure to argue with. He leaves the chain in much better shape than he found it and with a top-class management team to take it forward. There is a real place for high-quality bricks, mortar and web book retailers in the UK and Waterstone's is in prime position.

Walking to the event in the Waterstone's flagship Piccadilly store I heard a news item on my portable radio about a group of scientists who have mentioned to return sight to blind mice. I was delighted that the scientists had decided to publish their ground-breaking results in the very best place.

🗓 10 November 2006

Brave New World

Yesterday evening I tramped down to the hideous building housing the UK Government's Department of Trade and Industry.

The event was the launch of the Booksellers Association report on the digitisation of content, Brave New World. We had speeeches from the team who put together the report; from David Roche, President of the BA, CEO of Borders UK (whose website didn't work this morning, hence no link) and book trade personality of the year 2005; and from Victoria Barnsley, CEO of HarperCollins whose 'business' website is extremely helpful to professionals in the book trade and which links (rather quietly I thought) to 'consumer' sites.

The theme was that booksellers as well as publishers need to engage in the 'digital' revolution and that authors and publishers should facilitate a process of partnership.Everyone was saying the right things and the report itself is absolutely excellent and a credit to the BA and its authors. But nice words butter no parsnips. Here's my threepenny's worth.

1. Authors and authors' agents and societies need to trust publishers to protect and manage their copyrights in the digital age. There will be disagreements about rights and terms and consent and permissions and it is understandable that authors wish to have guarantees of protection and remuneration. However, if publishers don't act with speed and decisiveness there may be little future for paid-for content on the web. Delaying implementation while the minutiae of every author's contract are debated at a collective and individual level simply won't work. Digital sales are analogues of print sales and should be covered by existing contracts as far as possible.

2. Retailers need to invest in risk-taking. I don't think anyone knows what the future holds for electronic books but if bookshops wish to be viewed as the trusted source for literature and information they need to demonstrate that in their stores. They also need to negotiate terms with publishers which reflect the new reality rather than the former stock-holding and capital intensive past.

3. Publishers need to invest in a digital infrastructure for their books. We are building BookStore for ourselves and all publishers who wish to join. The working prototype was demonstrated at the Frankfurt Book Fair a month ago and literally scores of publishers have contacted us to discuss implementation in more detail. The first two Macmillan digital 'bookstores' to go live in January 2007 will be Macmillan Science and Macmillan New Writing. We shall be wanting to work with retailers, wholesalers, search engines to ensure that our authors' work is given the maximum possibility of selling in any format.

For the whole book trade I think the time has come to stop writing strategy reviews and planning systems. The time has come to invest, act, experiment and learn from the real world of publishing and selling.

11 November 2006

The Plimsoll Sensation

In the world of three for twos and micro-celebrity cut-and-paste instant books one category of publishing in particular is being punished. It is the serious work of non-fiction thoroughly researched, well-written and aimed at the general reader as well as the scholar.

Of course there are exceptions such as Norman Davies's recently published Europe at War which will undoubtedly set the tills ringing in the run-up to Christmas but is, as ever with Davies, a monumental work of scholarship as well as a rattling good read.

A more typical example of the genre is The Plimsoll Sensation by Nicolette Jones, the writer and freelance journalist. I have no idea how many copies Little Brown have sold to date in the UK (and no doubt they'll let us know in due course) but I'm sure it hasn't been easy to persuade bookshops to stock more than a token number. However the reviews have been spectacular and yesterday it won the Mountbatten Maritime Prize. It will go on to win more prizes and more great reviews because it is quite simply a fascinating book about a fascinating guy in a fascinating period of history. Amazon will no doubt continue to sell the book well but traditional booksellers will probably have already cleared their shelves for the next batch of 'sure-fire bestsellers'.

I'm beginning to sound like a grumpy old bookman, so I'd better sign off.

PS I was very pleased to link the Plimsoll Sensation to an excellent non-Amazon Internet History Bookshop. Offering a good service with specialist knowledge works as well on the web as it does in a traditional retail environment. I hope they succeed.

🐦 13 November 2006

Christmas is beginning

Great news this morning from Nielsen BookScan in Australia, the top five highest new entries in the Australian bestseller charts are all from Pan Macmillan and not a celebrity biography in sight:

1	The Great War	Les Carlyon	Macmillan	$55.00
2	The Valley	Di Morrissey	Macmillan	$32.95
3	The Unknown Terrorist	Richard Flanagan	Picador	$32.95
4	Circle of Flight	John Marsden	Macmillan	$29.95
5	Not Quite Ripe	Debra Byrne	Macmillan	$35.00

And we've got plenty more still to come. It should be a vintage year.

An interesting development in blogland and Wolves by Emily Gravett has been nominated already:

Bloggers Start Children's Awards

When a group of children's book bloggers got fed up with the lack of awards that recognized both a book's merit and popularity, they decided to make up an award themselves. Called the Cybils (which loosely translates to Children's and YA Bloggers' Literary Awards), the awards will be given out in eight categories (fantasy and science fiction, fiction picture books, nonfiction picture books, middle grade fiction, YA fiction, middle grade and YA nonfiction, poetry and graphic novels). The rules state that anyone can nominate a book, as long as it was published in English in 2006. The nominations close on November 20. After that time, a panel of bloggers with expertise in particular categories will bring that list down to five finalists. Once that list is compiled, judges (people such as librarians, teachers, homeschoolers, authors, illustrators and parents) will decide who wins. For more information about the awards and to nominate your favorite titles, click here.

🐦 14 November 2006

Crime and punishment

The British Government Home Office has issued a consultation paper. The purpose is to generate a debate about the issue of whether criminals should be able to profit from their crimes by selling their memoirs or similar. Macmillan has been involved in at least two books where this issue was raised. In 1999 we published Gitta Sereny's Cries Unheard, the story of the child murderer Mary Bell. There was outrage that Mary Bell might have received financial support from the author. More recently we published Jeffrey Archer's Prison Diary where the author donated the income from newspaper serialisation to a range of charities.

The publishing industry has been invited to comment on the proposals and Macmillan will be responding in detail by the deadline in February. I don't believe there is any attempt here to gag authors:

'The proposals are targeted only at the profit made by criminals from publications about their crimes. They are not targeted at anyone else's profits from such publications or at publishers and are not intended to prevent publications relating to serious crimes.'

However, there are bound to be varied responses to the proposals and it would be helpful to have people's views both from within Macmillan and elsewhere. I suppose Nelson Mandela's Long Walk to Freedom was written in prison and he earned money from it. Some people would regard George Bush's invasion of Iraq as criminal. Should he be banned from selling his memoirs? I sense an interesting debate in the offing.

Two scientific events today. I'm chairing a workshop this afternoon on the future of scientific research publishing. We have an opportunity to debate the direction of this vital industry with the benefit of a mass of hard data rather than soft prejudices.

Then to the other end of scientific publishing for the launch of Giant Leaps at the Science Museum in collaboration with The Sun newspaper. The marketing Director for this book, Tony Blair (who, incidentally, I've never met), has given us the following quote:

'I know better than most people how vitally important science is for our future, prosperity and quality of life. And it is getting more important by the day. So I wish I had paid more attention to science subjects at school. I have been trying to catch up since. I also wish there had been a book like this to awaken my interest in science and make me want to find out more.'

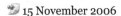 15 November 2006

Memoirs of a foxhunting man

Last year the British Parliament had two major items to debate – the war in Iraq and whether or not fox-hunting should be banned. The war continues and so does fox-hunting but the latter is now a crime. Yesterday's blog was about the latest parliamentary effort to prevent criminals profiting from writing books about their crime and there have been a couple of interesting comments. If this law is passed Siegfried Sassoon would not have been allowed to publish Memoirs of a fox-hunting man – not to mention the implied sexism in the title. Tim Howles (t.howles@macmillan.co.uk) is collecting views for our submission and I'd like people in Macmillan as a whole to let him (and this blog) know what they think.

In the euphoria of the 2005 Ashes victory, I rashly invested half my winnings (A$500) in a bet on England to retain them in the 2006/7 campaign in Australia. It seems that our captain won't be fit until at least the third match, our swing bowler is out altogether and now our star opening batsman has gone home suffering from depression. My investment looks extremely dodgy and the only description for me is whingeing pom.

I received yesterday an email invitation to a Christmas party. At the bottom was the following paragraph which seemed somewhat inappropriate (but probably legally quite sensible):

Any term contained in this email is intended solely as a basis for further discussion and is not intended to be and does not constitute a legally binding obligation. No legally binding obligations will be created, implied or inferred until a definitive agreement in final form is executed in writing and delivered by both parties. Without limiting the generality of the foregoing, the parties intend that there shall be no obligations based on such things as parol evidence, extended negotiations, oral understandings or courses of conduct (including without limitation reliance and changes of position).

16 November 2006

Three book people and a coincidence

I did a spell (approximately 1979-84) as head of reference publishing at Oxford University Press. Whenever I had what I thought was a brilliant new idea for marketing reference books someone would mutter (often under their breath) 'Tony Pocock tried that and it didn't work' or 'We've been doing that ever since Tony Pocock thought of it'. Tony Pocock was at that point sales and marketing director at Faber and teaching us lessons from afar. He died some three years ago and was rightly much lauded in obituaries for all he did to shake up the book trade.

In 1993 (when I was with the no-longer existing Reed International Books) I put out my back and was consigned to lying prone in bed. I was bored. Even reading a book was uncomfortable. I thought I might, however, be capable of picking up and reading individual pages of a typescript and the office duly sent over a recently-arrived manuscript destined to be published by Secker and Warburg. We had published this author's first three books to critical acclaim but disappointing sales and we were sitting on some quite large unearned advances. As I worked my way page by page through the manuscript I was impelled to ring the agent and ask if we could sign a contract for the author's next book at double the advance on the one I was reading – a very uncharacteristic move. I then shuffled off to the local bookmaker and tried to place £100 on this book to win the Booker prize – the bookie wouldn't accept the bet. He smelt a rat. The book didn't win the Booker but Louis de Bernieres and Captain Corelli's Mandolin went on to become global literary phenomena.

The third book person is John Suchet. He has been a TV journalist for most of his career and and my parents and his were close friends and we've stayed in touch over the years. John is proud of his journalistic career but I suspect he is even prouder of what he's achieved in writing books about his passion, Beethoven. The books are definitely not scholarly and they're not intended to be, but in a strange way they are more insightful than the most detailed scholarship.

The reason they're all featuring here today is that I've just discovered a common thread – they and I were all at the same dismal and tiny boarding school (Grenham House) in Birchington-on-Sea in our formative years (9-13) at different times. I can't remember literature being high on the agenda but maybe homesickness, freezing swims, sadistic teachers and meagre and disgusting meals encouraged us all into the book trade.

Picador Africa

In 2004 we launched the first Picador Africa titles. Last week we launched what will become our biggest selling title to date and I asked Terry Morris, Managing Director of Pan Macmillan South Africa, to write about it.

'Over three years ago, together with Picador UK, we contracted to publish *When a crocodile eats the sun* by Peter Godwin author of *Mukiwa*. The proposal was extremely powerful and on the basis of twenty pages we advanced the most we've ever done for the Southern African rights for a book. The manuscript was finally delivered and in October this year we released the book in this country under our Picador Africa imprint.

Quaking in our boots, the enormous print-run arrived in our warehouse and the author on our shores from Manhattan. The book has received an overwhelming response, not only from the media but from readers who have e-mailed us to tell us what an important book this has been for them. The Johannesburg and Cape Town launches were filled to capacity and the book has hit the number two spot on the best-seller charts this week (behind Screw it, let's do it it by Sir Richard Branson). It's been a privilege to publish this book in South Africa.

An excerpt from a reader:

I have just finished 'When a Crocodile Eats the Sun' . . . . .It is the most beautifully written, poignant book I have ever read. I finished it at 3am yesterday and promptly bought 3 copies to forward to colleagues this morning. More will follow for Christmas presents. I thank you for reaching me as you did. No doubt you will reach many more. I hope it sells out many times over.

Watch out Richard Branson – we're ready for the number one spot!'

Bloginfo

A main purpose of this blog from my selfish point of view is to learn how to generate traffic from the blogosphere by testing theories and then measuring results. A little while ago I was disappointed that having a title containing the names Paris Hilton and Jeffrey Archer didn't seem to have any impact. On the other hand, recounting the story of the Oxford poker school resulted in a 35% uplift in traffic mainly from gambling sites. More recently I blogged about an excellent mushroom book – its position on the Amazon bestseller list rose from 347 to 71 but it may be that the blog and the sales increase coincided with the beginning of the UK mushroom season. Apart from crude visitor numbers I also monitor the routes people have followed to reach this blog. The bulk come from links from other websites and blogs, quite a few from searches for charkin or charkinblog, but the most interesting ones are those referred from search engines where you can see what people were searching for. Here are some of the searches this morning (excluding the charkins etc). I rather feel most of them will have been disappointed when they got here.

John Marsden

Copies sold inheritance of loss

The great war

Not quite ripe

Dutch rugby association

Schappelle Corby

Yes but is it good for the jews

Waterstones returns

Racist jelly babies

Farewell speeches online

On the publishing side the big news of the day was of course the takeover of Blackwell Publishing by John Wiley for £572m. It is an indication of how times have changed that the bookshops have declined while publishing has dramatically increased in value over the last ten or twenty years. When I started Blackwell was principally a retailing name. I do hope that some of the profits from this sale might be ploughed into rebuilding Blackwells Bookshops as the leading college bookstore chain in the UK. It can and should be done.

And finally a sad moment. Sheldon Meyer of OUP USA died last week. I leave to others tributes about his great editorial skills. I'll remember him for giant dry martinis at lunchtime and for commenting when he received his honorary MA at Oxford that it was thoughtful of them to name the Theatre after him.

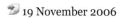 19 November 2006

Murder must advertise

I've done a couple of blogs about the British Government's efforts to stop criminals earning money from publishing books about their crimes. There have been good comments in from various people (disappointingly few from Macmillan employees) mainly politely (or impolitely) telling the Government not to interfere. The dangers of legislation would almost certainly exceed any potential benefits. The risks of unintended censorship and reduction of freedom of speech are inherent in any such legislation.

However, the case of O. J. Simpson's latest efforts highlights another angle. Maxim Jakubowski in his Guardian blog argues that booksellers should refuse to sell Simpson's book (which evidently tells the story of how he would have committed the double murder but which, of course, he did not). Maxim is owner of Murder One which is London's leading crime bookshop and he knows a thing or two about true crime and criminals (not personally you understand). Now, I'm not sure that any sort of censorship is appropriate but the irony of this case is that, under the proposed legislation, O. J. Simpson would fall outside the recommendations because he was found not guilty of the crime.

Regan Books (part of HarperCollins USA) are publishing If I Did It in the USA but HarperCollins UK say they will not. Presumably the UK were offered the rights and declined on grounds of taste. Certainly the only Simpsons mentioned on the UK site are Bart and his family (presumably no relation). I'm sure that both Maxim and HarperCollins UK will sleep more soundly for not being involved but censorship . . . ?

🔖 20 November 2006

Courtney Love and Lisa Scottoline

I see from my calendar that the Picador publicity department is organising events for this week's visit to the UK of rock legend Courtney Love whose 'official' site doesn't seem to have been updated since 1975. So maybe better to check out the Wikipedia entry which reminds me that she has been described as 'the most controversial woman in the history of rock.' That's quite a reputation to live up to – what about Marianne Faithfull?

Picador has published Dirty Blonde and it's attracting enormous media coverage. If you want to meet Courtney in person she'll be signing copies at Watersone's in Piccadilly on Friday at 6pm. In addition do have a look at this poignant extract.

By an extraordinary coincidence another Macmillan author, Lisa Scottoline, has also published Dirty Blonde in September. There is of course no copyright in the title of a book and I don't suppose there could be much confusion – except in our order processing department. I'll be tracking the sales of both these titles to see whether they each help sell the other and to see which one wins in the long run.

On a commercial note you may be interested to know that our earnings from Google ads on this blog has now reached the dizzying heights of $65.44. However, the money is not remitted until we reach $100 – get clicking on those ads.

And for a bit of literary reviewing shenanigans I commend Susan Hill's blog today.

🔖 21 November 2006

Per Saugman vs Ken Livingstone

John Wiley's takeover of Blackwell Publishing has already generated much speculation about what it means for scholarly publishing. Will it stimulate further consolidation (a renewal of the Springer and Informa deal)? What are the implications for the open access movement? What does it mean for the two bsuinesses? The main impact for me is to remind me of the importance of exceptional people in publishing.

Per Saugman was not the founder of Blackwell Scientific Publishing but he joined in 1952 when sales were £27,000 and retired in 1990 when sales were £27,000,000. And it wasn't just the sales increase. He created a business and published great books, launched important journals, made the STM organisation relevant, hired and trained the very best publishing managers, and entertained and educated the medical publishing community.

I remember one day I was pitching to take over publication of an important society journal. On the way to make the pitch I ran into Bob Maxwell who had been bidding on behalf of Pergamon Press. On the way out I ran into Per Saugman pitching for Blackwell. I was in my twenties and duly overawed by competing with these two heavyweights. Sure enough I didn't win the contract. I was told by the society that I'd come second. They had eliminated Maxwell when he'd threatened to sue them if they didn't choose Pergamon. They'd liked my proposal very much but Blackwells won because Per had sent them a hand-delivered letter immediately after the meeting confirming in writing everything that had been discussed thus proving both his efficiency and his probity. A very important lesson for a young editor.

Ken Livingstone, the Mayor of London, has become a publisher too. Another free newspaper dropped through my letterbox. It's The Londoner and it is absolute rubbish.

After a bit of badgering I've discovered that each issue costs £288,000. I'm still trying to establish whether that is the full cost, including overheads and distribution, and how many issues are planned each year. The reason for the questions is that I am paying for this newspaper through taxation and the newspaper is totally dedicated to the glorification of the politician who happens to be its publisher. It's too much like the old Soviet Union. I cannot imagine the amount of paper wasted in producing enough copies for delivery to every household in London. Why not ask the great Ken if he would focus on being Mayor rather than wallowing in self-aggrandisement paid for by the citizens of London. His email is mayor@london.gov.uk.

23 November 2006

Public libraries chapter 94

The activities of a number of key people in the UK book trade have raised the profile of public library management issues in the UK.

The debate is complicated with conflicting statistics being bandied about, insults flying, platitudes being uttered and tempers being frayed. I honestly believe all the parties want to ensure the existence of a healthy library service but more effort is being expended on analysis, argument and preening than on action. While this is going on there was an announcement yesterday about library closures in Devon. Interestingly the search page had prior news stories – 'Library visitor numbers increase', 'Library improvements considered' etc. Ha! In response, the authority has closed five libraries. And here's an extract about Hampshire libraries:

A third of librarians could be axed in Hampshire as library chiefs battle against a huge overspend. Hampshire County Council will ask for voluntary redundancies in the next two weeks to help save costs. And it is holding back £250,000 from its £2m book fund – meaning there will be no new books at libraries across the county until at least February.

I wish the civil servants, politicians and even the consultants who might be able to make a difference would own up to the problem, cease quarrelling and STOP THE ROT. Libraries which close do not reopen. Libraries which do not buy new books neither attract visitors nor fulfil their duty to society.

For more information on this and more go to the Good Library blog.

If I did it cover

The controversy which we discussed last week was subdued by Rupert Murdoch's intervention although I'm not sure there was any resolution of the principles being debated.

I am adding a new blog to the blogroll. It is by Martyn Daniels and is hosted by the Booksellers Association. I am sure it will be interesting. In yesterday's entry he discusses the fairness or otherwise of royalties payable on digital delivery of books. It is at present a purely hypothetical issue but we are establishing the ground rules for the future which makes it important.

'If artists hold back on digital rights and publishers don't equitably share the potential increased margin they potentially hold back the creation of the market which after all can't be built in a vacuum.'

The problem is that no 'artist' or publisher has ever believed that he or she is receiving a fair share. I remember a high-level meeting about this issue where we (publishers) presented what we considered to be a very generous offer including a first principle that whatever happened in the future 'the author should not be disadvantaged financially'. This principle was immediately rejected as being unfair to authors. This argument will run and run.

25 November 2006

Saturday meanderings

Publishing News has a regular slot for strange book titles. Yesterday's one seemed appropriate – How You Can Bowl Better Using Self-hypnosis. I wish, I wish that the England cricket management had issued our team with copies. For a concentrated precis of the humiliation so far treat yourself to this scorecard.

Extraordinary scenes at Waterstone's Piccadilly last night where fans had queued to buy signed copies of Dirty Blonde by the previously-blogged Courtney Love. In spite of her reputation (or maybe because of it) she was utterly professional and took real trouble to talk to fans and to answer questions intelligently and honestly. She has undertaken a huge amount of promotion this week and this BBC link only shows a fraction of the media exposure. What is more, the book is a treasure.

Bondomania is rife since the release of Casino Royale. Who knows what the film's box-office takings. At a much lower level I was delighted to see an advance copy of our Casino Royale specially adapted (and with audio CDs) for learners of English. It's part of our Macmillan Readers which has annual sales of millions of copies and which has helped enhance literacy and English speaking throughout the world. I remember reading Casino Royale (illegally) under the bedclothes at boarding school. It's great to know the tradition continues.

📷 26 November 2006

God of small things

Getting it right is as much about many small things as grand strategies. I probably irritate the hell out of colleagues with messages about apparently trivial matters.

A little while ago I did a presentation on the technological changes which have affected the dictionary business – relational databases, XML, on-line and CD delivery, voice recognition, corpus searching etc. I had picked up a small Langenscheidt dictionary as a prop and realised that the single most important advance from a casual user point of view was none of these things. It was the rounding of the corners of the plastic cover so that you didn't suffer cuts from the sharp edges. A small matter in some ways but a significant publishing decision.

One of the most important devices which has enabled the web to develop is the stapler. Imagine the chaos if we didn't staple documents printed from the web.

Keiko Oikawa

David Loftus

Similarly I've just been given a brilliant new cookbook, A year in my kitchen by Skye Gingell who is head chef at Petersham Nurseries. You can find some recipes from the book here but you might also buy the book. I have yet to test the recipes myself but I assume they all work. The design of the book is great as one would expect from

Quadrille Publishing. But what really struck me was that the book has three silk bookmarks so that one can index three recipes (starter, main, dessert presumably) simultaneously. Clever.

David Loftus

And finally a novelist who is steadily moving up the charts – C. J. Sansom. Winter in Madrid is just out in paperback – start there and then work your way back through the rest of his historical novels. The 'small thing' here is that his success has been

achieved by long-term editorial commitment and attention to to every detail of his publication. The 'big thing' of course is that C.J. can write and entertain.

On leadership

I've been reading proofs of a book close to my heart. It's called Beyond authority and was commissioned by the business editor at Palgrave Macmillan, Stephen Rutt. It is written by a brilliant leader, Julia Middleton, the CEO of Common Purpose (of whose UK trustees I am chair). You can hear and watch Julia talking about the book at the Meet the author website.

The book is about the real-life situations where leadership, reporting lines, ability to command or control simply don't exist. We may think we have authority but the truth is that rarely, if ever, is that the case. Traditional management theories relate to a world which doesn't exist, where organograms actually reflect power lines, where job titles are thought to reflect reality and so on. To lead successfully in the real world we all have to use other techniques – of influence, of example. of understanding, of belief but rarely of diktat.

I strongly recommend the book but the reason for mentioning it is that I'm recovering from the humiliation of both England's rugby and cricket teams' defeats over the weekend. In recent times both were triumphant. They are well funded, well trained, talented, committed. The main thing that has changed in both cases is the leadership. The captains of the teams are great players and great people but somehow they're leading losing teams. Perhaps I should send them (or more likely their successors) copies of Julia's book when it comes out in February.

27 November 2006

Hail to Rita

This is a plug. In the office this morning before leaving for New York I tore my trousers. Staples could only hold the seat together on a very temporary basis. Arrived at Heathrow Terminal 4 just in time to buy a new pair.

Went to the first shop (after deliberately avoiding Harrod's)to catch my eye, Hackett. Rita Vittorio (who has worked for Hackett for eight years) served me and rapidly found some appropriate corduroys. Unfortunately they were too long in the leg and there was no way I could find time or tailors in NY to fix them. Without hesitation and with a great smile she pulled out some needle and thread and shortened them on the spot. I'm posting this in the hope that Hackett realize that Rita is the tops at customer service; that the sort of thing she did makes a company great and profitable; and that they reward her.

If she is typical of Hackett employees then they deserve as much business as possible and I'll certainly be buying trousers there next time I have a similar disaster!

28 November 2006

New York

This comes to you from the offices of Scientific American on Madison Avenue.

'SciAm' has been part of the Holtzbrinck group since the 1980s and has grown every year since. The big challenges now are to maintain our print subscribers and advertisers while building for an Internet future. Fortunately, wherever technology leads editorial standards will drive reader loyalty and we have the best editorial team around – unsurprising perhaps given that SciAm is the world's leading scientific magazine for the general reader.

Apart from publishing every month SciAm is also involved in major awards such as SA 50 (for the 50 researchers, businesses and policy leaders who have made a difference) and the Weizmann Women and Science award won by Dr May Berenbaum pictured here (centre – n.b. British spelling).

And I've been reminded to mention the fast-growing magazine <u>Scientific American Mind</u>. More on New York and other things later.

🐦 29 November 2006

PEN at the ready, fingers on buzzers – it's quiz time

As Richard is currently laptop-less in New York, so has asked me to post about the Pan Macmillan effort at the annual PEN Quiz on Monday night.

For those of you that don't know, <u>PEN</u> is an international organisation which 'exists to promote friendship and intellectual co-operation among writers everywhere, to fight for freedom of expression and represent the conscience of world literature.' The fundraising quiz was organised by <u>Jonathan Heawood</u>, the director of <u>English PEN</u>, who, as always, did a wonderful job. The great and the good of the media and publishing worlds made up 36 teams, and rolled up to the Cafe Royal in Piccadilly to do battle. The teams included delagations from <u>The Times</u>, <u>The Mail on Sunday</u>, <u>Daily Mail</u>, <u>Daily Telegraph</u>, <u>Hodder</u>, <u>Penguin</u>, <u>Faber</u>, <u>Orion</u> and <u>Random House</u>. Quiz 'mistress' for the night was <u>Mariella Frostrup</u>, whilst the not so dulcet tones of <u>Piers Morgan</u> were employed for the raffle.

To properly set the scene, I should mention that <u>Pan Macmillan</u> were the winners of last year's quiz, in a tense tie-break situation. So, our reputation was on the line, and it was with some relief that we came in at third place, after <u>HarperCollins</u>, and quiz sponsors, <u>Colman Getty PR</u>. Those of us with a sweet tooth were particularly delighted with the third place result, as the prize was a box of luxury chocolates from <u>Hotel Chocolat</u>.

Congrats to all the Pan Mac team, which consisted of Booker-winning author <u>Alan Hollinghurst</u>, <u>William Fiennes</u> (author of <u>The Snow Geese</u>), <u>Tim Dowling</u> (author of The Giles Wareing Haters' Club, which Picador will publish next June), Tim Adams (Observer journalist and future Picador author, and James Walton, who won the tie-break for the team <u>last year</u>. There was some controversy at the time, with shouts of 'Ringer' flying about the place, but for the information of those who might wonder about the connection, he is the cousin of our Deputy Picador Publisher, Ursula Doyle.

In house team members were Richard Milner (team captain), Andrew Kidd, Camilla Elworthy, Ursula Doyle and Emma Giacon. Can't wait till next year . . . !

🦆 30 November 2006

The Business Press for the World

When you're wide awake at 3am in a New York hotel you tend to review the previous day's work. I and a number of colleagues spent the whole day in a meeting room in the wonderful and refurbished (thank goodness) Flatiron Building at board meetings of the various Holtzbrinck USA companies – St Martin's Press, Henry Holt, Farrar Straus Giroux, Picador, Tor, Audio Renaissance, Bedford, Freeman, Worth and others. It was an awesome display of American publishing and innovation. Although each of the businesses is independent and follows its own editorial and market development there were some common themes. Technology. The need for continuous improvement in quality and efficiency. Flexibility and the ability to move fast. Price pressures. The absolute requirement for growth. The size and vitality of the US market make it a world to itself. At the end of it I was completely shattered!

Of course, the business of America is business but it's not a monopoly. Europe, through business schools like INSEAD, is fighting back. Steve Rutt writes about our latest initiative.

INSEAD Business Press is a partnership between INSEAD, one of the world's leading business schools and Palgrave Macmillan. The combination represents a dream ticket with significant global reach and has the ambition to publish high quality, innovative and influential books that will inform debates for people in business and at business and management schools worldwide.

INSEAD was founded in 1957 in the Forest of Fontainebleau, not far from the famous chateau and has established itself around a unique global perspective and multicultural diversity that is reflected in research and teaching with two main campuses at Fontainebleau in France and Singapore in Asia.

There has been significant collaboration between INSEAD and Palgrave Macmillan on a number of projects including the INSEAD story, 'INSEAD: From Intuition to Institution by Jean-Louis Barsoux;

INSEAD Business Press represents a new level of partnership with the first three books on topical and compelling subjects, 'Service is Front Stage' by James Teboul, 'The Marking Enterprise' by Jean-Claude Thoenig and Charles Waldman and 'Mergers: Leadership, Performance and Corporate Health' by David Fubini, Colin Price and Maurizio Zollo.

Spring 2007 will see a new book by one of Europe's leading business gurus, Manfed Kets de Vries

and his team at the INSEAD Global Leadership Centre 'Coach or Couch: The Psychology of Making Better Leaders'

In a world with many business and management books the unique positioning of INSEAD Business Press is for rigorous yet accessible, perhaps bringing to mind the words of Albert Einstein:

'Everything should be made as simple as possible, but not simpler'

Charchive

< **December 2006** >

Mon	Tue	Wed	Thu	Fri	Sat	Sun
27	28	29	30	1	2	3
4	5	6	7	8	9	10
11	12	13	14	15	16	17
18	19	20	21	22	23	24
25	26	27	28	29	30	31
1	2	3	4	5	6	7

River deep mountain high

Yesterday the highest number of visitors came to this blog after searching for Riverdeep or Houghton Mifflin. This is because it was announced that the former had bought the latter for $3.5 billion. I know very little about Riverdeep but HM is clearly a great publishing company with a long tradition and excellent books but it's hard to figure the commercial logic of the price. HM has changed hands several times and, apart from the doomed Vivendi escapade, sellers have made money at every turn. Presumably the private equity owners will have extracted cash and no doubt hordes of professional advisers will have sent in astronomical bills for their wisdom. But who, in the end, pays for all this? Publishing is not an easy-profit business and bookbuyers (general or educational) are not flush with cash. I wish the team good luck but I fear Riverdeep might find the mountain rather high to climb.

Yesterday afternoon I visited Nature Publishing Group's industrial-chic new offices in Varick Street in downtown Manhattan.

Skyline Windows.

The offices are brilliant and by chance I was able to participate in a meeting with a hugely important medical society. It reminded me what the business is about and I was further reminded by Jonathan Eisen's blog where he commends Nature for its foresight:

Most surprisingly to me is that a reasonable number of my papers in Nature are freely available on the Nature web site as part of their Genomics Gateway program. Nature deserves serious kudos for doing this and they stand out compared to Elsevier journals (which do not seem to ever do this) and even Science. This is disappointing as Science is published by a scientific society but apparently does not seem to care much about access to publications. Nature, a commercial publisher, is in my opinion doing more for scientific openness than Science. Now, Nature has a long way to go, but I am SO glad I listened to their editors like Chris Gunter and Tanguy Chouard who made a big deal about the Genome papers being free. I did not think it was that big a deal, but in retrospect they were ahead of me in thinking about availability. Plus Nature clearly makes more of an effort to provide free online material than they have to – and certainly make more available than Science.

Not so long ago MPS technologies had a an idea for a new product. In this world of online information librarians are rightly insisting that publishers prove that people are actually using the material being purchased. Each publisher is obliged to supply statistical information to the librarians on agreed 'Counter-compliant' criteria. The problem is that each publisher supplies the information on spreadsheets in a slightly different way and librarians were having to spend time and scarce resource aggregating the data so that they could review it sensibly. ScholarlyStats was developed to automate that process and save libraries money. And yesterday it won the Best Library Product award at the International Information Industry Awards.

🐦 02 December 2006

Another great moment in classified advertising

A new month heralds a pile of packages of sales statistics and accounts for the previous month. The speed (and efficiency)with which these are produced is increasing all the time which is necessary, but it does mean that I tend to spend the first week of every month weighed down by statistics. My personal contribution to the statistics overload is to tot up visitors to this blog. So here goes.

In November we had 63,375 visitors, 16% up on October and bringing the year-to-date tally to 339,547. I don't have the software to tell me how many of these are unique. On a particular day I guess that most are unique but of course a highish proportion of people come in more than once a month (or never again!). I can also only guess how many are Macmillan employees and what the geographical split might be. I'll see if I can borrow some software from PublisherStats to improve the reporting.

If you click on nature.com today there is a huge banner ad 'Another great moment in science'. This doesn't refer to a scientific breakthrough or another Archimedes moment and it is unlikely to feature in the next edition of Giant Leaps. However it is a major moment in the world of classified advertising.

Traditionally classifieds (or small ads) are the bread and butter of magazines' and newspapers' income. They are not glamorous like flashy ads for perfumes but they do bring in the money. It has been a rather unsophisticated business. If you sell by the word, make the typeface small. If you sell by the inch make the typeface large. It is now, predictably, a battleground on the web and it is one of the reasons that newspapers are having to revisit their business models and their strategies. Perhaps the most signficant straw in the wind was last year's sale by Rupert Murdoch of the Times Educational Supplement which lives on classified job ads.

In any event, Nature has decided to gamble on making it free to post a job on its website. This means kissing goodbye to some revenue which is always hard to do. It also means that the Nature site becomes an even more essential tool of everyday life for the working scientist, thus pulling in more readers more regularly and allowing our advertisers better results, particularly if they decide to add to the free ads with more information and more sophisticated linking. It is fingers-crossed time because such a change is not without risk but in the web world the only certainty is that non-adaptation is fatal. Here's what EPS Newsletter thought of our move:

Until last week, recruitment advertising at Nature had followed a very traditional path: jobs placed by advertisers in the print title were also viewable online at no additional charge to the advertiser. That model has now been turned on its head. NPG believes that its core strengths now lie in the online environment, and has re-evaluated its recruitment advertising model to reflect this: advertisers can now place single or multiple job ads into the naturejobs.com database free of charge.

The naturejobs.com business is now structured around an upsell model whereby added value options that increase visibility and impact are sold to customers taking a basic free listing. Advertisers placing a single or multiple job adverts on naturejobs.com for free will be contacted by a member of NPG's sales team to be upsold a range of services including contextual advertising, where job ads will be placed alongside relevant content across the nature.com platform. This means, for example, that a job in the neuroscience field would be placed alongside articles on the niche site for the Nature Neuroscience journal and next to neuroscience articles published across the nature.com platform including Nature itself.

This has proved very popular with recruiters, as it increases the audience for the job ad and attracts passive jobseekers who would not necessarily have used the naturejobs.com site. Other added value offerings include job of the week placements, highlighted jobs, and the ability to add logos to a text ad. Advertisers placing multiple jobs online will be contacted by the sales team who will try to sell them a quarter or half page print ad to ensure that they achieve the maximum benefit. Print advertisers' job ads will still be placed online, with sales teams working to upsell the online services. Other services for print advertisers include lineage ads. This will enable Nature to target advertisers with lower budgets – previously, the only print options were to purchase a quarter or a half page.

Nature is one of the strongest science brands online, through its core Nature title and associated niche journals. The nature.com platform (which encompasses all of these titles) claims 35 million page impressions per month. Competition does exist. New Scientist is strong in Europe with a global print circulation of 170,000, while Science is a key player in the US (global circulation 130,000); at 60,000, Nature's print circulation is lower than either of these.

However, online it is a different story, and Nature is a much stronger competitor. NewScientistJobs.com claims 1.4 million page impressions against Naturejobs.com's 1.5 million, for example. Recruitment services from all three publishers allow users to create a CV online and offer features such as e-mail alerts and careers advice. Price is now a key differentiator, with NewScientistJobs.com charging UKP850 to post a single vacancy (UKP295 to NHS and academic advertisers) and ScienceCareers.com charging from USD425 for a single posting, to USD299 per posting for more than 50 ads. Upsells are, of course, also available from both players, with limited contextual placement available – recruiters with NewScientist.com can choose to place an ad alongside a specific upcoming feature, while Nature.com's contextual advertising option is automated across the platform.

Nature is already one of the premier titles which authors target when trying to publish a paper, and NPG intends that naturejobs.com should mirror this positioning, becoming one of the first places that science recruiters and jobseekers think of whatever their recruitment needs. NPG is also very aware of the challenges that B2B publishers and newspaper publishers have faced from services such as Monster and Craiglist, both of which already carry some science jobs, and sees this reversal of the traditional model as an early move against these potential challengers.

 03 December 2006

UK bestseller lists

Apparently this weekend is the beginning of the 'real Christmas' buying frenzy for retailers. And, as we all know, Christmas sales of books are the key to success for authors, booksellers and publishers. It's therefore no surprise that we publishers check out the bestseller lists more assiduously than ever. The lead titles have all been despatched to bookshops and now everything depends on the sell-through as measured by Nielsen Bookscan in the UK and elsewhere.

Pan is celebrating three of the top ten paperback fiction bestsellers.

By permission of Pan Macmillan, London.

By permission of Pan Macmillan, London.

By permission of Pan Macmillan, London.

And there are more bestsellers to come. However, I'd like to put in a 'blug' for our children's publishing. We have the fastest growing children's publishing group in the world and we're really proud of the quality of everything we produce. Do have a look.

Macmillan Children's Books

Priddy Books

Campbell Books

Henry Holt Books for Young Readers

Roaring Brook

Pan Macmillan Australia Children's Books

Farrar, Straus and Giroux Books for Young Readers

Macmillan Caribbean Children's Books

Castillo Literatura Infantil

I have no doubt I've missed some key children's links and my colleagues will remind me of any omissions. While researching these links I checked out whether we had a website for children's books in Namibia. We don't but I did discover a wonderful page of our publications in indigenous Namibian languages such as Khoekhoegowab. It is Macmillan's involvement in publishing such as this which cheers me on a Winter's Sunday morning in London.

 04 December 2006

O to be in England in December

This morning I'm driving to the Cotswolds in the West of England for a meeting with colleagues to discuss the future of scholarly publishing and how best to prepare for it. I guess the conversations will be about technology, changing business models, globalisation, threats to copyright, changing academic research priorities and methods, and budgets. The surroundings will be rather different and rather less contemporary – but none the worse for that.

Last week I wrote about the takeover of Houghton Mifflin by Riverdeep. The pretty obvious headline (variations on the Ike and Tina Turner/ Phil Spector song) was used by just about all the commentators. The best analysis, in my view, was by Luke Johnson in the Telegraph. I think this sums up Mr Johnson's views:

'Riverdeep has been a whirlwind buy-and-build in the educational software field. It went public on Nasdaq in 2000, went private in controversial circumstances after three years, and just a year later its private equity backers were bought out for more than twice their entry price.

Its worth appears to have risen from €349m, to €850m, to now perhaps €1.1bn, although underlying growth of the business has failed to match the vertiginous climb in valuations. Prior to this deal it had at least $380m debt of its own, much of it expensive notes at 9.25 per cent. To help fund the project, Davy is offering 200 of its high net worth clients a piece of the action, and have also brought in $200m of Middle Eastern money. Nevertheless, it sounds like the enlarged group will not cover its interest bill twice – wild stuff.

The entire tale has so many characteristics of our times: two companies with years of reported net losses – but no one seems to care; endless refinancings at higher values, while private equity firms book huge cash profits in record time; a very young Irish financier turning into an incredibly bullish industrialist; lucrative fees ($91m on this deal alone) at every turn for the advisers; and a financing structure built on mountains of debt, all at stratospheric multiples, with no hope of ever paying off the principal through operations.'

Incidentally, I first heard River Deep Mountain High in a sleazy and wondeful pub called The Criterion in the centre of Cambridge and it's never sounded better since. Unfortunately the Cri went bust and closed.

05 December 2006

The Strange Case of the British Airways Polonium Card

The British press has had a wonderful time over the poisoning of Alexander Litvinenko. Additionally British Airways has had three of its planes suspected of having carried Polonium and thus being a risk to travellers. I use BA a lot and they kindly sent me an email with a link to the part of their website listing the flights which might have been affected. I asked my secretary to check and all was well. But she added, 'British Airways say that they would have sent you a specific email if you were on one of the affected flights because you're an Executive Club Member.' In other words, if you don't have a BA airmiles card they won't bother to tell you you're at risk. Now that's what I call real customer service – and I'm going to apply for a Polonium card to replace my gold card just in case . . .

06 December 2006

Despair

I suggest that non-cricket lovers and anglophiles give this a miss.

When I went to bed on Monday night in the Cotswolds I calculated that the England cricket team would boringly bat until teatime on the last day of the test match in Adelaide thus scuppering any chance of a victory and ensuring a feeble but safe draw. Being an optimist I thought that maybe, just maybe, one of the batsmen would shine and we'd be able to get ourselves into a position where we had more than three hours to bowl Australia out and level the series. It was only when I woke at the ungodly hour of 3.30am that it occurred to me that England's batting might collapse and leave Australia a gettable target. I immediately realised that this was a wholly irrational nightmare and went back to sleep. On awakening I logged into BBC Sport and the excellent ball-by-ball commentary of Ben Dirs. This is what he had to say and there's nothing much I or anyone else can add:

18.53: That was the biggest load of rubbish I have ever seen. Lots of Aussies going berserk in Adelaide, lots of Englishmen looking like they've arrived home to find the French doors have been smashed and their new plasma TV's been stolen. Thanks for staying with me for the last 10 days – it's been a mix of emotions, but mainly depression and boredom, with a bit of anger and embarrassment thrown in. I'm off to Venice this weekend though, that should be nice, they don't even know what cricket is there. Bye

Ryanair of publishing

Every now and again I feel moved to do an update on Macmillan New Writing, our programme for finding new fiction talent which was memorably described as a Ryanair (cheap and basic) concept in Charlotte Higgins's piece in The Guardian. The publishing business model is quite simple. If we can avoid losing money on individual titles the occasional discovery will allow us to make a modest profit overall. We've managed the first part of the equation successfully. All the titles have performed decently but none of the authors has 'broken out' into the really big time. We think we may have found our first mega-seller and I've asked Will Atkins, the editor of MNW, to tell us about it.

'*Never Admit to Beige* puts Jonathan Drapes firmly on the map as one of Australia's most talented new writers.' – The Big Issue

On Wednesday night we launched Jonathan Drapes's novel *Never Admit to Beige*. There were canapés, inflatable palm-trees and (this being an Australian novel by an Australian author) plenty of wholly ungracious bragging about the cricket.

BBC Five Live's Simon Mayo Show has recently begun a Book of the Month slot and *Never Admit to Beige* is its December selection. It'll be discussed live on Five today from 3pm, with Jonathan and a panel of guest reviewers; there's also an online forum where listeners can comment on the book.

Never Admit to Beige is the fourteenth Macmillan New Writing novel to be published since our first books appeared in April. It's an anarchic comic romp across Australia's

Gold Coast, following guileless young Englishman Trigger Harvey as he searches, with increasing futility/desperation, for his lost luck. (Jonathan, incidentally, tells me he hadn't heard of his character's Only Fools and Horses namesake when he wrote the book). It includes shootouts with Japanese mafia, a run-in with a couple of coke-dealing OAPs, and probably the most violent round of golf in literary history. It's also turned out to be rather hard to classify – on its website, Five Live has a commendable bash: 'A kind of James Bond meets Inspector Clouseau with Men Behaving Badly'.

The Five Live Book of the Month slot is relatively new, so its impact on sales remains to be seen, but we've put through a pretty sizable paperback reprint, and Borders will be carrying the book in their Christmas 3 for 2 promotion. *Never Admit to Beige* is funny and loveable and bursting with energy; turns out it's also rather prophetic:

'Next Ashes series,' one of the novel's minor characters goads Trigger, 'you guys don't stand a bloody chance. Not if Warney's on form.'

08 December 2006

Society of Bookmen

Last night I attended one of the regular dinners of this society founded in 1921. It meets eight times a year at the Savile Club in Mayfair. The Chatham House Rule applies, so I cannot share with you what was said by whom and technically I cannot reveal the name of the speaker (but I do have his permission). It was Stephen Prickett and he gave a fascinating description of his current job which has one of the longest titles in my experience – Director of the Armstrong Browning Library and Margaret Root Brown Professor for Browning Studies and Victorian Poetry, at Baylor University, Waco, Texas, as well as Regius Professor Emeritus of English Language and Literature at the University of Glasgow, Scotland – phew.

But the most embarrassing moment was when neither of us could remember what he'd worked on for Macmillan. He edited the series 'Romanticism in perspective'.

If the Society of Bookmen has a rather traditional feel, the Centre for Creative Business could not be more 21st century. It is a partnership between the London Business School and the University of the Arts London which I represent on their committee. The strange thing is that both the Society and the Centre have very similar aims – to inspire, facilitate, network, enjoy and help sustain creative businesses, the former restricted to writers, booksellers, publishers and other members of the book trade, the latter a wider group.

Off to rainy Basingstoke today. Apparently there are rumours that Basingstoke can deploy nuclear weapons in less than an hour. I'd better check out this new element on the axis of evil.

And finally an excellent piece by Bryan Appleyard in The Times about the importance of popular science books. His last para says it all.

'These new, humble, wondrous books — and, indeed, that great TV testament to wonder, Planet Earth — are an unalloyed good. They restore the true faith, and will, in time, send children to seek out whatever maths and physics courses they can find amid the debris of the science faculties.'

From Russia with Love

Back in September I wrote about a Pan nostalgia website. Just for fun and with the polonium case in mind I reproduce one item.

This great website is run by Tim Kitchen and he wrote to me recently. It seems that people's interest in what his wife calls an obsession and he calls a hobby has encouraged him to do even more:

'I was going to stop at about 1963 when the number was added to the logo on the front cover and I do have all 1500 titles apart from two and these are all on the site. I then carried on with the later titles which still used PAN's eclectic number system. I definitely stop where ISBN comes in. Of the later titles I have over a thousand still to scan in with about 200 left on the wants list.'

On Thursday I attended a round table meeting at the Smith Institute where a group of very senior politicians, librarians, and managers met to discuss how best to ensure a first-class public library system in the UK. The debate was intelligent and constructive and clearly everyone is aware of the issues of efficiency, management and the need to deliver a service which the citizen wants. The Museums, Libraries,and Archives Council is the body charged with strategic oversight of libraries and they have produced a number of excellent reports over the years.

I have two concerns. First that, in spite of much protestation to the contrary, I'm not sure that books are really seen as central to the library system by some of of the participants. These are the objectives for libraries as set out on the MLA website:

- Provide safe, neutral, shared environments for people from all walks of life

- Support formal education and learning at all times of life

- Act as centres of creativity

- Serve as focal points for their neighbourhood

- Are at the forefront of universal access to the internet and e-government

No mention of books at all.

The second concern is hard to express and hard to prove. I have a feeling that many of the key figures in the library world believe that libraies are somehow too bourgeois and middle class and that they should be changed fundamentally for a 'more inclusive' system. However, most people in the UK **are** middle class or are aspiring to be middle class. I think libraries do serve the middle class and they should be encouraged so to do. By creating great libraries all citizens will use them and gain educational and cultural benefits. By artificially trying to change the customer base of libraries we risk losing everything.

The Soviet Union in the days of From Russia with Love showed how counterproductive it is to impose ideologies on people. I do hope the library world will resist any attempts to use it as an agent of political change.

10 December 2006

Military indiscretions

Yesterday I wrote about the problems facing libraries. I should have mentioned two links if you're interested in more information – Tim Coates's Good Library Blog and Karen Christensen's Berkshire Blog which is about much else as well, including the fascinating Love US Hate US debate about what the world (and Americans) really feel about the USA. And if you're in the least bit interested in the challenges and opportunities in book publishing in the coming decade I recommend this special report in Forbes magazine.

You may have noticed that I went to two meetings last week where the 'Chatham House Rule' was applied. It seems that more and more activities are subject to some degree of restraint when it comes to expressing opinions. I sometimes think that leakiness and ill-considered statements are at an all-time high but I was pleased to be sent a copy of a recently declassified letter from Eisenhower to General George Patton sent on 29 April 1944.

Dear General Patton

My attention has been called to a statement of yours in which you expressed an opinion as to the future political position of the United States, Great Britain and Russia. I have examined all available reports in the case, including that brought to my attention by your Chief of Staff, and I thoroughly understand that you thought you were talking privately, and moreover that your statements were made on the spur of the moment. Nevertheless, I must tell you frankly that I regard this incident with the utmost seriousness and you should understand thoroughly that it is still filled with drastic potentialities regarding yourself . . . .

I have warned you time and again against your impulsiveness in action and speech and have flatly instructed you to say nothing that could possibly be misinterpreted by your own subordinates or by the public . . . .

I am thoroughly weary of your failure to control your tongue and have begun to doubt your all-round judgment, so essential in high military position . . . .

I want to tell you officially and definitely that if you are again guilty of any indiscretion in speech or action that leads to embarrassment for the War Department, any other part of the Government, or for this Headquarters, I will relieve you instantly from command.

Sincerely,

Dwight D. Eisenhower

Commanding General European Theater of Operations

Phew. That's telling him. I wonder whether there was a reply and, if so, what it said.

 11 December 2006

Exact Editions

Exact Editions is a company set up by some old friends of mine about a year ago. Much as I dislike vacuous mission statements and straplines I think theirs is both straightforward and true – Bringing magazines into the digital age. Unlike many start-ups they don't have wealthy individual or corporate backers and, as far as I know, they don't have glossy business plans with absurd projections of growth and pretty pictures throughout. They are testing the market for online magazines by spending as little as possible on themselves and using brainpower and hard work to attract readers (and publishers) to their site.

And one of the founders, Adam Hodgkin, posts regular insightful pieces on their blog. Adam is by training a philosopher and the pieces tend to be pretty intellectual. Fortunately he is from the pragmatist school of philosophy which is important when involved in business.

The most entertaining thing about the site at present is the random nature of the magazines represented (inevitable with a start-up) – Baptist Times jostling with The Spectator and Green Parent and Today's Flyfisher for our attention. Actually, it's just like going into a traditional newsagent.

 12 December 2006

Microsoft money is put to good use

As Christmas is approaching I thought you might like to switch on the audio on your computer and click here.

On a much more serious note, millions of people in developing countries die each year from diseases that are treatable or preventable and three diseases alone – AIDS, tuberculosis and malaria – kill over five million annually. But standard diagnostic tests which could significantly reduce the death toll are imperfect. For instance, the standard TB test misses half of all cases. The Bill and Melinda Gates Foundation is committed to improving diagnostic health technology for the developing world and has worked with Nature to produce a special report which is available free online to everyone. It is a hugely important publication.

Last night I was fortunate enough to be invited by the private equity group Apax Partners to the Tate Britain for a party and a viewing of the Holbein in England show. The amazing success of private equity in recent years has always baffled me. They seem to make money appear out of nowhere and they continue to do so. I have had the trick explained many times but, rather like watching a brilliant conjuror, I still can't see how they do it!

Bestseller Lists

The latest top five paperback fiction bestsellers in the UK are:

1 The Devil Wears Prada – Lauren Weisberger HarperCollins 35,573

2 Looking Good Dead – Peter James Pan Bks. 27,654

3 Winter in Madrid – C. J. Sansom Pan Bks. 19,420

4 False Impression – Jeffrey Archer Pan Bks. 18,781

5 The Island – Victoria Hislop Headline Review 16,826

and it's great to see a really strong performance from Pan.

Almost as gratifying is to see another top five list where we don't appear.

1. Confessions of an Heiress – Paris Hilton

2. Made In Portugal – Jose Mourinho

3. Jordan: A Whole New World – Katie Price

4. Jade's World – Neil Simpson

5. Managing My Life – Alex Ferguson

I expect you've already guessed the criteria for this list – the most discarded books in Travelodge hotel rooms!

🐦 14 December 2006

Social networks old and new

On Tuesday I went to Jeffrey Archer's flat overlooking the Thames It must be one of the best metropolitan views in the world. I was there, along with a large number of his friends, for his and Mary's traditional shepherd's pie and champagne pre-Christmas party. It was, as ever, a place to spot politicians and other celebrities and this year the prize specimen was undoubtedly Margaret Thatcher who was just as you imagine her to be. It was a classic example of social networking.

And then on the dreaded early flight to Stuttgart (not a lot of social networking at Heathrow at 6.00am) which was looking good in that wonderfully German gemuetlich way.

On the plane, along with working on some board papers, I read the piece below by Karen Christensen and I have her permission to publish it here – she thinks it's too long and over-complicated but I think it's really worth the read. It describes a not-so-classic example of social networking:

'I'm a lover of old books who also blogs. I grew up in the Silicon Valley but have become a a skeptic when it comes to exaggerated claims made for the social benefits of human-computer interaction. I am fascinated by possibilities of Web 2.0 publishing, but I have shocked friends who are true believers by pointing out that not everyone knows the difference between a wiki and a blog. This article is an attempt to explain these different worlds.

The Evangelists

People involved in social media are almost fanatical about them, while traditional businesspeople seem to dismiss them as fad rather than seeing them as phenomena with truly transformative potential. You've no doubt read the evangelists' claims, heard the shorthand (Web 2.0, the 'long tail,' the 'tipping point'), and probably experienced the tent meeting atmosphere of a lot of conference keynotes. Bloggers who say that we should get rid of all editors and just let the people speak. Internet experts who think that publishers just print books. Overexcited journalists who write, 'When it comes to information, the balance of power has truly shifted to the consumer.' (One assumes the writer doesn't think his own job should be done by the magazine readers, though.) Web media producers who boast that they do everything online. (Surely not everything?)

When they paint a picture of the future as they see it-a future dominated by online interaction-social-media zealots appear to assume that teenagers (the age group most switched on to social media, and the one the zealots focus on) are going to be doing exactly the same things at 40 that they're doing today. They fail to take into account the fact that teenagers have considerably more free time than 40-year-olds. People with families and careers and community activities, however tech-savvy, can't spend all their free time downloading humorous video clips and chatting in MySpace. If a renowned professor and a high school kid get into a debate on Wikipedia, the student will win. He has the luxury of time, which successful professional people do not. Online, fanatics often rule.

The Skeptics

Then there are the detractors. I'm thinking of the senior business development person who said, 'Social what?' when I asked what her company, a major global publisher, was doing to incorporate social media into their online platform. 'Oh, sure, we're doing all that,' she eventually said, 'but that's just icing.'

In a way, she was right: users expect core content to be maintained, and when it comes to academic content and business information, stakeholders in the existing models will do everything possible to maintain the status quo. But times, and user expectations, are changing. The value added by that icing is going to be immense, and the companies that realize that using social software isn't just a sop to throw to consumers but something that can genuinely improve their businesses-with greater efficiencies, and far more market understanding-are going to be ahead of the game.

There are two types of detractor. Some are manifestly uninterested in the new technologies and are just hoping that the revolution doesn't happen until they've retired to Santa Fe or the Berkshires. They want to use the Web to connect to peers, but they don't really want any challenges thrown their way.. The others may be quite tech savvy and active on the Internet, but they don't understand the power – and difference – of social media.

Explaining Social Media

The online interfaces that make possible this brave new world are known collectively as social media. Weblogs (blogs) are an example of a social medium in which an individual addresses and receives feedback from a large audience-from the one to the many. Bulletin board systems (BBSs, or forums), relationship management media (sites such as MySpace or Cyworld, or even Mappr), massively multiplayer online role-playing games (MMORPGs), file-sharing systems (for music, photos, and videos), and wikis (for collaborative editing of webpages) are examples of social media in which many people interact with many other people-from the many to the many. Finally, and of particular interest to businesses, there are corporate feedback forums that let people give a company feedback on their experiences with the company's products-from the many to the one.

Interest in these media vary around the world. BBSs are, for now at least, the most important social medium in China, with an estimated 53 million people in China making use of them. They are easy to use and allow for anonymous communication, which, in a restrictive society such as China, gives people a feeling of liberation. The Chinese enjoy the social, community-oriented (as opposed to individualistic) nature of BBSs; in general Chinese people are not so eager to stand out. Blogs are extremely popular, too, but unlike in the United States, they tend to be personal, generally written just for friends and family.

What it's all about is new relationships, and in fact the webs of overlapping relationships we call community (or at least some semblance of it). This isn't for everyone, and some of the reasons for the surge in virtual community is that our world offers less in the way of actual community. Blogs, forums, and relationship management sites provide some of the benefits we used to find in real life public spaces like barber shops and even street corners. They let people:

* Stay in touch

* Discuss and debate

* Share content with friends

* Share opinions (with ratings and social tagging)

* Publish content (in the hope that others will find it useful or entertaining-and that expertise or talent will be recognized)

* Collaborate (in creative writing, building directories and information sources, and gaming)

Some of these are one-to-many, some many-to-many, and they can be designed primarily as expert to individual (allowing for questions and feedback) or as purely peer-to-peer. Even in peer-to-peer, leaders do arise, and certain people try to dominate. The online world is not without personal conflict and awkward social moments.

Hopes and Fears

So what do these new social media mean, for any media company? That the old top-down ways won't work with many audiences. The entertainment industry is already experiencing this, but close behind are any businesses that depend on a purveyor of abstract knowledge handing down words of wisdom from on high. People these days are much more interested in hearing from someone who has lived through the experience and can describe the problem and solution from a personal perspective-that is, they're interested in hearing from school-of-hard-knocks experts rather than ivory-tower ones. Of course, the danger with experiential expertise is that the stories are anecdotal; they may not reflect overall trends, and people relying on them may miss vital information that a person with 'book knowledge' but no experiential knowledge might be able to impart.

People have other fears, when it comes to social media. In the United States, there is much concern about predators online; in the United Kingdom and China, there is more concern about what is termed 'Internet addiction.' Although the evangelists of social media avert their eyes from the serious environmental impact of computing and mobile devices and from the social and economic consequences of diverting activity from local communities, corporate social responsibility may one day come to include not only improvements in remanufacturing and recycling capacity, but also responsible software and site design.

Many companies are trying to capitalize on the young eyes – and associated wallets – of those who congregate at MySpace and similar sites. But perhaps they should beware: many people don't like too much commercialization, and the MySpace crowd is likely to pick up and move if it feels too hassled-and companies may find themselves chasing their target demographic around cyberspace.

Companies engage with social media to differing degrees. Some love to wait and see. Others proudly announce a blog and then use it to post press releases. Others decide to add every kind of whiz-bang interface they can find, without ensuring that there really is a community-in-waiting. Virtual communities need some initial spark to animate them. Sometimes it's a political issue, or a crisis of some kind. Often there's an offline community, or many small communities, ready to come together in a new way. (There are risks: what if your community-in-waiting is a bunch of annoyed subscribers?)

The Promise and the Problems

An experience I had recently shows both what's wonderful about social media and what the drawbacks are.

At Berkshire Publishing, we use online project management software called Basecamp, and I wanted to post my Outlook calendar so staff, reps, and our publicist could easily access it, in real time. But Basecamp is built on open source, and Outlook is from Microsoft. I clicked on Help and found myself at a forum, hosted by Basecamp, where people discussed solutions to this problem. I was fascinated. The participants sounded so knowledgeable and cooperative: 'I tried your solution and it worked, except -' The discussion went on for pages, and I felt more and more hopeful. These guys would surely solve the problem, and I would be able to impress my IT guy with having figured this out myself.

But the more I read, the less certain I felt that there was a clear solution that I would be able to execute. Because, you see, there is no editor or publisher to delete the well-intentioned dead ends, to rewrite the explanations that are too long and complicated, and to test the final instructions. Because in a medium like this there are no final instructions.

Forums are full of good ideas and bad ones, and if it's your special subject, and you don't have anything else planned for a rainy afternoon, you might want to while away the time this way. But after first creating trust – key to any social network – the tech forum lost me because it didn't answer my question in a way I could understand. And that is good news for publishers, because it means that they will continue to have a role to play in the world of online and social media.

Part of what publishers do – and what our customers pay for – is to weed out most of the material we see. Most publishers reject 99% of the submissions they receive, and in general that's to the customer's benefit because it saves them time and money and gives them what they want without frustrating searches.

Perhaps the greatest challenge social media pose to corporate media companies is blurred boundaries between producer and consumer. Publishing companies may well need to be more than processors and enablers; the ones that have in-house creative and intellectual capacity and the ability to build active, ongoing relationships with creative people are most likely to take full advantage of social media.

Better technologies are also necessary if we are to have really effective, but affordable, interactivity. And the barriers need to be much, much lower: while the tech-savvy think that everyone can publish now, most people have absolutely no idea what a <strong> tag means and would no more edit a page in a wiki than try to drive a Mac truck. But one thing is certain: whether or not social media will turn out to be our bread and butter, it is far more than icing on the cake.

Karen Christensen is cofounder and CEO of Berkshire Publishing Group, to which readers have turned to for over a decade for award-winning titles on topics of international interest. Karen was senior editor of the four-volume Encyclopedia of Community and oversaw the publishing of Berkshire's two-volume Encyclopedia of Human–Computer Interaction. An expert on Chinese guanxi (business relationships) and online community building, she serves on the board of the content division of the Software & Information Industry Association, and spoke about social media in China at the first Global Information Industry Summit in Amsterdam in September 2006. She blogs here.'

15 December 2006

Reptiles and Untouchables

A reception I attended last night organised by the Publishers Association was held in the Reptile House at London Zoo.

It followed a PA International Division conference on the management and protection of global brands with contributions from Nature's very own David Swinbanks giving away all our secrets about brand extension.

Also there was Pan's very own futurologist author, Ray Hammond, whose monthly thoughts in Glimpses of the Future are normally unbelievable and then turn out to be feasible and then realistic.

At dinner afterwards the conversation turned, as it infrequently does, to soccer. Chelsea Football Club's successful manager, Jose Mourinho, refers to himself as 'the special one'. Check out his song on YouTube (fast forward through some of the spoken stuff at the beginning). Apart from his own specialness he also refers to nine of his eleven players as 'untouchables'. The question is who are the untouchables of the book trade, either individuals or organisations. Answers on a postcard, email or comment.

I'll start the ball rolling with Nielsen BookData (without whom we'd know even less about our industry than we do now), the Man Group (who have been so intelligent and generous in their sponsorship of the Man Booker Prize, and of course Jane Friedman of HarperCollins (who is publishing person of the year and responsible for just about every innovation our industry has seen).

Richard Doll

In the olden days, when I lived in Oxford and worked at <u>Oxford University Press</u> I was honoured to be made a Supernumerary Fellow of a very new Oxford institution, <u>Green College</u>. I was reminded of those days by the receipt of their alumni magazine, Green College News, this morning.

The creation of Green College was made possible by money from Cecil and Ida Green, the founders of <u>Texas Instruments</u>, and inspiration and vision from <u>Richard Doll</u>. He was convinced that, as medical sciences and adjacent disciplines exploded in importance, traditional Oxford colleges would simply not have the resource to offer scientists and scholars enough support. The only solution was a brand new college. He dedicated his later years to the college and ensured its success not just when he was Warden but in supporting the Wardens who succeeded him.

I spent time with Doll during the publication of a small book originally published by the <u>National Institutes of Health</u> as an extended journal article. We republished in paperback as <u>The Causes of Cancer</u> and sold quite a few copies. Neither Doll nor his distinguished co-author Richard (now Sir Richard) <u>Peto</u> would accept personal royalties. It was small but startlingly important and is still the starting point for discussion about the effects of smoking, food and other environmental factors on cancer incidence.

I have always regarded Richard Doll as an example of the very best scientist, very best scholar, very best university politician, very best person and not a bad wicketkeeper in his prime. I was therefore horrified by the recent attacks on him suggesting that his payment for consultancy by chemical companies threw <u>suspicion</u> on his research findings and statements. This piece by <u>Cristina Odone</u> puts another slant and finishes by saying:

Each age has its mores: we cannot expect the giants of the past to live by ours.

This is true but might imply he did something wrong. Rubbish. Richard Doll has saved more lives through his research than almost any other medical scientist in history. He lived frugally and his earnings went to support Green College and other causes. He nurtured students and encouraged colleagues. The character assassins should be ashamed of themselves and we should continue to be grateful for human DNA which occasionally produces simply great human beings.

The study was remarkable in many ways. First was its magnitude. Despite the fact that it started in 1951, when England was still recovering from the economic devastation of World War II, the field of epidemiology was just emerging, and 13 more years would pass until the U.S. Surgeon General's Report on Smoking and Health, Dr. Doll was able to recruit 34,439 of the 40,000 male physicians in the United Kingdom to participate in the study. Second was its duration. The study spanned 50 years, capturing the time in the subjects' lives when tobacco use was just starting to show an impact on mortality, and continuing through most of their deaths, when the risk of use again met the risk of no use. This is illustrated in Figure1, which approaches perfection and evokes accelerated heart beats and gasps for air among statisticians, much as Michelangelo's David does among artists. Third was its execution, which resulted in attrition of only 8.8% over 50 years, an average of 63 people or .147% per year. Finally are the results, which tell us that smoking cigarettes reduces life span by approximately 10 years, and increases the likelihood of death by 100% at age 50, 111% at age 60, 121% at age 70, 45% at age 80, and 26% at age 90 and will be the likely cause of death for two thirds of the people who smoke. It also tells us that quitting smoking adds 10 years to a person's life if they quit by age 30, 9 years if by age 40, 6 years if by age 50, and 3 years if by age 60.

🦃 17 December 2006

Why don't journalists check their facts?

Opening today's Sunday Telegraph and turning to the gossip column about books, Literary Life, (which I couldn't link to for some reason) I found the following:

'Congratulations to Claire Messud, the only British author to feature in the New York Times top five most notable works of fiction of 2006.'

If you may follow the NYT link you'll spot that is the top ten novels (although she does appear to be third and thus arguably could be described as being in the top five). But what surprise me was that she was described as British. I checked on Wikipedia:

'Born in the United States, Messud grew up in Australia and Canada, returning to the US as a teenager. Her mother is Canadian, her father is of Algerian origin, and her sister is French. Messud was educated at Yale University and then Cambridge, where she met her spouse, the British literary critic James Wood [1]. She has taught in the MFA program at Warren Wilson College in North Carolina and in the Graduate Writing program at Johns Hopkins University. Messud was considered for the 2003 Granta Best of Young British Novelists list, but none of the three passports she held was British.'

I double-checked with Andrew Kidd, described by Robert McCrum as the 'charming, sophisticated publisher of the cutting-edge paperback list at Picador', who confirmed that she is not British.

Why am I pointing this out?

I suppose firstly because I'm fed up with journalistic inaccuracy. It's pretty easy to check that sort of fact. Harder to check whether the £12m Jeffrey Archer is supposed to have received as an advance from Macmillan is correct because we don't disclose our financial arrangements with authors. What I can say is nobody should believe what they read in newspapers, particularly when it comes to authors' advances.

Secondly, because the story is a perfect illustration of globalisation in our industry. The New York Times is as important in the UK now as the London Times used to be. The nationality and domicile of an author is becoming irrelevant.

However, the really important thing is that Claire Messud's books are receiving the attention and praise they deserve. It's not too late to buy The Emperor's Children – just check out the reviews.

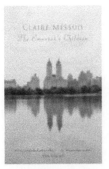

Incidentally, can anyone help me find a dvd of my favourite poker film, Big Deal at Dodge city (properly known as A Big Hand for the Little Lady)?

18 December 2006

Best books of 2006

We are all suspicious of lists, particularly lists based on subjectivity. The newspapers are full of Christmas choices of books. There might be an element of mutual back-scratching, of intellectual snobbery or exhibitionism, or simply puffery. Yesterday I blogged/bragged about one of our titles in the New York Times best of 2006 which is probably the most objective list.

I have since discovered that we publish three of the best ten and here they are.

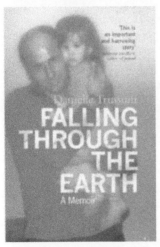

Danielle Trussoni's Falling through the earth, Rory Stewart's Occupational hazards and once again Claire Messud's Emperor's children.

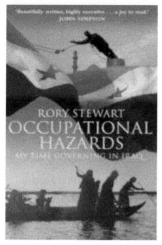

By permission of Pan Macmillan, London.

By permission of Pan Macmillan, London.

I hope all our independent bookselling colleagues are stocking these titles as an antidote to celebrity biographies!

19 December 2006

Chelsea Arts Club

For a while I was a member of the Athenaeum Club in London's Pall Mall. It is very posh.

There were, however, a number of drawbacks. The food was terrible, women were not allowed into the club except after 6 p.m. The last straw was to discover that 'members may not take off their jackets in the sitting room' – even when the temperature exceeds 30 Centigrade. I resigned.

A few years later I was invited to join the Chelsea Arts Club which is about as different as it can be. It is not posh.

The food is pretty good. Jackets are not compulsory. Women are welcome. Cats are also welcome.

One of the joys of membership of the club is receiving the monthly chairman's letter. Today's has a nice literary story:

There has, of course, also been a strong literary tradition at the Club with diverse writer and poet members such as A. S. Byatt, Roger McGough, right through to Laurie Lee, for whom we always kept a special supply of Ruddles County behind the bar! The Club has a bust of Laurie Lee sculpted by Lyn Bamber. I will never forget the story that one day Laurie was sitting for the sculpture when he asked 'can you do something about my pendulous lower lip?' to which Lyn reportedly replied 'I'm a sculptor darling, not a f***ing plastic surgeon'!

🦃 20 December 2006

Ashes 2006

Visitors to this blog may have noticed an omission in the last few days – no progress report on England's attempt to retain the Ashes, the every 18-month cricket battle between Australia and England. A little while ago I suggested that I'd be very happy if England was boringly 3-0 up in the series at this stage and I could claim my winnings (I bet A$500 at 2-1). I was nearly correct. The score is 3-0 but the wrong way round and I have had to concede the bet and any pride in the 2005 victory in England.

The defeat has been crushing but the strange thing is that, apart from the first match where England were completely dire throughout, the other two could have (or even should) have been won at various times. Apart from the obvious talent and professionalism of many of the Australian players I can't help thinking that a significant difference was about leadership. Somehow, England just didn't have it.

For more detail on all this disappointment go to the Ashes on cricinfo. In spite of this gloom – or maybe as an antidote – some cricket books are doing really well in Britain. My favourite, Wisden Anthology,was made Book of the Week in the Sunday Times and garnered this great review in the Guardian. I quote from the beginning of the ST review:

'If Wisden is cricket's Bible, here is the New Testament.'

The book, all 1300 pages and £40 worth, has reprinted and, hallelujah, a major bookshop chain has finally agreed to purchase some copies for sale at Christmas – better late than never. Perhaps they should have read my previous blog and taken note.

Finally on cricket someone sent me this rather unkind joke about England's cricketers.

Billy was at school this morning and the teacher asked all the children what their fathers did for a living. All the typical answers came out, fireman, policeman, salesman, chippy, captain of industry etc, but Billy was being uncharacteristically quiet and so the teacher asked him about his father.

'My father is an exotic dancer in a gay club and takes off all his clothes in front of other men. Sometimes if the offer is really good, he'll go out with a man, rent a cheap hotel room and let them sleep with him.'

The teacher quickly set the other children some work and took little Billy aside to ask him if that was really true.

'No,' said Billy. 'He plays cricket for England but I was just too embarrassed to say.'

📝 21 December 2006

Peer review

Walking to work this morning listening to BBC Radio 4 I tuned in to two pieces about Nature. They were triggered by the journal publishing the results of an experiment we undertook where we invited scientists to submit their papers for public (as opposed to the more traditional system of confidential reviewing) peer review. You can hear the debate at 7.25am here between the editor of Nature and the editor of an online scientific journal from the charity-supported Public Library of Science. There was also an earlier journalistic piece at around 640am.

Meanwhile, another experiment with collaborative editing got under way this week. A new online scientific journal called PloS ONE invites readers to post comments or questions about articles once they are published. PLoS ONE is published by the Public Library of Science, a nonprofit scientific publishing project aimed at creating a library of scientific literature that is accessible to the public.

It's great that a subject so apparently arcane as scientific peer review should be considered important enough to warrant two slots on the most important radio programme in the UK and a feature in the world's leading financial newspaper. What is not so great is that the discussions manage to confuse open reviewing with free access, comment with criticism, freedom of information with free information, an excellent system which catches nearly all attempted scientific fraud with a flawed system which allows fraud to happen, the desire to speak confidentially and openly as opposed to the apparently open but necessarily guarded alternative. In other words and as usual, a tricky and important debate has been reduced to a few soundbites of little value and significant distortion.

On a more immediately important subject, the disgraceful death sentence imposed on the health workers in Libya. Declan Butler has written a professional state of play piece. Do read it and do, if you can, support the resistance to this terrible injustice.

📝 22 December 2006

Against the Grain

Whilst there is no diminution in the debate about public library maladministration in the UK it is always encouraging to see some parts of the library business addressing the challenges of the future with determination and optimism. Against the Grain is a journal which 'links publishers, vendors and librarians' and consistently adds transparency and understanding to what can be fraught relationships. Just check out their latest contents list for a flavour. They also organise the successful Charleston Conferences and run a newsletter which has just landed on my desk, The Charleston

Report. A regular feature is a column called By the Numbers and I hope they don't mind my lifting a few statistics from it:

50% of web visitors don't scroll down to view the portion of a web page which is not visible on their monitor screen.

45% of people use Google for search, 28% Yahoo, 12% MSN and 6% ask.com. (What I find strange is that Google is not higher).

1.5 million people have joined the online social network Second Life already.

136 million people have registered with Skype.

And after all these wonderful numbers I was shocked to find a truly depressing number. One of our books which was identified as in the top ten best books of the year by the New York Times has managed to sell fewer than 1500 copies in the UK – an indication of the problems of publishing high-quality non-fiction successfully in a UK high street market dominated by celebrity biographies. Perhaps the fog-induced chaos at Heathrow Airport may stimulate book sales.

But publishers must remain optimistic and today is the birthday of the 32nd Nature branded journal, Nature Photonics. Its editorial team is spread between Tokyo, San Francisco and London and already it is attracting the very best research papers in what is one of the fastest-growing fields of scientific endeavour. Fingers, toes and optical fibres are all crossed.

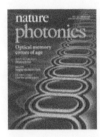

23 December 2006

Macmillan in numbers

There is a newish tradition at this time of year of CEOs emailing all staff reviewing the year just closing. Peter Olson at Random House is probably the star performer. Jack Romanos ('utterly charming, handsome and delightful') at Simon and Schuster has issued something similar and also Gail Rebuck. I'm never quite sure whether these letters are meant just for staff or for general consumption. Extracts always seem to make their way into the trade press anyway and so I suppose they are not confidential. The theme is usually the same (and I can be equally guilty). I offer this, copyright free, to all CEOs for use in any circumstances.

It's been a great year for us in spite of a number of market difficulties. Underlying sales and profits are at record highs (allowing for exchange differences, changes in GAAP, varying retail distribution criteria, enhanced accounting practices for advances and stock, intercompany tax movements, etc). Our competitors are struggling with the market conditions but we've managed to find solutions while maintaining our commitment to the highest standards of integrity and caring. All our authors are truly wonderful both creatively and as human beings. Incidentally, we also support environmental action, the developing world, inclusiveness, positive discrimination (where legally required) and fair treatment for all our stakeholders. India and China are really important places with many people and we are investing since our successful presidential visit. Next year will be even tougher but, thanks to the foresight of the senior management team, we'll probably survive. Thank you all from the bottom of my heart and have a wonderful holiday season with your friends and family. I loook forward to working with you to achieve our 2007 goals together when I return from (enter holiday destination) towards the end of January.

I decided not to put out such a letter this year. Instead here are a few milestones with round numbers. I'd be grateful if anyone from Macmillan would let me know of other statistics which should be included here to make the list more comprehensive.

Macmillan India processed over 1 million pages of text for publishers worldwide. We now employ more than 3,000 people.

Nature Publishing Group had 40,000 papers submitted – they accepted 3000. Nature itself rejected 11,000 of the 12,000 papers it received. The electronic version is now available on 10 million desktops and we've recorded 1.5 million podcast downloads.

Gill and Macmillan managed a 10% profit on general books in a market less than half the size of London.

College Press in Zimbabwe sold 500,000 books in spite of the dreadful conditions in that country.

Our co-venture with the leading Chinese educational publishers FLTRP sold 50 million copies of New Standard English in the year, taking the total to 150 million.

Macmillan Spain supplied 600,000 users with their new Bugs course.

More statistics to come in due course.

24 December 2006

Lord Ken of London

The death of Saparmurat Niyazov has triggered much about his absurd megalomaniac presidential decrees. It is a reminder of the personality disorders which can afflict those with power. It's pretty easy to laugh off the foibles of a central Asian dictator but power corrupts and the closer the power is to being absolute so is the degree of corruption.

Fortunately in business, reality is forced on even the most megalomaniacal by the market place. We can't force people to buy Wayne Rooney's memoirs, nor prevent them from buying Why don't penguins feet freeze?. Things become a little more difficult though in the public sector.

The democratic process in London elected a guy called Ken Livingstone as Mayor. There can be no arguing with the process but I'm beginning to have concerns about the degree to which he is being corrupted by power. He has appointed a Cartoonist Laureate. He appointed a 'Cabinet' although I can't find any reference to their meeting since 2002 (perhaps they disagreed with him). He built a new palace for him and his team on the Thames. Apparently it's already too small to house his staff and his ambitions and they are looking for a new opportunity to build a larger palace at Londoners' expense.

But what really triggered this outburst was the receipt through my letterbox of The Londoner which describes itself as a newsletter for Londoners. It is actually a propaganda document for the glorification of the Mayor and all his deeds reminiscent of <u>Pravda</u> in the good old days of Soviet imperialism.

After three months of email badgering (see below and read from the bottom up) I have now established that we taxpayers are contributing at least £3 million pounds a year to support the political ambitions of our Mayor. Harrumph. I'm waiting for him to change officially the names of South Ken, High Street Ken, Ken Salrise, The Ken Nington Oval, and Ken Tishtown.

Incidentally is a service level of 20 days to respond to an email adequate in the 21st century?

– – -Original Message – – -

From: Mayor [<u>mailto:mayor@london.gov.uk</u>]

Sent: 21 December 2006 15:40

To: Charkin, Richard

Subject: MGLA121206-3836: RE : RE: MGLA211106-1915: RE : RE: MGLA231006-8952: RE : The Londoner

Dear Mr Charkin,

Thank you for your further email. The cost quoted to you in previous correspondence is the total programme budget for The Londoner.

We use some freelance editorial contributors and designers to produce The Londoner and those costs are included in the £288,000 budget.

Yours sincerely

Nicola Golledge

Production and Commercial Coordinator

Dear Ms Golledge

Thank you very much. Perhaps I wasn't clear about the cost breakdown. Magazine publishers usually split costs between fixed and variable and show them separately. The cost you quoted is for all production and distribution (the variable bits). Are the fixed costs of editorial and design included in that figure too or accounted elsewhere?

Richard Charkin

– – -Original Message – – -

From: Mayor [<u>mailto:mayor@london.gov.uk</u>]

Sent: 12 December 2006 12:26

To: Charkin, Richard

Subject: MGLA211106-1915: RE : RE: MGLA231006-8952: RE : The Londoner

Dear Mr Charkin

Thank you for your further email.

We produce 10 editions of The Londoner each year. The print run varies very slightly from edition to edition, but on average is around 2,885,000 copies. The £288,000 cost quoted includes all production and distribution costs.

As The Londoner is a publication giving information about all the services in the GLA Group it is jointly funded by the Greater London Authority, Transport for London, The Metropolitan Police Service and the London Development Agency.

We do occasionally sell external advertising and will continue to do so in the next financial year.

Yours sincerely

Nicola Golledge

Production and Commercial Coordinator

Dear Ms Golledge

Thank you very much for this information. Can you also please let me know the print run, the frequency of publication and also whether the £288,000 per issue includes all costs – editorial, design etc overheads, print, paper and distribution. Also whether there are any income streams and whether there are intended to be in the future?

Thank you so much for your help.

Regards

Richard Charkin

– – -Original Message – – -

From: Mayor [mailto:mayor@london.gov.uk]

Sent: 20 November 2006 14:43

To: Charkin, Richard

Subject: MGLA231006-8952: RE : The Londoner

Dear Mr Charkin

Thank you for your email to The Londoner. Each edition of The Londoner costs approximately £288,000 to produce in total. This equates to a spend of approximately 10p per household. This compares favourably with other local borough publications, based on available information the average cost of local authority publications across London per copy per household is 18p. The Londoner costs 10p per copy per household- 7p cheaper than the average.

As The Londoner is a publication giving information about all the services in the GLA Group it is jointly funded by the Greater London Authority, Transport for London, The Metropolitan Police Service and the London Development Agency. Information about the budget for each of these bodies is available on the GLA's website. Please visit the link: http://www.london.gov.uk/gla/budget/current_budget.jsp for the Annual Budget 2006/07 and the information on the council tax precept.

We will not be publishing the budget in the newsletter, it is however in the public domain.

Yours sincerely

Nicola Golledge

Production and Commercial Coordinator

Dear Mr Charkin

Thank you for your further email requesting a response to your original enquiry (reference MGLA231006-8952).

Your email is currently with The Londoner team and is receiving attention. We aim to answer emails within twenty working days from the day following receipt. I have attached a link to our service standards http://www.london.gov.uk/gla/plu_service_stds.jsp

Yours sincerely

Catrina Holmes

Correspondence Desk Supervisor

Dear Mayor

It is now more than a week since I sent this. When might I expect a response?

Richard Charkin

– – -Original Message – – -

From: Charkin, Richard

Sent: 22 October 2006 09:44

To: 'mayor@london.gov.uk'

Subject: The Londoner

Dear Mayor

Will you please publish the total costs of producing, printing and distributing The Londoner? It could be a good vehicle for recruitment to the various London civic bodies but it would be interesting to see how the budget would work out.

Richard Charkin

25 December 2006

Harry Williams

Along with the last of the Christmas cards there arrived the Trinity College Cambridge Annual Record. It is a beautifully restrained piece of production, printed at Cambridge University Press with an elegant one-colour paper cover, 136 pages well-edited text and a handful of beautiful illustrations of the college, some of which are in colour. Trinity is indeed beautiful.

The last pieces in The Record are an obituary from the The Times and an address by the Bishop of London, Richard Chartres, about Harry Williams. I had missed notice of his death until I saw these.

I met Williams when, as a 16-year-old, I was invited to an interview to see whether I would be an appropriate member of Trinity assuming my exam results were satisfactory. I was studying biology, physics and chemistry and was applying to read medicine. It was therefore slightly surprising to be interviewed by someone who showed absolutely no interest in my clever rehearsed pieces about natural selection and cell differentiation. This genial old monk very courteously invited me into his rooms on Great Court.

He offered me my very first gin and tonic. If I'd thought of it I might have been expecting a sherry but G and T it was. We discussed rugby and the harshness of schools and the absurdity of exams. Then he offered me another G and T and more chitchat. We shook hands and two weeks later I had a letter telling me that I had a place provided I passed the exams reasonably well. When I started my rather undistinguished Cambridge career he was my 'moral tutor'. His broadminded liberalism was a huge relief to me.

I'm sure the interview wouldn't pass muster today where they have to be more 'rigorous', take into account 'balance' of admissions ensuring not too many middle-class people enter the college. I imagine, however, that what I enjoyed was what had been practised successfully quite some time as this list suggests.

The obituaries told me more about Harry Williams than I had known. I certainly didn't realise the impact he had on theology. I do, however, know that the interview with him and its result had enormous impact on my life and I am grateful to him for that.

26 December 2006

Management speak

Although we publish a large range of business books in Palgrave Macmillan and in Pan Macmillan I must confess to a deeply-held scepticism about the whole area of business studies and management education. In the early nineties I enjoyed a wonderful twelve weeks attending the Advanced Management Program at the Harvard Business School.

It was a privilege to be there and I made a lot of friends, had a wonderful time, and deepened my understanding of American corporate executive dynamics. I also learned what I was really bad at. Top of my incompetence list was office space planning. I'll keep the rest of the list to myself. However, I wasn't convinced that the academic basis of the curriculum was really as rigorous as it might have been and I came away believing that common sense was probably the best way to run a business profitably.

It was therefore with some surprise that I came across the Stanford Business School's Bob Sutton and his 'Ten Things I Believe'. I think I believe them too.

1. Sometimes the best management is no management at all – first do no harm!

2. Indifference is as important as passion.

3. In organizational life, you can have influence over others or you can have freedom from others, but you can't have both at the same time.

4. Learning how to say smart things and give smart answers is important. Learning to listen to others and to ask smart questions is more important.

5. You get what you expect from people. This is especially true when it comes to selfish behavior; self-interest is a learned social norm, not an inherent feature of human behavior.

6. Getting a little power can turn you into an insensitive self-centered jerk.

7. Avoid pompous jerks whenever possible. They not only can make you feel bad about yourself, chances are that you will eventually start acting like them.

8. The best test of a person's character is how he or she treats those with less power.

9. Err on the side of optimism and positive energy in all things.

10. Work is an over-rated activity.

27 December 2006

Macmillan blogs

I did a Google blog search on Macmillan mainly to discover whether any of our own websites are running blogs themselves. I couldn't find any (except the brilliant Nascent from Nature) but I'm sure that was my poor search strategy. There must be more.

However, the search did throw up a number of blogs from writers or commentators on Macmillan New Writing which we've discussed here from time to time. For a tiny upstart imprint MNW has certainly made waves, at least in the blogosphere and progressively elsewhere too. I don't think we've cracked the problems associated with publishing new fiction but at least we've found one channel which has the possibility of being commercially sustainable whilst retaining publishing integrity. Here are three blog links worth checking out.

http://macmillannewwriterpart2.blogspot.com/2006/12/some-things-and-quick-thing-about-old.html

http://davidthayer.booksquare.com/archives/2006/11/09/546/

http://girlondemand.blogspot.com/2006/10/in-defense-of-macmillan-and-other.html

One other link caught my eye.

This is the second book from the writing team of Clare ('not just another Bridget Jones') Naylor and Mimi ('youngest director of development for a Hollywood production company') Hare. The book will be published at the beginning of March which gives all of you time to enjoy first The Second Assistant (if you see what I mean). And now I have to declare an interest. They're both friends of mine as well as being a great writing team. We all know that word of mouth is what makes books sell. Do yourself, your friends and the authors a favour – get whispering.

28 December 2006

Publishing person of the year

At various times during the Christmas break I've been catching up on back issues of Publishers Weekly which is edited by the often controversial Sara Nelson. The magazine has improved significantly over the years and its banner now claims that it is 'The international voice for book publishing and bookselling'. It is definitely more international than before but some of the differences between US and British culture are still apparent.

It was great to see in December 11 issue that Jane Friedman was chosen as 'Publishing person of the year'. Given her excellent track record and her high standing in the industry this seems completely appropriate. PW covered the award well and I wasn't suprised to see that their excellent ad sales team had managed to 'persuade' a significant number of HarperCollins suppliers to take out sensibly congratulatory ads. I spotted Verso Advertising, Arvato, Command Web Offset, Quebecor, and Bowater all of whom deserve this further plug for their companies.

Unfortunately the ads don't appear in the online version and so I cannot show you the full page ad on page 5 which knocked me sideways and got me thinking of the differences between the USA and Britain rather than the similarities. You'll have to imagine the typography – here are the words.

Congratulations

Jane Friedman

Our Leader

Our Friend

Our Inspiration

From all of us at HarperCollinsPublishers

I wonder, did the cost of the ad come out of the corporate PR budget or was there a whipround all staff to raise the cash? In the words of the great Dorothy Parker, 'Pass the sickbag, Alice.'

29 December 2006

The law of unintended consequences

This letter was published in yesterday's Times.

Sir, It is time for the Society of Authors to discuss with the Publishers Association the payment of huge sums to celebrities, television reporters, sportsmen and politicians, whose books prove to be flops. Advance fees, which should be going to bona fide authors and young literary people who need financial help as they attempt to enter a difficult profession, are being flushed away. There should be a limit on these advances, and earnings should come only from sales.

British publishers appear to be bent on ruining English literature with this profligacy and poor judgment.

PETER KINSLEY
London SE15

I don't know Peter Kinsley and I don't know whether or not he is a writer, publisher, or reviewer. I sympathise with his irritation that large advances distort the market and draw funds away from young (and indeed not so young) writers. At Macmillan we have two experiments running where we pay no advances but do pay very decent royalties – Macmillan Science and Macmillan New Writing. We do, of course, pay advances and sometimes big ones (and sometimes to 'celebrities') in other parts of the organisation.

The problem with the Kinsley letter is his proposed solution and the consequences of the Society of Authors and the Publishers' Association meeting to limit advances.

1. Such a meeting is probably illegal and the participants might end up in jail for collusion (arguably a reasonable place for some publishers to be but not a first choice for most).

2. If 1 could be fixed here would the limit be set and who would decide who was a bona fide writer as opposed to a celebrity?

3. If 1 and 2 could be fixed who would monitor compliance and what sanctions would the group be granted? Can you imagine the Society of Authors discovering that a publisher had paid an author more than the stipulated limit and then having to take the publisher to court for being kind to authors?

4. If 1, 2, and 3 could be fixed what would happen to authors and publishers who are not members of their respective associations? Presumably they would be free to negotiate whatever terms they like. This would definitely lead to the demise of the two associations as their members deserted.

5. If 1, 2, 3, and 4 could be fixed what would we do about foreign authors or deals struck in foreign lands (e.g. USA)? Presumably we'd have to ensure the arrangement was global and would therefore require global monitoring and compliance.

6. If 1, 2 ,3, 4 and 5 could be fixed who would ensure compliance? I imagine we'd have to call on the services of the United Nations which would divert their attention from trying to solve the problems of the world.

QED

Incidentally, it's strange that people actually think publishers are bent on ruining English literature and that they deliberately exhibit poor judgement and profligacy. We're a pretty useless lot but I promise everyone it's not deliberate - it's just another unintended consequence.

PS I see that <u>Susan Hill</u> has also picked up on this letter and written a much better piece than this one. Do check it out.

📝 30 December 2006

Publishing risk

This press release arrived yesterday morning in the USA.

Advanced Marketing Services Files Voluntary Petition under Chapter 11 of United States Bankruptcy Code

Company Will Use $75 Million Loan Agreement to Fund Ongoing Operations; Customer and Publisher Service Will Not Be Impacted by the

Filing

SAN DIEGO – (BUSINESS WIRE) – Dec. 29, 2006 – Advanced Marketing Services, Inc. (the Company) (Pink Sheets: MKTS), a leading provider of customized merchandising, wholesaling and contract distribution services, announced today that it has filed a voluntary petition under Chapter 11 of the Federal Bankruptcy Code in United States Bankruptcy Court for the District of Delaware. The Chapter 11 proceeding does not include the Company's international subsidiaries in the United Kingdom, Mexico and Australia, and their operations will not be affected.

The Company also announced that, in conjunction with the filing, it has entered into a loan agreement for $75 million in Debtor-in-Possession (DIP) financing from Wells Fargo Foothill, Inc., subject to court approval. The DIP financing should provide sufficient liquidity to meet the Company's ongoing operating needs during the proceeding.

During the past few months, the Company explored a number of alternatives to strengthen the Company's financial base and resolve past legal and regulatory issues. Despite making some progress, the Company was unable to secure new financing and the current loan facility, which is used to finance the Company's operations, will not be extended beyond December 28, 2006.

'This move will permit AMS, with its investment banker, to continue to pursue strategic alternatives,' said Gary M. Rautenstrauch, President and Chief Executive Officer. 'Additionally, Chapter 11 protection will enable the Company to continue to conduct business in the normal course, make payments to vendors going forward and continue delivering quality service and products to customers.'

Forward-looking statements in this public announcement are made under the safe harbor provisions of the Private Securities Litigation Reform Act of 1995. All statements other than statements of historical fact are forward-looking statements that involve risks and uncertainties, including the following statements:

The DIP financing should provide sufficient liquidity to meet the Company's ongoing operating needs during the proceeding; and Chapter 11 protection will enable the Company to continue to conduct business in the normal course, make payments to vendors going forward and continue to deliver quality service and products to customers.

Certain important factors could cause results to differ materially from those anticipated by the forward-looking statements, including the following: The DIP financing is subject to certain terms and conditions. The Company's failure to comply with those terms and conditions could result in a default under the DIP financing loan agreement and, consequently, insufficient liquidity to meet the Company's ongoing operating needs during the proceeding.

What this means is that there is a possibility that all the efforts to publish books successfully – to work with authors to help create the right book; to design and produce it well; to generate publicity and clever promotional tricks to bring people into retail outlets; to ensure continuity of stock; to generate enough revenue and profit to continue to invest – will have been to no avail as the annual profit disappears into a bad debt black hole.

From the outside, publishing risk is seen to be all about making the right authorial bets. This is, of course, still important but even with the best authors there are still many nightmarish risks. Decisions about advances, marketing spend, size of initial distribution, legal, country economics, and last but not least customer bankrupcy.

It's a tough old world out there in this business. US trade publishers were, in general, showing a reasonable result for 2006. Two days from the end of the year they may have to revise their statements.

31 December 2006

Bye bye 2006

It's a grey day here in London as 2006 comes to an end. I've been back through a few of the emails people have sent me during the year to share with you.

When you're in deep SHIT, say nothing, and try to look like you know what you're doing.

Addressed to me personally.

The Salvation era is a phase when there is a reorganization and liberation of humanity . . . .(blah blah ed).

AS THE KING OF THE WORLD, IN THE INTEREST OF ALL HUMANITY, I HAVE ISSUED AND AM ISSUING DECREES, INCLUDING EDICTS AND PROCLAMATIONS TO PROVIDE NOURISHMENT TO ALL PEOPLE,

AND AM APPOINTING THE KING OF THE WORLD TO THE POSITION OF CHAIRMAN OF MACMILLAN, AND AM APPOINTING THE KING OF THE WORLD TO OTHER LEADERSHIP POSITIONS AS REQUIRED, AND AM ISSUING OTHER PROCLAMATIONS.

My executive directives as Chairman of Macmillan are as follows:

1) The opening of free food cafeterias all around the world.

2) At least a 200% increase in all pensions and salaries.

3) Improvements in shelter including more free shelters.

4) Construction of solar power plants.

5) Improvements in health care.

6) Freedom.

7) Additional humanitarian actions.

Cordially,

Steven Translateur, King of the World

A genuine letter from the UK Inland Revenue to a tax-payer.

Dear Mr Addison,

I am writing to you to express our thanks for your more than prompt reply to our latest communication, and also to answer some of the points you raise. I will address them, as ever, in order.

Firstly, I must take issue with your description of our last as a 'begging letter'. It might perhaps more properly be referred to as a 'tax demand'. This is how we, at the Inland Revenue have always, for reasons of accuracy, traditionally referred to such documents.

Secondly, your frustration at our adding to the 'endless stream of crapulent whining and panhandling vomited daily through the letterbox on to the doormat' has been noted. However, whilst I have naturally not seen the other letters to which you refer I would cautiously suggest that their being from 'pauper councils, Lombardy pirate banking houses and pissant gas-mongerers' might indicate that your decision to 'file them next to the toilet in case of emergencies' is at best a little ill-advised. In common with my own organisation, it is unlikely that the senders of these letters do see you as a 'lackwit bumpkin' or, come to that, a 'sodding charity'. More likely they see you as a citizen of Great Britain, with a responsibility to contribute to the upkeep of the nation as a whole.

Which, brings me to my next point. Whilst there may be some spirit of Truth in your assertion that the taxes you pay 'go to shore up the canker-blighted, toppling folly that is the Public Services', a moment's rudimentary calculation ought to disabuse you of the notion that the government in any way expects you to 'stump up for the whole damned party' yourself. The estimates you provide for the Chancellor's disbursement of the funds levied by taxation, whilst colourful, are, in fairness, a little off the mark. Less than you seem to imagine is spent on 'junkets for Bunterish lickspittles' and 'dancing whores' whilst far more than you have accounted for is allocated to, for example, 'that box-ticking facade of a university system.'

A couple of technical points arising from direct queries:

1. The reason we don't simply write 'Muggins' on the envelope has to do with the vagaries of the postal system;

2. You can rest assured that 'sucking the very marrows of those with nothing else to give' has never been considered as a practice because even if the Personal Allowance didn't render it irrelevant, the sheer medical logistics involved would make it financially unviable.

I trust this has helped. In the meantime, whilst I would not in any way wish to influence your decision one way or the other, I ought to point out that even if you did choose to 'give the whole foul jamboree up and go and live in India' you would still owe us the money.

Please forward it by Friday.

Yours Sincerely,

H J Lee Customer Relations

And finally from the archives of Qantas.

dear Captain
My name is Nicola im 8
years. old. this is my first
flight but im not scared. I
like to watch the clouds go
by. My mum says the crew is
nice. I think your plane is
good. thanks for a nice flight
don't fuck up the landing
LuV Nicola
Xx x x

Happy New Year everyone.

≤ January 2007 ≥

Mon	Tue	Wed	Thu	Fri	Sat	Sun
25	26	27	28	29	30	31
1	2	3	4	5	6	7
8	9	10	11	12	13	14
15	16	17	18	19	20	21
22	23	24	25	26	27	28
29	30	31	1	2	3	4

About this blog and more importantly India

This blog has now completed a full year. In December we had 60,400 visits down from 63,375 in November (the effect of the holiday season I hope rather than anything sinister). This brings the total for the year to 399,947, tantalisingly close to a milestone. With the statistics software I have I cannot tell how many of these are unique, nor how many are from Macmillan employees. Maybe next year our IT department can come up with a zero-cost way of answering these questions.

Nonetheless I am amazed and gratified by the volume of visitors and the amount of (usually) kind and constructive correspondence. The paucity of comments is a shame but I guess people have better things to do than populating this blog. I also wish more Macmillan people would contribute. There are some regular commentators, some of whom I've enjoyed arguing with. There have been only two comments which I've had to edit away for reasons of taste. It's worrying that the entries which generate the most and the most heated debate are those concerned with the British book trade and the relationship between publishers and independent booksellers. I accept that there are important issues here. I cannot accept, however, that these are more important than the impact of the digital revolution on publishing as a whole or the need to develop new structures for publishing to take account of globalisation and new reader tastes.

And while on the subject of literary taste I came across the following quote in a BBC report.

'It entertains, as sport must do, but it is without heft, or any substance, it is like a book picked up at an AH Wheeler & Co bookstand at Calcutta's Howrah Station and discarded on arrival in Delhi.'

I do not know the bookshop in question and I have never been to Calcutta. The sport in question is also irrelevant. You know exactly what the writer is trying to convey. The sport in question is, of course, cricket (the one-day version) and the journalist is Rohit Brijnath. His style of sports writing is hardly ever found in the British media. It is correct, old-fashioned English with flair and substance. It is discoveries like this which make me so enthusiastic about our investments in India. This is not a just a country for outsourcing or manufacture. This is a place of creativity, insight and literary adventure. Fortunately it is also complex and its rules of engagement will bamboozle all but the most determined would-be investors.

Macmillan has been part of Indian publishing since 1892 and we intend to make 2007 the best year ever with Macmillan India leading the rest of the group in growth and innovation. January will see our Gurgaon-based MPS Technologies launch of BookStore for the German Boersenverein and for Macmillan companies in the UK and Australia. More customers and more functionality are lined up for implementation throughout the year as we build on our lead over competitors. ScholarlyStats goes from strength to strength as librarians around the world discover the efficiencies and cost savings of using the system. On the text processing end of the business we are investing heavily in enhanced systems for all our clients and have built formidable resources for book as well as journal activities in Charon Tec and ICC Macmillan. On the publishing side we shall be publishing more and better than ever and investing in new markets in education both school and college, scholarship and science, Internet, fiction and non-fiction, in English and the vernacular languages. It will take the all the ingenuity and efforts of our 3000 people in India to make all this work and I have no doubt they will succeed.

Pan Bookshop Christmas

The list below is Pan Bookshop's top ten books sold by volume in the last four weeks of the 2006.It doesn't tally very well with the bestseller lists in the papers but neither, I guess, does the clientele.

1. Dangerous Book for Boys – Conn and Hal Iggulden

2. Previous Convictions – A. A. Gill

3. Suite Francaise – Irene Nemirovsky

4. North Face of Soho (volume 4 of Unreliable Memoirs) – Clive James

5. Amo Amas Amat – Harry Mount

6. Debrett's Etiquette for Girls – Fleur Britten

7. God Delusion – Richard Dawkins

8. The Kensington Book – Carolyn Starren

9. Made in Italy – Giorgio Locatelli

10. Daughter of the Desert (Gertrude Bell) – Georgina Howell

And the manager wanted me to mention two distinguished also rans:

Sorrows of the Moon – Iqbal Ahmed – privately published in 2004 but sold 100 copies in the shop this year.

Concorde – Frederic Beniada – at £40 this was in the top five revenue generators for the shop.

I have deliberately not linked any of these titles in order to encourage you to visit (at 158 Fulham Road SW10 9PR) or order by post or e-mail (panbookshop@btclick.com) from the Pan Bookshop.

On the blog transparency front I can now report that up to 31 December Macmillan has earned $109.73 from the ads carried on this site. The cash will apparently be arriving on 5 February, so look out for a major splurge.

And finally last week I wrote about Trinity, Cambridge, my entrance interview and subsequent undistinguished career. Someone has sent me this photo of the intake of 1967 which has me just two rows below my fellow new boy Prince Charles. His university career wasn't much more distinguished than mine but he's certainly got more press coverage.

03 January 2007

Predictions

At this time of year the media world is awash with predictions. The Booksellers Association runs a blog authored by (I prefer 'written by') Martyn Daniels. It's well worth investigating but just in case you're not up to clicking post holiday celebrations here are his predictions for our industry in 2007:

- Macmillan's audio MP3 player. Whether it is a promotional gimmick or the next audio format is immaterial as it will certainly create noise and stir others into action in this obvious format area.

- 508 compliance which may seem a million miles away to us Brits but signals a new impetus to audio, web site design and will help bodies such as the RNIB in its cause.

- New technology, in the form of OLED screens, or the Hearst reader.

- The announcement and initial roll out of a new distribution environment and services to support digital content within the existing channel.

- The start of real POD services based not on short print runs but distributed printing at affordable prices. Maybe a BOD (bind on demand) model to support customised printing.

- Richer and richer bibliographic services and the need for every publisher to engage in its provision, even if they don't sell digital content.

- Increased importance of Internet sales, emarketing and community engagement and participation. Success will be achieved increasingly by engagement and word of mouth than wallpapering web pages with books and offers.

- Omnivore fears will stoke more publishers to join their ranks but major publishers will continue to build their repositories and control their digital assets.

- Booksellers will increasingly sell old, used, new and digital side by side. Currency is only one aspect of selection and selection is what booksellers have always done best.

In my January 1 entry I published our blog statistics for 2006 including a challenge for our IT department:

This blog has now completed a full year. In December we had 60,400 visits down from 63,375 in November (the effect of the holiday season I hope rather than anything sinister). This brings the total for the year to 399,947, tantalisingly close to a milestone. With the statistics software I have I cannot tell how many of these are unique, nor how many are from Macmillan employees. Maybe next year our IT department can come up with a zero-cost way of answering these questions.

IT have now responded and it turns out that during the year we served 46,327 distinct hosts. Some hosts will represent many unique visitors but at least I now know that there have been a significant number of 'uniques'.

04 January 2007

More blog statistics

I'm indebted to Peter Collingridge for pointing me to a cost-free solution to analysis of visitors to this blog. I'm also grateful to Google and the Macmillan IT department for making it possible. Here are a couple of the charts available.

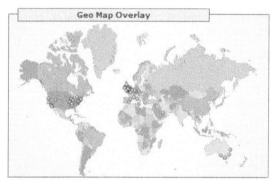

The surprise here is that I'd assumed a significant proportion of visitors were coming from India but the pattern is very similar to the standard geographical distribution of sales of an academic monograph.

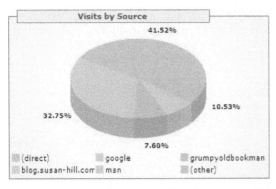

Visits by Source

41.52%

10.53%

32.75%

7.60%

(direct) google grumpyoldbookman
blog.susan-hill.com msn (other)

What can I say about this one? Thank you Susan Hill and thank you Grumpy.

On a very sad note I have just heard of the death of William Armstrong, formerly Managing Director of Sidgwick and Jackson and a great publisher and mentor to many. There will be in-depth obituaries in the trade press by people who knew him intimately. All I can say is that he never once lost his enthusiasm for publishing good books well and commercially. As a result of William's retiring style, there are no pictures of him on Google Images so I'll have to wait for the Bookseller archives to dig something up.

And finally, Publishers Weekly has reported on the AMS Chapter 11 which I wrote about last week. What I hadn't realised was the quantum of potential damage. Random House is owed $43m and the next four (Simon & Schuster, Hachette, Penguin, HarperCollins) around $80m between them. I'm not sure what the total profitability of these top five businesses in the USA is but I'd be surprised if it exceeded the sum of these liabilities. Let's hope that AMS keep their word and allow the non-US parts of the business to trade without depriving them of cash to pay suppliers.

05 January 2007

Independent bookselling in the UK

There is much gnashing of teeth in the trade press about the future of independent bookselling. Indeed, whenever I write anything about sales of books in the UK I get a lot of comments and correspondence attacking us (and other publishers) for undermining independent booksellers by granting too high discounts to chains, supermarkets and Amazon. The Bookseller magazine has carried many excellent articles on the subject but I think this angry and forthright letter published by them yesterday deserves to be widely debated and I've appended a few paragraphs from it. I don't agree with Mr Foster's conclusions (nor his views on the Booksellers Association) but I do think we need to address the issue more formally than through the Bookseller or this blog:

Independents are the key

I refer to Jonathan Spencer-Payne's recent letter (The Bookseller, 1st December) in which he forecast that there would be no independent bookshops in 20 years. While I agree with most of what he says, I do think he's being rather optimistic. I know of three which have closed relatively recently and two that are in difficulty in our region . . .

. . . The independents are the seedbeds of the business and the custodians of our literary culture. They subsidise the discounts given so generously by the publishers to the chains, supermarkets and internet booksellers. They are the de facto agents (unpaid) for Book Tokens, which are hidden by the chains (which prefer to sell their own vouchers), and they keep the wholesalers in business.

They are run in the main by sensible people who do not owe the banks hundreds of millions of dollars. They support a comatose and ineffectual trade organisation whose chief executive is never heard or seen promoting bookshops in the media.

When the independents go, the lot goes, and it'll be sooner than you think. The chains will never, ever be able to compete with the supermarkets and the internet. Happy New Year.

Philip Foster
Owner, The Tolsey Bookshop & Stationers
Tetbury, Glos GL8 8JG

06 January 2007

Weekend digitalia

Perusing the print edition of this week's Bookseller I came across this wonderful sentence:

Kate Mosse is the latest literary edition to Who's Who.

Was it generated by spell-checking software or . . . ?

Just about every publishing house is parading its digital credentials right now. Some have even worked out the difference between an e-book and a website. As part of our attempt to learn more about the new world Timo Hannay (creator of the outstanding Nascent blog and Nature's director of all far-out matters) has for the past couple of years organised a series of presentations for our people (and other guests) in London.

The speakers have included Jimmy Wales (founder of Wikipedia; the science fiction author Cory Doctorow (and co-editor of boingboing and a leading creative commons evangelist); Cory Ondrejka (CTO of Linden Lab which owns and manages the futuristic Second Life); and many others including stars from Apple, Microsoft, Google, Amazon and many more specifically scientific organisations at the cutting edge of the digital revolution.

Why do I mention this, apart from the desire to thank Timo, to encourage Macmillan people to come to future events and to show off how good we are at embracing the future? It's because if the book world is to play any part in this future it has to do more than pay lip service to digitisation, it has to begin to 'live' the future.

Our sister company in Germany, Holtzbrinck Networks, has just announced the acquisition of the largest student social networking website in Germany, StudiVZ. In a very short period it has attracted 30% of all college students in Germany, Austria and Switzerland to register and use it. Similarly in the English-speaking world Bebo has attracted millions of young people. It's easy to be cynical about these and other community developments and there's little doubt that some of the material published on them is sub-standard and even offensive but they represent a vibrant part of the reading and writing public and are therefore part of a publisher's core market.

I'm sure that books, booksellers and publishers will be around in ten years. I am equally sure that the most successful ones will be those who have invested early in digitising their authors' words, learnt how to protect and sell those words to new audiences, worked with existing and new distributors to find audiences, and kept their ears and eyes open to strange, wonderful and disturbing new people and new concepts. On the way we'll make mistakes and these will be showcased as evidence that the market is really about reading a novel in the bath or on the beach and nothing else.

I suspect that there will be two main criteria for success:

1. The ability to think and act innovatively; and

2. The ability to ignore the jeering from the sidelines.

Finally, a rather strange electronic New Year's greetings card from my friends at Random House. Switch on the sound for full effect. I wonder who the rocket is aimed at.

07 January 2007

Pride and prejudice

There's a story in today's Sunday Times about Jeffrey Archer's next book, The Gospel According to Judas, which he is writing along with the distinguished theologian and author, Frank Moloney.

I'm pretty certain that a significant number of people will demonstrate their unshakable prejudices about Lord Archer but I am proud to be publishing this book (on March 20th worldwide) and I know it is ruthlessly scholarly, entertaining and important.

Readers of this blog know that I don't like to let many days pass without getting in a reference to cricket (although recent events in Australia have suggested significant rationing is in order). You might think I'd find it difficult to manoeuvre a link there from The Gospel According to Judas. However, the Good Lord (and I don't mean Jeffrey Archer) is on my side in this instance.

Our senior managers are used to liaising with JA and find him exceptionally demanding but good fun. But there were some nerves about how to handle Archbishop Tutu, who had agreed to read the audio version of the book. Our South African company had booked a studio in Cape Town, hired sound engineers, and we flew out a director from the UK. After discussions with his PA, we set aside two days for reading, allowing breaks for his other duties. We thought it was tight.

In the event, he did it in one day, with a long lunch break for TV viewing. 'I have to catch up with the cricket,' he said. Here he is, reading and watching.

And, in line with his reputation, he charmed studio and publishing staff alike with his modesty and humour.

He said he was 'chuffed' to be asked to read the book – 'but having my kind of complexion you wouldn't have noticed that I was blushing.'

What did he think of the book?

'It's quite amazing, actually. I mean, it's so authentic. It sounds just like the kind of thing someone's son would do to try to rehabilitate their father's name. It seems to ring true. Lord Archer is gifted, but wanted to be quite sure that he didn't commit any 'oops', and so got this collaboration with an outstanding New Testament scholar. Everything there will pass muster.'

I suppose publishers' press releases can't be written in that relaxed style, but that's really just what we wanted to say.

08 January 2007

You've never had it so good

If you have half an hour – or even a few minutes – to spare, go to BBC Radio 4, switch on the volume control, scroll down to 'You've never had it so good' and listen to a fascinating programme written and narrated by Peter Hennessy about our former chairman, Harold Macmillan. If nothing else (but there is plenty else) it's worth it for his delivery.

Over the weekend I read the proofs of a book we are publishing in April. It is by the journalist and sports writer Matthew Engel and it is a selection from his obsessive collection of red notebooks. Every page had something on it which made me smile or think. Great lines such as 'Australia, the land that foreplay forgot' (Germaine Greer); 'In the history of the world, no one ever washed a rented car' (Lawrence Summers); 'After two years in Washington, I missed the sincerity and genuineness of Hollywood' (Fred Thompson); and so much more. Place your orders now.

I wrote yesterday about Jeffrey Archer's new book. Here is the cover. It is the first time his name does not appear on the front of one of his books.

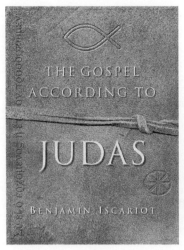

09 January 2007

Wheeling and dealing

I was sent this link today by the US media investment bankers DeSilva and Phillips. It is an in-depth review of mergers and acquisitions activity in the media sector. They conclude that:

'the year 2006 has turned out to be not merely strong, but also a year of extraordinary deal-making in both quality and quantity. A dollar volume of $20.5 billion in media transactions makes 2006 the strongest year since 2000, and close in volume even to that year's total.'

Within the report they predict that there will be trends towards the privatisation of public companies and the acquisition of US media companies by Europeans on the back of improved European economics and a strong euro. They also predict that 2007 will be even more active than 2006.

It is, of course, great to know that we are involved in an industry with so much activity. The trouble is that all this wheeling and dealing comes with significant costs – lawyers, bankers, accountants, disruption, redundancies, strategy consultants, headhunters, stockbrokers. At the same time the industry needs to invest more in transforming its activities from print to digital and customers are demanding ever better value for money. Somewhere there is a mismatch.

On a more parochial level it is remarkable that a blog I did recently about independent bookselling in the UK has generated 24 comments and quite a deal of heat addressed at publishers, supermarkets, Internet booksellers, and the Booksellers Association and its executives. It's good to see the debate and I understand the fears and concerns of independent booksellers. I do wish, however, that some of the commentators would try to understand the issues facing those they attack.

Publishers owe it to their authors to maximise sales of their books. In the 21st century this must involve sales through supermarkets, through Amazon, through chain bookshops as well as through traditional independent booksellers. The value chain and costs for each of these channels is different and complex. Publishers don't grant higher discounts than they need to and they certainly want to see the continuance of as many routes to market as possible.

Supermarkets need to serve their customers. Part of that service involves the supply of books as well as magazines, food, clothes etc. They also need to offer best value. They can achieve this by being able to sell very large quantities efficiently and that is certainly the case with best selling books. Publishers would be seen as very elitist if they didn't see the supermarket shopper as a potential customer for books.

Amazon and other Internet booksellers have generated new sales for authors by the re-invigoration of the 'long tail', by sophisticated algorithmic market research, and by heavy investment in customer service, technology and marketing.

The BA tries to represent all those organisations who sell books in the UK and Ireland. To shun certain booksellers because they are not 'independent' or 'traditional' would be daft. Of course it must be difficult for its executives to satisfy all its members all the time but that's true of every organisation from the local Parish Council to the United Nations. I think the BA gives booksellers a fantastic service and deserves 100% support from all interested in the security and development of the book market.

🌿 10 January 2007

E-commerce

In the 1990s when I worked at Reed International Books my office was in the spectacular art deco Michelin House building in Fulham Road. Apart from the publishing businesses, the building also housed (and still does) several other businesses. When we first moved in there was a deal with the Conran Shop whereby our employees got a discount at the shop and theirs got a discount on our books. Terence Conran rapidly realised he was getting the worse end of the deal and cancelled it. On the first floor was the glamorous Bibendum restaurant with a less formal Oyster Bar on the ground floor. Outside there is a fishmonger on the left and a florist on the right. It transpired that by far the most profitable and most stable of all the businesses was the florist which exceeded its budgets through the booms and busts of the economic cycle and all the other vagaries of retailing. Is there a lesson?

In those days the production director of the trade division (Heinemann, Secker, Methuen etc) was Peter Kilborn. He convinced me of a publishing rule which I now know to be immutable. If you want a thorough and sensible analysis of any publishing-related problem (or maybe any problem at all) ask your production

286

director. Anyway, since then he has worked constantly in the book trade and is now head of the Book Industry Communications organisation which we all know as BIC. BIC is the unsung hero of the book trade and it has been responsible for the successful implementation of many of the most significant industry initiatives. He has been following a number of the debates on this blog and is convinced that solutions lie in improving efficiencies rather than trading insults. I agree. He sent this contribution and I hope that this might move the debate from the sterility of differential discounts to the real gains to be made from technological investment and implementation.

Richard – and Macmillan Distribution – have long been supporters of electronic trading and I'm grateful to him for the offer of a guest blog on e-commerce and BIC's e4books campaign.

As an industry we have a good record of exploiting new technologies. Which publisher, small or large, doesn't use email or sell from a web site or use desktop publishing or use computerised accounting? Why then does supply chain e-commerce provoke so much hostile attention? Why are telephoned orders and paper invoices the sacred cows of our industry?

For instance, readers may be interested to look at Simon Edwards's article in last week's Publishing News (I cannot link to the article direct because the archive search isn't working properly – ed) about the costs and complexities of running a telephone hotline. This is a huge expense for distributors, both in terms of personnel as well as disruption to working patterns, yet they still feel the need to offer them for fear of upsetting both booksellers and their third party clients. And one of the biggest users of telephone hotlines is also the bookselling chain which has put the most resource into persuading its suppliers to trade electronically!

Nielsen's recent decision to stop sending out thousands of Teleorders by fax or post – to publishers who may or may not even still exist – and set up an order collection web site instead has met with a mixed reaction. This has to be a step in the right direction but sadly Nielsen can do little to persuade the thousands of publishers who still keep title records and product information in manual (even hand-written) form to submit it electronically.

There are many similar examples of old practice which give our trade a much higher than necessary cost base and of course lower profits. As an industry, we need a much better understanding of what the real cost is of doing business inefficiently – and how easily this cost can get neglected when it comes to negotiating booksellers' discounts or the terms under which distributors contract with their third party client publishers. For example, it is perfectly possible for one bookseller who trades electronically, returns very little and is altogether a model customer to get lower discounts than a bookseller who orders on paper, pays late and has high returns. Armed with some cost-to-serve analysis and a willingness to question the way we do business, much could be done to make the book trade more efficient, more profitable and more resilient.

11 January 2007

The thirty-nine steps

This comes to you from very genteel Henley-on-Thames where I'm staying at the contemporary posh Hotel du vin. The people here at the front desk disagree with my description – they prefer words like beautiful, comfortable and friendly. It is a great hotel but I'm fixated by the fact there were 39 stairs between the door of my room and the bed. A record I think, although someone will probably correct me.

I'm here for the Publishers Association international strategy meeting. In spite of the importance of the UK book trade, British publishers would not exist without their exports. And we do it really rather well in spite of having to contend with a very strong currency (vs our major competitor, the US dollar), threats from territorial erosion, piracy, dodgy dealers and restrictive practices in some countries.

The latest statistics show export growth of 14% in units and 10% by value with fastest growth in children's books and educational programs. Academic unit sales actually fell as a result of people switching to digital delivery but revenues held up. This year, subject to the usual provisos about political events and natural disasters should see further growth in Asia, Eastern Europe and the emerging markets in general.

The biggest issue (and cost) continues to be piracy and the Publishers Association (whose website will shortly reflect more obviously its merits!) leads the world's publishing industries in taking action where necessary and supporting legal and consitutional routes to the protection of authors' copyrights. It is expensive but vital. It is another example of a cost which commentators from within and without the industry tend to forget when calculating profits.

12 January 2007

Buchpreisbindung

A week ago I (perhaps unwisely) gave space to the cri de coeur of an independent bookseller. This was followed by several days of interesting and sometimes coruscating debate. I tried to steer things away from re-runs of the Net Book Agreement argument on the grounds that we no longer have retail price maintenance, it won't reappear, and there's little point crying over spilt milk.

However, some things never seem to go away altogether and the retail price maintenance debate is still a live issue in Germany. I wonder (again perhaps unwisely) if any of the commentators to this blog can offer advice to German publishers and retailers. For instance has the experience in the UK shown:

British consumers benefit from lower prices?

Supermarkets have significantly widened the market for books?

If the NBA had continued would supermarkets have even been interested in books?

Quality bookshop chains have thrived?

Independent booksellers have been able to carve out a price-insensitive niche?

Publishers have behaved responsibly in post-NBA dealings with retailers?

I think I can predict the responses but I'd love to be proved wrong. From a commentator in the USA a very interesting Q&A session with a mystery entrepreneur.

A very sad blog relating to the AMS bankruptcy in the USA which is likely to send small publishers into financial danger or disaster.

More statistics for the Macmillan year-end round-up – Numbers 1 and 2 in the back-to-university bestseller lists: Study Skills Handbook and Student Planner.

For those interested in cricket here is an extract from an email I received from a distinguished cricket journalist (you have to understand the game to get the joke/irony):

Sorry I haven't replied earlier but I have only just got back from Australia and what was probably a v close and competitive Test series compared with the ODIs to come!

And finally a show-off piece about a paper on stem cells which appeared in <u>Nature Biotechnology</u>. So far the paper has appeared in more than 1000 newspaper articles around the world according to <u>Google News</u> and any number of TV and radio mentions. Science may be difficult to understand but there is a huge demand for information about it and the reliability of that information is vital. We think our team offers just that reliability to scientists and the general public alike – and our press team knows how to make a scientific paper famous. That's a pretty good description of what all publishing is about – good content and good publicity.

13 January 2007

William Armstrong

It's curious that when I or others <u>write</u> about the problems of independent bookselling in 2006 there is always a flurry of vaguely nostalgic comments about the long defunct <u>Net Book Agreement</u>. And yet when I <u>invite</u> comments on that subject to help inform our German bookseller and publisher colleagues there is hardly any response. My view is best expressed in an extract from a letter in yesterday's <u>Bookseller</u> from the Chief Executive of the <u>Booksellers' Association</u>, Tim Godfray.

Moreover, it is ridiculous to suggest that the BA just watched the Net Book Agreement wither. With the PA, we played a leading role in successfully heading off an OFT investigation on two occasions, as well as winning a court case against DGIV (the European Competition Commission) in the European Court of Justice. But at the end of the day, the NBA was a voluntary publishers' agreement. Two leading trade publishers had by 1995 elected to have nothing to do with it; they were joined by other leading publishing houses who, faced by opposition from the competition authorities, the media, many politicians, and by one of our largest members, Dillons, decided it could no longer be sustained. It cannot be brought back. It is history. We have to move on.

I was unable to attend the funeral of the great publisher and friend of Macmillan, <u>William Armstrong</u>. He died on 22 December 2006. The funeral took place on 11 January at St Michael's Church, Highgate.

George Morley described the event for us.

'After the first appropriately Irish hymn, 'Be Thou My Vision', his daughter <u>Dido</u> – who used to work at Sidgwick with William before she became a successful singer songwriter – gave a touching, heartfelt and funny address, ending it by singing 'The Mountains of Mourne' a traditional Irish song beloved by her father. Next came William's cousin from Limerick, <u>Des O'Malley</u>, who told wonderful stories of William and his family, including an encounter between William's formidable mother and the B Specials. William's wide-ranging and often unusual literary tastes were apparent even as a young man, he told us, when he was very keen on the Venerable Bede who was 'not very big in Ireland then.' The priest of St Joseph spoke next and even managed to work in a reference to Bede's story of the sparrow's flight through a great hall being a metaphor for human life. William's widow, Clare, then read John

Donne's 'Death Be Not Proud', followed by a family friend, who read a poem about William that she had written. Another hymn – Lord of the Dance – preceded Patrick Janson-Smith's encomium to William's long and successful career, reminding us that he had presided over Sidgwick & Jackson's golden age, publishing – among many, many other successes – Edward Heath's bestselling books about music and sailing, Shirley Conran's book of household hints, for which William coined the title and thus ensured its success – *Superwoman*, Shirley's novel *Lace*, Judith Krantz's *Scruples*, Bob Geldof's *Is That It?*, the memoirs of Ron & Reg Kray, Boy George's *Take It Like A Man*, whose title, PJS said, had to be explained to him by younger members of staff and, of course, General Sir John Hackett's *The Third World War*, which was entirely William's idea. Mary Mount, ex Sidgwick work experience, now Editorial Director of Viking and family friend, read Philip Larkin's 'On an Arundel Tomb' and the congregation sang the final hymn, 'The Day Thou Gavest, Lord, Is Ended.' William's son, Rollo, came next, speaking about his dad lovingly, wittily and warmly, before Dido sang Patrick Kavanagh's On Raglan Road, which she had sung to her father when he was dying and which he always claimed was about his great-aunt Hilda O'Malley. The service ended with the Pie Jesu from Faure's Requiem and the usual prayers. Afterwards, the family and many of the congregation followed the cortege to Highgate Cemetery where William was buried, but not before Clare, Dido and Rollo had thrown tennis balls into the grave with him, reflecting William's abiding love of a fiercely competitive game of tennis.'

And I am grateful to Patrick Janson-Smith for his permission to quote from his eulogy.

'William O'Malley Armstrong was a good friend of many years' standing. I met him through publishing and so it is of his distinguished career in publishing that I will speak.

Insofar as I am aware, William began his publishing career at Purnell, where he edited a partwork on World War 2, but it was in 1968, when he joined the then independent publishing house of Sidgwick & Jackson, that he began to attract the trade's attention. For over a quarter of a century, through several changes of ownership. William presided over what was, without question, Sidgwick's Golden Age, publishing enthusiastically across a wide range of subjects, from poetry and politics to hard rock and even harder criminals' memoirs . . .

Milestones in William's illustrious career would have to include Edward Heath's extraordinarily successful books on sailing and music, of which it was said: The unsigned ones are the valuable ones . . .

In conclusion I have chosen an anecdote, mildly censored, that, to me, best sums up his human qualities:

I was going to lunch one day when William hailed me over. He was at his desk reading a tabloid newspaper.

'It says here that my son Rollo was cavorting on a beach in Ibiza with someone called Helena Christensen . . . . why is THAT in the newspaper?'

'She's a well-known supermodel, William.'

'Oh really . . . .So it's a GOOD thing?'

May the road rise up to meet you,

May the wind be always at your back,

May the sun shine warm upon your face,

and the rain fall soft upon your fields,

and until we meet again,

May God hold you in the palm of his hand.'

🗓 14 January 2007

Cheers and boos

I came across an interesting website, Publishing Hub, sponsored by the Oxford International Centre for Publishing Studies, Specifically I can recommend a podcast interview with David Attwooll of the electronic publishing consultancy Attwooll Associates. Here's a picture of David whom I've known for decades.

Chris Jennings, pagetoscreen.net.

As you can clearly see from his physiognomy he is an optimist and he sees the opportunities in publishing – a key characteristic for success. Perhaps less characteristic of publishers is that he doesn't just want to succeed in his own endeavours, he revels in the success of others. Cheers to David.

This article from the Independent newspaper is entirely different. It is an attack on Jeffrey Archer's forthcoming The Gospel According to Judas. The journalist, Boyd Tonkin, has decided it's worthless before reading a word. He's rather thrown by the fact that Archer has had support from the likes of theological giants such as Cardinal Martini, Desmond Tutu and Frank Moloney. He can only explain this away by suggesting that they are simply being Christian in supporting a repentant sinner. Boyd, how about the possibility that they might think it a good idea to work with a best-selling author to make Christianity more relevant and interesting to a wide audience?

He then tries another tack. The Christian establishment shouldn't suppport someone who committed perjury (for which, incidentally, he served a long prison term). Boo to Boyd.

Fortunately not everybody is so negative, so partial, so mean-spirited and the world's media have welcomed the forthcoming event with enthusiasm – I won't bore you with the five pages listing the coverage but here is a balanced piece from Publishing News.

The book and audio version will be available on 20th March. I'm sure you'll be able to order from all good booksellers but perhaps you should try the excellent Bedside Crow or Keeble Antiques who, as independent booksellers, give personalised customer service rather than relying on discounting books.

And to end on a recommendation, Andrea Camilleri. His detective books set in Sicily have made him Italy's most popular novelist. Picador has just launched his sixth in English, described here in the Independent. The (anti)hero Montalbano is definitely the grumpiest detective in fiction and makes even our correspondent, Clive Keeble, seem restrained.

Les francais

There's a wonderful news <u>story</u> this morning about a suggestion by the French Prime Minister in 1956, <u>Guy Mollet</u>, to the British Government that France and Britain merge. And when that idea was scotched by the British Prime Minister, <u>Anthony Eden</u> he then applied for membership of the British Commonwealth. This triggered a memo just released which stated that:

'The PM told him on the telephone that he thought in the light of his talks with the French:

- 'That we should give immediate consideration to France joining the Commonwealth

- 'That Monsieur Mollet had not thought there need be difficulty over France accepting the headship of her Majesty

- 'That the French would welcome a common citizenship arrangement on the Irish basis'

We publish an excellent series of books with the generic title, <u>What If?</u> which address just this sort of thing but I don't think even they had the nerve to think this was within the realms of possibility. But just think, what if France and Britain merged? No European Union? A state-driven British economy. The English language 'purified' and kept pure. A much better rugby team. Windsor Castle moved to Versailles. No net book agreement in France! Les Tuileries converted into a cricket ground. Extraordinaire.

Back to publishing, this is the week when news comes in from round the Macmillan world about the final reckoning for 2006. There's one stand-out piece of good news from just about everywhere and it is the success of both <u>Macmillan Children's Books</u> and <u>Priddy Books</u>. The latter was set up only a few years ago and it is already the leader in information books for young (and not so young) children. There are always arguments about whether children's books can cross cultures. Sometimes yes, sometimes no. In the case of both these businesses just about every country has welcomed their titles as if they were created specially for their children. It's great to see genuinely innovative publishing teams succeed in this tough old world.

South African triumphs

Another quote from Matthew Engel's forthcoming <u>Red Notebooks</u>, this time by <u>Adlai Stevenson</u>: An editor is one who separates the wheat from the chaff and prints the chaff.

As the sales figures for 2006 flow in from all parts of Macmillan I thought I'd share with you over the next few days a more international representation of the non-chaff bestseller lists from our various companies.

First, South Africa where Peter Godwin's <u>When a Crocodile Eats the Sun</u> is second only to the perennial <u>Guinness World Records</u>.

3. <u>Wilbur Smith's Triumph of the Sun</u>

4. David Baldacci's The Collectors

5. Jeffrey Archer's Cat o' Nine Tails

6. The Google Story

7. Jeffrey Archer again with False Impressions

8. The 80th birthday edition of the condensed version of Nelson Mandela's Long Walk to Freedom

9. Our Iceberg is Melting

10. Scott Turow's Ordinary Heroes

Here in the UK it has been an interesting week for national statistics (a contradiction in terms?), with the simultaneous launch by the UK Office for National Statistics (ONS) of their new Personal Inflation Calculator to much media attention, and the launch, to a perhaps somewhat less frenzied press interest, of a new ONS journal publication – the monthly *Economic and Labour Market Review* – which Palgrave Macmillan publishes on behalf of the Office for National Statistics.

The two were launched together on Monday evening at an event hosted at the DTI conference centre in Victoria Street, London. The personal inflation calculator, which has been heavily trailed in the media already, is explained in detail in the new *Economic & Labour Market Review*. A definitive article on the new calculator can be accessed for free here.

17 January 2007

Wholesalers

Today we received the news that the British wholesaler Bertrams is being acquired by its competitor Entertainment UK. I suppose consolidation is inevitable. Publishers will no doubt disagree on whether the potential benefits of greater efficiencies might or might not be outweighed by the risks of reduced competition. I would be very interested in the views of retailers, particularly independent booksellers, who rely on high-quality, cost-effective service from wholesalers.

Yesterday I published the top ten bestsellers from Pan Macmillan South Africa. Now it's the turn of Ireland and Gill & Macmillan.

1. The Pope's Children

2. This is Charlie Bird

3. Overheard in Dublin

4. New Complete Geography

5. Impact

6. New Concise Maths 1

7. The Past Today

8. Wednesday's Child

9. Inis Dom 3

10. Ireland and the Ryder Club

This is a fair reflection of the diversity of publishing. I do hope consolidation doesn't ever reduce such choice.

18 January 2007

Who killed Napoleon Bonaparte?

One of our most important investments has been the development of the Nature Clinical Practice stable of journals for practising clinicians which we launched in 2004. We undertook a great deal of market research and consulted literally hundreds of eminent physicians about their information needs. I don't think a single one would have identifed the cause of Napoleon's death as a very high priority but now Nature Clinical Practice Gastroenterology and Hepatolgy has cracked it with the publication of the snappily titled and open-access available Napoleon Bonaparte's Gastric Cancer: a clinicopathologic approach to staging, pathogenesis, and etiology. A pithier description will be found here and in any number of tabloid newspapers around the world.

And while on journals from Nature Publishing Group I couldn't resist this extract from Michael Crichton's genetic bestseller, Next:

'Good,good. Make those changes, shoot it back to me, and I'll submit it to Nature. I think this deserves a better platform than Science, which is a little down at heels these days. I'll call over to Nature and make sure the editor understands the importance of this paper, and see that we get immediate publication.'

What greater praise could we receive?

Continuing our round-the-world review of Macmillan bestsellers we reach Macmillan Publishers New Zealand.

1. The Lovely Bones

2. The Collectors

3. Triumph of the Sun

4. Cat o'Nine Tails

5. Science World 9

6. Camel Club

7. Macmillan New Zealand World Atlas

8. My Story: Schappelle Corby

9. Science World 10

10. <u>The Gruffalo</u> whom I couldn't resist showing:

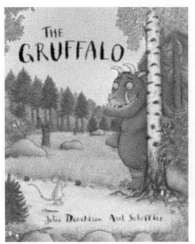

And Chris Baty, who runs Pan Macmillan NZ, sent me these words to accompany the list – thanks Chris:

'Kiwis could be regarded as an ornery bunch. Despite being at the bottom of the world and there not being many of them, they have a habit of determinedly doing things their own way. And this was the way of New Zealand in 2006. Many retailers would say it was the worst year in a very long time.

As with many parts of the world, 2006 launched to rapidly and frequently rising petrol prices, which continued until the last quarter. With little in the way of public transport – even in the bigger cities, freight being road based, and NZ being a long way from all markets, it meant the impact on the country was sharp. The extra money ordinary folk spent on fuelling their cars to get to work, was the equivalent of the cost of at least one or two books.

Combine this with the Reserve Bank raising the rates of interest each quarter in their efforts to take the steam out of the housing market, which has seen unprecedented growth in the past 2 years to the point where a very average house in Auckland, NZ's largest city in the north, is going up at the rate of $540 per day! Part of the New Zealand dream is that one owns one's own home, so a high percentage of the population does just that. Despite their best efforts, the Bank has failed miserably to shatter this dream. Kiwis continue to buy and sell property unabated taking bigger and bigger mortgages at increasing interest rates (floating mortgage rates are 9.55%). The government wails at the amount of money invested in the non-productive housing sector, but for individuals, it is the only reliable investment return they have found. Most ordinary people invest for their old age, of course, but when there is no national superannuation scheme offering tax incentives or employer contributions, why would a madly individual Kiwi not go for something more reliable which they can manage themselves.

Furthermore, when the country's annual surplus comes in at $40 billion and way more than the government planned in their wildest dreams; when there is a huge skills shortage and record employment levels (unemployment is below 4%), business confidence is on a real high, one could be forgiven for thinking these individual Kiwis would have stopped believing their government who steadfastly claim an overheated economy. And certainly they would not do anything the government exhorted them to, in regards to economic wellbeing.

And mostly this is true – with one exception! The Reserve Bank has cajoled, begged, bullied and threatened New Zealanders to stop spending money, particularly on the 'plastic fantastic' (credit cards). And of all the things they chose to be obedient on, it was shopping at Christmas – especially for books. They indulged minimally!

And so Kiwis maintain their proud tradition of being perverse! Internationally they are best known for it in the sports arena, but they are like it at home too.

Talking of sports arenas – just watch them this year at the Rugby World Cup, the America's Cup, the Netball World Cup, the Bledisloe Cup (rugby), the Tri-Nations (rugby), and the Softball World Cup. They assure us that local perversity was, of course, proven yet again when they let England win the cricket a few days ago! Anyway they invite you all over to see for yourselves – there will be plenty of cups for everyone this year; there just may not be enough chairs!'

🐦 19 January 2007

Booksellers and digitisation

Yesterday I attended a meeting organised by the <u>Booksellers Association</u> to discuss the opportunities and threats posed to the book trade as a whole by the shifting sands of technology and consumer behaviour. The meeting was conducted under the Chatham House rule but it was agreed that the findings and discussions will be widely communicated as soon as the materials are put in order. I shall not jump the gun but, while listening, my mind kept going back to an interview which I <u>blogged</u> a few days ago. It generated a lot of <u>comments</u> from independent booksellers as the 'mystery entrepreneur' challenged many preconceptions about our industry and bookselling in particular. However, it was the last question and answer which has (understandably) made me think hardest:

WW: What about Publishers? Aren't publishers part of the problem? Shouldn't they be part of the solution?

MC: My guess is that somewhere in that solution will be the elimination of 'publishers' as we traditionally know them. The only other industry consisting of massively over-compensated mediocre performers who have utterly outlasted their utility and raison d'etre and exist only by virtue of an entrenched, self-protective, bullying autocracy that gangs up against threats posed by obviously more efficient methods that would, could, should and will eliminate them—is Wall Street.

Well, that's telling us. The only consolation is that, for all its sins, I'm pretty certain that Wall Street will survive – and so shall publishers.

Our virtual tour of Macmillan bestsellers takes us to Palgrave Macmillan in the Flatiron Building in New York who have just ended the best year in their history thanks to brilliant publishing and assiduous marketing.

1. <u>The Statesman's Yearbook 2007</u>

2. <u>Grants Register 2007</u>

3. <u>The Battle for Peace</u>

4. History of Africa

5. The New American Workplace

6. Purpose

7. Patten.

8. Brandsimple

9. Open Target

10. Samuel Adams

And finally today I'd like to point you to our latest significant investment, the creation of a completely new university-level science publisher, Nature Education. A quote from its newly-appointed publishing director, Vikram Savkar, says it all:

'Instructors and students are thirsty for learning environments that move beyond traditional textbooks and even course management systems to provide a highly interactive and personalized experience that simultaneously builds understanding, inspires career and research aspirations, and connects the student to a worldwide community of likeminded thinkers. With its excellent content, brand, global reach, and community of practicing scientists, NPG and Macmillan are superbly positioned to catalyze and capitalize on a radical shift in education.'

🗓 20 January 2007

Occam and his razor

I attended another meeting yesterday focussing on the problems besetting the British public library system. Tim Coates has written about it on his Good Library Blog. I was delighted to see his reference to my old friend William of Ockham. Not much is known about his life except that he was born in Ockham in Surrey and the medieval church there has had a stained glass window of him installed.

The paintings of him aren't very helpful but here's a colourful one looking rather like a cartoon monk.

What I really like about him is the vagueness of it all. His name is spelt several different ways. According to this brilliant article in the Internet Encyclopedia of Philosophy he wasn't the originator of his famous philosophical razor concept, nor did he even use the word 'razor'. The concept is written in Latin – *entia non sunt multiplicanda praeter necessitatem* – and can be interpreted in any number of subtly different ways.

'All things being equal, the simplest solution tends to be the best one.'

'Simpler theories are, other things being equal, generally better than more complex ones.

'Don't multiply entities beyond necessity.'

'Plurality should not be assumed without necessity.'

'It is useless to do with more what can be done with less.'

The amount of hot air being expended on library funding, management and objectives might be significantly reduced by the application of old Bill Occam's razor and a review based on these five Occamesque observations from Tim Coates.

- The library service is for people and its only purpose is to respond to their needs (currently it does not do this adequately)

- It is essentially about reading (currently it is not sufficiently so)

- Its operation must be simple (because at present it is too complex)

 – Those responsible for providing the service are those who work in the libraries (currently they are not able to be).

 – Those accountable to the public are councillors (currently they do not account).

And please may we ignore for this exercise other bons mots such as 'The devil is in the detail' or Einstein's 'Everything should be made as simple as possible, but not one bit simpler.'

Bill's contemporary version is 'Keep it simple, stupid' and I suggest that all library acronymic participants adopt this as their mission statement.

⏳ 21 January 2007

Bangalore

I'm off to Bangalore later today. We employ around 1500 people in Bangalore and 3000 plus in India as a whole. The business is divided into several divisions and the divisions into units. This is essential for manageability but inevitably introduces complexity.In the two days I am there I'll be attending thirteen separate board or executive meetings, each dealing with a separate strategic business unit. And when I leave I bet we'll have created some new ones too.

One of the key technologies impacting the book industry is on-demand printing and Ingram's Lightning Source is a leading supplier. A Macmillan production manager visited their factory recently and brought back this photo. When he asked the plant manager what went on in that particular department, the response was R&R. Now we know.

⏳ 22 January 2007

Letter from Bangalore

As the plane prepared to descend the BA steward reminded us to clear the area around our seats of ALL materials – 'including books and other debris'. I sometimes think we're in the paper recycling industry but debris . . . ?

Of course the big news story here is Shilpa Shetty and Big Brother.

The media in Bangalore and across the sub-continent are having the time of their lives attacking British TV, British racism, British manners, and celebrity idiocy – and affirming the superiority of Indian culture. I agree with them.

The other headlines today were all about the riots in East Bangalore where an 11-year-old boy was killed and a curfew imposed. In the West we hear a great deal about violence in the Middle East (of course) and we make a great deal out of, for instance, the riots in Paris. We tend to view India as a vibrantgrowing democratic economy. India has issues too and they are not far below the surface.

But the more positive side of India is evident in today's Bangalore newspaper where the bulk of the ads are from Australian universities trawling for the best students. The world is, indeed, flat.

⏳ 23 January 2007

Orissa

I wrote a little while ago about the funeral for William Armstrong. Here is a link to an excellent obituary in The Independent.

The riots in Bangalore have subsided. The row over Shilpa Shetty is simmering but not explosive. Today's big news is that the Indian cricket manager, Greg Chappell, has been assaulted for failing to select anyone from Orissa State in the Indian team. When he took the job I can imagine Chappell had a few concerns – selection, fitness, opposition, poitical tension – but I don't suppose being beaten up at an airport was one of them.

The other thing he would never have predicted is that the <u>BCCI the Indian cricket board</u> would grant TV rights to an operation which has resulted in the most popular sports entertainment for a billion people not being available to half of them. That is even worse than not selecting anyone from beautiful Orissa.

🔖 24 January 2007

Recommendations and refreshments

As we all know, India is almost perfect. The economy is booming. The human resource is adaptable and plentiful. The food is outstanding. However, every institution can improve and I have four recommendations to put to the Indian Parliament.

1. Move the time zone 30 minutes forward or backward so that dimwitted and jet-lagged foreigners know what the time is when they wake up. Try subtracting 5 and a half hours from the local time.

2. Abolish lakhs (100,000) and crores (10.000,000) except for literary and poetic use.

3. Introduce the New Rupee which is 100 Old Rupees.

4. Persuade British Airways to invest in more than one phone per check-in staff.

I estimate these amendments would increase India's GDP by at least one percentage point.

I am indebted to <u>Tim Coates</u> for the following costs of borrowing a book from libraries in various parts of London. The cost is derived by simply dividing the total costs of library provision in the area by the number of loans. Both the absolute costs (it would be cheaper simply to give the books away?) and the variations suggest that there are huge savings to be made which could lead to enhanced book stocks and even better service.

Camden £11.50
Greenwich £7.14
Hackney £10.07
Hammersmith £6.63
Islington £10.46
Kensington £8.54
Lambeth £10.29
Lewisham £5.77
Southwark £6.89
Tower Hamlets £9.90
Wandsworth £3.64
Westminster £5.91

And finally the mission statement from the only cafe in Bangalore Airport:

To be the best cafe chain by offering a world class coffee experience at affordable prices.

I'm thinking of adapting this for the Baldons Cricket Club which has been obliged by some new regulation to invent a constitution. To be the best village cricket team offering excellent teas at affordable prices. Shame about the pavilion and the pitch.

🦉 25 January 2007

Prospect and property

Prospect magazine is the brainchild of David Goodhart, its editor. It was launched in 1995 and has been described as 'more readable than the Economist, more relevant than the Spectator, more romantic than the New Statesman.' They have just launched a blog and I was invited to contribute a piece on scientific publishing. In the process of writing the piece I rediscovered the difficulties of explaining a complex situation in very few words and of typing more than one sentence on a Blackberry in the departures lounge at Bangalore Airport.

One theory of success in publishing is that the chances of survival are directly linked to intelligent property policy. Faber's ownership of its offices in Queen Square, Souvenir Press's office in Great Russell Street have helped the companies through difficult times. John Murray's wonderful Albemarle Street offices allowed it to hold on to its independence for more than two centuries.

This article from the New York Times suggests that our Nature team in New York are following an equally sensible property policy.

🦉 26 January 2007

Australia Day

It's Australia Day down under and the Aussies are enjoying it in the traditional way – humiliating England in a cricket match.

It seems appropriate therefore to complete the global review of our bestsellers with Pan Macmillan Australia's top ten.

Guinness World Records 2007

The Valley – the latest from Australia's highest selling female writer.

My Story – Schapelle Corby's chilling story of her imprisonment in a Bali jail.

The Great War – Les Carlyon's new classic history has sold over 90,000 copies in hardback in Australia – how many serious history books achieve those numbers proportionately anywhere else in the world?

Cat on the Mat is Flat by the brilliantly funny Andy Griffiths.

Circle of Flight by the best-selling author for teenagers ever in Australia, the legendary John Marsden.

Cat O'Nine Tails – the first Pom in the list – Jeffrey Archer on top short story form.

The Unknown Terrorist – a simply brilliant novel from Richard Flanagan.

Seven Ancient Wonders from Matthew Reilly, Australia's (and progressively the world's) leading adventure writer.

Triumph of the Sun by the ever popular Wilbur Smith.

I reckon that side would beat any team in the world and, in addition to the authors, the success is down to exceptional publishing people. I have a nasty feeling that the Pan Macmillan Australia publishing team would also beat the current England team at cricket too.

And while on the subject of publishing teams, last night we had a very special party at our Kings Cross offices. It was to celebrate the careers of two of our top management team who are retiring. This blog would become very boring if I recorded and commented on every retirement but Mike Barnard and Geoff Todd deserve special mention. Neither of them has featured heavily in the pages of the Bookseller. Neither claims to have the secret of publishing. Neither is interested in bullshit. Between them (for over thirty years each) they have ensured that the machine which makes Macmillan tick is in good working order. The accounts come out on time and are accurate, royalties are paid, books are produced beautifully and economically, offices function and conform to the law, IT systems work and don't cost the earth, distribution is the best in the industry. Since I joined Macmillan, I've had to worry about many things but I've also known I could trust the machine to function because it had two such high-quality operators. They are also exceedingly decent and fun people. Thanks guys.

Crime shouldn't pay?

Back in <u>November</u> I wrote about a British Government consultation aimed at preventing criminals profiting from their crimes through publication earnings. The deadline for responses to the <u>Home Office</u> is 9 February. At Macmillan we have taken this potential threat to freedom of expression seriously not least because we have been threatened on several occasions including around the publication of <u>Cries Unheard</u> by <u>Gitta Sereny</u>, the story of <u>Mary Bell</u>.

By permission of Pan Macmillan, London.

There was also quite a ruckus over the publication of Jeffrey Archer's <u>Prison Diaries</u>.

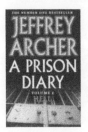

By permission of Pan Macmillan, London.

As a result we commissioned a Macmillan employee, Tim Howles, to discuss the issue with editors and lawyers internally and externally and generate a response. Here is the opening part of it – the full document will presumably be uploaded to the Home Office website in due course.

In principle, do you think that a new measure is necessary? Please say why or why not?

Response:

> The response of the Macmillan Publishing Group to this consultation paper is as follows:

> i. The Macmillan Publishing Group supports in principle the need to avoid causing undue offence to victims and to the families of victims of serious crime due to the publication of writing by the convicted offender that refers directly to the crime;

> ii. However, the public interest is ultimately served most by safeguarding the freedom of expression and by protecting the right to receive information about serious crime;
> iii. For this reason, the first concern of the Macmillan Publishing Group is that no proposal would prevent the publication of such writings. This includes any mechanism that would tend towards either direct prohibition (such as the introduction of criminal or civil liability for the publisher) or

indirect action (such as making the writing of relevant material less attractive to criminals or too expensive for the publisher to contemplate);

iv. The Macmillan Publishing Group believes that proposal options (1), (2) and (3), as set out in the consultation paper, are unacceptable, since they would all in practice equate to a prevention of the publication of such writings;

v. The Macmillan Publishing Group strongly asserts that no new measure is necessary. This is on the grounds of cost (these options would be expensive and time-consuming to implement), efficiency (they would be hard to define and implement) and public interest (the market should be the ultimate arbitrator of what is acceptable);

vi. Therefore, the Macmillan Publishing Group strongly believes that proposal option (4) should be pursued in order to allow market forces to determine whether or not the publication is read.

I cannot believe that the Government would be silly enough to try to enforce unenforceable and constrictive legislation in this area. The problem is that Governments sometimes do silly things in response to tabloid headlines. The book trade should help the Government not to be silly on this occasion.

As part of my 'academic' duties I sit on the board of a partnership between the London Business School and the University of the Arts London. It is called the Centre for Creative Business and its aim is to help organisations which focus on the development of creativity also to cope with the demands of business. They run an excellent and heavily subsidised course, Building the Creative Business, and you can download a prospectus here.

28 January 2007

Schoom

Years ago a doctor friend of mine asked me to look at manuscript of short stories by his brother. I was not overkeen (brothers of friends with manuscripts to sell are a publisher's cross to bear by and large).Anyway, I agreed and these were the first words I read:

'Tell me something,' said Morris, my father-in-law to be. 'What would a guy like you make?' 'A guy like me,' I replied, 'would make about the same as I do.'

These were the opening lines of Schoom by Jonathan Wilson which we published under the now-defunct Limetree imprint. He has gone on to publish several books with Random House in the USA. He sent me an invitation to a reading of his latest book A Palestine affair published by Five Leaves Publications which was originally published in 2004 by Random House USA.

The reading is 7.00pm 28th February at the Gallery at Swiss Cottage Library, 88 Avenue Road, London NW3 (where I used to swot for my A levels).

Why am I writing this apart from bringing your attention to a brilliant but not very famous writer (whom I happen to know and like)? It is to ask why on earth in a global marketplace a global publisher like Random House doesn't just publish a book like this everywhere in English in the first instance. One of their excellent editors in New

York clearly liked the book. They've invested in it. They've got to know the author. They've copy-edited it, proofread it, designed a jacket for it, they've loaded it onto their computers, they've had it printed, deposited the stock in their warehouses, they've promoted it, entered it in their catalogues. And then they decide not to 'publish' it in little places like Britain, Australia etc.

This is not to pick on Random House – we frequently do just the same – but what sense can this make?

By permission of Pan Macmillan, London.

I can't resist quoting from a review of Exile by Richard North Patterson. You can read the full review in the The Times.

EVERY NOW AND THEN — but a lot more rarely than that implies — you come across a thriller so important that it absolutely demands to be read. This is one . . . .

. . . His recent books, however, have taken a more political stance, drawing on such contentious issues as abortion, US gun laws, the death penalty and now, most controversially of all, the Israeli-Palestinian conflict . . .

. . . Patterson has done stupendous research, is admirably level-headed, eschews sermonising and patronising. Now, more than ever, as this conflict holds the world to ransom, this is a thriller that deserves to be a bestseller.

Finally, a few extracts from an interview with me in the American librarian journal Against the Grain which doesn't (yet) publish its articles on the web but which is well worth reading if you are in the least interested in developments in electronic publishing and the academic community.

Richard Charkin, chief executive of Macmillan, one of the world's leading educational, scholarly, and general publishing companies, is known for a willingness to take risks, even to the point of starting to blog earlier this year. We turned to him with questions about innovation in publishing, the book supply chain, and electronic publishing. The most surprising thing about his comments is that there is not a single word here about cricket or The Ashes, but you'll be able to follow England's fortunes, as well as news about UK and international publishing here.

Q: What's the most exciting new thing Macmillan has done since you've been there?

A: The transformation of <u>Nature</u> and its sister journals from a paper-based magazine company into a global electronic scientific information and navigation service. Sales have tripled and annual investment has increased more than tenfold. Every single part of the value chain has been inspected for 'fit for purpose' in the twenty-first century and abandoned, replaced, or improved. Most importantly, we have never ceased taking risks, launching new products, experimenting, and promoting talent.

Q: One of your most controversial innovations is the <u>New Writing</u> program. What makes it different, and why has it ignited so much anger from other publishers and literary agents?

A: Macmillan New Writing is a program that gives a voice to new authors who are talented but who might otherwise not get into print. We offer standardized terms that are modest at the beginning but place the commercial risk on the publisher rather than the author. The author receives no advance but also pays nothing (unlike typical arrangements with vanity publishers) and benefits from a royalty arrangement that is generous and open-ended. The author is published in standard book format and distributed through our normal Macmillan channels and through <u>MNW</u>. We review only adult fiction, take only electronic submissions, and look only at complete manuscripts-and there's still a 99 percent rejection rate.

When it comes to the negative reaction we've had from some quarters, I suppose that when a system is established it's very hard for its practitioners to accept that it may be flawed and that something much simpler (and actually more old-fashioned) might be a better model. In fact, we just applied Occam's Razor. What are the essential elements for spotting new talent? What are the bits that are counterproductive or uneconomic? Let's keep the former and abandon the latter. We've had general break-even. One or two titles have done better than par, but the real success will come only when we find an author who really breaks through in sales or esteem, and that's still to come. However, the key thing is that when searching for the new superstar we don't lose money-and that we have achieved. We have also rewarded our authors fairly, which is important.

Q: Given all our exposure to new ideas, one might think publishers would be innovative and likely to try new things. But publishers aren't known, to put it gently, for being innovative. Why's that?

A: I disagree. I think there is a misconception here about the role of the publisher. Where publishers are conservative is in their desire to publish 'safe' content – in other words, high-quality authors in a traditional format – novel, reference book, textbook, etc. However, content production is not the primary role of the publisher. The primary role is content dissemination, and here publishers have been innovative. For instance, the complete invention of a new business model – the site license – in scientific publishing. Or Westlaw and Lexis-Nexis. Or <u>xrefer</u>. Or <u>One Stop English</u>. I could go on but won't.

Q: What needs to change in publishing?

A: How many pages am I allowed? Get closer to readers as well as to intermediaries. Stop saying, 'I bought this book' rather than, 'I've been granted a license to publish this book.' Stop and turn around the movement to disintegration of rights. Improve profitability in trade publishing. Have more multilingual people on staff. Have more genuine all-rounders and more genuinely specialist people. Get less arrogant and accept that publishers are no more than a link between writer and reader and that there are plenty of others in the chain adding at least as much (and frequently more) value. Reduce the number of times a book is handled between printing machine and reader (currently around twenty-five times in my estimation and another twenty-five times on the way back for 35 percent of books that are returned). Buy into on-demand printing at point of use – library, bookshop, corporation. By the way, this is one reason why journals are more profitable than books. The process for journals publishing is much simpler.

Q: How about Google and Amazon – threat or opportunity?

A: Both are both. The biggest threat is the threat to copyright. There is a balance in society between the need to protect the inventor or creative talent and the need for society to benefit from their works. The Internet has a significant inclination toward the rights of the user and tends to undervalue the rights of the inventor. Google and Amazon don't always realize the consequences of their actions, in terms of maintaining this balance. The opportunity they offer is, at very low cost, to publicize the existence and help people find and buy books, in e or print form.

Q: You're now a blogger. What has that taught you, do you expect to continue, and what do your publishing colleagues say about it?

A: How to do accents on letters (but I've now forgotten). How to insert a hypertext link. What words generate extra traffic. Which statements generate comments and which ones don't. My colleagues by and large think I'm mad or a showoff or a fool.

Q: Are publishers an author's natural enemy, and is that the real reason for open-access journals?

A: No, readers are the author's natural enemy because most of them don't want to read a particular author's work, however good it is. There have always been open-access journals – they're usually called 'controlled circulation' (or 'organs of state propaganda'), and normally they are rather substandard. I'm sure that Public Library of Science and others are excellent, but I don't think they are the result of anti-publisher sentiment but rather a legitimate desire to make available everything to everyone for free. The problem is there is no such thing as a free lunch, and a good value one can be pretty sustaining.

Q: This article is for Against the Grain, which is read by academic librarians, publishers, and vendors. Anything else you'd like to talk about related to libraries?

A: Library acquisition budgets should be increased significantly as the productivity of librarians improves. But I would say that, wouldn't I?

29 January 2007

Authors and readers

I've been challenged by a commenter for this exchange in a recent interview with me.

Q: Are publishers an author's natural enemy, and is that the real reason for open-access journals?

A: No, readers are the author's natural enemy because most of them don't want to read a particular author's work, however good it is. There have always been open-access journals – they're usually called 'controlled circulation' (or 'organs of state propaganda'), and normally they are rather substandard. I'm sure that Public Library of Science and others are excellent, but I don't think they are the result of anti-publisher sentiment but rather a legitimate desire to make available everything to everyone for free. The problem is there is no such thing as a free lunch, and a good value one can be pretty sustaining.

Of course the question related to scientific authorship and the open access movement. My answer was slightly tongue in cheek and could be interpreted more widely. However, thinking about it more, perhaps there is some truth in it.

I remember Per Saugman, the early creator of Blackwell Scientific Publishing (sold recently for £600m), gave me a tip for authors demanding a higher royalty (the advance had not been invented!). His argument was that the publisher doesn't pay the royalty, the book purchaser does. And does the author really feel that his readers would be willing to pay significantly more for the book? Normally authors settled for the existing royalty and price on the grounds that the reader wasn't overkeen to pay the extra.

And then there's the nearly universal authorial complaint that their publisher isn't marketing hard enough. We all know that the best marketing is word of mouth. If sales aren't high enough it might be the publisher's marketing budget but it's more likely it's those pesky readers not spreading the word hard enough.

Sometimes readers even have the temerity not to like a particular book. Or they may find it of no interest. Or they just can't be bothered. Hard for the publisher to explain to the author whose world frequently revolves round the latest book.

Publishers are not authors' natural enemy. Authors and publishers and booksellers might do well to join forces and try to ally themselves with readers too. Perhaps that is the explanantion for the success of the Richard and Judy Book Club. Last year one in four of all books sold in the UK were recommended by R&J, an extraordinary statistic and evidence of the power of understanding the reader. Here are Britain's leading book marketers posing in front of a tiny proportion of the books they've been helped sell.

🎇 30 January 2007

The British Library

The last couple of days have seen a number of articles about the potential threat to the finances of the British Library as a result of the current Government spending review. This article sums things up pretty well. I should declare interests. Apart from being a great fan of the BL I also sit on one its advisory committees and I love the Eduardo Paolozzi sculpture of Isaac Newton in its piazza.

Fortunately the Library has a very strong and vociferous bunch of supporters who will be arguing for its budget for reasons of culture, scholarship, history etc – for instance here. It does seem crazy that the while the 'creative economy' is being heralded as one of Britain's fastest growing and world beating industries that we should be contemplating cheese-paring at its heart.

I would like to add one thought only and it's to do with geography. In November 2007 the Channel Tunnel rail link will open at St Pancras and will deposit 50 million passengers a year literally a stone's throw from the British Library. The library will be not only a magnet for British citizens but for the whole of Western Europe. Apart from the clear cultural benefits to Britain, the possibilities for generating revenue for the economy are enormous. Don't let's miss the chance by administering pointless cuts now.

Australians have a particularly direct way of describing politicians with whom they disagree about such things. Former Federal Treasurer and then Prime Minister, <u>Paul Keating</u>, was a world-class insulter and here are his references to opponents in 1984 alone: harlots, sleazebags, frauds, cheats, blackguards, pigs, mugs. clowns, criminals, stupid foul-mouth grub, corporate crook, rustbucket, scumbag, rip-off merchants, constitutional vandals, perfumed gigolos, gutless spiv, stunned mullets, barnyard bullies, pieces of criminal garbage – courtesy <u>Sydney Morning Herald</u> and <u>Matthew Engel</u>.

From one great national and international institution to another, <u>Google Corporation</u>. The spat over copyright and the Google library program continues and the lawyers are getting even richer. Meanwhile the story is beginning to make it into the broader press. Here's an excellent <u>article</u> from the New Yorker. The sentence below sent a shiver up my spine. The sooner the publishing industry can develop ways of working with Google on the basis of copyright licences and the sooner Google can accept that copyright is a genuine asset which cannot be appropriated without permission the better for all parties.

'The law is supposed to resolve issues like these—between self-interested parties with reasonable claims and legitimate arguments. But the rules of copyright are so ambiguous, and the courts so slow, that the judicial system serves largely to implement the law of the jungle.'

31 January 2007

Pleasurable Kingdom

About a year ago we published the hardback of <u>Pleasurable Kingdom</u>, a wonderful book by <u>Jonathan Balcombe</u> which argues that animals can feel pleasure. Here's the jacket which demonstrates the thesis.

The book hasn't (yet) made the bestseller lists but it has sold decently and its paperback release in July will give it further impetus. When we first published we focussed attention on the core markets of UK and USA but I was delighted to see just this week that the Macmillan machine burst into action in India last week to support the author on a tour and to ensure great press coverage such as <u>this</u>. It sometimes takes time for a book to reach its potential audience and it definitely takes patience. It also takes determination. Special thanks to Kalpana Shukla and her sales and marketing team in India. It's not always the obvious books which need marketing support.

But a forthcoming best selling book which will definitely be receiving the full marketing works is in house now and being prepared for worldwide publication this

Autumn. It is the latest thriller from <u>Ken Follett</u> entitled World without End. It is a sequel to his record-breaking <u>Pillars of the Earth</u> and I have absolutely no doubt that it will outsell all the other 20-odd books called World without End! Thank goodness there's no copyright in a book title.

Incidentally, today is a big day here at Macmillan because we promised various people that they would have an up and running digital <u>BookStore</u> by the close of play today. As with all deadlines we are right up against it and teams in the UK and India are working frantically hard to deliver. I'll report tomorrow on whether we've kept our promise.

For those of you who not yet seen it and for everyone who loves gossip, intrigue and a publishing soap opera please go to <u>Even Bitches Have Feelings</u> and enjoy the story of Judith Regan, Rupert Murdoch and O. J. Simpson. I think that the whole animal kingdom should find pleasure in this – with one or two notable exceptions.

≤ **February 2007** ≥

Mon	Tue	Wed	Thu	Fri	Sat	Sun
29	30	31	1	2	3	4
5	6	7	8	9	10	11
12	13	14	15	16	17	18
19	20	21	22	23	24	25
26	27	28	1	2	3	4
5	6	7	8	9	10	11

Happy birthday to BookStore

As this is the first of the month, I bore you with blog stats. In January we had 73059 visits, compared with 9036 in January 2006 (when we'd only just started) and 60,400 visits in the previous month (December 2006). This brings the total number of visits to 473,006.

I got into trouble yesterday for mentioning the deadline on the go-live date for BookStore ahead of its implementation. 'Supposing we'd had to delay – how embarrassing.' Quite. The best way to ensure compliance in Britain is not to threaten violence or offer bribes, it is to wave the possibility of embarrassment. In any event it worked and here is a relieved piece from MPSTechnologies commercial director, David Sommer. I should, however, add that, as with all babies, this is not the finished article. We are already working on improving speed, enhancing functionality, developing new formats and business models. It took over 500 years for the printed book industry to reach its present status. Let us have at least a few weeks to establish the e-book industry!

'Well – it has happened. MPS Technologies launched BookStore yesterday – on time. Macmillan Science and Macmillan New Writing are the first two publishers to go live with over 30 eBooks in a variety of formats. See their sites at: http://www.macmillansciencebookstore.com and http://www.macmillannewwritingbookstore.com

BookStore provides publishers with a customizable platform to better serve the needs of their readers and authors and enabling them to:

- Market, sell and deliver eBooks in the 3 main downloadable eBook formats as well as read online access

- Remain in control of their content and protect authors' copyright

- Build a direct relationship with readers and reach new readers

- Experiment with flexible business models to slice and dice access to content in new ways

Both sites allow users to browse inside the books' content, without compromising the control that Macmillan has over its digital content.

Authors at both imprints are enthusiastic about their work becoming available digitally and giving many more people the chance to search, sample and purchase these critically acclaimed books in a flexible, future-proof and eco-friendly way.

By permission of Pan Macmillan, London.

This is a major milestone for Macmillan's digital book strategy, but is just the start of the journey. There is a long way to go in terms of enhancing BookStore, adding functionality and meeting the needs of our publishing clients. We really would welcome your feedback on the sites please send comments (good or bad!) to: ValuableBookStoreFeedback@mpstechnologies.com

For more information, contact Lisa Hayden at Macmillan Science (l.hayden@macmillan.co.uk), Sophie Portas at Macmillan New Writing (s.portas@macmillan.co.uk) or Rupert Bacon at MPS Bookstore (r.bacon@mpstechnologies.com).

02 February 2007

Print is dead. Long live the book.

My piece yesterday on BookStore prompted my good friend, colleague and author Jeff Gomez to remind me of the blog he's set up to support his forthcoming book, Print is Dead, which we are publishing in print and electronically later this year. Jeff is responsible for the electronic publishing and marketing of much of Holtzbrinck Publishers, our sister company in USA and he knows what he's talking about.

And another sister company has just launched a new service to showcase the fruits of Chinese science to the world. It is Nature China. This has been made possible by the generous sponsorship support of AstraZeneca and is another example of the development of multiple business models to support the dissemination of scholarly material.

Yesterday I was asked in the comments for more detail on our visitors. Here are two pretty pictures showing which websites feed this blog and which countries during January. I hope they are helpful.

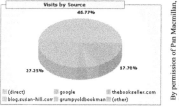

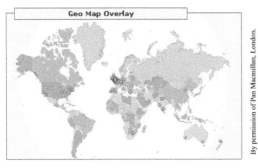

03 February 2007

Vive les anglais

The British novelist, Peter James has won the Prix Coeur Noir, France's leading award for crime fiction. Or as the PR agency Midas headlines its release: French beaten on home turf for major literary prize by plucky Brit. You can read him in English and German too.

I mentioned the party we held on Australia Day to celebrate the careers of Geoff Todd and Mike Barnard, two long-serving Macmillan directors. I'm not sure they'll thank me for this but here are photos of them at the party. Geoff is the Burns lookalike, Mike with the guitar.

Finally, to round out the Macmillan top sellers for 2006, here is the list of our top twenty English language teaching courses in unit sales order. For obvious commercial reasons I'm not publishing the actual numbers but I have been allowed to say that the first course in the list had sales of 50,513,200 in the year. The others were slightly less, but some pretty impressive numbers nonetheless. It's hard to link each of these individually but you can see a good selection at Macmillan English.

Position	Region	Title
1	China	New Standard English
2	Africa	Primary English
3	Mid East	English for Palestine
4	Mid East	Sunrise
5	Lat Am	Explore
6	Mid East/Asia	Way Ahead
7	Spain/W.Eur	Bugs
8	Lat Am	Rally
9	Caribbean	Essential Primary English
10	Lat Am	Bounce
11	India	New World Interactive
12	India	New Fun with Grammar
13	Spain	Story Magic
14	W.Eur/Asia/Lat Am	Inside Out
15	Asia/Mid East	Smile
16	Mid East	English for Agriculture
17	Asia/Lat Am	Skyline
18	Asia/Mid East	All Aboard
19	Lat Am	LINKS
20	Mid East	Explorers

04 February 2007

Of code-breaking, spies and unsung heroes

On a more serious level there have been many books about the British Government's intelligence centre, GCHQ, in Cheltenham. I hope I won't be arrested for showing this picture of its latest office building.

I was reminded about spy publishing by the arrival yesterday of a copy of Thirty Secret Years by my former boss and friend, Robin Denniston. The book is about his father, Alastair Denniston, who was in charge of the code-breaking team at Bletchley Park during the war. There are many historians who reckon that this project was a defining contribution to the outcome of the war.

I don't suppose the book will be another Spycatcher in terms of sales, not least because the Government has probably learned a few lessons about censorship attempts, but it would be great to see Robin and his far-sighted publishers, Polperro Heritage Press, succeed. It is a fascinating account of the back-room teams of intelligence and a social history of a special period of world history. The book is underpriced in trade paperback (in my opinion) and so order now!

Alastair Denniston worked in secret on behalf of Britain for thirty years. Neither the Times nor the Guardian published an obituary of him although belatedly the Dictionary of National Biography has put the record straight. On a much less important stage he reminds me of all those people in publishing who ensure success but never get any recognition. So a salute to the code-breakers of publishing as well as to Alastair Denniston.

Neologism of the day – 'frenemies', to describe the likes of Google or Amazon. They are our best friends but could easily become our worst enemies.

05 February 2007

World Book Day

I've had a bad blog morning. I wrote a pile and then the server lost it. Grrr. So I'm running late today.

Anyway, World Book Day on March 1 approaches and it's their tenth anniversary. For some reason this always leads to a plethora of lists and this year the Bookseller (check out their excellent new web design) has asked a random bunch of readers like me to list their 'top ten books people cannot live without.' Of course any such list is pointless and subjective but I list mine for what it's worth. Incidentally I notice that this week's Bookseller poll shows that 59% of voters think that discounts will rise faster than book prices (29%) and book sales (10%) – we're an optimistic bunch.

1. Wisden Cricketers' Almanack – although you might do best to wait until the 2007 edition is published, along with Spring, towards the end of March.

2. Oxford English Dictionary – I treasure my 20-volume set but really the online version is more sensible, less expensive, and does a better job.

3. Summer Lightning by P. G. Wodehouse, the master who created an England which probably never existed but should have.

4. Billy Bunter's Brainwave by Frank Richards whose real name was Charles Hamilton and who was not only the least politically correct novelist (and one of the funniest) but also the most prolific – 80 million words in a lifetime is going some.

5. The darling Buds of May by H. E. Bates – for humane comfort.

6. A Handful of Dust – by the dreadful but brilliant Evelyn Waugh and well worth reading this review from 1934.

7. A Fine Balance by the magical Parsee writer, Rohinton Mistry.

8. A-Z of London – although I fear that more and more it's being replaced by UK Streetmap.

9. Times Atlas of the World for obvious reasons.

And finally

10. A Kid for Two Farthings by Wolf Mankowitz – because we all need some schmaltz in our life.

Do let me know your lists.

06 February 2007

More on lists

When compiling yesterday's list of essential books I came across this book review archive from Time magazine. It is completely riveting and a wonderful example of how the Internet can enrich the history and understanding of literature and books. If you have a spare thirty minutes just dip in randomly at your favourite or least favourite books.

A commenter on yesterday's entry about lists observed quite rightly:

'This question always frightens me. I have a lurking fear that someone will hold me to it and strand me on the proverbial desert island with only the ten I unreflectively cited.'

This reminded me of an occasion when a very distinguished colleague was invited to appear on Desert Island Discs. As it happened, he was not in the least bit musical or knowledgeable about music and hadn't the faintest idea which eight pieces of music to choose. Clearly, however, it was vital that the list would impress listeners, particularly those of high intellect with whom he would normally mingle, with his erudition and good musical taste. He therefore asked his loyal team of workers to make suggestions. They did so and the list included the likes of Mozart, Beethoven, Mahler etc which sounded impressive and which he happily adopted as his own. What he didn't know was that every piece had been chosen because it was flawed in some way – the performer was hopeless, or the piece hackneyed, or it was musicologically unsound – such that his lack of musical nous was clear to the very people he was out to impress. A cruel, hopelessly disloyal but effective trick. The redeeming feature was that I'm not sure he ever realised.

Walking to work this morning (cold but clear) past the British Library, whose architecture was knocked by a commenter last week, I had to stop and admire the development of St Pancras station next door. It's very definitely not contemporary architecture but it is a wonder nonetheless.

07 February 2007

Macmillan Digital Audio

Audible is the brainchild of Don Katz, a former journalist who recognised early the potential market for downloadable audio and built a company to serve that market. He has been immeasurably helped by an exclusive contract to serve Apple's i-tunes audio bookstore. More importantly, it is clear that downloading audiobooks is a much better technology than fiddling about with multiple CDs or tapes and that the next generation of in-car entertainment systems will include the ability to download on the road. The market potential is immense.

Macmillan has a very strong audio list and we now have an agreement with Audible UK to make it available throughout legitimate territories. We're gradually loading up all our titles and first out of the blocks are Wilbur Smith and Colin Dexter's brilliant Inspector Morse novels. I suspect that Desmond Tutu's reading of the The Gospel According to Judas coming out on 20 March might be the Spring bestseller.

From the future to the past. I am a member of the UK Literary Heritage Working Group and we have today launched a website. Our job is to emphasise the importance of literary archives as part of Britain's scholarly, cultural and educational heritage. While part of our remit is to develop ways of capturing digital archives it is also vital to hang on to manuscripts and papers from great contemporary and not so contemporary writers.

Last night we had a small gathering in my office to welcome a new member of our team, Vikram Savkar, and the beginnings of a completely new venture, Nature Education. Rather than reproduce our press release I've copied in a piece from the leading industry newsletter from Electronic Publishing Services. Another journey begins for our teams.

319

* Nature Publishing Group has launched Nature Education, a new division that will produce educational resources and tools for science students and teaching staff. What is the new division's strategy for this market?

by Kate Worlock, Director

****

In recent years, Nature Publishing Group (NPG) has proven itself to be one of the most innovative scientific publishers, with experiments around open peer review and the launch of services such as Naturejobs.com (the first free scientific recruitment facility online), Nature Network Boston and Connotea. The company has also demonstrated its desire to move into new markets – the launch of Macmillan Medical Communications and its Dissect Medicine service moved NPG into a strong position in medical publishing, building on the success of its relatively new Nature Clinical Practice medical journals division.

The latest sector to be addressed is education. Clearly Nature's content, through its scientific journals, is already widely used by science professors, but Nature Education aims to provide tools for both teachers and students to facilitate access and use of this existing content, as well as content which is to be created specifically for educational purposes. The new Publishing Director at Nature Education, Vikram Savkar, who was most recently at Pearson, has recognised the difficulties in addressing the undergraduate textbook market, and believes that 'instructors and students are thirsty for learning environments that move beyond traditional textbooks and even course management systems to provide a highly interactive and personalised experience'.

While Nature Education is the group's first attempt to address educational needs directly, there are plenty of valuable best practices that the new division could draw on from elsewhere in the group to support its activities. For example, Nature has been working, through services like Nature Network Boston and Dissect Medicine, to develop community applications, and through Connotea to understand how tagging can add value for the end users. It seems likely that Nature Education will follow in the footsteps of these services to create Web 2.0-style offerings likely to appeal to today's science students, who have been educated in a very PC- and internet-centric manner. Nature has also recognised the importance of personalised learning, highlighted in the recent 2020 Vision report on teaching and learning in the UK. While this focuses on the K-12 age range, there is no reason why the teaching methods discussed could not apply effectively to other age groups.

© Electronic Publishing Services (EPS) 2007

EPS is an Outsell, Inc. company

08 February 2007

Sales conference

There are many shades of sales conference. I'm just off to the annual Pan Macmillan one. After a couple of years of hauling everyone to London we decided to move to the seaside – Eastbourne on the South Coast of England.

We've invited a stellar cast of authors and booked the <u>Grand Hotel</u> built in 1875 and almost certainly still using the original plumbing. I believe tonight will be a black tie affair which is definitely in keeping with the surroundings.

The only problem is that at 3 o'clock this morning it started to snow. Train schedules are at risk. Roads will be blocked. It doesn't take much to bring Southern England to a halt but I'm pretty sure our teams will battle through. I'm setting off now and hope to be 'enjoying' the beach later today rather like this lot. Not quite Bondi Beach but the best we can do in England in February.

📃 09 February 2007

They also serve

The snow didn't reach Eastbourne, the sun came out, all but two of the Pan Macmillan sales conference guests arrived, the <u>hotel</u> was great, speakers were entertaining and on schedule, the food was edible and <u>Andrew Marr</u> reminded us what an extraordinarily interesting history the British have lived since the end of World War II and how lucky we've been – but will the luck hold? <u>We British</u> is published in May alongside a BBC TV series. Keep an eye out for it. It could be the most important history book for a very long time.

But the bulk of the morning session was dedicated not to books being published by us but by other publishers who have chosen to use our sales and distribution operations rather than build their own.

There are two schools of thought about this. When I worked at Reed International Books the view was that if we were good at something (e.g. logistics) the last thing to do would be to share that expertise with a competitor or potential competitor. At Macmillan we take the opposite view. If we do something well we should offer that service to others in order to build more scale and to allow us to invest to ensure we are always one step ahead. An additional benefit is that having outside clients who are free to walk away encourages all our service divisions to adopt a customer-friendly approach to their business for internal as well as outside clients.

We've had enormous success in <u>India</u> with information processing, fulfilment and software development, in <u>China</u> with our print sourcing and distribution services, at <u>Macmillan Distribution</u> in the UK and elsewhere. We are now positively developing sales support for client publishers using the highly-regarded Pan Macmillan team. And here are some of the publishers who are innovating, investing and creating great books without having to build their own sales operation. An additional benefit for us is that all this brings us into contact with some of the best people in the industry without our having to hire them.

<u>Spy Publishing</u> – the best reference works for boutique and luxury hotels.

<u>The Friday Project</u> – the best of the web into the best of books – and more.

<u>CAMRA</u> – beer is the new wine and the Campaign for Real Ale is out to ensure improving standards of beer and pubs.

<u>Think Books</u> – linked to magazines published for not-for-profit organisations such as the Campaign for the Protection of Rural England.

<u>Rodale</u> – the number one health and fitness publisher.

Tokyopop – the market leader in the mushrooming Manga market.

Viz books – related closely or not to the perennial Viz magazine.

10 February 2007

Pan-demonium

Last December I wrote about an experiment we were undertaking in classified advertising and I was asked to keep readers abreast of progress. The idea was to allow recruiters to place job advertisements on Nature Publishing Group websites free of charge and thus become the number one site for scientists seeking a job. Yesterday we achieved that objective when for the first time Nature carried more jobs than its principal competitor – 2872 jobs are showing at this moment, just four more than Science but commercial competitions (and cricket matches – see yesterday's triumph for England) are often won by very narrow margins.

I've come back from our Eastbourne sales conference very buoyed up by the quality of the Pan Macmillan publishing programme and by the tremendous energy and imagination of the team. General book publishing in the UK and elsewhere has never been easy but I suspect it's never been more difficult. Retail consolidation, price deflation, royalty advance inflation, territorial and other copyright abuses, library budget constraint, and competition from other media are very real threats. However, there are opportunities and great books to be written, edited, sold and enjoyed. It feels as if our team has more than its fair share this year.

This year we are celebrating Pan's 60th anniversary although if you've clicked on that link it appears we should have celebrated two years ago! I think this was the first Pan paperback cover.

And here was the record of its tenth birthday celebrations.

Pan went on to challenge Penguin and to build its reputation as a highly commercial mass-market publisher with strengths across the board but particularly in popular fiction. That was achieved by teamwork, hard work and a nose for a book. During the 1980s I think it's fair to say that Pan's mantle was challenged successfully by a resurgent Corgi Books under the inspired leadership of Paul Scherer, Mark Barty-King and Patrick Janson-Smith.

All the signs are that Pan is the fastest growing paperback imprint of the moment and that the mix of established bestsellers and new arrivals is making its impact on retailers, literary agents, translating publishers and, most importantly, authors. It's great being a 'destination' publisher for popular novelists, even if it's only by a very narrow margin. Congratulations to everyone at Pan for this fantastic achievement. Here are a just a few of our recent and sure-fire future successes.

And if you'd like to hear Gerry (G.M.Ford) go to http://www.bbc.co.uk/radio4/today/listenagain/ and scroll down to 8.30 a.m. and the chilling interview with Angus Stickler about the Peckham murder of a teenage boy.

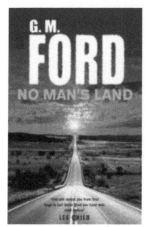

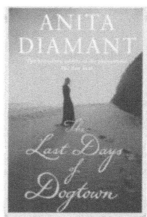

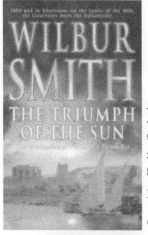

In God and Shakespeare we trust but not in spam

A minor but strange 21st century misunderstanding. I was e-mailing a senior American scientist about a nomination for a publishing award organised by Booktrust, the very respectable independent charity which encourages the discover and enjoyment of reading. I didn't get a reply although the scientist is well known to be efficient and courteous. We chased him by phone and it transpires that he'd deleted the email because 'Booktrust' in the subject field suggested it was spam. It must have been the 'trust' bit. In the Internet world, as in the world of advertising, words seem to take on opposite connotations – essential means 'don't need it', great value means 'shoddy', cutting edge means 'won't work', easy to assemble means 'impossible'. And of course publishers have been known to transgress in book blurbs . . .

Later this week I'm going to write a little more about the new Shakespeare project we've developed with the Royal Shakespeare Company. As it's a Sunday you might have time to check out this fascinating interview with its editor, Jonathan Bate. You can find out more here and this is a poor reproduction of what is a brilliant jacket.

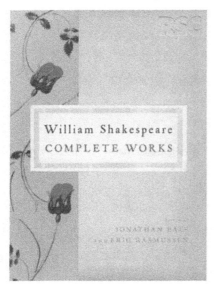

Bookselling to the Stars and the Creative Economy

You learn a little every day (sometimes a bit too much) about blogs and blogging. In response to the Pan-demonium piece a bookseller wrote to point out an omission from my list of current great Pan books. This will take you to his excellent review of Bella Pollen's Midnight Cactus.

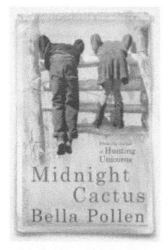

By permission of Pan Macmillan, London.

The bookseller in question is Mark Farley and he writes the Bookseller to the Stars blog. There is no link that I could find to where he works and a Google search on his name is unrevealing, although I suspect his bookshop is in West London. But none of that matters. His blog is brilliant and it's everything a bookseller's (or book trade person's) should be. I am green with envy.

Later today I'm going to be discussing the British Government's Creative Economy Programme at the Work Foundation, an organisation led by the well-known and successful author, Will Hutton. He has been invited to pull together the results of seven working groups and to write the first (and presumably the most important) part of the Green Paper which will emerge later this Spring. The process is described here. The problem as I see it (but doubtless I am wrong and will be corrected) is that the creative economy cannot be driven by Government to any great extent.

Traditionally, political repression has been a stimulus to creativity but I don't think that's what Will and his team have in mind.

So what is the point of all this? A colleague suggested that the only way the Government could help aspiring artists, writers etc would be to advise them on how to avoid paying any income tax. I'm not sure that's what Will and his team have in mind either but it would certainly be worth a try and I'll suggest it. Any other ideas?

13 February 2007

More on government and publishing

The Publishers Association has now posted its response to the Government's consultation process, 'Making sure crime doesn't pay'. It comes to pretty well the same conclusions as Macmillan. I hope that the Government listens and shelves these proposals to further limit freedom to publish and freedom to read.

On an unrelated Government issue, The Creative Economy Programme, which I mentioned yesterday when I met the team responsible for producing the main part of the Green Paper. It was a very interesting (for me, I cannot speak for them) session. I tried to make the following points from a publisher's point of view (obviously I'm even more unqualified to comment on other creative industries):

We are a global technology-driven industry not a craft industry.

We do not seek Government subsidies in the main and have shown that we can thrive without mollycoddling or intervention.

We do not need civil servants telling us how to improve our productivity or how 'to make us fit for purpose'.

British publishing leads the world in various sectors, most notably in scholarly, educational and children's publishing, something we should be very proud of and protect.

Government's role in supporting our creative economy should be to improve book, journal, and electronic information provision in school, public and university libraries – which means more efficient purchasing and management rather than bigger total spend.

To ensure that the schools market in particular remains competitive and is not distorted by cross-subsidies (as in the case of BBC Jam) or corporation tax breaks in the case of certain 'charitable' publishers.

And to help ensure the protection of authorial and territorial copyright.

All the other stuff about regional incentives, diversity, creative grid etc seemed to me well-intentioned, politically correct, expensive and pointless.

One paragraph from the Infrastructure working party executive summary particularly caught my attention – and not just for its jargonlish:

Progressive creative senses of place are formed, and creative people are stimulated, by connectivity of concentrations of infrastructure and activity. A key challenge is to position cultural and creative infrastructure at the heart of place and community, which will allow our cities and regions to flourish as creative hubs that work collectively and with London and the South East for UK creative competitiveness.

I found myself wondering whether the creativity of the impressionists in Paris in the late 19th century would have benefited from the support of the Department of Culture Media and Sport. They seemed to be pretty creative with just a touch of absinthe.

14 February 2007

The Bognor Declaration

Back in the old days of 2003 a group of scientists and scholars held a conference and issued The Berlin Declaration on open access to knowledge in the sciences and humanities. In short it proposed that research information should be published free of charge on the Internet and that all models for doing that should be investigated and sustained.

Yesterday a large group of publishers and learned societies published their own Brussels Declaration. I had rather unhelpfully suggested that Brussels sounded a little too 'European' and countersuggested Bognor or even Basingstoke. Here is the very important declaration:

Brussels Declaration on STM Publishing by the international scientific, technical and medical (STM) publishing community as represented by the individual publishing houses and publishing trade associations, who have indicated their assent on the website link (it was too long a list for this blog).

Many declarations have been made about the need for particular business models in theSTM information community. STM publishers have largely remained silent on these matters as the majority are agnostic about business models: what works, works.

However, despite very significant investment and a massive rise in access to scientific information, our community continues to be beset by propositions and manifestos on the practice of scholarly publishing. Unfortunately the measures proposed have largely not been investigated or tested in any evidence-based manner that would pass rigorous peer review. In the light of this, and based on over ten years experience in the economics of online publishing and our longstanding collaboration with researchers and librarians, we have decided to publish a declaration of principles which we believe to be self-evident.

1. **The mission of publishers is to maximise the dissemination of knowledge through economically self-sustaining business models.** We are committed to change and innovation that will make science more effective. We support academic freedom: authors should be free to choose where they publish in a healthy, undistorted free market.

2. **Publishers organise, manage and financially support the peer review processes of STM journals.** The imprimatur that peer-reviewed journals give to accepted articles (registration, certification, dissemination and editorial improvement) is irreplaceable and fundamental to scholarship.

3. **Publishers launch, sustain, promote and develop journals for the benefit of the scholarly community.**

4. **Current publisher licensing models are delivering massive rises in scholarly access to research outputs.** Publishers have invested heavily to meet the challenges of digitisation and the annual 3% volume growth of the international scholarly literature, yet less than 1% of total R&D is spent on journals.

5. **Copyright protects the investment of both authors and publishers.** Respect for copyright encourages the flow of information and rewards creators and entrepreneurs.

6. **Publishers support the creation of rights-protected archives that preserve scholarship in perpetuity.**

7. **Raw research data should be made freely available to all researchers.** Publishers encourage the public posting of the raw data outputs of research. Sets or sub-sets of data that are submitted with a paper to a journal should wherever possible be made freely accessible to other scholars.

8. **Publishing in all media has associated costs.** Electronic publishing has costs not found in print publishing. The costs to deliver both are higher than print or electronic only. Publishing costs are the same whether funded by supply-side or demand-side models. If readers or their agents (libraries) don't fund publishing, then someone else (e.g. funding bodies, government) must.

9. **Open deposit of accepted manuscripts risks destabilising subscription revenues and undermining peer review.** Articles have economic value for a considerable time after publication which embargo periods must reflect. At 12 months, on average, electronic articles still have 40-50% of their lifetime downloads to come. Free availability of significant proportions of a journal's content may result

in its cancellation and therefore destroy the peer review system upon which researchers and society depend.

10. **'One size fits all' solutions will not work.** Download profiles of individual journals vary significantly across subject areas, and from journal to journal.

And while on copyright matters, here is an excellent example of what can happen when copyright is watered down.

15 February 2007

Back in India

This comes to you from a meeting room in Bangalore. My head is buzzing from the discussions about the implications of the digital revolution for our educational companies around the world – represented by India, Ireland, South Africa, Japan, Mexico, Argentina, Spain, Egypt, Australia. More on that later.

One of the fun things of running this blog is to see what routes visitors have taken to get here. Most seem to come from other sites or from this url bookmarked but a good chunk come from search engines. Here are some of the searches people were undertaking when reaching here. I suspect they may have been disappointed in many cases.

Primary English teaching India

Inflation calculator

Les anglaises

Good library

Amanda Ross hate (!)

Peter Hennessy Krays

Jonathan Wilson Swiss Cottage

China luxury hotels

How foreigners view India

16 February 2007

Second Life Again

I asked Pan Macmillan's intrepid editor, Jon Butler, to bring me up to date with the mysterious Second Life phenomenon. Here's his piece.

'Imagine a world in which land can be bought for less than a dollar, and the only planning restrictions are those of its inhabitants' imaginations; an online tourist destination where you can spend the morning shopping for virtual designer clothes before heading off to a live virtual gig by Suzanne Vega or Razorlight – and if you're still not exhausted (or broke) after all that, you can dance the night away and perhaps take a new friend back to your personal spaceship for virtual coffee or . . . well, you get the idea.

As many of you will no doubt know from several recent articles in the traditional press and a previous posting here, Second Life is a virtual online world populated entirely by the people who create it, much like Wikipedia. What started as a small operation in San Francisco in 2003 has clearly reached something of a 'tipping point', with 3.5 million people inhabiting the virtual 'metaverse' , and new users arriving at the astonishing rate of 1 million a month. All with their own hopes and dreams, hobbies and interests . . . and all with very real money to spend – a fact not lost on a host of big companies and brands, keen to reach consumers in new and exciting ways. As a result, you can now test-drive and own the new Toyota, try on the latest Adidas trainers and watch U2 perform (almost) live on stage, all from the comfort of your bedroom.

Happily for Macmillan and other publishers, the site also offers an exciting opportunity to reach new readers – through author events hosted by virtual bookshops such as the in-world 'Shakespeare and Company' or even by allowing customers to try a book out, by lifting it down from a virtual bookshelf, sitting in a virtual chair and turning the pages with their own virtual hands.'

Penguin and the small indie publisher Snowbooks have already begun to experiment with Second Life as a forum for attracting new readers, and I'm pleased to say that Macmillan is now in on the act too, on several fronts. Nature magazine is busy terraforming its own island, 'Second Nature', within Second Life, an island which we hope will become a hub of virtual scientific activity; and as befits the discovery of a whole new country, on 20 April 2007 Boxtree will publish the fast, fun Unofficial Tourists' Guide to Second Life, by Paul Carr and Graham Pond. Prior to the release of the physical edition of the book, we hope to recreate it within Second Life itself – available to all to browse for free under a Creative Commons licence – before tying it into Macmillan's growing presence in the e-book market. With all this activity, the successful launch in January of over 30 titles in a new e-book store for the Macmillan Science and Macmillan New Writing lists and more online bookstores for Macmillan Australia and Pan Macmillan penciled in for later this Spring, I think it's fair to say that there's Second Life in the old dog yet.

17 February 2007

There are networks and there's Nature Network

Greetings from (according to the signs) the world's finest airport, Kuala Lumpur. It may be the world's finest airport but I'd much rather be downtown admiring what's left of its colonial architecture.

But no, I'm on a three-hour stopover which gives me time to review the latest emails. This, with occasional bracketed additions from me, is a piece by Sara Abdulla, the only begetter of Macmillan Science, all about her latest venture.

Nature Network was launched on Valentine's Day. It is Nature Publishing Group's new free global online scientific (what a lot of adjectives) networking website. It offers a pioneering Web 2.0 (whatever that is)toolkit which will help scientists everywhere to meet like-minded researchers, hold online discussions, showcase their work via personal homepages, share information with groups (open or private), comment on content and tag it. Participation is free to all. As with all interactive initiatives launch is the beginning, not the end, of the road and we'll be rolling out upgrades regularly in response to users' needs.

This website is yet another example of our commitment to stimulating and facilitating scientific communication. (It's a far cry from my early days in journal publishing where the objective was simply to get the damn things printed in order to stop contributors complaining at the length of time the process was taking.)

Science's next generation – postdocs and junior faculty – are particularly enthusiastic about the new opportunities for informal and open online exchange. And Nature Network also features local hubs, offering all the global tools plus local area news, blogs, jobs, and events (no mention of dating but surely . . .).The first local site is Boston which we've been trialling for the last eight months. It now boasts all the tools of the global platform and supports, celebrates and connects scientists in the city, with rich daily editorial coverage of Boston-area research and researchers, Boston bloggers, a calendar of Boston-area lectures, seminars and conferences and listings of local (not pub) jobs for scientists.

Coming in late March is London – and then . . . the world. Having launched this network on the world of science we now wait for the interesting part. What will scientists do with it? We won't know for six months but we will share the results.

18 February 2007

Dateline Sydney

Had an interesting contretemps at Kuala Lumpur airport where I was siphoned off by passport control for extra surveillance. Apparatchiks took my passport and fiddled with their computers for around an hour while I was becoming pretty nervous and irate about the possibility of missing the plane. Not to mention getting some pretty suspicious looks from the bureaucrats. I was convinced by a fellow traveller that the issue related to the Australian Government's fear of anything and anybody coming into Australia from Asia. Much righteous indignation on my part. It transpired that my visa had elapsed (the expiry date on the visa which said 2015 related to my passport not the visa itself – poor signage) and God bless the guy in the visa office in Canberra who fixed things for me in six minutes on a Saturday morning. Close shave.

Top ten titles from around the Macmillan world are still coming in and I've now received the list of downloaded articles from Palgrave Macmillan journals. Total downloads for 2006 were just a tad under one million and, perhaps unsurprisingly, the list was led by Michael Porter with Competitiveness in a globalised world: the microeconomic foundations of the competitiveness of nations, regions and firms in the Journal of International Business Studies. Less obvious was number three on the list, The time factor in liner shipping services, from Maritime Economics & Logistics. Maybe not the sexiest title in our list but I guess time is the key factor in running a liner service.

I am grateful to Don Katz of Audible.com for these links from the ever-changing world of digital publishing. I'm not sure I agree with most of it – hence last week's Brussels Delaration.

Chr. Science Monitor: Scholarly journals taking a beating, could be going obsolete

Wednesday, January 24th, 2007

For years researchers have wondered how long traditional journals can survive the competition from the internet with its quick reflexes, interactive forums, communal peer review on the fly, and ever-expanding formats for sharing information. Plus, electronic publishing is cheaper. Science journalists have wondered about the same things, especially about what will happen to embargoes and the usual instinct to place most confidence in peer reviewed literature. The Christian Science Monitor's Gregory M. Lamb offers a nicely done update on the issue and the underlying trends behind it. His online version includes links to some of the major actors, including the Public Library of Science.

Read it;

LATE ADDITION (Jan 25) – RELATED NEWS: Nature.com Jim Giles reports that several big journal publishers including Elsevier and Wiley have met with a well-known 'pit bull' of a public relations man, apparently via the auspices of the American Assoc. of Publishers, to launch a campaign against open-access publishing of scientific papers — such as the NIH's PubMed and PLoS. Their new adviser usually helps celebrities and, it says here, worked to help one of the Enron execs who later wound up in prison.

LATE ADDITION #2 (Jan 26)

- Wash. Post's Rick Weiss wades in with a story heavy on sources sympathetic to the open-access mode of publishing. He writes that the publishers are waging battle 'against medical associations and advocates for the ill.'

- Scientific American online's David Biello has an extensively detailed history and analysis of the legal issues, economic factors, and legislative maneuverings of this struggle. In here we hear the old-line publishers worrying that open access amounts to 'socialized science,' just one snatch of pithy fightin' words from both sides.

🌏 19 February 2007

Gung Hay Fat Choy

Even though this is dated 19 February (in Sydney) it's still the 18th in some parts of the world and I feel justified in wishing everyone a happy Chinese New Year (of the pig).

While I was in India I learned from one of our colleagues, Amit Bhatia, about the Hole in the Wall project. There is some debate in Britain and elsewhere about the efficacy of using computers to support education. After all the investment that's been ploughed in, can we measure any positive impact? Well, it seems to work in India.

The Hole in the Wall Project.

A computer was placed in a hole in the wall near a slum and the local children were simply allowed to play with it. Unsupervised, they worked out how to operate it as well as play. There are now thirty such holes in the wall and the educational development of the children is being monitored and calibrated. Fascinating.

And while on Amit Bhatia I should mention his amazing Indian Shakespeare film of Othello and the Meena Project to improve the status of girl children in India which we publish for UNICEF.

📝 20 February 2007

Author publicity tours

I read the other day that the head of HarperCollins worldwide, Jane Friedman, was the inventor of the author tour as a way of selling books. I had always been led to believe that the honour went to Alewyn Birch of Granada who sent many a poor author to Australia to drum up sales. This was so successful that Alewyn used to promise author tours in order to increase initial orders even when there was absolutely no chance. However, I have been reminded that Macmillan sent Rudyard Kipling to Australia in 1891 (along with Rolf Boldrewood) and we even paid to get him into the members stand at the Melbourne Cup. I think this must predate Alewyn and Jane.

Hubris

Australia is a great country. Australians are great people. Australians are the best cricketers in the world. Australia humiliated England in the most recent Ashes series (by far the most important biennial challenge in sport). But last night, when New Zealand beat their one-day team for the third time in a row, following on England's victory before that, the word which came to mind was hubris – and it was interesting to be in Melbourne to observe. However, these defeats may have served to harden their resolve and I wouldn't bet against Australia in the forthcoming World Cup.

Yesterday's posting on views from offices has generated a few comments and links about the view from our Kings Cross offices. Joy Moore from our Cambridge MA office thought you'd like to see this, which she keeps on her desk as a memory of her first exciting visit to the headquarters of the world famous Nature Publishing Group. It would be great to have some more (and even perhaps prettier) views from Macmillan offices.

I am a great fan of the London College of Communications and am attending part of their Innovation in Publishing conference on 15 March. It's open to all and should be a fascinating event.

I thought you'd like to know that Google have just deposited £55.18 in the Macmillan bank account as our share of the revenue from the ads which appear on this blog. Not a great return but I promised transparency. The most interesting thing to my commercial mind is the length of time the money has taken to reach us. The income was generated over the whole of last year and no doubt Google bill advertisers immediately. They have therefore kept the cash for an average of 6 months. Sounds familiar!

22 February 2007

Heartsick

Before you do anything else today click here to hear about a thriller to be published by Pan Macmillan in August. Don't forget to turn on the sound.

Apart from working with Macmillan in Melbourne I've also been seeing colleagues at Melbourne University Publishing whom we sell and distribute in Australia and on whose board I serve as a non-executive director. I was, therefore, doubly delighted to see this article in the university newsletter – and the smiling editor of Nature, Phil Campbell – all about Nature's awards for mentoring scientists.

I'm still awaiting photos of Macmillan views worldwide. It's a big shame the windows in our Dubai office obscure the view – see yesterday's comment from the wonderful Sheila Hutton.

23 February 2007

Kurdistan

I've written about Macmillan's efforts in Iraq before – here and here.

I don't suppose many of us know very much about the Kurdistan. Some Western politicians are doing their best to wreck the Middle East but there is some hope while initiatives like this blossom. I'm delighted that we are involved. Apologies for the formatting.

Matt Salusbury talks to Kurdish Ministers
English Language Gazette, March 2007

A new English language American University in Iraq is planned – but not for Baghdad.

It will be based in the outskirts of Suleimaniyah, a city in the comparatively safe Kurdish-controlled region in the north, which is seeing and expansion of ELT.

In an interview for the ELGazette the Kurdistan Regional Government higher education minister Dr Idriss Hadi Salih said a charter had been awarded for a Suleimaniyah-based private American University to be opened 'next year or the year after'.

The university aims to reverse the brain drain of Iraqi intellectuals. It will be part-funded by $10.5 million (£5.32 million) from US agencies – believed to be the biggest donation for an Iraqi educational project. Teaching will be in English. It aims to specialise in IT and engineering, but will open with a small intake for intensive foundation English courses in the spring.

The American institution will follow the region's first English-language university, the Kurdistan University Hawler, already running foundation English courses accredited by the University of Bradford. Science, maths and medicine at state-run Kurdish universities are now switching to teaching in English.

The expansion of the sector has led to a shortage of university teachers. The ministry now runs scholarships 'for the significant amount of teachers from Baghdad' moving to the safety of Kurdistan 'for security reasons'. There is a special programme to fill posts with teachers from other parts of Iraq with a good enough standard of English to teach Kurdish-speaking university students who don't speak Arabic. Dr Salih, predicted that continued expansion of the university sector would fuel the teacher shortage.

Minister for primary and secondary education Dilshad Abdul-Rahman said, 'we receive 10 teachers a day' who are 'seeking refuge' from Baghdad. Kurdistan takes primary and secondary teachers and pays their salaries for 'humanitarian reasons'. They can't use these teachers because they can't teach in the Kurdish language.

Kurdistan is introducing an overhauled English-language school curriculum, assisted by Macmillan, which has an office in the regional capitalErbil. A staggered system introduces the new curriculum one school year at a time. Books 7 and 8 – the first and second year of secondary school – are ready, as is the material for six-year-olds in the first year of primary school. The Macmillan programme includes cascading training and training for trainers, but there is still a shortage of English teachers and a dire shortage of school buildings, with some urban schools teaching in three shifts.

© Matt Salusbury.

JOB ALERT ELT and subject teachers are urgently required for short or long-term paid assignments in the safe and stable Kurdistan Region. Qualified and interested? Email your CV here.

24 February 2007

Oh to be in England now that February is here – or not

Yesterday's posting on Kurdistan has generated this link to an account of being a teacher-trainer in Iraqi Kurdistan – fascinating.

There has been some competition for the worst views from Macmillan office windows in the UK. Strangely those with wonderful views don't seem to have submitted any photos.

I'm preparing to leave Melbourne for Delhi this morning. For those of you suffering a Northern Hemisphere Winter you'll be pleased to know that it's chucking it down here. There's been a terrible drought in Victoria and there's no international cricket on at the moment so I guess everyone will be pleased.

25 February 2007

Alumnization

I feel like an irrational Cantabrian grumpy old man as I write this from a hotel room in Delhi. I received an e-mail from the Cambridge Alumni office which pretends to be about communicating with former students but is actually about raising money from us on the lines of the major American universities. On the face of it this is a perfectly reasonable thing to do, so why do I feel irrational and grumpy?

The University of Cambridge doesn't need the money. Many of the colleges (and particularly Trinity which I attended) have invested in property for several centuries – and property has probably been the best long-term investment ever in the UK, with no signs of any significant threat. Wikipedia estimate of Trinity's endowment is £700m for instance.

Of course, and in spite of statements to the contrary, the British Government has to ration funds for education – and particularly for the funding of high-quality as opposed to broadly inclusive institutions. The Government is also attempting to dictate admissions policy on the quite reasonable 'he who pays the piper' principle.

On the other hand, there has never been more investment in scientific and scholarly research and Cambridge's leading position in a number of fields has allowed it to build significant income from corporate, industrial, philanthropic and government research funds.

I suppose I'd be less grumpy about being 'schnorrered' if I thought that the money would go to maintaining and developing a world-class university. My suspicion is that whilst Government controls the purse strings the ethos will be to favour access over excellence and, if that's the case, then the Government should fund. If Cambridge were to kick themselves of Government subsidy habit and set themselves up on the private Harvard model then I'd happily send them a small cheque and even stop objecting to being called an alumnus.

More on India later.

🦫 26 February 2007

The jewel in the crown

Not only is my body clock at sixes and sevens (London-Bangalore-Sydney-Melbourne-Delhi in a just a few days) but so is my blog clock, so this is Monday's posting although it's Sunday for many readers. Yesterday's post which was Sunday (!) elicited an interesting comment from Alok Bhatt who works at MPSTechnologies in Gurgaon, one of India's high-tech hubs and growing at an extraordinary rate.

He wants to know what I think of India. What can I say without resorting to platitudes and cliches? So I thought I'd simply analyse Sunday's Times of India in the hope that it might throw some light on what's going on here.

The main part of the paper has 32 pages. A quarter of the front page relates to an interview with the captain of India's cricket team, Rahul Dravid where he argues that cricket isn't important enough to be on the front page of a newspaper unless India were to win the World Cup (which begins in a couple of weeks). That is a typical example of an Indian contradiction – a front-page story arguing against being on the front page.

There are four full pages about cricket at the back, a quarter page of cricket nostalgia, a full page on thinking positive and its psychological impact on cricketers, a full travel page on the Caribbean for Indian cricket fans going to support their team, a full page interview with Dravid, a quarter page story about how Dravid wins the hearts of young fans in Delhi.

Approximately 40% of the editorial content of the paper is dedicated to cricket – and the World Cup doesn't begin until 11 March.

And for the rest there are high-quality articles about every aspect of Indian life, business, economics, religion, politics and sex. As Alok says in his comment, India is a giant laboratory experiment. The best way of following it is to bookmark the Times and/or the Hindu and check in several times a week.

I think that India is the most exciting place on earth but that doesn't really answer Alok's question. My personal view is that the success or otherwise of the 'Indian experiment' is one of the most important factors for the health and wealth of the whole world. If intelligence and decency and ambition are keys to success, then India will succeed. If, however,the experiment is derailed by prejudice, corruption and greed, then Gods help us all.

I'm backing England for the World Cup but when we are eliminated (as we surely will be) my support will move to India without hesitation for the simple reason that Indians care more about this than any other nation and they've earned that success.

🥀 27 February 2007

The Pan Asian Tiger

I'm still in Delhi where excitement levels are building for the upcoming world cup of cricket. The front page of yesterday's Times of India review had a photo of Rahul Dravid holding a copy of Tony Crozier's excellent <u>Wisden History of the Cricket World Cup</u> with his deep assessment of the work: 'I love the pictures in this book', exclaimed Dravid, promising to say more after he had read it.

I imagine the Times Literary Supplement will be keen to publish his final and decisive verdict.

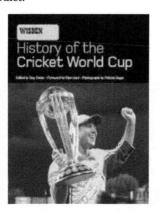

It's coming up to five years since we launched <u>Pan Macmillan Asia</u> under the leadership of Dan Watts. It is now an established part of the Asian book trade and of Macmillan. Here is Dan's history of the adventure.

May 2007 marks five years since Pan Macmillan first opened offices in Hong Kong. It's been quite a journey and the time has flown by more quickly than I could have imagined. Looking back we've enjoyed some significant milestones. The Asian markets and our business have changed since the late nineties when I covered the region as an export rep out of London. Indeed, the prospects for trade publishing and English language sales in Asia are looking brighter that ever. It seems timely therefore to take a moment to reflect on the journey that's brought us this far and what lies ahead for Pan Macmillan in Asia.

I began my foray into bookselling in Asia in 1999 after relocating to London from Pan Macmillan in Melbourne. At that time I was responsible for Pan Macmillan UK's export sales to The Middle East, The Indian Subcontinent and Asia Pacific. India represented the biggest sales territory and was certainly perceived to be strategically the most important area for our English language sales and most efforts were focussed here accordingly.

At the time two thirds of our sales were accounted for by Singapore/Malaysia. Otherwise HK, Thailand and Japan represented other significant territories. We had no export sales to China, Korea or Vietnam and negligible sales to The Philippines, Taiwan and Indonesia. Most British publishers still referred to Asia Pacific as 'The Far East' and the sales efforts were largely channelled through single market distributors in the countries with strong colonial histories.

Macmillan Children's Books represented a mere 10% – 15% of our sales at this time compared to over 50% today. The English language children's book boom was still far from being anticipated. China's recent economic growth was just starting to make waves in the west although it was still thought to be many years before we'd be selling any English language trade books there. Little optimism prevailed with regards to HK which had sunk into gloom in the wake of the hand back to China two years prior. Korea was only just beginning its drive for international competitiveness and Japan was barely starting to show signs of shrugging off its decade long recession. Political tensions between Taiwan and China were at their height and Singapore was looking at a recession as it watched its electronics manufacturing industry slowing disappear to cheaper labour markets like China. Generally the region had been heavily shaken by the 1997 Asian Economic Crisis.

Despite the prevailing negative mood, we were approaching the end of the century and times were changing. The 'dot com' bubble was starting and the world was facing an information technology revolution from which Asia Pacific would be one of the biggest beneficiaries.

Pan Macmillan's export sales doubled in 18 months through a combination of opening up new markets, and breaking down old distributor arrangements in existing territories. We started to realise the cross over potential of children's books through the educational sales channels and the wider economic recovery had begun. Potential for English book sales outside the non-commonwealth territories was becoming apparent. The positive growth trends continued steadfastly and East Asia soon came to represent around 2/3 of our revenue from greater Asian territories.

In 2002 we made the decision to take advantage of Macmillan's infrastructure in Hong Kong by adding a small Pan Macmillan sales office to the existing production and publishing offices. I relocated to Hong Kong in May of that year and hired an assistant sales manager and a marketing assistant in addition to our Japan rep, Shino Yasuda. The aim was to provide a better service to our growing database of customers, expand sales into emerging markets through local skills and service combined with the unique ability of providing regional marketing and publicity services.

In the same year, Holtzbrinck Publishers were reviewing their existing arrangements for export sales into Asia from the USA. Considering Macmillan's new local position they soon changed their representation arrangements from a third party sales agent to use the services provided Pan Macmillan. The combination of Pan Macmillan and Holtzbrinck Trade sales made Pan Macmillan in Asia a formidable presence for general books in the regional markets.

In 2003 Hong Kong, and many other countries in the region, were hit with the terrifying phenomenon of the SARS outbreak. Air travel, tourism, the hotel industry, the restaurant industry all practically ground to a complete halt. Could this spell the beginning of another Asian Economic crisis? Our business was hit hard, as was our lifestyles. (Can you imagine commuting to work every day wearing a surgical mask?) Paranoia completely swept the region.

Despite the sudden impact of the SARS outbreak we did manage to grow the business over the next two years. UK and USA sales continued to flourish. We began representing a growing number of third party publishers such as <u>Granta</u>, <u>Rodale</u> and <u>Walker Books</u> on a commission basis. We started selling <u>Pan Macmillan Australia</u> books into the region and managed a number of regional, high profile author tours including <u>Wilbur Smith</u>, <u>Daniel Mason</u>, <u>Matthew Reilly</u>, <u>John Banville</u> and <u>Alan Hollinghurst</u>. We were generating regional publicity and promotion in a way that had never been done by any of our competitors. Janet Chan and Jade Lui who had joined me with the initial move to HK had now developed a mature approach to the business and had become invaluable members of the team.

In 2005, as a result of Richard Nathan's strategic review of the Holtzbrinck Group's business in Asia, it was decided that Pan Macmillan Asia would cease to become a sales branch of the UK instead to become a stand alone, commission based, business centre. Assuming responsibility for our own profit and loss provided the incentive to take the business beyond simply a rep office towards a local publishing operation.

It was fortuitous that year that the well known literary agent and sinologist, <u>Toby Eady</u> approached David North with the idea of partnering with Pan Macmillan to create an Asian focussed publishing program. Thus, the idea of Picador Asia was formed. Toby's experience with oriental writers such as Jung Chang and his contacts in China provided us with a wealth of publishing opportunities within China and the greater region. The aim was to acquire Asian literary talent from our offices in Hong Kong for publication locally and within the group around the world.

A year later we published our first title, *February Flowers*, by Fan Wu and have consequently slowly put together program of Asian writers through Toby and from within the resources of the group to bring about a schedule of around 6 – 8 new titles a year from 2007.

The books have not only been successful in the English language but have also proved popular internationally as well. *February Flowers* has now been sold in 13 different languages and Picador Asia's second title *The Eye of Jade* in 15 languages included a $250,000 deal with Simon and Schuster in the USA as part of a two book deal.

By permission of Pan Macmillan, London.

In this time the export sales business continued to grow so did the team with an increasingly diverse international flavour. Keren Cheung switched allegiances from Macmillan Education to join the Pan Macmillan team. Claudia Buzzoni left

Macmillan Australia for a stint in Hong Kong and Ilangoh Thanabalan left our Singapore Distributor, Pansing to work with us in Hong Kong.

We also continued to expand through acquisition of further third party sales agency contracts including Lonely Planet, Houghton Mifflin, Kingfisher, and Guinness World Records to mention a few. A weak US dollar provided a boost to our US business resulting in a 50% increase in export sales in 2006.

Our marketing efforts have also intensified. More author tours of more big names gained even better exposure for our titles. Lord Jeffrey Archer completed a hugely successful tour of Singapore, Andy Griffiths toured the region and completed a marathon of school visits and next month we'll host a four city tour for Julia Donaldson. We're regularly securing interviews with CNN, The International Herald Tribune, The Asian Wall Street Journal as well as a larger number of local publications. We've developed our unique website as a bookseller resource and producing our own unique quarterly catalogue.

In April this year we'll open a new sales office in Beijing in order to capitalise on both the growing export sales opportunities in Greater China but also to develop co-publishing ventures in the mainland. We have plans to launch a direct sales channel in China in the form of a Book Club and are discussing a possible joint venture with FLTRP in Beijing to launch a Chinese Language Children's books program under Macmillan Children's Books China.

Other plans under development include a possible partnership to manage some limited local distribution of our locally published titles. We're looking to expand our copyright activity and facilitate further local production, direct deliveries and printing.

The Chinese Economic phenomenon continues with full force and is driving aggressive optimism throughout the region. Japan is firmly bouncing back from its economic woes and the Korean Children's Book boom is back in full swing. With the Beijing Olympics just on the horizon regional confidence has not been stronger. The spread of the internet is facilitating the spread of the English language and with that is coming a seemingly endless increase in demand for English language books of all varieties. We've achieved quite a lot in five years but there's still so much more that can be done. I hope that in another five years I'll be able to report much more than I have today.

28 February 2007

Potpourri

Back in London and in no state to compose a coherent posting. So a few bits and bobs from my inbox.

Congratulations to HarperCollins for discovering a new business model for success on the web. The only trouble is that they had to sack the innovators.

I suspect many of you are aware of this latest piece of neuroscientific research but I share it with you just in case.

fi yuo cna raed tihs , yuo hvae a sgtrane mnid too. Cna yuo raed tihs? Olny 55 plepoe out of 100 can.

i cdnuolt blveiee taht I cluod aulaclty uesdnatnrd waht I was rdanieg. The phaonmneal pweor of the hmuan mnid, aoccdrnig to a rscheearch at Cmabrigde Uinervtisy, it dseno't mtaetr in waht oerdr the ltteres in a wrod are, the olny iproamtnt tihng is taht the frsit and lsat ltteer be
in the rghit pclae. The rset can be a taotl mses and you can sitll raed it whotuit a pboerlm. Tihs is bcuseae the huamn mnid deos not raed ervey lteter by istlef, but the wrod as a wlohe. Azanmig huh? yaeh and I awlyas tghuhot slpeling was ipmorantt! if you can raed tihs forwrad it.

Good news from the Pan Bookshop who have reignited their blog. Let's hope they can keep it going, and more importantly keep on selling books.

And as I'm back in London I thought I should mention a new initiative from Common Purpose (of which I am Chair). Go check it out here.

Finally, I've received two rather disquieting promotional emails. This one suggests I'm rich, which I'm not.

And this from Sunset Overseas suggesting it's time for me to shuffle off into retirement, which I'm not, I hope.

< March 2007 >

Mon	Tue	Wed	Thu	Fri	Sat	Sun
26	27	28	1	2	3	4
5	6	7	8	9	10	11
12	13	14	15	16	17	18
19	20	21	22	23	24	25
26	27	28	29	30	31	1
2	3	4	5	6	7	8

01 March 2007

World Book Day 10

It's just under a year since I last wrote about World Book Day which celebrates its tenth birthday today. It has been a huge success in the UK. I wish it would take off elsewhere to the same extent. Perhaps we should plan to celebrate its twentieth birthday in Beijing. Anyway, a few facts from the UK.

Record numbers of retail outlets are taking part this year. The total number is around 3300 stores. Every major retailer and library authority in the UK is supporting Quick Reads 2007, to encourage non-readers to pick up a book. 47,000 World Book Day packs for primary and secondary schools and preschools have been sent out this year, all with World Book Day £1.00 tokens for every child on the roll. More than 90% of schools celebrate World Book Day in some way. Over 400 stores around the UK are using World Book Day to work with their local communities to collect Books for Hospitals. And more, plenty more.

And I recommend you click here with the volume on to hear a song by Julia Donaldson which celebrates her World Book Day book.

It will be a good day for books if J.K.Rowling succeeds in her case against eBay. She has won the first round with an Indian injunction won by Akash Chittranshi, the lawyer who represents the Publishers Association anti-piracy activities in India. Some publishers (particularly some general book publishers as opposed to academic or educational publishers) think that spending money on anti-piracy activities shows little benefit. Here is an example of where it does and with implications way beyond India and eBay. Essentially, web retailers will have to take responsibility for ensuring there is no distribution of illegally created or imported copies of books through their services. Such a shift will protect authors, copyright and the free movement of legal copies – hooray. I've never met J.K.Rowling but I think the global book trade should thank her and not just for Harry Potter.

Good news today for Palgrave Macmillan who have signed an agreement with the hugely important International Monetary Fund for the publication of the IMF Staff Papers from April this year.

I think this photo wins the futile advertising of the month award. The bus stop is round the corner from Nature's Kings Cross, London offices in Caledonian Road. Apart from the Nature team (who already subscribe to Science) there can be no potential readers of this excellent but very high-level journal at this bus stop. The poster is there (at significant expense) presumably simply to irritate the Nature team (I can think of no other explanation). What it does suggest is that 'not-for-profit' publishers (Science is owned by the learned society, AAAS) can be more liberal with their subscribers' money than privately-owned ones.

It's the first of the month and so time for charkinblog stats. In February we had 66527 visitors, down from January's record 73059. My rather feeble excuse is that February is three days shorter than January. I guess I'll have to be a little more controversial or undertake a free marketing campaign to get the numbers moving again. Total visits to date are now 539533.

02 March 2007

Ray Fidler

A couple of days ago we threw a party to wish one of Pan's greatest stars a very happy retirement. Ray Fidler had chalked up 39 years and 4 months service. It is a real testament to Macmillan that an earlier smaller gathering of friends and colleagues held on Tuesday evening established over dinner that between the 13 of them they had 282 years service.

At the party last night David North managing director of Pan Macmillan reflected that following the summer of love in 1967 Ray had sought out the easiest job in Britain, choosing to join the commercial powerhouse in paperback publishing Pan Books.

At this time only Penguin and Pan really existed as paperback publishers. Pan was then jointly owned by Macmillan, Heinemann and Collins. Ray started as an assistant in the accounts department, went on to serve the company in a number of administration, sales and distribution roles before settling in for the past twelve years as Sales Operations Director.

Ray was presented with the customary book 'Fidler on the Proof' signed by all his colleagues and an i-pod, at which point he asked is it already loaded with Snow Patrol?

Ray thanked his colleagues and friends for making it such fun over the years and was looking forward to spending his time following Reading FC, watching cricket and working on his allotment. Thank you, Ray, from all of us.

A propos of absolutely nothing, I loved this quote from the guy organising Anna Nicole Smith's memorial service: 'It will be something very beautiful, very private, very over the top and very pink.'

03 March 2007

The other side of Kings Cross

Over the last week or so I've published a few photos of views from people's offices around the Macmillan world (I'm still waiting for a view from the Flatiron). There can be little doubt that Kings Cross has so far won the competition for the least attractive but this from the other side of the building show a rather different perspective.

Most of us are aware of the Oracle of Omaha, <u>Warren Buffett</u>, and his famous annual letters to shareholders. I confess thought that I had never actually read one. It is an extraordinary letter – give it a <u>go</u>. It may not be great literature but it is an example of great straightforward capitalist writing.

04 March 2007

Eoin Purcell

Eoin Purcell works in publishing in Ireland and in addition he runs an excellent <u>blog</u>. I had an enjoyable lunch with him in London a little while ago which may explain why he rates my blog at number 11 in his top twenty blogs on books, media and publishing. The lunch was only fish and chips in the local pub. Perhaps I should have invested more . . . In any event his list is interesting and should sit on most publishers' bookmarked favourites. For those who don't click on links and in the hope that Eion doesn't sue me for breach of copyright here is his top ten.

1/ *Publishing 2.0*
Scott Karp really does think and it shows. His posts are clear, concise, well written and interesting. If he is driven more perhaps from the revenue perspective his commentary only benefits from this.

2/ *if:book*
The Institute of the Future of the Book's blog. The <u>Ronseal</u> of Book blogs [It does what it says on the tin], this site is really a hub for changes and possibilities on text and its future. Well thought out, at the forefront of change and tools for change this blog is for theory and application what Scott Karp is for the economics and revenues.

349

3/ *Buzzmachine*
Jeff Jarvis is the real deal. In a phrase he likes to use himself, he 'gets it!' Never afraid to try (witness his own video reports) always encouraging and enthusiastic his blog is one of the most important in point possible directions for the news media (especially the changes necessary for print media).

4/ *Open Access News*
I don't think you can discuss the changes in media and print without considering Open Access and its potential. If you care about these topics then you need to read Open Access News written by Peter Suber.

5/ *Booktwo*
Though not new, Booktwo is new to me. That aside it is an essential link to the changing technology and media environment. Somehow James manages to get his hands on great links and info before anyone else. And he works at one of my favourite publishers Snowbooks.

6/ *Medialoper*
Medialoper is one of a pair of blogs (booksquare being the other) that I love and read daily. It is not simply the links and nods to others in the area of change that Medialoper provides freely, Medialoper as a blog takes a much more considered perspective and avoids the breathlessness that can at times enter the discussion about the future. I like that.

7/ *Plagiarism today*
Jonathan Bailey has built an impressive body of material regarding copyright/plagiarism and the abuse of content on the web. In so many ways his site allows the reader and the less well informed to not only keep up to date with developments in protecting content from scrapping etc. but also the theory and debate that underpin modern copyright.

8/ *Personanondata*
If you want to know more about the possible tie-ups between the powers in publishing, the potential for data in the digital future or the likely trajectory of digital text in the education market, Michael Cairns' blog is the spot for it. Relatively new on the scene it is one of the best in terms of analysing and discussing change both real and possible. His knowledge of the US market is hugely useful in making sense of company announcements and strategic decisions.

9/ *PaidContent*
Who doesn't like PaidContent, a blog that has industry access, runs meet ups and generally functions like an institution much older than it actually is. Not only is PaidContent a blog about the changing nature and economics of Content it is itself a paragon example of that change.

10/ *Invisible Inkling*
Ryan Sholin started this blog as a student of journalism and has developed it since. His posts are insightful and useful for those wondering what the people entering careers in the media are thinking.

Entrepreneurs

I was told a wonderful (probably mythical) story about the film producer and director, Otto Preminger. While making the epic, Exodus, in Israel he needed a huge number of extras and the budget was tight. He managed to recruit five thousand by the simple ruse of offering to allow people to appear in a Hollywood movie for a fee of only ten shekels a day. A true entrepreneur.

He came to mind when I was reading the rather interesting proposal in this week's Bookseller to turn the new Harry Potter publication day into a celebration of independent bookselling. The article requires a subscription to view and so I haven't linked but perhaps a kindly Bookseller executive might cut and paste the piece into the comments section below.

The proposal came from Matthew Clarke of the Torbay Bookshop in the West Country of England. I knew Matthew and his wife Sarah (always Randall to me) in the old Oxford University Press days. I have never been to their shop but what they're doing seems to me a fantastic exemplar of entrepreneurism in action. Check out their website. They're offering just about every service a book lover could want. I bet it's not easy making a living in an English seaside town but it looks to me that they are succeeding.

And a final bit of entrepreneurial thinking. Hinkler books is a value-for-money children's publisher in Melbourne. They were spawned from the former Budget Books owned by Reed International and managed by Robert Ungar. Hinkler is now managed by Robert's son, Stephen, who has taken the almost treasonable (under Australian law) act of advertising in the Bookseller for Pommie publishers to go and work in Australia, presumably because they are better than the equivalent Aussies. As he says in the ad, candidates will have their own flip-flops, visa and air ticket . . . Sounds irresistible for budding British publishing entrepreneurs.

06 March 2007

Women in publishing

When I began in this strange industry in the early 1970s it was dominated by men. Women were allowed to take significant roles in children's publishing as their minds were considered 'well tuned to understand children's tastes'. Publicity and rights departments were well stocked with women and there was an occasional brilliant woman editor. By and large, however, management was masculine. That has all changed, thank goodness, and women hold leading and very senior positions across the industry. Two of the big four general publishing houses in Britain have female chief executives (Gail Rebuck at Random House and Victoria Barnsley at HarperCollins). At Macmillan, well over half our divisional directors are women and a number of our overseas companies have women managing directors (e.g. South Africa, Mexico, Brazil, Russia, Peru, Poland etc). The trend will continue.

The industry has benefited enormously from this change but it clearly has effects on the women themselves. Here's an interview with Jane Friedman, head of HarperCollins worldwide. A more typical insight into the life of a publishing supermum can be found on this baby juggling blog from Pan Macmillan's e-publishing guru, Sara Lloyd. And here is a great piece from the Girl Friday blog of Clare Christian of the Friday Project.

Thanks to Adam who spotted my non-deliberate spelling mistake in yesterday's title (which is now corrected to spare my blushes).

Off to see T. Blair deliver a speech on the creative economy. I can hardly wait.

Finally, I'd like to congratulate Ghana on its celebration of fifty years of independent rule. Macmillan has been publishing specifically for the Ghanaian market since 1965 through its local company, so another eight years before we can celebrate our half century. Greetings to all our team – and have a great day.

07 March 2007

Blair's creative legacy

Yesterday I mentioned that I was off to hear Tony Blair speak on the British creative economy. I waited for a bus to take me there but when it arrived it was full. Immediately behind it was a number 14 which takes me in the direction of my office. I decided to give Tony a miss but here is his speech in full. For those of you who would prefer an abstract, what he said is that arts are important, that before he came to power Britain was in a shocking state culturally, that he invested in the arts which are as a result flourishing as never before, and that he has commissioned a Green Paper which will make things even better. In the words of Macmillan's former Chairman 'You've never had it so good'.

Yesterday saw Microsoft attack Google for its cavalier approach to copyright as reported here. It is true that Microsoft's dealings with libraries have always been respectful of in-copyright works and it is certainly in Microsoft's interests to support the legal protection of intellectual property. There are those who are suspicious of every move that Microsoft makes but I feel comforted that we publishers seem to have a rather substantial ally in our efforts to protect our authors' rights and a business model which not only rewards creativity but also encourages freedom of expression.

It was fascinating to read that one of Reed's former star authors, Naomi Campbell, is set to start mopping floors. When we published her 1996 novel Swan (Five girls and a dream to die for!) there were those who said that she hadn't actually written the book. Maybe she won't actually mop the floors either.

There has been a debate today about whether independent educational establishments should continue to enjoy charitable (hence tax-free) status. There are apparently new much tougher public benefit tests which the organisations have to prove. There is much information about all this at Charity Commission's website. It will be interesting to see whether some publishers who are exempt from UK corporation tax on the grounds of their educational remit will find the new tests to their liking and how long it takes the Inland Revenue to wake up to this tax-raising opportunity.

08 March 2007

High stakes at the Savile Club

There is a rule in fiction publishing. Publishers should never encourage their authors to meet each other. It can only end in unionisation, jealousy, and collegiate authorial carping. We broke the rule last night at the Savile Club (although we were in a slightly less palatial room than this one).

The event was a Society of Bookmen (yes, bookmen not bookpersons) dinner where the guest speaker was Brian Martin, the author of North. He spoke about the problems of finding a publisher when your work might not fit into a currently popular genre. He was one of the first (if not the first) authors in the Macmillan New Writing series, a project for which we received a significant roasting from established literary commentators.

The project was, of course, a risk but not as risky as having five of its authors at the same dinner. Somehow we survived.

A little while ago I reprinted an interview from the excellent journal for publishers, vendors and librarians, Against the Grain. I've just received the printed copy and it looks great but more importantly the issue is full of fasinating and entertaining articles. Here is just one example – an alphabetical fable about Article and Book (aka Ant and Bee) meeting Google written by Margaret Landesman of the Marriott Library at the University of Utah.

My route to work this morning took me past one of the great bookshops of the world, Hatchards, which has managed to retain (and enhance) its identity in spite of ownership changes and varying corporate philosophies. Hooray.

I was surprised to be told by a reader yesterday that one of the Google ads which appeared here was for a product to fight insomnia. I'd have thought that the blog itself would suffice.

And the Otto Preminger story the other day reminded an old friend of the wonderful Dorothy Parker line:

'The two best words in the English language: Check Enclosed'.

Copyright debate

Yesterday evening I attended a debate organised by the Authors' Collecting and Licensing Society and held at the British Library. The speakers were distinguished – three writers, one media executive, one book publisher and an MP – the auditorium was full of intelligent and interested people, the chairman was the excellent John Humphrys. Unfortunately and worryingly, the debate was trivial, shallow, anecdotal, self-serving, smug and boring. Apart from that it was okay. In an era where technology and social change are challenging copyright more fundamentally than at any time since its inception, the debate was typified by an anecdote about a magazine sublicensing an article to another magazine in Australia without informing the author. It was really a moan session between authors and publishers. Authors and publishers are on the same side when it comes to copyright and intra-trade squabbling will only serve to weaken the vital case for the retention and adaptation of copyright as a rewarder and guarantor of literary and other creativity. Harrumph.

On the other hand, this eloquent essay by Peter Brantley at the University of California Berkeley Library describing second thoughts about accepting Google's offer to digitise their books is much more germane. And I'm grateful to Michael Cairns and his Persona Non Data blog for this link.

The guy on the right of this photo is Peter Collins who, amongst many other responsibilities, is in charge of advertising at Nature Publishing Group. He is hard to recognise here because his shirt is white and tucked in.

Back in December I wrote about our experiment of allowing recruiters free advertisements in the online editions of our journals while charging for premium upgrades and word-associated links. I described it as 'another great moment in classified advertising'. The photo shows Peter, representing the Nature Jobs team, accepting the first prize in the Online Recruitment Awards Ceremony, a tribute to innovation and another great moment in classified advertising.

Yesterday's papers printed obituaries of two very different people both of whose inventions have changed millions of lives around the world – Robert Adler with the TV remote control and more importantly for me Alejandro Finisterre who designed, built and eventually patented table football.

Stop press: Try this link for an outstanding headline.

Warehouses and other things

While all major publishers are constructing digital warehouses along the lines of our BookStore project there's still demand for physical books and they too need secure and efficient housing. This photo of our new warehouse in Mexico City gives some idea of the scale of our business there. The books will be moved in from several warehouses belonging to Macmillan de Mexico and Castillo in order to consolidate, improve productivity and enhance service levels to the schools, the Government, distributors and booksellers throughout Mexico and elsewhere in Latin America.

Elsewhere in the world one of our sales people was surprised to see this sign in the usually respectable Germany. Apologies for any offence caused but it deserves to be shared.

And, on this pictorial Saturday, another landmark building on my way to work, the British Museum, and here is a picture of the wonderful new Reading Room furnished with books purchased from publishers at terms negotiated by Paul Hamlyn. He was a tough negotiator but he believed in paying for 'content'.

Incidentally, in deference to Clive Keeble's comments yesterday, I think I've avoided a direct link to the site on which I found this image. You learn something every day in this blogging business.

Here's a quote from a review in today's Times of the too young, too pretty, too successful Nell Freudenberger's first novel The Dissident published by Picador. She might be as described but she is clearly the real thing as a writer too.

To discover a young writer not disappearing into postmodern doodling or navel-gazing but training her formidable acuity on big themes – authenticity and copying, truth and lies, posterity and the present – is news indeed.

Freudenberger's novel unfolds into that rare thing, a work of poetics itself, a meditation on the nature of representation in art. The fact that she does it with such wit and compassion, such generosity of mind and heart, is miraculous.

11 March 2007

Lloyd George and Churchill

There's nothing like an intellectual spat to liven up a Sunday morning. Later this week we are publishing Lloyd George and Churchill by the Cambridge historian Richard Toye.

By permission of Pan Macmillan, London.

During the course of his research for the book he discovered a previously unpublished 1937 document by the soon-to-be British Prime Minister Winston Churchill. The document can be interpreted as suggesting that he was less sympathetic to the Jewish predicament than future events would have suggested. In any event the world's most famous Churchill scholar, Martin Gilbert, has come out fighting on behalf of Churchill and the press are having fun – The Observer, The Independent and The Times have all run stories and I'm sure there's more to come. Google News has already found 31 stories. Of course, if you want the really definitive biography of Churchill there is nothing better than Roy Jenkins's Churchill which is underpriced at £9.99 for a 1000-page paperback!

Whilst on the political theme, I attended a launch on Friday at the German Information Centre in London of Palgrave Studies in European Politics Series. The drinks and speeches were preceded by a day-long seminar on current and future agendas for the European Union. I must confess that I'd rather the EU had no agenda but that's clearly a personal and narrow-minded view. What is much more important is that we publish freely and participate in the debate. If you click here you'll be able to see Palgrave Macmillan's voluminous politics catalogue and get some idea of the contribution we are making. This is publishing of the highest importance.

The great unread

This article in the <u>Independent</u> reports on analysis of a survey undertaken by <u>Kevin Killeen</u>, co-author with Peter Forshaw of the Word and the World.

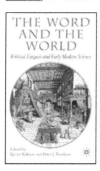

To summarise, the survey of a thousand people (in Britain, I assume) found which books were most owned and least finished.

In fiction the winners are: Vernon God Little by DBC Pierre; Harry Potter and the Goblet of Fire by JK Rowling; Ulysses by James Joyce; Captain Corelli's Mandolin by Louis de Bernieres; Cloud Atlas by David Mitchell.

In non-fiction: The Blunkett Tapes; My Life by Bill Clinton; Beckham by guess who; Eats, Shoots and Leaves by Lynne Truss; Wild Swans by Jung Chang.

I have sympathy with the non-finishing readers. I have a house full of unfinished books. However, I think the survey is flawed. Best sellers are bound to lead the way. These books probably also have the largest number of finishers.

My suspicion is that the total number of books purchased and never finished is enormous and may well represent more than 100% of the total profits from publishing rather like <u>Colman's Mustard</u> whose business model is based on what is left on the plate.

Finally, I am grateful to Clive Keeble for pointing out this excellent <u>article</u> on digitisation of archives from the <u>New York Times</u> and his contention (correct in my view) that digitisation is not a complete alternative to hard copy preservation.

🐦 13 March 2007

Julia Donaldson on tour

A few weeks ago I <u>wrote</u> about one of the earliest author tours (Kipling in Melbourne in 1891). This morning I was sent evidence of one of the most recent – Julia Donaldson in the <u>Children's Bookshop</u> in Christchurch, New Zealand.

Here she is in the overflowing shop conducting the children in the Gruffalo Song and you can hear it <u>here</u> courtesy of Radio New Zealand. Some authors go to a long way to reach their readers and we go a long way to support them. If you weren't in Christchurch at the time you can find 112 titles by Julia on Macmillan Children's Books <u>website</u>.

Whenever I think of New Zealand, rugby comes to mind. I was slightly shocked to see in the email about Julia that they don't rate England's chances in the forthcoming World Cup (incidentally this is a link to the unofficial site, the official site isn't working). They are probably right but the discovery of four world-class newcomers on Saturday when England beat France at least gives us hope. But the more miraculous rugby development is the emergence of Italy as a serious competitor. Italy today, Netherlands tomorrow, Germany soon after and then the big one, Russia. I'd love to attend the first Russia-New Zealand test match.

14 March 2007

Talent

Macmillan runs a graduate recruitment scheme and has done for more than thirty years. We are the only publisher in Britain (and maybe in the world) to have consistently and systematically tried to bring into the industry high-calibre people without a specific job vacancy. It has been a great success within Macmillan (five of our current crop of managing directors are from the scheme and 25 are not – it is not the sole qualification) and within the industry (two of the top six British publishers are run by ex-Macmillan graduate recruits and they occupy many other top slots).

I have just interviewed six of this year's applicants and I'm confident that the traditon of excellence will continue. The industry continues to be attractive for the best and the brightest but we need to maintain that by being and being seen to be innovative and relevant. Sometimes that is a bit of a challenge.

The new head of the HMV Group (which owns Waterstone's), Simon Fox, has had to open his tenure with a profits warning and announcement of a significant number of store closures as described here. I'm sure that there are cost savings to be made in the book supply chain and we are going to work with the new team to find and implement them. Right now a book is handled around twenty times between printer and purchaser and every handling costs money and introduces the chance of error. While we're doing that (which inevitably involves introspection) it's vital that Waterstone's (along with all other retailers) don't forget to look outwards at their customer base and its expectations. I do hope 'more emphasis on novels, cookery and children's books and less on 'academic and humanities' areas' doesn't mean what I think it means – further homogenisation of the bookshop experience. Mind you, if it does, then independent booksellers should be able to benefit from filling the gap.

Debating the future

The New Statesman has published the <u>proceedings of a round table discussion</u> about the future direction of public libraries. I took part in the discussion hosted by the <u>Smith Institute</u> between 16 individuals including MPs, advisors, librarians, agency directors and representatives of various interest groups. As you would expect it was a lively discussion, but no one disagreed that libraries do need to adapt for the 21st century so that they continue to play a vital part in local communities and in our culture.

Meanwhile a perhaps even livelier <u>debate</u> around the <u>Macmillan Science</u> publishing model is currently taking place on the forum pages of our own <u>Nature Network</u>. Passions are running quite high in this discussion about the terms on which publishers and authors should engage in order to ensure maximum PR, marketing and sales of a book whilst giving the author a reasonable income and publishers a reasonable profit.

16 March 2007

BBC Jam jam

Good news for British educational publishers. The <u>BBC</u> has decided to suspend its subsidised entry into on-line educational publishing, <u>BBC Jam</u>, under pressure from the European Union. It's good news because an organisation like the BBC is able to discourage new entrants by its very (and not-for-profit) presence just at the point when the market shows signs of taking off. Britain leads the world in e-learning and this can become a significant export market apart from its benefits within the UK provided the publishing is driven by competition and student and teacher satisfaction. The volte face has been achieved by a very long period of argumentation by a number of groups but I want to highlight the role of the the Educational Publishers Council of the <u>Publishers Association</u>. There are some publishers who resent coughing up their annual subscription and some are not members on the 'what's in it for me?' grounds. This ought to be a reminder to everyone of the value of having a committed and professional trade association battling for all of us when it really counts.

Yesterday morning I was in Oxfordshire with a group of Macmillan managers trying to plot our strategic path in various markets and in various formats. We ran three case studies and the aim was to ensure that managers only reviewed a case outside their normal job. It was extremely revealing and the results will show in the not too far future. Here is idyllic Sandford-on-Thames.

Next stop was rather less idyllic – Elephant and Castle in South London.

I was there for the Publishing Innovation conference organised by the MA students of the London College of Communications. I was on a panel with some very distinguished book and magazine publishers, the head of non-fiction for BBC Radio and an old friend and literary agent. The theme was that consolidation of publishing leads to focus on bestsellers at the expense of innovation or new writing – and an undertone that small is beautiful, bigger is bad, 'conglomerates' stifle 'independents' and so on. I think it's all pretty straightforward stuff but it can certainly generate a lot of disagreement and there were some forceful views aired. I disagreed with much of what was said ('sales people should not be allowed any input into publishing decisions'; 'the Richard and Judy Show is a wholly malevolent influence', for instance) but one of the speakers reminded us all how lucky we are to be able to have open debate (she had just returned from China). And this is an opportunity to remind one of the panellists that it's about time he joined the PA if he really wants the publishing industry (and his company in particular) to prosper.

17 March 2007

Controversy

My comments yesterday on the demise of BBC Jam have stirred up a hornets' nest of firmly-held opinions and a bit of rancour too. I suppose that's the point of a debate and the point of feedback. This blog is particularly pertinent. A couple of additional points about the issue.

Macmillan is described by one commenter as a 'profit-chasing shareholder-saddled commercial monster'. This is rubbish, not least because we do not publish for the UK education market and therefore have no profit to chase by the elimination of BBC Jam from the market. And we are not a public company and therefore not shareholder-saddled. Sorry to disappoint some prejudices.

Second, one of the commenters rightly points out that UK publishers have benefitted from ELCs (electronic learning credits) funded by the Government. I would argue strongly that stimulation of a market place by encouraging new entrants is very different from funding a producer to achieve a potential monopolistic position in that market place.

This debate will run and run. The important thing to my mind is that publishers grasp this opportunity to invest more in developing and marketing excellent educational resources for schoolchildren. I am sure they will.

One of the best independent bookseller sites is Crow on the Hill. They have asked me to mention Shaggy Blog Stories which I am assured is very funny. It's great that it is supporting Comic Relief but the bit that impressed me the most is that they produced the book in seven days from start to finish. And not a bad cover either.

Finally for the warehouse lovers among my readers here's the latest picture of the Mexican warehouse as it develops. The racking might well be displayed as contemporary sculpture at Tate Modern.

The age of the train

The traffic around our London offices in Kings Cross has been disrupted for a couple of years by the reconstruction of St Pancras station. This article in today's Observer tells how the new Euroterminal will open for business on November 14 this year. It's well worth clicking through to a wonderful slideshow of the development. When complete I think London will have one of the great stations of the world, not to mention making Macmillan the equal most convenient publisher (along with Hachette Livre UK) for the European mainland.

Also in the paper is a piece by Rachel Cooke on the strategy of the retail chain, Waterstone's. She reminded me of last year's battle to block the takeover of Ottakars:

'When writers and publishers opposed HMV's proposed takeover of Ottokar's on the grounds that it would lead to fewer titles being available on the high street, not even the biggest pessimists among them can have thought it would come to this so quickly; the £63m bid, which resulted in the combined group's taking a 24 per cent share of the market in books, only took place last May.'

Actually, I believe that the new strategy of improving the supply chain, selling off unprofitable stores and applying modern management techniques to bookselling is the right one. What I question is whether apparently moving the stock and brand profile closer to that of W.H.Smith can be the right thing to do.

I'm off to Rome tomorrow staying in the Piazza Nicosia, close to the Vatican in case we get an urgent call to meet the Pope. I am there to meet once again Father Frank Moloney who you can read about here. More on all that later.

Today, in Britain at least, is Mother's Day and you could do worse than check out The Bad Mothers Club as antidote to the pink ribbons and cheap flowers – oh and incidentally get a copy of Stephanie Calman's Confessions of a Bad Mother from your local independent bookseller.

Small guys rule

It was a weekend of high depression (contradiction in terms?) for an England sports supporter. An appalling display against Wales at rugby set the tone (England lost), an underwhelming performance against Canada at cricket (yes, Canada and cricket in the same sentence, we couldn't even bowl them out in 50 overs, but at least we won).And then, on a much more serious note, the former England player and Pakistan coach, Bob Woolmer, died yesterday.

But as Alok commented yesterday, there was good news too:

'Ireland has caused one of the major upsets of Cricket World Cup by beating Pakistan on St. Patrick's Day. On the other hand, Bangladesh handed out India its worst & humiliating defeat while trying to overcome the tragic loss of one of their young test cricketer.

Inspiration of two different but slighly similar sorts (St. Patrick's Day is also believed to be Death Anniversary) turned minnows into tigers.'

If only the Ireland rugby team hadn't faffed around in the last seconds of their game against Italy they would have won the Six Nations Championship (France sneaked it by a last-minute try against Scotland by a guy called Elvis).

For those of you interested in history in the making, take a look at the history feature on the website of Palgrave Macmilan USA. It represents an extraordinary list of books on topics of immediate interest, most of them rather disturbing.

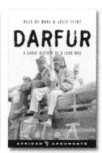

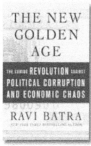
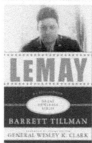

🔖 20 March 2007

Roman adventure

I attended an extraordinary event last night at the <u>Ristorante due ladroni</u> (two thieves). We were there to celebrate the simultaneous publication in nine languages (Italian, German, Serbian, Polish, Spanish, Portuguese, Brazilian Portuguese, Dutch, and English – an almost unique achievement in itself) of <u>The Gospel according to Judas</u> by <u>Jeffrey Archer</u> and <u>Frank Moloney</u>. Only the French (of the obvious language groups) have so far failed to come to the party. There is a major press conference today with the world's TV, radio and newspaper journalists turning up in force. Some news <u>stories</u> are beginning to filter through already.

By permission of Pan Macmillan, London.

I have absolutely no doubt that some reviewers will sneer at Jeffrey. There may be Christians who will be offended at the idea of a 'new' gospel – and by the 'disgraced Tory peer' (as the press nearly always describe him) to boot. But you only have to listen to his co-author, who is a very distinguished theologian and very close to the centres of influence in the Church, to realise that this book is special. And that Jeffrey is no Satan.

You can read an extract (in English) <u>here</u>.

More later as the day develops.

🔖 21 March 2007

More from Rome

I promised <u>yesterday</u> to update you on the Roman adventure but was frustrated by technoproblems. The Foreign Press Club in Rome where we launched <u>Judas</u> wouldn't let me use their computer. The BA lounge at Rome airport doesn't have a screen. The public PC was surrounded by YouTube-loving users. My computer at home couldn't find the correct server at 5.30am and I've just lost today's story by pressing the wrong button at the wrong time! Grrrr.

So, in brief we held a press conference and about seventy people attended including camera crews and journalists. The authors gave excellent reports on the. Questions from the floor were numerous and not as barbed as I had anticipated. The responses were straightforward and witty.

Within minutes we had our first <u>review</u> by someone who had actually read the book.

'And it came to pass that Jeffrey Archer, being an ennobled novelist and fallen politician, set forth to defend Judas Iscariot, the man who ratted out Jesus Christ for 30 pieces of silver.

The odd thing is that Archer's defense, written in Biblical verse and published today as "The Gospel According to Judas, by Benjamin Iscariot," is an engaging work worthy of reflection as Easter approaches.'

The downloadable audio version read by Desmond Tutu made the front page of Audible almost immediately.

Within hours the story was global.

As I said yesterday, there will be carpers but so far the reception has been positive and the idea that a 'new' Gospel can encourage more people to take a serious interest in Christianity over and above the Da Vinci Code hoopla is catching on. Archer's co-author, Frank Moloney, said yesterday that the authors' job was done; the book has a life of its own; it is up to the public to decide whether they approve.

Incidentally, one journalist commented that Archer was likely to make more money out of this than Judas's thirty pieces of silver. My inflation charts don't go back that far and I'm not sure how much the pieces of silver weighed but it could be that earning more than Judas is tougher than you might think. This is publishing after all, not Hollywood.

The dynamic duo are in London today (to compete for space with Gordon Brown's last budget speech) and in Dublin later this week.

22 March 2007

A Google Summit

A colleague of mine attended an invite-only 'publisher summit' held by Google yesterday. She had to sign an NDA (non-disclosure agreement) simply to enter the building, but, subject to that, here are some impressions of the meeting:

Google's offices in London are like those of a start-up in corporate giant's clothing. 'Cool' kids wander around amidst the animal print bean bags, retro artwork and free jelly bean kiosks but this all takes place over several floors of the most beautiful and enormous new building in the heart of Belgravia.

Today's 'summit' was the first in what Google says will be a series of meetings to 'engage with the publishing community', understand its business concerns and generally try to put to rights the damage it has done to its relationship with newspaper, magazine and book publishers in recent years.

Google gives the impression of a company running to catch up with itself, its creative technology focus having taken it so far and so fast that it is only now drawing breath, and of a company having swiftly to develop an internal communications infrastructure and external PR strategy on the hoof. In his slick opening presentation, VP European Operations was spot on about 'sectoral trends', but the rest of his delivery really just went over what we have heard so many times about Google's focus on the user experience and how 'monetisation' is not at the forefront of Google's plans. Hmmmm. So far, so on message.

Googlies throughout the day displayed staggering levels of disingenuity about the potential impact of the company's activities across the media and content creation landscape. There were repeated assurances that Google has no 'hidden agenda', that they wish only to work with 'publishing partners'. But in this they fundamentally miss the point and misunderstand publishers' fears. For intention is not always directly related to effect and it is the vagueness about potential future developments that almost worries publishers most.

For a company committed to openness and accessibility of information, the word 'secret' is bandied around with alarming frequency. Perhaps more alarming is the appendage 'yet . . . ' at the end of so many sentences, as in, 'we have no plans to do that – yet.'

But the team that met with us today did at least show a willingness to listen, an empathetic attitude, and a desire to effect change. Increasing transparency, more sharing of information and constructive engagement with publishers was pledged. Interesting new initiatives were outlined (I could tell you but I'd have to shoot you. I signed the NDA). But actions speak louder than words and the proof of the pudding is in the eating and all that. How Google now follows up will be key.

While on digital matters do have a look at this link about digital text.

Today sees the launch of Nature Network London 'looking lovely, on deadline, with 500 events in the calendar and a juicy roster of stories'. It is set to become the daily must-visit site for scientific Londoners. Thanks and congratulations to the team.

On more domestic matters, there are some in our London offices who might be described as reserved in their love of the Kings Cross area. However, there is a house on the street where we live (Crinan Street) which is on the market for £2.85m. If you have a spare few million and want to live within fifty yards of our office take a gander here.

And finally a big thank you to Picador for an excellent party last night to celebrate its brilliant 2007 publishing programme, its galaxy of authors, its supportive booksellers and its dedicated and creative team. It would be unfair (and dangerous) for me to pick out any one of the distinguished authors I met at the party and so let me just point to one who wasn't there. Congratulations to Nell Freudenberger whose novel, The Dissident, has been long-listed for the Orange Prize. Fingers and toes crossed.

23 March 2007

Crime and punishment

It's been a very strange week for cricket, the game for gentlemen. For those who don't follow the game the story is that one of the weakest sides in the world (Ireland) beat one of the strongest (Pakistan). It was about as likely as Jeffrey Archer winning the Booker Prize. The Pakistan manager, a former English international, Bob Woolmer, was found dead in his hotel room the next morning. Various theories emerged – a heart attack, stress of losing, depression, suicide, match fixing – but it now appears he was strangled. Who would have thought that cricket would lead the sporting world in murder?

While on crime I was delighted to receive this from the Publishers Association's head of e-crime (shouldn't it be head of anti-e-crime?), Rob Hamadi. Another example of why all publishers should be members of the Publishers Association (whose website will improve, I promise).

'I have recently returned from the North of England, where I was assisting police by analysing evidence seized during a raid on an address for another matter. The seized items included a large quantity of recordable CDs and DVDs containing audio books including Star Wars, Stephen King, Harry Potter, James Bond, Narnia, Dan Brown, Michel Thomas and a quantity of old BBC radio material.

The occupant of the address has admitted to operating a number of ebay accounts, some of which are known to me as having been responsible for the sale of quantities of counterfeit audio books in the UK. From the information provided and other evidence seized I have been able to link the individual to several other accounts, and hence to the large scale sale of counterfeit audio books. For example, using one piece of paperwork seized during the raid I was able to link the offender to an ebay account (which he had not admitted to operating) for which I hold evidence of receipts of almost £2000 corresponding to sales of 92 counterfeit copies of Harry Potter audio books in the 30 days leading up to 15 July 2006.'

On a happier note I'm delighted to record that Wilbur Smith's latest book, The Quest, has been launched ahead of everywhere else in South Africa and has entered the bestseller list there at number one (six times more sales in the week than Richard Branson at number 2).

For those gagging for more about the Publishing Innovation Conference I wrote about last week but which was drowned out by the reaction to my BBC Jam remarks go to the excellent Girl Friday blog.

24 March 2007

When ideas matter

Publishing, thank goodness, is heterogeneous. Mass-market, school and college textbooks, scientific research, literary fiction, poetry, music, religious, popular science are all important genres and have their own sets of editorial and commercial characteristics. One hugely important area is high-quality non-fiction of the sort that Macmillan has been engaged in since the days of Keynes's General Theory of Employment and other seminal works. We are still highly active in this field and I have asked Airie Stuart of Palgrave Macmillan in New York to share some of her thoughts with us.

The market for serious non-fiction has changed dramatically over the last couple of decades. The success of authors such as Stephen Greenblatt, Jared Diamond, Malcolm Gladwell and Thomas Friedman are evidence that there is a potentially large readership for challenging ideas, historical narratives and counterintuitive analysis. For publishers of these kinds of books, the continued success has brought with it a whole new set of challenges.

Over the last couple of decades, the primary aim of most literary agents has been to sell books to the highest bidder, with marketing and editorial considerations taking a back seat. And who can blame the agents? Publishers enable them. If editors see something they like, they often pre-empt for a huge sum of money or get swept up into auction fever, with little consideration for the profit and loss reckoning that will come two years later.

Many editors evaluate proposals at face value; if they don't see what they like they pass and move on. This is, of course, often a function of time constraints in the face of the volume of submissions and day to day tasks. Yet the downside is that editors are rarely able to give much thought and time to reshaping and developing a proposal with an eye toward the larger trajectory of an author's career. What if an author is doing fascinating research in one area but wants to write about an altogether different one that many others are writing about? What will happen to the all-important sales track if an author's second book idea is not as strong as his first? What if an idea is not fully developed? When is it worth it to overspend for a trophy author? How does one pay sensibly when even assistant professors with dissertations they want to turn into books are represented by top-tier agencies?

These scenarios and questions are endemic to the publishing of serious, commercial non-fiction. And not every company can, or should, take the easy path to answering them. We certainly can't take that approach at Palgrave Macmillan.

When you publish upmarket non-fiction there needs to be a different model for how authors and editors interact. For serious works, the role of the commissioning editor is different than that of the buying editor. 95 percent of the time we are not acquiring a book or proposal at face value. We might get in a proposal and think the author should take a different approach, as we did with Purpose or The War of Ideas.

We might find a hidden gem in another language and find a special translator for it, like we did with This has happened, a holocaust memoir and finalist for The National Jewish Book Award. We might get a proposal in slush mail and take a leap of faith with an author we know we'll have to work hard to develop, like we did with Anne Morrow Lindbergh. We might go to an author with an idea, like I did when I went to Abe Foxman, head of the Anti Defamation League and told him the time was ripe for a book on the rise of myriad forms of anti-Semitism. When we get a proposal we meet with the authors and we tell them our own ideas about their work, we talk to them about their careers and what they need to do to grow. And when they come back to publish with us again after a successful go-around the first time, we might suggest ideas for their next book, like we did in the case of _New Golden Age_.

I'm proud to say that our authors actually receive royalty checks. In this kind of give-and-take we are not just victims to the going rate, the frenzied auction or the travesty of overpaying for books left and right that might not earn out. And we have the fulfillment of knowing that we've brought something to the table, too.

And because it's Saturday and you might like something to cheer you up here is a picture of a bunch of rogues at a dinner in Rome waving copies of a book in a variety of languages with the authors seated at the front. To further my embarrassment here is a link to me pretending to interview one of our authors for a podcast. I don't think the BBC Today team need fear for their jobs.

📃 25 March 2007

Cricket lovely cricket?

About this time of year every year I dust down my ageing dinner jacket and wonder whether I can put up with the agony of cramming myself into it for the annual Wisden dinner. This year I decided to pluck up courage and buy a new one so that I could enjoy the dinner and its associations with Spring and a new Summer without acute discomfort. But this year's event looks like being overshadowed by the unsavoury and deeply depressing case of Who Killed Bob Woolmer (and why). The cricket section of today's Times gives some indication of the understandable domination of the issue. Forgive the strange typography.

The best we never had

Bob Woolmer had few equals as a coach, but his native country were never to benefit

Endless talent, endless problems

Ivo Tennant, who was working with the former England batsman on a new book, says his friend had been charmed by the nation

'I believed that Cronje never fixed any match'

Woolmer found it impossible to believe that the captain of South Africa would contemplate an involvement with bookmakers

Autopsy reveals Bob Woolmer was murdered

Jamaican police confirm British-born Pakistan coach Bob Woolmer was strangled to death and launch a murder probe

Bob Woolmer 1948–2007

Man of the world

As Bob Woolmer's biographer, I was privileged to tell the story of a man who fulfilled himself as a outstanding coach

Woolmer: the boys' own pragmatist

I played for England with Bob Woolmer, but it was as a coach that I came to respect him

Cricket paying high price for naivety

Due to recent events, questions are being asked of the ICC's handling of corruption and whether they have reverted to complacency

Bob Woolmer: obituary

'Citizen of world cricket' who was a highly respected coach of South Africa and then Pakistan

A search on the ever useful Wisden Archive gives even more information about Woolmer's career. Anyway, Wednesday (or is it Thursday morning) sees the publication of Wisden 2007 which is still under wraps but is sure to be yet another triumph for its editor, Matthew Engel, who is also publishing his Extracts from the Red Notebooks this week. Rarely have I enjoyed a set of proofs so much. Do grab a copy of the book – and simply enjoy.

By permission of Pan Macmillan, London.

The (publishing) scene in Britain

There's an excellent article in the 12 March issue of Publishers Weekly by Edward Russell-Walling. I think the strapline says it all:

'A dodgy retail scene and an increasingly celebrity-oriented culture are leaving little room for reason.'

The special feature is there to forearm (forewarn?) publishers coming to the UK for the London Book Fair next month. The Fair itself leaves little room for reason but at least it has moved from last year's disastrous experiment of housing it somewhere between Tower Bridge and the Western outskirts of Moscow. This shot is of Olympia. The fair moves to Earls Court but I don't suppose the aerial view ill be much different.

Photo copyright www.shotsmag.co.uk.

Visitors will, as the feature suggests, find a very strange atmosphere. Publishers are, by and large, faring quite well (or they say they are). On the other hand, trade publishers continue to be squeezed between the highest levels of discount to retailers in the world (I can't prove this but I think it's true) and the highest relative level of author advances in the world (again I can't prove it but I think it's true). In parallel, they are having to make investments in a digital future with no proven business model to support it. They are having to battle with their American colleagues about territorial rights and in particular the necessity of acquiring exclusive EU rights. And there is effectively retail price deflation driven by th esupermarkets.

The retail environment is consolidating and there may be more on the horizon with the recent Borders announcement and advances for celebrities and best-selling authors show no sign of abatement.

And yet the parties will continue to be lavish. The Book Fair will be a triumph. Deals will be struck. The book world will continue as ever to defy gravity.

Meanwhile the Cricket World Cup continues to amaze and I'm very glad I didn't respond to the comments on an earlier posting. My favourites to win, India, are out. As are Pakistan in strange circumstances. For the good of the game, I'm now going with New Zealand.

It's Spring Party Time

Here's a spot the author competition from Picador's author gathering last week. Photographs are courtesy of <u>Duncan Soar</u> who may (or may not – I'm investigating) be related to the great Macmillan publisher, Adrian Soar.

And more, many more.

And this evening sees the launch of Wisden 2007. More on that later as the press release is still under embargo and I'm not sure I can take any more free advice from Clive Keeble. It is strange that, for a publisher who shoots itself in the foot constantly (as Clive suggests), Wisden seems to manage pretty well, increasing sales and profits every year and producing a brilliant, highly complex and beautiful book on schedule and to amazing reviews. What's more, sales through wholesalers and independents are holding up fine.

Last night wasn't meant to be a party. I was having dinner with a colleague from New York and then Niso and Wilbur Smith showed up by coincidence and the dinner turned into a pre-publication celebratory party for The Quest to be published in the UK in early April but already at number one in South Africa.

The Wisden embargo is now lifted and I am in the happy position of being able to share with you this year's index of unusual occurrences. Enjoy but you'll have to buy the book to get the real flavour.

Batsman given out in Test while congratulating century-maker.... 1221

Batsman gives himself out lbw in Lord's final................................. 904

Brothers open for opposing sides in one-day international............1303

Century scored entirely in boundaries 756

Collies on county stand-by for goose attack.....................................637

Commentator showered with glass for second time in same seat 931

Counties play extra time as tie-breaker...945

County asks to bowl only at one end 932

☀ 28 March 2007

The honourable company of master mariners

Last night's event was held courtesy of the Honourable Company of Master Mariners on board what was once HMS Wellington and is now (for reasons too complicated for me) HQS Wellington. Fortunately it is moored safely on the Victoria Embankment in London.

The event was the Wisden annual dinner and the discussion was at least as much about murder as cricket – unsurprisingly. I was seated between the journalist Leo McKinstry who had the awful job on writing up the story (and staying up all night to watch as the trgaedy unfolded) of the last Ashes rout and Kamran Abbasi who, apart from writing about cricket is editor of the Journal of the Royal Society of Medicine and Chief Executive of OnMedica. The conversation veered from cricket to politics to medical publishing but the real treat was seeing Alec Bedser graciously receiving a leather-bound Wisden from 1947 when he was a cricketer of the year.

Nearly enough cricket but one more picture, from the jacket of this year's edition. For those of you who don't know, the greatest slow bowler of all time retired from international cricket and this is Shane Warne after his last game (winning against England of course).

Finally, on digital publishing, I promised my old friend Anthony Watkinson that I'd link to UCL's first conference on e-publishing <u>here</u>. The theme is 'Books and journals: models in flux' and there could hardly be a more central issue for our industry. It's on 28-9 June in London.

📅 29 March 2007

<u>Springtime in Stuttgart</u>

Here is an extract from an email received. Can you, from the language or content, guess the nationality of the writer?

'It was good for me to have a word during the daytime (I am sorry that you had to ring me twice early morning). I am completely drunk and I could not speak to you properly. Speak to you soon again.'

I'm back in Germany (that's not a clue) and my colleagues in the 'Controlling Department' have agreed to guest for me.

Einfahrt verboten!

At the moment Stuttgart is all about coloured stickers. Motor vehicles need a sticker to entry the so-called 'environmental zone'.

The colour scheme reflects the emission stage to which the vehicle was originally certified. Vehicles without a sticker are to be denied entry in such zones. On days with particularly poor quality air local authorities are supposed to permit entry only to vehicles with selected sticker colours.

That's the new law in Stuttgart and it seems that I will not get a sticker at all! Which means, in future I will run to work . . .

Congratulations to Jackie Kay on her triumph at the Nibbies last night. I was in Germany and therefore had the perfect excuse not to be there. More on Jackie later . . .

30 March 2007

Diversity

Yesterday's competition has elicited only two public responses (although several private ones). No correct answer yet although Cricklewood might be considered warmest.

Also yesterday I promised more on the Scottish Nigerian writer Jackie Kay as described by the head of Picador, the delightfully American Andrew Kidd.

'Jackie Kay triumphed last night at the British Book Awards, taking home the Decibel Writer of the Year Prize. The Decibel is "for a writer of fiction, narrative non-fiction or poetry who is of African, Caribbean or Asian descent and has made the greatest contribution towards or impact on the literary year". Novelist, poet, story writer, playwright, Jackie is a wonderful and unique talent, and the book for which she was shortlisted is the story collection, *Wish I Was Here*, a touching, funny, lively and profound study of the vagaries of the human heart. But this splendid book is in fact only one of many of Jackie's achievements over the last year. Last Sunday, Radio 3 broadcast her play, "The Lamplighters", which brought to life the voices of African women during the age of enslavement. It was immediately hailed as one of the best and most original works to be inspired by the anniversary of British abolition. Many congratulations to this treasure of a writer.'

Yesterday was a proud day for Macmillan for other reasons too. After many months of hard work we were able to announce that we are the first book publisher to embrace fully black empowerment in South Africa. Many publishers have paraded their enlightened attitude to diversity in publishing and have even appointed diversity comunications managers. We don't do that but we are delighted to take a lead in what is a genuine attempt to remedy past mistakes and build a stronger and fairer business environment for the future.

Here is a story from one of Macmillan's most intrepid sales people, Hispanophile Jim Papworth in Jamaica.

'The story behind this is that it was my very first trip to Jamaica with colleagues from Macmillan Caribbean. It had been drummed into me on the flight over on just how big cricket was in Jamaica (and the Caribbean) and that any match took preference over almost anything else. This lecture was so I would not feel aggrieved if, during a sales meeting, there happened to be any match, anywhere, on telly. If a game was on, anything I may want to contribute to the meeting would be at best ignored, at worst get me thrown out for having the insolence of travelling 6,000 miles lugging Macmillan catalogues just to interrupt the game !

When I arrived at the Pegasus Hotel (where last week's murder took place) one Sunday evening, I went up to my room, opened the balcony, stepped out and the game in what is now the hotel car park, was my very first proper glimpse of Kingston.'

Cricklewood. America, Scotland, Nigeria, South Africa, Jamaica – diversity is us.

And here's a link to an interesting interview from the US Today programme.

31 March 2007

In praise of older monks . . .

. . . , the patience of IT help desks around the world, and courtesy of Ann Michael who sent me this link. The worry is that I recognise myself as the technophobic monk.

I've just been sent this picture of the Publishing Innovation Conference I wrote about on 16 March. We don't look like innovators. That could be the problem.

The best futurologist in the UK is Ray Hammond and the best insights into future technologies can be found in his monthly newsletter, Glimpses. The April issue jus out has the usual mix of wondrous things – sugar-powered batteries, ethics for robots, air-conditioned vests, poetry-writing software etc – but, being a doting grandfather this item caught my eye. It all sounds fine except for the headline in the catalogue. It may be tempting at 3.00 a.m. but we don't really want to put the babies to sleep forever, do we?

'The plush toy features a digital audio player loaded with womb sounds. Apparently an internal microphone was placed into a living womb while music played in the outside surroundings.

Put your new baby on a bender of sloshing fluids, heartbeat, and muffled music and he or she will be out faster than you can say 'sweet dreams'. And what happens when baby wakes to find he's been duped by a giant mouse? No worries, a 'baby mood switch' will sense the baby's cries and generate an audible 'curiosity trigger' to make baby forget why he was crying in the first place. Another cocktail of womb music and he's back to sleep. Feed, cuddle, repeat. Magic.'

April 2007

≤   ≥

Mon	Tue	Wed	Thu	Fri	Sat	Sun
26	27	28	29	30	31	1
2	3	4	5	6	7	8
9	10	11	12	13	14	15
16	17	18	19	20	21	22
23	24	25	26	27	28	29
30	1	2	3	4	5	6

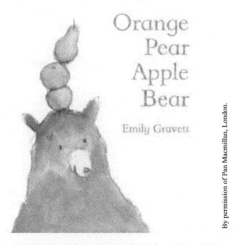

By permission of Pan Macmillan, London.

📓 01 April 2007

April Fool's Day

I was going to run an April Fool story but somehow there are so many bizarre things going on in the world that almost anything is believable. A friend of mine advised me the other day that if you want to fabricate an absolutely unbelievable fact and have people suspend credulity all you have to do is open the sentence with 'Did you know that in America . . . '

Here are some totally credible (and true) statistics. Visits to this website in March numbered 81424, 22% up on February (which was a lousy month) and way up on last year's February of 18724. This means the total number of vists is now 620957. An average day is 2500 visits, a rotten day 1500 and a great day is around 3800. I'm looking forward to breaking the 4000 barrier.

If you have any time today do read this interview with Emily Gravett and in particular follow the link to the audio slideshow.

In yesterday's comments on this blog, Tim Coates asks:

'Are we too interested in the technology and the future rather than the inventiveness and thought of the past to which the internet might give us access? We confine our study of the past to a small list of accepted historic work. Should we be looking for more?

Are we obsessed with the technology rather than the opportunity?'

Very fair questions. But before we can do more we need, as publishers, to secure the present and I have permission to reproduce this article by Nick Clee (published in the Times Literary Supplement but not available online) which summarises some of the issues facing the book industry:

At a pace evocative of Jarndyce and Jarndyce, two lawsuits with significant implications for the future of copyright are making their way through the US courts. The Association of American Publishers and the Authors Guild are suing Google, alleging that the internet search company is engaged in 'massive copyright infringement' in its project to digitise the book collections of leading libraries. A victory for Google – or an extension of legal wranglings to a point beyond which its opponents run out of funds – would raise the threat, the book industry believes, of a severe compromise of authors' and publishers' rights.

Google runs two book scanning schemes as part of what it calls Google Book Search. The Google Books Partner Programme is an association with publishers, allowing browsers to search texts under conditions agreed in licences that Google and the publishers sign. No one is protesting about that – although some publishers, for reasons we shall see, are determined that they, rather than Google, should digitise the texts. The problems are with the Google Books Library Project.

Google is digitising the collections of libraries including Princeton, the University of California, Harvard, Stanford, the New York Public Library, and the Bodleian. At some of these institutions – New York and the Bodleian among them – Google is digitising only out-of-copyright works. ('I've asked the Bodleian how it knows that only public domain works will be involved,' Hugh Jones, copyright counsel of the Publishers Association, tells me. 'I've never had a reply to that.') At other libraries, Google is making digital files of the entire collections, copyrighted books and all.

Publishers can prevent the copying of the protected works; but only if they follow Google's procedures for opting out of the scheme. Some say that this is like being told to complete an 'I should prefer not to be robbed, thank you' form in order to protect you against burglary.

Google would be genuinely upset by this analogy. We respect copyright, the company protests. We show users only 'snippets' of copyrighted works. 'We believe a tool that can open up the millions of pages in the world's books,' Google says on its Book Search pages, 'can help remove the barriers between people and information and benefit the publishing community at the same time.' In legal terms, Google cites the 'fair use' provision of US copyright law, which allows copying of works without the copyright holder's permission under certain conditions. Copying a work in order to promote scholarship, and indeed to promote book sales, is fair use, Google argues.

Perhaps it is. That is for the courts to decide, eventually. If they rule in Google's favour, they will have judged the company's digital files to be 'transformative', giving the copyrighted work 'new expression, meaning or message'. But if a file is transformative, does not that term imply a new copyright? (I asked Google this question, but did not receive an answer.) And would the libraries, who receive copies of the files Google digitises, have copyrights in their digital files? What, then, would prevent the sale of these files at some point in the future? Perhaps not even another lengthy court case.

Again, this is a suggestion that would distress Google. Selling things, apart from advertising, is not our business, it says. We're good guys. One of our mottos is 'Do no evil'. But who knows what Google's business will be, or what its ownership will be, in 10 years' time?

These questions are just some of the many that are worrying rights holders in the digital era. 'With every new technological development our copyright becomes more precious,' Maureen Duffy told an Authors' Licensing & Collecting Society seminar on copyright earlier in March. (Unfortunately, the seminar drifted away from this point, and got bogged down for too long in a discussion of authors' contracts – another concerning issue, to be sure, but one that may be rendered irrelevant if larger threats to copyright are realised.)

Another threat concerns territoriality. Look up the 2006 Man Booker Prize winner, The Inheritance of Loss by Kiran Desai, at Amazon.co.uk. The top result is the Hamish Hamilton hardback edition, available for £10.18. Below it is a mass market paperback edition, at £4.08. This turns out to come from Grove Atlantic in the US. True, you will have to wait from one to three weeks to receive it. But the point is that, if you live in the UK, you should not be able to get hold of it at all: Hamish Hamilton holds the exclusive rights. Order books through the 'Used and new' Amazon Marketplace, and you may receive pristine US editions in just a couple of days.

Researching this piece, I looked up a series of titles, of all kinds, on Amazon. In every case, I found US editions sitting alongside UK ones. Publishers have met Amazon, with lawyers present, to complain about the listings, and have received a sympathetic response. "We have systematic measures in place to ensure we don't infringe, and where [those measures] fall down, we have a notice and takedown process,' a spokesman for the online retailer said. There is little evidence of a clean-up yet, however; it appears that considerations of territorial rights are not built into the data, and that manual correction of the records would be too laborious.

Some digital enthusiasts would say that territorial rights will become irrelevant as the internet becomes the primary medium of text distribution. The suggestion that electronic devices will supersede books among readers of such genres as fiction and biography may, despite advances in technology, arouse scepticism; but it is clear that digital distribution will become the norm elsewhere. In areas of academic and professional publishing, it already is. What will be the role of publishers then?

In scholarly publishing, there is an influential movement in favour of 'open access' business models, by which research is made available for free. Susan Hezlet, publisher of the London Mathematical Society's journals, told the Guardian: 'If all publicly funded published research was made available free on the internet, publishers would all go bust and no one would manage the peer review, editing and distribution processes.'

Publishers fear becoming redundant in general publishing, too. Some authors and agents – the agents believe that they will retain their mediating role, even if publishers become extinct – argue that most authors will simply post their works online. Companies that perform editorial, marketing and distribution functions will become unnecessary. Stephen Page, chief executive of Faber and president of the Publishers Association, took these predictions seriously enough to devote a lecture on World Book Day (1st March) to countering them. Publishers' taste and marketing skills would become more important than ever in the digital-dominated future, he said. Moreover, publishers would have the increasingly urgent task of 'ensuring that authors' copyrighted works are sold and not given away'.

Piracy will certainly be widespread on the internet. Protecting texts against it is a huge problem, not only because of the skills of the hackers, but also because digital rights management (DRM) systems are unpopular with consumers. However, it remains likely that most people will continue to buy texts from official sources. Let us hope simply that the dominant official source for books is not Google. Or else we shall all have to find another way of earning a living.

📃 02 April 2007

Open or closed data?

I gave out the latest statistics for visitors to this blog yesterday. And now the really important data – monthly ad revenues from Google were $34.94 and the accumulated earnings since the last payment are $122.79. Quite a long way until it becomes Macmillan's principal revenue generator. I was, however, rather put out to discover that our finance department are recording the revenue in the management accounts of our Fiction division. I've asked them to move it immediately into non-fiction. Hardly any of this blog is fiction.

Here's part of a comment by Ann Michael yesterday:

'While protecting what is ours is certainly a fair course, sometimes you have to wonder whether that protection is akin to fighting the ocean tides. I don't have all the answers but it seems to me that working with the tide is more constructive than working against it!'

I couldn't agree more and that is why we set about building BookStore openly and in full consultation with Google and other search engines and with other publishers and booksellers. We've made great progress but it has not been easy. For all sorts of reasons (some good some not so good), Google finds it difficult to work with others unless the others agree to work exactly as Google dictates. We continue to believe that Google wants to 'do no evil' and that it wishes to remain light on its feet, responsive and innovative but sometimes it does not appear that way.

Incidentally, I think Ann's open letter to the Harvard Business Review is worth studying for anyone in the business of trying to make a living out of online publications.

By permission of Pan Macmillan, London.

This is my prediction for the book with the most press coverage this week. I'm still slightly worried since I discovered I'd eaten in one of the restaurants visited by the poisoners. Strangely, the poisoning doesn't rate a mention on the restaurant's website.

Shakespeare in the Spring

The RSC Shakespeare

'...a glorious edition of one of the world's most important books...' ~ Dame Judi Dench

Our new RSC Shakespeare website goes live today in anticipation of the imminent publication of the new RSC Complete Works. It is absolutely brilliant. We are already reprinting the book which, when it comes to a large-format 2552 page monster, is a harder task than usual. I wanted a Shakespeare quote about Spring or April as the heading but got diverted by this Browning piece of nostalgia for an English Spring – corny but true. The sun was out this morning and Spring was in the air but not too many chaffinches along the Euston Road.

Oh, to be in England
Now that April's there,
And whoever wakes in England
Sees, some morning, unaware,
That the lowest boughs and the brushwood sheaf
Round the elm-tree bole are in tiny leaf,
While the chaffinch sings on the orchard bough
In England – now!

While on matters English and Springy, Matthew Engel's Extracts from the Red Notebooks is now out and we can all enjoy what Bill Bryson describes as 'marvellous'; about which Jeremy Paxman wrote 'If you don't pick this up and either smile or laugh outright, you'd better check your pulse'; and of which John Cleese characteristically said 'I'm thoroughly fed up with this sort of anthology, but, if you REALLY need one, this is the best I've ever seen'. I agree.

And given today's Shakespearean theme, I turned to the 'Stagestruck' chapter in the book to light upon this hugely politically incorrect advert for repertory actors in 1950:

'No fancy salaries and no queer folk.'

Competition and books

Last year the British book trade spent a huge amount of time and money on the referral of the Waterstone's takeover of Ottakars to the Competition Commission. I mentioned it frequently – e.g here – not least because I was at the time President of the Publishers Association and thus charged with leading our team during the investigation. Ultimately publishers lost the argument and the takeover went ahead, albeit at a significantly lower cost to Waterstone's owners HMV than had originally been proposed. Apart from the money the other issue was diversion. Instead of publishing, promoting and selling books the industry underwent a prolonged period of navel-gazing.

Yesterday saw another referral to the Competition Commission – Woolworth's proposed takeover of the wholesaler Bertram Books. Apparently the investigation will take several months to complete and presumably once more substantial amounts in lawyers' and economists' fees. At least we can hope the trade will not be diverted from its primary objectives.

So back to books. One of our most successful publishing programmes of the last decade resulted from a collaboration between Macmillan Education and the brilliant lexicographic team at Bloomsbury. We have sold more than two million copies of the dictionaries emanating from this collaboration and are on the point of launching a new edition of the flagship Macmillan English Dictionary. Along with the usual launch parties in various parts of the world (the London one is at Globe Theatre with Andrew Marr metaphorically cutting the ribbon) we are releasing 7500 red balloons each labelled with one of the 7500 most frequently used words in the English language. The person who finds a balloon the furthest distance from its launch pad will win a round-the-world air ticket. So watch out for red balloons. And why red?

Obvious, isn't it?

There are many difficulties and complexities in the dictionary market. The one thing I can say for absolute certain is that it need never be referred to the Competition Commission. It's about as competitive as it's possible to imagine.

Incidentally, I was interviewed for BBC Radio Five Live about why CEOs write blogs. My answers were, I fear, deeply inarticulate but fortunately the interview was broadcast before 6a.m. and so the audience will have been pitifully and mercifully small.

P.S. Here's the link.

05 April 2007

Passover and Easter

In the run up to this period of Judaeo-Christian festivals I thought some of you might be interested in this Seder night summary.

Here is just a taste of the article:

Four questions:
1. What's up with the matzoh?
2. What's the deal with horseradish?
3. What's with the dipping of the herbs?
4. What's this whole slouching at the table business?

Answers:
1. When we left Egypt, we were in a hurry. There was no time for making decent bread.
2. Life was bitter, like horseradish.

3. It's called symbolism.
4. Free people get to slouch.

🦉 06 April 2007

Wouldn't it be nice?

Happy Easter. It's a holiday here in Britain, Spring is bursting out all over, the sun is shining, all is for the best in the best of all possible worlds. In this spirit of optimism and taking my cue from various correspondents recommending improvements for the book trade and in the spirit of the classic song (click for brilliant original video on youtube) from the Beach Boys I offer some proposals and maybe commentators would like to add their own suggestions.

If returns of books never happened and bookshops still stocked large quantities to ensure that they never ran out and were able to display properly;

If all bookshops could carry all the books ever published and still find them when a customer asks for the most obscure, particularly when that customer is also the author of the title;

If all books were priced low and all outlets charged the same price in spite of the huge differences in costs of distribution and display – and no cheating would occur;

If authors insisted that publishers sold to all retailers on the same terms even though this would certainly result in their latest title not appearing in the bestseller lists because supermarkets would not stock;

If literary agents recognised that a publisher's commitment to an author is about more than the size of the advance against royalties and would feel embarrassed rather than proud when earned royalties fail to repay the advance;

If new technology entrants to the book industry respected all its traditional customs and practices without diluting their commitment to change or competing directly with an existing participant;

If e-books could be sold with no form of rights protection because customers would never ever try to copy the work illegally;

If book reviewers criticised a book on its merits rather than on prejudice (e.g. this review);

If all governments recognised the importance of public libraries and doubled expenditure on information and not on bureaucracies;

If publishers would spend less time in meetings and more time helping to create better books, sold more effectively, and generating more royalties and readership for their authors . . .

Wouldn't it be nice? And then we'd be happy.

Being Jewish and bolshie.

These are the first words of Matthew Engel's article on the front page of today's Weekend Financial Times. He explains how he came to compile the Extracts from the Red Notebooks which we have just published. I've warbled on about it before and so I won't warble anymore. Just go find a copy.

On the subject of Jewish bolshie-ism (and I'm not sure that the phrase isn't a tautology), I've just finished a novel by a long-standing friend (I have to put that in or risk being accused of concealing connections), the wonderful Charlotte Mendelson who you can see and hear here. The new book is When we were bad which I wolfed down in an afternoon. Being the uncultured publisher that I am, my only suggestion was that she create a glossary of Yiddish for those readers not brought up in Jewish culture. The meaning of most Yiddish words is pretty clear from the context and from films and sitcoms but the subtleties of difference between a shmendrick and a shlemiel could do with some elaboration.

By permission of Pan Macmillan, London.

I was going to mention a few other forthcoming books and then I received my monthly Pan Macmillan newsletter which does a much better job than I could. You can sign up for it at www.panmacmillan.com but here is a sampler. We have a busy few weeks at Pan.(And don't ask me why html has decided to centre the newsletter !).

Wilbur Smith returns to ancient Egypt

Wilbur Smith, one of the world's bestselling authors, is back this month with *The Quest*, a spectacular new novel set in ancient Egypt. *The Quest* follows on from *River God*, *The Seventh Scroll* and *Warlock*. You can read the first chapter here, and enter a competition to win a copy of the book, along with a signed hardback edition of Wilbur's previous book *The Triumph of The Sun*. *The Quest* is also available on audio here.

Double lives are not just for single girls . . .

. . . as mum-of-two Sadie discovers in *Any Way You Want Me*, Lucy Diamond's tale of motherhood and infidelity. Read our <u>interview</u> with Lucy this month in which she talks about the difficulties of being a 'having it all' mum:

'I think there's massive pressure on women these days to 'have it all' – to be this mythical perfect mother, who snaps back into shape weeks after giving birth (like the celebs do), holds down an amazing job, has a fantastic social life, as well as bringing up happy, confident, super-intelligent children. It's enough to make anyone feel a failure. I certainly didn't feel I was managing to do any of those things back when I started writing *Any Way You Want Me* – and felt obliged to refute this 'yummy mummy' myth, and tell it like it is!'

<u>Listen to our interview with Graham Swift</u>

Booker Prize-winner Graham Swift returns to Picador this month with his masterful and compassionate new novel <u>*Tomorrow*</u>. You can listen to Graham himself interviewed about the book on the <u>Pan Macmillan podcast</u> this month, and read an extract <u>here</u>.

Also this month on panmacmillan.com

Hear Jeffrey Archer talking to Macmillan Chief Executive Richard Charkin about *The Gospel According to Judas,* and listen to a <u>clip</u> from the audio book read by Archbishop Desmond Tutu.

Get a sneak preview of Ken Follett's <u>*World Without End*</u>, the long-awaited sequel to <u>*The Pillars of the Earth*</u> to be published in October this year.

Charlotte Mendelson's new novel <u>*When We Were Bad*</u> is not published until next month, but you can enter our <u>competition</u> now to win an exclusive signed proof copy.

Read an extract from Claire Messud's Booker-longlisted
The Emperor's Children, out this month in paperback.

Martin Sixsmith draws on his long experience as the
BBC's Moscow correspondent, and contact with the key
London-based Russians, to dissect Alexander
Litvinenko's murder in *The Litvinenko File*.

Listen to an extract from Meg Cabot's new book *How to
be Popular* on the Pan Macmillan podcast.

You can find all this and more this month on
panmacmillan.com. And if you have any questions or
feedback about any of our books, please email us on
webqueries@macmillan.co.uk

Best wishes

All at Pan Macmillan

🗓 08 April 2007

Popular science

Popular science is a strange genre in publishing. Every now and then, a book takes off
– for instance, The Selfish Gene way back in 1976 (which which I betted would not
sell 5000 copies) or A Brief History of Time which must rate as one of the most
bought least read books of all time.

Immediately following one of these success there is a flurry of popular science
publishing, large advances are paid, marketing campaigns are launched and most of
the books sink with little trace.

There are, in my view, two reasons for this. The first is to do with a flaw in the
industry itself. There is an assumption that a talented publisher can publish almost
any genre successfully. This may be true on the arts and humanities but it is not true
in science (or quite a few other genres for that matter) where understanding of the
subject and the market is essential. Simply paying big advances for famous names
doesn't work.

The second reason is less easily fixable – a general distrust and lack of interest in
science.

Fortunately, the Royal Society has made the public understanding of science one of
its priorities and has taken over sponsorship of the Booker Prize of science, what was
known as the Aventis/Rhone-Poulenc and is now more straightforwardly known as
Royal Society Prizes for Science Books.

The judges have just announced their longlist and I am delighted that Macmillan has
two titles in the running for the world's most prestigious award and they are both
favourites of mine which I've mentioned here before.

We published Giant Leaps in November in asociation with the Science Museum and The Sun newspaper, together with the marketing support of a once powerful politician. If you're at a loose end over the holiday weekend why not try the Giant Leaps quiz?

The second is less in-your-face but none the worse for that. Lonesome George by Henry Nicholls is the story of a bachelor giant tortoise in the Galapagos who is the last of his line and has yet to find love. And check out some of the reviews at this link.

Both of these books saw the light of day through the efforts of people who care about the dissemination of scientific knowledge rather than the traditional lemming-like me-too publishing we all see too much of. Thank goodness quality publishing still exists.

09 April 2007

Media revolution?

There is the beginning of a debate about the future of reference books on Tim Coates's Good Library Blog. It was started by a recent posting about our dictionary for learners of English, Macmillan English Dictionary, which we're about to launch in a second edition along with website and CDRom. Clearly reference books are changing in relation to the web but that doesn't mean either that they are doomed or that the print version is redundant.

But that debate seems rather small beer compared with the recent flurry of articles about the media revolution. Forbes Magazine,for instance, tries to analyse the winners and losers:

'Advertising on TV will vanish as we know it as home media servers take over command of home entertainment and step past it. Movies will quickly lose the DVD sales income that help inflate their budgets beyond what the cinema can recoup. Cinemas themselves will be under threat as home screen sizes grow to theater-sized proportions. Even the venerable book will be threatened when some time in the near future a 'digital ink' media becomes as cheap and cheerful as paper. Why buy a *Harry Potter* book when you can download it for free from a book p2p network to your cheap digital paper?

Right or wrong, the audience cannot be relied upon to pay for media as they do if they absolutely have to. If content can be purloined, a large proportion of the audience cannot see why it shouldn't be. This is not surprising; people buy what they must and are still left wanting more. There seems to be little doubt that there is no practical solution. As such the media model as we know it is on its way out.'

And Outsell, who have merged with EPS (Electronic Publishing Services) have an article entitled 'Google – the threat to median and information'. To quote from it:

'When Eric Schmidt stated Google's goal to reach $100 billion, Google had hit $8 billion in revenues. Consider that Microsoft at that time was at about $50 billion in revenues. Google's management said, in effect, 'We'll be twice the size of Microsoft in the future.'

The very detailed research article costs $295 to non-subscribers and should be required reading for everyone in the publishing business. Their list of essential actions might be debatable but I wonder how many organisations are even debating them. Here are the conclusions. Some of the phraseology and vocabulary may sound alien to traditional publishers and the actions might appear millions of miles from what we do to stay in business today but . . .

'Google's software is more capable than many recognize. Its pockets are deep and the scalability of its technology unprecedented. Google can innovate endlessly and with little incremental cost. Do publishers pack up and go home? No, there is ample room providing they pick their spots on the battlefield. It's important to focus on six key areas:

1. Take Action to be Ahead of Aggregation and Back-Office Services

2. Fill Gaps and Provide Context

3. Use New Editorial Models

4. Think Beyond Vertical Search

5. Expand Acquisition and Partnering

6. Upsell, Go Upmarket, and Focus on Annuities

Take Action to be Ahead of Aggregation and Back-Office Services

Companies delivering basic forms of aggregation continue to be at risk from the Googleplex juggernaut. As we've written over the years, the ability to add unique value to content *or* provide unique data in the content is essential for staying power.

Fill Gaps and Provide Context

Product developers must focus on how users consume media and information providers' content in their workflow. Important gaps in content streams must be filled with new product content. This can be created through new editorial models, acquisition and partnering, or all of the above.

Use New Editorial Models

Focus on new editorial processes and people. New content creation methods that allow for some semblance of agility, or automation that allows cost-effective content creation at the bottom so more editorial focus and value-add can be applied to the top, are essential. This goes beyond outsourcing or re-engineering processes. It is about wholesale change of core knowledge processes.

Think Beyond Vertical Search

Vertical search offers no panacea in the face of Google's launch of personal search and what it is capable of accomplishing with its technology. In our opinion, publishers and providers must own unique and proprietary data at their core for long-term differentiation. Further, they must be able to marry that core to value-added analysis and the integration of their own analysis with external content. Publishers who 'own a space' will want to think beyond their four walls to create a comprehensive user experience. But first they must have unique assets at their core that go beyond editorial.

Expand Acquisition and Partnering

No publisher and provider, not the biggest or the nimblest, can mirror the technical wherewithal of Google. It is being applied on several fronts – content creation, distribution, and monetization. One can't fight all these battles on all these fronts. Acquisitions, divestitures, and partnerships will be even more essential for future success. Focus on core. Allow others to do what they do best. In our opinion, publishers and information providers will be even more prolific partners than we've seen in the history of this industry or any of its segments.

Upsell, Go Upmarket, and Focus on Annuities

As we've advised throughout the last decade, the market is commoditizing because of major disruption from firms like Google. We've labeled Google the Wal*Mart of our industry, and we are only one of six industries in its sights as it seeks the $100 billion mark. It is essential to continue focusing on value-added services, core content, and service differentiation. Protect annuity revenue streams first, whether they come from advertisers or paying subscribers. Ensuring a recurring revenue stream from existing customers is the first focus of the day. From there, upsell, cross-sell, partner, and remain focused. Many of the verticals served by publishers and information providers are so narrow and niched, or so reliant on specific types of information, that they won't register on Google's radar screen or customers will insist on continuing with a more authoritative source. In Outsell's opinion, just as local shopkeepers or big-box stores have had to counter Wal*Mart's thrust into their communities, publishers and information providers of all types will have to counter Google. Its presence is too large for the community to stay static.'

🐦 10 April 2007

Li Pengyi

There's a lot of tosh in the book trade press (and indeed in the general media) about 'the most powerful person in publishing'. In Britain, the accolade usually goes to Amanda Ross who co-produces the Richard and Judy Show and manages its hugely successful book club. In the USA I guess Oprah Winfrey fills the bill. Once upon a time, the chief buyer at Waterstone's, Scott Pack was deemed to be Mr Big (incidentally his blog is well worth following). Of course, none of these people, however influential, is really powerful. Their impact is rather limited in scope (perhaps a dozen books a year out of 100,000 new titles published), in geography (typically very national) and in genre (fiction and some narrative non-fiction).

I received an email this morning from an old friend and business partner, Li Pengyi, President of FLTRP (Foreign Language Teaching and Research Press) in Beijing. He has a new job as Party Secretary and Vice-President of the China Publishing Group which is an umbrella group for a dozen publishers, printers and distributors including, for instance British publishers' principal trading partner for finished books, CNPIEC (China National Publications Import and Export Corporation).

Given China's importance to the twenty-first century world and, in particular to publishing, and given the centrality of this new job, Pengyi gets my vote as the most powerful person in publishing 2007. He is also one of the most professional. Any other contenders?

While on matters Chinese, we are holding the London launch of Picador Asia tomorrow which Dan Watts wrote about in February. One of the launch titles is The Eye of Jade by Diane Wei Liang which brightened my weekend and which taught me more about contemporary Beijing than any number of learned articles.

By permission of Pan Macmillan, London.

THE EYE of JADE

Diane Wei Liang

🕮 11 April 2007

In praise of Wilbur

Last night we had a Macmillan 'family' dinner to celebrate the launch of <u>Wilbur Smith's</u> 31st (I think, it's hard to keep up) novel, <u>The Quest</u>. Do have a look at Wilbur's <u>website</u> and in particular his autobiography. He may be most celebrated for his best-selling novels (he is right now number one in South Africa, Australia and New Zealand and our fingers are crossed for the UK this weekend) but he is much more.

At the other end of the book publishing spectrum, one of the main <u>news items</u> this morning has been about the changes in family life in Britain. In particular that one on four children is being brought up in a single-parent family. This research has been published by Palgrave Macmillan in the 37th (Wilbur will have to put his skates on to catch up) edition of <u>Social Trends</u> created by the UK's <u>Office of National Statistics</u>. There is hardly any good news in the data – more obesity, more time being ill, less ability to fund house-buying etc. Ah well, we'll all have to escape to fiction for some good news.

🕮 12 April 2007

More on China

Exactly a hundred years ago this year (and approximately 99 years before some large American publishers descended on the <u>Beijing International Book Fair</u> 2006 to teach Chinese publishers how to do business) Macmillan appointed F.G.Whittick as travelling representative in China. A year on the headcount was doubled by the appointment of M.E.Taur as his assistant on $40 per month (not bad for those days) but this didn't work out and Taur was 'demoted' to being a 'mere' translator. Selling Macmillan's very British and rather imperial titles in China proved tough and so a local publishing programme was established including 'Arithmetic for Chinese Schools' and in 1912 a Chinese school atlas.

In 1979 the programme was revived after a visit by <u>Harold Macmillan</u>, then aged 85 but still determined to do a publishing deal and to muse on the 'unheard of possibilities we must be ready for.'

This century of hard (and often unprofitable) work is beginning to pay dividends now with the establishment of <u>New Standard English</u> as market leader in the Chinese

English Language Teaching market; <u>Nature China</u> as the premier shop window for Chinese science; <u>Nature Asia</u> which makes English-language scientific information available Chinese, both simplified and traditional, as well as Japanese and Korean; <u>Macmillan Production Asia</u> which sources print and associated products for Macmillan and many other publishers; and much else.

The latest venture in this centenary year I mentioned earlier in the <u>week</u> and I can now link to a page all about <u>Picador Asia</u> which we launched at the excellent <u>Asia House</u> with the help of our Chinese literary adviser and make-things-happen guru, <u>Toby Eady</u>. It is a great initiative with great books, great authors and a continuation and enrichment of a great tradition of learning from China rather than lecturing to China.

Here are the first two authors in the list, <u>Diane Wei Liang</u> and <u>Fan Wu</u>.

Yesterday I wrote in praise of <u>Wilbur</u> and in the hope that his clutch of number one best selling positions (in Australia, South Africa, New Zealand) might be added to in the UK. I can now confirm that <u>The Quest</u> is indeed the best selling novel in the UK this week, way ahead of number two.

And finally and with no particular logic I thought I'd show you this <u>link</u> which popped up as a Google ad here recently. It is quite extraordinary but perhaps I'm simply being old-fashioned.

🐦 13 April 2007

Geri Halliwell

It's an open secret that one of the most innovative and most important parts of general book publishing is in the children's arena. We are very proud that <u>Macmillan Children's Books</u> has been in the forefront of creativity for the last decade and has grown faster than almost any other children's publisher, matched only perhaps by our colleagues at <u>Priddy Books</u>.

Yesterday we announced a major coup in children's publishing, the <u>Ugenia Lavender</u> series from <u>Geri Halliwell</u>. Coverage of the announcement has been <u>extensive</u> and there is much more to come. Congratulations to everyone in the team who has worked so hard to win this programme and thanks in advance for all the work that still needs to happen.

One of the best books published by <u>Picador</u> is John Lanchester's <u>Debt to Pleasure</u>. He is also a journalist and has written an extremely interesting and cogent <u>piece</u> on copyright in a digital age. It's a shame he spoils it by arguing for a legally imposed (but almost certainly legally unenforceable) minimum royalty rate which would have no effect but to increase rancour and bureaucracy.

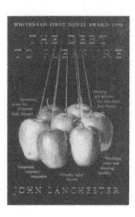

🌱 14 April 2007

Of balloons and electrons

I ran into a little trouble recently when I <u>posted</u> about a competition to promote the <u>Macmillan English Dictionary</u> by releasing red balloons and offering a round-the-world air ticket to the competition winner. In spite of the balloons being biodegradable there was still the issue of carbon dioxide emissions from the plane. In any event, things went ahead and I'm not really too ashamed that the competition has got off to a great start with this launch from Bucharest.

And this one from Madrid.

And while on matters green, you can hear <u>Archbishop Desmond Tutu</u> reading <u>The Gospel according to Judas</u> via audi download without harming a single leaf of a tree. Give it a whirl. On the same theme, Pan Macmillan launched its first <u>e-list</u> with nine titles. There are many many more to come but we wanted to act fast and start learning as soon as possible. I don't suppose we shall make any money on this first list but we and our authors have to engage in the digital world and find the new opportunities and we won't do that by sitting on our hands.

And finally a link to an article in <u>The Spectator</u> all about developments at the <u>Royal Shakespeare Company</u> and the be-all and end-all, the alternative title for our new <u>Complete Shakespeare</u>.

Have a good Spring weekend. I'm preparing for the <u>London Book Fair</u> which, glory be, has returned to West London and within walking distance from my home.

🔖 15 April 2007

Print is dead?

One of my favourite columnists is <u>Matthew Parris</u>. His latest <u>piece</u> is entitled 'So much for world progress. We have failed. We're stuck.' It promotes the contrarian view that there has actually been little progress in the last fifty years in the West (accepting that developing countries have seen significant change). He also referenced this <u>link</u> to the February 1950 issue of Modern Mechanics magazine predicting how the world will be in 2000. The predictions are, by and large, wrong. Here is one paragraph which is fairly typical.

'When Jane Dobson cleans house she simply turns the hose on everything. Why not? Furniture (upholstery included), rugs, draperies, unscratchable floors — all are made of synthetic fabric or waterproof plastic. After the water has run down a drain in the middle of the floor (later concealed by a rug of synthetic fiber) Jane turns on a blast of hot air and dries everything. A detergent in the water dissolves any resistant dirt. Tablecloths and napkins are made of woven paper yarn so fine that the untutored eye mistakes it for linen. Jane Dobson throws soiled 'linen' into the incinerator. Bed sheets are of more substantial stuff, but Jane Dobson has only to hang them up and wash them down with a hose when she puts the bedroom in order.'

This got me thinking about our ability to predict and how hopeless we probably are. We all remember predictions for the paperless office. Ha. Remember when libraries were going to get rid off all books and replace them with microfilm? Ha.

However, sneakily things do change (usually in an unpredicted fashion) and book publishing is changing. Last year we commissioned Jeff Gomez who is head of internet marketing at Holtzbrinck Publishers USA to write a book about these changes. It's called 'Print is dead' and will be published in print form this Autumn (or Fall). As part of writing the book Jeff has set up the brilliant Print is dead blog and I was particularly taken by this quote from Woody Allen:

'More than any other time in history, mankind faces a crossroads. One path leads to despair and utter hopelessness. The other, to total extinction. Let us pray we have the wisdom to choose correctly.'

16 April 2007

Mergers and acquisitions

I have just received a copy of Green College News, the alumni magazine of Green College, Oxford where I was once a supernumerary fellow (whatever that means). The college was set up by Sir Richard Doll with money from Cecil Green, the founder of Texas Instruments. Doll was then Regius Professor of Medicine and was committed to growing the Oxford faculty of medicine significantly (which has indeed happened, spectacularly successfully). Many of the established colleges were sniffy about offering college facilities to all these new medics ('we'll be over-run . . . ') and so he established Green to abosrb some of this growth and to offer a new sort of Oxford college. He succeeded.

The sad news reported in the magazine is that Green is to merge with Templeton College, an institution set up to specialise in management and business studies. The move is justified on the grounds of scale, cost, academic strategy and available capital (Templeton sold some land and they could use the cash generated to develop further the Green College site in the centre of Oxford).

So, why sad? I'm not sure but I'll bet that academic politics has played a part and that this merger was driven by that more than anything else. The new entity will not differ significantly from the other colleges. The medical and management strands of the individual colleges will be lost. And I'll bet the synergies promised do not emerge. It all sounds like the mergers that happen in publishing on a fairly regular basis where two and two end up making three.

On a more positive note, warmest congratulations to Joe Wikert whose Publishing 2020 blog has won the 2006 Annual Litty Award for Best Publishing Blogger from the Book Chronicle. I'm not surprised.

And finally today is the first birthday of Macmillan New Writing and I asked its editor, Will Atkins, to bring us all up to date with this heinous (in the eyes of some people) creation.

Macmillan New Writing – 'The Ryanair of Publishing'™ – is a year old this month. We launched in April 2006 with six debut novels, and have published one per month since then. News of the imprint's creation was greeted with scepticism from some quarters of Literary London: apparently Macmillan was not only 'abdicating cultural responsibility' but taking advantage of 'impressionable young authors'.

So what was all the fuss about? The business model is simple: we consider unsolicited novels from unpublished writers; we don't pay an advance but we do pay a good royalty. (Nicholas Clee lamented in a recent *Bookseller* piece that royalties from sales of his own recently published book were 'lower than they would have been under the terms of the Macmillan New Writing list.') Anyhow, suffice to say some commentators found this rather modest, rather old-fashioned way of publishing distasteful.

In other respects, MNW works in the same way as any conventional publishing imprint: the books are edited and produced to the same standard as other Pan Macmillan titles; jackets are designed by Pan Macmillan's design department; publicity is handled by a dedicated publicist.

The criticism that greeted MNW's launch twelve months ago doesn't appear to have been taken seriously by writers (and it has, in any case, been outweighed by far more positive coverage since then): around 7,000 completed novels have now been submitted, of which we have published eighteen. The latest, Brian McGilloway's superb police procedural, *Borderlands*, was launched last Thursday at a packed event in Derry.

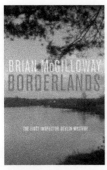

By permission of Pan Macmillan, London.

Not only does publication of *Borderlands* coincide with MNW's first birthday, we believe it also marks the emergence of a major new voice in crime fiction. Set on the border between Northern Ireland and the Republic, the novel follows Inspector Benedict Devlin as he investigates a series of murders on his home patch; it's a hugely accomplished piece of writing, deftly plotted, and distinguished by intelligent characterisation and a powerful sense of place. As Marcel Berlins said last week in the *Times*, 'Brian McGilloway's command of plot and assurance of language make it difficult to believe that *Borderlands* is his debut . . . his characters convince, and he skilfully conveys the cloying atmosphere of a small rural community.'

MNW will publish the sequel to *Borderlands*, *Gallows Lane*, next April, and Brian has recently been signed up by Macmillan to write a further three installments in the Inspector Devlin series. A German edition of *Borderlands* will appear next year, followed by the translation of *Gallows Lane*.

One of the principal aims behind MNW's creation was to find a sustainable way of publishing debut novelists, some of whom we hoped would find a long-term home with Pan Macmillan's mainstream imprints. With Brian McGilloway's recent signing to Macmillan, that is starting to happen, and we're confident that it won't be long before other such deals occur. In addition to second novels by several MNW 'debutantes', a nuumber of MNW originals will be reappearing as Pan paperbacks over the coming year, starting with Edward Charles's superb In the Shadow of Lady Jane in August (and look out for Edward's second novel, Daughters of the Doge, next month.

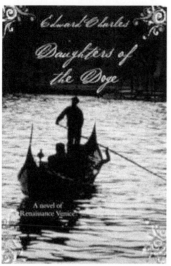

As for taking advantage of vulnerable young authors – ask Brian Martin. The urbane and erudite author of the critically acclaimed literary thriller *North* (to be published by Pan in paperback in September) describes himself as 'rivalling Mary Wesley' – in that he published his first novel at the age of 68.

17 April 2007

London Book Fair 2007 day 1

Yesterday was the first day of the LBF in its new home, Earls Court Exhibition Centre.

Just to remind you why we're here. In the old days the Fair was down the road in West London at Olympia. The organisers persuaded the industry that we had to move – Olympia was too small, it was being turned into a casino, we needed much more modern facilities, We transferred to a new purpose-built facility in the Far East of London. It didn't work. It was hard to get to, not enough women's loos, lousy catering etc. But the organisers were adamant. We had to stay.

And then a team from the Frankfurt Book Fair appeared, like the US Cavalry, over the horizon with an offer to launch a new London Fair in the Spring at Earls Court. The industry was delighted and the press releases were ready to go when all of a sudden the original organisers, Reed Exhibitions announced that the Fair was moving to Earls Court under their management and ownership. The owners of Earls Court had done a quiet deal with Reed thus leaving the Frankfurt bid scuppered. Perfidious Albion was the phrase which came to mind.

Nonetheless, the Frankfurt team were incredibly restrained and dignified; the Reed team were magnanimous and professional; and the Fair is back in West London which suits most exhibitors and visitors.

The new venue is excellent – spacious, well lit and comfortable. The catering is okay but hideously expensive. The management and support staff of the organisers are terrific. There is a smile back on the face of the Fair.

And here's a pic of our stand this year, taken by hotshot photographer Tim Godfray:

My only remaining concern is to ask what it's all about. My back-of-an-envelope calculations suggest that the elimination of all trade book fairs (LBF, BEA, Bologna, Delhi, Guadalajara, Tokyo, Cape Town etc) might reduce total industry costs by several billion dollars. Makes a boy think.

18 April 2007

London Book Fair Day 2

A busy Macmillan stand at the book fair with a pensive blue-shirted loner in the centre (photo courtesy of Keith Martin, Senior Lecturer in Publishing at the London College of Communications).

Our big announcement was one which filled me with pride – the news that Peter Ackroyd was moving his future publishing to Macmillan. I was involved in his last big and successful publishing deal when I was at Reed (and the lists were later sold to Random House) and so somehow it feels more like a continuation than a change. He is one of Britain's great literary talents and his new projects are humdingers. More on Peter here.

And this happy event was matched by the announcement that long-time Picador author Cormac McCarthy has won the Pulitzer Prize for Fiction with The Road.

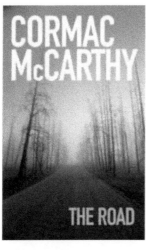

By permission of Pan Macmillan, London.

These two important literary events follow a <u>debate</u> after a recent blog about our publishing <u>Geri Halliwell's</u> children's books. I think the knockers are wrong about Geri Halliwell but that notwithstanding I also think that a healthy publishing campaign thrives on diversity and at Macmillan we are nothing if not diverse in what we publish, how we publish and where we publish.

Here are the red <u>Macmillan English Dictionary</u> balloons taking off from Sao Paulo, Brazil and Beijing, China.

London Book Fair Day 3

I didn't go to the fair yesterday. One and a half days is enough for anyone. However, this extract from the nearly always reliable Publishers Lunch says it all better than I could.

So it turns out, all previous Reed studies notwithstanding, that people like spring, and it's a good time to come to London for business. The good weather and abundant blossoms of lilac and cherry and profusion of other colors and smells is just another bonus.

It turns out that people like having the book fair in the same basic part of central London, in the same type of space as Olympia, only larger and with more amenities (including everything from 'salt beef carvery' and a Ben & Jerry's ice cream stand to short taxi cab lines manned by two guys in top hats and tails).

It turns out that beige decor and clearly-marked booths and aisles work nicely.

And so it turns out that London Book Fair organizers have recovered well from last year's disastrous relocation to Anaheim-upon-Thames's Excel and comfortably settled back into Earl's Court as if nothing ever went awry.

Of course it also turns out that such happy circumstances, excellent for transacting business, are less suited to snappy coverage. But that's ok. As turns out to be the case more often than not these days, the lack of a particular book or two masquerading as the 'book of the fair' (in fact you were hard pressed to even find a few 'medium' books this year) leaves a lot more oxgyen for the quieter, earnest and successful meeting and dealmaking that's been taking place all over for the past three days.

Other Turns

It turns out that the dollar is now officially worthless (reaching its lowest point against the pound in 15 years) and complicated conversion math is no longer necessary here since everything costs at least twice what it does in New York. Which also gives us a sense of how British and European conglomerates feel about the earnings of their American publishing subsidiaries.

It turns out that the location of our News Desk at the rear of the Rights Center was along one major pathway – which leads to the designated smoking room. It also turns out – as we knew already in our hearts – that people like cookies (smokers in particular) and you can never go wrong in having a steady supply available. (Though it also turns out that finding a proper cookie in London that it something other than a flavored buttered biscuit is quite a challenge.) But as for the two people who stole my nice metal Publishers Lunch lunchboxes from my stand . . . .

For more in-depth reporting do go to day one and day two from the Bookseller – and there is a day three but I couldn't make the link!

Here is the final picture from the great balloon escapade for the Macmillan English Dictionary launch and no prizes for identifying the location:

20 April 2007

A week in publishing

It's been a hell of a week.

It all started on Saturday with the traditional get together for the <u>international</u> publishers of <u>Wilbur Smith</u>. The evening was made particularly cheerful because his latest book, <u>The Quest</u>, was number one in the UK, NZ, South Africa and Australia simultaneously for the first time ever.

On Sunday I hosted a gathering for publishing friends attending the <u>London Book Fair</u> and for Macmillan visitors from the USA, China, Australia and South Africa.

Monday and Tuesday were taken up with breakfast meetings, announcements, negotiations, debates etc at the London Book Fair but we managed to hold a retirement party for Howard Scott who is going to travel the world in a mobile palace. It is probably fair to say that Howard is not as celebrated as many other known-by-their-first-name book trade characters such as Gail or Tim or Vicky or Nigel but he may have achieved as much. His knowledge of IT systems and his willingness to share his skill and time with the industry as a whole has resulted in the UK having one of the best supply chain systems in the world and, while I'm no logistics expert, I'll bet Howard was the key.

Tuesday evening was a celebration of <u>Ken Follett</u> and the planning for his sequel to <u>Pillars of the Earth</u>. October sees publication of <u>World without End</u> and there is a little doubt that this is going to be the major commerical fiction event of Autumn 2007.

On Wednesday I travelled on the inordinately expensive <u>Virgin Trains</u> to Manchester for a meeting of the Council and Editorial Board of the <u>British Journal of Surgery</u> to discuss the challenges and opportunities in the world of medical publishing. For those of you not up to speed in scientific and medical publishing here is a snippet of information. The cost of accessing and reading a research paper has fallen from around at least $10 to less than $1 over the last decade. As a result and as a result of much easier search and retrieval, readership has increased more than tenfold. This allows faster, wider and more effective communication of inportant clinical information. It is definitely a reason to be cheerful and also a reason for all publishers to take the digital revolution seriously. Another reason to be cheerful is the amazing <u>Juniper</u> restaurant just outside Manchester.

While on matters digital, do check out this <u>link</u> where two publishing blogger stars talk about our world on the BBC – <u>Danuta Kean</u> and Macmillan digital guru and mum, <u>Sara Lloyd</u>.

Thursday saw the official launch of RSC Complete Works of Shakespeare in the vaults of the RSA. We have already reprinted this monster of a book and we shall have to place a further reprint today. The book has reached number 9 on Amazon briefly which is remarkable for a work of scholarship. We have a hit on our hands but it is only the beginning for an alliance with the Royal Shakespeare Company which aims to bring Shakespeare in multiple formats to schools, universities and homes throughout the world. The editors have done a magnificent job and we intend to beat every sales record to support them.

Of course there has to be a disaster in such a cheerful week and it was dutifully supplied (as usual) by the England cricket team's elimination from the World Cup. As my ever kindly cricket-loving colleagues from Gill & Macmillan pointed out the Irish team managed to score more runs against South Africa than England. Baldons CC for which I've played for more than thirty years may not be as good as England but at least we try.

📁 21 April 2007

A maiden century for Picador

On June 20 1997 Picador printed an initial 15,000 copies of the paperback editon of Bridget Jones's Diary by Helen Fielding.

This week we placed the 100th reprint of the main edition (excluding tie-ins, specials etc). I think we should all stand and applaud Helen – and Bridget.

I received an email yesterday from Evan Schnittman who is Oxford University Press's Vice-President of Business Development and Rights for the Academic and USA DIvisions – crazy title but not so crazy guy. He has written a number of articles on the excellent OUP Blog and I think it's worth checking out this particular link on Google Book Search (now apparently known as GBS, presumably after the great Irish writer – or maybe not). I'd be interested in any feedback on his pricing ideas.

Here is another blog worth looking at, and not just because it features a few Macmillan-related items. Jon Reed knows a great deal about digital publishing and he is clearly also a brave person in calling his business Reed Media in spite of the risk of a trade mark infringement suit from the mighty Reed Elsevier gorilla. His name is, of course, his defence.

Which leads me to a Charkin anecdote. My father established a small chain of shoe shops under the brand 'Peter Knight'. His main competitor was 'Peter Lord' owned by the then mighty Sears Holdings run by Charlie Clore. They sued Peter Knight for 'passing off'. In court the judge asked my father why he had named the shops Peter Knight if it wasn't to make them sound like Peter Lord. My dad's reply was that the name came from an old family saying ' Make sure you pee tonight before you go to bed.' We lost the case but Peter Knight lives on as a dormant company 'P.K. Holdings'.

This weekend sees the Second Life Book Fair. I haven't the faintest idea what it means but you can probably discover more from this, published today. The authors, Paul Carr (aka Montag Alacrity) and Graham Pond (aka SweetSweet Mincemeat), will be signing virtual copies of the book in-world and we will be giving out some virtual freebies . . . but you'll have go in-world to find out what.

By permission of Pan Macmillan, London.

🔁 22 April 2007

Kate Greenaway

I'm off to the airport in a while at the start of a rather long and complicated trip (London-Mumbai-Mexico City-Buenos Aires-London in ten days) and so apologies in advance if my postings become even more erratic than usual.

I've just received the news about the latest Greenaway Prize shortlist for the best children's illustrated books of 2007. We are delighted to be the publishers of two of the six titles.

They are Emily Gravett's Monkey and Me:

By permission of Pan Macmillan, London.

And Chris Riddell's <u>Emperor of Absurdia</u>:

By permission of Pan Macmillan, London.

The winner will be announced on 21 June. There is also an interesting vote for the best children's books of the last seventy years. Worth looking up the rules <u>here</u>.

Lest anyone thinks I am Macmillan-obsessed I've been forwarded a clever bit of viral marketing about a Penguin US title, <u>The Starfish and the Spider</u>, having an on-line abstracting service <u>Get Abstract</u> produce a useful but incomplete summary of the book and having that widely distributed. The theme of the book is that if you cut off a spider's leg, it's crippled; if you cut off its head, it dies. But if you cut off a starfish's leg it grows a new one, and the old leg can grow into an entirely new starfish:

• The spider, with its brain, head and body, represents hierarchal order. In contrast, the starfish, an undifferentiated neural network, represents decentralization.

• Starfish organizations are far more flexible and adaptive than spider organizations.

• Decentralized starfish organizations do not require CEOs or extensive headquarters operations.

• Starfish organizations can change readily.

• In the starfish organization, norms of behavior matter more than codes of conduct.

• Centralized organizations become even more rigid when attacked, while decentralized organizations expand and adapt.

• Starfish organizations stand on five legs: circular structure, a catalyst which 'initiates a reaction,' an ideology, a pre-existing network and a champion.

• If you want to promote your product in some innovative way, put a catalyst to work.

• Remove the catalyst from a starfish organization and it will continue to thrive, but insert property ownership into a starfish organization, and it will become a spider.

• Companies now are becoming hybrids, with traits of both spiders and starfish.

It all sounds okay to me in spite of the inevitability of losing my job in the new starfish structure. I wonder whether my friends at <u>Penguin</u> will send me a copy to hasten my demise. Incidentally, we don't have an 'expensive headquarters operation', so we pass that test at least.

Furthermore, in all probability for reasons of the complexity of spider organisations the book doesn't appear on the Penguin UK website at all!

🦋 23 April 2007

Mumbai

Mumbai is now rated one of the most exciting cities in the world but this is about as close as I get. Meetings today start in the hotel at 8.45 (4.15 a.m. UK and Charkin body clock time) and continue all today and tomorrow. Macmillan India has more than 3000 employees, more fifty separate locations, a quotation on the Mumbai and National stock exchanges, several semi-independent subsidiaries, a printing press and goodness knows how many forms to be filled in under pain of severe punishments. The meetings are not just to monitor the progress of the business but also to comply with the very high standards of Indian corporate governance.

I am grateful to the fascinating Charleston Report magazine for librarians for these two factlets.

In January 2007 MySpace recorded 31.5 billion unique page views per month. A colleague did the maths on this and said it was highly improbable but I am reporting what I read.

Also in January the US record industry sold 34 million albums. In the same period in 2002, album sales were 50 million, a 30% decline in five years. There are those who think that the book industry will be protected from change because we (some people) like reading books in the bath or on the beach. This is true but perhaps a third of readers might like to switch to an alternative medium or delivery route and a similar 30% drop would be a devastating blow to a relatively low-margin industry unless we find ways of joining in the new world.

The highlight of the flight to India was reading in one gulp Tomorrow by Graham Swift. It is an amazing achievement but I think the key to enjoying it is to read it in the same time frame as the story is told (a few hours during the night) and a flight to Mumbai is ideal although, as the author pointed out to me, a 747 is not quite the same as a bedroom in Putney.

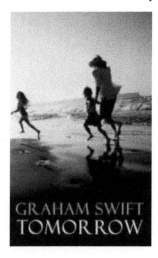

By permission of Pan Macmillan, London.

🗓 24 April 2007

Investors meet

Yesterday afternoon we held a session for the shareholders of Macmillan India at the Oberoi Hilton Towers in Mumbai for an Investors' Meet (not quite sure why it's a meet rather than a meeting but local terminology must win out).

Amazingly, 133 people turned up – mainly from investment banks and investor groups. We presented the company and then took questions for the best part of ninety minutes and then descended on what is known in these parts as High Tea. This had originally confused me. I couldn't work out why we'd want to conclude with a session on IT. There again, India is confusing – what with lakhs, crores and 4.5 hours time difference.

The good news here is that educational (and trade and academic too) sales are booming and that gradually, ever so gradually, the scholol system is being liberalised thus allowing private publishers (as opposed to state governments) to publish and sell books to state schools. Already this is forcing standards and value up.

I leave Mumbai for Mexico City (via New York) tonight. Fortunately I am armed with a pile of books to while away the time between reading Latin American accounts and eating and sleeping. I think the journey time (if I've calculated the time differences correctly) is 25 hours, probably nearer thirty door to door. Perhaps I should write a book rather than read one.

🗓 25 April 2007

More on the Second Life Book Fair

I'm in the air somewhere right now, so this report on the virtual Book fair that took place in Second Life last weekend comes from Pan Macmillan's intrepid Press Officer, Emma Giacon:

On Sunday night we held an event for The Unofficial Tourist Guide to Second Life, at the Second Life Book Fair. (As blogged previously here) There is a thriving book community in SL, as we've been discovering, and our event had a good number of people and generated interesting discussion about publishing/the digital world.

The format of the event was much the same as a Real Life one – the authors participated in a Q&A session with Falk Bergman , who has created books in SL for several authors and publishers. For SL literate readers of this blog, his bookstand can be found here . The discussion was then opened up to the floor, and we had intelligent and polite questions. We gave away free, in-world copies of the Guide, which residents can read when they are logged in to SL, and also some funny little branded hats, which you should be able to see in the pics. A branded hat might sound strange, but SLifers love a freebie, particularly one they can wear! Of course, we knew that the experienced SLifers already in-world were not our target audience for the Guide, but our aim is that they'll go and tell all of their 'newbie' friends how brilliant and useful it is!

This has really been an interesting experience, despite various technical problems to begin with. I certainly think that we will pursue other in-world opportunities. Our colleagues at Nature are ahead of the game as they already own two islands, but expect to see a more permanent Pan Macmillan presence at some point soon!

PS, my favourite audience comment came when someone suggested that the SL Book Fair should take the place of Frankfurt . . . Not sure what other people think, but it would definitely reduce our carbon footprint!

26 April 2007

Mexico City

Most of yesterday and a bit of the day before was spent on a thirty hour journey from one very large, very hot, very congested, very polluted, very exciting city to another. The main difference is that Mexico has the added joy of high altitude and consequent breathlessness.

I won't bore you with the tedium and discomfort of the trip but here's a personal recommendation. If you can possibly avoid using Delta Airlines, do.

Board meetings about Mexico and Latin America in general start later today. The good news is that it appears that the recently elected Mexican Government seems to have recommitted itself to addressing the acute educational problems of this country with vast numbers of school-age children and a need to develop fast. Our two main Mexican ventures, Macmillan de Mexico and Ediciones Castillo are both crucial to educational development here and our discussions will involve how to serve this market even more actively. More later.

But while I'm away, things continue to develop in Europe. This article from the Irish Examiner tells how the major TV channel, RTE has teamed up with Gill & Macmillan to find undiscovered writing talent in Ireland. Without wishing to over-generalise I can't help feeling that this could open up the organisers to the largest wave of submissions in the history of publishing. Every Irish person has at least two books in a drawer and is confident that the world wants them. If, however, a new Irish star is found the Guinness will be on me.

My favourite headline of the week comes from the Guardian:

Tale of a sexless tortoise shortlisted for science book prize

It refers, of course, to my favourite book, Henry Nicholls's Lonesome George. They know a thing or two, these shortlisters.

I'm off for a jetlag busting walk in neighbouring Chapultepec Park (pre-Colombian hill of grasshoppers). Mexico City is not all pollution and concrete.

Mexico City day 2

The last time I was in Mexico I was shown a dilapidated multi-storey car park-type building which I was assured would make wonderful offices for our two comanies here. I was a tad sceptical but the cost seemed sensible and the location was a vast improvement over either of the two original offices. The work has amazingly gone almost to schedule, the building has been transformed and we now have the best publishing building in Mexico City on the best terms. A truly Mexican economic and architectural miracle although from the outside it still looks a little like a car park.

As I mentioned yesterday our main objective in Mexico is to publish for schools whose quality enhancement is vital for the future of Mexico economically and culturally. I was interested to hear some statistics from the British Government. Apparently one in seven children in UK primary schools does not have English as a first language. That's 800,000 children. Late last year we published an innovative reading scheme for the Middle East but based on the methodology used in British classroooms. It is Macmillan English Explorers and we've now begun a marketing campaign for it in the UK. Another example of globalisation in action.

One of the recurring themes in English Language Teaching publishing is to come up with new titles for series – Access, Horizons, Streamline, Contact, Turn Around etc. I was, therefore, delighted to discover that one of our most successful ELT courses ever (over 13 million copies sold) had the gloriously boring and incomprehensible title, Basic Junior Active Context English. Can anyone beat that for the least memorable title in history?

For the latest on Second Life which we mentioned earlier in the week you could do worse than check out Jo Scott's latest blog about Second Nature. It's mysterious but fascinating.

28 April 2007

Small world, big world

Another overnight flight, another rotten airline, this time AeroMexico. To quote from their chief executive in the in-flight magazine –

At a time rife with positive changes, I would like to reiterate our ongoing commitment to excellence for our passengers with a modernised fleet and corporate image and its attractive new routes such as Mexico City to Buenos Aires.

I can only think that they must have used up all their resources on the corporate image because the plane on the Mexico to BsAs leg was at least forty years old, the service was dreadful, and the only thing that was really essential – sleep – was denied by the flight team switching the lights on every hour to ensure maximum disruption.

However, my heart lifted on arrival in Argentina. The city of Buenos Aires is great. The sun was shining, there is very little pollution and the traffic is a breeze.

Of course the technology did not work. Neither Blackberry nor WiFi nor Internet connection but thanks to the team and especially Carola at Design Ce hotel who, against all the odds on a Saturday, managed to find me a working computer on which to write this. And the point of the title of this blog is that the designer and owner, Ernesto Goransky, owner, designer and manager of this hotel studied at the Architectural Association in London and knew one of my cousins and a number of acquaintances. If you are ever in Buenos Aires this place gets my vote for trendiest design and most helpful people.

29 April 2007

A book fair with a point

I'm not in Buenos Aires for its book fair but, as I was here and so was it, I wandered in to have a look. It is amazing. It runs for three weeks, is visited by a million people and is packed more or less continuously. Publishers and booksellers offer books for sale (rarely at anything less than full retail price) and people queue to pay – in cash. It is open until 2 a.m. It is a joy to see books absolutely central to a country's culture and, perhaps most encouragingly, a significant commitment to ensuring that the next generation grows up with a love of reading. I'm not famous for being a fan of book fairs (expensive, introspective, self-satisfied, cliquey) but this one is a triumph.

There's an interesting article about the music industry and digital rights management in the excellent technology section of the Guardian newspaper. After years of resisting pressure to reduce the security embedded into digital music downloads, the industry is now moving to DRM-free offerings at higher prices. I won't try to recapitulate the arguments (read the article) but I do think it's strange that book publishers seem to be moving towards stricter DRM control just as the parallel music industry is moving beyond that debate. I'd be very interested to hear from people (within or without Macmillan) what they think.

For those of you who want another angle on Argentina (from Noel Coward and Nina), you might want to check this out.

🌱 30 April 2007

You really can't win

It's very strange being at the other end of the world and reading articles like this in today's Guardian newspaper. It quotes the head of the UK retail group Woolworths as saying that publishers had 'whipped independent booksellers into a frenzy' about Woolies' proposed takeover of the wholesaler Bertram Books. This frenzy had then led the booksellers to complain to the Competition Commission in an attempt to block what might be considered a potential monopoly in book distribution to the independent trade.

This report is very strange for three reasons. Firstly, publishers normally stand accused of never supporting independent booksellers (see any number of comments on this blog from various independents). Secondly, unlike in last year's Wottakars case, I'm pretty sure that the Publishers Association has taken a rather passive stance. And thirdly, and most strange, I think I can safely say that publishers have never been able deliberately to whip independent booksellers into a frenzy about anything. Sometimes by mistake of course . . .

Now back to reality. I have a day of meetings ahead of me in various parts of Buenos Aires. Our companies here are Macmillan Argentina (who have the great but only occasionally true slogan 'With Macmillan you have all the answers') which serves the English Language Teaching market and Puerto de Palos which publishes books in Spanish for children, schools and the genral market.

During the dreadful Argentine economic crisis of 2002 several international publishers abandoned their companies. I am glad for all sorts of reasons that Macmillan did not. Of course we had to adapt the business to the economic horrors of the time but we hung in, thanks to the committed local team, and we are now on a significant expansion path. Nothing is straightforward in Latin America (or anywhere?) but there is a strong recognition of the importance of education and we are determined to be at its centre.

Should you ever be in Buenos Aires do try Los Pinos restaurant for basic Argentine cooking in an authentic setting (sounds like a travel brochure but I couldn't think of alternative words) with a melancholic and nostalgic atmosphere. The other thing is that the meal costs less than £10 a head including top quality wine.

Charchive

≤   **May 2007**   ≥

Mon	Tue	Wed	Thu	Fri	Sat	Sun
30	1	2	3	4	5	6
7	8	9	10	11	12	13
14	15	16	17	18	19	20
21	22	23	24	25	26	27
28	29	30	31	1	2	3
4	5	6	7	8	9	10

🔖 01 May 2007

Puerto de Palos

Here is the office of <u>Puerto de Palos</u> in Buenos Aires. I love it for its turrets, for its scruffiness and for its anonymity. The problem is that the wiring is pre-historic, the offices are tiny and not very well ventilated and some of the corridors and staircases are, to put it gently, a little unsound by modern standards. The guys outside might be issuing the certificate of safe business premises. They might equally be from the local branch of the protection of businesses society. Or even the management eyeing up a potential real estate opportunity.

As this is the first of the month I share with you the blog statistics for the previous month. In April we had a disappointing 68227 visits. This is down from March's record 81424 bringing the total visits to 689184. Any ideas for boosting traffic (apart from the obvious ones) gratefully received.

I'm returning to London this morning, just another seventeen hours travelling. Thank goodness for books.

🔖 02 May 2007

Back in the UK

Arrived back in London this morning having missed the <u>Booksellers Association Conference</u> which was held in Harrogate this year. Apparently there was a dearth of booksellers which rather misses the point. It would be awful if it were to become just another get-together for publishers.

However, the good news from Harrogate is that Pan Macmillan's brilliant rights director, Chantal Noel, was voted rights professional of the year. I'm amazed she hasn't won it before but better late than never. I tried googling Chantal for a photo, only to discover there is another <u>Chantal Noel</u> who is not in the least like ours.

And another friend was voted young publisher of the year – <u>Clare Christian</u>, managing director of <u>The Friday Project</u>.

Trivial fact of the day. I was discussing the differences in style between American and British dictionaries – in partcicular between <u>Webster's Third International</u> and the <u>Oxford English Dictionary</u>. The American approach is to be far more descriptive (for

419

instance, check out Webster's definition of 'hotel'). The British approach is to describe a word accurately with as few words as possible. I believe the greatest (and least helpful) example of this was in the sixth edition of the <u>Concise Oxford Dictionary</u> where the brilliant but pedantic editor, <u>John Sykes</u>, defined 'aspirin' in two words, analgesic febrifuge.

03 May 2007

Customer service

A little while ago I <u>blogged</u> about a letter to the <u>Harvard Business Review</u> complaining about their policy on on-line subscriptions. They have now <u>responded</u> and turned a complaining reader into a loyal customer and, as Ann Michaels rightly says, that's good marketing.

Another way of creating loyal customers is equally obvious (and equally often forgotten). It is to encourage customers to tell you what they think – and tell each other. We are launching a new blog today with the somewhat inelegant (to my eyes) title <u>connect2mec</u> which is there to help teachers of English keep in touch with us, share ideas with each other and find out about the latest available lesson plans, study aids and how to best integrate <u>Macmillan English Campus</u> into a blended learning programme within their institution. Here's the team.

By permission of Pan Macmillan, London.

And here's a <u>press release</u> about <u>Editorial Estrada</u> which was issued this morning in Buenos Aires.

Ángel Estrada y Compañía S.A. has reached an agreement with Macmillan Publishers Limited

Buenos Aires, May 2007. On April 30th, Ángel Estrada y Compañía S.A., a company with 130 years' tradition in educational publishing in Argentina, reached a non-binding agreement with Macmillan Publishers Limited pursuant to which Macmillan will acquire the company's publishing business through the purchase of the shares of Editorial Estrada, S.A, a company controlled by Ángel Estrada y Compañía S.A.

Completion of the purchase of Editorial Estrada S.A. by Macmillan Publishers Limited is subject, among other conditions, to legal and financial due diligence, at the end of which both parties will agree the final price of the transaction.

Ángel Estrada y Compañía S.A. will continue to operate, concentrating on its school and business stationery division.

The Securities Exchange Commission and the Stock Exchange have been informed of this agreement.

Press Relations in Estrada:

María Eugenia Fernández Blanco
RRWW Comunicaciones
mefernandezblanco@rrww.com.ar
Ph: (+5411) 4556-0099

Contact in Macmillan:
Christopher West
Ph: (+5411) 4717 0088

Ángel Estrada & Cía S.A. was founded in 1869 and is Argentina's first publishing company. Its stationery brands include Arte and Rivadavia:the latter has been in the Argentine market for 90 years. The company has two business divisions: school and business stationery under the brands Rivadavia, América, el Nene and Arte; and high quality, creative educational texts and complementary teaching materials. The stationery factory in La Rioja province dates back to 1982 and the company has a modern distribution facility in Spegazzini, in Buenos Aires province, which distributes its products nationwide.

Macmillan Publishers Limited was founded in 1843 and is part of the German media group Verlagsgruppe Georg von Holtzbrinck GmbH. The Macmillan group has been established in Argentina since 1998 and is a market leader in textbooks for teaching the English language.

04 May 2007

That was then but this is now

I was cheered up on the way to work this morning to hear about about a BBC6 competition to establish the worst pop song lyrics of all time. The one that stands out and deserves everything it gets is from a song by ABC with the same title as this posting. Here is the last verse for your Friday enjoyment.

More Sacrifices than an Aztec priest,
Standing here straining at that leash,
All fall down,
Can't complain, mustn't grumble,
Help yourself to another piece of apple crumble

There's a bit of momentum in the UK book world at the moment in support of independent publishing. Both Waterstone's and Borders have announced schemes to support independents such as free window displays, front-of-store promotions at no cost etc. There are, however, a couple of problems.

First, what is an independent publisher? Is it defined by membership of the Independent Publishers Guild? If so, what would happen if, for instance, Random House were to join the IPG? Is the word 'independent' a euphemism for 'small'? If so, is Faber, as an example, small enough? If it means 'privately owned and funded' can Macmillan benefit from these excellent opportunities? If it means 'free to publish non-mainstream books' then Picador should be a candidate.

Second, assuming that there is a finite amount of money and prime retail space then a benefit to one sector of the industry must be a disbenefit to the rest. In other words a publisher such as Hachette Livres is being forced to subsidise some of its competitors by one of its distributors. Is that a sustainable or acceptable situation? I hope UK booksellers either recognise that Macmillan is an independent publisher and warrants the same generous treatment as the officially-designated independent publishers or allow us to negotiate lower discounts in view of our having less-favoured treatment.

05 May 2007

Gordon Ramsay

I was told by a restaurant critic that a sure way of increasing visits to a website is to mention Gordon Ramsay. Hence today's title. I'll let you know if it works.

My career has been blessed by the colleagues I have worked with and for. Perhaps one of the most important times was in the eighties working at Oxford University Press in various roles with Robin Denniston as my boss. He is the son of Alastair Denniston who was a key figure in British intelligence during the war and has recently published a biography of his father entitled Thirty Secret Years which I wrote about a little while ago. Robin has also published some fascinating extracts from his childhood diaries in the Daily Telegraph.

Now, for publishing historians and current and former Macmillan employees this link opens up a treasury of nostalgia. The team working in the Macmillan Archive in Basingstoke, with the help of Macmillan India, have digitised all back issues of Macmillan News (the Charkinblog of its time?) and these are now searchable and deliverable as pdfs. Random browsing throws up gems even for non-Macmillan people. Give it a try. I wish OUP would digitise and make available Robin Denniston's (see above) newsletter from the olden days.

I'm off to Johannesburg tomorrow if I can find a way to Heathrow through the Chelsea and Arsenal fans (witnessing what might be the decider for the soccer premiership title) who will be blocking the streets near my home at just the time I need to leave. A few weeks ago I wrote that Macmillan South Africa was participating fully in black empowerment. We have now announced an imaginative scheme to establish a virtual training campus for South African teachers. I have been sent photos of the launch event. Most of them are very high-quality shots of the distinguished speakers but I thought this picture more entertainingly sums up the spirit of modern South Africa.

By permission of Pan Macmillan, London.

🦃 06 May 2007

Magic Moments

The first record (78rpm) I remember listening to was <u>Magic Moments</u> by <u>Perry Como</u>. Not only was the melody (<u>Burt Bacharach</u>) addictive but the lyrics (<u>Hal David</u>) were superb. Imagine how I felt when, after <u>blogging</u> what I thought was the worst pop lyric couplet of all time:

Can't complain, mustn't grumble,
Help yourself to another piece of apple crumble

I came across a letter in <u>The Times</u> claiming this masterpiece from Magic Moments to be a competitor for worst couplet. I think it is up there with the very best. You need to hum the melody for best effect:

The way that we cheered whenever our team was scoring a touchdown,The time that the floor fell out of my car when I put the clutch down

I promised to share the results of yesterday's <u>Gordon Ramsay</u> traffic enhancement experiment. I'm afraid it's inconclusive. We had 2152 visits yesterday compared with 2612 the day before (a Friday) and compared with 1850 the previous Saturday. I couldn't detect any surfers searching for GR and getting RC but there's hope yet. Maybe Gordon Ramsay has a long tail.

Back to books or maybe it's just another magic moment. <u>Richard Wiseman</u> is a scientist dedicated to explaining science (and in particular psychology) to the general public. It's a tough assignment, not least because much media coverage is both slight and wrong. However, his new book <u>Quirkology</u> looks like it will break down all resistance. Stephen Dumughn has described part of the publication process in <u>The Digitalist</u> blog which is only available to Macmillan UK web users. So here it is for the world.

Ok, I want you to try something for me. Put down your afternoon cup of tea and draw the capital letter Q on your forehead. Done it? Good. Believe it or not, that simple test will tell you something profound about your personality. If you drew the Q with the tail on the right side of your forehead (ie as you would see it) then you are a self-centered personality type (not as bad as it sounds). If you drew it with the tail on the left, you are other-centered.* Intrigued? For more detailed results click <u>here</u>.

Welcome to the world of 'Quirkology', a world I feel I've been inhabiting for the last 6 months or so as we have built up to the publication of the book Quirkology today. Using simple experiments like the one above, behavioural scientist Professor Richard Wiseman has spent 20 years examining the quirky science and psychology behind our everyday lives, and the results are truly fascinating. How can you tell when someone is lying? Why do incompetent politicians win elections? What is the best chat-up line? Can you really be born lucky? Does frowning make you miserable? Richard knows all the answers to these questions and tons more like them, and the results will certainly surprise and entertain you.

The non-fiction team here were so fascinated when the book proposal of his work came in last year we fell over ourselves to publish it. And we're very glad we did – Quirkology is currently getting the kind of pre-publication trade buzz and media attention that comes along all too rarely. The book is proving to be a dream to promote – packed full of hooks and angles that instantly pique people's interest. And we've had a lot of fun with the marketing of it – we've got the book trade to take part in experiments all the way through the sell-in period and even turned the book jacket itself into an experiment. The hub of the marketing is the website we've built specifically for the book at www.quirkology.com. Here you can read more about the book and the author, take some simple tests (like the Q test above) and watch the video of Richard performing the 'colour-changing card experiment' which really has to be seen to be believed. If you do you won't be alone – the video has had over 26,000 hits on YouTube since it went up two days ago.

But the key to making this work has been Richard himself. The man is a human dynamo – one of those 600 ideas before breakfast guys, all of them good. Together with his incomparable publicist Dusty Miller, they have been blitzing the media with a series of Richard's projects, generating what you could genuinely call 'blanket' coverage. Stories running at the moment include a study into how your surname affects your life with The Telegraph, why men write the best personal ads with The Times, extracts from the book including the search for the world's funniest joke with The Guardian and myriad interviews, features and offshoot stories across national TV, Radio and the rest of the press. The latest story to break has been Richard's study with the British Council into comparing the pace of life in 32 cities around the globe, with major coverage in The Times again (twice) and the BBC. With more stories expected (we're currently trying to place a sports story on the science of penalty-taking) the media storm looks let to continue. All the latest stories will be on the website, which will be continually updated throughout the summer in the run-up to Richard's major TV series with the BBC in the autumn – a fascinating 20 part series developed from Richard's Quirkology ideas. Watch this space . . .

*Of course, if you drew the Q with a pen and not your finger then you are a bit of an idiot in either case.

07 May 2007

More on Mexico

I've just arrived in Johannesburg, but thought you might like to see some more pictures from my Mexico trip.

As you can see below, Macmillan is taking global warming seriously. Our company there has organised to have its own energy-saving train for freighting books from the docks to the new warehouse in Mexico City and for onward despatch to bookshops and schools:

It's an impressive set-up, with heightened security to ensure no books are inadvertently filched by visiting executives . . . .

On another note, we're always pleased when our colleagues from Germany go travelling and ask to visit our local offices. Andreas Kirschkamp from the 'Controlling Department' in Stuttgart paid a visit to India recently and met up with many of the team there.

He received even more than the typical Indian hospitality. He and I agree that this might have something do with his similarity to Michael Vaughan, the England cricket captain.

08 May 2007

Wanderers

Board and strategy meetings today in our Johannesburg offices.

At long last we have a respectable Macmillan South Africa website. The first item is the announcement of our black empowerment initiative which we have been working on for more than a year. We decided to take this step as part of our partnership with South African education.

And it's not just South Africa. We are the largest publisher in the Southern Africa region with significant operations in Botswana, Swaziland, Lesotho, Mozambique, Namibia and, of course, the unfortunate Zimbabwe.

For some reason mention of Zimbabwe reminds me of my former boss (a short-lived experience), Robert Maxwell. There was a wonderful BBC documentary of parts of his life starring David Suchet (who,incidentally, was my dormitory captain at my first boarding school) in the title role. His performance was chilling and accurate – well worth getting to see the programme.

What's in a name?

I am waiting for some photos of the school I visited yesterday in Soweto. I'll post them for a simple reason. The picture below is most people's image of the township. The reality, as you will see, is different. More anon.

Our new rep in the Free State is called Macmillan Mareka. Apparently a first name of Macmillan is not that rare in South Africa, particularly among people born shortly after Harold Macmillan's Winds of Change speech in Cape Town in 1960. But I still think it shows commitment to the cause. Perhaps all our reps should be called Macmillan.

Back in the UK now and saying farewell to my term as an officer of the Publishers Association at their annual general meeting in a few minutes. So must rush. I wouldn't want my term extended in absentia.

If you have a few minutes to spare and you're interested in the importance of design, check out this video. I love the guy's name, Jesse James Garrett – but still not as good as Macmillan Mareka.

10 May 2007

Shakespeare in Bogota

Yesterday a bomb exploded in Erbil, Kurdistan region of Iraq. Fortunately none of our staff or friends working there was hurt but it does underline the risks that people are taking to bring education to the people of Iraq as I've described before.

On a lighter note, Pan Macmillan are celebrating a number one. Not a book but a video which was made to support the book's marketing. I mentioned Quirkology a few days ago but I had absolutely no idea that the card trick video would reach number one (yesterday for a few hours) on YouTube (and it's still number three as I write with 250,000 hits in a week – 390,000 now, four hours later). I believe this is a first for any publisher's promotional video but I am sure someone will correct me if I'm wrong.

Most of my readers are probably aware that I am not inordinately fond of book fairs. However, they exist and some of them even generate demand for books. Macmillan will do almost anything to achieve a sale and here is a picture of the RSC Shakespeare at the Bogota International Book Fair (to my shame, it wasn't until searching for that link that I discovered that Bogota has been declared Book Capital of the World – we should be told more).

And while on book fairs, I promised a colleague that I would mention the ever-increasing Cape Town Book Fair. The fair has been so successful that they have had to double the floor space in order to accommodate more and bigger stands. Is this growth in book fair activity in spite of or because of the Internet, I wonder?

There was a unique event last night at the Chelsea Arts Club. We were there to honour and thank Ronnie Williams (OBE, not the comedian) on his retirement from being Chief Executive of the Publishers Association. Some indication of the respect in which he is held is attested by the attendance of eleven past and future PA presidents (in chronological presidential order, Philippa Harrison, Adrian Soar, David Kewley, Simon Master, Anthony Forbes Watson, John Clement, Henry Reece, me, Stephen Page, Mike Boswood and Ian Hudson). Trevor Glover meant to come but was delayed at a concert. I'm not clear what the collective noun for eleven PA presidents is but would be happy to publish any (or more or less any) suggestions.

🦅 11 May 2007

Kim Scott Walwyn

Kim was a friend and colleague of mine at Oxford University Press during the 1980s. She was a great person and a great publisher. She died at a ridiculously young age but her memory is kept alive by the annual award of a prize which recognises the professional achievements of women in publishing. The shortlist was announced in April and last night I went to St Anne's College in Oxford for the award celebration overseen by Tim Gardam who was Kim's husband and is now Principal of the college. To my – and I suspect many people's – delight Annette Thomas, Managing Director of Nature Publishing Group won in what was a very strong field (as reported in the Guardian today). It is a tribute to everything that she and the fantastic team at NPG have achieved over the last few years. I am certain that Kim would have approved of the choice.

While on success, I'd like to point you to this anniversary review of Macmillan New Writing and I can assure you that this is not the result of backscratching or any other underhand measure.

For those of us who remember the glory days of sales to Nigeria in the 1970s this vignette from an old Nigeria hand returning to one of Macmillan's outlying offices will ring a bell.

'A reassuring scene, though: a dusty entrance lobby with pealing lino tiles and segments of spaghetti-type wiring; battleship grey paintwork (always so encouraging I find); a receptionist reading a two-day old copy of the Daily Times plus a grubby Mills & Boon novel; a fading picture of the late Supermac hung at a rakish angle but so high up you had to positively seek him (o tempora! o mores! o winds of change! – nothing had changed in this lobby for years); the MD's ante-chamber crammed with cheap Asian wall clocks and support staff with little to do pending the arrival of the MD but read newspapers and seek soul-mates on the web; and the car park full of sound and fury, drivers and reps, but little if any sign of coordinated activity . . . '

And to finish, a sort of review of this blog which leaves me wondering whether to be flattered or offended.

🐟 12 May 2007

Stuck in deepest Suffolk

It transpires that technology is less developed in Suffolk than in Patagonia. As a result I've asked 'Woman Publisher of the Year' NPG's Managing Director Annette Thomas to write a few words . . .

Site licenses have revolutionised the way that researchers access content and numerous studies have shown that there is now more access to more content and at lower prices than ever before. But this all a bit heavy for a Saturday morning, so on to the point of this posting.

Every summer Nature Publishing Group's site license business unit holds their annual sales conference. For the past 3 years we've gathered together at the Ocean Resort and Spa on the New Jersey Coast.

Like most sales conferences the days are filled with a mix of work and play and everyone has a good time. The meeting is organised by the excellent Geoff Worton who heads up our world-class sales team.

This year we've changed venues and we'll be meeting at the Hudson Hotel in NYC. It looks very posh (and expensive) but I've been assured that we've negotiated a very good rate.

Yesterday I received the agenda of the meeting and to my shock/horror/surprise/ delight I no longer have top billing on the program. Apparently Richard will be attending and I've been relegated to introducing him. What to say? What to say? I'm appealing to readers of this blog to send me their suggestions.

Have a lovely weekend

Annette

🦋 13 May 2007

The future of reading

As I'm still stuck in the technological black hole that is deepest darkest Suffolk, I've asked our Digital Publisher Sara Lloyd to expand on the email she pinged off to me last week after reading her Friday copy of Guardian supplement g2 . . .

To adulterate a joke made by that funny doctor bloke Dr Phil Hammond on Have I Got News for You last night, 'a qualification as 'Head of Digital Publishing' for a major international publisher is really no substitute for clairvoyancy'. I'd like to start from this point to avoid jokes made at my expense later; predicting the future has always been wrought with hazards and I lay no specialist claims to being able to do so.

However, I did get just a teensy weensy bit excited to read Andrew Marr's feature, 'Curling up with a good eBook' in g2 on Friday. This much loved and respected journalist, broadcaster and writer was given one of the latest eReaders, an Irex Iliad, to road test for a month. It was a case of 'bibliophile, or perhaps bibliomaniac, meets book-killer', as he so Andrew-Marr-ishly put it. You can read the article for yourself, but the results were surprising, in some ways. This key proponent of the book as beautiful object / thing to be read in the bath argument and sniffer of dusty covers in second hand bookshops was 'reluctantly impressed' with his ebook. He could even see a future in which he'd choose the e-version of 'a dozen new novels or biographies' to replace his bulging book bag when travelling, and he could certainly see the advantage of this when combined with an ability to download all the newspapers, magazines and other 'throwaway' content that he needs to digest on a regular basis.

For me the existing ereaders on the market still don't cut it. The 'killer device' – an iPod for books – isn't with us yet, but I think this generation of ereaders could be the beginning of a quiet revolution. As major Internet and computing players enter the fray to carve out a piece of the ebook market which they all believe could be round the corner and the 'download generation' graduate into the consumers of tomorrow, the ground has got to shift. Hasn't it?

🦋 14 May 2007

Boepakitso

A few days ago I mentioned a visit I made to a school in Soweto. Here is a picture of Boepakitso Primary School.

A fairly typical and functional piece of architecture and scene by any standards. What it doesn't show is the commitment, verve and vision of the teaching staff and the enthusiasm of the children. The school is partly supported by the Read Educational Trust which is our partner in South African publishing sector's first black empowerment transaction.

For those interested in statistics, our promotional video for Quirkology which I wrote about last week has now been viewed 769,427 times. Now, if each view sells a book . . .

After my technology-jinxed weekend in Suffolk I'm glad to be independent of guest bloggers but concerned that the guests succeeded kicking traffic numbers up and I suspect fooled readers into expecting higher standards of writing and insight than I can manage.

While on the standard of writing, here is an Observer review of my pick of the moment. Do get hold of a copy of When we were bad and find a few hours to read it. See if you agree with the reviewer and me.

🦃 15 May 2007

The reading debate continues

I'm often slightly disappointed that this blog receives most comments on subjects affecting British independent booksellers. Of course there are important issues and I'm always pleased to hear from booksellers but there are other controversial matters for the book world. I was therefore pleased to see that Sara Lloyd's excellent guest piece on the future of reading has generated some thought-provoking and insightful comments from a range of people. Do join the debate if you can.

The last couple of weeks have seen the building blocks for a new educational publishing landscape. The Pearson acquisition of what I know as Heinemann Education in the UK and Commonwealth and Harcourt Assessment in the USA (for $950 million); the sale of Thomson Learning (for $7.7 billion) to a private equity consortium (presumably with the intention of buying out the remaining bits of Harcourt Education); and the continuing speculation about the fate of Wolters-Kluwer's education divisions; all point to radical change in response to perceived technology shifts in teaching. The bets being placed are enormous but the rewards (and risks) are high.

If e-learning really establishes itself in schools (as I am sure it will) there will be an inevitable knock-on impact on the way adults will read and acquire information and hence the importance of the debate about the future of reading. It may take longer for some of the predictions about e-books etc to come true but the book trade simply has to come to terms with these new media before it's too late and we lose a generation of readers. Hence Macmillan's commitment to BookStore.

🦃 16 May 2007

Wisden Walk

I've been trying (without success) to arrange to join a bunch of friends from Wisden in a walk across Southern England starting on Saturday in support of the Teenage Cancer Trust. The Trust was set up in memory of Laurie Engel, the son of Wisden editor, Matthew Engel. Royalties from Matthew's latest book, Extracts from the Red Notebooks also go the fund. I'm sure the team would welcome any companions on the walk which is described here and where you can also contribute.

A propos last week's posting about the Kim Scott Walwyn prize won by Annette Thomas here is a link to an article in the Guardian by Hermione Lee about it.

Over at Pan Macmillan, there are celebrations for the success of James Herbert's latest paperback The Secret of Crickley Hall. In hardback the book reached number one in the best seller list and it is sitting at number two in paperback, a smidgeon behind the number one (whose title I won't mention). There was a time when Pan only had to compete with Penguin for paperback sales and those days are beautifully chronicled on this website. Things are much tougher today but it is great to see that Pan's tradition of mass-market fiction brilliantly packaged and marketed continues. A couple of covers to compare now and then. The 1961 price was 2/6d (old money). The 2007 price is £6.99 although many outlets will be selling the book at a lower price. Inflation doesn't explain the whole of the increase.

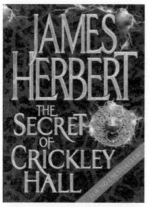

text on the side

By permission of Pan Macmillan, London.

17 May 2007

Happy Birthday Waterstone's

This is the first Waterstone's bookshop at 99-101 Old Brompton Road in South Kensington, London. It was founded by Tim Waterstone in 1982 with the redundancy money he received when he was sacked by W.H.Smith. The chain has developed extraordinarily to become Britain's largest bookseller and Tim tells some of the story in his book Swimming against the Stream.

Yesterday evening Waterstone's and its current owners HMV threw a fabulous party to celebrate 25 years of bookselling and to honour our top authors of the last quarter century and the twenty five for the next quarter century. I was delighted that Macmillan scored a 12% 'market share' of the future with Emily Gravett, Charlotte Mendelson and C.J.Sansom being selected. For more on the list follow this link.

Who knows what the next twenty-five years of retail bookselling will bring (as evidenced by the debate on this blog) but Bill Gates seems to think he knows:

'Reading is going to go completely online. We believe that as we get the smaller form factor, the screen has gotten good enough. Why is reading online better? It's up to date, you can navigate, you can follow links. The ads in the online reading are completely targeted as opposed to just being run-of-print, where many of the readers will find them completely irrelevant. The ads can be in new and richer formats. In fact the only drawbacks of the digital form are the things associated with the device: how big is it, heavy is it, how many hours of power does it have, how much do I have to spend to buy it? But those are things that once you achieve that threshold, in terms of the convenience and the cost, then you see a dramatic change in behavior. Today, for people who read newspapers and magazines, even the most avid PC user probably still does quite a bit of reading on print. As the device moves down in size and simplicity, that will change, and so somewhere in the next five-year period we'll hit that transition point, and things will be even more dramatic than they are today.'

So now we know.

Today sees the beginning of Summer in England. It is grey, rather damp and not very warm but it is also the first day of the first cricket Test Match of the season and England take on West Indies at Lord's Cricket Ground.

The other event to take place today will be the announcement of Gordon Brown as Britain's next Prime Minister. I am no political expert but it does seem surprising that someone can take over the leadership of a country (the mother of parliamentary democracy I believe) without a ballot of the people, the parliament or even his own political party. I have nothing against Brown but I hope his self-appointment doesn't encourage any other country to impose democracy on us by invading what is a country with a huge armoury of weapons of mass destruction, a danger of splitting (Scottish Nationalists now govern in Edinburgh), a strong breeding ground for militant Islam, strategically placed geographically and with extraordinarily valuable assets – and an unelected leadership.

18 May 2007

Vorsprung durch Technik

I'm not sure how many readers of this blog understand German (beyond the title above) but I think this pdf courtesy of Der Spiegel is saying some pretty nice things about Nature, its commitment to innovation and the quality of the team.

Later comment by editor:It turns out that this pdf link will not work outside the Nature firewall and Spiegel Online understandably charges for articles, so here is a taster within 'fair usage':

'Timo Twin irrt leicht orientierungslos über den Strand, dann zickzack den Hang hinauf. „Na endlich, ich wusste doch, dass es hier irgendwo ist', sagt der Mann im roten T-Shirt. Über einem weitläufigen Platz prangt groß wie ein Bauschild das Logo seines Unternehmens, weiß auf rotem Grund: „Nature'. Timo Twin ist in seinem neuen Reich angekommen, auf einer Insel im Online- Rollenspiel „Second Life'. Der Name der Insel ist Programm: „Second Nature'. Der Avatar sieht dem Timo im realen Leben nur entfernt ähnlich – dieser ist ein großer Mann Ende dreißig mit leicht rundlichem Harry-Potter-Gesicht. Er heißt Timo Hannay. Und er ist so etwas wie der Vertreter der Wissenschaftszeitschrift „Nature' in der virtuellen Welt.'

The British Department of Trade and Industry has just released figures for 2006 exports of books and a comparison with previous years. It makes fascinating reading on the soon-to-be-revamped Publishers Association website. In spite of all the changes in the global economy and the growth of the English language the traditional English-speaking and Commonwealth markets still dominate. And for all the hooha over China we sell ten times as much to the Republic of Ireland with a population of 4 million as to China with a population of 1.3 billion.

Clearly, however, markets such as China and India will grow and I was delighted to read in the Economic Times of India that territorial protection of copyright has been upheld by a Delhi High Court injunction preventing re-export of low-priced Indian textbooks. Whilst this restricts Indian export sales it allows publishers to produce low-cost editions for the very poor without fear of those editions entering the more affluent American market. In time, of course, global prices will equalise but in the meantime territorial copyright protection is vital for the development of publishing and education in emerging economies. Supporting these developments is the International Publishers Association whose new website has just been launched and where it is good to see that annual Freedom Prize has been awarded to a Zimbabwean publisher.

Harold Macmillan, Earl of Stockton.

I was doing a little research in the fascinating Macmillan News Archive and came across the 10 February 1987 issue which is all about HM's death – his funeral in Westminster Abbey, reminiscences and obituaries from around the Macmillan world. It's worth a look. As is this is interview with Peter Cook who is almost better than the real thing. A wonderful Cook as Macmillan quote from a description of a summit meeting with JFK:

'We talked of many things, including Great Britain's position in the world as some kind of honest broker. I agreed with him when he said no nation could be more honest, and he agreed with me when I chaffed him and said no nation could be broker.'

Back to the present and an irresistible parable about advertising today from a superb blog – Logic+Emotion – about marketing and design which was brought to my attention by Ann Michael.

I cannot resist posting this entry on the Future of Publishing from The Millions – a blog about books because it is entirely sensible in its review of Macmillan New Writing and because it helpfully lists all the titles available in the USA even though no American publisher was interested in the series.

20 May 2007

In praise of independent-minded publishers

There was a mini-debate on the meaning of independent publishing here a couple of weeks ago. I think it's a fairly meaningless (but sometimes helpfully self-serving) concept. Independence doesn't come from size or type of publication or ownership structures. It comes from the minds of people. On Friday I attended a birthday party at the Stationers' Hall.

It was to celebrate forty years since the formation of Kogan Page, 'Europe's largest independent publisher of business titles'. There is a story in The Times where they interviewed its Chairman, Philip Kogan. There's a letter from him in their latest catalogue but no pictures on Google Image Search.

I am a huge admirer of Philip and the company he founded. Not because of the books he's published. I'm sure they are good but it's just not my field. Not because he hasn't sold the company. I'm sure if someone had offered enough . . .

I admire him and the company because they have never ceased to innovate in order to stay in business and never ceased to enjoy the business we're in. Philip's daughter, Helen, is now in charge and it seems that the company is in great shape for now and the future. If that's what is meant by independent publishing, I'm all for it but I prefer to think of it as simply a matter of independent-minded publishing.

At Macmillan I think we're still pretty independent-minded too. Here is our most recent innovation – a blog for teachers of English. Everyone is welcome to contribute, so please do.

And of course, congratulations to my local team, Chelsea Football Club, on winning the FA Cup thanks, as so often this season, to the magnificent Didier Drogba. The celebrations in Chelsea last might were long and noisy and I think we can expect more today.

⟡ 21 May 2007

The literary tourist

We published <u>The Literary Tourist</u> by <u>Nicola Watson</u> in October 2006 as a scholarly book. It has received first-rate reviews and has been a moderate commercial success albeit with a short print run and a high price.

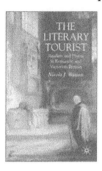

<u>Susan Hill</u> has issued a challenge on her <u>blog</u> for us to produce a cheaper edition in order to garner more sales through general-reader purchase. Her opening line is 'Great book, pity how it's published'.

This is an old chestnut. I cannot think of an academic author (or interested reviwer) who doesn't think that their book will find a wide audience if only it were priced and marketed like the latest <u>Jilly Cooper</u> (£3.99 for 1000 plus pages from Waterstone's). Sometimes the author is right but it is very rarely the case that a book written for scholarly reasons becomes a best seller. We shall be issuing a paperback of this excellent book in due course and, given the interest and potential market, I am sure it will do well. It may sell several thousand copies but I'd be amazed (and delighted) if it sold the tens of thousands that would have justified original publication as a general book.

Apart from this specific case, the challenge raises the question of pricing of academic books in general. Susan's commentators are horrified at the idea of paying £45 for a 250 page book. Compared to discounted <u>Harry Potter</u> of course £45 seems expensive. But is it? Try comparing the price with a shirt, a meal in a London restaurant, a ticket to a major sporting event, a train ticket, an hour of a lawyer's time. I think academic books are amazingly good value. They are permanent. They are valuable. They are great value for money. They are the fruit of extensive research and application. They are fundamental to the scholarly process. They reach a global audience and are readily available through libraries for those who cannot afford to purchase. They are fit for purpose and worth every penny. Thank goodness academic publishers have worked out a way of continuing to publish academic works commercially in spite of library budget constraints and falling print runs.

Last week I <u>wrote</u> about an article about Nature in <u>Der Spiegel</u>. I couldn't link to the article because it was 'subscriber only' and so a gave a brief quote in German. <u>Adam Hodgkin</u> kindly sent me this Google translation:

'Timo twin errs easily orientationless over the beach, then zigzag the slope up. „Well finally, I knew nevertheless that it is here somewhere ', says the man in the red T-Shirt. Over an extensive place prangt largely like a building sign the Logo of its enterprise, knows on red Reason: „Nature '. Timo twin arrived in its new realm, on an island in on-line game of roles „Second Life '. The name of the island is program: „Second Nature '. The Avatar sees only far away similar to the Timo in the material life – this is a large man end of thirty also easily roundish Harry Potter face. It is called Timo Hannay. And it is like that something like the representative that Science magazine „Nature 'in the virtual world.'

The piece is now open to everyone in English on Spiegel Online International. Here is a flavour. As a colleague remarked, it's hard to decide whether this makes much more sense than the Google version.

'Twin has arrived in his new realm, on an island in the online role-playing game Second Life. The name of the island is fitting: Second Nature. The avatar bears only a vague resemblance to the real-life Timo, a tall man in his late 30s with a slightly round, Harry Potter-like face. His real name is Timo Hannay, and he is something like the representative of the scientific journal Nature in the virtual world.'

22 May 2007

Reading in the Bath

Invariably when there is discussion of the advantages and disadvantages of print versus digital delivery of books, someone says: 'Ah, but you wouldn't want to read an e-book in the bath.' I am therefore most grateful to New Yorker Chris Steib who has undertaken a controlled scientific experiment comparing his Sony Reader and a print copy of Thomas Pynchon's The Crying of Lot 49. The Reader won!

I must thank Jeff Gomez and his Print is Dead blog for stimulating the experiment in the first place and then bringing it to my attention. Jeff's book (in print and digital editions)with the same title comes out in November.

I had a meeting yesterday with the person responsible for the OUPBlog. They manage approximately two postings a day, which puts me to shame – and they are very interesting. My only defence is that most days the blog is written by one of their illustrious authors while I'm pretty much a sole trader with the occasional and much-appreciated support of some Macmillan colleagues.

I've just seen the latest account from Google ads, a majestic $122.78. Here's my question. Do the ads upset any of you in any way?

23 May 2007

Litvinenko

We heaved a sigh of relief yesterday when the Crown Prosecution Service issued its press release and where Sir Ken Macdonald stated:

'I have today concluded that the evidence sent to us by the police is sufficient to charge Andrey Lugovoy with the murder of Mr Litvinenko by deliberate poisoning.

'I have further concluded that a prosecution of this case would clearly be in the public interest.

This was the same suspect as <u>Martin Sixsmith</u> had fingered in his book <u>The Litvinenko File</u> which we published about a month ago. Goodness knows where the

diplomatic stand-off between Russia and Britain will end but one side-effect is that the book's sales have already accelerated in the 24 hours since the announcement.

I asked <u>yesterday</u> whether anyone objected to the ads on this blog which have earned (I had pointed out to me) $254.12, not the figure I gave which was just the latest instalment. Nobody seems to mind and so I'll continue. The money will, I promise, be put to good use.

A little while ago I <u>wrote</u> about the differences in style between British and American dictionaries. British entries try to define a word as accurately as possible with as few words as possible. Analgesic febrifuge as a definition of aspirin in the COD is an extreme of Britishness. The American style is more discursive and descriptive and here is an extreme of American-ness from <u>Webster's Third New International Dictionary, Unabridged</u>:

Main Entry: ¹**ho·tel** <u>Pronunciation Guide</u>

Pronunciation: ()h|tel
Function: *noun*
Inflected Form(s): **-s**
Etymology: French *hôtel,* from Old French *ostel, hostel* – more at <u>HOSTEL</u>
1 *archaic* **:** a city mansion of a person of rank or wealth
2 a : a house licensed to provide lodging and usually meals, entertainment, and various personal services for the public **:** <u>INN</u> **b :** a building of many rooms chiefly for overnight accommodation of transients and several floors served by elevators, usually with a large open street-level lobby containing easy chairs, with a variety of compartments for eating, drinking, dancing, exhibitions, and group meetings (as of salesmen or convention attendants), with shops having both inside and street-side entrances and offering for sale items (as clothes, gifts, candy, theater tickets, travel tickets) of particular interest to a traveler, or providing personal services (as hairdressing, shoe shining), and with telephone booths, writing tables and washrooms freely available.

(By permission. From *Webster's Third New International® Dictionary, Unabridged* ® 2002 by Merriam-Webster, Incorporated (<u>www.Merriam-Webster.com</u>).)

Wormsley

I spent some of yesterday at Sir Paul Getty's cricket ground at <u>Wormsley</u>.

This panorama doesn't really do justice to the beauty of the place on an early English Summer's day.

The cricket was incidental to the fun and hospitality of the <u>Wisden</u> cricket day for advertisers, sponsors and contributors. I didn't play (saving myself for a needle match on Sunday) but did manage to suffer silly sunburn.

A controversy waiting to happen has just surfaced in the USA. It relates to an author's right to have the rights in her/his book revert if the publisher fails to keep the book in print. <u>Simon & Schuster</u> have eliminated this reversion clause from their boiler-plate contract. I can see their point. The existing clause refers to a simpler world where the definition of in print or out of print was clear. Today, publishing is global. If there is a copy in, say, an Australian warehouse, is the book still in print? If a book is immediately available by print on demand, is it in print? If a book is available digitally or by chapter, is it in print? However, I can understand an author's legitimate desire to ensure that a publisher does not simply 'sit on' the rights to a book. We need a new approach to rights reversion which recognises the new world in which we operate but which also recognises the decencies and fairness (in both directions) of the old. Some of the complexities are elaborated by <u>Peter Brantley</u>. This one will run and run.

🐦 25 May 2007

German books

I was at a <u>supervisory board meeting</u> in Stuttgart yesterday. There was a display of recently-published books from our various companies – <u>S.Fischer</u>, <u>Rowohlt</u>, <u>Kiepenheuer & Witsch</u> and <u>Droemer Knaur</u>. The books were beautiful. Imaginative jackets, high-quality text design, good paper, strong binding – in short treasurability. The other thing I noticed was that the hardbacks carried neither price nor barcode – and they looked much better for it. Apparently, hardbacks are individually shrink-wrapped (is that eco-friendly?) and then stickered with price etc. In-store, the bookseller will unwrap one copy for display purposes and keep the rest pristine. The other thing I noticed was that prices compare more than favourably with British ones.

How come there is so much more quality in German book production and design than in the British (and some other country) equivalents? I'm sure independent retailers will cry 'retail price maintenance' but I'm not sure. Perhaps it is simply a greater reverence for the written word which permeates the educational system and into the book industry. Whatever the explanation, I think there's a lot British publishers can learn fronm Germany about how to make a book a desirable object as well as a leisure 'product'.

If you're interested in getting a sense of German books and can cope with the non-English signage, go to Lovely Books, a social network for book-lovers which our team in Germany has launched in beta version just recently and which is building up a significant number of literary registrants.

Stop press: The German Parliament has recognised the centrality of publishing and publishers to the development of scientific research. More German commitment to quality.

26 May 2007

Chris Patten – East and West

Soon after I joined Macmillan in 1998, I was summonsed by the literary agent, Michael Sissons, of what is now the pfd international literary and talent agency. He was representing Chris Patten who had recently overseen the transfer of Hong Kong from British to Chinese control.

Patten had agreed with HarperCollins UK a contract to write about his time in Hong Kong and his views of the Chinese authorities. Sissons had just been informed that HC were withdrawing from their contract under instructions from Rupert Murdoch. The assumption was that Murdoch did not wish to upset the Chinese authorities while he was negotiating a licence to broadcast TV across Asia. HC claimed it ws because the book was boring.

We were delighted to be invited to take over the contract for publication of East and West and HC apologised unreservedly for calling it boring. We sold more than 100,000 copies in our territories. Random House sold a goodly quantity of the US edition and there were several translations. Reviews were excellent. A publishing success all round.

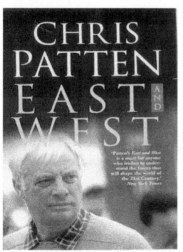

I was therefore surprised to read yesterday that Rupert Murdoch, whose business acumen and commitment to freedom of speech I admire enormously, told the Financial Times that the reason he over-ruled publication not because the book was boring, nor in order to kowtow to China, but because he thought it wouldn't sell. Even the greatest can make mistakes in predicting book sales.

Women in the board room

There was an interesting article in The Times last week about the commercial importance of women directors. The article was based on the research described in A woman's place is in the boardroom by Peninah Thomson and Jacey Graham.

I think we all understand how important it is to recognise that the previous waste of half the intellectual and business talent of the world has been ridiculous and yet the 100 top public companies in the UK boast only twelve female executive directors. The authors list a series of reasons, described as 'problems' and one of my female colleagues pointed to this one, which rings true with me too.

Problem: A major reason why women don't reach senior levels is because, as individuals, they don't think that they're good enough. They also tend to assume that by doing a good job and working hard, recognition will follow. This does not happen, and is not helped by women's awkwardness in discussing their own merits, especially as men excel at telling the world how great they are. Worse, women are also inclined to broadcast their limitations.

I had an annual treat last night – a visit to Glyndebourne Opera House for a weird and wonderful production of Verdi's Macbeth. The three witches emerging from 1950s-style caravans will remain with me a very long time. Reviews have been mixed but The Guardian liked it and so did I. The other weird and wonderful thing about Glyndebourne is that people actually dress up in black tie etc in order to have a picnic in the garden and in the rain. Strange lot, these Brits.

We had an interesting comment from Vanessa at the Fidra blog about the pricing of scholarly books. She says:

Or is it that publishers can get away with charging £45 for an academic text because they're mainly bought via library budgets rather by individuals putting their hands in their pockets?

Clearly she is right that libraries are more likely to pay £45 for a book (however good it is) than individuals. What I slightly object to (I am a very sensitive soul) is the phrase 'get away with'. It implies a degree of crookedness. Nobody in his/her right business mind charges less for something than the customer is willing to pay. A very wise publisher of law books, Gordon Graham now of Logos but then head of Butterworth's now (sadly) known as Lexis-Nexis used to regale training courses with two pieces of wisdom;

In order to stay in the publishing business charge more than customers **want** to pay but no more than they can **afford** to pay.

And:

In order to keep your job in a corporate environment always show profits slightly ahead of your boss's expectations but always hold back a bit for next year.

🐦 28 May 2007

Hay-on-Wye

'Hay-on-Wye? Is that some kind of a sandwich?' A wonderful quote from the great playwright Arthur Miller when he was invited to attend the second Hay Festival of Literature in 1989. The festival now pretentiously describes itself as the 'Woodstock of the Mind' (first dubbed that by Bill Clinton in 2001) and has sponsorship from The Guardian, a blog, a haycast, more than 100,000 visitors and the cream of the literary elite. I am not there and to my shame I have never felt the urge to go.

As a result of Hay and a bank holiday, books are in the news today. I wanted to share with you the business news on the Today programme of the BBC this morning but the link hasn't yet been posted (try going to 'listen to today's programme in full' and click on fifteen minutes after the beginning – 6.20 a.m. UK time). There were interviews with independent booksellers bemoaning the impact of Internet bookselling; an interview with David Roche about the profit impact of Harry Potter on retailers (with a plug for Borders UK); and a promotion piece for HarperCollins and its eco-friendly policy as explained by Vicky Barnsley. I wanted to ask Vicky why, if using recycled paper is a good idea for titles in her Fourth Estate list, does she not apply the policy to the much longer print runs enjoyed in the core HarperCollins lists. There must be a good reason.

During these various pieces two surveys were cited. One poll showed that most people would like to see independent booksellers survive. The other showed that most people would like forests to survive. Well I never . . . Motherhood and apple pie – we're all in favour.

And while on radio, literature and publishing, I recommend you find an hour to listen to this week's Private Passions where the guest is co-founder of Bloomsbury and brilliant publisher Liz Calder. Her choice of music is eclectic with a Latin-American tinge. Brilliant.

And finally, you might enjoy this link to the Afghanistan part of the Jewish Virtual Library. With only two Jews left in the whole of the country, they managed to fall out with each other. Very Mel Brooks.

🐦 29 May 2007

News from Macmillan Spain

I'm in New York this week but I wanted to share some news from Macmillan Spain, where we are developing our local publishing programme and have just launched three flagship literature collections for children.

The launch has been well received with coverage in the Spanish press and on children's publishing forums. As most of it is in Spanish I'm copying an English translation of the piece in Diario Siglo on 10 May:

The new Spanish imprint, Macmillan Infantil y Juvenil (Macmillan Children's Publishing), that was presented today in Madrid, is be represented by three flagship collections: 'Librosaurio', 'El mundo de Rita' (Rita's World) and 'Pepe en Inglaterra' (Pepe in England). This is how it was outlined by Jeremy Diéguez (Managing Director of Macmillan Spain) and Elisa Ayuso (Publishing Director), who stated that the official launch of this new publishing venture would take place on 2nd June coinciding with the Madrid book fair.

This imprint (which will be launched in both Castilian Spanish and Catalan) arises with the aim of 'promoting creativity and offering quality books to children, future readers who we have to inspire', stated Elisa Ayuso. In her opinion, the success of this collection lies in the right choice of subjects, contents, authors and illustrators.

In the Librosaurio series the latter two have a particular prominence. In this way, Spanish authors and illustrators the likes of Alfredo Gómez Cerdá, Marinella Terzi, Vicente Muñoz Puelles, Rocío Martínez, Carlos Romeu, Sara Rojo, Paz Rodero, Tesa González, Juan Kruz and Juan Berrio, share the limelight with foreign authors Christine Nöstlinger (Austrian), Enrique Pérez (Cuban), Lawrence Schimel (American), Claudia Ranucci (Italian) and Fréderique Loew and Nathalie Choux (French).

TWO PECULIAR CHILDREN

The collection 'El mundo de Rita' (Rita's World), with text and illustrations by Mikel Valverde, has an eight year old as the main character. She is a short, dark-haired girl with a variety of situations and problems common to children of that age, who travels the world accompanied by her uncle Daniel.

The publishing house has made use of its experience in English language teaching to create 'Pepe en Inglaterra' (Pepe in England), written and illustrated by Gordon Reece and which narrates the exploits of a Spanish boy on arriving at this country. 'It is a way for the readers to take their first steps in English in a playful and effortless manner', assured Paz Barroso, one of Macmillan Spain's editors, explaining that illustrations of the characters with speech bubbles in English are inserted throughout the story of Pepe's adventures.

Lastly, Jeremy Diéguez pointed out that despite the existence of quality titles for children and young people, this is 'a good moment' to launch a series like the one proposed by Macmillan, as 'the Spanish market is very open and tolerant of books of English origin'.

A print run of between 4000 and 6000 copies of 54 titles (of which 34 in Castilian are to be launched this first year and 20 of them in Catalan) is foreseen.

 30 May 2007

Connectile Dysfunction

Pedalling away on the exercise bike in the hotel gym here in New York I found myself watching this on the TV. Somehow it captures my frequent sufferings at the hands of mobile technology.

New York is looking great in beautiful May weather and the Flatiron Building which houses most of our US-based colleagues is looking close to its best after much renovation.

The only problem is that city appears to be overrun by British publishers. For instance, I bumped into sixteen visitors in the Palgrave Macmillan offices from small Northern British independent publishers such as Carcanet Press here to learn more about the American market and to visit Book Expo America ('Where the world gathers to get a great READ on the industry' – yuk). It was an intelligent and lively bunch of committed publishers but I found myself wondering (in a disgusted of Tonbridge Wells sort of way) why the North-West Regional Development Agency was spending British taxpayers' money on subsidising these very competent publishing people to discover America. It's a strange old world.

The other large and visible contingent comes from Google who are, as ever, telling the publishing industry and the world at large how lucky we are to be helped by them. There is an excellent piece about the recently-launched Google Universal in the latest Outsell newsletter (terrible branding for what used to be the clearly-labelled Electronic Publishing News). Here are the last two paragraphs for a flavour and a warning to publishers.

And in this lies the opportunity for other search engines and publishers as well. Google's apparent abandonment of a vertical approach appears to open a door for others who are working on honing down their results to address a narrower field of content – be it based on subject, content type, or locale. But complacency here is not advised. Google will be applying the full force of its engineering to hone algorithms to decipher this vertical intent all from one screen. The opportunity for others to gain new users is now, before these results are improved significantly enough to keep some narrower audiences from looking around.

Yet amid this short term opportunity is perhaps an even greater threat. What Google's new universal search provides is ultimately a platform for aggregating disparate pieces of information and displaying them in a unified view tailored to an individual's unique needs. In short, it plants the seeds for Google to become an agile publisher and one that is able to cross nearly every type of content and medium. And it gets worse. With this change, searchers are now being exposed to pay-per-click (PPC) advertisements alongside web results that include video and news. This is a significant development as previous concerns over Google's approach to copyright were largely quieted because the company did not run display ads along those sites like News and YouTube which caused the most concern. That line was quietly crossed last week by monetizing all web content – regardless of copyright – and the debate will now rest entirely on the definition of fair use. If publishers do not act aggressively now, they may soon be faced with a very large direct competitor able to monetize content it does not pay to produce.

The red phone box

I wrote about <u>Wormsley cricket ground</u> last week and Andrew Hall has kindly sent me this great photo of the back of the pavillion complete with a proper English phone box. It makes me homesick although this view from my hotel window compensates quite a bit.

The <u>video</u> promoting Richard Wiseman's <u>Quirkology</u> passed a million views on <u>youtube</u> yesterday. An extraordinary piece of book marketing which is generating global sales.

By permission of Pan Macmillan, London.

Similarly, this article about George Lucas using Starwars fans to create mash-up versions of his films raises issues about how best we book publishers can encourage reader involvement in the editorial process. It really is a brave new world.

Meanwhile, in the old world I have to go off to my next batch of board meetings – for St. Martin's Press, Tor and Scientific American. Pip pip.

Charchive

≤ **June 2007** **≥**

Mon	Tue	Wed	Thu	Fri	Sat	Sun
28	29	30	31	1	2	3
4	5	6	7	8	9	10
11	12	13	14	15	16	17
18	19	20	21	22	23	24
25	26	27	28	29	30	1
2	3	4	5	6	7	8

🐦 01 June 2007

Jacqueline Wilson goes to America

The first of the month brings statistics. This blog enjoyed 81296 visits in May, up from the disappointing 68227 in April and taking the total visits to 770480. We should pass the million before year end.

Last night I went to a 'desserts party' at the right-on Housing Works Bookstore in SoHo. We were there to celebrate our US children's publishing and to meet a number of the world's best children's authors. I was particularly pleased to meet Jacqueline Wilson who is an enormous success in the UK but, for no good reason, has not yet cracked America. Roaring Brook Press is now publishing her and I'm betting that they'll do the trick although the US market can be a fickle beast.

By the way, Roaring Brook are the publishers of one of my favourite children's books Lemons are not red which sadly and inexplicably (I'm sure there is a good explanation but it will be convoluted!) is not published by Macmillan Children's Books outside USA.

Now I'm off to the BEA to be horrified at the cost of the event, perplexed by the volume of new books, amazed at the creativity, baffled by the economics and cheered by meeting old friends and enemies.

🐦 02 June 2007

The heist

This is a typical scene at Book Expo America. A lot of people milling around aimlessly. But check out the picture below.

There's no computer where a computer should be to the left of the gentleman's arm. You will also notice that there is no sign saying 'please do not steal the computers'. I confess that a colleague and I simply picked up two computers from the Google stand and waited in close proximity until someone noticed. This took more than an hour.

Our justification for this appalling piece of criminal behaviour? The owner of the computer had not specifically told us not to steal it. If s/he had, we would not have done so. When s/he asked for its return, we did so. It is exactly what Google expects publishers to expect and accept in respect to intellectual property.

'If you don't tell us we may not digitise something, we shall do so. But we do no evil. So if you tell us to desist we shall.'

I felt rather shabby playing this trick on Google. They should feel the same playing the same trick on authors and publishers.

On a more positive note (but not making me feel less shabby nor Google less guilty) Google threw a great party in their amazing New York offices, for which I am very grateful.

🗓 03 June 2007

The Shorter Unabridged

While moseying around Book Expo in New York on Friday, I came across a wondrous sign on the OUP USA stand. I managed to persuade a passing Japanese with a camera to snap the sign and gave him my email address to send me the photo. It hasn't arrived, but fortunately the OUP website has the same phrase in its description of the Shorter Oxford English Dictionary:

The world's most comprehensive, thorough, and up-to-date unabridged dictionary, the Shorter Oxford English Dictionary is an essential resource for every library.

I encouraged the sales guy on the stand to look up the word 'unabridged in the Shorter' and of course it means unshortened . . . . But it's still a great dictionary.

Here's a worrying statistic from one of our international sales people. A campus bookstore manager showed him a breakdown of the shop's sales in the first three months of 2007 (the peak college season in that country) and 45% of revenue came from selling mobile airtime to students (and at very low margins).

As I've just spent thirty hours travelling from New York to Chennai (lesson – avoid Emirates like the plague) I'm a little behind with the news but I think this Irish initiative to find new non-fiction writers deserves a mention. The biggest problem was for the editor having to sift through more than 2000 submissions and now there's talk of making it an annual event.

The other bit of news I've only just tripped over is the decision by Reed-Elsevier to sell off its defence exhibition business because of pressure from various pacifist organisations and individuals. I'd be very interested in people's views on this. The danger is a form of creeping censorship where it is very difficult to draw the line between moral and non-moral activities when the activity is entirely legal. I suppose (and hope) that Reed-Elsevier's decision was entirely pragmatic – by selling they can make more money than by not selling. At least that is consistent with their philosophy. Any other reason would be a big worry for shareholders.

04 June 2007

Scrobbled

As I come to the end of another week of travelling, I was amused by the latest addition to Dan O'Connor's Department of Neologisms, the noun 'Scrobbleizer' , which is apparently a tool that automatically creates a list of your favourite well-paid corporate bloggers. God forbid that I should ever be scrobbleized.

In other news I was interested to read this by blogger Robert Nagle on the attractions, and disattractions, of the current crop of eReaders, focusing on the Sony device.

And finally, despite the initial sensation of shabbiness that attached itself to me after the Google heist at Bookexpo on Friday, I have been buoyed by the support of the blogging community, for example in the comments on this blog here, as well as here and here. Although I have to admit I haven't Scrobbleized them yet.

PS. Just found this link on The Register with 24 comments to date, mostly, but not all, supportive. One guy wants me to be banned from the USA for the crime. It could be worse.

05 June 2007

Turf Wars part 2

Last year at Book Expo America there was, apparently (I wasn't there), a high-octane debate about European territorial rights as described here. It was acrimonious and achieved nothing except to indicate that publishers were typically more excited by the internal carving up of their markets than expanding and developing the overall size of the market for books and writing.

Being a traditional industry we therefore decided to repeat the exercise and had a session last Friday which I did attend. I wanted to link you to a news story about it and was delighted when Google News proffered Turf Wars: How to grow your lawn the organic way as the lead story on the subject.

British publishers stayed away from the event in droves – nothing to gain, nothing to say – and I don't blame them. However, Kim McArthur, one of the panellists, leant on me to attend to back her plea for a bit of common sense on the subject and so I did.

I think I am neither a British patriot, nor hypersensitive, nor particularly petulant but the presenters I listened to were so one-eyed, anecdotal and insulting that I walked out of the meeting rather than hear more. I've never done that before. I quickly regained my composure and returned to support Kim and the legitimacy of British publishers to protect their and their authors' commercial position on legally-acquired rights.

I'm not wedded to the concept of 'splitting' the world between American and British editions and I think the future will ultimately belong to global marketing of a single edition. However, where territorial rights have been acquired and paid for, they should be protected and without European exclusivity, the UK market exclusivity is under threat, particularly in a digital age.

The idea that this is a ruse to protect British imperial machinations is complete nonsense. And it seems to come from those who think for instance that the Commonwealth either does not exist (it does and it is growing) or that it is a proxy for the British Raj (which it definitely is not). When such prejudice colours people's arguments there is little hope for rational debate.

I won't be going next year.

Off to our Chennai meetings now. They start after a puja at our printing plant. I am not sure whether this is a religiously appropriate image but it is very Hindu and I'll change it if people will send me better ones.

www.4to40.com

452

🦋 06 June 2007

Macmillan India

I was in Chennai on Monday for the Annual General Meeting of Macmillan India Limited. We presented the 2006 results and gave some guidance about 2007. You can see a number of presentations here . In short, sales were up more than 40% while profits were flat as a result of increased long-term investment and the need to offer extremely competitive prices to customers. Of course there are some shareholders who would rather we reduced investment and increased dividends and the picture below shows the board with a dissenting shareholder seated in front of us. It's a shame the picture doesn't show the other hundred shareholders who supported the board and its investment policy on their behalf.

Here is a sad tale of the times in which we live.

A colleague went to the US this week and carried with him a luxury Harrods Christmas pudding to present to the family he was staying with. (A little early in the year, perhaps, but that allows time for a teaspoonful of whisky to be added each week to enhance the flavour on the 25th.)

At Dulles airport in Washington the package was confiscated by security at the gate for a transfer flight to Norfolk, Virginia. 'We just don't know what you've been putting in the pudding,' he was told.

And back in the UK and to books, just to say that we are celebrating, along with Andrew Marr, his number one position in the non-fiction best seller list with A History of Modern Britain. Just as I was beginning to wonder whether a serious book could ever displace footballers' wives' memoirs etc, along comes a quality winner. Hooray.

By permission of Pan Macmillan, London.

07 June 2007

Pocket problem

An old friend and colleague came to visit me yesterday to discuss her new publishing project, Pocket Issue books. This a series of well-written, beautifully produced (with illustrations by my favourite cartoonist Andrzej Krauze), well-priced at £4.99 books on well-chosen subjects of contemporary interest.

The problem is that support from the book trade is unlikely to exceed a few hundred copies, the cost and energy for marketing is very high, and thus expenditure will almost certainly exceed income unless she can find alternative ways of generating significant sales. Any ideas would be welcome – and even a few orders for the books.

The Google heist posting of last week is still generating considerable comment here and elsewhere. I am being characterised variously as a fool, a child, a luddite, a crook, or a counter-revolutionary. Hey ho. At least it has generated debate, not least as to whether physical property has greater rights to protection than intellectual property. I don't know but somehow this photo from Book Expo America courtesy of Publishers Marketplace says something about the relative sizes of Google and a very large publisher.

And while on Google matters, I was checking out the excellent Google Scholar platform, which is an example of how search engines and publishers can work together within copyright to allow readers to find what they want, scholars to communicate better, and still have a viable business model.

But that's not my point. I noticed the tag line, 'Stand on the shoulders of giants'. This comes from a letter by Isaac Newton to his contemporary Robert Hooke:

'If I have seen further it is by standing upon the shoulders of giants.'

The quotation is frequently used as an example of scientific humility. It transpires that Hooke was one of Newton's greatest rivals and enemies and was rather small and deformed. Read the quotation with the emphasis on the word 'giants' and you will see that Newton and his quotation were not in the least bit humble. Truth is a strange thing. For more on Newton try this paper by Nobel-prize-winning physicist Sheldon Glashow.

08 June 2007

Society of Bookmen

The Society of Bookmen founded by Hugh Walpole (and I cannot find a decent link for you although a Google search reveals quite a lot about its members) had a dinner last night where the guest speaker was Michael Grade, Executive Chairman of the

British commercial television company <u>ITV</u>. As a matter of fact, he has run nearly every bit of the British TV industry at one point or other. I am not allowed, under the <u>Chatham House Rule</u>, to reveal what he said but I can reveal that the evening was a sell-out, he left the audience wanting more, and now I have the tough task of finding the next speaker. It's very hard following <u>Jessica Kingsley</u> who has done such a brilliant job as Chair(man) of the Society. All suggestions welcome.

Working my way through some sales reports yesterday, I noticed that <u>One Unknown</u> by <u>Gill Hicks</u> was selling exceptionally well in Australia. I hadn't read the book. I now have and I recommend it to all of you.

Macmillan Egypt held a training seminar for teachers of English at the <u>Meridien Hotel Cairo</u> yesterday. 900 people turned up, we catered for 300, the hotel ran out of food. The tribulations of success.

I have a new statistics package for this blog. This rather bad reproduction shows the weekly pattern with a huge spike this week. Yesterday was the highest day ever with 8406 visits. It seems that my visit to New York may have triggered this upsurge.

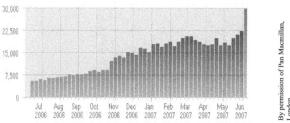

By permission of Pan Macmillan, London.

🗓 09 June 2007

Things Japanese

First a confession. Yesterday I wrote about the <u>Society of Bookmen</u> and mentioned the concept of Chatham House Rules. There is, of course, only one <u>Chatham House Rule</u> and I have edited away my solecism.

Last week was the twentieth anniversary of <u>Nature Japan</u> which is now correctly known as Nature Asia-Pacific. They celebrated by holding a forum to promote networking in the region and David Cyranoski, the Asia-Pacific coorespondent for <u>Nature</u> has written about it for us:

Tokyo was the setting on Wednesday for a Nature-hosted forum to promote networking in the Asia-Pacific. With representatives from 10 countries, the forum was a first attempt to make researchers from the region sit down and think about what benefits might be had by working together. The forum was timed to coincide with the 20th anniversary of foundation of Nature Publishing Group's (NPG) representative company in the region, which recently changed its name from Nature Japan to NPG Nature Asia-Pacific, a sign of the importance Nature places on the region.

Why hold such a forum? Americans and Europeans network well and collaborate often, through both formal and informal arrangements, and create things like the

European Molecular Biology Organisation (EMBO) which give them a bigger-than-the-sum-of-the-parts presence. Edison Liu, head of the Genome Institute of Singapore, raised the key question for Asia using SARS as an example. During the SARS scare, despite the virus's Asian origin and mainly Asian path, research was coordinated by the US Centers for Disease Control and the World Health Organisation and much of the work took place in Europe and North America and even the significant work done in Hong Kong was funded by the National Institutes of Health. Liu asked: Why are large scale scientific interactions by Asian scientists most commonly with the West or at least coordinated by the West?

There are many answers, none fully satisfactory, but taken together, they add up to a powerful set of obstacles: culture, language, nagging political problems sometimes expressed in violent demonstrations or saber-rattling diplomacy, etc. There is also a tendency for Asian scientists, their funders, and everybody involved in science to think that everything important is really happening in the United States and, to a lesser extent, Europe. The upshot is that, for example, stem cell biologists in Beijing are more likely to know what is happening in Boston than in Tokyo or even Shanghai for that matter.

There have been a lot of hesitant steps toward collaboration, and a few notable successes.

Liu gave an example of the Pan-Asian SNP Initiative, a look into migration patterns and ethnic diversity in Asia through a study of DNA variations. It had to overcome two huge obstacles—an unwillingness to send genetic samples overseas and a tremendous disparity in wealth, infrastructure, and scientific know-how among the ten countries represented. They were able to do it. In another talk, Nobel laureate Ryoji Noyori discussed the success of pulling regional scientists together to found Chemistry: An Asian Journal.

Will there be more? It would be natural because of proximity and because economic power and infrastructure are balancing out. It would also be natural in fields such as: global warming/atmospheric chemistry, since China and India especially are going to be the biggest environmental threats given their growth and some of the nearby wealthy countries will have a vested interest in working together; stem cells, because scientists in the region share a significant level of expertise and relatively lax ethical regulations (with the exception of Japan); infectious diseases, because they often have an Asian origin and carry a greater threat to the nearby countries like SARS or avian flu; 'Asian' diseases, such as Bechet's disease, which strike primarily in Asia; the whole range of fields of material sciences, nanotechnology, and photonics in which Asian countries have a huge, and likely soon to be dominant, presence.

Could Asia-Pacific countries ever make a sum bigger than its parts? Will Asia ever be able to pull its weight as a scientific power alongside North America and Europe?

Certainly NPG and most other Western STM publishers are betting that the region will become an even bigger player than it currently is with their investments in local journals and, in the case of NPG, the placement of editorial staff in the region for the journals Nature Nanotechnology and Nature Photonics, a first for Nature journals. NPG Nature Asia-Pacific has seen its staff more than double to over 50 in the past two years, with offices opened in Hong Kong, Melbourne and Delhi, and the forum also offered an opportunity for staff from around the region to get together and celebrate while pursuing a common cause.

Nick Drake

I left school at the end of 1966 and didn't start university until the following Autumn. I enrolled at L'institut britannique in Paris in January 1967 but soon got bored and joined a friend with a car on a trip to Morocco. We stopped off in Aix-en-Provence to pick up a couple of other guys, one of whom was called Nick Drake. We had many adventures and spent time together later at Cambridge and in London. He died in 1974 having made a couple of records. Since then he has become a cult figure. It's bizarre to think that forty years after I met him he would be posthumously releasing a new album; that there would be a new biography of him; and that his sister, Gabrielle, would be publishing a letter and podcast to him for the world to read and hear.

There is an excellent article in the latest issue of Logos about the insularity of the world's book trade press. I'll ask the author's and publisher's permission to run it here in due course. Meanwhile, here is a genuinely non-Angloamerican trade press website, Publishing Today, from China. I particularly like their bestseller list which contains only one 'Western' title but which also has some of the best names for publishing companies I can imagine. I think the British Machine Press has a nice ring to it.

And finally, I wrote about my discovery of the Unabridged Shorter Oxford English Dictionary and here, courtesy of Terry Lee who just happened to be passing with a camera in hand, is the evidence. Messrs Onions, Fowler, Burchfield etc would be turning in their graves.

Models in flux: books and journals

The heading of this piece is also the title of a <u>conference</u> being held at the <u>Centre for Publishing</u> at <u>University College London</u> on 28-9 June. I'm doing the last session so you'll be able to enjoy the conference and still avoid me quite easily.

For in-depth discussions of publishing models in flux you can't do much better than Peter Brantley's <u>personal blog</u>. His latest posting on <u>On scholarly communication and university presses</u> is both intelligent and thought-provoking for both publishers and librarians – and it's garnered some interesting comments too.

Today sees the possibility of one of the great upsets in cricket (and sporting) history. If the West Indies score another 154 runs without losing five more wickets (they have scored 301 for the loss of five so far) they will record the highest ever score to win a test match in the history of the game. You can follow the action <u>here</u> from 11.00 a.m. UK time if you're not working. I am an England supporter (goodness knows why) but I, along with most of the cricketing world, would love to see the West Indies achieve this record. It would do wonders for the game as a whole and it would cheer the worldwide West Indian community.

Poker and genes

Last October I carried a piece about the <u>Oxford poker investment committee</u>. It was just a piece of nostalgia really but it had a dramatic effect on the numbers of visitors coming to this site. It would appear that mention of thw word poker had even more impact than the unlikely combination of Paris Hilton and Jeffrey Archer, as described <u>here</u>. It is, therefore, with some anticipation that I can reveal the publication later this week of <u>Swimming with the Devilfish</u> and an interview with its author, <u>Des Wilson</u>. He uncovers the truth about professional poker but does he fully understand the utter ruthlessness of amateur poker players?

By permission of Pan Macmillan, London.

From poker to heredity (which is a form of poker after all) I have a note from the team at <u>Nature</u> about last week's issue.

As well as a superb issue with a focus on stem cells, to be marketed at the <u>International Society for Stem Cell Research</u> annual meeting and to help showcase our new online web portal stem cell reports, we had two mega stories to boost.

Firstly, two papers published online that show that fibroblasts can be reprogrammed to an embryonic state which eliminates the need to use embryos – the finding is described as being akin to Dolly in accomplishment by a stem cell researcher in our <u>news pages</u>.

We also published one of the biggest genetic association studies completed to date which identified more than 20 genetic markers associated with 7 major diseases.

This issue and these papers generated headlines around the world, including two US and two UK front pages, as well as volumes of print, broadcast and online coverage. Highlights include the <u>BBC</u> <u>twice</u>, the <u>New York Times</u> <u>twice</u> and the <u>Guardian</u> <u>twice</u>.

And many, many more – not bad for a serious journal of science.

For those not following the cricket yesterday, it ended in predictable anti-climax. England <u>won</u> but credit goes to the West Indies and to our new star, Monty Panesar.

13 June 2007

PaperBooks

Comment number 16 on a recent <u>posting</u> came from Keirsten Clark of the publishers <u>PaperBooks</u> which, to be honest, I'd never heard of. She writes:

We are attempting an unusual and innovative way of marketing each of our titles on pub day – even if it means we are keeping the number of our titles down. We want to give our first time authors the best chance we can so are trying to look beyond (but not ignore) in-store promotions and huge discounting. Our first campaign – a Book Drop around central London – for The Angel Makers by Jessica Gregson seems to have got off to a good start.

I think many publishers, large and small, are trying to do this and it's great to see that this experiment seems to be working. All power to PaperBooks. The problem is that, even if it is a mega-success the quantities sold are unlikely to exceed a few thousand. In order to attract and reward competitively the very best-selling authors it is necessary to sell hundreds of thousands of copies and 'guerrilla' tactics just won't succeed on a consistent enough basis. We have to work out, as Keirsten implies, how to knit together the very different and sometimes conflicting business models of the supermarkets, high street chains, Internet and traditional independents.

Why hasn't it happened? Is it because publishers are simply stupid? Or might it just be that it's a really tricky problem?

Spanish children's party

I <u>wrote</u> about the launch of our new Spanish-language children's list. Unlike most publishing launch parties there was very little warm white wine, no smoked salmon rolls and Salman Rushdie wasn't there. Instead, the Spanish book trade – retailers, wholesalers, distributors, book reviewers, authors, illustrators – brought their children to a games and storytelling party in Madrid. It was a huge success and here are some photos to tell the story.

I also mentioned an article by Gordon Graham about the international trade press. It was published in the excellent forum of the book community, Logos, and I have their and the author's permission to republish it here.

THE LAST WORD

The provincialism of the book trade press

56 LOGOS 18/1 ©2007 LOGOS

The Last Word

For more than fifty years I have been a follower of, and an occasional contributor to, Publishers Weekly in the US and The Bookseller in the UK — and have given similar respect to The Bookseller's challenger, Publishing News, since it was founded in 1979.

Like most of the industry they served in the 1950s, the first two journals were then familyowned — Publishers Weekly by the Melcher family (of Bowker) and The Bookseller by the Whitaker family. Both of their histories went back to the 19th century. Both were quiet monopolies. Books were announced rather than advertised. They both attained the position of being trade oracles. Publishers believed themselves to be the most valuable constituents of the two journals, with booksellers forming a second stratum. However, both journals were making significant income from libraries through Books in Print and other bibliographic publications.

In the second half of the 20th century there came to these journals, as to their publisher patrons, the corporate age. Corporations love quiet monopolies (though they seldom say so publicly) and believe that if they can acquire such companies they can make them more profitable. So the heirs of old companies are persuaded to sell out. Bowker went first to Xerox, and later to Reed. Whitaker went finally to the Dutch conglomerate VNU (now rebranded as http://www.nielsen.com/). Neither of these corporations is much interested in book publishing. But they do know how to publish business- to-business magazines. Publishers Weekly and The Bookseller (as well as Publishing News) are now models of glossy design, with liberal use of colour. News columns concern mainly personalities and company finances. 'Product' is described in author interviews and feature articles.

In brief, all the weaknesses of the fuddy-duddy 1950s have been corrected. Except one. These journals are still essentially local sheets. This would be understandable if they were serving local markets defined by language — as do Boersenblatt in German or Livres Hebdo in French — or by geography like Australia (Australian Publisher and Bookseller) or Canada (Quill and Quire).

But Publishers Weekly and The Bookseller are the major professional periodicals of a world industry. It was understandable that they overlapped very little fifty years ago. To the international reader with a global view today, local news is no longer the heart of the matter. In the Whitaker days, David of that ilk used to say: 'We are a parish magazine.' He is still right. Exports are a kind of bonus. Students of the fortunes of the book who confined their reading to these journals would assume there is nothing of significance going on in Asia, Africa or Latin America.

In the five issues of Publishers Weekly from mid-January to mid-February 2007, only a halfpage was devoted to the UK, one page to Canada and three to other countries. In The Bookseller over the same period, just over one page was devoted to the US and six pages to other countries. This fragmentary coverage, averaging a page per issue, does not reflect the world reach of English-language publishing; nor the fact that the US is the UK's largest export customer and the UK the US's second largest after Canada; nor the fact that ownership of publishing today is said to be multinational.

The Bookseller shows more consciousness of the rest of the world than does PW by designating one page per issue 'International'. It consists of snippets from freelance correspondents in Europe and the US. PW's long-time American-in-Paris correspondent, Herb Lottman, has not been replaced and its occasional international supplements — all adbased, the copy written to describe the publishing houses in the regions covered — seem to have faded away.

The only occasions which stimulate spurts of international coverage are the book fairs, principally Frankfurt, London and the US's BookExpo (the latter two with the same owner as PW's), where the journals themselves exhibit and produce daily newssheets.

Although corporate publishers subscribe to the concept that book publishing in English is a world business, in practice, once rights are sold, even within a corporation, American books become British and British books become American; and local imprints, no matter who owns them, aim their publicity at their home markets, and the trade journals reflect this.

Yet these journals are also no doubt uneasy about the fact that trade publishing, the highprofile sector of the publishing industry, is being challenged by the Internet and eroded by the boundary-less marketing of the Amazons and Googles.

By contrast, the world market for specialist books and journals, a large part of which is now digitized, is served by specialist journals such as Booklist published by American Library Association, and by established periodicals like Scholarly Publishing, STM Newsletters, Serials, Against the Grain, Publishing Research Quarterly, etc. Specialist journals such as these have loyal supporters. In them the reader is king. Published both online and in print, they have little or no advertising.

In essence, the issue is not national vs international; it's reader-based vs ad-based. Thinly disguised ad-generating vehicles naturally reflect the intent of the advertisers in the readers' columns. Whatever the reason, when the world's trade journals drop through my letterbox these days, the old tingle of anticipation is missing. I think my fifty-year affair is fading. I know what you're thinking. But you're wrong. I'm the one who is moving with the times.

Gordon Graham

15 June 2007

A bit of nostalgia

I was at Barts Hospital last night for the party to celebrate a number of literary prizes administered by the Society of Authors. The full list of winners will be published later today. The event was held in the beautiful Great Hall. It made a welcome change for a book trade party to see authors outnumber publishers by 50 to one.

The last time I was at Barts was when I was editor of Oxford Medical Publications (which is celebrating its centenary this year. Happy birthday OMP). I was working with the authors (A. E. Mourant, Ada C. Kopec and Kazimiera Domaniewska-Sobczak – and I remembered the names and spelling to this day) on the second edition of The distribution of the the human blood groups and other polymorphisms. It was over 1000 very large pages crammed with incomprehensible (to me) statistics and symbols. It was typeset in hot metal and then photographed for litho printing. We had galley proofs, page proofs, revised page proofs, ozalids and I know not what else. The typesetting cost was more than £100 per page. The book was a monster. We published in 1976 at £55 (roughly equivalent to £250 in today's money). It received a rave review on the op-ed page of the Times ('Here's a book to throw at racists'), amazing coverage in the medical press and we sold more than 2500 copies in the first month (probably not many thereafter, it is true). Those were the days when a serious book was reviewed seriously, priced seriously, stocked seriously and sold seriously.

Whilst on this nostalgia theme I was slightly sad yesterday to hear that Les Editions Grund depuis 1880 has been taken over by Editis ('Where creativity meets culture' –

should there be a competition for the most hifalutin publishing strapline?). Not sad because anything terrible will happan. Editis are an excellent company and will treasure the Grund business. Sad because Alain Grund and Monique Souchon have played such important roles in French and European publishing and in particular for children's books. They are staying on and Editis have promised full editorial independence but I fear it just won't be the same.

But we must loook to the future and I see that this blog has a new competitor The Charkin Group committed to saving lives at sea. I didn't know there were Charkins in Nigeria but you live and learn.

And finally for Londoners, a recommendation. King's Cross where we have our London offices is not traditionally renowned for the quality of its restaurants. At various times it has led the world indices for availability of crack cocaine and ladies of the night, but not for food. However, things are changing fast and the latest indication of this is the opening of Camino Cruz del Rey (geddit?). All very chic but great food.

📖 16 June 2007

Munich

I'm in Munich at a conference this weekend. It doesn't get much better.

I came across a wonderful orange juice description on the unopenable-without-squirting-everywhere carton on the plane coming here – 'slightly pasteurised orange juice'. Now, I know you can have gently carbonated water and lightly simmered peas but . . . I suppose they only wipe out half the germs.

I try not to use this blog as a press release distributor but sometimes linking to a release makes sense. This one is all about our efforts to develop scientific publishing in <u>China</u>. It's a big deal for us and a big deal for scientific communication and what's more it's been made possible by sponsorship from the pharmaceutical company <u>AstraZeneca</u> for which we are hugely grateful.

17 June 2007

<u>Honours</u>

Britain has an absurd, out-dated, elitist, imperial, patronising and hugely loved and revered honours system. Twice a year or so, the Queen publishes a list of the great and not so great who have been awarded what is technically known as a gong – a peerage, a knighthood and various forms of orders, medals and companions of the British Empire. The liberal establishment tends to sneer and there's probably a real element of honours in exchange for political favours delivered – and even sometimes the sniff of money playing a part. But nonetheless, the recipients – the real ones who deserve their recognition – by and large appreciate it.

The latest list contains some celebrity heroes – <u>Salman Rushdie</u>, <u>Ian Botham</u>, and the wonderful <u>Barry Humphries</u> aka <u>Dame Edna Everage</u>. But the gongee who gets my vote for most deserving and most decent is less well-known outside the world of Shakespeare scholarship – <u>Stanley Wells</u> whose <u>Shakespeare for all time</u> we published – and who edited the magnificent <u>Oxford Shakespeare</u> which we are now challenging with the new <u>RSC Shakespeare</u>.

Yesterday was busy. The Mayor of Munich <u>Christian Ude</u> told our annual <u>Georg von Holtzbrinck</u> conference that Munich is the second largest publishing centre in the world after New York. Sounds like nonsense to me but I guess it depends how you define large – numbers of titles, sales, profits, review inches. My own similar but unprovable statistic is that Oxford is the single most profitable publishing centre in the world (ahead of New York etc) when you include Elsevier, Harcourt International, Blackwell Wiley, Oxford University Press, Informa, Macmillan Education and a host of smaller but highly successful businesses.

In the evening we were entertained at the headquarters of the <u>Max Planck Society</u> where the President, <u>Professor Peter Gruss</u>, argued strongly for the open access availability of scientific research.

In between we were treated to great presentations by our sister companies based in Munich – <u>Droemer Knaur</u>, <u>Holtzbrinck Networks</u> and <u>eLab</u>. Take a look <u>here</u> to get a feel for the investments we are making in the digital world. It's beginning to look impressive.

Climate change and stem cells

This link will take you to the original mission statement (although I don't think that particular piece of jargon was current in 1869) of Nature. For those with click fatigue here is the essence of the objectives it was seeking:

> FIRST, to place before the general public the grand results of Scientific Work and Scientific Discovery ; and to urge the claims of Science to a more general recognition in Education and in Daily Life ;
> And, SECONDLY, to aid Scientific men themselves, by giving early information of all advances made in any branch of Natural knowledge throughout the world, and by affording them an opportunity of discussing the various Scientific questions which arise from time to time.

Now, Nature is better known for the second of these aims and that has been the core of its, and its associated journals', success. However, it has never lost sight of the the the first objective and today sees the launch of two free websites on two of the hottest topics around today.

Nature Reports Climate Change and Nature Reports Stem Cells both address highly contentious issues within the community and both have significant social, ethical, economic and medical implications for all of us. There is a range of content aimed at the non-specialist as well as the scientist. Both sites allow comment and discussion and we are building facilities for social networking and community involvement. Nature intends to be at the centre of scientific debate in all spheres.

It was a beautiful day In Munich yesterday. The afternoon was spent playing and eating Bayerische style – and milking cows (picture to follow!).

And the evening was special with a concert and dinner at mad King Ludwig's Nymphenburg Palace.

The concert was given by seven members of the Vienna Philharmonic and there was a fascinating ta about the importance (or possible obolescence) of classical music by the conductor and pianist Daniel Barenboim. It was quite a day.

Bavarian rhapsody

The controversy over the Google heist posting has quietened and there are the signs now of some sensible debate emerging. This piece from Even Schnittman writing on the OUP Blog is an example. There's also rather a good piece in Frankfurter Allgemeine Zeitung marred only by their describing me: 'von Statur einem Möbelpacker ähnlich . . . ' – not quite sure what it means but I suspect the worst. One lesson I've learned from the affair is that increased visitor traffic (visits leapt several fold for a few days) doesn't necessarily translate into increased ad revenue. Dammit!

I know some of my readers are more interested in the ins and outs of the British independent book trade than significant events in the world of scientific information. I am also aware that I've blogged about things going on at Nature Publishing Group a lot recently. But I can't help it. They keep coming up with really interesting new projects and ideas. Here's the latest, Nature Precedings (no, it's not a spelling mistake) described here by Timo Hannay:

'Nature Precedings is a free online service that enables researchers rapidly to share, discuss, and cite their early findings.

Written scientific communication takes place mainly through journals, but the web provides new, complementary opportunities for more rapid, participative and informal approaches. Nature Precedings accepts contributions from biology, medicine (except clinical trials), chemistry and the earth sciences. Submissions are screened by a professional curation team for relevance and quality, and are usually posted online within hours. The service is free of charge to both authors and readers. It has been created in collaboration with an outstanding group of partner organisations: British Library, European Bioinformatics Institute, Science Commons, and Wellcome Trust. You can find out more at Nascent, Nature's own blog, and on O'Reilly Radar.'

20 June 2007

Go to work on an egg

There is an organisation with the snappy name Broadcast Advertising Clearance Centre who have informed the equally snappily named British Egg Information Service that their proposed marketing campaign featuring today's title as its slogan should not run. Read the story here. In essence, the watchdog is concerned that the campaign does not promote adequately the concept of a varied diet. What a load of nonsense but it does give me the opportunity to link to these wonderful original egg commercials by Tony Hancock – brilliant. I hope this blog doesn't count as broadcast advertising. If it does, I could be in big trouble now.

I spent yesterday with the senior management team from our Latin American companies. We were reviewing performance and working on three-year plans. As you can imagine, given that there are some forty business units spread across a dozen countries publishing more than a thousand new titles a year, there were plenty of numbers – sales, stock, overheads, cash collection etc. But one line stood out. Our total number of full-time employees (excluding temporary sales staff etc) has risen in five years from 273 to 772 and we plan to grow more. That's real investment. Here's wishing all our Grupo Macmillan employees (including of course the ones in Spain) mucho suerte.

21 June 2007

Macmobile and Natureplex

At Macmillan we try to encourage and facilitate a decentralised, entrepreneurial culture. There isn't a company in the world which doesn't try to do that (or says it is trying to do it). But how do you measure whether you're succeeding? I've just tripped over one indicator of success.

It is the discovery that one of our businesses, ICC Macmillan, based in Portland Oregon has developed a service to allow publishers a simple way of selling their content through mobile phones and PDAs. The announcement is here. Why is this an indicator of decentralised, entrepreneurial success? Because the press release was the first I'd heard of it. It sounds great.

It's not just me that thinks the innovators at Nature are outstanding. This is an extract from the latest Outsell Newsletter:

* Nature Publishing Group has now launched so many innovative Web 2.0-style initiatives that the development floor of its London offices is being referred to as 'the Natureplex.' Scintilla, a new information filtering and personalisation aggregator, is the latest service to launch, and indicates not only Nature's understanding of the ways in which scientists work, but also how the range of services might start to come together . . .

. . . And no self-respecting Web 2.0 service is complete without some form of social element – indeed, Nature.com users already have social services available through the Nature Network sites that currently serve London and Boston. Like Scintilla, these services offer the opportunity to set up groups (either around a lab or institution, or around a topic), and it seems likely that, since these services operate off a common user database, facilities of this sort will start to tie together so that the Nature offerings form a contiguous whole rather than a patchwork quilt. Patching these offerings together is more easily said than done – troublesome items, according to Scintilla developer Euan Adie, include issues such as data protection and user privacy. As the latest in a series of innovative services Connotea, Postgenomic, Nature Precedings, Scintilla, whose name means spark of inspiration, shows that inspiration is one thing that the NPG development team certainly does not lack.

22 June 2007

Crie de grrrr

This arrived at my inbox yesterday.

Dear Mr Charkin,

I intended sending this as a comment to your blog. But I didn't want to use my name, which might have embarrassed my agent. Also, there wasn't an obvious opening. But if you would care to respond on the blog, while keeping me anonymous, that would be fine.

I realise that you are a busy globetrotter and top company executive, with a lot more on your mind than the anguish of would-be writers, but I wonder if I could drag you back for a moment to the business of publishing – or not publishing – first novels.

I have a number of friends who are successful novelists. They started years ago and have have continued ever since, winning a loyal following over the years and attracting, for the most part, postive reviews. I have also met several writers, Robert Harris and Sebastian Faulkes among them, who have gone on to great things.

In my own case, and I am now in my late fifties, the story has been very different. I have written six novels so far, none of which has been published. The first two probably deserved their fate. The subsequent four, were, however, above average (if I say so myself) and could easily have sat alongside the products of my more successful pals.

I don't say this vaingloriously. The agents I have had over the years – two in the United States, three in Britain, were all convinced that I had the talent to make it to the top. Each in his (or her) turn assured me that the book they were representing would get published, make me good money and provide the basis of what would be a successful literary career.

Of the five, three are very big in the trade. My present agent is even, I might say, a leading luminary, much quoted on the state of the business and the difficulties of marketing.

In an email to me this morning, he said it was 'tragic' that my latest offering had not made it. He couldn't understand it, he said. And even though he much likes both of my latest proposals, he now fears that they may not be saleable.

Time after time, the responses from publishers have been that my writing is first class, my plots fascinating, my structure solid and resourceful. There has been criticism, of course, but most of it centred on detail or the foibles of individual characters.

In the most recent case, one leading publisher (not from Macmillan, I hasten to add) said that my main character was someone he recognised immediately. He had laughed out loud, he said. I had got the particular corner of London life that I was after exactly right. Sadly, he added, his sales people were not convinced that there would be a big enough market for what I was offering. So, in the end, he felt he had to decline.

One of the country's top publishers, who years ago produced a non-fiction book of mine, told my agent that I was a 'wonderful' writer Another, a former Fleet Street colleague, said she was sure I had what it took to succeed in fiction. Yet both turned me down, as did the head of popular fiction at one of your principal rivals, who said that he loved the book himself but was unable to persuade his sales team of its virtues.

What is going on? I don't expect to become rich and famous. I don't expect to be annointed in the Guardian as the new Evelyn Waugh. But I do believe that I write accomplished fiction and deserve my place, for a week at least, on Waterstone's Big Tables.

Is it because I write, mainly, about men in their fifties? Is it because I have left it too late to break through? Is it because these days I lack a proper media 'platform' that would guarantee me notice from the critics? I don't know, but I feel sure my age has a lot to do with it.

What really gets my goat is the sheer volume of truly awful fiction that *does* get published, only to go nowhere. In every such case, the publisher concerned must have thought, yes, this one is in with a chance, and the sales people must have agreed. The fact that they turned out to be wrong does not appear to embarrass them. Water under the bridge, dear boy . . . publishing isn't an exact science. Well, if these books are allowed to fight their corner (and lose money hand over fist), why not mine? At least once.

I might add that I am sticking with my latest agent, who is a prince among men and seems determined to get me published. But it has been hard pounding for both of us.

Your thoughts on the above would be much appreciated.

Best wishes,

Puzzled of London

What can I say? It must be deeply frustrating for the correspondent. We set up Macmillan New Writing with precisely this type of author in mind. The list is doing fine but the numbers wouldn't make an accountant's eyes light up with excitement. If we had to publish these books under the currently traditional model – advances, hype etc – the accountant would throw him/herself out of the window. Even so and even though we have had success, other publishers haven't followed suit. Why not?

Publishing fiction is tough. There are arguably more wannabe authors than readers. Of course there is rubbish published but there are more fine novels published every year than anyone could possibly read. Readers also have to be picky. We all enjoy only a limited amount of leisure time and we are likely to think twice before spending it on an unknown author. This posting on Susan Hill's blog highlights another set of issues. Even if an author does get published and does become successful there appears to be little loyalty to the publisher who took the original risk. The big profits frequently go to an author's second or third publisher and some of the most successful publishing houses deliberately and intelligently ignore first novels in order to pick up the third or fourth from an author after much of the hard work is done.

Perhaps the answer does lie in Lulu or simply web publishing under a Creative Commons licence. At least such publication allows an author some exposure. But it will do little to stem the flow of so-so or worse novels being published which will make it even harder for the reader to discern the good from the bad and encourage even less reading experimentation.

Anyone else want to contribute their thoughts?

23 June 2007

Cri de grrr from Vienna

Please note the change in spelling from yesterday's post, which generated some interesting and alarming comments. I do hope that Chip Dale has made it up with his cat although I'm not quite sure why he should have been so depressed. More authors are being published than ever. Whilst it may be harder to find publication through the traditional 'literary' publishing houses there are many alternative ways of being published and many new and innovative companies. Glass half full or half empty? There have always been bad books as well as good books. There have always been potboilers and ground-breakers. I believe there has never been a more interesting time in the history of the book trade and authors are in the perfect position to take advantage of all the new ways of reaching readers either with traditional publishers or through new routes.

I'm here for the wedding of a friend and it's the whole works – morning suit, evening dress, hats, reception, waltzes. I'm not really used to all this dressing up and the FAZ description of me as having the look of a Möbelpacker (furniture mover) is feeling distinctly accurate. Must run and pick up my morning coat and make my way to the Schottenkirche where the wedding takes place – beautiful.

🦃 24 June 2007

Brits take beating in turf war

I was re-reading this article from the Bookseller about the debate in New York on the subject of territoriality. It is a fairly obstruse argument and ultimately revolves around whether or not it is a good idea to have both American and British editions of the same book available for sale in a particular market. I attended most of the debate (I stomped out at one point when one of the speakers had become plain offensive) and what surprised me was the heatedness of the language. Phrases such as 'atavistic protectionisn', 'last gasp tactics' and 'imaginary empire called the Commonwealth' were a bit over the top.

The issue seems pretty simple to me. If authors and agents wish to have separate US and British editions of their book (as opposed to a single global publisher) that is their choice. If having both editions available in a country increases sales (which I don't believe) then both editions should be available in all countries and British and American publishers should open their home markets to allow any editions from overseas to enter and compete. I cannot quite see American publishers being happy about this. Nor would I be. I think that exclusivity is good for authors and retailers and the health of th eindustry. In which case American and British publishers should do everything in their power to protect territorial exclusivity, including granting exclusive EU rights to British publishers, rather than the very dangerous open-market Europe of the past.

Or am I being simplistic?

The wedding in Vienna was sensational, ending up with a wonderful party at the Schönbrunn Palace below. Old Europe certainly knew how to build palaces and knows how to celebrate weddings. I cannot, however, resist recording that the groom's mobile rang just as the bride was making her wedding vows. What a moment.

🦃 25 June 2007

On-demand printing

There has been much discussion recently about the definition of 'in print and 'out of print' in a world where one copy of a book can be printed at a time. That debate will, I suspect, run and run until everyone gets tired. What is much more important is the technology development itself. I was delighted to see this press release last week.

The New York Public Library has installed an on-demand printing machine in its Science, Industry and Business section where library users will be able to print out-of-copyright works for free.

It's too big. It's too expensive. It's too slow. It's too limited. I'm sure it's too noisy. But later versions will be smaller, faster, cheaper. The advantages are huge. With the help of publishers digitising their material and making them available readers will be able to find, create and read a vastly larger selection of books. Physical distribution costs will be reduced significantly. Authors will be paid via a licence fee and a new income stream opened up to them. Libraries themselves might decide to use this to generate income for themselves and thus be able to fund more purchases for their traditional collections.

And the machines need not be restricted to libraries. Why not have machines installed in large bookshops – or even small bookshops as the prices drop.

In a perfect world, returns could be virtually eliminated saving trees, energy and money. This is a huge opportunity for transformation of our industry. For it to to become more concrete we need publishers to invest more rapidly in their digitisation and storage programmes; authors and their agents to cease fretting about the issues surrounding rights reversion; libraries and booksellers to take a few risks while the technology develops; and the industry to work together to develop a new and equitable business model.

Not much to ask . . .

🐦 26 June 2007

Collective licensing

Yesterday I gave a talk at the Annual Meeting of the Publishers Licensing Society (PLS) whose job is to distribute money received from licensing organisations to publishers. It is a parallel organisation to the Authors Licensing and Collecting Agency (ALCS). Both organisations are excellent and vital. They are both facing challenges as we move into the digital world. It's not going to be easy. Will publishers be happy to see a third party doing deals with the digital content they control? The organisations were set up to ensure fair payment for the use of copyright material from photocopying etc. A collective licence was clearly the best way to deal with that. But is it the best way to deal with digital delivery of content which can be tracked much more readily? I definitely don't know the answer but I do know that working together through these organisations is a better way forward than every author and every publisher trying to set rules.

And today, on a similar theme, I am attending the first international conference of ACAP whose acronym hides the incomprehensible but important words 'Automatic content access protocol'. It sounds arcane but it is an essential development if copyright holders are to work successfully with the major search engine companies. I quote from the conference programme:

At its first major conference on 26 June in London, ACAP (Automated Content Access Protocol), is presenting its work so far in developing a standard by which the owners of content published on the World Wide Web can provide permissions information (relating to access and use of their content) in a form that can be recognised and interpreted by a search engine 'spider', so that the search engine operator is enabled systematically to comply with the permissions granted by the owner. ACAP will allow publishers, broadcasters and any other to express their individual access and use policies in a language that search engine's robot 'spiders' can be taught to understand.

It is not an easy road and some of the technical stuff is jaw-breakingly dull but ACAP has managed to bring together most parts of the media industry (newspapers, TV, radio, publishing) to work with search engines. The result, if we can get there, will be that search engines will be able to find relevant pieces of information and allow the content holder to control access and charge if desirable. That is beneficial to all and allows full copyright control.

As today's posting is a bit serious and acronymic I thought I'd end with this link. Many people have suggested that I suffer from ADD but I thought they meant attention deficiency disorder not this alternative translation.

🐦 27 June 2007

History corner

Nature, along with many other publications, runs a regular feature reprinting clips from 50 years ago. This one from 22 June 1957 caught my eye:

'Far from causing a decline in reading, as was once predicted, it is now becoming evident that television has led to a greatly increased sale of books dealing with topics which have proved popular on the screen. This is perhaps most evident in archaeology, but it is becoming noticeable in other fields too. The growing sport of undersea swimming has reinforced the demand for books about sea life, the publication of which has received a further fillip from the film and television successes of Hans Hass and Jacques Cousteau. We cannot blame the publishers for trying to satisfy this demand, but we can blame them for publishing books seemingly written in haste merely to profit from this fashion.'

The messages are clear and still relevant.

New technology does not necessarily kill old technology and can in fact enhance it.

Publishers are profit-chasing idiots (or at least blameworthy profiteers) and always have been.

I'm off to France next week. I notice that the Blackberry has been deemed a subversive instrument by the French Government. I trust that British citizens will still be allowed to carry such a dangerous object. If not, this could turn into a French prison blog.

I notice that the UK Treasury-funded report on the creative economy has just been published. It is very long but I will find time to read it, if only for the pleasure of establishing the ratio of waffle to content. I'll try to summarise its recommendations for you in due course but perhaps some of readers of this blog would like to have a go too . . .

🐦 28 June 2007

On-line learning

Most educational publishers and many other businesses have invested heavily in building software platforms to present materials for schools and universities. The amounts of money invested have been astonishing in some cases. Financial and pedagogical successes have been limited.

At Macmillan we have focussed on a subset of education rather than the whole curriculum and we have concentrated on building a system which uses technology in the context of the traditional classroom and with the teacher absolutely playing the central role. The subset is the teaching of English for non-English speakers and the project is known as the Macmillan English Campus (MEC). Today we announce a new edition which will further strengthen our leadership in this important and fast-growing market. Everyone at Macmillan is proud of what we've achieved not only in creating a brand new business but in showing that online education actually works – both students and teachers have confirmed that our language is learnt faster and better using MEC.

While innovations such as MEC are flourishing, other parts of the publishing industry are still enmired in legal actions and arguments about copyright in a digital world. We have to find solutions and we have to be flexible. This announcement about so-called 'orphan works' is another example of our industry's efforts to adapt and take leadership in the digital world.

Bookshop news

Two stories from yesterday's PN Online depressed me.

The first was about HMV's 'disappointing results'. The headline affecting the book trade is that Waterstone's like-for-like sales were down 4.1% in spite of all the price promotions, marketing activities, Richard and Judy hype and some brilliant books being published. Apparently, this year has started better and we all want the new team at Waterstone's to succeed. My concern is that the Chairman's statement doesn't seem to address the fundamental need to sell more books at economically viable prices:

'The strategy has three important strands: protecting our core business, saving costs aggressively and growing in new channels and related products. The environment for entertainment and books retailing will remain highly competitive. However, with aggressive plans, focused leadership and the continued commitment and dedication of our employees, our resilient brands will strengthen their market positions and performance as they comprehensively satisfy the preferences of our customers.'

The second story relates to a much smaller chain, Fopp Music Books + Film who are fighting to avoid bankrupcy and the closure of its 46 stores. Fopp has tried to innovate with very contemporary shops and eclectic purchasing but it doesn't look like it's working.

Add these two stories to the continuing drip drip of independent bookshop closures and the picture for book retailing in the UK does not look pretty. It's a little too easy to blame the lack of retail price maintenance, or competition from supermarkets and the Internet, or the existence of a returns system. It is also simply too easy for bookshops to demand ever higher discounts (or marketing bungs) from publishers. A vibrant high street book trade is vital culturally as well as economically. We must fix it – and fast.

29 June 2007

Bookshop news 2

Further to this morning's post this link just hit my inbox.

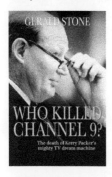 30 June 2007

Extra extra read all about it

There is an old publishing adage. Books by journalists about journalists don't sell. The infighting between newspapers is endlessly fascinating to the protagonists but to nobody else. It is therefore surprising when booksellers liken such a book's impact and sales to that of Harry Potter.

The book is Gerald Stone's Who killed Channel 9?. Clicking on this and a few of these Googlenews links will give you some idea of the furore the book is generating among the sensitive souls of the Australian media. Last year Macmillan Australia published Schapelle Corby's My Story which dominated the best seller lists. I suspect they have this year's winner too.

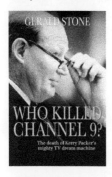

Incidentally, my favourite Kerry Packer anecdote is the one about him driving back from a successful day at the races with a bunch of mates and a bulging wallet. They stopped at a cafe for a bite and the owner said he was just closing for the night and couldn't serve them. After a certain amount of 'discussion' with the owner they drove on to the nearest pub and ordered some sandwiches. When the bill for £15 arrived Packer counted out £1000 in cash, including the tip. The publican was delighted and amazed. 'What have I done to deserve this?' 'Nothing yet,' responded Packer, 'But you know the cafe down the road? Tomorrow morning just go and tell him what a lucky thing happened to you.'

And while on Australia it was great to see the inauguration of a new Prime Minister's Prize for Australian History which was won jointly by Les Carlyon's The Great War (which has sold more than 100,000 hardback copies in Australia alone – hard to imagine such numbers for a serious British book about World War I) and Peter Cochrane's Colonial Ambition published by Melbourne University Publishing of which I am proud to be a non-executive director. Australian publishing is in excellent health.

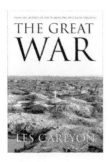

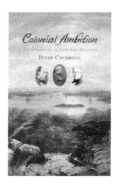

The Labour Government in Britain, through a wholly undemocratic process, has appointed a new Prime Minister to lead us and he started his new job this week. So far so good. He showed excellent taste in an <u>interview</u> (scroll down to open book and click) on the radio where he chose <u>The Snail and the Whale</u> as one of his five favourite books of all time. Quite right, Gordon.

By permission of Pan Macmillan, London.

476

≤ July 2007 ≥

Mon	Tue	Wed	Thu	Fri	Sat	Sun
25	26	27	28	29	30	1
2	3	4	5	6	7	8
9	10	11	12	13	14	15
16	17	18	19	20	21	22
23	24	25	26	27	28	29
30	31	1	2	3	4	5

Darwin

I attended the final sessions of the <u>First Bloomsbury Conference on E-publishing and E-publications</u> and was asked to make predictions for the future of the industry as a wrap-up. This is, of course, a completely impossible and futile task. I don't think I was particularly helpful or insightful but the event took place in the Darwin Theatre at <u>University College London</u> which gave me the excuse to quote the great man. As readers of this blog may have ascertained, I'm not a great lover of mission statements or management dicta ('passionate about gardening', 'do no evil', 'for the love of it' etc) but I do think that <u>Charles Darwin</u> got it right when he wrote:

'It is not the strongest of the species that survives, nor the most intelligent that survives. It is the one that is the most adaptable to change.'

If Macmillan had to adopt a by-line perhaps that should be the one.

One of the good things about working on this blog is that I've made acquaintances through it. I was waiting for a lift in Sydney earlier this year and a guy in jogging kit came up to me to ask whether I was the Richard Charkin who blogs. Similarly in New York recently. But even better is that people send me books from time to time just out of friendliness, I think. This arrived from the author, <u>David Silverman</u>. The book, <u>Typo</u>, is published by <u>Soft Skull Press</u>, an independent house in Brooklyn. Its subject matter is unpromising – 350 pages about a typesetting company going bust. It is absolutely brilliant. Everyone in the publishing business should read it and most people in any sort of business should too. It's currently at number 51754 at Amazon.com and 241540 at Amazon.co.uk. Do yourself a favour and read it. Charles Darwin would have approved.

As this is the first of the month I continue the tradition of boring you with the blog statistics from the previous month. June saw 136,064 visits, up from May's 81,296. It was the highest month by far and brings total visits since launch to 906,544 – the million mark beckons. The June numbers were boosted by the coverage of the <u>Google</u> <u>heist</u> posting. A 'normal' week has about 20,000 visits. The week of 3 June had 42,809. Things are back to normal now, as the chart below shows.

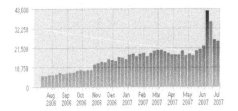

This shows the geographical breakdown by continent for June. Blue is Europe, purple North America, green Asia, yellow Oceania and red South America.

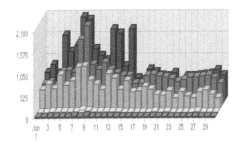

The top five countries were USA (21654 visits), UK (9841), China (5655), Germany (3550) and France (3048). I found the China and France scores higher than I'd have expected and suprised how relatively few visits we get from India (1839), Canada (1069), and Australia (866).

02 July 2007

Keep on rolling

We've just anounced that we'll be publishing <u>Ronnie</u>, the autobiography of Ronnie Wood of the <u>Rolling Stones</u> on 20th October this year. It promises to be 'interesting' to say the least. It may not sell as many copies as Harry Potter but it'll certainly cause a big stir and bring both teenagers and grandparents into bookshops to discover what keeps those stones rolling.

By permission of Pan Macmillan, London.

This title more or less completes our Autumn list for trade books in the UK. It is a spectacular programme. Already Pan Macmillan has seen its market share increase significantly in the first half of 2007, with growth in fiction, non-fiction, Picador and children's books. The second half looks even stronger with great titles from all our traditional best selling authors; new authors such as Kate Morton (whose House at Riverton has been picked as a Richard and Judy Summer read); and the long-awaited Borat (Kazakhstan's sixth most famous man) book. It's going to be a good Christmas for Macmillan.

03 July 2007

Triumph of form over content?

The debate runs and runs on the future of the book. But are publishers too hung up on wondering what the 'killer device' will be that launches a thousand eBooks? Publishers are constantly getting excited about the potential for the ipod to become an eReader, as illustrated by this video. On Peter Brantley's excellent Book 20-1 list there have been heated exchanges over Manolis Kaneidis's 'BlueBook' prototype (a paper book with circuits embedded in each page and with text printed with conductive ink), as reported here. It strikes me that Adam Hodgkin's insights about all this over at the Exact Editions blog are spot on. He suggests that the obsession with the hardware is wrong-headed. I couldn't agree more. Publishers should be focusing on digitising their content and ensuring that it can be accessible via a web-based interface. The Apple iPhone, which does not incorporate specific eReader software but does feature a 'humble familiar web browser', could leapfrog the various eReader device offerings to become the consumer's eReader of choice. Many don't know it yet but I also believe publishers will need to ensure they have the capability in place to deliver content streams via subscription – and not just in the academic and STM sectors in my view. At Macmillan I am glad that we are developing BookStore to enable publishers to deliver on these needs.

On another note entirely, one of the things I like about blogging is the interesting co-blogger contacts that you make. One such is Eric Neu. Eric, who works in e-business for a publisher in Brussels, has posted this 'mini-interview' with me on his blog. It's nice to see my words up in French. They sound so much more interesting.

🌁 04 July 2007

Scientists date too

Okay, I know I'm boring about Nature Publishing Group and its initiatives but, I ask you, how could I not post this link from the Guardian all about our recently launched Nature Network London? The writer of the column has (quite rightly) picked up on the dating (sorry, I mean relationship building) aspects of social networks such as facebook. I'm sure NNL (as it will be known, I'm sure) will be addressing the needs of scientists in this arena shortly – probably via the Holtzbrinck-owned and highly successful Parship (lousy name in English, great service).

While on the subject of social networks and their importance I have been musing on the concept of an *anti-social* network. I suppose the mafia was an early adopter in the field but you'd think there was a significant opportunity using modern networking technology to create establishment alternatives. Throw off your ASBOs (anti-social behavious orders for those of you not in the UK), meet your peers, build gangs, exchange safe-breaking tips, see ads on the best stolen goods handlers in your local area . . . The opportunity is huge but I suspect someone is already there, as usual!

Another aspect of techno-networking is tagging, which I don't understand in spite of having just been tagged myself. So far, nothing terrible has happened but I (as usual) fear the worst.

I'm on holiday for a few days, so the blogs might be even worse than usual. Sorry.

🌁 05 July 2007

Blogiquette

I don't suppose many people come to this blog more than once a day (most only once in a lifetime) and even fewer will have noticed a change yesterday. In the morning, this comment appeared:

'Same old names on this comments board, I see.

Just goes to show you really are better off reading a quality publishing publication than the electronic fast food junk. The blogroll is one consonant too long methinks.

Sven Eriksson'

I don't disagree with the sentiment and I don't take offence but I do object to the author's anonymity. If s/he wants to make a point s/he should be identified. So in future I'll take down all anonymous comments asap. I hope you don't think this is unwarranted censorship.

Another day another launch. This evening in Madrid sees a celebration for Nature Publishing Group Ibero-America a project we've been working on for a year. It is another part of the Grupo Macmillan jigsaw as we develop materials of all sorts for Spanish- and Portuguese-speaking markets. And the timing could not have been better . . .

This announcement was made yesterday. Two scientific journals, Science and Nature, shared the hugely important Prince of Asturias Foundation Award for Communication and Humanities. These awards are the Spanish equivalent of the Nobel Prizes and are far and away the the most revered distinctions in Spain and the

Spanish-speaking world. A further coincidence is that Nature and Science were meant to be asserting authority over each other with the traditional annual cricket match. It rained and therefore a draw was declared which seems appropriate in the circumstances.

Other winners of these awards this year are <u>Al Gore</u>, <u>Bob Dylan</u> and <u>Amos Oz</u>. We're mixing in good company.

Here are three reasons why Nature is so important in the world of science.

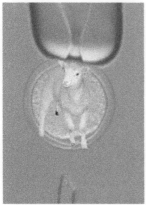

Tyrranosaurus Drip

Julia Donaldson, along with the brilliant illustrator, David Roberts, has come up with a modern classic published this week. I just received this message from the book's editor Suzanne Carnell and I believe her:

Do have a read: children love it – and so will you. If you've got kids, this is one you'll positively enjoy re-reading on a daily basis. I'm extremely proud of this book and, as Gordon Brown (who last week chose The Snail and the Whale by Julia Donaldson and Axel Scheffler as one of his top five favourite books) might say: I recommend it to the House!

Two of the most important serial best sellers in my life are Wisden Cricketers' Almanack (of which I am a non-executive director) and Harry Potter which Macmillan Distribution is proud (and worked to the bone) to distribute for Bloomsbury. In the normal course of events these publications have little in common but at the premiere of the latest Potter film, its star Daniel Radcliffe pulled a copy of this year's Wisden out of his pocket (big pocket) to get cricket celeb and cover adorner (see below) Shane Warne to sign the book. Aaaaah.

07 July 2007

Parallel universes

It sometimes seems that the book trade is operating in several parallel universes – authors, agents, general publishers, educational publishers, specialist publishers, independent booksellers, supermarkets, wholesalers, second-hand booksellers etc.

What I didn't know until this morning is that the first scientific proposal for the existence of parallel universes is fifty years old today. It was part of a PhD thesis developed at <u>Princeton</u> by <u>Hugh Everett III</u>.

You can read about how this young quantum physicist came up with the concept <u>here</u>. This special feature of Nature also heralds the return of <u>Futures,</u> a weekly series of scifi short stories. This is where fact and fiction meet and where the parallel universes of Nature and <u>Pan</u> overlap.

Back to reality and our monthly statement from Google Adsense. June generated $43.47, the second highest month ever. Total income has reached the heights of $338. Unfortunately it seems that the value of the dollar against sterling is declining almost as much as the account is increasing. More seriously, the strength of sterling is posing significant problems for British exporting publishers. One more thing for us to worry about.

08 July 2007

Write it right

I have always admired writers. All of us write (I answer some fifty emails a day; the rest I delete) but some write better than others. There are, of course, great writers and their talent is hard to teach in spite of the best efforts of creative writing courses. But most of us just want to write clearly and accurately. I fail on a regular basis given the number of times people manage to misinterpret a message from me. The need to write clearly is one of the keys to success as a university student and we published <u>Write it Right</u> by John Peck and Martin Coyle a couple of years ago.

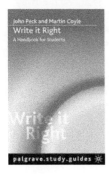

The reason I mention it here is that we have issued a free audio download version of this and several other study guides via the Palgrave Macmillan website. College textbook publishing has had to adapt as publishers move from being a supplier of books to being a partner in education. Booksellers used to be the key 'customer'. Over the last twenty years the focus of attention has moved to the lecturer. I suspect the focus has to shift yet again, and this time the key customer is the real thing, the student.

09 July 2007

Ni hao, tovaritch

Simon Greenall is one of the most successful authors in the Macmillan English list. He has sent in this latest briefing from one of the farthest reaches of our marketing efforts and I thought you'd be interested. Thanks, Simon.

We're in Heilongjiang province, in north-eastern China, where the regional Ministry of Education has adopted New Standard English for Senior High Schools, the textbook series published jointly by Foreign Languages Teaching and Research Press (FLTRP), Beijing, and Macmillan Education. We're here to do some teacher training sessions, organised by the Ministry. It's a substantial adoption too, 200,000 copies of each book every year, so over eleven books . . . well, you do the math. Other provinces, both larger and smaller, are already using the series, more will do so next year, we hope, and at last I'm beginning to understand the concept of critical mass.

The capital city is Harbin, home of the Ice Festival, although it's now midsummer, and around 30 degrees most of the time. More importantly, as far as I'm concerned, it's the hometown of Ivy (Wang Jianbo), my friend and our director of textbooks for the schools department of the press. She is directly responsible for the books which sell around 50 million copies sold every year (some kind of record?), and is justifiably proud to be returning home to give a presentation on the project for which she has worked so hard.

In Harbin, we have an audience of 500 teachers cramped together in auditorium which is steaming at 8am in the morning, so you can imagine what it feels like when I finish my presentation three hours later. They all have their Macmillan/FLTRP textbooks in front of them. Strange to think that books which were written with authors in small towns in the UK end up here, so far away.

In the evening, after the usual welcome dinner, we go shopping late in the evening in Harbin's main pedestrian streets. The Russian Far Eastern border is not so far away, so Harbin has many Russian-style buildings, including Saint Sophia, an Orthodox Cathedral, and shops selling Russian goods. We then walk along a causeway far out into the Songhua River, at this point two kilometres across, and watch hot air lanterns drift into the night sky over the water.

One feature which astonishes me about China is the size of the cities, an impression which usually strikes me only as we arrive on the outskirts, as we catch a 180 degree glimpse of the built-up area. Harbin was described to me as a small city but turns out to have over a population of 8 million.

The next day we travel six hours by train to Jiamusi, a city of half a million further along the Songhua River. How could I have remained so unaware, in the comfortable west, of such huge centres of population in China?

Jiamusi on a Sunday afternoon is relaxed, full of people enjoying themselves on the boardwalk alongside the river. People stare at me – there are not many Caucasian visitors – but in the most kindly, friendly way. One older woman greets me in Chinese and Russian, 'Ni hao, tovaritch!' (Hello, comrade!).

Every day lunch and dinner follow a very similar pattern. According to socio-cultural conventions, there is only one place for me to sit, which is for the guest of honour, and I comply obediently. But there is always a ritual tussle for the second place ('No, you must sit next to our guest' . . . 'No, I insist it must be you!'). We sit down, wait for the food, and begin drinking. We all negotiate the choice between Great Wall Red Wine (excellent), local firewater (no opinion, can't drink it) and local beer (Harbin beer is hoppy, light and more-ish, Jiamusi beer is even better).

Then the toasts follow. The first toast is always by the host, and everyone joins in. We raise our glasses, tap tap on the lazy Susan turntable and touch glasses. The next toast is usually from the host to me, the honoured guest, Gambay! and continues with short speeches to everyone around the table, thanking them for their co-operation, respecting their professionalism, welcoming their contribution, admiring their good looks . . . Then each person shows his glass to each other after the toast, to show how much they have finished, usually the whole glass, although they keep their eye on the other person to make sure they don't make them drink too much

Well, I don't drink much alcohol, and despite two years of Chinese classes, most of all this goes over my head. So, from time to time, basking in the warm glow of friendship but unable to keep up, I lose concentration and sink into my own thoughts. I snaffle some more food from the lazy Susan . . . thinking . . . it's 11am in the UK, my son back home has got his last A level exam today, maybe I should text good luck wishes . . . and suddenly, I realise I'm the object of yet another toast of welcome, and I'm back into action with another glass . . . tap, tap, Gambay!

The turntable turns, the food keeps coming, and we eat and drink, and promise everlasting friendship. And we mean it.

Next morning in Jiamusi, Ivy and I give presentations to 300 people, The same warm feelings of welcome and greeting, of kindness and interest.

And so it goes.

We travel back from Jiamusi to Harbin on a butt-numbing coach, faster than the train, but good fun. We stop for ten minutes in the middle of the journey, the road-side food sellers are waiting with fruit, tortillas-style wraps filled with vegetables, kebabs and corn on the cob. Ivy buys two corns cobs, tells me to eat slowly as they may hurt my stomach, and the coach sets off again. We're watching a Jackie Chan movie on the coach video as we get back to the big city.

In Harbin we have lunch in a Russian restaurant – we could be in central Europe – and we go then to the airport, for my flight back to a steamy Beijing. Ivy has two more weeks on the road, I'm back to the Beijing office for more meetings. And we say goodbye.

Seven years of working in China, with Macmillan and FLTRP . . . . . When I'm there, I feel that I'm in a safe and kind society, where the values of family, of hospitality, of respect for others' views, are strong. We can learn a lot from 'Ni hao, tovaritch!'

Books lovely books

About six months ago some colleagues in Germany launched a community site for book lovers Lovely Books. It is a great success and because imitation is the sincerest form of flattery (and because we asked prior permission) we have copied it. Yesterday saw the launch of the beta version of the English-language lovelybooks.com. The more people who sign up and use the site the better it will become. Do please give it a go and feed back too. Here's a shot of the German version.

I was castigated recently by a commenter, Alan Kellogg, for the pricing of a pdf in Nature. I had actually linked to a free pdf – Nature makes some of its content available free of charge as well as the bulk being available on subscription or 'by the drink' – but he latched on to the price of associated articles:

'$30.00 for a file of an article? A file you don't need to print, bind, or mail? A file the customer can download. A file you don't need to replace because the customer is getting a copy?

You can find 300 page PDFs on the web for $10.00, and the publisher make a profit. How long is the typical Nature article?'

I think he is missing the point about value of information. It cannot be measured by price per page. It cannot be measured by the cost of paper or replaceability. It can only be measured by its usefulness to the reader and to some extent in relation to the cost of producing it. In the case of articles in Nature we have a rejection rate of well over 90%. This is an extremely costly process requiring teams of skilled scientists separating the wheat from the chaff and publishing only the very best and most pertinent articles. $30 is not a reflection of the length of the article, it is for the knowledge that the article in question is reliable and in part it reflects the cost of NOT publishing the rejected articles.

Finally, a very strange postscript to the blog linking the new Harry Potter film and Wisden Cricketers' Almanack from the Daily Telegraph:

'He [Daniel Radcliffe] has, he says, been plagued by strange dreams lately, although he cannot lay the blame at Harry Potter's door. "I've dreamt I'm being stalked by an England cricketer. I don't know what prompted it – although I've been watching huge amounts of cricket – but for some reason Andrew Strauss was being paid to stalk me. I woke up with a cricket bat in my hand." '

bLink

This is going to be the shortest posting for a while but it might just be the most important. Click on this link to Jeff Gomez's excellent Print is Dead blog. Perhaps Manolis Kelaidis is to the digital world what Allen Lane was to mass-market paperbacks, Paul Hamlyn to colour illustrated books, or Robert Maxwell to scientific publishing.

12 July 2007

The beautiful game

I've been finding it terribly difficult obeying the embargo on one particular press release this week, but I'm finally allowed to tell you that Pan Macmillan is publishing Cristiano Ronaldo's first and only official book, MOMENTS. Pan will be publishing partner to Pedro Paradela de Abreu of Ideias & Rumos, who launched the book in Portugal last Saturday.

MOMENTS is one of those books that everyone in the business feels a bit of a thrill about publishing; even those with little interest in 'the beautiful game' can see that such a unique insight into the world of football's biggest star has got to be a hit. Pan's non-fiction publisher Richard Milner tells me that in the book, Ronaldo shares thoughts on some of his best moments on and off the pitch. It's a sumptuous book too, with over 150 photographs to accompany the text.

Meanwhile, in other excitement, the Pan Bookshop is planning a big 'summer extravaganza' on Friday 20th July. They sent me this report about their plans:

For those of you who for some reason haven't picked up on this yet, this is the day of the midnight Harry Potter launch. There will be more written about books and bookshops than any other day this year and the bookshop has sensibly thought to take advantage of the acres of print to promote other aspects of bookselling.

In the morning there will be various entertainments for the under fives; at tea time we have two top-notch authors for older children and in the evening the adults will take over. The centre piece of this part of the day will be a history event to celebrate what a great year it has been for history books. Also featuring will be the ever wonderful and wise Isabel Losada plus advice on getting your novel published from the very experienced Michael Cady. A blues band will play until the shop closes at 10pm, only to reopen at midnight for Harry Potter and the Deathly Hallows to go on sale.

I'm pleased to say that the book will be sold at full cover price; independent booksellers like the Pan Bookshop may not be able to compete on price but they can certainly compete on the individuality and creativity of their promotions, and those in the queue for their copy of this much-awaited book will be entertained royally by the sounds of it. We hope to see you there.

The long and winding digital road

Yesterday I was on the breathtaking Peninsula de Magdalena in <u>Santander</u>. I was there with a colleague to join the annual meeting of the <u>Federacion de Gremios de Editores de Espana</u> (the Spanish Publishers' Association equivalent) to discuss the threats and opportunities for publishers in the digital world. We concluded that, in spite of all the difficulties and the length of the road, it's time for book publishers to take a walk on the digital wild side, build digital infrastructures, shake up traditional workflows, develop new marketing techniques and join the 21stcentury.

Meanwhile, across the Atlantic in Sao Paulo, our Macmillan English team is attending the annual <u>LABCI</u> (English language teaching) conference. You can read all about it on the <u>MEC blog</u> and here is the tourism ministry in Sao Paulo but our royal tradition (last week the Prince of Asturia award)continued with a mention of <u>Macmillan English Campus</u> by <u>Princess Anne</u> in her conference-opening address.

And finally on this mini world tour to Tokyo where there has been huge press <u>coverage</u> for an article by Emperor Akihito which has been published in <u>Nature</u>. Yet more royalty. What is going on?

It's hard to keep up with it all.

Apron strings

This is the Macmillan team at the <u>LABCI</u> conference in Sao Paulo which I mentioned yesterday.

You can read more about the day and see a video of the opening ceremony (uploaded on youtube acrobatically by Emma Shercliff (centre of the photo) on their blog. What it doesn't explain is why they are all wearing aprons. It might be in defiance of a project we intiated a couple of years ago known as apron strings. The idea was (and is) that businesses such as Macmillan Brazil should cut the apron strings from the UK and set off on their own adventures. We've made good progress but it seems that there must still be some resdiual affection for the mother ship.

In jolly old England last week the unions at the Royal Mail Group held a further one-day strike, thus confirming the sense of Amazon's decision to cease using them for the delivery of parcels. However, the clever people at Publishing News used this as an opportunity to launch their new and excellent digital version. It's an ill wind . . .

I've been asked by a friend to help with a glossary of Yiddish terms. Can anyone help with the spellings of these words, better (and funnier) definitions, and corrections to howlers. Thanks so much.

Afikomen – apiece of matzoh hidden during the Seder for children to find

Auf ruf – a blessing on a prospective bride and groom before the wedding day

B'racha (*plural* b'rachot) – a blessing

Beth Din – Rabbinical court

Bimah – a platform in a synagogue on which the Torah is read

Bris – a circumcision ceremony

Broigus – angry/a row or grudge

Bubeleh – my little one, darling

Challah – plaited white bread

Channukah – eight-day festival of lights in December

Charoset – mixture of apples, nuts, spices and sweet wine, symbolising the mortar with which Jewish slaves built the houses of their captors.

Chuppah – a canopy under which wedding vows are taken

Cossackski – a kicking dance with arms crossed and legs bent, derived from the great friends of Jews, the Cossacks.

Frummer – a religious person

Goyisher – a non-Jew

Haggadah (*plural* Haggadot) – the story of the Jews' exodus from Egypt, read aloud at Seder

Halachah – Jewish law

Hametz – food containing yeast, which must be removed from the house before Passover begins

Hillel sandwich – a little piece of horseradish between pieces of matzoh

K'nayn hora tu-tu-tu – expression said superstitiously to ward off the evil eye: please God

Kadimah – summer camp

Ketubah – a legal marriage document

Kiddush cup – cup for wine used during the blessings recited on the Sabbath and festivals

Kippah (*plural* kippot) – skullcap worn by observant male jews, and some female rabbis

Klezmer – folk music from Eastern Europe

Kvetch – to complain or moan

Leo Baeck – London's rabbinical college

Mah Nishtanah – the beginning of the Four Questions asked during the Seder

Maror – horseradish, symbolising the bitterness of life under slavery

Matzoh – thin sheets of unleavened bread

Matzoh-kneidl or matzoh balls: dumplings for chicken soup

Megillah – a complicated palaver

Mensch – a decent person, a good egg

Meshuggener – a mad person

Milchedik – food classified as dairy by Kosher laws

Minyan – the ten male Jews required for religious services

Mitzvah – a good deed, and a religious obligation

Nu? – So? Well? And?

Pesach – Passover: at which Jews commemorate their ancestors' escape from slavery in Egypt

Rebbitzin – rabbi's wife

Schlemiel – a clumsy, foolish or unlucky person

Schlep – to haul or move laboriously

Schloompy – frumpy, drippy, droopy

Schmendrick – a particularly puny schlemiel

Schmooze – to chat, or chat up

Schmuck – a stupid idiot

Schmutters – rags, clothes

Schnorrer – a scrounger

Schtick – a routine

Schtum – quiet

Schtuppable – fuckable

Seder – a ceremonial feast, with prayers, on the first and second nights of Passover.

Shabbat – the Sabbath

Shiva – a period of mourning

Shul – a synagogue

Tallith – a prayer shawl

Tchotckes – a little silly plaything

Tefillin – leather boxes with straps containing biblical passages, used by Orthodox men for prayer

Tochus – a bottom

Torah – the five books of Moses

Yahrzeit – the anniversary of a death

Yeshiva – rabbinical college; cf. *Yentl*

Zaftig – juicy, sexy

 15 July 2007

HarperCollins

The trade press is a strange thing. An editor moving from one publishing house to another warrants headlines. As does a publisher signing a contract with an author for a book which will be lucky to sell 5000 copies. Or a discount promotion in a bookshop chain. Here is a recent and fairly typical Publishing News home page. The fourteenth item is News in Brief and the eighth and last story in that section is:

DAVID Worlock has been named Non-Executive Chairman of HarperCollins UK, and Ian Bedwell is appointed International Business Development Director. Worlock is currently Chief Research Fellow at Outsell Inc and his career has included roles at Thomson Corp and Pearson. Bedwell has enjoyed a long career at VNU, which he left earlier this year.

I think it it possibly the most important news item in the whole issue.

It is not my job to be generous about competitors and I have been known to be a tad dismissive of some strange bits of self-promotion (for instance, here). However, this appointment of David Worlock by HarperCollins UK shows that at least one British trade publisher is beginning to understand the importance of the digital revolution and the need for fundamental change.

I first met David several centuries ago when he was setting up Eurolex, a pioneer legal database business, for Thomson. He was a digital native then and he still is. I also heard an excellent talk last week by another HarperCollins executive, Brian Murray, who is Group President of the company worldwide. My guess is that HC are putting into place the management building blocks to take decisive action when it comes to finding new markets for books in electronic form. Building platforms from which to sell (e.g. BookStore) is an essential, quite tricky and quite costly first step but the real difficulty is re-engineering a workforce used to the old ways of doing things. That's where people like David and Brian come in.

And Macmillan has people like that too!

16 July 2007

How to get rich

In the echo chamber that we sometimes inhabit as publishers, one often repeated concern is that we employ far too many English Literature graduates. I refer you, then, to a piece in The Times today by the sports writer Simon Barnes, which neither encourages nor refutes this view particularly, but which is definitely very amusing and thought provoking on the subject of English Literature degrees and their purpose. The précis version, for those with too little time to read it, is that young people today are under far too much pressure to follow degrees which 'transform them into an effective economic unit', that this is not helped by educationists developing courses that 'look like short cuts to a sexy job' (e.g. sport, journalism, fashion) and that it's a real shame that we can't go back to the days when a good old English Literature degree gave students the time and the excuse to 'suss out the meaning of life.' Barnes suggests that modern education prepares people for wealth but that the old approach made you richer. Or, in other words, that reading is the route to a more developed world – and self – view. I hate to hark on a familiar theme, but there's much here to compare with the problems intrinsic to high street bookselling today; the best-seller, trend-following culture making some people a lot wealthier, for sure, but almost certainly making us as a nation poorer from a cultural point of view.

17 July 2007

Corrigendum

On Sunday I wrote enthusiastically about the report of a new Chairman of HarperCollins UK. It turns out that the story was a mistake caused by Publishing News's assumption that HCUK could only mean HarperCollins. This email from David Worlock's daughter, Kate:

Even though it was lovely to see a picture of my esteemed father in your blog today (and I'm sure he appreciates the compliment too!), the news has in fact been misreported. He's been made non-executive Chairman of HCUK, a producer of online event management software (http://www.hcuk.net/home.asp), rather than HarperCollins. However, since people seem so keen on the idea, perhaps we may soon have HarperCollins knocking on the door as well.

Apologies if anyone was upset by the misreporting but I can't help feeling that HarperCollins could do a lot worse . . .

As it's Summertime and many people flock to France for their holidays, this video is worth watching, both to improve your French and to get an understanding of the French view of the digital future – deux oiseaux avec une pierre.

And here's another vision of the future, developed by the Laverna Group and described by them as:

'The Felix kiosk is a multi-level marketing device running on ADSL networks and offering a range of functions including Everyone's a Winner game, Mobile Top-up, Digital Purchase library and ATM. Certain kiosks may also include an Instant print Photography unit.'

Perhaps independent booksellers should look at installing one by the cash register.

Independent booksellers should also be interested in the row between Bloomsbury and the supermarket chain, ASDA. This is what a forthright Bloomsbury have had to say:

Asda's latest attempt to draw attention to themselves involves trying to leap on the Harry Potter bandwagon. This is just another example of their repeated efforts at appearing as Robin Hood in the face of controversy about their world wide group which would suggest they are perceived as more akin to the Sheriff of Nottingham.

Asda may grandstand all they like in their attempts to use poor *Harry Potter* to lure the public into buying a bag of their groceries but they seem to attribute no value to Bloomsbury's very serious environmental mission, clearly stated, in printing this Harry Potter book for the first time on part recycled paper which costs more not less;

and to fuel surcharges. As people are slowly realizing, there is a price to be paid by the consumer for environmental best practice.

It is self-evident that most multiple retailers deliberately to choose to sell Harry Potter at a significant loss in an attempt to attract customers who will buy their other products, such as a £20 bag of groceries. Loss-leaders were invented by supermarkets and have nothing to do with Bloomsbury Publishing or Harry Potter and we deeply regret being dragged into their price wars.

(By permission of Bloomsbury Publishing.)

18 July 2007

Summertime fun

Our trade publishing around the globe is having a run of successes. Today on Channel 4 at 5.30 Kate Morton's The House at Riverton published by Pan Macmillan, which is one of Richard and Judy's Summer Reads, will be reviewed on the Richard and Judy Show by celebrity reviewers Matt Baker (of Blue Peter fame) and Jo Whiley. In Australia, Who Killed Channel 9?, the book I blogged about a week or so ago, is at No 1 after its first full week of sales. And in other trade publishing news, I'm pleased to see that the war of words between ASDA and Bloomsbury over the forthcoming Harry Potter launch was closed yesterday with Bloomsbury receiving the apology they deserved from the Walmart-owned supermarket chain, as reported here by The Bookseller.

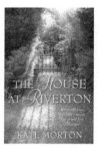

By permission of Pan Macmillan, London.

Meanwhile, I was amused by the BBC's feature on the man whose Internet life begins to eat up his entire business and personal life, so much so that he now pays someone else to be him online. Could it be time for me to employ a full-time 'digital biographer'?

19 July 2007

Richard and Judy, God bless them

I was sent this link by the managing director of John Wisden. You have to be a little patient but the denouement is worth the wait. I don't think that the scene is from our Basingstoke customer services department but . . .

The Richard and Judy book club isn't everybody's cup of tea. I was at a meeting where a distinguished publisher blamed it for the decline of almost everything in the book trade – a mite extreme I thought. Clearly it (and other similar ventures elsewhere in the world) tend to make a very limited number of titles best sellers and this might to some extent draw sales away from other equally worthy books. On the other hand the TV show itself has done more for the profile of books and reading than anything else I can remember (except perhaps the Harry Potter phenomenon).

It's not surprising I feel positive about R&J. Here are some quotes from yesterday's show about Kate Morton's The House at Riverton:

'I really enjoyed it' 'Completely my sort of book' 'It's like Titanic without the boats' 'It keeps you guessing – I couldn't put it down' 'A page-turner' 'An excellent book' 'If you like lying on your sun lounger for hours getting lost in another world, you'll love this book'

And Judy said: 'It's a corker . . . probably my favourite of all the Summer Reads'

Thinking about fiction I remembered that Tim Coates wrote this a few days ago in the comments section of this blog. Nobody has responded. I think what that council is proposing is outrageous, illogical, counterproductive and wrong. What do you think?

Hampshire County Council, in England, is proposing that its 54 public libraries should no longer stock works of fiction.

The argument is that 'people buy fiction in book shops now – there is no need for libraries to do the same job'.

The proposer is Yinnon Ezra, who is head of the library and leisure service and he is supported by his council and his chief librarian, Richard Ward.

Is this an action your readers would endorse?

You can read more about this and other attacks on libraries on Tim's Good Library blog. I don't suppose it will ever happen but wouldn't it be great if R&J launched a campaign to save public libraries from the ravages of inefficient bureaucracy and political correctness.

A book which will definitely not make the R&J club is Thirty Secret Years by my former boss, Robin Denniston. I wrote about it back in May when it was first published. It is great to see that a serious book from a serious but small and independent publisher Polperro Heritage Press has been picked up and reviewed sensibly in the Spectator. All is not lost.

🦋 20 July 2007

Happy HP7 night

The last few days have seen a series of almighty rows about HP7 and I've mentioned the book a couple of times (and so have Clive Keble and others in the comments) here and here. I've had any number of journalists ring up and ask me to opine, all of which I declined on the grounds of ignorance of the detail of the row and also because Macmillan Distribution is Bloomsbury's client and has a hard enough job ensuring the security and efficient delivery of the millions of copies of HP7 without me muddying the waters. (And here I simply have to say a big thank you to all at MDL who have contributed to the toughest logistical exercise in book distribution history and who, in spite of the pressures, have managed to maintain their customary high levels of service for all the other things they do. You know who you are. Fingers crossed that nothing goes wrong today and that you can take a well-earned mini-rest and enjoy the sense of a job well done).

However, tonight is the night and I cannot resist expressing some views. Harry Potter is the most amazing literary phenomenon of all time. I don't have the numbers (nor does anyone I suspect) but I reckon that more people have bought (or will have bought) Harry Potter books than any other title. The Bible may have printed more (it's been going a sight longer) but the majority of copies are given away rather than purchased. I cannot think of anything else that comes close. Even Mao's Little Red Book must have been overtaken.

Its impact on our and other industries has been phenomenal. Of course, Bloomsbury as the original English-language publisher has benefitted but think of all the foreign-language publishers, all the sales agencies, all the rep commissions, the printers, papermakers, freight forwarders, mail delivery organisations, Hollywood, retailers large and small, journalist desperate for copy, literary agents who owe J.K. Rowling and the editorial team at Bloomsbury a huge debt of gratitude.

There will always be carpers and knockers but we should rejoice that a whole generation of children around the world have been introduced to books and reading. It is the job of the rest of us now to turn those children into long-term readers and book buyers.

On a much more local level, Sky News have decided to host a Potter party at the Pan Bookshop in Fulham Road, London. All our regular and not so regular customers are welcome and the shenanigans begins at 10 p.m. Enjoy.

🦋 21 July 2007

Floods and things

Yesterday, England suffered some pretty bad floods which caused the usual amount of chaos and disarray. Amazingly however, there was play in the India-England cricket match.

This is, of course, not the first flood to hit Britain and Nature reports this week on the flood which created the English Channel 200,000 years ago – and you can listen to the podcast version too.

In spite of the floods we managed to distribute HP7 successfully. The acid test is that Macmillan distribution has hardly been mentioned in any of the coverage. Phew – and thanks again to the team.

🐭 22 July 2007

Nigeria, Test Match Special, Razorlight and Spiderman

A little while ago on this blog I quoted from a memo written by an old friend working for us in Nigeria:

'A reassuring scene, though: a dusty entrance lobby with pealing lino tiles and segments of spaghetti-type wiring; battleship grey paintwork (always so encouraging I find); a receptionist reading a two-day old copy of the Daily Times plus a grubby Mills & Boon novel; a fading picture of the late Supermac hung at a rakish angle but so high up you had to positively seek him (o tempora! o mores! o winds of change! – nothing had changed in this lobby for years); the MD's ante-chamber crammed with cheap Asian wall clocks and support staff with little to do pending the arrival of the MD but read newspapers and seek soul-mates on the web; and the car park full of sound and fury, drivers and reps, but little if any sign of coordinated activity . . .'

At the bottom of the email he mentioned that his stepson had become a rather successful musician with a band I'd not heard of at the time, Razorlight. On Friday this week, when tuning in to Test Match Special to get the latest score in the cricket, I found myself listening to a tea-interval interview with a cricket-loving rock star, Jonny Borrell. Usually these interviews are with former international cricketers rabbitting on about the good old days blah blah. The rock star was interesting, interested, insightful and funny. I'll bet he's a good musician too. He's also got a film-star girlfriend, Kirsten Dunst of Spiderman fame.

It's a strange series of connections.

Back to books and Harry Potter in particular. I was sent this Seth Godin link.

'By now, the Harry Potter hype machine has told you all about the pre-shipped copies, the scanned book and the spoilers. No doubt it'll sell a few copies, and no doubt the reported $20 million on security (not to mention fedex expense) was both useful and ineffective.

The interesting thing for me is how the Net changes what it means for something to be a secret. Five hundred year old technology (books) is just too slow for the Net. The act of printing, storing and shipping millions of books takes too long for a secret to ever be in a book again.

My solution? A hybrid. Publish the first edition of the book without the last three chapters. Take your time, save the $20 million. Every purchaser then gets access (hey, everyone gets access) to the last three chapters on launch day.

Books are souvenirs. No one is going to read Potter online, even if it's free. Holding and owning the book, remembering when and how you got it . . . that's what you're paying for. Books are great at holding memories. They're lousy at keeping secrets.'

Save to del.icio.us (13 saves, tagged: books marketing security) • Digg This! (6 Diggs, 1 comment) • Email this • Stumble It!

What do you think?

Corporate flogging

It's a dank, grey Monday morning here in London. I hope this video from David Vaine helps to start your week with a smile.

And for something a bit more serious, check out this One Laptop Per Child talk by Nicholas Negroponte. I was brought up to speed on this last week at a strategy meeting of our African managing directors who are beginning to grapple with the issues of digital education in unbelievably poor countries. It's hard to argue against the scheme which is potentially of huge benefit to schools and education. I see two problems. First, $100 for the hardware is too much for many developing countries. Second, the focus on technology is detracting from the need for better materials for computer-assisted learning. At Macmillan Education we are working with OLPC to help with the latter. It would be a disaster if all the efforts to develop and distribute millions of laptops to schools ended up with unused hardware lying redundant in the corners of classrooms.

The latest quarterly update from Book Marketing Limited landed on my desk this morning. I think I may have mentioned the Travelodge survey on what British people prefer to do in bed but it is well worth repeating.

1. Reading 44%

2. Watching TV 23%

3. Going to sleep 21%

4. Making love 16%

5. Listening to music 14%

Reading is nearly three times more popular than making love.

Finally. a reality check on book prices. I decided yesterday to spend a couple of hours at Lord's Cricket Ground to see Kevin Pietersen score yet another century (which he duly did). The cheapest ticket available was £70 compared with Wisden Cricketers' Almanack at £40 (recommended retail, frequently sold for less) for 1664 pages and hundreds of hours of use. Go figure.

Mind Candy

We have a tradition here in Kings Cross of inviting interesting people to come and speak to the staff about interesting developments, usually of a digital kind. A little while ago we had a fascinating presentation from the Mind Candy team. One of the presenters, Adrian Hon, has a blog called Mssv which is shorthand for massive apparently. His pieceyesterday on the death of publishers is well worth reading even though he has a few side swipes at Macmillan and even though I disagree with much of what he has to say.

Meanwhile, Pan Macmillan's summer of successes rolls on, with Colm Toibin's Mothers and Sons winning the Edge Hill Prize for the Short Story 2007 and Jackie

Kay winning the Outstanding Contribution to Literature Award at the Grazia O2 X Awards last week.

More importantly, today is a day to celebrate the release of the wrongly incarcerated and prosecuted nurses in Libya. I am proud that Nature took such a proactive stand on their behalf as described here and that the world of science as a whole stood up for justice.

🐦 25 July 2007

Libraries go social

The Charleston Report, a newsletter about the US Library Market, has been landing on my desk – and over the last ten years – my desktop, for more years than I care to remember. Its focus is of course now primarily on changes brought about within the market by the impact of digital, and it always highlights some interesting tidbits. If the latest edition is anything to go by, it seems social networking trends have hit libraries jus as much as other markets, with reports that:

1. 50% of faculty members across the US believe social networking sites will change the way students learn according to a recent Thomson survey

2. video advertising through sites such as YouTube is now a significant trend as shown by a survey by the Online Publishers Association (OPA) which reveals substantial statistical data on the attitudes and behaviours of Internet users towards online video

3. OCLC has added a social networking feature to WorldCat.org, to allow users to create their own profile and create personalised lists of items catalogued in WorldCat, then share them with colleagues

4. the 'Infotubey' award winners have recently been announced – 'Infotubeys' being awards given to libraries for exemplary content posted on YouTube. Information on winners can be viewed here.

And the social networking theme continues as I have just learned that Pan Macmillan has developed a facebook page for its forthcoming title HEARTSICK, with the aim of generating publicity for the book in advance of publication on 3 August. The group has 150 members and counting, perhaps lured by the promise of a free advance book proof (while stocks last) to everyone who joins the group. Facebook fans might also like to look up the facebook group dedicated to our new book lovers' community site, lovelybooks, here.

On an entirely separate theme our Australian publishing deserves another mention today as Les Carlyon's brilliant book The Great War, published by Pan Macmillan Australia, won Australian Book of the Year last night at the 2007 *Australian Book Industry Awards* (ABIA), as reported by the Australian News here.

🐦 26 July 2007

Liberty, Justice, HIV and Libya

This blog is usually about one or other aspect of publishing and books. Today is different. I celebrated the release of the six foreign health workers from Libya and the threat of the death penalty a couple of days ago. Our editorial team, and in particular our senior reporter Declan Butler, at Nature played an active part in the campaign to secure their release and Declan has written this piece as a guest blog explaining more of the background. As I said before, I am really proud of Nature's part in achieving a modicum of justice and grateful for Declan's contribution.

The liberation of six foreign health workers, held hostage in Libya, is a welcome denouement of this tragic affair. Today, the 5 Bulgarian nurses and a Palestinian medic woke up in Bulgaria, free at last from the threat that one morning, they might have woken only to be led out, blindfolded, tied to a stake, and executed by firing squad.

But the moral price of securing release of the hostages has been high.

The EU humanitarian aid package for over 400 infected Libyan children accidentally infected at a Benghazi hospital is desirable and commendable. But Libya's tying it to the six's release, in effect a ransom, sets a dangerous precedent for future unjustly condemned prisoners.

How much more ransom was really paid in the murky deal between the European Union and Libya will probably never be known. The $400 million in 'blood money' paid to the families of the infected children from an opaque international fund – which paved the way for the end of the crisis – may in fact have largely been paid by Libya, as part of a complex face saving deal. But Libya extorted concessions on debt relief, and many other fronts. The EU has also promised returns by normalizing its political and economic ties with Libya.

Moreover, Libya set the tempo for the prearranged choreographed diplomatic script. The sequence of the sorry spectacle went like this.

The Supreme Court upholds the death sentence to play to domestic opinion by being seen to stand up to the West, and to avoid calling into question the farce of a trial conducted by its judicial system.

The families then get bought off to gracefully pardons the medics. The Supreme Council then stalls for days, keeping the West waiting at its feet, before finally commuting the death sentences to life imprisonment, and opening the way for extradition of the six to Bulgaria.

Instead of extraditing the medics immediately, Libya continued its bad faith, knowing that with the West so close to resolution of the crisis, it could still try to raise its price. Right until the final hour of their release, Libya haggled as if the nurses were carpets in a Tripoli souk, and used delaying tactics, to win further concessions.

In short, the West has been forced to appease Libya, and ultimately reward it for taking six health workers hostage for eight years. This all is difficult to swallow. The six were not given a fair trial, prosecution evidence was fabricated, and scientific evidence that would have exonerated the medics ignored. Their trials were a kafkaesque mockery that trampled on justice.

But that outcome was perhaps inevitable. From the outset, the six were pawns, caught up in global geopolitics. Once sucked into that quagmire, respect for fundamental human rights such as the right to a fair trial, became just one element in a wider basket, that included Libya's renunciation of weapons of mass destruction, it's utility as an ally in the war against terror, not to mention that Libya's coming in from the cold opened up to for Western economic interests the goldmine of the world's largest unexplored oil reserves.

Once the case had become politicized, it was inevitable too that the solution would have to be political. The campaigns by Nature, human rights groups, scientific organizations and lawyers, acknowledge this reality, and that the only real pressure point available was to raise international public opinion and awareness to force Western governments to do more to resolve the case.

As well as defending the fundamental principles of a fair trial, and the right for relevant evidence to be heard, the focus on calling for the scientific evidence to be heard was considered by the defence as its best card in the run up to the end of the trial last autumn.

Had Libya accepted to have had the scientific evidence heard in court, the prosecution case would have collapsed like a pack of cards. But as was most likely, they refused to do so, it would also expose with clarity that the trial was anything but fair, and provide a fulcrum, a focus, to leverage public opinion, and consequently political opinion.

The massive international outrage after the 19 December death penalty verdict was in large part prompted by the fact that science had demonstrated the emptiness of the prosecution case, leaving the world in no doubt that this was an appalling miscarriage of justice. The scale of the outrage led to more intense diplomatic activity, in particular by the EU.

The human rights case was also not entirely lost. After the verdict, the EU broke temporarily with its policy of 'silent diplomacy' – refraining from public criticism of Libya's handling of the case and relying on behind-the-scenes discussions – and condemned in no uncertain terms the human rights violations, and abuse of scientific evidence in the case. This, combined with the fact that Bulgaria became a member of the European Union at the start of the year, led to pressure for a speedy resolution of the case.

The United States meanwhile has been absent from the case, and mute on the human rights abuses in the case. Its absence though was perhaps a good thing after all, given the current administration's own abysmal record on human rights, which deprive it of moral authority.

Unbelievable perhaps though, that the administration couldn't find anything better to do on 11 July, the day the Libyan Supreme Court upheld the death verdict, than to announce it would appoint an ambassador to Tripoli for the first time in more than 25 years.

Realpolitik all along meant that the six could probably never have hoped that the international community would force Libya to give the six a fair trial. That the medics are free at last is already a major victory, and hat's off to the EU and British diplomats who worked patiently to put together a solution to the case – they are right to be livid with France and the Sarkozy family's shameless attempt to steal the limelight and take all the credit for the release.

The 1998 outbreak was a triple tragedy — for the six unjustly imprisoned, and for the infected children and families. Exoneration of the medics must be the next step. And as Vittorio Colizzi, an AIDS researcher at Tor Vergata University in Rome, Italy, who campaigned for scientific evidence exonerating the medical workers to be considered by the Libyan courts, says: 'We must not forget the children.' The third victim was the stuggle to have nation states abide by the fundamental international principles of justice and human rights enshrined in treaties to which they are, on paper, parties to.

For further information: Nature Focus on the case.

Why are trade books different?

My old friend <u>Adam Hodgkin</u> posed a question in a comment <u>here</u> which I think is worth a discussion.

I would be interested in the Macmillan view on why it has been possible to develop really excellent and profitable digital publishing for the Nature audience, and the commercial digital market still doesn't look at all convincing for trade publishing in general.

The first thing to say is that Macmillan doesn't have a view. Macmillan is made up of several thousand people all of whom have different views on more or less everything, thank goodness. This is my view.

1. Scientists are by their nature early adopters of technology and thus have had no problems moving from communicating in print to communicating digitally.

2. Scientific publishing has been intrinsically more profitable than trade book publishing. This allowed the major publishers and societies to invest the significant sums needed to create electronic delivery and storage platforms for scientific information. These platforms are a cornerstone for the creation of a new business and communication model.

3. Budgets for the acquisition of scientific information already existed and coud be readily transferred from print to digital acquisitions. These budgets were and are controlled by a professional cadre of librarians whose job is to ensure the best and most economic retrieval of information. They are the key partners to ensure highest standards.

4. The people who work in scientific publishing are by and large fascinated by the challenges of delivering often obscure information to a global audience and have embraced digital technology.

Trade book publishing has very different characteristics.

1. The general public has adopted some new technologies very quickly but to most people a book is a book – sheets of paper between covers, usable without batteries and readily portable.

2. Trade book publishing is usually a low-margin business and any spare cash has tended to be spent on investing in new authors and new marketing campaigns rather than long-term technological platforms. This is changing now with the emergence of solutions such as <u>BookStore</u> but this late movement hasn't helped a business model to develop.

3. Apart from the less-than-healthy public library market, there are no institutional budgets for the purchase of trade books and so no easy way of pump-priming the market.

4. The people who work in trade publishing are driven by the desire to find a great new author, to mix in the world of literature, to win literary prizes. Delivery mechanisms and complex technology are simply not high on their agendas. This is also changing but it will take time.

And I suppose the final reason why trade books will find it harder to establish a digital model than scientific journals is that not all books are purchased simply to be read. They are purchased as gifts, as furniture, as status symbol, as insurance against boredom. None of these reasons is adequately solved by a digital version. A scientific paper is only purchased for its content.

However, none of this means we should not be investing in digital delivery of trade books. We owe it to our authors to invest in every means of finding an audience for their works. We owe it to them to hold their copyright material securely and to fight on their behalf to protect their rights. We need to serve readers in whatever way they choose. We need to work with public libraries to make digital and on-demand editions of books available through them. We need to use digital versions to promote books and to create digital libraries for research and study.

Trade books are different now but I'm convinced that the technological gap between general book publishing and scientific publishing will narrow – and the pace is gathering.

To finish today's blog on the future of books I thought I'd share a thought sent to me by an old colleague of mine in France. Apparently the most interesting analysis of publishers' and authors' rights issues and their interaction with the concepts of digital libraries, open access and public domain is to be found in the 1763 La lettre sur le commerce des livres by the always brilliant Denis Diderot. Apparently it has never been translated into English and it should be. Can anyone help?

I can't resist this quote (of no relevance whatsoever to books or publishing) from the man himself:

Il y a un peu de testicule au fond de nos sentiments les plus sublimes et de notre tendresse la plus épurée.

🍃 28 July 2007

Cricket rocks

It's Saturday. The sun's out here in France. England are being humiliated by India at Trent Bridge and I believe the state of terrorist alert has fallen from red to amber. Incidentally, here is the official terrorist position.

The English are feeling the pinch in relation to recent terrorist threats and have raised their security level from 'Miffed' to 'Peeved'. Soon, though, security levels may be raised yet again to 'Irritated' or even 'A Bit Cross'. Londoners have not been 'A Bit Cross' since the blitz began in 1940 and tea supplies all but ran out. Terrorists have been re-categorized from 'Tiresome' to 'A Bloody Nuisance'. The last time the British issued 'A Bloody Nuisance' warning level was during the great fire of 1666.

I stop there because the rest of the joke was too anti French, German and Spanish for me to risk losing friends.

Back to cricket and Jonny Borrell. Here is the link to the teatime interview with him. I have pinched the BBC headline as the title of today's blog as an example of a contradiction in terms.

Of course, we all know that Australia rules the cricket world but I was delighted to hear that Macmillan Education Australia won both Primary Publisher of the Year and Secondary Publisher of the Year at the annual Awards for Excellence in Educational Publishing in Melbourne last week.

Publishers' Returns

Ask a typical manufacturer what his returns percentage is and he'll probably tell you his profit return on sales. Ask a publisher and he'll seethe about the perecentage of books sent back to his warehouse by retailers.

I'm not sure which publisher uttered these famous words when conducting a visitor round his warehouse and seeing a parcel of books ready for despatch:

'Gone today, here tomorrow.'

Perhaps someone can enlighten me as the who and the when. I'm not sure the official histories of publishing identify the first person to say to a bookseller: 'I know you don't think you can sell a dozen but take them anyway and, if you're right, I'll take back the unsolds and give you full credit.' Whoever it was unleashed a trade practice which not only decimates publishers' and booksellers' margins but it eats up retail space, diminishes the need for buying and selling skills, and doesn't do the environment much good either.

In Australia a few years ago, several publishers introduced backlist firm sale. This seems to be working fine and there is now a movement in the UK to do the same which I applaud. I also applaud Bloomsbury's returns limit on Harry Potter.

But what saddens me is that we seem to make no progress on the total elimination of returns. One of the arguments for the abandonment of retail price maintenance was that it would allow retailers to remainder without the absurdity of sending books back to the publisher, the publisher shipping them to a remainder merchant and the bookseller then buying the books back at remainder price for sale on the 'cheap' table. I ran an experiment with Waterstone's in the early 1990s where they were granted an extra couple of points of discount in exchange for no returns (except damaged books). It worked pretty well except that change of management and ownership meant it was discontinued. Why not try it again? We have nothing to lose except tons of credit notes, complexity, carbon dioxide and lazy buyers.

The Friday Project

When I worked at Reed Elsevier we had a policy of not selling any spare capacity in our distribution business to third parties. The logic was that we shouldn't help potential competitors to grow in any way. At Macmillan, we take the completely opposite view. We are happy to see competitors grow while using our services and helping us to become more effcient too. As a result we offer all sorts of services to our competitors – typesetting and text processing, copyediting, website development, Asian print sourcing, advertisement design, sales and distribution in USA, UK, Australia, New Zealand, South Africa, Ireland, India etc. It's a big set of businesses employing more than 4000 people worldwide and the scale we achieve from serving others as well as ourselves allows us to compete effectively with much larger publishing operations.

This is a preamble to a mini-review of one of our UK sales and distribution clients, the start-up company The Friday Project. It's been a fascinating ride for them and for us. The Pan Macmillan sales team represents their books to the trade and Macmillan Distribution services their orders.

turning the best of the web into the finest of books

Their strapline 'Turning the best of the web into the finest of books' is fine but it doesn't lead to commissioning focus. The catalogue is all over the place which is both its charm and its problem. The business has had its ups and downs. Good sales months followed by less good ones. Good books selling really well such as Blood, Sweat and Tea. Other good books not finding their market. But the key directors, Clare Christian and Scott Pack, have soldiered on and TFP is now a thriving publishing company with a stable workforce, a pipeline of new books, a backlist and one of the best websites (and blog sites) in the industry. I just hope that we can continue to work with them until they're big enough to kick us in the teeth and do their own thing.

Back-office support for independent publishers is not as glamorous as publishing itself but it can rewarding and companies like TFP can grow to be the likes of Quadrille or Bloomsbury. Fingers crossed for all small publishers.

31 July 2007

Celebrity biography

I've had to say no to a unique launch party for a celebrity biography on Thursday (out of the country). It's unique because the average age of the invitees is somewhere in the eighties and the main tipple will be tea. And it's unique because this celebrity biography is about a not very famous person who deserves to be more famous as opposed to the normal book about a famous person who has little to say and not much talent.

The biographee is Alice Herz Sommer (do listen to this Woman's Hour interview) and the book is A Garden of Eden in Hell.

By permission of Pan Macmillan, London.

Alice was born in 1903 (work it out) and is still going strong. She suffered in a Nazi concentration camp but continued to play piano throughout the ordeal. She is still playing today and you can purchase a CD of her music from reinhard.piechocki@t.online.de .

I doubt that sales of this book will exceed those of Wayne Rooney, Jordan et al but somehow I feel it's a little more deserving.

Yesterday saw the annual Science v Nature cricket match which Nature duly won. If only the England cricket team were as reliable. Incidentally, Nature took the first three wickets with the first three balls of the Science innings. Is that one for next year's Wisden?

≤ **August 2007** ≥

Mon	Tue	Wed	Thu	Fri	Sat	Sun
30	31	1	2	3	4	5
6	7	8	9	10	11	12
13	14	15	16	17	18	19
20	21	22	23	24	25	26
27	28	29	30	31	1	2
3	4	5	6	7	8	9

Carpe diem

India duly won the latest cricket <u>test match</u> against England and thus cannot lose the three-match series and have a very good chance of winning it by drawing or winning the last game. They bowled and batted very well and deserved the victory.

The England management will have various explanations and will point to various turning points over the five days of the game. However, I think the series was forfeited by England on the mid-afternoon of the fourth day of the previous game. England had built a lead of more than 350 with their star batsman, Kevin Pietersen, with a century to his name. Instead of launching an all-out attack on India they batted sedately and unproductively for an extra hour to add a few more runs and reduce the chance of India winning. As a result they had no opportunity to bowl at India before the tea break. The forecast for the following day suggested rain. The England lead was almost impregnable. There was only one reason to bat on – the fear of losing. In the end, the rain did arrive on Monday just in time to save India. Had England not been afraid of losing they would definitely have won the game – and demoralised India and almost certainly won the series. A great example of knowing when to be brave and seize the moment. It's sad that England failed but great for India and for cricket – and I hope (but doubt) that the lesson will be learnt.

Incidentally, the same applies to publishing. Carpe diem.

It's the first of the month. In July this blog had 84682 visits, a come-down from the amazing June statistics caused by the <u>Google heist</u> post. However, total visits to date have reached 991,226, within spitting distance of a golden blog award.

Fear and hope

One of the best sources of news about future developments is <u>Ray Hammond's</u> monthly digest, <u>Glimpses of the Future</u>. This month's issue contains this piece (based on research originally published in <u>Nature Neuroscience</u>) which perhaps is relevant to my posting of <u>yesterday</u> about the England cricket team's fear of losing. But would Cdk5 count as performance enhancing?

A Cure For Fear

Are you afraid of fear itself? MIT biochemists <u>have identified a molecular mechanism behind fear</u>, and successfully cured it in mice.

Researchers from <u>MIT's Picower Institute for Learning and Memory</u> hope that their work could lead to the first drug to treat the millions of adults who suffer each year from persistent, debilitating fears – including hundreds of soldiers returning from conflict in Iraq and Afghanistan.

Inhibiting a kinase, an enzyme that change proteins, called Cdk5 facilitates the extinction of fear learned in a particular context, <u>Li-Huei Tsai, Picower Professor </u>of Neuroscience in the Department of Brain and Cognitive Sciences and colleagues showed.

And as a follow-up to another recent posting about <u>Alice Herz Sommer</u> here is an interview with her which appears on the <u>Pan Macmillan website</u> It's not quite in the league of Mel Brooks's and Carl Reiner's <u>2000 year old man</u> but what is?

What do you remember best from your childhood?

The best memory of my childhood is playing music with my brother Paul. I was not yet ten years old and he was only a little older, and evening after evening my mother said, 'Come on children, get playing.' She would sit down next to the stove and we'd play anything that came to our mind – Schumann most frequently, I think. We had a huge repertoire.

What is your happiest memory?

The happiest moment of my life was the birth of my son on June 21, 1937.

What is your saddest memory?

The sudden, unexpected death of my only son, Raphael, in November 2001. Living with this painful memory is a daily challenge.

What is your favourite time of day?

I think it is the morning – the three hours that I play the piano.

Where is your favourite place in the world?

My favourite place in the world is in the middle of nature – anywhere.

What is the most important thing you have learned in your long life?

Don't expect others to make you happy. Happiness does not come to you through others. You find happiness if you have a challenge in your life – and you fulfill it.

What advice would you give for a healthy old age?

Discipline! Especially if one reaches old age. You need to be disciplined. A routine to keep to. Time for your tasks. And time for physical exercise. Even it is just a daily walk.

Who is your favourite composer?

When I was young it was definitely Schumann. He is just adorable. Now I am older I love Beethoven and Schubert. Beethoven – because his music is deeply human and universal, and it represents endlessness. And Schubert, because his music makes you feel you are talking to God.

Do you still play the piano?

Every day! For almost 100 years. Despite my two crippled fingers I will keep playing until my last hour.

What advice would you give a young musician today?

You've got to work with phenomenal passion, and unbelievably hard! Otherwise it comes to nothing and you won't succeed.

Digital copyright – again

This link is to an article in yesterday's New York Times. The piece is entitled 'Content makers are accused of exaggerating copyright' and is about a complaint made by the Computer and Communications Industry Asssociation to the US Federal Trade Commission. Here are the first two paragraphs of their complaint. You can read the full attack on their website home page.

The Computer & Communications Industry Association (CCIA) announced today that it has filed a Federal Trade Commission complaint on behalf of consumers against Major League Baseball, the National Football League, NBC/Universal and several other corporations. CCIA alleges that the named corporations have misled consumers for years, often misrepresenting their rights through deceptive and threatening statements. The complaint, part of CCIA's newly sponsored DefendFairUse.org initiative, is aimed at exposing how media and sports organizations have systematically misled consumers with regard to their legal rights to use content, and to protect those rights in the digital age.

'Every one of us has seen or heard that copyright warning at the beginning of a sports game, DVD or book,' said Ed Black, CCIA President and CEO, during a press conference at the National Press Club. 'These corporations use these warnings not to educate their consumers, but to intimidate them.'

A glance at the association's list of members shows how powerful they might be. Clearly, the main battlegorund is video where the owners of rights to sporting events etc are getting fed up with the constant abuse of these rights and are taking legal action against the owners of youtube, for instance. This seems to be a counter-attack. However, book publishers are caught up in the row – Penguin and Harcourt.

Thankfully Macmillan has not been named and we have no need to waste money on hordes of lawyers to defend us against these absurd charges. The warnings at the front of books are the result of legal advice and are what they are – neither misleading nor intimidating. It is ridiculous to imply otherwise and the CCIA should perhaps look at the legal small print which comes attached to the software its members sell – 'people in glass houses' comes to mind.

Copyright in the Internet age is indeed a complex and challenging issue for everyone but this sort of action does nothing to help. It merely siphons money to lawyers and creates antagonism where none need exist, provided that the legitimate rights of content creators (authors in the case of publishing) are respected and valued.

Our publicity triumph of the week relates to this story about the potential for treatment of patients in a minimally conscious state. So far we've had the front pages of The Guardian and Telegraph, a big banner in the Times and articles in the New York Times, Washington Post and LA Times, not to mention coverage on NBC nightly News, ABC News, the CBS Early Show and much else – not bad for 'hard science'. Of course, the story of an unconscious person 'waking' after six years is pretty amazing and newsworthy but it requires real skill to have the story reported (more or less) accurately and globally through all media. Congratulations to the whole team.

VAT on print

Britain enjoys a zero rate of value-added tax on newspapers, magazines and books (and children's clothing). Elsewhere in the European Union varying rules apply but books are frequently taxed (e.g. Ireland – corrigendum – silly me, see comment below). The EU, in its predictable way, would like to simplify (i.e. dictate standard terms) tax rules across Europe and the European Commission has opened a political debate on the subject. Fortunately the British Government has promised to resist change to the current system and we can only hope this is a promise they intend to keep.

But I have a further question. If it is important not to tax reading (which I support) why does the Government think that taxing on-line reading makes sense? Readers have to pay VAT on on-line subscriptions and purchases of digital downloads. If we could liberate these from tax it could make a huge difference to the speed of adoption of digital information and make very little difference to budgetted tax revenues.

The Guardian reports that being a librarian is among the least stressful jobs (along with postmen and hairdressers). I can well believe it but perhaps a little bit more stress would improve the library service? It's worth checking out Katherine Rushton's blog about this (and other library matters in the future).

Et alors?

I've been immersed in a fascinating newspaper aimed at ex-patriate Brits living in France – French News. The main story is, as you might expect, 'Traditional dinner keeps French slimmer.'

But there's plenty of other stuff. France's suicide rate is double that of Britain's. There is detailed analysis of the new President Nicolas Sarkozy's tax-reducing policies and how it affects British immigrants. I enjoyed this headline in the La Vie est Belle section: Supervising his erection in the Haute-Vienne, Barry Cornell finds he has to contend with tradesmen who speak French, Welsh, Yorkshire and Latin.' I was pleased to note Le parti du plaisir led by ex-stripper Miss Cindy Lee has promised to create a network of nudist camps across France if elected next time around.

However, I was most pleased to discover in the sports section that 'Et alors' is the equivalent of 'Howzat' and that on Sunday 26 August on the Damazan Cricket Club ground there will be the finals of Siddalls Cup between Tarn and Toulouse.

Penguins stopped play

I am absolutely clear that I am incapable of writing a book. So are most people (incapable of writing a book that is). It is extremely difficult. It is even more clear that – and I know it – I couldn't write a great book. Great books are rare and wonderful and require a slice of genius. However, there are some books which I half-think I should have had a crack at writing. I've just read one such.

The <u>book</u> is about a team of (almost entirely) useless cricketers known as the Captain Scott XI, named after the (failed) great explorer and against whom the <u>Baldons Cricket Club</u> (for whom I have played for more than thirty years) battled annually. The author, <u>Harry Thompson</u>, tragically died before the book was published. I remember him as a highly competitive, irritating and rather untalented opening batsman (not unlike me). He has, however, written the book I would love to have had the talent to write.

It is not just about low-quality cricketers touring the world. As a producer and writer of, amongst other things, <u>Have I got news for you</u>, he knows how to put the boot into the likes of <u>British Airways</u>. However, he is also wise. In one scene, the team is enjoying the low cost of food and drink in Buenos Aires. A bottle of <u>Malbec</u> which would cost £20 in London was selling for £2. Rather than buy the £2 bottle they wondered how a £20 bottle of Malbec in BsAs would taste. Out of this world, of course. And a good strategy.

It's an excellent and funny book published by <u>John Murray</u> and I'm sure they won't mind my pointing out the mis-spelling of 'genius' in the <u>blurb</u> of the hardback.

PS on book prices. The average price of a meal for one in the new restaurants in London as recommended by food critic <u>Fay Maschler</u> is £41. Makes Harry Potter,even at full price, a real snip.

🔖 08 August 2007

Man Booker Prize longlist

The lottery has begun. Thirteen out of 110 entries have got through to the next round, the shortlist of six to be announced on September 6. Picador has one title on the list, <u>Self Help</u> by the youngest writer on the list, <u>Edward Docx</u>. Fingers crossed.

By permission of Pan Macmillan, London.

Of course the list can be interpreted any which way. The Bookseller's headline 'Indies shine on Booker's dozen' isn't really borne out by the facts. I'm not sure that two out of thirteen is a particularly high strike rate. And where are the darling 'indies' such as Faber, Canongate etc? A more appropriate headline might be 'Triumph for conglomerates as Random House bags four'. The Guardian went for the shock giant-killing story but I'm not sure that Ian McEwan and A.N.Wilson count as complete outsiders. The Chairman of the Judges, Sir Howard Davies, goes for the quick win approach by describing the list as 'diverse', which means absolutely nothing but wins political correctness brownie points for implying racial diversity.

The one thing I'm pretty sure about is that the dreadful shock as described in the Guardian article will soon pass and editors and literary agents wil be assuring each other that the literary manuscript in hand will definitely win next year's prize.

'The news will produce as much shock among literary agents as authors – and the editors who entered them with some confidence for yesterday's long list.'

You may have noticed the Google-supplied ads to the right of this column, although very few of you click on them to judge by my earnings from this source. I occasionally click if one catches my eye and I clicked on Manuscript Editor Online yesterday. It's a service offering scientists help with preparing their manuscripts for publication but it's a shame they can't spell 'ophthalmology' in their main catalogue. It makes you wonder. Grumpy old ex-copyeditor speaking – and I know this column is anything but literal-free, but still . . .

09 August 2007

SciFoo and South Africa

How many times does something have to happen for it to be an annual event? In September 2006 I wrote about the first SciFoo camp. It's just happened again (which makes it a tradition in contemporary time scales) and Timo Hannay has blogged about it. For those of you who don't know what I'm talking about just follow the link and be (a bit) enlightened and here is a para from Timo's blog with some more direct links:

'SciFoo '07 was wonderfully intense, mind-expanding and surreal. Organisationally, it was a bit less stressful than last year's inaugural event (at least for me), mainly because we knew it was going to work to some degree. Indeed, the success of SciFoo '06 lead to a fair amount of anticipation this year, best described in words by

Jonathan Eisen and in pictures by Pierre Lindenbaum. (See also Pierre's cartoons from the event itself.)

Such is the variety and (relative) anarchy of the event that there's no such thing as one SciFoo experience, only 200+ personal experiences. To give a feel of the occasion, read Henry Gee's opening post and have a look at Bora's photos, photos, and more photos.'

On the other side of the world, everyone at Macmillan has been delighted for the Pan Macmillan team in South Africa who have just been voted International Publisher of the Year at the awards evening in spite of being one of the smaller operations. In particular, our team was commended for its commitment to children's books, excellent service and good pricing structures. I would offer an additional personal accolade. Pan Macmillan are the crew everyone wants to succeed because they are so professional and so pleasant too. Here they are, small in numbers, showing but perfect in performance, showing off their Oscars.

By permission of Pan Macmillan, London.

A propos of absolutely nothing, I am ashamed to admit that I have only just discovered (pointed to by a friend) Uncyclopedia, the content-free competitor to the ultra-serious reference websites. I particularly liked their definition of wiki:

The term 'wiki' derives from the Hawaiian 'wiki-wiki' which means 'some random guy on the Internet said it, so it must be true.'

10 August 2007

Books and threats

I was in Surrey yesterday attending part of the brilliantly organised Palgrave Macmillan sales conference. Do click on the link which will take you to their US site which naturally enough has a slant towards books published originally in the USA but which are of global interest. The blandness of offerings from the much of the retail trade can sometimes undermine confidence in the publishing of high-quality, challenging and non-TV-related titles but a day at that sales conference and a trawl through the websites here and in the USA dispelled all that. And the surroundings were pretty palatial (but economic) too.

I used the opportunity to discuss with our sales and publishing people some of the concerns, threats and opportunities of the digital age. Of course, Palgrave Macmillan, being an academic publisher, has fewer concerns about territorial erosion than a general trade publisher would.

Nonetheless there are real challenges and the principal one in my opinion is the devaluation and commoditisation of information. 'Free' does not always (or often) mean better but somehow the Internet has encouraged the view that information should be free. The row over the Google heist showed that many people value physical objects such as laptop computers far more highly than the information, wisdom, entertainment the computer might contain.

Another area where 'free' is considered ethically superior is within the open access debate which has been reignited recently by Yale University science libraries' decision not to continue funding BioMed Central's open-access publishing experiment on the basis that the business model was not viable in the long run. BMC have responded robustly and the debate will continue but it is just one example of the turbulent waters in which publishers are having to swim.

All this simply underscores the importance of the value of copyright, not just to authors and publishers, but to students, teachers, researchers, readers and to all developers of new ideas. Thank goodness there are powerful laws and organisations protecting creativity.

11 August 2007

Good news week for libraries

This week's Bookseller has a headline which may mark a turning point for the better in the sad saga of the decline of the British public library system: 'Tim Coates to save Hillingdon £260,000'.

Tim has reproduced the article in full on his Good Library blog but here is an extract:

Library campaigner Tim Coates has designed a major overhaul of Hillingdon libraries that is projected to increase opening hours and book stocks, and save £260,000. The plans have been approved by the borough council and are expected to be implemented from September. They will see all 17 libraries in the borough entirely refurbished, Starbucks coffee made available in every branch, opening hours extended and the supply chain simplified.

Tim has made himself rather unpopular among the mandarins of the public library service by pointing out uncomfortable truths, by challenging politically correct but absurd views on the role of libraries, and by being consistently rude and abrasive. This unpopularity has from time to time set his campaign back. There are those in positions of power who would vote against absolutely anything Tim suggests.

However, perhaps his approach is correct. Perhaps campaigners need to be obnoxious from time to time. Perhaps civil servants and politicians need to be insulted. In any event I believe the tide may be turning for the public library service and that Tim's ideas will be seen to be sensible.

The objective is to have libraries better stocked with books (radical idea), open when people want them to be open (seems sensible), in a safe and clean environment (sound thinking), managed by front-line librarians (they understand how libraries work) and at no extra cost to the taxpayer (phew). All pretty straightforward but there are those who want to see libraries as something else – as tools of social change, as outreach centres, as vehicles for diversity – just take a few minutes to scroll through some of the stories on the Good Library Guide and be horrified.

Here is a reminder of the simplistic but hard-hitting Occam's Razor version of his views which I originally wrote about in January:

- The library service is for people and its only purpose is to respond to their needs (currently it does not do this adequately)

- It is essentially about reading (currently it is not sufficiently so)

- Its operation must be simple (because at present it is too complex)

– Those responsible for providing the service are those who work in the libraries (currently they are not able to be).

– Those accountable to the public are councillors (currently they do not account).

🔖 12 August 2007

Letter from Australia

Until today I was unaware of Tower Books, an independent distributor in Australia. Neither do I know its director Michael Rakusin. He has just written a letter to the major bookshop chain, Angus & Robertson, which you can read about in the Sydney Morning Herald blog complete with 176 comments, so far. A&R are demanding lump sum payments from small and medium-sized publishers if they want to continue to be stocked.

This letter is to be treasured and I reproduce it here in full for your enjoyment and appreciation. I can think of other potential recipients of such a letter. It's also worthwhile going to Sydney Morning Herald link to view the original letter from Charlie Rimmer, particularly the last line: 'If you would like to discuss this with me in more detail, I am delighted to confirm an appointment with you at 1.00 p.m. on 17th August for 10 minutes at my offices at 379 Collins Street, Melbourne.'

6 August 2007

Mr Charlie Rimmer
ARW Group Commercial Manager
14th Floor, 379 Collins Street,
Melbourne, VIC 3000

Dear Mr Rimmer

We are in receipt of your letter of 30 July 2007 terminating our further supply to Angus & Robertson. As you have requested, we will cancel all Angus & Robertson Company orders on 17 August and will desist from any further supply to your stores.

I have to say that my initial response on reading your letter as to how you propose to 'manage' your business in the future was one of voluble hilarity, I literally burst out laughing aloud. My second response was to note the unmitigated arrogance of your communication, I could not actually believe I was reading an official letter from Angus & Robertson on an Angus & Robertson letterhead.

My reply to you will perforce be a lengthy one. I hope you will take the trouble to read it, you may learn something. Then again, when I look at the level of real response we have had from Angus & Robertson over the past six or so years, I somehow doubt it.

The first thing I would say to you is that arrogance of the kind penned by you in your letter of 30 July is an unenviable trait in any officer of any company, no matter how important that individual thinks himself or his company, no matter how dominant that company may be in its market sector. Business has a strange habit of moving in cycles: today's villain may be tomorrow's hero. It is quite possible to part from a business relationship in a pleasant way leaving the door open for future engagement. Sadly, in this case, you have slammed and bolted it.

More to the point, however, we have watched our business with Angus & Robertson dwindle year upon year since 2000. We had to wear the cost of sub-economic ordering from you through ownership changes, SAP installation, new management, and stock overhang. In summary our business with you has dropped from over $1.2 million at the end of 2000 to less than $600,000 in 2007.

You would be quite correct to question whether our offering to the market had changed in any way. The answer can be derived from the fact that during the same period our business with Dymocks, Book City, QBD and Borders continued to grow in double digits, our business with your own franchise stores has grown healthily, and our overall business during the same period has grown by more than 50%.

Six years ago we were allowed to send reps to your company stores and do stock checks. Then these were 'uninvited' and we had to rely on monthly rep calls to your Buying Office. Subsequently even that was too much trouble; your Buying Office was too busy to see us, so we were asked to make new title submissions electronically. Every few months the new submission template became more and more complex. This year, we have been allowed quarterly visits to your Buying Office at which we were to be given the opportunity to sell to all your Category Managers. At the first, we did indeed see all of the Category Managers – but they didn't buy any of the titles offered. At the second, one Category Manager was available, and again no purchases resulted. At the last (only last week), two Category Managers attended. Through all of this, your overworked and under resourced Buying Department never got to see, let alone read, an actual book. While one may be forgiven for believing that Angus & Robertson is actually a company purveying 'Sale' signs, I do believe you are still in the book business?

That Angus & Robertson is struggling for margin does not surprise me. It amazes me that the message has not become clear to your 'management': there are only so many costs you can cut, there is only so much destiny you can put in the hands of a computer system, there are only so many sweetheart deals you can do with large suppliers. After that, in order to prosper one actually has to know one's product and have an appropriately staffed buying department. Most importantly, one has to train sales people of competence. You will never beat the DDSs at their cost cutting game, you will only prosper by putting 'books' back into Angus & Robertson. And it would seem to me paramount to stop blaming suppliers for your misfortunes, trying ever harder to squeeze them to death, and actually focus on your core incompetencies in order to redress them.

How a business that calls itself a book business is going to do without titles such as the Miles Franklin Prize winning book or titles like Rich Dad Poor Dad (according to this week's Sydney Morning Herald it is still the fifth best selling business title in Australia nine years after publication) is beyond me. And how in good conscience Australia's self-purported largest chain of book shops proposes to exclude emerging

Australian writers who are represented by the smaller distributors, is an equal mystery.

We too have expectations Mr Rimmer. We have had the same expectations for many years, none of which Angus & Robertson have been willing to deliver:

—That we are treated with equal respect to the larger publishers within the obvious parameters of commercial reality;
—That your Buying Department is able and willing to assess our books with equal seriousness to those of the big publishers and buy them appropriately;
—That you recognise the fundamental differences between the smaller distributors and the larger publishers and stop demanding of us terms that we are unable to deliver;
—That you would support and help develop Australian literature.

Had you made any effort to meet these expectations you would have found the niche we should have occupied in your business, as have all other book shops, and you would have found our contribution to the profitability of your business would have been dramatically different.

In summary, we reject out of hand this notion that somehow, even giving you 45% discount on a Sale or Return basis, with free freight to each of your individual stores, where we make less than half of that on the same book, puts us in the 'category of unacceptable profitability'. We have seen Angus & Robertson try this tactic before – about 12 years ago Angus & Robertson decided that unless we gave them a 50% discount, they would not buy from us any longer. We refused. Angus & Robertson desisted from buying from us for seven months. We survived, Angus & Robertson came back cap in hand.

We have seen Myer effectively eliminate smaller suppliers. We survived and prospered but look at the Myer Book Departments today.

We have seen David Jones decide that it had too many publishers to deal with and to exclude the smaller suppliers. We survived and prospered but look at the David Jones Book Departments today.

David Jones and Myer sell other goods; Angus & Robertson does not.

That the contents of your letter of 30 July are both immoral and unethical, I have no doubt. That they probably contravene the Trade Practices Act, I shall leave to the ACCC to determine. (Five percent interest PER DAY !!!)

If you wish to discuss any of the contents hereof you may call my secretary for an appointment at my office in Frenchs Forest. I shall be marginally more generous than you and at least allow you to pick a convenient time.

Michael Rakusin
Director
Tower Books Pty Ltd
Carpentaria, Alexis Wright : Winner of 50th Anniversary Miles Franklin Literary Prize, 2007

Copy: Graeme Samuel, Chairman, ACCC
Rod Walker, Chairman, ARW Group
Ian Draper, ARW Group Managing Director
Rickard Gardell, Managing Director, Pacific Equity Partners
Simon Pillar, Managing Director, Pacific Equity Partners

Barbara Cullen, CEO, ABA
Maree McCaskill, CEO, APA

13 August 2007

Letter from America

Just over a month ago I wrote about a book I had been sent out of the blue by the author, David Silverman.

I raved about it and so have a few others. As a result I've been in e-mail correspondence with the author and he has kindly agreed to write a guest blog about the contemporary American author tour. Here it is and very grateful I am.

'Are you going on a book tour?' friends asked me, and I'm sure, being nice.

'Why yes, I am going to the Midwest.'

'Don't you live in New York City?' they asked, eyeing my newly purchased corduroy jacket querulously.

Kansas City, Kansas

My first bookstore. Since my book takes place in the bordering state of Iowa, I expect a band, or maybe a microphone, or at least a couple chairs.

The store manager says she will 'set up the table' and offers me 'something from the café.' I've already eaten, and by her reaction when I say 'no thanks,' I sense that more experienced authors know to make the most of the café.

I sit in the middle of the store. I have a small pile of books and a pen. You can't miss me.

But the store's few patrons and the local knitting group avoid me. They dodge to the left through the dollar books. They shoot to the right, wedging between mysteries and large-eyed puppy calendars.

No one makes eye contact—as if I were a wolverine. Are they afraid I will lacerate their jugulars with a book? After four hours of reshuffling my pile of books, I wonder if I that might improve sales. Perhaps the transformation of writer to wolverine occurs regularly at book signings.

Ultimately, three high school students befriend me. They smile, but don't buy. It hits me, they can't afford it. I slide a $10 bill under the cover and make my first sale. Since I earn a $1 per book, I've just lost $9.

Omaha, Nebraska

I take photos of the behinds of people who exit without looking at me. The store manager tells me the last author only had a couple of dozen people come. His name was Newt Gingrich.

Later, I sell three books to three drunk men in the Holiday Inn bar. This triples my sales.

Des Moines, Iowa

I worry that my ex-employees will show up with sharp sticks and poke me for writing 'snarkily' about them. No one shows up. I get an organic turkey melt and caramel mocha latte from the cafe.

At the Holiday Inn, the angry clerk assures me, 'All the rooms are booked. You have no room. This desk is closed.' I sleep in the parking lot, hiding under my corduroy jacket to avoid the security guard.

In Sum

I drove over a thousand miles in three days, spent several hundred dollars, and slept in a Chevy.

Let's face it, the world has gone online, and, unlike the book tour, my online publicity has led to sales everywhere from California to Scotland. It's also been free.

So does any hope remain for old school feet on the ground? The answer came a few weeks later, at the B&N in my hometown of Kingston, NY.

I shook out my corduroy and worried the store manager would resent having put out so many chairs. But then people started to show up: high school classmates, parents of a college friend, other friends, and some guy—at random!

I am given a microphone. They laugh. I sell some books. And I remember that any publicity is good publicity.

A sample of my book Typo: The Last American Typesetter or How I Made and Lost $4 Million is here.

Or just buy it here.

And lastly, my website.

David Silverman

August 12, 2007

🐦 14 August 2007

August meanderings

It must be August. Yesterday's piece about author signing sessions in bookshops elicited this comment:

'It's early in the day but booksignings are best compared to sex ; sometimes more enjoyable than others, but seldom a total failure!'

Hmmm.

In the excitement of August I failed to record the millionth visit to this blog. It appears to have happened on Saturday 4 August with a VAT on print entry and some excellent comments. I can't tell exactly who the visitor was – there were 2804 visits that day, slightly below par but not bad for a weekend. So, whoever paid the millionth visit, welcome and I hope you return.

More good news on the public library front following on last week's. CILIP, which is a horrible acronym for the equally horrible-sounding but actually brilliant Chartered Institute of Librarians and Information Professionals, has come out all guns blazing in an attack on local and national politicians for the decline in support for the library services and an apparent disregard for the views of the poeple who know best, the librarians. Hooray, sense may be beginning to prevail. Here's a quote from CILIP's letter to the government minister responsible:

'A number of Public Library Authorities are planning drastic reductions in the number of professional staff they employ, and some are even planning to hand over control of library services to local community groups without any professional expertise at all,' explained Bob McKee, CILIP Chief Executive. 'We hear talk about improved customer service and greater community management, but this is just spin-doctoring to cover up the reality of budget cuts and job losses. The truth is that without adequate professional expertise the quality of service will be reduced and the future of the service put at risk.'

Finally, hooray for the cricketers of India who won the test match series against England convincingly and properly. England's pusillanimity on the Sunday of the first test match was the trigger but then the Indian team made the most of everything that followed. The old colonial power has been put in its place by the new stars – and quite right too.

🗓 15 August 2007

India Today

Yesterday Pakistan celebrated sixty years of statehood. Today India revels in sixty years of independence. Much will be written about the sub-continent and most of it will be much better informed than my thoughts.

I've been visiting India for twenty-five years, always (apart from the occasional day or two by the beach) on publishing business. My first visit was to the Delhi offices of Oxford University Press India in Ansari Road where they (and just down the road the editorial offices of the educational and higher education divisions of Macmillan India) are still situated.

My principal memory of that first visit was the large number of typists in the office. It was apparently cheaper to create file copies by retyping letters than by using carbon paper. Remember carbon paper? I was a medical editor at the time and India was responsible for the sale of largest number of preclinical textbooks through the British-government much missed ELBS scheme (notice that the debate was about what better scheme the Government would devise to replace ELBS – ha ha ha). We used to sell 60,000 copies of each volume of Cunningham's Manual of Practical Anatomy in India – those were the days.

Macmillan India has been operating since 1892, way before Independence but always in the Macmillan tradition of publishing independence. We now employ well over 3000 people in I don't know how many locations (probably more than a hundred if one includes showrooms etc). Pan Macmillan, Palgrave Macmillan and Nature Publishing Group all have operations in India in addition to the activities of the main Macmillan India operations.

We have high-tech offices in Gurgaon, Delhi, Bangalore, Chennai and elsewhere where we typeset, process text, copyedit, fulfil subscriptions, build websites, develop software, innovate. The growth is astounding, the challenges enormous and the results excellent.

In the days of the Raj, India was always referred to as the jewel in the crown. For Macmillan it still is. I wish everyone in Macmillan India (and everyone in India) a great celebration and I hope I'll be there (just) to celebrate your century forty years hence.

 16 August 2007

Did you know?

I am indebted to the Pan Macmillan internal blog, The Digitalist, for this link to a site about the future of education. I'd recommend that you switch off the sound unless you're into meaningless electronic musical drivel but the graphics are terrific and the messages clear.

I'm off to a meeting right now but will later today add a spot of nostalgia.

And the nostalgia comes courtesy of Alysoun Sanders who runs the Macmillan Archive in Basingstoke. If you take the trouble to checck out the links you'll also be introduced to the riches of the old newsletters which are a treasure house for historians of publishing.

Macmillan's involvement in India from pre-Independence days to the 1990s can be found in articles that appeared in Macmillan News, the company newsletter that ran for 30 years from 1961.

294 Bow Bazar Street, Calcutta

At the time of independence Macmillan had 3 branches in India based in Bombay, Madras and Calcutta. K R Clemens Manager of the Calcutta branch, worked in India during the three and a half decades that bridged the last years of British India 'with its endeavours and its last vestiges of pomp and circumstance, and the first twenty years of the independent Republic of India' and succeeded C A Parkhouse who had been in India with Macmillan since 1913. Clemens saw changes, which were 'great and far-reaching' calling for 'constant adjustments'. On his retirement in 1968 he commended 'the co-operative effort that has always existed' within the company.

Mrs. Parkhurst with Mr. and Mrs. Stagg

David Green who succeeded Mr Stagg as Manager of the Madras (Chennai) branch also tells his story of post-independence publishing and the growth of local publishing and nationalisation of school textbooks and the opening of showrooms in Bangalore, Hyderabad, Coimbatore, Trichinopoly and Rivandrum. The 'Stories to Remember' series that began in 1954 are still on the Macmillan Education list.

In January 1970 the newly formed public company, Macmillan Company of India Ltd with its headquarters in Chennai took over the role of the 3 branches and in 1972 the main offices were moved to Delhi.

By 1979 the process of indianisation was fully implemented and the company has continued to grow and to expand into areas that were never envisaged by Alexander Macmillan when he first embarked on plans to publish a series of books especially for India more than 140 years ago in the 1860s.

🐦 17 August 2007

Publish and be damned

From time to time, somebody asks me how on earth or why on earth we published a particular book. The easy thing to say is that I wasn't involved in the decision (which is true in 99% of cases) but that feels like a cop out. Ultimately, if the book carries the Macmillan or Picador (or whatever imprint) name I am responsible to some degree. I try to explain that it seems to me that there are three main criteria for deciding whether to publish a particular book, in no particular order;

It is a good book – well-written, accurate, timely etc;

It is by an author whose career we want to be associated with in the long term;

It might make money.

I don't think all three criteria have to be fulfilled on every occasion but it's usually a good idea if two of them are. I believe the bulk of what we publish passes this test. If none is fulfilled by a particular book, then the only response to a complainant is 'we got it wrong.'

What I hope we never do is make editorial decisions based on internal prejudices. There is a row brewing in the USA as described in this New York Times article. The Israel Lobby and US Foreign Policy is published by Farrar, Straus and Giroux next month. The article from which it was derived which describes how the Jewish lobby effectively controls US policy was attacked for implied anti-semitism but the team at FSG clearly think the book is important and defensible irrespective of criticism. And all power to their elbow.

Meanwhile, just a few blocks away from FSG (Union Square, New York City), the team at Palgrave Macmillan USA (Flatiron Building) are preparing for the publication of The Deadliest Lies: the Israel lobby and the myth of Jewish control which argues just the opposite as described in the NYT article.

I have no doubt that there are many people who think that one or other of these books should not have been published. Personally, I think they both fulfil all three criteria and I am proud that they are both published by companies within the Holtzbrinck Group of which Macmillan is a part. Freedom to express opinions, however controversial, is part of our role as publishers.

18 August 2007

Dear Bill

One of Macmillan's most loyal and most entertaining authors, Bill Deedes, died yesterday. For more about him just follow this link to today's vast number of news stories. Even better, sample one of his books the most recent of which has just come out in paperback with the author aged 94.

By permission of Pan Macmillan, London.

Two links for those interested in the future of educational publishing. University Publishing in a Digital Age is a report written by an old friend and former head of Oxford University Press USA, Laura Brown, principally about the university press sector in the America. It's a strange thing but, whilst British university presses are among the most successful and vibrant publishers in the world, their American equivalents by and large are tiny and very traditional. I think this is because the Britsh ones (OUP in particular) have been forced to stand on their own feet by virtue of the relative poverty of their owners. The American ones have traditionally received some form of support from their very wealthy owners. Subsidies don't work. Anyway, Laura's report is an excellent overview and it's well worth reading the conclusions and summaries if not the whole very long thing.

The second link is to a very basic and almost empty landing page for CourseSmart. The reason for mentioning it is that it is a very rare beast – an alliance of publishers working together to find solutions to the delivery of digital information to students. I wonder whether there should be similar initiatives elsewhere in the world . . .

19 August 2007

Earthquake in Peru

One of the most difficult parts of being part of a very international business is trying to be aware of the problems affecting each of our businesses, both commercial and environmental. Clearly on September 11, 2001 everyone rushed to establish whether their colleagues, friends and family were safe. It becomes harder when the disaster is less globally newsworthy or in a more distant culture or geography. The earthquake in Peru is an example. We have a small but hugely committed Macmillan Education business in Lima. Thank goodness all our team are safe but of course they all know people caught up in the tragedy and the after effects could be as bad as the disaster itself.

Obituaries of Bill Deedes are still flying off the presses. I particularly liked this tribute by Alan Watkins in today's Independent on Sunday where he quotes the wonderful Deedesian mixed metaphor: 'You can't make an omelette without frying eggs.' I couldn't agree more.

20 August 2007

Popular science and missions

There is a school of thought (particularly prevalent in the UK) which says that 'educated' people must be able to discuss literature and politics (and maybe business, wine, food, sport etc). Equally however, it is considered quite cool (or certainly not shocking) to claim almost total ignorance of science. 'Popular science' is frequently a contradiction in terms.

Of course, issues like climate change, the Internet, genetic engineering, and health issues have started to make basic scientific understanding a 'must' but the level of discussion among even 'well-educated' people is pretty embarrassingly poor.

Macmillan Science has published some great books trying to address this. The latest is Ten Questions Science Can't Answer (Yet) by Michael Hanlon.

Books like this make a difference but in addition I'd like to point you to News at Nature. Without any dumbing down, this site allows non-scientists to discover what's happening at the cutting edge of research. It is really the most authoritative and accessible source of scientific news and fulfils the first part of Nature's two-pronged mission 'to place before the general public the grand results of Scientific Work and Scientific Discovery; and to urge the claims of Science to a more general recognition in Education and in Daily Life'. This comes from the first page of the first issue in 1869. A more recent mission statement can be found here although an editorial about it has started a bit of a flurry in the blogosphere (which incorrectly is commenting about an amended version of the 1869 statement – oh what fun we have):

First, to serve scientists through prompt publication of significant advances in any branch of science, and to provide a forum for the reporting and discussion of news and issues concerning science. Second, to ensure that the results of science are rapidly disseminated to the public throughout the world, in a fashion that conveys their significance for knowledge, culture and daily life.

21 August 2007

Prime Minister's question time

I see that Tony Blair has appointed the hotshot Washington lawyer, Bob Barnett, to get a deal for his memoirs. There is little doubt that this will be an important and big-selling book and that the forthcoming auction will be interesting, to say the least.

There are many variables and imponderables in calculating what advance to offer. When will the book be published? How good will it be? How revealing or otherwise? How much would a newspaper pay for serialization? What might be the scope and size of translation rights? How well might the book sell in the UK and USA? How much would the publisher have to set aside for security and management diversion?

As an aid to all the publishers who might be bidding can I invite you to suggest:

1. How much should be the top offer for world rights?

2. How much will be the top offer for world rights?

3. Which publisher will triumph?

Over to you.

And here is a link to an amazing tribute to Bill Deedes.

22 August 2007

On retailers becoming publishers

Once upon a time, when I was a medical editor at Oxford University Press (incidentally did anyone else notice this rather intriguing headline Oxford Publishing Sold last week?) I came across an internal memo from earlier days saying something like 'since Blackwell's have failed to achieve higher discounts from scientific and medical publishers they have decided to go into publishing themselves'. This signalled the foundation of Blackwell Scientific Publishing which, after various mergers and acquisitions, was sold last year for £600m, many many times more valuable than the wonderful bookshop which spawned it.

The concern at the time was that Blackwell would favour their own publications when it came to retailing, thus disadvantaging other publishers. I don't think this ever happened and in any event the Blackwell shop was never a dominant part of the overall market for scientific or medical books.

However, I was reminded of this by an announcement from Amazon yesterday. I urge you to follow this link to a blog by Timo Hannay commenting on the announcement.

Please read his thoughts, read the press release from Amazon's CreateSpace, read Timo's piece again. Sit down and think about it from a book publisher's point of view. Is Timo right? Could Amazon succeed where Blackwell were only partly succesful (albeit £600m richer)? Interesting times.

On a lighter note I was at a meeting yesterday which included a number of academics. One of them reminded me of a marvellous quote which he attributed to C.P.Snow but which appears to belong to Henry Kissinger. Either way, it's a great quote and applicable to many situations:

'University politics are vicious precisely because the stakes are so small.'

The stakes in the publishing business right now are not small, so let's hope the politics are therefore not vicious.

23 August 2007

England 1 Germany 2

For the last few months there's been a German intern working for us just outside my office. He goes back to university to finish his studies tomorrow and so we're giving him a drink or two this evening to say thanks for all the good work he's done and for being so understanding of our strange British ways. As I was leaving the office yesterday evening he asked whether the drinks would still be on if England lost yesterday's friendly soccer game. Of course the drinks are on and of course England lost. Anglo-German soccer relations have been normalised since that great game in 2001. I see that Brown and Merkel were at the game. What was their score?

But it's good to see that the BBC have given headline space to Christian Schweiger's Britain, Germany and the Future of the European Union which we published late last year and which argues that our two countries are the ideal partners in Europe (although I think the natural German assumption that the EU is a good thing in itself is not so widely held in Britain).

I was disappointed that yesterday's blog about Amazon's new initiative CreateSpace generated only two comments so far – it's not too late. I'll be interested to see how this all develops. I wonder how author-friendly the Amazon contract is. I wonder what will happen when one of on-demand authors is sued for libel. I wonder what will happen if one of the books is a pirate edition. I wonder where the quality control will come from. Perhaps someone at Amazon/CreateSpace would like to address these issues.

Although it's August and Britain tends to go on holiday there is still plenty of activity at Macmillan. Yesterday we announced our intention to acquire Frank Brothers in Delhi. Together with our existing businesses this will make Macmillan the number one educational publisher in India and underscores our commitment to education and business there.

24 August 2007

Death of the publisher?

The Amazon announcement which I wrote about earlier in the week is generating a great deal of debate. Mark Thwaite, who is managing editor of The Book Depository has contributed an interesting piece with good comments to the Bookseller blog with the same title as I've used here.

I have also been granted permission to reprint an excellent article about it by Dan Penny at Outsell. The only place where I fundamentally disagree with Dan is his worked example showing that an author would earn a royalty of $12.35 on a $25 book. The truth is that a 100-page paperback work of fiction will not sell for $25. If you do the maths at a more realistic $10, the author would receive $1.85 per copy. A more typical extent for a $10 novel would be 200 pages and in this case the author would actually have to pay Amazon 15 cents a copy sold, if I understand the deal correctly.

'* Amazon has launched its CreateSpace Books on Demand service, which allows authors to upload content and publish direct. How radically might this change the publishing landscape?

Important Details: CreateSpace is Amazon's new name for CustomFlix Labs, Inc., which it acquired in 2005. The new service will compete with Print On Demand companies such as Lightning Source, Xlibris and Antony Rowe, which have agreements with many STM publishers. Amazon severed its existing link with Lightning Source in 2006, in anticipation of this new service. However, CreateSpace is not partnering with publishers, but is instead inviting authors to contribute content directly.

CreateSpace has been offering customers single CDs and DVDs on demand since 2002, and it is envisaged that its new service will provide books in just the same way, aiming to ship books within 24 hours from when they are ordered. Customers pay the standard paperback price for a book, set by the author, with no setup fees or minimum orders. For authors, books must be uploaded to CreateSpace as PDFs, and he must then purchase and approve a proof copy of his book before titles can be produced on demand.

Amazon's share of each sale is calculated by taking a fixed charge of $3.15 per copy, plus a charge per page ($.02 per black and white page or $.12 per color page), plus a percentage of the list price (30% for sales through Amazon.com). For example, a 100-page black and white book sold on Amazon with a list price of $25.00 would earn an author a royalty of $12.35 per sale.

Implications: Timo Hannay at Nature suggests that this announcement 'may just prove to be the publishing news of the decade.' By accepting content direct from authors, the traditional middle-men are excluded, mirroring online self-publishing services like Lulu and as Hannay says, opening the way for Amazon to become 'the ultimate clearing house for books of all kinds (and much else besides)'.

But it may be a long time until this new world becomes a reality. Certainly the advantages of CreateSpace are clear – its speed of distribution, and its low cost. Authors using the service will also see its royalty rates compare favourably to those associated with traditional publishing models.

There are also a number of challenges which Amazon faces, and perhaps the main one will be looking after its content creators. Blogs about CreateSpace have expressed dissatisfaction with the time it takes to put uploaded content for sale on Amazon (officially, 'up to 21 days', but sometimes longer), and higher profile authors will want to see a certain level of marketing activity surrounding their book. At present, Amazon runs promotional e-mails by grouping together books that correlate according to individuals' purchasing habits. It's unclear whether CreateSpace books are to be included in these campaigns – but even if they are, authors may find that that their books are frequently squeezed out because they lack the head of steam that traditionally published books build up through newspaper or television reviews and printed bookshop sales. It's doubtful too whether the majority of authors will be as skilled as seasoned publishing organisations at producing high-quality metadata to elevate their books in search results listings.

This is the central question – is the CreateSpace initiative, and others like it, going to create excessive amounts of network noise that will make finding high-quality content more difficult than it is today? Searching for a book on Amazon is straightforward at the moment, but once books, journals, articles, blogs and websites merge into one big amorphous blob of information, picking out the best content will not only get more difficult, but will start to become more highly valued as a service. Online peer-ranking will be important, but this is easier to do well in vertical sectors than it is across the entire international publishing landscape. Brand and long-standing author loyalty will continue to count.

In today's Wal-Mart world there may be room for specialist shops that offer higher quality products and better service – but only for those that know their products and customers better than anyone else. Online, that's where Amazon's data advantage threatens the traditional publishing industry the most – so that's where the battle must be fought.'

I think this is the appropriate time to mention a seminar being organised by Book Marketing (BML) on the afternoon of 21 September at the offices of DLA Piper at 3 Noble Street, London (application forms from BML and more info here) entitled provocatively 'Dinosaur or Dynamo: does the bookseller have a role in the digital era?'

25 August 2007

Print on demand

Yesterday's posting about the latest Amazon initiative to offer would-be authors a print-on-demand publishing solution generated some interesting comments. Clive Keeble, in an earlier comment wrote:

'I long for the time when the entire Picador backlist is reproduced at a regular price in POD format instead of all this RPU bore : heck, then I'll even open up an account with MDL. Its up to the established publishers to ensure that they have control of the market place.'

The head of Picador, Andrew Kidd, responded:

'Regarding Picador and POD, I wholeheartedly agree. We are moving forward with digitisation of our backlist, and as costs and technologies improve it should not be long before the bad-old-days of RUC are behind us.'

Great. Print in demand is a good thing. However, Susan Hill thinks the quality isn't good enough and so dismisses it. But there is a bigger problem. Anne-Lise Pasch wrote:

'When books are no longer reprinted, do the rights return back to the Author from the Publisher? If so, wouldn't a sensible step be to retain digital rights to push onto 3rd-party services such as Amazon's POD, and thereby extend the 'shelflife' of a title from disappearing into obscurity?'

Great again. Why haven't publishers done it? Well, academic publishers have and are managing to extend the lives of scholarly monographs significantly. General book publishers have been much slower. The first and most obvious and most solvable reason for this is cost. Print on demand has been significantly more expensive than conventional printing. Expensive scholarly books can stand that extra cost and still be commercially viable. £5 paperback novels cannot. But that will change and cost will become a much less significant barrier.

The real barrier now is the publisher's relationship with authors. Ironically, there are authors (and authors' societies) who value their books going out of print because this triggers a reversion clause allowing them to annul the original publisher's contract and resell the titles to the publishing market-place. With print on demand there is no such thing as 'out of print' and thus no opportunity to revert rights. In actual fact, there are very few instances of authors benefitting from the reversion clause because usually there is a very good reason the title went out of print – there was no demand – but one can understand why an author would not want to be shackled to a publisher who cared not a jot for their books. There is a lot of noise around this issue and the various trade and author associations are trying to find a way through with little success so far. Meanwhile, technology advances and Picador still doesn't have its full backlist available using traditional AND print on demand. It is very frustrating, not just for Clive Keeble but for publishers too.

And while on Picador I was delighted to see a spread from Grafik 150 celebrating the 150th issue of the influential design magazine of the same name, featuring covers from Picador proof copies.

The featured covers are from Picador proof copies. Henry Hobson has written:

'After being given one of these as a random present, I have become more and more obsessed with them. Picador's proof copies, or advance reading copies, have an understated beauty about them which you just can't find in most "designed" books . . . .However, the main inspiration comes from the books' plainness – the empty unfinished covers can't fail to inspire. Knowing that they'll never make it onto a retailer's shelves, they feel like they've been made for my eyes only.'

I agree but wonder why we don't dispense with the designed covers and simply publish with the beautiful proof covers even if it destroys Mr Hobson's my-eyes-only reverie.

Hobby horses

I suppose we all have hobby horses. Some independent booksellers who comment on this blog regularly seem to be obsessed by Amazon's discounting policy and the thought that publishers are encouraging it by granting bigger discounts. I cannot speak for other publishers (and it would of course be wrong to discuss such matters between ourselves) but we grant the lowest possible discounts to all distributors and retailers. It would be madness to do otherwise. Of course, we could choose not to do business through certain channels which use discount to their customers as a marketing tool but that would result in our turning away around 80% of our business. I imagine our authors would be less than pleased at a reduction of 80% in their sales and their omission from best seller lists and they would abscond. That would leave us with a reduction of sales of 100%. Not a great way to run a business but at least we couldn't be accused of failing to support small independent book shops.

However. my hobby horse is public libraries and their apparently unstoppable demise through lack of investment in books. Major parts of Macmillan's business operate in a town called Basingstoke in the county of Hampshire 'rolling green hills, tranquil villages and ancient forests'). It is a relatively prosperous part of the UK. The library service is the responsibility of Hampshire County Council through its Libraries and Discovery Centres department. They have set up a Library Review Panel to:

- Assess progress of the service in meeting the challenges

- Gain current perspectives of national professional organisations

- Discover how other library authorities are meeting challenges and/or reversing trends

- Assess progress with the 'Discovery Centre' approach

- Inform future thinking

All well and good but they might save a lot of time and money if they simply looked at their own audited accounts sent to me by the industrious Tim Coates.

The number of books held in stock has declined by 24% over the last eight years.

Spending on books has fallen by 35% before taking into account anything for inflation.

Total library spending has increased by 43%.

Spending on books as a percentage of total spend has fallen from 13.6% to 6.23%.

The cost per visit to to libraries has increased from £2.03 to £3.28.

What does this mean? The libraries under their management stock fewer books and thus attract fewer visitors. At the same time they have been spending more money on the management of the libraries. The result is that they have become less efficient at what they do and cost the taxpayer more than they should.

What should the Library Review Panel recommend? Transfer responsibility for individual libraries to well-qualified, knowledgeable and committed librarians, cut out the local government (and central government for that matter) back-office strategy committees and bureaucracy, and spend more money on books and clean and safe buildings. Abolish themselves. I'm sure it's much more easily said than done but we need action now not words.

This excellent piece by Katherine Rushton in The Bookseller tells the national story much better than I could. I've just spotted this great piece in today's Observer by Rachel Cooke and I reprint just one paragraph to give the flavour:

'It would not be exaggeration to say that this piece of wimpish guff makes me feel physically ill. The person who made it clearly has no idea how parlous the situation is. I do not have the space to go over all the closures, recent and mooted, here. So let me give you just one recent example. Earlier this month, a man called Yinnon Ezra, who is head of leisure services at Hampshire County Council and also, more interestingly, a recently appointed board member of the MLA, blithely announced: 'We have to ask whether fiction should remain in libraries when most people buy books.' When asked whether it disagreed with this statement, the MLA (the central government quango with responsibility for libraries) refused to do so.'

27 August 2007

Baldons Cricket Club

Today is a Bank Holiday in the UK and I hurt all over. I have just discovered why it's called a bank holiday (courtesy of the Wikipedia link above):

In 1871, the first legislation relating to bank holidays was passed when Sir John Lubbock introduced the Bank Holidays Act 1871 which specified the days in the table set out below. Sir John was an enthusiastic supporter of cricket and was firmly of the belief that bank employees should have the opportunity to participate in and attend matches when they were scheduled. Included in the dates of bank holidays are therefore dates when cricket games were traditionally played between the villages in the region where Sir John was raised.

Which allows me to explain why I'm in agony. Yesterday I played my first game of cricket of the season. For one reason or another (mainly the weather and a tricky travel schedule) I have missed all this season's games of Baldons Cricket Club. I have played for this lot for thirty-three years and it shows.

536

The club represents two villages, Toot Baldon and Marsh Baldon (known by those from Toot as sin city). There is a church and a pub in each village. Above is the Marsh church.

Yesterday's game was fairly typical. We won the toss and managed to reach a paltry 142 having been bowled out in a couple less than the allowed forty overs. I contributed my usual two runs coming in at number 9 in the batting order. We had a great tea and then waited for the inevitable humiliation as the young, fit and clearly professional openers from Aston Tirrold set about getting the runs required with no loss of wickets and an early drink in the pub. Miraculously, our bowlers performed like international superstars and the visitors were all out for less than 100. And then to the pub. The good news was that their innings lasted for only thirty overs. I was keeping wicket and I'm not sure I could have moved an inch today if it had gone to the full forty. Here are some action photos of a previous game taken by Terry Trinder. The wicket-keeper is not me but is a successful publisher.

This one is there as much for the cottage in the background as for the cricket.

And this is our captain, Mark Denning, with hayfield for losing balls in background.

Back to the book world tomorrow.

🥢 28 August 2007

Livres Hebdo/Publishers Weekly Ranking of the Global Publishing Industry

I spent part of the Bank Holiday weekend catching up on back issues of the trade press and came across this article Publishing's World Leaders in the constantly improving and Internet-friendly Publishers Weekly and co-sponsored by Livres Hebdo whose copyright this is. I have permission from them and the producer Ruediger Wischenbart and I would have put a (c) with a circle round it next to Livres Hebdo 2007 but I can't work out how to find that symbol.

I post the chart here as a reminder of the range, internationalism and relative size of the world's major publishers and to give perspective to some of the discussions on this blog.

Rank	Publishing Company (Group or Division)	Parent Company	Parent Country	2006 $ Revenues	2005 $ Revenues
1	Reed Elsevier	Reed Elsevier	UK/NL	7,606.30	7,217.60
2	Pearson	Pearson plc	UK	7,301.00	6,807.00
3	Thomson	Thomson Corp.	Canada	6,641.00	6,173.00
4	Bertelsmann	Bertelsmann AG	Germany	5,995.60	5,475.60
5	Wolters Kluwer	Wolters Kluwer	NL	4,800.90	4,386.20
6	Hachette Livre	Lagardère	France	2,567.50	2,137.20
7	McGraw-Hill Education	The McGraw-Hill Cos.	US	2,524.00	2,672.00
8	Reader's Digest	Reader's Digest	US	2,386.00	2,390.00
9	Scholastic Corp.	Scholastic	US	2,283.80	2,079.90
10	De Agostini Editore	Gruppo De Agostini	Italy	N/A	2,089.10
11	Holtzbrinck	Verlagsgruppe Georg von Holtzbrinck	Germany	N/A	1,594.84
12	Grupo Planeta	Grupo Planeta	Spain	1,319.50	N/A

13	**HarperCollins**	News Corporation	US	1,312.00	1,327.00
14	**Houghton Mifflin**	Houghton Mifflin Riverdeep	Ireland	1,054.73[1]	1,282.10
15	**Informa**	Informa plc	UK	1,271.14	N/A
16	**Springer Science and Business Media**	Cinven and Candover	UK/Germany/Italy/France	1,201.20	1,088.10
17	**Kodansha**	Kodansha	Japan	1,180.92	1,253.85
18	**Shogakukan**	Shogakukan	Japan	N/A	1,176.63
19	**Shueisha**	Shueisha	Japan	N/A	1,093.95
20	**John Wiley & Sons**	John Wiley & Sons	US	1,044.19	974.00
21	**Editis**	Wendel Investissement	France	981.50	1,008.96
22	**RCS Libri**	RCS Media Group	Italy	937.82	921.18
23	**Oxford Univ. Press**	Oxford University	UK	786.11	858.65
24	**Kadokawa Publishing**	Kadokawa Holdings Inc.	Japan	808.60	809.90
25	**Simon & Schuster**	CBS	US	807.00	763.00
26	**Bonnier**	The Bonnier Group	Sweden	769.56	N/A
27	**Gakken**	Gakken Co. Ltd.	Japan	682.89	756.99
28	**Grupo Santillana**	PRISA	Spain	635.44	545.22
29	**Messagerie Italiane**	Messagerie Italiane	Italy	629.20	N/A
30	**Mondadori** (book division)	The Mondadori Group	Italy	571.35	552.50
31	**Klett**	Klett Gruppe	Germany	520.00	458.12
32	**Cornelsen**	Cornelsen	Germany	451.10	450.97
33	**Harlequin**	Torstar Corp.	Canada	407.03	449.54
34	**WSOY Publishing and Educational Publishing**	Sanoma WSOY	Finland	401.70	N/A
35	**Médias Participations**	Media Participations	Belgium	381.16	391.56
36	**Les Editions Lefebvre-Sarrut**	Frojal	France	342.29	293.80
37	**Langenscheidt**	Langenscheidt	Germany	338.00	N/A
38	**Weka**	Weka Firmengruppe	Germany	327.47	333.84
39	**Groupe Gallimard**	Madrigall	France	309.40	330.14
40	**Westermann Verlagsgruppe**	Medien Union (Rheinland-Pflaz Gruppe)	Germany	303.94	294.84
41	**Kyowon**	Kyowon	Korea	N/A	303.68
42	**Weltbild**	Verlagsgruppe Weltbild GmbH	Germany	299.78	291.46
43	**La Martinière Groupe**	La Martinière Groupe	France	296.40	334.10
44	**Higher Education Press**	Higher Education Press	China (PR)	N/A	266.50

| 45 | **Egmont** (book division) | Egmont International Holding A/S | Denmark | 260.00 | 232.70 |

N/A = Not Available.

1 = For first nine months of 2006.

Note: Figures are based on sales generated in calendar 2006 or—in cases with a fiscal year—from fiscal 2006. Data is from publicly available sources, in most cases annual reports. No attempts have been made to estimate sales in 2006 for companies that have not yet released updated figures. The listing was compiled by international publishing consultant Rudiger Wischenbart.

Source: Reed Business Information and Livres Hebdo

As a follow-up to the <u>Death of the Publisher?</u> (I wish I'd headed it Death of a Publisher? – so much more literary) there is an excellent essay on the <u>Exact Editions blog</u>. Adam Hodgkin points out that these print-on-demand operations are likely to have a major democratising impact for authors which will result in millions more titles being published. I agree but the inevitable consequence of that will be the even greater need for publishers to continue to act as quality arbiters. My fear specifically about the <u>Amazon</u> initiative is that the huge additional numbers of unrefereed titles available for sale and promised exposure on Amazon by Amazon will obscure other potentially more relevant titles thus diminishing the customer experience. The bad will drive out the good.

29 August 2007

Cormac McCarthy

He's done it again, this time Cormac has won the <u>James Tait Black Memorial Prize for Fiction</u> for <u>The Road</u>. What I really hope is that this leads to a greater readership for all his <u>books</u>. Here are two.

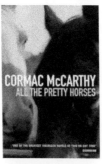

By permission of Pan Macmillan, London.

By permission of Pan Macmillan, London.

Moving on from the successful to the not so successful, I am immensely grateful to Danuta Kean for this helpful link on how to cope with rejection while maintaining dignity and courtesy.

I am very pleased to see that a poll in today's Bookseller on 'Who should run the library service?' has Tim Coates way out in front with 52% of the votes, followed a long way back by local authorities(21%), librarians (13%), the Government (11%) and the MLA (Museums, Libraries and Archives Council, the quango charged with leading the transformation of the library service) in last place with not a single vote. Not a resounding vote of confidence in the responsible institution.

And finally a plug for a book published not by Macmillan but written by a Macmillan employee. It is Eating the Sun: How plants power the planet by Oliver Morton who is the Chief News and Features Editor at Nature. I'm not sure how it's come about that he's being published by HarperCollins under the Fourth Estate imprint rather than by Macmillan Science but I guess that's the way the cookie crumbles and a good book is being published by a good publisher. Give it a go. It's a fascinating read.

🐝 30 August 2007

Royalties

We've just completed our annual IT strategy day which is becoming an ever more important prelude to the budget round which follows. One of the issues is how to simplify our royalty system without compromising its accuracy and reliablity.

At one point in my career the royalty system being used didn't work properly. The angst, fury, management time, author damage and cost were staggering and I never want to suffer that again.

The problem is that the concept of royalties is a fair one but that the changes in our business have made it, in its present form (a percentage of the UK published price of a book), unwieldy and unrealistic.

The percentage is linked to a price which applies in only a minority of cases. It doesn't apply to all sales overseas; it doesn't apply to nearly all sales made in supermarkets, Internet bookshops and many bookshop chains.

In educational and academic publishing houses the system has been radically simplified by the almost universal application of royalties based on publishers' gross income rather than retail price.

However, literary agents and many authors' organisations have set themselves against this because they fear that somehow a change would work against authors' interests. I don't think there is anything to fear and there is an enormous amount to be gained from the simplification, transparency, auditability, and shared motivation to reduce average discounts to retailers. How about agreeing new equitable royalty rates based on real money not a notional recommended retail price?

🦉 31 August 2007

Edinburgh International Book Festival

Yesterday's posting about royalties has generated some really interesting comments, largely from the USA. Do check them out and join the debate.

I wrote about Oliver Morton's new book a couple of days ago and invited him to contribute a guest blog here. Being the journalistic professional he is, it arrived on deadline and here it is:

'I don't know much about book festivals, but you don't have to know much to be knocked out by the Edinburgh International Book Festival, which closed on Monday night. I'd been there before a few years ago, for an on-stage interview with Jim Lovelock that was a sold-out success, and this time I was there to plug my own book, Eating the Sun, at two events. But the thing that struck me, both times, was the enthusiasm of both organisers and punters, the stunning number of people and topics that they manage to get into 17 days (700 events, 650 authors, pdf programme) – and the stamina that those 17 days must require. Organiser Catherine Lockerbie, who has that stamina in spades, found time to give the Daily Telegraph a taste of what the weeks are like.

Good things: endlessly friendly and helpful staff; generous sponsorship in kind (and doubtless otherwise) from Highland Park, which may not be 'the best spirit in the world' (among other things, forget not the Ott) but which is undeniably wonderful; a terrific bookshop; excellent chairs at the events who knew their stuff and worked hard to do their best by the speakers and by the audience; Carol Ann Duffy's closing poetry recital; my co-presenters Martyn Amos and Nick Harberd; bumping into Ken Macleod (great short story published in Nature|recent Nature feature, both subscribers only); speaking in the Spiegeltent, which had a really great vibe to it – much more Moulin Rouge than the venue for your average talk on 'The future of nature'; pretty much everything else.

Bad things: not being able to go to all of it; one slightly underlit lectern; err . . . that's it.'

≤ **September 2007** ≥

Mon	Tue	Wed	Thu	Fri	Sat	Sun
27	28	29	30	31	1	2
3	4	5	6	7	8	9
10	11	12	13	14	15	16
17	18	19	20	21	22	23
24	25	26	27	28	29	30
1	2	3	4	5	6	7

01 September 2007

Why royalties?

The posting on author royalties continues to generate interesting comments but perhaps the most challenging response comes from Evan Schnittman on the excellent OUPblog. He argues for a single payment for all standard publishing rights in a title for a defined period – and then spoils the purity of his propsal by introducing 'kickers' for higher than anticipated sales, which is a royalty by any other name, but let that pass. I'm not sure I agree with everything he says but his penultimate paragraph bears reading:

'The state of book publishing requires a radical change to the standard business practices that have existed for decades. This has to happen from within the core assumptions of the most basic elements of the business. Retail price vs. gross earnings are just window dressing on the real problems of trade publishing.'

The author of Typo, David Silverman has uploaded a video about booking a hotel room – it's a joy.

It's the first day of September which means Autumn is with us. It also means I have to compile the monthly statisitics for this blog. August was a relatively quiet month (unsurprisingly) with 77284 visits against 84682 in July but 80% up on August 2006's 42944. It brings the total visits to the site to over the million at 1,068,510.

02 September 2007

Puff the Magic Dragon

This interview with Pete Yarrow, co-writer of Puff and co-author of Puff,the Magic Dragon book which we've just published took me straight back to 1963. I couldn't find an original version so here is a much more recent performance

Puff, the magic dragon lived by the sea
And frolicked in the autumn mist in a land called Honah Lee,
Little Jackie Paper loved that rascal Puff,
and brought him strings and sealing wax and other fancy stuff.

I was at a boarding school with little heating and little entertainment bar sport. The highlight of the week was the Sunday afternoon singles chart lists on the radio. The Beatles were riding high, Presley released Devil in Disguise, Gerry and the Pacemakers released the best-ever football anthem You'll Never Walk Alone and who could forget Brian Poole and the Tremeloes and Do You Love Me? (now that I can dance)? In the middle of all this edgy stuff came the sweetest little song from a clean-cut American folk trio.

I'll bet that as soon as you saw the title of this blog you started to hum the tune in your head. I also bet that most of you never knew how to spell Honah Lee – and what on earth is it? Buy the book (and CD) and find out.

Finally, just in case you missed this wonderful advertisement for Western education . . .

🗓 03 September 2007

The Economist

I spent some time over the weekend reading Inside the Googleplex in this week's Economist. It gives a fascinating insight into the workings of and issues facing the 21st century's commercial giant. In the editorial, the conclusion is:

'One obvious strategy is to allay concerns over Google's trustworthiness by becoming more transparent and opening up more of its processes and plans to scrutiny. But it also needs a deeper change of heart. Pretending that, just because your founders are nice young men and you give away lots of services, society has no right to question your motives no longer seems sensible. Google is a capitalist tool —and a useful one. Better, surely, to face the coming storm on that foundation, than on a trite slogan that could be your undoing.'

I could not agree more.

Having digested the Google stuff I then moved through the rest of the issue and realised (for the umpteenth time) that this magazine must be the best weekly print publication in the world for the general reader and we all know that Nature is clearly the best for the scientific reader. Both these magazines have British roots but both have adapted to become genuinely global. I suspect they do more for British prestige around the world than almost anything else, including hugely expensive prime ministerial visits. Hooray for British journalistic standards.

And now the Economist Group is launching a new quarterly sister magazine called Intelligent Life. You can find out more about it here. If it's as good as its sibling, it will surely be a huge success.

🗓 04 September 2007

One Stop Staff Room

It's exactly one year to the day since the launch of Staff Room, the subscription-funded part of the world's largest ELT website, onestopenglish which has more than 400,000 registrants. Most of the subscribers are teachers of English as a foreign or second language and they come from every part of the world with Germany and Mexico leading the way. The testimonials for the service are glowing and, unlike many web propositions, people are willing to pay for the content. But the Staff Room is just the most recent development of onestopenglish which was launched in May 2001.

For a flavour of onestop try this trailer to The Road Less Travelled, a soap opera for learners of English. Whatever next?

And here's a link for lovers of nature and the underdog.

🗓 05 September 2007

The Almost Moon

The Almost Moon is the title of Alice Sebold's new book which Picador publishes a month from now.

By permission of Pan Macmillan, London.

Her previous book The Lovely Bones was one of Picador's best sellers of all time and everyone who has read the new one reckons the author has written another masterpiece. As part of the build-up to publication the UK marketing team is running a competition with signed advanced proofs as the prize. It seems that proofs have become more valuable than the finished book. Strange but true.

I spend quite a bit of time (mainly unsuccessfully) trying to explain why publishers are not all evil, stupid or mad. It doesn't help when publishers shoot themselves in the foot. PRISM is a lobbying organisation and describes its mission as:

The Partnership for Research Integrity in Science and Medicine – the PRISM Coalition – was established by The Executive Council of the Professional & Scholarly Publishing Division of the Association of American Publishers (AAP) to educate policy makers and the American people about the risks posed by government intervention in scholarly publishing. The coalition is guided by the PRISM Principles, which affirm the key role that publishers play in peer review, access and dissemination, and preservation of knowledge, and which advocate sustainable business models to ensure continued investment and innovation in these essential contributors to scientific objectivity and integrity.

All well and good. Unfortunately this lobbying appears to many people to be anti-scholar and anti free flow of information and may actually set back the debate by antagonising many researchers and indeed many publishers too. It has already generated articles like this. Maybe publishers are evil, stupid or mad.

06 September 2007

Routes to market

One of a publisher's jobs is to ensure that an author's book reaches as many people as possible. We achieve that through publicity, marketing campaigns and most importantly through visibility in retail environments. I classify (and I think most other people would do so too) these environments into independent book shops, chain book shops, libraries, supermarkets and the Internet. Each of these environments has its own characteristics in terms of type of customer, cost base, cost to service, range, and service levels. Each is important.

Publishers are frequently under attack for favouring one channel over another and of being short-sighted in allowing different prices to prevail in different sectors etc.

You only have to run a search on this blog for 'Keeble' and click to some of Clive's comments to get a sense of the debate. In essence, independent booksellers feel that large discounts granted by supermarkets rob them of sales of mass-market titles, large discounts granted by Internet booksellers rob them of sales of higher-priced 'quality' non-fiction sales, and large discounts granted by high-street chain booksellers rob them of everything else.

I recently checked out the UK sales of two recent best sellers. The first is a mass-market fiction title in paperback. **The chains represented 50% of sales, supermarkets 35%, Internet 9%, independents 5% and libraries 1%(rounded up).**

The second is a serious TV tie-in hardback non-fiction title. **Chains were again 50%, Internet 30%, independents 11%, supermarkets 8% and libraries once more a little under 1%.**

In making these calculations I assumed that the bulk of wholesalers' sales are to independents and I included small chains (a few outlets rather than scores or hundreds) in the independent sector. In other words, I don't think I have understated the independent share of the overall market for these books.

These numbers can be interpreted many ways and I'd welcome feedback. What it says to me is that the industry needs all these (and maybe other) channels. Certainly the independent market share is a concern but if we had not offered these books through the Internet and supermarkets (by not trading with them on acceptable-to-them terms) and, say, independent sales had doubled as a result (unlikely because neither of the titles would have made the best seller lists without supermarket and Internet data), our authors would still have been significantly worse off. The result of that would have been the loss of these authors in the future and consequent medium-term damage to our business. We have to find ways of creating a viable independent book shop sector but not by impeding other routes to market.

On a lighter note I am indebted to David Silverman for alerting us to this French version of Puff to sit alongside the book and CD we publish tomorrow. Enjoy.

07 September 2007

Guest Speaker

Back in June I mentioned that the Committee of the Society of Bookmen (which doesn't have a website and so I've linked to an interesting article by Hazel Bell on 'The fellowship of the book' which gives a little of the Society's history) had appointed me its Chairman for a year. Last night was the first dinner with me holding the gavel. I am not meant (under the terms of the Chatham House Rule) to mention the identity or affiliation of the speaker or the participants but I can tell you that we had a terrific talk on the issues of being both a Picador novelist (When we were bad) and a publisher (Headline Review) – oh to hell with Chatham House, it was the multi-talented Charlotte Mendelson. Not only was she entertaining and insightful but she reduced the average age of the diners substantially.

Kate Eshelby.

The next meeting is scheduled for the Thursday before the annual Frankfurt Book Fair and we have a leading American mega-publisher as guest. The pre-Frankfurt frenzy of e-mails arranging meetings, flyers advertising new gizmos for transforming the books business and the Fair itself reminding us all to attend has begun. I was particularly taken by this piece of information from the organisers:

35,000 sausages, 18,000 sandwiches: caterers Accente have 1,200 staff in action to provide for everyone at the Book Fair.

I suppose the statistics are meant to be impressive but I am merely concerned. I normally spend five days at the Fair every year and calculate that I get through at least ten sausages in that period. Last year nearly 300,000 people attended. I think they may have seriously under-estimated sausage demand.

08 September 2007

Le rugby

Last night saw the opening game in the Rugby World Cup. I happened to be in Toulouse airport going to a friend's wedding and stopped by the bar with a TV. The silence was golden as it became clear that Argentina were going to beat France. It doesn't mean much in the mathematics of the competition but it certainly makes things interesting. England will probably be next for humiliation.

On the publishing front, the highly successful Macmillan Digital Audio has moved into educational audio with the launch of downloadable Macmillan Readers. This is a series of classic novels with limited vocabulary for learners of English. It will be a fantastic resource for adults as well as students. Try out the samples at least.

In another digital development, an organisation called Live Ink maintains that rearrangement of words can make screen-presented text more readily ingested. I'm not sure, but if you check out this version of Moby Dick they seem to have created an automatic method for turning prose into poetry. I'm sure Melville would have been impressed.

And finally, a plaudit to a competitor. It is fifty years since the launch of Sputnik and New Scientist magazine has produced a wonderful web celebration here if you click on the 'gallery' icon.

09 September 2007

What is it about Jerusalem?

I attended a wonderful wedding at a church on the top of a hill in Southern France yesterday.

The first church was built on this site around 1000 A.D. and it's been adapted, augmented, and fiddled around with ever since. It has, however, always been a church and a very beautiful one too.

The ceremony involved two English friends and the opening hymn was William Blake's Jerusalem.

And did those feet in ancient time
Walk upon England's mountains green
And was the holy lamb of God
On England's pleasant pastures seen

And did the countenance divine
Shine forth upon our clouded hills
And was Jerusalem builded there
Among those dark Satanic mills

Bring me my bow of burning gold
Bring me my arrows of desire
Bring me my spears o'clouds unfold
Bring me my chariot of fire

I will not cease from mental fight
Nor shall my (my) sword sleep in hand
'Til we have built Jerusalem
In England's green and pleasant land
'Til we have built Jerusalem
In England's green and pleasant land

After the service I asked the Deacon whether he thought that hymn had ever been sung in that church in the past thousand years. The answer was no. I remembered that some German colleagues expresssed ignorance of the hymn at a previous service in England. An American I quizzed told me that she'd never heard it or of it until she came to live in England. Here it is for those who don't know it.

Of course, the hymn IS very English but it is so powerful that I'm surprised it seems not to have crossed national barriers at all. Any explanations?

Graham Robb

Returned from France late yesterday evening to find a note from the police to let me know that someone had smashed the driver's window of my locked and alarmed car, legally parked in a 'safe' street. They didn't steal anything but it'll cost me several hundred pounds to fix assuming no collateral damage (not worth losing a no-claims bonus) and . . . .grrrrrr.

While in France I was chatting to a nomadic writer. He doesn't own a house and survives by house-sitting for friends around Europe and earning enough from his writing to pay for his car, computer and books. Not a bad life. He was telling me how he has just finished The Discovery of France by Graham Robb and that it was so good he was going to read it again straight away. What an endorsement. There are more extraordinarily glowing reviews from the more traditional reviewing media here.

By permission of Pan Macmillan, London.

The book (essentially a social history of France since the beginning) is clearly a work of enormous scholarly importance but it fascinates too. I didn't know about the stilted shepherds (and postmen) of Les Landes. They could move over rough land at 8 mph which is significantly faster than the average speed of traffic in London today. How about the Mayor of London introducing incentives for stilt walking?

And I love these lines he quotes from <u>Madame de Genlis's</u> phrasebook for stagecoach travellers:

'The wheels are on fire . . . I am suffering greatly. I am going to vomit. Give me the vase'.

That's how I felt when I got to see my car last night.

11 September 2007

On Beauty and Libraries

Last night I visited the <u>London Library</u>, shamefully for the first time. It is a really beautiful building and the writers I spoke to there all raved about its utility and importance.

While the publishing industry is rightly involved in debates about our digital future, the economics of retailing or public library funding, it is easy to forget the importance of aesthetics. I am indebted to <u>Nat Torkington</u> of <u>O'Reilly Radar</u> for this <u>librophiliac link</u> to some of the most beautiful rooms in the world. I cannot think that any other human activity (sports, aviation, theatre, art etc) could have created quite so many wonderful rooms as reading has (although I guess opera houses might come a close second). For purely personal reasons, my favourite is the <u>Wren Library of Trinity Cambridge</u>.

But for splendour, how about <u>Melk Abbey Library</u>? And more, so many more.

A few days ago I <u>published</u> some statistics about the proportion of new books sold through independent booksellers in the UK – only 5% of a paperback and 11% of a hardback. Many people have explained these low percentages as being caused by discounted sales through Internet bookshops. I have therefore done some research in Australia where Internet sales represent only 0.4% of the total (compared with 9% for the paperback and 30% for the hardback in my previous example). Even if you allow for people buying from the US or UK Internet sites, the proportion would be very small. These figures reflect sales across hardbacks, paperbacks, fiction and non-fiction (in brackets are my previous numbers, paperback then hardback) – chains 56% (50,50); supermarkets 29% (35,8); Internet 0.4% (9,30); independents 11.5% (5,11); libraries 3% (less than 1 in each case).

I wouldn't claim that these statistics are definitive, hardly anything in publishing is, but they do suggest that picking Internet booksellers as scapegoats for the woes of independent bookselling is ill-founded. It seems that, in the absence of significant Internet bookshops in Australia, customers are buying more books through chain booksellers than in the UK. It's also interesting to note the significantly higher proportion of sales to library suppliers. Perhaps the Australian Government is showing more respect for libraries, books and education than the British bunch. Good on 'em.

12 September 2007

Duckworth

It's party time in the London book world and last night was no exception. Off to the very chic <u>October Gallery</u> for the annual celebration of the existence and future publishing of <u>Gerald Duckworth and Co Ltd</u>, hosted by its owner (also owner of <u>The Overlook Press</u>), Peter Mayer.

Since then the company has healed itself and, in spite of market difficulties, is re-established as a home for both general and scholarly authors – still quirky, still small but very definitely alive and kicking.

While Duckworth chugs along perfectly well publishing books traditionally, the debate about the future of the book continues to swirl around the web. <u>Here</u> is yet another (and rather good) discourse on the possible scenarios. Who will be the new publishers? The social networking sites, Amazon, Google . . . ? Or maybe <u>Duckworth</u> or <u>Macmillan</u> will survive by virtue of doing a few things well – spotting an opportunity,finding good authors, encouraging them to write books people want to read (rather than the other sort), editing, packaging, promoting, investing, doing deals for the author and then paying royalties. When someone at <u>my space</u> can do all those things as well as Peter Mayer, then we have something to fear.

13 September 2007

On branding

Once upon a time I was in charge of the reference division of <u>Oxford University Press</u>. It was at a time when <u>Collins</u> had declared a 'dictionary war' to fight over market share in the UK trade market. These 'wars' broke out on a fairly regular basis and still do. Collins had many advantages. They had more clout in the trade because of their fiction and mass-market lists. They had more marketing money. They could even afford to use <u>Frank Muir</u> in TV ads. All we had was our brand which reeked of authority, reliability and seriousness. The problem was how to broaden the appeal of the brand without besmirching our name or spending money.

We got lucky. A daily word quiz programme called <u>Countdown</u> was being launched (and twenty-five years later it's still going strong) and they had the idea of using live lexicographers as adjudicators. We were invited to supply these boffins and, after negotiations about clothing allowance (lexicographers aren't by and large renowned for dress sense) and attendance fees, we agreed. Oxford dictionaries were promoted every day to a mass audience on TV and the TV company were paying us for the honour. It was (and still is) wonderful branding.

I was reminded of this as I passed Piccadilly Circus on the way to work this morning.

The McDonald's ad in the centre must cost a fortune. This morning it was replaced by the words 'Oxford English Dictionary' and a series of sentences saying why McJobs are really good things. The reason is that the McDonald Corporation has taken offence at the OED definition of 'McJob' – 'an unstimulating, low-paid job with few prospects'. They are running a petition to have the definition changed and are advertising it on their absolutely main site. Has there ever been a better exposure campaign for Oxford? Whoever decided to include McJob in the dictionary deserves to win the industry branding idea of the year award.

 14 September 2007

Avoirdupois

There are many types of war. Some are fought on matters of principle. Many, I suspect, are fought on matters of comfort. For the last few decades Britain has been squabbling with the Common Market, the EEC, the EC and the EU (or whatever name it wore at the time) over matters of comfort not principle. There have been victories (France and Holland voting against the constitution for instance was certainly seen as a cause for rejoicing) and setbacks (Common Agriculture Policy for instance).

This week saw a resounding victory. The European Union has given up on its efforts to force Britain to adopt the metric system universally. We can continue to buy a metre of 3 by 1 inch timber. We can continue to have cars using petrol at so many miles per litre or kilometres per gallon. We can continue to buy a pint of milk or a half of lager.

By permission of Pan Macmillan, London.

I am told that the non-fiction editorial department of Pan Macmillan had early knowledge about this decision and with enormous foresight arranged for About the size of it by Warwick Cairns to be published to coincide. As Alexander McCall Smith says about it:

'A full and convincing account of why our well-tried and trusted traditional measures make human sense'.

This is one of the many new books hitting my desk at the beginning of the Autumn season. It really feels to be an impressive list. Here are just a few of the top titles (five fiction, five non-fiction) as selected by our top salesperson. A prize for anyone who guesses the correct order by sales value as measured at the end of December.

<u>Chameleon's Shadow</u> by Minette Walters (pub September 20th)

<u>World Without End</u> by Ken Follett (pub date October 4th)

<u>The Almost Moon</u> by Alice Sebold (pub date October 16th)

<u>Stone Cold</u> by David Baldacci (pub date October 19th)

<u>Rhett Butler's People</u> by Donald McCaig (pub date November 6th)

<u>Not Quite World's End</u> by John Simpson (pub date 5th October)

<u>Moments</u> by Cristiano Ronaldo (pub date October 5th)

<u>Ronnie</u> by Ronnie Wood (pub date October 12th)

<u>Borat</u> (pub date November 2nd) – take your pick of title – the book comes in two parts – 'Borat's Guide to the US and A' or 'Touristic Guidings to Glorious Nation of Kazakhstan'

<u>Musicophilia</u> by Oliver Sacks (pub date November 2nd)

As a rule I'm rather negative about publishing parties but I'd love to see all these authors in the same room.

CORRIGENDUM. I had Borat's subtitle slightly wrong – it is actually:

Touristic Guidings to Glorious Nation of Kazakhstan/Minor Nation of U.S. and A.

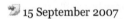 15 September 2007

The Empire Strikes Back

A dark day for England's sporting teams yesterday as Australia <u>thrashed</u> us at cricket and South Africa completely <u>annihilated</u> our rugby world cup team. It's presumably related that I woke up with the sad <u>I think it's gonna rain today</u> on my mind. A great song but lousy performances by the English sportsmen – and a brilliant performance by South Africa, they might just challenge New Zealand for the championship.

On a more serious note, I was delighted to see this hugely important supplement to Nature on <u>Neglected Diseases</u>.

I think the editor's opening paragraph sums up the issue:

'We have never had such a sophisticated arsenal of technologies for treating disease, yet the gaps in health outcomes keep getting wider. This is unacceptable.' This plea to close the gap between rich and poor nations was made last month by Margaret Chan, director-general of the World Health Organization (WHO), in her first major address on primary health care. Few would disagree. The tragedy is that it joins a litany of similar unheeded appeals by WHO directors-general, stretching back almost 30 years.'

This supplement is open-access on the web, free to all subscribers and distributed very widely beyond, thanks to its sponsors. Everyone at Macmillan – and particularly the two thirds of our people who work in developing countries – should be proud that Nature is engaging so actively in this area.

16 September 2007

Trevor Glover

Trevor Glover died last week. He worked for Penguin in Australia and the UK, he was President of the Publishers Association and then became Managing Director of the eminent music publisher Boosey & Hawkes. There will be formal obituaries in the trade press next week.

I got to know him best during the 'reversion wars of the early nineties when he had returned from Australia to run the London office of Penguin and was having to live with the Rushdie fatwa affair. I was responsible for building a paperback list to support the trade hardback houses then owned by Reed International, William Heinemann, Secker and Warburg and Methuen. One way to improve the list was to publish authors whose books had previously been licensed to third-party paperback publishers, frequently Penguin. (This is a normal part of life today but at the time was considered in some way evil, or at least underhand.) The licence on a very important, albeit not huge selling, author (whose identity you'll have to guess) came up for renewal and we told Penguin that we would revert unless they coughed up a very very large advance for an extension of the licence. Trevor called to ask if our absurd request was for real which it was. He quite rightly refused to pay the advance and we prepared to publish the books ourselves. A few weeks later he called again. He'd been thinking about what it would be like to be the head of Penguin responsible for losing this particular author. He realised that Penguin without that writer on its list just wouldn't be the same and he agreed to the ridiculous refresher advance. The book trade and the world without Trevor just won't be the same either.

Peter James, whose latest hardback Looking Good Dead is his best ever, sportingly contributed to my best seller competition of last Friday even though he doesn't have a book in the list (the latest one was too early, the next one too late to be included).

Incidentally, there is no charge for entering the competition. The prize has yet to be decided but it will, I'm certain, be worth winning. Nobody is excluded, so please go to here and enter your list as a comment, not forgetting to enter the anti-spam code underneath the comment box.

Because it's Sunday I think I'm allowed a 'use of English' moan. I received this from the Chelsea Arts Club:

'Roger, as you all know, has now decided to take things a little easier in the Isle of Wight but I would ask you to join with me in thanking him . . . '

When did the redundant 'with' become the norm? Why is it there? Who started it? Why not launch a campaign for the elimination of redundant prepositions?

17 September 2007

Runners and riders

The game I started last Friday to guess the order by sales value of ten of Pan Macmillan's Autumn best sellers has generated a few entries and so I'd better clarify the 'rules'. The winner/s will have listed the correct order by invoiced sales value up to 31 December 2007 of these ten books. More information on each is available through the highlighted links. It would be helpful if entries could be made as 'comments' on the original posting. No more entries after the end of September so that I can then post progress on the 'runners' as the Autumn season develops. If we get too many winners I'll introduce some sort of tie-breaking competition.

Chameleon's Shadow by Minette Walters (pub September 20th)

World Without End by Ken Follett (pub date October 4th)

The Almost Moon by Alice Sebold (pub date October 16th)

Stone Cold by David Baldacci (pub date October 19th)

Rhett Butler's People by Donald McCaig (pub date November 6th)

Not Quite World's End by John Simpson (pub date 5th October)

Moments by Cristiano Ronaldo (pub date October 5th)

Ronnie by Ronnie Wood (pub date October 12th)

Borat (pub date November 2nd) – Touristic Guidings to the Glorious Nation of Kazakhstan/Minor Nation of U.S. and A.

Musicophilia by Oliver Sacks (pub date November 2nd).

The competition is open to everyone including Macmillan staff with insider information. The prize is still under discussion but will definitely not be of a size that would require this bit of nonsense to be registered under the Competitions Act of 2003 or any such bureaucratic nonsense.

And for your musical treat today try Farewell to Stromness by Peter Maxwell Davies. I prefer the piano version by the composer but couldn't find it. It's still pretty good in any version.

18 September 2007

Bookshops matter

One of the most innovative publishers in the world is the computer book publisher O'Reilly. They have been at the cutting edge of collaborations with Google and

Amazon, with copyright-lite experimentation etc. It is therefore with great delight that I spotted this paragraph from O'Reilly Radar about the sales of computer books:

If you wonder whether it matters to publishers whether books appear in stores given that they can be ordered online, try breathing through a straw. You can get all the air you want if you lie low, but you'd better not try any strenuous activity. Retail distribution is like the alveoli in our lungs – it increases the surface area for respiration, except in this case, rather than oxygen binding to hemoglobin, it's customers binding to possible products to purchase. People go to Amazon and other online retailers with specific purchases in mind. Despite all Amazon's brilliant work on collaborative filtering and recommendations, a computer screen just doesn't match up to a physical bookstore when it comes to browsing and the chance discoveries that spark an unplanned purchase.

What more can I say? I think the Booksellers Association should invite Tim O'Reilly to give the keynote address at their next conference.

In the staff canteen in our Kings Cross offices yesterday I got into a conversation about the death of the musical. I argued, for no particular reason, that a more obvious case was the dearth of listenable operas since Puccini packed it in. I was, of course, reprimanded and corrected by my younger and betters and thoroughly shamed by the fact that we have just published a book as a result of a contemporary opera.

By permission of Pan Macmillan, London.

David Frost's brilliant book about his confrontation with Richard Nixon follows the extraordinarily successful opera Nixon in China and the play Frost/Nixon. So drama and opera (and I'd argue musicals too) still flourish.

19 September 2007

Stuttgart

Here's a traveller's tip. If you're ever in Stuttgart try to get a room at the not-very-posh but very stylish Der Zauberlehrling. Click on hotel, then XXL, and then on the room of your choice. The restaurant is also very good.

I'm here for a board meeting and to catch up with several of my German colleagues. The pace of change in the infrastructure and politics of Germany may not be particularly rapid but the speed with which digital technology is being adopted is awesome.

Our owners, the Holtzbrinck Group, have been investing strongly in fast-growing, innovative, technology-driven media businesses and the success is palpable. Social websites such as StudiVZ (which I'm only very gradually learning how to pronounce) are attracting millions of registrants and tens of millions of visits. The trick book publishers must learn is how to persuade these visitors to read (and pay for) books and other high-quality information rather than simply communicating with each other. It won't be easy but the prize will be great.

Sites such as Lovely Books in the UK and in Germany are just the beginning of a new approach to making people aware of books and sharing opinions. While this is happening we must also work closely with our traditional partners, the bookshops (see yesterday's posting), to ensure that this new generation of readers can also enjoy physical as well as digital browsing. I've yet to be convinced by any of the current crop of e-book readers (why woud anyone want yet another lump of metal to carry around?) but there is little doubt that the Internet as a marketing tool is vital and that we'd better learn how to use it fast.

20 September 2007

The Special One

I woke up today to find my neighbourhood in mourning at the departure of Jose Mourinho as manager of our local soccer club, Chelsea FC. He's been the most admired (and fancied, I suspect) member of the Chelsea set-up. It'll be interesting to watch the team's fortunes without his leadership. I fear the worst but meanwhile enjoy this clip.

And now to the other championship race, the competition to predict the order by sales value of the Pan Macmillan top ten new titles this Autumn. Entries are still coming in on the original posting. The cut-off date for entrants is the end of this month, so get to work and encourage your friends to join in. So far, analysis shows that people are more confident about picking the least likely to succeed than the most likely. Rhett Butler's People just pipped Musicophilia at the bottom of the table. The only other title picked for tenth position was Cristiano Ronaldo's Moments but it was also put in first position by the same number of people. Number one spot is occupied by Borat but seven of the ten titles have also been nominated. The only title which has not been nominated at either number one or number ten is Ronnie Wood which, arguably, is the one most likely to be a runaway success . . . or not.

What will be Pan Macmillan's Special One?

21 September 2007

Bits and bobs

One of Picador's best writers, Charlotte Mendelson, also works as an editor for one of Picador's principal competitors, Headline Review, part of Hachette Livre. Two of Sphere's – also part of Hachette Livre – potential best selling writers, Jon Butler and Bruno Vincent, work for Pan Macmillan in editorial. Their new book has the very serious and tasteful title, Do ants have arseholes?, and will doubtless sell tens of thousands of copies. Never let it be said that I only mention Macmillan titles but I do expect a pourboire from the Sphere marketing department.

Last Friday's blog has amassed 38 comments so far (which is a pretty good bag by my standards) but my favourite comes from Vladimir in Kazakhstan:

'Dear Prime Minister (we remember Christine Keeler was your friendly girl – even news in our country). Is not a race with Borat in November December. So kindly what about it?'

I'd be happy to respond but I'm not quite sure what the question is. Can anyone help?

For crossword fiends here is a link to a clever marketing idea to promote the sixth edition of the Shorter Oxford English Dictionary. I'm delighted to see that they've taken absolutely no notice of my strictures on the use of the word 'unabridged' when applied to a 'shorter' dictionary: 'Each entry offers everything you would expect from a leading unabridged dictionary . . . ' except that it is abridged!

And finally, I've found myself wondering whether Alan Greenspan's warnings about the impact of the credit squeeze might equally be applied to author advances which have risen faster even than London house price inflation . . .

22 September 2007

Some Experience Necessary

From time to time I've written about a forthcoming book with an ironic title Print is Dead by Jeff Gomez (this links to his excellent blog), who is about join Penguin USA in a senior electronic publishing role.

I asked him to describe what it felt like to be on the receiving end of being published rather than the doing end of publishing and, being the professional he is, he has delivered on schedule and to commission. Thanks, Jeff. If only all authors . . .

In the 1991 film The Doctor, William Hurt plays an arrogant young physician who becomes ill with throat cancer. As he begins to go through the health care system – - as an ordinary patient and not a hot-shot doctor – - Hurt is shocked by how clinically he's treated; he feels like an object instead of a human being. The experience forces him to reflect on how a profession whose stated goal is to help people can end up treating them as little more than a commodity. By the end of the movie, of course, he has acquired a new and added perspective on his profession.

As someone who works in publishing who has recently been through the process of writing and editing a book, I've been thinking of this film a lot over the past couple of months. That's not to say that my treatment during the past year (it was last September that I signed the contract to write the book, and it's now been printed and will be in stores in November) has been anywhere near as traumatic as what William Hurt faces in *The Doctor*. In fact, it hasn't been a bad experience at all. But it has indeed been important and instructive, and it's an experience I wish more people in our industry could have.

One of publishing's dirty little secrets is that, increasingly, it's not about the books. Or maybe, it's *too much* about the books (meaning books as objects, or even books as a number on a balance sheet). In the publishing process we find ourselves sometimes getting removed from the ideas and stories found in our books; the words that provide the power to deliver amazing and transformative experiences to readers (and are therefore the kinds of books we read growing up that made us want to get into this business in the first place).

One of the reasons this happens is because people who work in publishing, for the most part, have not had the experience of writing and publishing a book. They know the physical process, and they know the business inside and out, but they don't know what it means to slave over an idea, or live with a single character or theme, for a number of years. They don't know what it's like to see their name on a dust jacket, not to mention - after all that hard work - getting a hideous review on Amazon. (Having been through both experiences, I can safely say that one is better than the other).

They also don't know the feeling of having a signing and showing up to an empty bookstore, reading to just employees and in the end not signing anything but some stock. True, some editors and publicists have witnessed these kinds of things from the wings, while escorting their authors around town, but it's a much different experience when you're the one standing in front of all those unoccupied folding chairs.

In Oliver Stone's 1987 film Wall Street, Michael Douglas's infamous character Gordon Gekko at one point says, 'Today, management has no stake in the company.' What Gekko meant was a financial stake; people who were Vice Presidents didn't own company stock, and thus were sometimes not terribly motivated to make the company perform well since it wasn't their own fortunes on the line. Well, in today's literary world I would make the comparison that, in publishing, we are like those Vice Presidents Gekko described.

Not because we don't care whether or not our companies do well (we of course have a vested interest in the well-being of our companies; without them, we wouldn't have a job). But rather, it's not our names on the dust jacket, spine or title page. Our hopes and dreams don't (usually) ride on the success or failure of any particular book. In fact, the same way that hundreds of sentences create a novel, the dozens or hundreds of books we're associated with throughout our tenure at any one company form our career. Our reputations don't rest on one book or another. And yet, for many authors - especially first-time ones - this is *it*. This is what they've been dreaming of for much of their lives, and we shouldn't take that for granted or treat it cavalierly in any way.

That's not to say that we don't root for our titles, or that editors don't evangelize their writers internally and externally. They do, and I've seen many editors do everything that they could to get the word out about a book that they loved. But still, at the end of the day, it's a business. It's a business we love, and one we wouldn't trade for anything else, but it's still business. And the fact is, the books we sell aren't our own words.

Because, while we can imagine what it's like and try to empathize, it's just not the same until it happens to you. It reminds me of when I was having dinner years ago with a friend who's a famous writer, and we got to talking about <u>Spy</u> magazine. (This was during the interregnum when *Spy* was off the shelves for a few years before coming back to life.) My first novel was about to come out, and I was lamenting the fact that *Spy* wasn't around to make fun of me. My friend looked up from his meal and warily said, 'It's not as fun as you think.' At the time, I just waved his comment aside with a grin. Well, when my second novel came out, in 1997, *Spy* had returned and, lo and behold, they made fun of me. And guess what? My friend was right.

Beyond this general feeling, I think we as publishers tend to use our experience and knowledge in a way that automatically puts the author at a disadvantage. We're the ones who know the trends, the sales curves, and - more importantly - the fiction buyer at <u>Barnes & Noble</u>. We think we know best, and we make decisions based on this fact. But we're not the ones who wrote the book. And sometimes, during various parts of the publishing process, authors are made to feel more or less powerless.

For instance, I've had <u>five books</u> published, and I've never had major input on a cover. In fact, for my first novel, I had a terrific fight with my publisher and - even though I loathed the cover beyond belief - they went ahead and printed it. (True, I was a first time author, but I have since commiserated with other authors, ones who have sold many more books than I ever did, and they have confirmed similar experiences.) And so, back then, I was that crabby author on the other end of the phone; the one who caused an editor's eyes to roll towards the ceiling. Later in the day I was the subject of a snarky story told in the elevator on the way down to lunch ('Guess who *still* doesn't like his cover?').

I was a problem, a nuisance, a bore; a know-it-all and someone who didn't know anything (both at the same time!). And yet I was also a writer, an author whose book they had paid for and put on the cover of their catalog. I remember at the time being immensely confused, thinking, 'How could they want my novel, but not my advice?' And now the shoe is on the other foot. For instance, I've been on the phone with authors who were complaining about their websites, and this time it's *my* eyes that roll. I tell stories about them the way that my previous publishers used to talk about me.

It reminds me of a scene in <u>Annie Hall</u> (yes, for someone in publishing, I know I watch too many movies), where <u>Woody Allen</u> and <u>Diane Keaton</u> are both on screen in separate therapy sessions. The off-screen doctors ask them each a question ('Do you sleep together much?' 'Do you have sex often?'), and even though the questions are essentially the same, their answers are different. Keaton replies, 'Constantly, three times a week,' while Allen answers, 'Hardly ever, three times a week.' While this exchange is a wry commentary on how, within a romantic relationship, two people can have the same experience but reflect on it differently, I can see a correlation to our industry. Because, during the typical publishing experience, we always think we're doing everything we can to help our writers. Meanwhile, they think we're not doing enough.

All of which goes to say that, while I doubt every person who works in publishing will find the time to write and publish a book, I think that if everyone tried more often to envision what it's like to be an author, we would be better off. After all, we spend so much time these days crunching data and trying to look at our products from the point of view of consumers, reviewers, and booksellers; we should try to also imagine what it feels like to be a *writer*.

🦫 23 September 2007

Literary silliness

About once a year (or actually much more frequently) the London literary world shoots itself in the foot and confirms what the 'real world' believes, that it is composed of a bunch of snobby interbred reactionaries. This piece describing current events at a leading literary agency is a classic of its type. For those of you who can't be bothered to follow the link (and who can blame you?) here is a taster:

'On the surface we all get on brilliantly, but on a personal level we all f***ing loathe each other,' as the editorial director of one of the country's largest publishing houses cheerfully confided yesterday. 'I'll tell you everything but it's career death if I go on record. In my view what's happening in publishing in the past few days is a catastrophe. Everyone is horribly excited.'

And while all that backstabbing and gossip is going on there is a real literary issue. The British Government, not content with appearing to stand by while public libraries are allowed to wither (although perhaps that is about to change), is now threatening to undermine the forward-thinking digital programme at the British Library. Lynne Brindley, the Library's Chief Executive, has written courageously and forthrightly about the issue in today's Observer. The irony is that, while the Google Library Project absorbs a huge amount of attention and legal bills in order to be allowed to digitise books which the publishing industry is separately arranging to digitise without subsidy, one of the world's great libraries is being forced to beg to be able to digitise and thus protect and make available the very books which need to be digitised and need to be funded. It drives me to distraction.

🦫 24 September 2007

Second Nature

There are some (many?) things I simply can't get my head round. One of these is Second Life in spite of having been involved in the publication of Graham Pond and Paul Carr's excellent Unofficial Tourists' Guide to Second Life (where I reckon the apostrophe is in the wrong, or at least less correct, place). So, rather than mislead you I asked our resident expert, Jo Scott aka Joanna wombat, to update us on developments in this weird world.

'Since last November, one large green wasteland floating somewhere on the outskirts of Second Life has been transformed into the multi-island archipelago of Second Nature. Second Nature is our flagship island, and over the last few months, has become home to a wide variety of scientists. We have decided that Second Life is so experimental that we can't possibly know what scientists will actually find useful, so the best thing is to let them find out for themselves. The upshot is, any scientist with an idea for a project in Second Life is welcome to come to us and experiment on our island. The result is an island full of interactive and developing exhibits, from full scale city modelling, to a ride through a giant cell to a scientific art exhibition. To see all of these, do come and visit Second Nature.

In the meantime, we have been experimenting with meetings. Following the SciFoo unconference, several attendees led by Jean-Claude Bradley have been holding regular SciFoo Lives On sessions in Second Life: a topic is chosen by wiki and anyway, attendee or not, may come and present on, or simply discuss the topic, just like a SciFoo session. Not to be left behind, we have organised a weekly series of events. The format is simple: a scientist comes to our island, gives a short talk about his work, and then takes questions from the audience. The first was given by Dr Phil Holliger on how to evolve polymerases to repair ancient DNA, and that was followed last week by Professor Graham Martin on cormorant vision. Both were really well attended and the feedback has been really postive, so we're definitely going to keep doing them, and one day, we may even learn how to work the slide projector properly! The next talk is this Thursday, featuring Professor Philip Gibbard from Cambridge University, talking about how massive floods cut Britain off from the mainland with the creation of the English Channel. All talks are free and no specialist knowledge is required, so please do come along. Any questions, IM Joanna Wombat . . . '

On the subject of social networks and cyberworlds, I have just been sent a copy of The Bookaholics' Guide to Book Blogs (apostrophe also in wrong place in my opinion) compiled by Rebecca Gillieron and Catheryn Kilgarriff, published by Marion Boyars, which is owned and run by the Catheryn. This blog has a very small mention but it is much more to do with genuinely bookish rather than corporate-ish blogs.

The link with social networks is that I used to work with Catheryn's dad, Arthus Boyars. He is, according to Wikipedia a poet, but I always viewed him as the advertisement sales manager of Early Music magazine for whose profitability I was responsible at one point – and thank God for Arthur and his ad revenue in those difficult days.

And in parallel, Marion Boyars old business partner was John Calder and together they ran Calder and Boyars for a decade. Calder became a stalwart defender of retail price maintenance and on one occasion personally challenged in court the decision by various publishers in the Uk to abandon it. He summonsed me to the Royal Courts of Justice in the Strand as a witness. I was first on after the lawyers had spent an hour talking their very special language. I was pretty nervous. There was this grand old man of the book trade with lawyers and judges all around waiting to demolish me by clever argumentation and cross-examination. The opening exchange ran something like:

'Mr Charkin, in your affidavit you describe yourself as a publisher.Where did you go to uiversity? Trinity, Cambridge. What did you study? Natural Sciences. There you are, m'lud, the man claims to be a publisher but he studied science.'

Unspoken but clear meaning . . . I rest my case! Fortunately the judge didn't quite see it that simply.

I suppose the Catheryn, Arthur, Marion, John Calder, net book agreement is my idea of a social network.

Open access experiment

Here's an interesting promotional experiment. My friends at <u>Exact Editions</u> have worked with the US reference book company, <u>Berkshire Publishing</u> to make available their huge <u>Encyclopedia of World History</u> free online for a limited period of time. This has happened before with journals – and <u>Nature</u> uses the technique quite frequently but I'm not sure I've heard of its being used for books in any significant way. It will be interesting to see whether this helps or hinders sales. It's even got a mention in <u>Open Access News</u> although the first comment about monographs selling better when made available free permanently seems a bit off the wall to me.

Last week I mentioned the death of <u>Trevor Glover</u>. There have been some excellent obituaries in <u>Publishing News</u> and in <u>The Times</u>.

Got back late from Germany (again) last night. The plane was meant to leave Stuttgart at 7.00pm and arrive in London at 7.50pm. It left at 9.00pm and arrived at 10.00pm. Home by 11.00pm. The crew couldn't understand that the passengers were more interested in getting home for the evening than in the fact that we were terribly lucky to be flying a brand new Airbus. 'It still had the plastic wrapping on the seats' they told us excitedly. That was British Airways. This morning I'll be testing the other great British transport success, South-West Trains to Basingstoke. Will it be on time? Will it be a brand new train? Can't wait to find out.

Study Skills

In the academic and publishing calendar in Britain this time of year is known as BTU (back to university). According to recent <u>research</u>, British students work less than their continental European counterparts. You can read the full report <u>here</u>. I'm sure it is true but I have some counter-evidence.

The highest Macmillan entry in today's Amazon <u>bestseller list</u> is none of the titles from the Autumn bestseller <u>competition</u>. It is <u>The Study Skills Handbook</u> by Stella Cottrell. Maybe British students are learning how to work smarter rather than longer and this book is the key. I certainly hope so because student life without the pub would be a real drag.

I am indebted to <u>David Silverman</u> for this <u>link</u> to one of the most bizarre website ideas ever – everything should taste like bacon. I know what they mean but . . .

Pip Pip

This went out an hour or so ago.**Richard Charkin moves on after ten years at Macmillan**

26 September 2007: Macmillan announced today that Richard Charkin will leave his post as CEO after exactly ten years with the company. He will take up a new position as Executive Director of Bloomsbury plc on Monday 1 October 2007.

Richard commented, 'It is exactly ten years since I accepted the job as Chief Executive of Macmillan and it has been the best ten years of my career. I have been able to work in a company with strong values and traditions owned by a family committed to quality, innovation and autonomy.

The decade has seen significant growth in all our diverse areas of publishing and we have been able to do this mainly organically but also with some excellent acquisitions. We are in the middle of a digital revolution and Macmillan has embraced the changes without losing sight of the importance of our authors, our staff, our customers and our history.

This success is down to everyone at Macmillan everywhere in the world. I hope I have been able to contribute to it a bit.'

Stefan von Holtzbrinck, CEO of Holtzbrinck Group, the owners of Macmillan, paid tribute to Richard's contribution to the company.

He said, 'Richard and I joined Macmillan at more or less the same time and from the beginning it was an inspiring, creative and successful relationship. It is a great joy for me, my sister Monika and all of us at the Holtzbrinck Group to see Macmillan thriving in every way which is the result of strong leadership and a loyal and successful team.'

Mike Barnard, who retired from the main board of Macmillan in May after 35 years, will return as Deputy Chairman to maintain momentum until a new CEO is appointed.

What it means is that I won't have to think of something to write about every morning on this blog. Just for the record we've had 1,137,267 visitors and generated $338.37 in advertising income. More importantly I've made new friends, learned tons and had fun. Thanks to all of you and pip pip from charkinblog.

Index

Acknowledgements

Thanks to Nicholas Blake, Beth Cleall, Wilf Dickie, Lucy Foley, Caitlyn Miller, Mark Richmond, and Stuart Wilson.